THE CENTRAL SCHOOL OF
SPEECH AND DRAMA
UNIVERSITY OF LONDON

H
Kin

Duc
du Mai

Mary

William III
Prince of Orange
Stadholder
of Holland
King of England

Louis XIV
The Other Side of the Sun

CHRISTIANISSIMUS ☙ LUDOVICUS MAGNUS REX

S. Thomassin delineabat et   Sculpebat. Cum Privil. Regis

Louis le Grand

Louis XIV
The Other Side of the Sun

Prince Michael of Greece

Translated by Alan Sheridan

Orbis Publishing, London

© 1979 Olivier Orban
English translation © Alan Sheridan 1983
First published in French by Les Editions Olivier Orban 1979

English language edition first published by
Orbis Publishing Limited, London 1983

Phototypeset by Tradespools Limited, Frome, Somerset
Printed in Great Britain by Eyre and Spottiswoode
ISBN 0-85613-514-3

Contents

CHAPTER I

An Unhappy Father

As night was falling in Paris on 5 December 1637, a man and a woman were talking quietly together in the dimly lit parlour of the convent of the Daughters of St Mary, in the Rue Saint-Antoine. The woman, one of the sisters of the convent, remained hidden in the shadows behind a grill. Her visitor on the other side was none other than the King of France, Louis XIII. The beautiful young nun was once known to the world as Mlle de La Fayette, and before she withdrew from society she had been the king's greatest love. Now the only way left for him to satisfy his passion was to come secretly to confide in her at the convent. The lonely, tormented, inhibited king believed he had found peace when he had discovered this girl among his wife's maids of honour. She was sweet-natured and loyal, selfless and honest, and she felt genuine love for him. But she was also an innocent, and soon fell victim to the intrigues of the Court, to the jealousy of the queen and, above all, to the scheming of Cardinal de Richelieu, the cunning, ruthless dictator of France, for whom she represented an obvious potential danger. In the end she had succumbed to pressure and retired to the convent. On hearing the news, the king, usually so undemonstrative, had thrown himself on to his bed and openly wept.

This love, which had never been physical, survived the unhappy girl's brave decision. They had gone on seeing one another, despite the impassable barrier of the cloister wall, but even this meagre happiness was threatened. Richelieu became increasingly concerned about the influence of the young nun, and various ecclesiastical intermediaries were appointed to persuade the two lovers of the impropriety of these visits, which became increasingly rare. The storm that struck Paris that winter night formed a fitting background to one of their last meetings. No one will ever know what they talked about, but when they parted it was already too late for the king to return to Saint-Germain-en-Laye, where he was expected. There was always the Louvre Palace, of course, but the furniture and hangings had been removed from the king's apartments.

As it happened, the queen was in Paris and her apartments would be ready to receive the king, but Louis XIII had no intention of spending the night in the same bed as his wife. Louis had avoided the performance of his conjugal duties for most of his married life, and twenty-three years of marriage had still not produced a child. After the queen's second miscarriage, he had given up trying. Haunted by his own impotence, he had no wish to embark on further attempts that would merely have confirmed his misfortune. In any case, his inclinations lay with his favourites, boys from whom he demanded a degree of understanding and tenderness that they were incapable of providing. For her part, his wife, the Spanish king's daughter known as Anne of Austria, sought consolation in a life of frivolity which seemed innocent enough but sometimes had far-reaching consequences. (After all, France had been at war with the country of her birth since 1635, and Anne, however unwittingly, was seen as the focus for discontented elements both inside the Court and outside the country.) More seriously she had indulged in political intrigue and plotting against Richelieu. All this had the effect of irrevocably widening the gap between herself and her husband, while the throne of France still lacked a direct heir. The nobility calculated the effects of such a stormy succession; France grieved and offered up prayers to God; Europe sniggered.

Time passed at the convent of the Daughters of St Mary while the king refused to spend the night with the queen. But it is possible that Louise de La Fayette, with characteristic candour, urged him to do so. Did Louis XIII resign himself to the inevitable, or did he suddenly find enough courage within himself to carry out his distasteful duty? Was the presence of his wife in Paris on the very day he was there entirely fortuitous, or was there a plot behind it? In the event, the king finally made up his mind to dine, and to sleep, with the queen.[1]

On 20 January 1638 the news burst like a bomb: the queen was pregnant. Louis XIII was transformed; he even began to show some tenderness towards his wife. But fifteen years of discord and rancour could not be effaced so easily; once the initial enthusiasm had worn off he took to avoiding her company again. This attitude, together with the king's well-known tendencies, were enough to give rise to wild rumours: surely the child must be a bastard. Contemporaries, like posterity, were to invent the most various and most preposterous fathers for the child who was to become Louis XIV. The Comte de Brienne, an intimate at Court, lent credence to these suppositions and insisted in his writings that he had not only heard them repeated in Louis XIV's presence, but that the king had said nothing to deny them.[2] It would however have required extraordinary skill on Anne of Austria's part to escape from protocol, Richelieu's spies and the all too easily aroused suspicions of her husband, to have a liaison that appears to have left no trace whatsoever.

The long-awaited Dauphin, born on 5 September 1638 at a quarter to twelve noon in the Château de Saint-Germain, was most certainly legitimate. Cannon were fired, church bells rang out, fireworks were set off, messengers were despatched to take the fantastic news to the four corners of Europe. The king fell on his knees, followed by the whole of

France, but he had to be reminded that he also had a wife, the baby's mother, and it took the admonitions of the Church to persuade him to kiss her before the assembled Court.

Of the entire population of France only the Dauphin's nurses were to be less than enthusiastic about this unexpected birth: his teeth appeared well before the normal time and he wore out seven wet nurses in six months. The surgeon Dionis, however, maintained that it was their fault: in his opinion, they should have had enough milk to satisfy his appetite thus preventing him from virtually turning into a vampire. And the Swedish ambassador commented gravely: 'France's neighbours should beware of such precocious voracity.'[3]

When the child no longer needed a wet nurse, it was his father's turn to complain: 'My son is extremely stubborn: I am determined not to bear with his ill temper.' The Dauphin was still only two years old at the time. Louis XIII's irrepressible hatred of his wife was already poisoning relations between father and son, although it does seem that relations between the parents improved at least long enough for a second son, Philippe, to be born in 1640. Abominably mistreated in his own childhood, Louis XIII had no idea how to treat children himself. All his life he had repressed his own feelings; he now intimidated his son, perpetuating the same process, but regretting it bitterly at the same time: he was only too well aware that he was adding to the catalogue of stillborn relationships that had marked his life. On one occasion, the queen returned home from hunting with the Dauphin, when they were surprised by the king, who sprang out at them like a fleshless ghost, his head surmounted by an enormous nightcap. Not unnaturally, the terrified child ran howling into his mother's arms. His father lost his temper: 'I am very displeased with my son. As soon as he sees me he cries out as if he had seen the devil and goes rushing to his mother. He must be cured of these ill humours and taken away from the queen as soon as possible.' It gave Louis great pleasure to threaten his wife in this way, but he had little idea of the effect it would have on the two children. Paradoxically, he was, in fact, very fond of them, especially the elder, whose least smile represented a joyful triumph: 'My son played with me for over an hour. I gave him some toys to play with; we are the best of friends. I pray God that it will last.' When a smallpox epidemic broke out at Saint-Germain, he forgot his love of solitude and ordered the children to be sent to him immediately at Versailles, to the small castle that had become his favourite retreat. He even became sufficiently self-denying to consider allowing his wife to join them, 'but I am afraid the large number of women would spoil everything for me if the queen were to go there'. This unloved iceberg of a king could be incredibly pathetic and clumsy.[4]

On 4 December 1642 he lost the collaborator whom posterity has often chosen to see as his tyrant. Richelieu's death lifted the steel yoke that Louis XIII had chosen to bear for eighteen years, out of a sense of duty and love for his country. His first action as a free man was to liberate others. He opened the prisons, recalled exiles, expressed regret in public for past cruelties and sought means of stopping the war that was ruining France. Was this belated revenge or a need to come out from behind the figure of the dead dictator, was it remorse aroused by a painful conscience or was it simply demagogy, as the queen's friend, Mme de Motteville, suspected?

Richelieu had appointed his own successor: he could not have been more different. The touchy, proud aristocrat, the ever resourceful, tireless genius, the domineering ruler who was as hard on himself as on others, the international star, riddled by fear yet feared throughout Europe, chose Mazarin – an unknown Italian turncoat of humble origin, a cunning flatterer, a cynic who laughed at those who despised him, a corrupted corrupter, a past master at dividing, manipulating, winning over, seducing, reassuring. The tragedian, capable on occasion of the sublime, left the stage to a comic buffoon. For the moment, Giulio Mazarin remained in the shadows as the tragedy for which he was so ill-fitted pursued its course, the last act being the rapid decline of the king.

At forty-one Louis XIII was an old man. Tuberculosis and the criminal aberrations of his doctors, added to a neurotic's continual frustrations and emotional crises, had quite simply worn him out, and towards the end of February 1643 he retired to bed in the Château de Saint-Germain and never got up again. The disease galloped apace; soon the king's fleshless body was covered with yellow and white spots like a leper. On the advice of doctors, the minister Chavigny was given the task of informing the king of his desperate state and making the necessary arrangements.

The king flung his arms around the astonished minister's neck; in all his life, he declared, the best news that he had ever had was learning that he was about to lose it. Chavigny took advantage of the situation to intercede on behalf of the queen, reiterating her constant denials of the terrible accusations laid against her. 'In my present state, I must pardon her, but I must not believe her ...' And as he spoke, Louis XIII was whittling down the power which would go to his wife at his death. Anne of Austria was to become regent, but she could take no important decision without the advice of a council whose irreplaceable members the king had already carefully chosen. The queen received this affront like a slap in the face, but her counsellors advised her to bow before the inevitable, wait and see how things turned out. On 20 April the royal proclamation was read out before the royal family, the nobility and members of the *parlement*, all assembled in the dying man's bedchamber. They heard that as a final act of revenge the king had forced his wife to make a solemn oath to abide by the decision that deprived her of power. She agreed, probably realizing that it mattered little, since she represented the future while he already belonged to the past.

Having finally put some order into his affairs, indistinguishable as always from those of France, Louis XIII could indulge the morbidity and bitterness that now assailed him. 'People come to see whether I shall die soon,' he remarked, observing the glittering courtiers fluttering around his bed. 'If I could come back I would make them pay dearly for wishing that I were dead,' he added, guessing the impatience of tomorrow's men. Then, resigned once more, he pointed to the spires of the abbey of Saint-Denis, site of the royal sepulchre, which he could see from his window: 'That's where I shall be going soon.' He expressed anxiety about the condition of the roads: 'My body will soon be jostled along, for the roads are bad.' And, to make quite sure that his hearse did not get stuck in the mud, he recommended that the procession avoid a particularly bad patch.

While the king skilfully displayed his detachment before death according to the custom of the time, intrigue was well afoot not far from his bedchamber. Stifled by fifteen years of dictatorship, princes and nobles were becoming more and more excited at the idea that power would once more be on the market. Nothing seemed to be moving yet, but a lot was happening underground, so much so that Queen Anne ordered the guard to be doubled and the castle gates to be locked to avoid the abduction of her children. Richelieu's way with dissent was to behead anyone who stepped out of line, but now that the king was dying the spectres of plots, kidnappings and sedition came rushing back.

The atmosphere grew heavier as the king moved towards death. Everyone – not least Louis himself – impatiently awaited his end but his body still refused to comply. In the view of a horrified eyewitness, he was ill-cared for, ill-served, almost abandoned. In his own palace the king of France could not even get a bowl of warm broth.

May arrived, and with it the final agony. One morning Louis ate a dish of mushrooms with great relish, then ordered his first gentleman of the bedchamber to join him in singing a duet. However, the next day, he motioned to his doctor to approach: 'Tell me, I beg you, how many hours I have still to live.' 'Sire, Your Majesty may have two or three hours left at the most.' 'Then I thank God and consent with all my heart.'[5]

His thoughts wandered off. He looked back over his reign, the tasks begun over and over again and never completed, the war that had lasted for eight years and which he would so much have liked to bring to an end before he died. The Spanish army was still threatening the kingdom on its northern frontier, and it was only being held by a young man of twenty-two, his second cousin, the Duc d'Enghien. Suddenly the king became feverishly excited, demanding his pistols. He fumbled around pitifully, apparently looking for his weapons, then grabbed his wife's fan – she was sitting at his bedside. 'What's he going to do with it?' she asked, quite taken aback. The king rambled on: 'Do you not see, M. le Duc d'Enghien is leading a great battle against the Spaniards, good Lord, how he leads them!. . . They are defeated, they are all dead or taken prisoner, apart from a few runaways.' He was radiant.[6] Five days later, the Duc d'Enghien, known to history as the Grand Condé, was indeed to carry off the crushing victory of Rocroi, but Louis XIII was never to see the fulfilment of his premonitory vision. He died that same day, 14 May 1643.

Some weeks later, the funeral took place at Saint-Denis with all the theatrical pomp of monarchy and death combined. Allegorical ornaments and draperies disguised the ancient medieval abbey. A pyramid of candles rose up beside the enormous catafalque. The entire Court, the ambassadors, the members of the *parlement* and of the great institutions of state were all there. At the appointed moment, the princes of the royal family presented the offerings of candles from which gold pieces were suspended. The king's chaplains moved forward to receive them, but the monks of Saint-Denis rushed forward at the same time, and the astonished onlookers were treated to an ecclesiastical brawl around the remains of the dead king. The fighting was so violent that the Cardinal Archbishop of Lyon, Richelieu's brother, who was officiating at the ceremony, was very nearly burnt to death.

After the funeral service the long, glittering cortège descended into the burial vault. The guards in their white and gold uniforms carried the coffin which was covered with cloth of gold. When everything was in place, the dignitaries approached one by one and laid down the insignia of their offices and the emblems of monarchy. 'Monsieur le Duc de Luynes, bring the hand of justice. Monsieur le Duc de Ventadour, bring the sceptre. Monsieur le Duc d'Uzès, bring the royal crown.' Then, three times, the King-at-Arms let forth the fateful cry: 'The King is dead, pray for his soul.' Everyone knelt; there was a minute's silence; then the same King-at-Arms was the first to rise: 'Long live King Louis, fourteenth of that name, by grace of God King of France and of Navarre, my lord and master.' As the crowd of people rose, the cry was repeated throughout the vault, then throughout the packed church, 'Long live the King', punctuated by trumpets, tambourines and oboes, and without further ado everyone removed the black crêpe that covered their golds and silks.

To the surprise of her friend Mme de Motteville, Anne of Austria showed a genuine sorrow at her husband's death, in spite of the fact that he had consistently ignored and despised her.[7] The feeling was short-lived, befitting those first few days of widowhood, but it was also the sign of a good heart and perhaps even of regret. She was the only one in the entire Court to show such feelings. Everyone else who, only the day before, had been standing stiffly to attention round the deathbed now relaxed and wasted no time in trying to attract the attention of the new regent, shamelessly abandoning their master's corpse to the curiosity of the mob. The feelings of the five-year-old child who had become king of 'the most beautiful kingdom after heaven' were ignored.

★

The day after his father's death, Louis left Saint-Germain for Paris. Anne was urged to show the child, the symbol on which her power depended, to the people. The courtiers, anxious not to remain among the shades of the past, departed with him, deserting the castle in which a remarkable reign had just come to an end. The entire capital took to the streets, and some curious inhabitants went on foot or by coach as far as Nanterre to await the royal procession. They were not disappointed. The king had only to appear before them to win all hearts. Any fears as to the weakness of his constitution were confounded; with a tubercular father one could never be sure, of course, but thankfully the child was handsome and healthy. Fully aware, even at the age of five, that he was on display, he put on a noble bearing and an 'air of greatness' that aroused the acclamation, applause and blessing of everyone on the way. The two bugbears – Richelieu and Louis XIII – who for so many years had bullied, puzzled and terrorized France had gone, replaced by an elegant, dignified woman, and a radiant, impressive-looking child. Together they seemed to bring hope of peace, prosperity and happiness for all; that at least was how the jubilant crowd saw the image of monarchy presented to it.

There remained, however, one small matter to be settled: to quash the dead king's last testament. Everyone agreed, for no one wanted to go on living under the rule of the two dead dictators, through their creatures in the Council of Regency. The queen wanted the power that was hers by right; the French tradition that queen mothers acted as regents during their sons' minority stretched back to the middle ages. The party at Court which had consistently worked against Richelieu, overtly or otherwise, took the queen's side but had every intention of manipulating her, while the *parlement*, which alone could abrogate the will, expected, under weak rule, to increase its own importance and to legitimize what it saw as its rights.

The *parlement* of Paris was not a representative body like the English parliament but one of the sovereign courts of justice. Its members, the *parlementaires*, were lawyers (known as presidents), whose positions were theoretically in the gift of the crown, but which in practice were purchased in perpetuity by the members and which passed from father to son by hereditary right. Consequently dissident members could not be removed from office. The Parisian *parlement* was the most important of several regional *parlements* in France and acted as a court of appeal and as an administrative arm of the crown, registering edicts and commissions. As such it sometimes tried to limit the power of the monarchy by exercising its right to refuse to register a decree it felt was at odds with the ancient traditions and laws of the realm. When this happened the only way the French king could insist on registration of a disputed edict was to appear before *parlement* in person at a *lit de justice*. This was to cause major problems for the regency, and indeed would lead in a few short years to civil war, but for the time being crown and *parlement* were in accord, and the *lit de justice* was a formality for appearance's sake, a way of deflecting possible criticism levelled at Mazarin and the queen for overturning Louis XIII's will.

The session in the Great Chamber of the *parlement* in the early summer of 1643 was simply a ceremony agreed in advance. During Chancellor Séguier's speech, Anne of Austria, a moving sight in her widow's weeds, could observe at leisure the princes of the royal family, sitting not far away. They formed three formidable and rival clans. First, there was Gaston, Duc d'Orléans, Louis XIII's very different brother, a pleasure-loving fop, ambitious but weak-willed, cowardly, unstable and treacherous. By his own wife he had only one daughter, known as the Grande Mademoiselle, the richest heiress in France, who even at sixteen proved to be a much stronger character than her father. This commanding young woman, self-willed and romantic, might have done great things had she not also been so muddle-headed and naïve. She did not care for her distant cousin, the Duc d'Enghien, hero of the opposite camp, perhaps because she was jealous of him. With his fiery eyes and his nervous tics the Duc d'Enghien looked, and in many ways was, a rather dotty genius. In 1643 he was still content to win battles, leaving political intrigue to his father, the Prince de Condé, who had only three more years to live. His mother, Charlotte de Montmorency, who at sixteen had been the last love of an almost sixty-year-old Henry IV, had grown old herself as a respected dowager whose only concern was to protect and to promote her family. In addition to the hero of Rocroi, she had another son, the Prince de Conti, and a daughter, Anne Geneviève de Bourbon, a marvel of beauty and, as yet, of virtue, who had been married for a year to the Duc de Longueville.

The third clan was less important in rank, because its head, the Duc de Vendôme, was only a royal bastard, the offspring of Henry IV's love for Gabrielle d'Estrées. Its influence resided in the Duc de Beaufort, Vendôme's son, a hothead capable of anything, an utterly reckless, irresistible, irresponsible adventurer, who, like so many of his contemporaries, was happy to mix love and politics.

These princes, brought up in mutual enmity and accustomed as part of their birth-right to oppose the monarchy, were for once in agreement with it. The Prince de Condé needed a little persuasion, as usual, but the decision was quickly ratified by the *parlement*; there would be no more Council of Regency, and Anne of Austria would after all become queen regent.

Victorious at last, she gloried in the gratitude now shown her and savoured the sweetness of revenge. She recalled to Court those who had supported her during the dark years: the Duchesse de Chevreuse, a dear friend and the most formidable intriguer of the century; Mlle de Hautefort, a former trusted adviser of Louis XIII but also a faithful ally of the queen out of hatred for Richelieu; the gentleman of the bedchamber, Pierre La Porte, who had been arrested when a plot in which Anne of Austria was implicated was uncovered and who had always refused to speak even when threatened with torture. On the other hand, the regent wanted to remove the Duchesse d'Aiguillon, Richelieu's famous niece to whom Corneille had dedicated *Le Cid*, from the governorship of Le Havre. Similarly, she rid the ministry of the detested dictator's creatures – the Chavignys and the Bouthillers – to the delight of the *parlement* which had 'begged her most humbly to dismiss the ministers of the late tyranny' at the *lit de justice*.

It seemed certain the same fate would await the prime minister, Mazarin. He had done everything possible to incur the regent's disfavour; he had been created by Richelieu who had noticed him, taken him on, sent him on delicate missions and finally rewarded him with a cardinal's hat although he was not a consecrated priest. Expressly recommended by his dying patron to Louis XIII, he had taken over as first minister, a post the late king willed that he should keep. It was even said that he had written in person the declaration depriving Anne of Austria of the effective power of the regency. Mazarin himself was under no illusion as to his fate; he had only to contemplate the void that had suddenly opened up around him. He was friendless; only the Marquis de Chouppes came to see him and found him alone, packing his bags. He had made up his mind: he would leave before he was ignominiously kicked out. Chouppes tried to reassure him: surely the queen would not let him leave? Mazarin laughed; he knew the queen only too well. To remain in her favour, he would have to flatter her and humble himself. As it was more than he was capable of, he decided to return to Rome. He had set out long ago on his tortuous career as a humble employee of the Princes Colonna, and he would now return a cardinal, with a glittering past. He was sure the queen would choose to replace him with her favourite, the Bishop of Beauvais, for whom she had just demanded a cardinal's hat.

At this moment the Bishop of Beauvais himself arrived at Mazarin's apartments, on behalf of the queen regent, bearing orders neither to resign, nor to leave the country: 'Her Majesty offers Your Eminence the only post befitting his dignity, that of Prime Minister.'[8] Mazarin hurried to the Louvre where Anne of Austria confirmed the news. She had had to sack a few ministers, of course, she told him, and as for the Bishop of Beauvais, she had never dreamt of giving him the government of France. 'She accompanied this speech with a thousand flattering things', and they set to work at once. Thus Richelieu's invention, convinced of disgrace in the morning, found himself, by the evening, more powerful than ever by grace of Richelieu's worst enemies. Anne of Austria's intimates could hardly believe their ears. The Bishop of Beauvais made a 'modest' complaint but she silenced him; for the moment, at least, she needed someone who knew about politics and who therefore had served during the previous reign. She had chosen Mazarin because he was a foreigner and therefore had 'no interest, no support in France'.

It was true that he had been Richelieu's creature, but in Richelieu's time Mazarin had always been careful not to displease the queen. He was the only one of all her torturer's collaborators she could tolerate; he even reassured her. Similarly he skilfully concealed his plans from the arrogant lords and petulant ladies of the Court, behaving in their presence with a humility that flattered them, and convinced them they had nothing to fear from him. A few days of regency had been enough to reveal to the queen the terrifying reality of power. It did not consist in giving orders, in satisfying a few whims or doing as one liked. Power consisted in being confronted, besieged, assailed day and night by a multitude of problems each more complex than the last; in being constantly forced to take serious decisions and to remain bound to a crushing task. Excessively modest, according to her friends, and all too ready to admit her own limitations, she had convinced herself that she was incapable of governing. At the first council of ministers over which she had presided, she had committed a gaff that revealed the extent of her ignorance to all. As a reward to her *femme de chambre*, she had proposed giving her a modest property belonging to the crown that went by the name of 'Les Cinq Fermes'. The ministers burst into laughter and explained to her that this term referred to the five enormous estates that provided the income to support the entire Court.[9] But what terrified her most was the prospect of having to abandon the life of luxurious idleness that she had imagined she would now be able to enjoy in peace and quiet. Her solution was to get a prime minister quick and, since Mazarin was still in the saddle, let him stay there.

The cunning Italian understood at once what was expected of him. He began by getting rid of the importunate individuals who besieged her, filtering her audiences and erecting protective barriers around her. He made a habit of coming for a private conference each evening. As the ladies of honour and Court intimates chattered in a drawing-room, Mazarin and the queen worked in an adjoining study with the doors open, unheard but in full view. In half an hour or so he would explain the affairs of state, simplifying and reducing them as much as possible. He initiated her into the ways of politics making clear what had hitherto been obscure to her.

Everything about Mazarin was calculated to shock the bigoted but generous-spirited regent. He was suspicious and miserly in the extreme, utterly lacking in morality but devoid of malice; a churchman who never read his breviary and who preferred cards to devotions. But Anne appreciated the extraordinary rapidity of his brilliant mind; his efficiency and experience made up for her own laziness and ignorance. Finally allaying the queen's suspicions of any possible encroachment on her own authority, the skilful Mazarin transformed into consultations what were in fact simply instructions. Her conscience at rest, since she believed it was she who was governing the country, the queen was left free to involve herself in her devotions or more frivolous pursuits while he exercised true power.

The Court was not as easily taken in as the queen. Despite the assurances, flattery, fine words and lies that he distributed to all and sundry, the nobles realized that they had found their master. They went and protested to the queen and demanded his removal. At first Anne was evasive: 'I must employ him for some time yet. He is very learned in the affairs of the kingdom, of which I have still not had the time to acquire a perfect knowledge.' The Vendôme clan, who imagined themselves to be Anne's preferred party, tried to exert pressure on her. The queen changed tack and replied with a sharp refusal. She expected everyone to respect her choice of prime minister and would tolerate no demur.

The Duchesse de Montbazon, pillar of the Vendôme clan, indulged in a few insolent words to the queen; she was exiled.[10] The Duc de Beaufort was planning to assassinate Mazarin; he was arrested.[11] The Duchesse de Chevreuse, sister-in-law of the first and a friend of the second, decided to intervene. Trusting in her long friendship with the queen and in the complicity that had linked them together from the time of Richelieu, when they had vied with one another to be the greater conspirator, she went and pleaded with the queen; was this the way to treat old friends? By way of reply she was told not to meddle in anything and especially not in politics. It would be better for her, the queen concluded, if she found somewhere far from the intrigues of the Court and enjoyed a well-earned rest.

Soon it was the turn of Mlle de Hautefort to enter the lists. She had always taken the queen's part against the king when she was his confidante. She decided on the kind of frank attack that so often terrified Louis XIII, and took the opportunity one evening when she was left alone with the queen helping her to undress. As she was taking off Anne's shoes, she advised her not to forget her old friends. No sooner had the words passed her lips than the usually gentle queen flew into a violent rage. She had lost all patience with these continual criticisms and was extremely angry with Mlle de Hautefort. Having said all that she had to say, she threw herself on her bed, ordered Hautefort to draw the curtains and not to open her mouth again. The astonished woman threw herself on her knees, trembling, protesting, begging forgiveness, but in vain. Next day she received an order not to appear before the queen again.[12]

Without doubt, Mazarin was winning. First he had kept his job, then he made himself indispensable and the attacks on him merely bound him to the queen all the more. It was simple enough for him to demonstrate to her that if she gave in to the demands of the nobles and removed him, she would be their prisoner for ever. In the end, without deviating from the deference he owed her, he profited from these daily interviews to introduce an intimacy into their relationship that she found most agreeable. Even his enemies admitted that he had an extraordinary power to please. Mazarin's gaze was described as sometimes fiery, sometimes caressing, his manner of speaking gentle, insinuating, almost amorous. Considered to be handsome, tall, elegant and well preserved (he was in his forties, born in the same year as the queen), he felt capable of charming anyone, men and women, friends and enemies, even France itself. And Anne was the embodiment of France in her position of supreme power. This eminently feminine woman, still something of a coquette in early middle-age, was not averse to compliments, though she had renounced all sexual activity after having been deprived of it practically all her life. Now too proud of her rank to lower herself, she did not even dream of seeking lovers. She was quite satisfied with this discreet, inconsequential courtship which Mazarin, as a good Italian, knew how to introduce into even the most professional relationship. They shared a common desire for happiness, she because she had never known it, he by nature. (He disliked unhappiness so much he would enquire whether anyone who wanted to approach him was happy before he would receive him or her.)

Most observers, however, were not content with the true innocence of this relationship. So close a collaboration, so evident a complicity, so exclusive a favour were not long in setting tongues wagging. The less malicious were content to describe the blinded queen as utterly in thrall to her minister. But soon lampoons began to appear on the love of 'Jules and Anne'. Later came the rumour of a secret marriage between the widowed queen and the cardinal who was not a priest – a rumour to which Louis xiv's own sister-in-law gave credence.[13] Envious courtiers went over to the attack. Old friends who had been brushed aside sent delegations of priests to protest. Was not the queen afraid of offending God in having a liaison with her prime minister? The gallant Chevreuse even sent a future saint on a mission of protest, a man celebrated throughout France for his piety and charity, none other than Vincent de Paul.[14]

The imperious Hautefort acted more directly. One day, in the queen's presence, she had the impudence to allude to the connection that was on everyone's lips. Anne burst into laughter at the idea that she might be Mazarin's mistress. He did not like women in that way, she protested, he had quite different tastes. But at first she had blushed to the roots of her hair. She had just discovered where her own naïvety combined with the malice of the world could lead. With tears in her eyes, she explained to her good friend the Comtesse de Brienne the nature of her attachment to Mazarin: 'I admit that I am very fond of him; but my affection does not go as far as love, or if it does without my knowing it, my senses play no part in it and only my mind is charmed by the beauty of his mind. Is that a crime? Do not flatter me and be assured that if there is a shadow of sin in that affection, I shall renounce it this very moment before God.'[15] It was a friendship that Mazarin had succeeded in making emotional, and which might have led to a liaison if the virtue of the one and the tastes of the other had not restrained them. But was it a crime? Because she was not guilty, Anne could not imagine what absurdities people would read into her friendship for Mazarin and took no precautions to prevent them. She refused to do anything about the rumours and she made no attempt to distance herself from Mazarin. She felt that a queen should not be deterred by tittle-tattle, especially when she was beyond reproach.

Mazarin might have exercised absolute control over the regent, but he was unfortunately far less successful in mastering the financial problems of France. He inherited a catastrophic situation from Richelieu: no budget, expenditure completely out of control, declining revenue and, to top it all, a quite insane fiscal system. Moving from one expedient to another, responding to every deficit by further borrowing, the State lurched from one partial bankruptcy to another. The revenue of the next few years had already been eaten up, ruin threatened at every moment and, in the midst of this unprecedented confusion, vast fortunes were made too quickly to be honest. Mazarin was not the man to bring order into such a situation. His skills were rather those of the conjuror and juggler. Time after time, the storm threatened.

In addition to practically empty coffers Mazarin also inherited provinces seething with discontent. Harassed by taxes, old and new, exploited by their betters, the terrified lower classes rose in revolt, tired of paying the price of administrative disorder. The order that Richelieu's dictatorship had tried to establish had often been disturbed by unrest in the provinces, and whole areas thought to be entirely under the dead cardinal's control were in fact on the verge of revolution. The west and south were in open rebellion, and the old demons were once more on the rampage as the protestants took advantage of the situation to arm themselves, demand their former privileges and resume contacts with foreign powers.

The government, at its wits' end as usual, launched a new tax, known as the *toise*, calculated on land area. The *parlement* was incensed, the people groaned, riots broke out in Paris and spread rapidly to the provinces. Everything became a pretext to challenge authority. When the parish priest of Saint-Eustache· died, the Archbishop of Paris appointed a successor but the parishioners refused to accept him and demanded the dead priest's nephew, a certain Merlin. Archers were sent to put a stop to the agitation but were soon put to flight. The church was occupied and the alarm bell rung. The rebels planned to go and burn the chancellor's house down for not taking Merlin's part even though he was a parishioner of Saint-Eustache. In the end a delegation of fishwives obtained an audience with the regent and demanded their candidate as parish priest, on the grounds that the incumbent had traditionally been a member of the Merlin family. Meanwhile propositions and counter-propositions concerning the *toise* appeared almost daily, each class trying to escape the proposed tax by various amendments. *Parlement* became openly insolent and the government, in a sudden display of firmness, had to exile the ringleaders.

In the midst of all this, the Duc d'Enghien had the excellent idea of winning another battle, more decisive than the preceding ones, at Nordlingen. This gave the government the strength to arrange a *lit de justice*, at which it tried to impose its will on a less than willing *parlement*. On 7 September 1645 Anne of Austria, superbly elegant in diamonds and huge pearls set off by black voile, the young king at her side, headed a dazzling procession from the Louvre to the (present) Palais de Justice. Swiss guards and bodyguards lined the streets as princes and lords, musketeers and light cavalry followed the royal pair. In the great hall of the *parlement*, the king was hoisted up on to a pile of cushions decorated with gold lilies. The young monarch gravely greeted the assembly, turned for a moment to his mother who was sitting beside him, then in a loud voice articulated the ritual words: 'Gentlemen, I come here to speak to you of my affairs. My chancellor will convey to you my will.' Thunderous applause greeted this performance by the seven-year-old child. Then the chancellor expounded the royal 'will', which confined itself of course to a demand for money, and was answered by the first president of the *parlement*. It was a day of compromise: the government abandoned the *toise* and *parlement* accepted other new taxes; but before sealing this agreement the government had to hear some bitter truths. The advocate general Omer Talon described the misery of the people to the queen and, on his knees, pathetically asked pardon for himself. On her return to the palace, Anne reacted in a way that did her credit: 'I highly approve of the firmness of his speech and the warmth with which he defended the people. I esteem him for it, for we are flattered all too often.'[16]

CHAPTER 2

An Abandoned Child

In his speech on that September day in 1645, the first president of the *parlement* referred constantly to 'the king's declarations', 'the king's affairs', 'the king's party', just as the chancellor before him had spoken of 'the king's council', 'the king's armies', 'the king's pleasure'. Similarly each article in the gazettes, each page in memoirs or correspondence speaks of 'the king's authority', 'the king's command', 'the king's people' or tells us that 'the king is sending his armies' or 'the king orders his *parlement*'. But who was this omnipresent, omnipotent king who concerned himself with everything and who governed an entire people? He was a seven-year-old boy. Displayed on great occasions, surrounded with pomp, dressed in resplendent clothes, at *Te Deums, lits de justice,* Court balls and, before long, on the battlefield, Louis XIV was the embodiment of a myth. But what happened when, the celebrations over, his silk and gold clothes put away, the mythical character became a child once more? How did he live? In what surroundings? Where and with whom did he spend his days? What was his timetable? Of those innumerable memoir-writers who left whole volumes on the period, who describe in detail the lives of the queen, Mazarin and so many others, and whose successors were to analyse in the minutest detail the life of the aging Louis XIV, of all those observers, some good, some bad, all of them long-winded, there is hardly a sentence about the everyday life of the child who was the focal point for the entire nation. There is very good reason for this, for most of the time he was left alone, abandoned to a degree scarcely credible not only for a king of France but for any child. His many governesses left him in the hands of their own *femmes de chambre*. He would scrounge food from the pantry, maybe begging a piece of omelette which he would take away to devour in a corner with his brother. No one showed the slightest concern about his diet, no one showed the slightest concern about him in any respect. There was no one even to keep him company and he was left largely alone in his apartments. Innumerable doctors, courtiers, servants, guards were appointed to wait on him; in theory he was to be surrounded, served, protected at every moment of the day, yet he, the king of France and of Navarre, could fall into a pool in the grounds of the Palais Royal and no one would be there to fish him out.[1]

Sixty years later he was to recount the episode with undiminished bitterness. Sometimes, however, he did have a playmate, the little daughter of his mother's *femme de chambre*. Usually they played *'la madame'*, a game they invented themselves. The girl played the part of Queen Marie and he was her servant. He carried her train which they had made themselves, pushed her in her chair or held a torch in front of her.

The queen regent, his mother, did in fact see quite a lot of her children. They lived near her in the Palais Royal, which she preferred to the Louvre on the grounds that it was more comfortable. They visited her every day in her apartments between ten and eleven o'clock in the morning – she always woke late. She would give an audience for urgent matters while still in bed, then have her breakfast in her dressing-gown before dressing, assisted by her women, but also by her eldest son. It gave the boy great pleasure to see her do her hair and watch her hands, famous for their perfection, playing endlessly with the long, light-brown waves. Since she had become a widow she had given up wearing make-up which accentuated the pallor of her complexion. She wore only black, but remained elegant at all times. She was a tall, majestic woman, well-preserved rather than beautiful, for she had put on weight. Her mouth remained small and red and her green eyes had retained that gentle gaze that was apparently so disarming.[2]

She led a quiet life and preferred to remain in her own apartments. Audiences, meals, devotions, daily meetings with Mazarin – all took place there. Her children were both present and absent. She did not want them around when she was praying or receiving her ministers or in any way occupied. Inevitably her position as regent combined with her natural idleness meant she had little time for them. In the evening, when she relaxed with her ladies of honour, they were in bed. They had their own timetables, meals and recreations, at which she never put in an appearance. So she saw them, without seeing them.

Anne of Austria was a profoundly good woman who loved her children. Sometimes she stroked and teased them, sometimes she punished them, sometimes she would smack them without rhyme or reason but she was guided more by affection that reflection; she never worried about what they were doing when they were not with her. For her it was enough to know that they had their own programme of activities, their governess, their servants.

As the children grew older they were allowed to make friends with a few carefully chosen boys of their own age. Louis-Henri de Brienne, son of the Minister of Foreign Affairs, was seven or eight when he came to play with the king for the first time. The sub-governess, Mme de La Salle, received him at the head of a whole string of children. She had stuck a man's hat with black feathers on her head; a sword was slung round her waist and she was carrying a pike. She was the Sergeant Major. She put a musket over young Brienne's shoulder and, at her command, 'one, two, one, two', the children drilled like soldiers, before the enchanted, applauding king. Even when he was quite small he would beat angrily on an enormous drum like those of the Swiss guards and many of his toys were reminders of war. Brienne gave him a tiny cannon made of gold, drawn by a trained flea, and Louis reciprocated with a cross-bow that had once belonged to his father. He loved nothing better than explosions and the smell of gunpowder. Soon he was given his first rifle and he couldn't wait to learn to fire it. But the children came to play with the king only during their free days – indeed, after a week at school, Brienne began to find it boring having to carry a rifle and march up and down the parquet floors.[3] The rest of the time the king had no other company but that of maids and servants.

Soon everything was to change. On his eighth birthday, he had reached the age when he was to be trained to be a man. One morning he was taken away from his governesses and handed over to his guardian, the Marquis de Villeroi, his tutor, the Abbé Hardouin de Péréfixe, two sub-guardians and two gentlemen. The faithful La Porte, appointed first *valet de chambre* by Anne of Austria in reward for his earlier services to her, replaced the *femmes de chambre* and slept in the king's bedchamber for the first time. As he was putting Louis to bed, the boy asked him timidly to tell him fairy stories as the women had done each night before he went to sleep. La Porte was moved by the little boy's vulnerability and obliged. He even replaced 'Queen Marie' in the same pathetic game of master and servant – but he regarded it as quite improper and used the game to set things straight. One day during the game, he deliberately sat down in a chair and put on his hat. Since Louis had got him to play the master, he would show him how a master behaved. The boy reacted swiftly. In an instant he understood the insult and became the master once more. He went and complained to his mother of La Porte's insolence, but she told him that it served him right for playing servants.[4]

Practically, however, nothing had changed. The king lived in the same solitude and the same deprivation. La Porte was horrified to discover to what a state of neglect the king had been reduced: there were holes in his sheets, his dressing-gown reached only to his knees and his coach was so ancient that it was liable to fall to pieces at any moment. None of the innumerable servants took the slightest notice of the child. Utter laxity reigned supreme. When La Porte complained to the servants, they grumbled but did nothing.[5] The mythical personage of the king, before whom ministers, ambassadors and members of the *parlement* knelt, meant nothing, to them he was no more than an abandoned, vulnerable child. They refused to obey his every whim, told him to go off and play somewhere else, and the neglected child naturally ran to his mother. Confusing the respect justly due to the king and the indulgence of a mother, Anne of Austria refused him nothing. She showed him an outrageous preference over her younger son and during the disputes between the two brothers, she automatically took the side of the elder to teach the younger brother submission.[6]

The difference in Anne's treatment of the two boys may well account for Philippe's later well-attested homosexuality. Much has been made of the fact that he was dressed as a girl well beyond the normal time (boys wore dresses until the age of five at that time) and that while Louis was banished to his own apartments for the good of his education, Philippe remained with his mother and her female companions to be taught docility and other feminine attributes during his entire childhood. In a way there was sense in it; for a start Anne did not want Philippe to represent any sort of threat to Louis in later life, as Gaston d'Orléans had been to Louis XIII. It is possible that Philippe's upbringing in the company of women may have predisposed him to transvestism which he frequently indulged in as an adult, but the opportunity for homosexuality was openly available at the Court for him to take up when he reached his teens. On balance, Philippe probably had a more enjoyable childhood than Louis since he was not subjected to the pressure – and isolation – of learning how to be king.

His upbringing was also less emotionally confusing than Louis' as well. What was a child to make of the constantly fluctuating attention and rejection that he experienced at the hands of his mother? Naturally, the queen's ladies followed her example. Each would vie with the other in spoiling the pretty boy who would one day be their master. They lavished attentions upon him, played with him and went into ecstasies of admiration at the slightest thing he said or did. The boy was, of course, delighted and acquired a taste for feminine company that never left him. He demanded their presence even on the battlefield. He was stiff and formal in the company of men, but with women, whom he imagined to be weak, he was relaxed, warm, agreeable.

Anne was surprised, even disturbed, by the assiduity of her son's visits. His continual presence was almost an embarrassment to her. She did not understand that he came to her apartments to find what he could not find in his own rooms: she herself never set foot there. She did not understand that he had come in search of something that every child needs at that age: simply motherly love. She was quite unaware that when the boy's tutors had retired after solemnly attending the *coucher du roi,* Louis would get up and, without a word, slip into La Porte's bed so as not to have to sleep alone.[7] But with the best will in the world a *valet de chambre* is no substitute for a mother. Louis' lack of affection was soon to shrivel up his heart, and would lead to the later insensitivity which amazed his contemporaries.

Here was a child who daily passed from the pomp of royalty to the sordid circumstances of a character from a novel by Dickens. On ceremonial days he was smothered in satin, feathers and embroidery; he was taken out as if he were the Blessed Sacrament, and at the mere sight of him the crowds would become delirious with enthusiasm; his least gesture, the most ordinary remark, would be commented upon and praised to the heavens. Afterwards he would find himself, like Cinderella, back in patched clothes, eating food cadged from the servants. The first experience gave him a lasting sense of the importance of spectacle – if one had to be a spectacle in order to dominate and submit others to one's will, then let it be so, especially if one had an innate liking for it anyway. The second experience toughened him. Discomfort, hunger, fatigue, cold, sickness were not to exist, often to the dismay of those around him. Having become the most spectacular monarch of his century, he also remained its most Spartan.

One had to be Spartan to live at the Court of Anne of Austria, which was understaffed, badly run, and impoverished almost to the point of penury. But it was well-behaved, which was probably why it did not attract a great many people.[8] The poles of attraction, where real society amused itself, were the palaces of the millionaire princes, the Duc d'Orléans and the Condés. They were the ones with the fabulous inheritances and extensive revenues, while the State coffers, indistinguishable from those of the king, were always empty. The princely families lavished their prodigality, displayed their luxury and supported their innumerable hangers-on. The service at Court was so bad that the queen was not even in a position to receive people properly. When she wanted to entertain the ambassadors from Poland, an argument broke out between the *maîtres d'hôtel*: the boiled meat planned did not appear and the first course was missing. No one was there to meet the Poles, who had to grope their way through the dark to the staircase.[9] Anne scolded everybody, then would burst out laughing: she maintained that nothing would ever work in France, whether important or trivial. She rediscovered this healthy sense of humour every evening when her lady friends would fight with the women who served them over the leftovers of her dinner; the former had nothing else to eat, so they helped themselves out of the queen's dirty plate and even devoured the bread she left; the latter were furious, watching the food disappear that they were in the habit of keeping for the next day; and the queen regent would double up laughing.[10]

Despite these inconveniences the Court was not without its charm. There was a friendly atmosphere, protocol was lax, and the prevailing tone one of spontaneity and gaiety. The queen and her minister shared a taste for entertainment and spectacle – one more thing they had in common. While theatrical performances could be frightful they were generally so successful that one ill-tempered priest, the Curé de Saint-Germain, fulminated against the theatre which he saw as little better than hell. Fearing that the flames might spring up all around her, Anne consulted her bishops, who reassured her; so she would go off to a show at the Palais Royal every evening. The zealous priest returned to the fray: armed with a formal condemnation of irreligious spectacles by the doctors of the Sorbonne, he turned up at the theatre and presented it to her. Not entirely convinced, the queen consulted the learned doctors once again, and without batting an eyelid they came up with the contrary opinion just in time for Mazarin to introduce into France a new kind of spectacle that the Curé would surely find diabolical. The capture of Dunkirk by French troops gave the cardinal the excuse to put on the first opera ever produced in France.[11] Luigi Rossi's *Marriage of Orpheus and Eurydice* was a major production with complicated special effects, continual set changes, magnificent costumes, all serving as a background to a score in the then fashionable Italian manner, interpreted by a Diva, Signora Leonora, imported specially for the occasion. It was an undeniable success. The fashionable world applauded, the religious frowned and the jealous criticized. But *Orpheus* lasted six hours at a stretch and the spectators at first agreeably surprised, eventually became bored, some of them even dozing off. The only spectator to stand the entire course, and the only one who might have been forgiven for not doing so, was the boy king.[12] When everybody else had had enough, he was still listening conscientiously to the end without showing a trace of fatigue. Such stamina could not fail to impress.

The courtiers scrutinized the serious, proud, nine-year-old child, who never lost his dignity or his incredible gravity for a moment. Under the eyes of those he knew were trying to strip him bare, he stiffened and closed up. He noticed everything, but said little: 'He was even prudent enough to say nothing, lest he did not say it well.'[13] He had nothing of the brilliance of his younger brother, Philippe; indeed, he expressed himself in a rather awkward way, but since what he said was of little account, nobody cared very much. If he was treated in a rather off-hand manner by his mother, perhaps preoccupied with her own affairs, he would say nothing, but his silence was accompanied by an appropriate expression on his face. 'Even when playing and amusing himself, the young prince hardly ever laughed,' his companion Brienne remarked. His mother's friend, Mme de Motteville, was surprised by this and the Venetian ambassador remarked upon the fact in a report. He had very little to laugh about, and was anyway discovering what could be gained from this attitude: when his face displayed no emotion and he said nothing, everyone would look at him with anxious curiosity. He realized that the severe, indecipherable mask he had adopted to hide his own fear itself inspired fear in others. At the age of nine he discovered the aura of impressive and vaguely terrifying mystery beneath which he was able to conceal both his unhappiness and weakness.

The disconcerted courtiers seized on the slightest clues. In 1647 a ball was given at Fontainebleau for some visiting foreign princes. Suddenly the usually silent child announced to his mother that he very much wished he were grown up. She asked him why, and he replied that he wanted to be able to rule alone. This remark caused a flurry of excitement. What did it mean? Who had put such ideas into his head? Who was behind it? Who was manipulating him? Anne questioned him unremittingly and an investigation was ordered; the guilty party would have to be brought to justice. (The culprit turned out to be a German gentleman who had simply remarked that his own sovereign, the

Landgrave of Hesse, was fortunate because he was young, handsome and ruled over his own states.) Thus the child king was to remain an enigma for everybody, his mother included, and a formidable enigma for the cardinal prime minister.

Mazarin was not very good with children. The subtle egoist was not interested in the very young; his charms did not work on them. He reserved his seductive powers for adults since children did not count; seen simply as a child, the king was no exception. But there might always be intriguers who could use the king against the cardinal. No precaution was unnecessary; Mazarin surrounded the boy, now ten years old, with a veritable spy network. Having appointed himself superintendent of the royal education, he could keep a watch on the child's guardian and tutors. He examined everything that the child read and was taught in the greatest detail. From the noble Marquis de Villeroi to the laziest of manservants, every member of the royal entourage was turned into a spy; either they wrote reports, which were then sent to Mazarin, or they reported to him direct the slightest thing said or done by the young king. Mazarin selected the children who came to play with Louis and limited their number more and more. The king must remain absolutely innocent of any pernicious influence: in other words kept away from anything that might, directly or indirectly, lead him to doubt the benefits of Mazarin's omnipotence.[14]

And yet, despite all these precautions, Louis had declared that he would like to be old enough to rule himself! Mazarin was beside himself and vented his fury on the unfortunate Villeroi. What was the use of appointing a man one could trust as the king's guardian and then having to listen to the king expressing such wishes. In fact, it was Mazarin himself, not Villeroi, who was to blame. He had won over everyone around the king but forgotten to win over the king himself. Of all the measures that he had taken he had forgotten the most important: to persuade the child to like him. With the acute sensitivity of his age, the young king was perfectly aware of the cardinal's indifference. Seeing him pass in the midst of his glittering cortège, he turned to La Porte and said, with bitter irony, 'There goes the Grand Duke!'[15] All the attention, respect, anxiety of the courtiers, spongers and flatterers went to the minister and not to the child who was well aware that he was the real master. One evening he was sitting on his privy in his dressing-gown when he was warned that Mazarin had just entered his bedchamber to attend the king's *coucher*. The king did not budge. The cardinal was getting impatient, but Louis refused to hurry. The cardinal declared that he had not time to waste and left, followed by his cortège. The king, hearing the commotion, remarked, 'He makes a lot of noise wherever he goes . . .'[16] The minister had given in and Louis had won. Only La Porte knew how much Louis hated the man who never had time for him but who monopolized the attention if not the heart of his mother.

It may have been partly to cheer him and soften him up that Mazarin brought from Italy several delightful companions of the boy's own age.

Through his two sisters, Mazarin had a string of nephews and nieces, and of these Paolo Mancini and his two sisters, and one of the Martinozzi daughters, had already joined the Court. While the courtiers observed these dark and petulant children with amused curiosity, the king gave them a chilly reception. At his *coucher* he obstinately refused to hand the candlestick – a great favour – to the Mancini boy to hold, for his hatred of Mazarin extended to his nephew.

Mazarin was also in charge of the king's education. But needless to say affairs of state took precedence and the boy was left to fend for himself. The result was an education which was strangely inadequate. He was taught Latin well enough (he particularly excelled in translation), a little mathematics, Italian and Spanish; he was encouraged in sporting and artistic pursuits: swimming, dancing, drawing, the guitar,[17] but his education stopped there. No history, no geography, no economics, no law, all of which were necessary if he were to assume the responsibilities that awaited him – not to mention the general cultivation of his mind. 'He had hardly been taught to read and write,' declared the Duc de Saint-Simon, exaggerating somewhat. However it was generally thought that Louis had been left in crass ignorance and, as a result, he would say things as an adult that were unthinkable for an educated man, gaffs which merely increased an inferiority complex that nothing could remove.

Yet he was willing enough. He would hang on La Porte's lips when his guardian put him on his knee and told him in secret the history of the kings, his ancestors and predecessors. And the child shook with fury when the faithful *valet de chambre* predicted that he would be a second Louis the Idle if he did not work harder.[18] This reference of La Porte's to the Merovingian king reputed for his laziness haunted the boy, since much later he was to write in his memoirs: 'Even from childhood, the very mention of the *rois fainéants* . . . troubled me . . .'[19] And it was a fact, as his companion Brienne was later to maintain, that the young king was rather lazy, though he concealed this fault beneath a no less deep desire to learn.[20] How could such shortcomings develop in a child surrounded by devoted servants, a loving mother and an overlord – Mazarin – anxious to educate him?

During Louis XIII's lifetime Anne of Austria, constantly threatened with being separated from her children, insisted that no one was better qualified than her to educate them. When confronted with her responsibilities, however, she soon realized her inadequacies, became anxious and, again, handed over the whole thing to Mazarin, reserving only the children's religious education for herself. She excelled in this domain with the help of Spanish and Habsburg fanaticism. A faith that was unquestioned, which would stand no deviation, which demanded of everyone the same adhesion, practice that was continual and ostentatious and which assured the satisfaction of conscience, such was the demanding, intransigent, omnipresent and bigoted religion that Anne inculcated in her son. She was incapable of teaching him anything else, whereas Mazarin, trained in the school of study, taste and experience, could.

However, Mazarin's shortcomings in devising Louis's education could have had other reasons aside from pressure of work. When a properly educated king had reached adolescence, he might well find that he could do without his prime minister. He might think about things and gain in self-assurance, thus running the risk of challenging the authority of that same prime minister. He might prepare himself for the day when he could rule alone – and a study of history would provide him with plenty of examples. So Mazarin showed marked displeasure at the secret history lessons that La Porte lavished on the child.[21] It seems therefore that there was a deliberate intention on the part of the prime minister to leave his ward in ignorance. He wanted to turn the young king into an honest man with a basic education, who would nevertheless remain dependent on him. The king's guardian and tutors were given the strictest instructions not to spoil this fine programme with excessive zeal.

Villeroi, the boy's guardian, was appalled. He was bitterly aware of the inadequacies of Louis's education and detected his pupil's desire to learn, his openness of mind, his good intentions. But he was forced to leave the ground fallow. He could not do anything, for he was merely a blind instrument in the hands of the cardinal prime minister. However, he lost no opportunity of bringing to the king any man 'who excelled in some science or art' and he tried to educate the young king indirectly by recounting his life, and by describing events and persons he had known. Villeroi was cultured and intelligent, kindly and well-intentioned, but he was also a courtier of boundless flexibility who found himself in an impossible position. On the one hand, his duty was to do as Mazarin told him; on the other, he did not wish to upset his pupil, his future master. Indeed his compliance sometimes cost him dear. One day the child was amusing himself, jumping up and down on his bed. Villeroi did not dare to tell him to stop. The inevitable happened . . . the king fell and banged his head against a rail. Little harm was done, but Villeroi was so paralysed with fear that he sat for a quarter of an hour, unable either to move or speak.[22] This culpable indulgence, combined with real kindness, made the otherwise neglected child very fond of his guardian. Villeroi took advantage of this fact to introduce his own son François, six years younger than the king, as a companion. The king instantly adopted the boy and, to the end of his days, displayed a very special attachment to him.

A grumbling La Porte, on the other hand, tried to dissipate the poisoned vapour of adulation that was already rising round the child-king: Louis would be the master, he repeated, only when he was worthy to be so. But he was wasting his time. The boy carefully copied out, in his tall, firm handwriting, the sample writing that had been given to him: 'Homage is due to kings: they do as they please.' He was nine years old when he translated from French into Latin the sentence: 'So I must always remember that I am a king.' Already, ambitious courtiers with an eye on the future were slipping in their doses of flattery. What child would not be delighted when his tutor wrote to him: 'God has given you an advantage ... that majestic presence, that almost divine air and bearing, that height and beauty worthy of the empire of the world that attracts all eyes and the respect of all those to whom Your Majesty shows himself.'[23]

It was natural, then, that Mazarin should try to stifle this pernicious chorus. In the long term, flattery might give the king a false idea of his importance, to the detriment of his prime minister. Mazarin also wanted to give his ward a solid moral base. He wished to keep him in ignorance, but he also wished him to be 'virtuous', and his tutors were instructed to stress this aspect. But stifling the boy's natural generosity does not seem to have been very conducive towards virtue. Mazarin did not even let Louis have a *sou* to give to the beggars who swarmed the streets of Saint-Germain and whose very sight terrified the child. The cardinal's meanness went further; he confiscated the hundred *louis* that the Minister of Finance had set aside for the king's pocket money, and when the king went to ask him for part of it to pay back a servant who had bought him a pair of gloves, he refused. La Porte remembered that the child blushed and stammered when he admitted later that he would not be able to pay back the money borrowed.[24] This ridiculous debt profoundly humiliated him, as did the feeling of his own powerlessness, especially as flatterers led him to believe that he alone was master. How could he resist flattery when it offered so comforting an illusion before such a bitter reality? What contradictory feelings the boy must have felt, shamelessly neglected and ridiculously praised, spoilt and humiliated, and always, in the last resort, alone.

One evening in 1647 he complained of feeling ill. The next day he had a fever, and two days later smallpox appeared. It was only the mild, infantile form of the disease and the queen took it philosophically: at worst only the king's looks would be affected. She took up residence in his apartments while the courtiers, terrified of contagion, deserted the royal palace. The disease seemed to follow its normal course, so the queen went out to attend mass at Notre Dame one morning without worrying. But then the king suddenly fainted and the fever increased alarmingly. Next day his condition grew worse and the day after that everyone gave up hope. If the king died and Anne was prevented from taking on the new regency, the Duc d'Orléans would assume power as regent of France and, why not, king. All that was needed was to remove the younger son Philippe and long live Gaston I! Such views were openly voiced at a scandalous reception given by the duke at the Luxembourg.[25] For his part, Mazarin was so worried that he contacted the Abbé Rivière, Orléans' powerful favourite; the Abbé would get a cardinal's hat if he persuaded his master to bring back Anne of Austria's regency after the young king's death. Meanwhile, at the Palais Royal, the doctors were simply awaiting the child's death. It was a miracle that he had survived at all after the four bleedings that they had given him. Anne was beside herself, though in public she had to conceal her fears. Almost stifled with grief, she sat at the bedside of her unconscious son. Then at last at midnight the fever subsided, and the smallpox marks appeared. The child was saved, and only the prescriptions of the doctors could now delay recovery. So great was the relief at knowing that he was safe that in a great outburst of reconciliation the plotting and intrigue about his succession were forgotten.

Throughout his illness the king had once more impressed all his attendants. His patience and courage, the gentleness he showed his mother and his servants, were clearly those of an older child. His cool bravery in the face of death belonged to the image that the seventeenth century in general and the aristocracy in particular attributed to their leaders. Now the boy attained heroic stature, even if custom – and the theatre – forced it upon him. Already, as a child, Louis XIV revealed the courage in adversity that gave substance to his haughty mien.

Hardly had he recovered, however, than his talent was requisitioned for another spectacular performance given by the monarchy, for a new *lit de justice*, on 15 January 1648. He was puffy and red-faced: the disease had obviously impaired his looks and he had lost that lily-white complexion that Mme de Motteville found so useful to his role. But the government could not wait much longer; it had to make an urgent request to the *parlement* for new credits for the war. The soldiers, unpaid for months, had deserted and returned to Paris, forming gangs of looters that terrified the city. To this was added political unrest that had been springing up for several weeks: violent demonstrations against taxes, calls to revolt. In Paris shots had been fired on the constabulary.

It was in this climate that the monarch once again had to listen to the words of Omer Talon: 'You are, Sire, our sovereign lord ... but your glory requires that we be free men and not slaves. To be king of France is to reign over men of heart, over free souls and not over convicts ... For ten years now, Sire, the countryside has been in ruins, the peasants reduced to sleeping on straw, their furniture sold to pay taxes, which they still cannot pay and, so that Paris may live in luxury, millions of innocent souls are forced to live off bread and bran ... The wretches own nothing but their souls and these only because they could not be sold at auction ...'

The courtiers were outraged by this subversive tone. The government refused to take it seriously however: what it needed was money, not criticism. So it reintroduced a tax paid by magistrates: the *paulette*. The gentlemen of the law reacted at once and the members of the *parlement*, though excused the *paulette*, joined them. The machine finally broke down; the government issued orders, the *parlement* protested, contradictory propositions were offered, useless conferences took place, individuals were exiled, and others recalled from exile. The princes entered the fray, blaming each other, and the Duc de Beaufort, who was still held prisoner at Vincennes, took advantage of the chaos to escape, using acrobatic techniques worthy of an adventure story. The people, at its wits' end, called on the *parlementaires* to help; they answered the call at once.

Stubbornly retrogressive in their thinking, determined not to bear any new tax whatsoever, constantly and resolutely negative in attitude, the members of the *parlement* saw themselves as Roman senators, destined to cleanse Mazarin's Augean stables. Faced with this flood of demands, the cardinal was ready to drop everything, as was his way: retreat before a frontal attack, then undermine, divide, wear down the enemy. And, anyway, Mazarin was a timorous man. '*Mio fratello e un coglione* ('My brother has no balls') – make a lot of noise and he'll run away', one of his brothers once said of him. But this time Mazarin had to take account of the queen. She was determined not to give up the smallest crumb of the royal authority that she held in trust and she intended to hand it over intact to her son. Despite the infinite latitude she left her minister, despite her sense of her own inadequacy, she reacted strongly. Mazarin soon lost his temper. What did that lazy woman know about affairs of state? Why couldn't she leave everything to him as usual? Anne of Austria stuck to her guns, though without losing her gentleness of manner. Mazarin was unable to understand that the queen despised the middle-class *parlementaires*; for her, there were only two ways of dealing with them: exile and prison.

But could she still use these two weapons? The people, convinced that only violent change would relieve its misery, would not hear of it. As Louis XIV passed on his way in great pomp to yet another *lit de justice*, for the first time no cry of 'Long live the King' was heard. It was bad enough that Mazarin should be cursed and the queen hated, but that their unpopularity should extend to the child, the potent symbol of monarchy, was really serious. What was more to the point, the coffers were empty. The king's cooks, tired of not being paid, went on strike, and the queen had to pawn the crown jewels and borrow from private individuals to pay the more urgent debts: the Princesse de Condé came up with 100,000 *livres* and the immensely rich Duchesse d'Aiguillon, Richelieu's niece, also lent money – and not without some ironic pleasure – to the queen who not so long ago had wanted to exile her.

Powerless to act in these conditions, the prime minister could only make concessions to the *parlement*, which came too late and which were merely admissions of weakness. Giving free rein to their audacity and imagination, the *parlementaires*, with the members of the other sovereign Courts, passed a declaration consisting of twenty-seven propositions intended to strip the monarchy of much of its administrative, financial and judicial powers, and which would turn it virtually into a parliamentary monarchy. To consider such a development at that time was revolutionary indeed. At the time the government could do nothing except agree to discuss these propositions at meetings in which the *parlement* openly poured scorn on it. Then, on 21 August 1648, in the early hours of the morning, a citizen of Arras arrived in Paris. A great battle had taken place on the outskirts of his city, he declared, for he had heard the cannon. He did not know whether it was victory or defeat, but he had not seen any Frenchmen deserting the field. It was a good sign, and Mazarin sent a messenger to awaken the queen with the news. Doubts remained, but she was convinced at once that it was a victory, and if so, it could get them out of their difficulties. All day she was on tenterhooks awaiting confirmation of the news. At midnight, as she was undressing to retire to bed, the Comte de Chatillon arrived with a despatch from the front. The Duc d'Enghien, who had become Prince de Condé at the death of his father and who was doing everything he could to earn the title of 'Le Grand Condé', had just crushed the Spanish at Lens; there were three thousand dead, an 'incredible' number of wounded and five thousand enemy prisoners. The Palais Royal erupted with joy, but it was no less a person than the boy king himself who remarked, 'Those gentlemen in the *parlement* will be very angry at the news.' The *parlementaires* were simply sowers of discord, traitors to the nation; that, at least, was what the child heard around him every day. If they were democrats, there was no point in listening to them. In the opinion of his mother, what was needed was strong government, without concessions and without limitations.

The queen regent ordered a *Te Deum* at Notre Dame to celebrate the victory of Lens. At the very time Court and City were assembled in the cathedral, a lieutenant of the guards, the Comte de Comminges, was visiting a member of the *parlement* named Broussel, an honest, elderly man who was, in the opinion of the Grande Mademoiselle, an old fool. But what she and others in the Court did not realize was that he had become the idol of the Parisian crowd, and his reputation was high in the *parlement*. He was recognized and applauded by ordinary people in the street simply because he was known to have criticized the government.

The street in which Broussel lived was very narrow, so the Comte de Comminges left his coach at the corner, continued the rest of the way on foot and knocked at the door. A servant boy let him in. Comminges ran up the stairs four at a time and found Broussel eating with his family. Comminges informed the president that by order of the king he was under arrest, along with two other presidents, de Blancmesnil and Charton, who together were considered to be the ringleaders of the opposition. Broussel looked worried and mumbled an excuse: he could not move, he had taken a purgative. Couldn't they wait before taking him away? His old servant woman rushed to the window and shouted for help: they were arresting her good master, they were going to take him away. Windows opened, doors banged, neighbours came out, the street filled with people, and before long a riot had broken out. Comminges, alarmed, threatened Broussel with death if he did not follow him, incontinent or not. He dragged him away from his family, pushed him down the stairs and pulled him into the street, protected against the vociferous and threatening crowd by a few guards. He had just enough time to hoist him into the coach, and had to go a roundabout way in the neighbouring streets, at the risk of being stopped at every moment by the crowd. With great difficulty, Comminges and his prisoner finally arrived at Saint-Germain, where the queen regent had decided recalcitrant *parlementaires* would be detained.[26]

Paris had already taken to the streets, demonstrating and setting up barricades. At this point Monseigneur Paul de Gondi, the future Cardinal de Retz, came on the scene. More vain than ambitious, the prelate had been waiting for just such a moment. Going out into the packed streets in cape and mantle, blessing the crowd for all he was worth, he preached peace and tried to calm the more violent demonstrators, but without much success. Paris preferred to vomit its hate for Mazarin and Anne of Austria than to listen to Monseigneur de Retz, so night fell without bringing any change, and he repaired to the Palais Royal to ask that Broussel be freed. His request was, of course, refused and Paris and France had entered a period of anarchy known to history as the *Fronde*. (The word literally means catapult or sling, the weapon of the street mob, and it was first used as a term of insult. But as the years of civil war progressed, the *frondeurs* adopted the term and were proud to wear sashes or belts embroidered with a little *fronde* emblem.)

After the first day of unrest, Chancellor Séguier, accompanied by his brother, the Bishop of Meaux, and his daughter, the Duchesse de Sully, left his town house at five the next morning, bound for the *parlement* with instructions to calm the situation. At the Pont Neuf a group of rough-looking Parisians stopped his coach. 'Free Broussel or else …,' they shouted. The chancellor wisely ordered the coachman to proceed by a different route. He just had time to knock at the nearby house of the Duc de Luynes; everyone was asleep, except an old servant woman who sized up the situation immediately and hid them in a small wooden shed. The demonstrators broke down the doors of the house, waking the Duc de Luynes who appeared, terrified, in his nightshirt. Monsieur le Duc was reassured that they wanted neither him nor his wealth but simply the chancellor, who was hiding in his house. They would like to make a proper search. 'Prisoner for prisoner,' yelled the demonstrators, who wanted to exchange the chancellor for Broussel. The chancellor, hearing everything from his hiding place and convinced that his last hour had come, made his confession to his brother the bishop. At this point a marshal and two companies of Swiss guards arrived to rescue the prisoners who were then conducted home. As their coach passed the Pont Neuf once more the frustrated demonstrators fired on them. A few soldiers fell, shot dead, and a bullet went through the Duchesse de Sully's arm. The crowd then proceeded to ransack the duke's house.

At the Palais Royal the regent received a delegation of *parlementaires*.

They, too, demanded Broussel's freedom but she refused categorically and left them, slamming the door. The first president ran after her, begging her to change her mind, but the queen still refused, and the *parlementaires* trooped back, downcast. In the Rue Saint Honoré, they were stopped by a barricade. 'Where's Broussel?' they were asked. Demonstrators pointed their pistols at the first president, jeering at him, threatening him. The *parlementaires* quietly turned back and returned to the Palais Royal to ask once more that Broussel be freed. Beside herself with rage, the queen was then forced to give in and Broussel was released. The delighted crowd brought Broussel to Notre Dame for an improvised *Te Deum*, ridiculing the pomp of state ceremonies. The old man had the tact to avoid it and left by a side door, returning home to the protection of his supporters.

Calm had scarcely returned when two cartloads of gunpowder intended for the guards entered Paris by the Porte Saint-Antoine. The crowd immediately jumped to the conclusion that they were going to be shot down, so the disturbances started up all over again. About seven in the evening a new riot broke out, nearby in the Rue Saint Honoré. The crowd besieged the Palais Royal with the intention of setting fire to it. The queen was warned: there were not enough guards to defend the palace. Mazarin was so scared that he was useless. He had changed into a grey costume in order not to be recognized and had given orders to have his horses ready for immediate departure. The new captain of the guards, the Marquis de Jarzé, did nothing to raise morale: 'Madame, there are only a handful of us here and we shall die at your door.' Anne of Austria paled and the seriousness of the situation finally dawned on her. But in the midst of the general confusion she refused to show the slightest weakness, alone remaining calm right through the long night. But she was not the only one. The king, too, kept his *sang-froid* which was truly extraordinary for a child. His younger brother Philippe, on the other hand, trembled with fear and refused to remain alone in his room. The older boy took him under his wing, drew his tiny sword to defend him if need be, and calmed him with encouraging words.[27] A king should never be afraid, even at ten years old; or if he is, he should hide it.

At last day broke and calm reasserted itself. And whereas in Paris things got back to usual, hundreds of kilometres away, in Germany, the bells were ringing and heralds announcing at the street corners that a European peace had just been signed. By concluding the so-called Treaties of Westphalia on 24 October 1648, the representatives of France, Sweden, the Teutonic Holy Roman Empire and the German princes put an end to a war that had lasted for thirty years, which gave it its general name of the Thirty Years War. France gained important territories in Alsace and Lorraine, but she kept an enemy, Spain, which rejected the peace. Nor was there peace in Paris, where the *parlement,* its appetite whetted by its earlier successes, returned to the attack from September onwards with a whole new set of demands. The example of

England did not help: a foolishly absolutist king, Charles I, had set himself against a parliament that would not compromise its principles and actually raised armies against the sovereign, defeated him, took him prisoner and tried him for crimes against the constitution and democracy. In short, republicanism was in the air and the contagion might spread to France. One had only to look at the growing pressure exerted by the *parlement*. The queen could not stand much more: 'Truly, if I consented to such demands and allowed the authority of the king to be eroded to such a point, my son would become no more than a playing-card king.' Anything but that.

The way things were going in Paris, however, did not bode well. On 5 January 1649 Mme de Motteville went to sup at the Palais Royal. She found the queen in her small study, quietly watching the king at play. Motteville had no sooner sat down than the Duchesse de La Trémoille came over to her: 'There's a rumour going around Paris that the queen is leaving tonight.' The queen had announced that next day she would visit her favourite convent of the Val-de-Grâce, and the palace was beginning to empty. Courtiers only made cursory appearances before leaving to dine at the Gramonts'. Soon no one was left in the room except the queen, her eldest son, Motteville, her sister and another lady. Anne calmly suggested cutting the Twelfth Night cake. Mme de Motteville dismissed as nonsense the idea that the queen was leaving Paris that night. The ladies waited to see her in bed before saying goodnight, then went themselves to bed. Mme de Motteville had scarcely left the palace before she heard the gates shut for the night. Cardinal Mazarin was in his apartments and went on playing cards with his friends.

At four in the morning there was a knock on the door of Motteville's apartment. Still half asleep, she went to answer it. It was one of her friends, a servant in Mazarin's employ. The queen, the king and the entire royal family had fled Paris and were on their way to Saint-Germain, he announced. He himself had come to fetch her with a coach and six, to take her to rejoin the court. Motteville was too tired, refused the offer and went back to bed.

The moon was still shining as the sky grew pale. In the royal coaches galloping on the road to Saint-Germain, everyone was gleefully retelling the details of his or her flight. Villeroi had let the king and his brother sleep until three o'clock, then he got them up, dressed them and took them to the gate of the palace gardens where they were to await the queen and the coaches. The Orléans, Condés and the Prince de Conti soon joined them. Shortly before, Mazarin had sent his nieces and, some say, his treasure out of Paris. Everything was working perfectly, everything, that is, except the small matter of accommodation.

On arrival at Saint-Germain they found the place empty and cold. The windows were all broken and the freezing January wind blew through the entire building from one room to another. First they went to mass, then the day was spent seeking out and questioning new arrivals. The establishment was in a parlous state: no furniture, no servants, no clean clothes, for no proper packing had been done, so as not to arouse suspicion. The king of France in his Château de Saint-Germain did not have a clean shirt to put on. The courtiers argued over a few bales of straw that they had cadged for themselves in the city, the price rising dizzily in a few hours. Prudent as always, a few days before Mazarin had arranged for four camp beds to be sent to Saint-Germain intended for the queen, the king, Philippe and, of course, Mazarin himself. The rest would have to fend for themselves. The Duchesse d'Orléans slept on straw and the Grande Mademoiselle, installed in a superb bedchamber, all gilt and tapestry, but without a fire in the chimney or glass in the windows, had to share a mattress on the floor with her sister, a rather restless sleeper.[28]

The news of the royal flight spread through Paris from six o'clock in the morning, causing confusion and anger everywhere. The bourgeoisie exploded with insults and curses against the régime, while the aristocracy thought only of leaving. But the mob prevented them and very soon the gates of Paris were guarded by hostile volunteers: 'No one leaves.' At the Palais Royal, demonstrators prevented the king's baggage from leaving and then the old instinct arose at the sight of carts overloaded with fugitives: 'At them! Go for them!' And in a moment coffers and chests were thrown onto the pavement, broken open and emptied.

Aware that they had gone too far, the parlementaires were worried. Feigning surprise, they sent a deputation to Saint-Germain. Why had the queen fled Paris? Was there anything that had displeased her? When Anne refused even to receive them, the parlementaires returned, no longer downcast but determined. Since there was no way of being heard, they had no option but to resist. They began by drawing up an insolent decree declaring Cardinal Mazarin a public enemy and ordering his prosecution.

Government and opposition had become two entrenched camps. With the government were half the royal family, a large part of the aristocracy, the army and one general, Condé. On the side of the rebellion was another general of the same calibre, the Vicomte de Turenne, the parlement, the capital and its bourgeoisie and several important aristocrats who, seeing an opportunity for political influence, made their presence felt and became the stars if not the leaders of the movement: the Duc de Beaufort, of course, revenging his detention, Monseigneur de Retz, and the Duc de Bouillon, Turenne's brother.

The government's aim was nothing less than to lay siege to Paris, starve it out and bring it to heel. But there were not enough troops for an effective siege and it had to be content with sending patrols to block the main outlets. In Paris, however, steps were being taken to place the city on a defensive footing. It was decided, then, to take the Bastille (even then a key position), which was still held by the royalists. The Rue Saint-Antoine was filled with coaches belonging to ladies who had come to admire the exploit. Old cannon were trundled out, a few shots were fired off at random and the governor of the formidable fortress, the Sieur du Tremlay, asked to capitulate. The *parlement,* encouraged by this initial success, raised an army, but as it had no money it had to levy extraordinary taxes. Having already sold off the cardinal prime minister's art collection at auction, Monseigneur de Retz in person managed to drag before the *parlement* a man who knew where the old skinflint had locked away his gold and silver table services. They were worth 900,000 *livres* in all. Next to be dealt with were his supporters at Court, who were nicknamed the 'Mazarins'. They were taken prisoner, then ransomed quite shamelessly, but the notion of 'Mazarin' broadened considerably and soon the rich bourgeois, who were far from being supporters of the Court, also found themselves heavily taxed which soon gave rise to violent protests. Carried away by zeal and a desperate desire to be noticed, Monseigneur de Retz mounted the pulpit in the church of Saint-Paul and before a huge congregation proposed seizing private individuals' silver tableware and melting it down. He went even further, suggesting that the same should be done with the gold and silver valuables of the monasteries and convents. The well-to-do thought that he had really gone too far, especially as the populace was getting more and more out of control. They were ransoming royalists or those of them who were worth it, ransacking and looting their houses. The blockade of the city was beginning to have its effect. The winter was particularly hard, so much so that the Seine froze over. Supply convoys were regularly intercepted, the price of bread rose daily, and with it the temper of the mob. House searches and confiscations, threats and molestings became ever more common, in flagrant disregard of the law. The mob, enraged by hunger, dealt harshly with all those suspected of being royalists. Some tried to flee in the most varied disguises. Mme de Motteville tried her luck along with her sister, but the volunteers guarding the Porte Saint-Honoré pushed them back roughly. The crowd became threatening and the two women ran back, not stopping till they had reached Saint-Roch. There they rushed into the church, kneeling breathlessly before the high altar where high mass was being celebrated, and followed by the crowd which continued to insult them. The parish priest arrived; he had difficulty making himself heard, but he eventually managed to calm the crowd and led the two women back to their apartments.[29]

By contrast, another of the great ladies of the aristocracy moved in this purely revolutionary atmosphere like a fish in water. Anne Geneviève de Bourbon Condé, Duchesse de Longueville was a superb, fair-haired woman, celebrated for her glowing complexion and her magnificent eyes, blue 'like a pair of turquoises'. A sensual, lazy woman, she suddenly emerged from the respectable idleness in which she had hitherto confined herself. Convinced by her lover, La

Rochefoucauld, that she had a role to play, she threw herself into the rebellion to spite the royalist general, her brother Condé, whose incestuous mistress it was murmured she had once been. An amusing idea occurred to her: she would prise from the Court her other brother, Conti, also accused of being her lover. And while she was at it, why could she not also remove her husband from the royalists? Conti and Longueville responded to the beautiful woman's first appeal, quietly left Saint-Germain and galloped to Paris, where they were received in triumph. Meanwhile, her other brother, Condé, cut to the quick, was determined to be revenged. He set out at the head of his army to attack Charenton, one of the few points at which Paris could still be entered. Despite a heroic defence on the part of the garrison, he continued on his way, seized the village and massacred everyone in it, villagers and soldiers alike. As the prisoners were thrown into the Seine, he shouted after them: 'Go and see your *parlement!*' Then, somewhat calmer, he drew up his troops in battle order opposite the *parlement*'s army which had come, rather too late in the day, to the assistance of Charenton. But the soldiers that the *parlement* had raised at great expense had no stomach for a fight. Condé, for his part, had had Charenton and two thousand corpses to appease his anger. So the two armies, after eyeing one another for a time, withdrew without a fight.

As the siege bit deeper, Paris was starving, and it could be felt at every social level. To make matters worse the Seine flooded, turning the streets into canals. Queen Anne made the absurd gesture of selling a pair of diamond earrings, and having the proceeds secretly distributed to the poorest Parisians who every day cursed her name.[30]

The leaders of the rebellion, following the old tradition of all dissidents in the past, called on the help of a foreign enemy, on this occasion the Spanish. Seizing the opportunity, Spain sent an emissary to Paris and arrangements were made for him to be received in the *parlement*. There were still some men with consciences however: 'Is it possible, Monsieur, that a prince of the blood royal of France should offer a seat upon the *fleur de lys* to a deputy of its most cruel enemy?' exclaimed de Mesme to the Prince de Conti, as Retz smiled on ironically. Similarly, wise spirits were aware that with or without the help of the Spaniards the adventure could not fail to end in disaster. Discreet contacts began to take place between representatives of the majority of the *parlementaires* and emissaries of the government.

Official negotiations between the *parlement* and the Court opened in March 1649 at the Château de Rueil. But the *parlementaires* obstinately refused to speak to Mazarin, whose removal and arrest Paris was still demanding. As if to give weight to this demand, at the very moment when talks about peace were beginning, the furniture and library lovingly collected by the cardinal were being sold off in the streets of Paris. Finally, after laborious bargaining, an accommodation was worked out and the *parlementaires* at last sat opposite Mazarin.

At this point, news arrived that made the *parlementaires* much more conciliatory. Turenne, who had wanted to help the rebellion in the middle of a war, was deserted by his soldiers, who, under the command of a German royalist general, moved over to the service of the government. The wheel had turned full circle for the *parlementaires*. With little real force to back them, they might go on haggling about details, but on 11 March 1649 Mazarin sent a messenger to the queen announcing that agreement had almost been reached.

That was not the end of the matter however. The *parlementaires* who had attended the conferences were ill-received when they returned to Paris. To compensate for this vilification, the leaders of the rebellion began to pile one extravagant claim upon another. They were not opposed to a settlement, but the government would have to pay the price: lucrative offices, wealthy abbeys, accumulated pensions, enormous tips, various decorations and honours, nothing satisfied their appetite. The queen wept with rage; people who had wanted to dethrone her son were now asking for rewards. Meanwhile it was learnt that enemy troops, called to the assistance of these same rebels, had entered France. Public opinion, which had had its fill of war, finally turned against those members of the aristocracy whose only aim was to satisfy their own interests. Indifferent to this change of heart the nobles continued to make more staggering demands until they reached the point that they themselves were riddled with division and mutual mistrust. It was only then that an agreement could be made between the government and the rebels. On Ash Wednesday 1649 the queen was attending the office of *Tenebrae* in the chapel at Saint-Germain when a messenger brought her news that a real settlement had been concluded.

Eventually the Court prepared to return to Paris. What a spectacle awaited them as they approached the capital: whole villages abandoned, everything looted and pillaged. The countryside was little more than a desert, but at Saint-Denis a crowd assembled and the horrors of war gave way to the street decoration of a joyful return. Even those who had taken up arms against the king and the ordinary people who had cursed him night and day now turned out to welcome him. The enthusiasm accorded well with the temperature. In the unbearable heat and the stifling dust of August all that could be heard were shouts of 'Long live the king'; there were cheers for the queen mother. People held out their hands to her, rhapsodized on her beauty, swore that they loved her in spite of everything. Even Mazarin was welcomed, and praised for bringing Louis back. Sceptical at the sight of these demonstrations, Mme de Motteville concluded that the cardinal must have paid dearly for his own welcome. The crowd was so dense, so enthusiastic, that soon the royal coach was cut off from its escort and the procession could not move forward. Crammed with six other persons into the queen's coach, the Grande Mademoiselle, dripping with sweat and dead with fatigue, grew increasingly bored and ill-tempered. It had taken them five hours to cover the three and a half or so miles between Le Bourget and the city gates.[31]

CHAPTER 3

The Struggle for Power

In view of the sympathetic welcome accorded the royal family by the Parisian crowds another *Te Deum* was arranged at Notre Dame. The enthusiasm of the capital for its monarch was given a further boost, and among those who cheered the loudest were the fishwives of the Marché Neuf, the very same who had shouted loudest against the government. In an attempt to carry the young king themselves, they mounted an assault on the coach and as they all attempted to grab him they tore his silk clothes to shreds.

This enthusiasm did not prevent the most violent tracts from circulating. Some of them declared that the people had a just right to wage war on their kings and to change laws and dynasties by force of arms, and such subversive ideas could be read in the capital at the very moment that the embodiment of a seemingly immutably absolute monarchy was being welcomed by all. Authority, however it manifested itself, was being openly mocked. In the regions most affected by penury, people refused to pay taxes and controlled foodstuffs like salt were being sold freely without the constabulary daring to intervene. Customs offices were attacked, the royal forests were being stripped by thieves and smugglers had never been so prosperous. Like the country, the Court was also sinking into bankruptcy: the crown jewels were still being held by moneylenders, and there was nothing left to pay anybody. Pages had to be sent back to their families, servants refused to work and plates sometimes remained empty because tradesmen's bills were not paid.

Money was scarce, but it went on being spent as before. On 5 September, for the king's eleventh birthday the city of Paris decided to arrange a magnificent entertainment in his honour. Food was as abundant as in the old days and the ladies, on the express instructions of the queen, wore all their jewellery. Dancing took place during the day, which was extremely curious for a formal ball. But this was on the queen's orders; she feared the night, knowing what a tempting target she was for possible assassins among the temporarily pacified rebels. A measure of confidence was returning, however, though it was still difficult to tell who could be trusted. The provinces, sensing that they were no longer under the control of Paris, were seething with unrest.

Normandy reacted first, despite Mazarin's efforts. In Provence, the *parlement* at Aix remained in open struggle against the Comte d'Alais, the governor of the province. Reims, exasperated with the governor of Champagne, quite simply took him prisoner. Then Bordeaux revolted against its governor, the Duc d'Epernon, who fired four thousand cannon shots on the city. The rebels attacked the government's representatives, who hit back at the rebels: Spain, called in by the rebels, benefited, while France paid the bill. Epidemics spread rapidly in the unhealthy atmosphere. In three months the plague had caused 17,000 deaths at Rouen alone, while at Marseille 12,000 deaths were estimated.

The Spaniards had to be added to the epidemics. After a month the inhabitants of the northern cities chose to flee into the woods and to live off roots rather than live under their occupation. For their part, the government's troops had no wish to go short. Mazarin found an extremely simple way of feeding his troops: he left them to loot the regions they passed through. An order was given to generals and governors to allow their soldiers to act as they thought fit – for the good of France. German mercenaries were particularly good at this. Torturing priests, burning the soles of peasants' feet to extract money from them, raping girls between eight and twelve years old under the eyes of their parents were part of their daily activities. They often showed imagination. Slaughtering an old woman in her bed, they replaced her with a goat, which they dressed in her bonnet, then summoned the priest to administer the last rites to the animal.[1] Notwithstanding, Mazarin congratulated their commander, Erlach, on his victories and the queen of France begged him to remain at the head of her army.

There was indiscipline, too, at Court. The Marquis de Jarzé claimed to be in love with the queen, and duly sighed, grew thin, languished. Anne of Austria knew nothing of the whole business, but the cardinal prime minister was informed and, to everyone's surprise, manifested a fit of jealousy. It was not that he was in love with her himself, Mme de Motteville explained, but that he was 'like a miser when someone wants to deprive him of his treasure'. He informed his 'treasure' of de Jarzé's passion and the queen laughed in his face. He insisted, however, that she dismiss her first *femme de chambre,* Mme de Beauvois, whom he accused of having fabricated the whole affair, and the queen did so, much to Mme de Beauvois' astonishment. Anne of Austria had been irritated by the whole incident. Seeing her 'admirer', she remarked in front of everybody: 'Really, Monsieur de Jarzé, you really are quite ridiculous. They tell me you are playing the lover! Just take a look at this handsome young gallant! I pity you with all my heart!' Jarzé turned pale, then green, mumbled something and staggered out in disgrace. But the Prince de Condé was a friend of Jarzé's and took up his cause. He took him into his own house, declaring that the queen no longer knew what she was doing and that he would see that his friend was respected; he even demanded that she receive Jarzé and forgive him.[2] The *parlement* and the *Fronde*, eager for just such an opportunity, joined in the fray.

The Duc de Beaufort, President Broussel and Monseigneur de Retz carefully laid their plans. One night they took the doublet of a fellow *frondeur* called Joly, stuffed it with straw, fixed it on a wooden dummy and fired a few pistol shots into the empty sleeve, while Joly himself made a small wound on his own arm with gunflint. Next morning, as Joly was walking through the Rue des Bernardins, an explosion was heard and Joly fell to the ground, shouting, 'Quick! A doctor!' The story spread quickly: he was wounded, dying; it was an assassination attempt. His followers moved through Paris, spreading the news that the government was assassinating a former *frondeur*. Broussel suggested locking the city gates; the Marquis de la Boulaye and his friends ran through the streets, crying, 'To arms, down with the traitor Mazarin!' But the subterfuge was a bit crude, and most people were not taken in.[3]

Far from discouraged, the conspirators went back to work. That same evening a merchant warned one of the Prince de Condé's equerries that there were plans to assassinate his master as he was crossing the Pont Neuf. To check, Condé sent his empty coach across the bridge and, sure enough, shots were fired on it. Who was responsible? Who could tell who was a friend or an enemy in this confusion? The Court was buzzing with the most sinister rumours, of plans to assassinate the Duc d'Orléans, Mazarin, even the queen herself. Mazarin forbade the queen to leave the palace without a strong escort, having just learnt of several dinners attended by *frondeurs,* at which toasts had publicly been drunk to Oliver Cromwell – Cromwell, the republican! But it was not so much these aristocratic *frondeurs* that Mazarin most mistrusted, but the Prince de Condé himself. His ill temper, cleverly maintained by his sister Longueville, his unpredictable jealousies, his endless demands, his megalomania, made this unenthusiastic 'friend' of the government a dangerous enemy.

On one January morning in 1650, the Royal Council was meeting as usual. The Duc d'Orléans, Condé and Conti entered the Palais Royal, as well as their brother-in-law, the Duc de Longueville, who rose from his sick bed because they were going to discuss business that was of particular interest to him. As it was reported that the queen was suffering from a migraine, the doors of her apartments were shut so that she was not disturbed. Condé's mother visited her, sat at her bedside and asked endless questions about her health. Anne of Austria, it seemed, turned pale, then became excited and began to stammer, and the anxious princess believed her to be very ill. Condé then came in, but finding the queen in the company of his mother went out in search of Mazarin, whom he found in the corridor and attacked at once with a list of complaints. Mazarin listened patiently, but they were interrupted by the arrival of the Prince de Conti. Everyone was now present for the council and Mazarin sent a valet to warn the queen that they were ready. Her Majesty would be waiting for the members of the council in the gallery, they were informed, and Condé went first, followed by Conti and Longueville, then the rest of the ministers. Guitaut, captain of the guards, came in through another door. Condé thought that he had come to ask him a favour and went up to him. 'Yes, Guitaut, what is it?' 'Monsieur, I have an order to arrest you, together with Monsieur le Prince de Conti your brother, and Monsieur de Longueville.' 'Me, Monsieur Guitaut, you are arresting me ...?' – a short silence followed – '... in heaven's name go back to the queen and tell her that I must speak to her.' The queen, who had not really been ill, had meanwhile taken the young king from his lessons and led him by the hand to her chapel. There she made him kneel down, told him of her decision and enjoined him to pray God for the success of the operation.

In the gallery Condé was still waiting to know whether the queen would see him. It was beginning to dawn on him that things were serious: 'I admit that all this surprises me, I who have always served the king so well and believed that I enjoyed the friendship of Monsieur le Cardinal.' Guitaut returned with the news that the queen would not receive the prince, and he resigned himself to his fate: 'Well, so be it. We will obey, but where are you taking us? I hope it will be somewhere warm.' In January, this 'warm' place was to be the Château de Vincennes.[4]

Summoned to the Palais Royal but having a good idea what awaited her there, the Duchesse de Longueville fled and managed to reach Normandy, her husband's fief. Turenne, the Duc de Bouillon and La Rochefoucauld just managed to escape arrest. The Duchesse de Bouillon, about to be arrested in her bedchamber, had just enough time to slip into the cellar, where trusted friends tied her up with rope and pulled her into the street through an air vent. When the Princesse de Condé, the hero's wife, was warned that she was about to be arrested, she put one of her maids in her place in the bed and managed to pass unnoticed between the guards, fleeing with her young son. As for the princess's mother, Anne of Austria's friend, she left without leaving any trace.

When it was announced that the princes had been arrested, Paris lit bonfires to celebrate, tables were brought out into the streets and a great deal of wine was drunk. Whenever she appeared Anne of Austria was cheered, and there were even cries of 'Long live Mazarin' as the prime minister passed by. The triumphant government organized tours through the more turbulent provinces that were both a military and a propaganda exercise. The king, the queen, the Court and the army travelled first to Normandy, where the Duchesse de Longueville was trying to transform latent rebellion into civil war. But the governors of the cities rejected this *pasionaria* and the monarchy was able to make a triumphant entry into Rouen. An order was sent to the duchess to relinquish Dieppe. However, she was apparently ill in bed and sent word that she would obey the order as soon as she was better; the government sent troops to aid her recovery. The duchess made inflammatory speeches to the Dieppe notables, but they refused to follow her in her adventure. As she was about to be besieged in the city castle, she managed to leave it through a small unguarded postern, and one of the most precious and voluptuous ornaments of the Court found herself running through the fields in mid-winter towards a quiet harbour, from which she could flee the country. Eventually, she managed to get hold of a small boat, but her attempts to clamber aboard were thwarted by the elements. Nothing remained but to climb up behind a peasant on horseback and gallop through the stormy night in search of asylum. For two weeks she wandered from hiding place to hiding place. Meanwhile, her cousin, the queen regent, returned to Paris, convinced that the duchess had succeeded in leaving the country and relieved in the knowledge that the seductive trouble-maker was out of the way.

Anne's stay in Paris would be shortlived, however, for they would soon have to deal with Burgundy. There things were more serious. Already ravaged by the European conflict that had just ended, the province was now a veritable battlefield where the young king had to face a horrifying spectacle. The magnificent procession of the Court was followed by a comet of misery, suffering and death: sick or maimed soldiers, peasants dying of hunger, haggard women holding their skeleton-like children. The chorus of complaints and prayers was never ending. [5] But the king of France could not respond to his subjects' pleas, for he did not have a *sou* in his pocket.

Meanwhile the royalist troops were laying siege to the rebel-held city of Bellegarde. Indeed the siege seemed to go on forever, thanks to the torrential rain that drowned the royalist camp, and Mazarin, who came to visit the site, was nearly killed by a bullet that wounded the man next to him. In the midst of this depressing atmosphere, a rumour spread through the army: 'The king is coming. The king is here.' Louis XIV had indeed come to raise the spirits of his troops and to undergo baptism by fire. The commandant of Bellegarde obliged by shooting on the royal procession, but immediately recognizing his mistake, he sent a few hasty, unconvincing apologies. During the gunfire, the boy remained quite impassive. He knew that he had been brought here to set an example and his courage, noted enthusiastically by all around him, paid off as usual. The royalist soldiers never tired of acclaiming their king, while the rebel soldiers lost their heads, starting to shout 'Long live the king'; they were not far short of arresting their officers and handing them over to the royalists. Indeed, after a few days, Bellegarde asked to surrender and the soldiers of both camps made peace amid general rejoicing.

The same day in Paris the Princesse-mère de Condé, who had disappeared since the arrest of her family, made a dramatic appearance in the *parlement,* and in moving terms asked for justice for her children. In the west the Duc de La Rochefoucauld gathered troops and publicly raised his standard against the king, while the Duc de Bouillon sent one of his gentlemen to Madrid to ask the king of Spain for credits. The arrest of the princes had certainly not put an end to opposition. Its efforts were directed at Bordeaux, which was still in conflict with its governor, the Duc d'Epernon. Exhortations, encouragements, promises of help – especially money – were lavished on the Bordelais, who duly declared war on the king. With remarkable timing, a powerful Spanish army then appeared on France's northern frontiers, whose second-in-command was Turenne, one of the bravest French generals.

The government took advantage of what seemed like a period of calm in the capital and set out for Bordeaux in an attempt to bring the rebellious city to heel. The Spaniards did not invade France quickly enough and the Paris *parlement* did not intervene energetically enough; the Bordelais were soon forced to negotiate. As the negotiations were proceeding the Maréchal de La Meilleraye, the commander of the royalist army, was 'pacifying' the region. One day he attacked a castle whose governor – who 'was not even a gentleman' – dared to hold up His Majesty's troops. Lacking a sense of humour, La Meilleraye had the impudent man hanged, which aroused cries for vengeance in Bordeaux. The Duc de Bouillon, the Bordelais commander, picked out from among the royal prisoners a captain of the Navailles regiment who was playing cards with some ladies from the city, had him hanged on the spot and left his body dangling from the wall. When Anne of Austria saw it, she broke off negotiations and war resumed.

The young king had to entertain himself as best he could while all this was going on, and on one occasion, while watching the queen's horses being exercised, young Brienne noticed tears running down Louis' cheeks. Brienne took his hand. 'What is the matter, dear Master, are you crying?' he asked. 'I will not always be a child, but say nothing,' the king replied. 'Those Bordelais wretches will not lay down the law to me for long. I shall punish them as they deserve.' For a brief moment, his true feelings had broken through his legendary composure. He was bitterly aware of his humiliation, the humiliation of the monarchy that he embodied. Those rebels would see what was coming to them when he was grown up. But he soon took hold of himself: 'I don't want anybody to see my tears. Say nothing about it, do not abuse the trust I have placed in you.'[6] At the time Louis was just twelve years old.

Bordeaux continued to resist, but it was vital that it should be taken soon for the Spanish were almost at Reims, and Paris, filled with refugees, was in a dangerously unstable state. It was a race against the clock. The Maréchal de La Meilleraye intensified his attacks, while Mazarin let it be known that he would not be against the idea of reopening negotiations. The Bordelais nibbled at the bait and sent Gourville, a friend of the Condés, as their representative, a man who was as cunning a negotiator as Mazarin himself. Mazarin offered the hand of his own niece, Mademoiselle Martinozzi, to the Prince de Conti, which would have the piquant effect of making the granddaughter of a Sicilian cook a princess of the blood royal of France. But this was not the only trick he had up his sleeve and he equivocated about it. Nevertheless both parties were at the end of their tether and Bordeaux at last concluded a grudging peace with its king, as could be seen during Louis' official entry into the city. There was a huge crowd on the wharves, but their faces were solemn and there were few shouts of 'Long live the king'. The dinner arranged by the city for the king was particularly bad and the firework display that followed a feeble effort; it was hard to decide whether this was an indication of poverty or a calculated insult.[7]

The return to Paris was painful. The queen was ill with a fever brought on by her worries. Still greater political worries awaited her on her return to the capital. While Mazarin dashed to the frontier to try to stop foreign invasion, the *parlement* increased its pressure, protesting more and more strenuously against the 'illegal' detention of the princes Condé, Conti and Longueville. The principal target of the *frondeurs* was still the Duc d'Orléans, whom they wished to detach from the royal party, of which he was the last bastion. For some time now this professional weathercock had shown himself to be distinctly less enthusiastic about the king's cause and held an ever more attentive ear to the criticisms levied against the government. On returning from the front, Mazarin invited him to dine with himself and the king, on 6 January 1651. There were some forty guests, all men, and a great deal was drunk. Gaston, Duc d'Orléans, asked the Marquis de Roquelaure, always the life and soul of any party, to do his stuff; the marquis was in good form, told stories and did imitations. He was so funny that the young king actually burst out laughing, which caused universal amazement.

The drinking continued, and the talk was of absent friends, *frondeurs* of course. Gaston, much the worse for drink, made cruel fun of them. Others looked surprised, for it was said that Gaston was on the point of abandoning Mazarin for the *Fronde*. Encouraged by Gaston's example, the Chevalier de Guise set about the Duc de Beaufort and Monseigneur de Retz. Here, in his opinion, were two completely worthless gentlemen and he started into a smutty song about them. By now all the guests were drunk and each tried to outdo the other with songs against the *frondeurs*. Mazarin rose; the king must not hear these obscenities, the prestige of the Crown and the innocence of childhood forbade it. He himself would dearly have liked to stay; such vicious attacks on his worst enemies, even when sung by raucous, drunken voices, were sweet music to him. But his dignity forbade it and he considered it ill-advised to listen to drunkards pour derision on those who took him as their target, so, leaving the guests, he withdrew with the king. The nonsense that the Duc d'Orléans poured out about the *frondeurs* was to ring pleasantly in his ears for a long time to come.[8]

But the very next day, 7 January 1651, the Duc d'Orléans agreed to intercede with the queen with a view to freeing the imprisoned princes; he had gone over to the opposite camp after all. The delighted *parlementaires* hastily put together a delegation that would go to the queen without waiting for her to recover so she was obliged to receive them in bed. Thoroughly emboldened, the first president, Molé, was in no mood to beg, ask or hope. He demanded and threatened instead; respect had paralysed the king's subjects for too long; it was now time for them to examine the causes of the disorder in France, to call the government to account. The young king, who was standing near his mother, trembled. Molé continued, daring to call government policy 'unfortunate', an adjective that nearly made Mazarin explode with rage despite his proverbial self-control. Molé ended his speech and left, followed by a chorus of curses from the queen's bedchamber. Louis burst out, 'Had I not been afraid of angering you, mother, I would have silenced the first president and sent him packing, not once but thrice.'9 It was the bravado of a still powerless child, but it was recorded and remembered.

The opposition now stepped up its attack on the government. Delegations arrived every day at the Palais Royal to demand the princes' freedom. All that remained now was for the Duc d'Orléans to deliver the final blow by demanding that the queen should dismiss Mazarin. The government was in its death throes, and, well aware of this, *parlement* wanted to arrest the cardinal and bring him to trial.

At last an official announcement proclaimed that the princes would be freed, although Anne refused to give in entirely, insisting that they declare their support for her first; she wanted to release allies, not enemies. But her conciliatory move came too late; the Parisian mob were baying for Mazarin's blood. The cardinal was terrified; in his fear he came up with the expedient of leaving Paris to travel to Le Havre and release the princes himself. Anne agreed eventually, but right to the last moment she had tried to avoid relinquishing her minister. In the face of such stubbornness, more rumours were spread of a secret liaison, even a secret marriage, between the queen – who really was virtuous – and the cardinal – who disliked women. They did not want to admit that, in spite of pressure from all sides, she had held on to a minister whose policies they regarded as disastrous. For, although Mazarin excelled in foreign policy, his handling of internal affairs was often clumsy – he was content to pursue a day-to-day policy, with no concern for the future or overall strategy. Diplomacy and duplicity could not always replace firmness. Above all he was incapable of grasping France's real problem, the profound need for social and economic reform. The people, crushed by poverty, exasperated by injustice, had clung to the *parlementaires* and nobles of the *Fronde,* who were equally incapable of providing solutions, but who at least were able to give the illusion that they were by attacking the government. There had to be a silent *Fronde,* without which the active *Fronde* would be reduced to what it seemed, a ballet of crazy, criminal plots motivated by passion and greed. Bogged down in their wretched intrigues, sustained by their selfish ambitions, the *frondeurs* had failed to form a common solid front. The régime was fortunate that, in spite of its weaknesses, it had only a conglomerate of incompetents to confront; otherwise, it would not have lasted much longer.

Once the accursed Italian had left, the whole of France rejoiced and the queen wept secretly in the arms of her friend, Mme de Motteville: 'I believe I am obliged to defend the minister whom they have taken from me by force ... I know as well as you do that he has faults and that he has made many mistakes. But I also know that he has always striven to serve the king and myself to the best of his ability; that he has conducted those affairs that he has been left to conduct in splendid fashion; that the first five years of my regency were happy ones and that having been betrayed by those whom he obliged, it is hard that this iniquity should go against him; and this, it seems to me, obliges me to have all the more pity on him.' After the fine words of a queen came the cry of an anguished woman: 'Would that it were always night; for although I cannot sleep, silence and solitude agree with me, because during the day I see only people who betray me.'[10]

These same people were waiting impatiently for the queen to free the princes. There was no hurry, she replied – a dangerous delay in the circumstances. On the evening of 9 February 1651 at the Palais de Luxembourg, the Duc d'Orléans announced that one of the king's officers had come to warn him that the queen was planning to flee Paris that very night with her son. Gaston realized that without the dummies of the monarchy in his hands, he would have little power, so he stirred up the city: 'The queen is going to flee, the king is going to flee.' The temperature of the capital, always ready to rise, reached danger point and yet again the Parisians went out into the streets. 'To arms, to arms,' they shouted, 'they are taking the king from us.' It was almost midnight. Anne of Austria had already retired to bed when she was warned that the demonstrators were approaching, but she immediately doubled the guard at the gates of the Palais Royal. Gaston's plan was nothing less than to seize the king – or such was the rumour that was repeated to the queen mother. She sent for her most faithful supporters, but no one came, while at that very moment Monseigneur de Retz was suggesting that she should be locked up in a convent. Once again she rose to the occasion and quelled the fears of her trembling women; she was sure it would turn out to be yet another flash in the pan, the mob would calm down as quickly as it had been aroused. Capitaine des Souches, of the Duc d'Orléans' Swiss guard, was shown in. He conveyed a message from the Monseigneur, begging the queen to put an end to the disorder by denying the news of her departure. It was pure invention, the queen cried; she pointed out that she would hardly be preparing to flee while the king and his brother were asleep in bed. Des Souches dared to question whether the king was really asleep, and refused to leave the Palais Royal until he had seen Louis in bed. The

49

queen shrugged her shoulders and, turning to the king's guardian, Villeroi, ordered him to take this Doubting Thomas to the king's bedchamber. Villeroi did so, raised the curtain around the bed, brought a candle close to the child's face and allowed des Souches to take a long hard look at it.

As he left the Palais Royal, des Souches met the demonstrators, and reassured them the king was actually asleep and would not leave. 'We want to see him for ourselves,' the crowd shouted, and invaded the Palais Royal. Remaining ice cool, Anne ordered that all the gates and doors be opened, and the king's bedchamber was soon packed to capacity. The curtains around the bed were raised. There lay the king, the very image of childhood in all its vulnerability and innocence. The excited demonstrators were instantly won over, declaiming their love for the child; they wished him happiness, prosperity, long life, glory. They could hardly take their eyes off that small face with its closed eyes. One can only conjecture whether Louis was really asleep, with all the noise in the streets and the palace, all the endless comings and goings in the neighbouring apartments, even in the room itself, or whether he was only pretending while the crowd stared down at him as if he were some curious animal. Either way, thanks to the young king's slumbers, the riots subsided. The burghers withdrew on tiptoe, but they left several of their number on guard. The queen had two of their number brought to her and chatted with them, discovering that one of them, 'Du Laurier, at Your Majesty's service', knew the Court well, for he had been a servant of His Majesty's *maître d'hotel*. The queen and her ladies gave a sign of recognition and everyone relaxed. Most of them wanted to go to bed; it was three in the morning and they were all exhausted. The queen suggested celebrating mass before retiring, but it was two hours before the Court chaplain would be saying mass, so, to pass the time, several ladies started to play cards. Mme de Motteville, lying on a carpet, felt her eyes closing. Five o'clock sounded at last, the queen put on a dressing-gown and led her entourage off to the chapel. To thank Du Laurier and his companion for their kindness, she took them to see her personal treasure and they stood for some time admiring the glittering jewels.[11]

In the morning the monarchy found itself once again the prisoner of Paris. Guards stood at the city gates searching everything, even forcing women to remove their make-up lest the king had assumed female disguise. People were forbidden to go hunting or to leave the city even for a walk. It was almost impossible to leave the Palais Royal. Every evening, Capitaine des Souches paid a visit on behalf of the Duc d'Orléans to check that the king and queen were still there, and would come back several times during the night, demanding to be shown the king. Louis had only the palace garden to play in, where he had had a miniature fortress built so he could play soldiers. He would divide his friends into two armies, a pathetic game for a young king to be playing, while a prisoner in his own capital. It was also dangerous; young

Brienne nearly blew himself up with a keg of gunpowder, but he was no less keen to fight, as was his inseparable companion, Paolo Mancini, Mazarin's nephew, whom the king had hated from the moment he had arrived in France and who now joined in all his games.[12]

Meanwhile Mazarin had arrived at Le Havre. He entered the Prince de Condé's cell and humbly announced that Condé, Conti and Longueville were free. He had insisted on being the first to bring them the good news. Condé grasped him in his arms. 'I shall always be the good servant of the king and queen,' he said and, with a gracious smile to Mazarin, added, 'and of you, too, Monsieur.' Condé was in no hurry to leave; he was hungry, he said, and would eat there, in the prison; would Mazarin care to join them? The three princes sat down with their former jailer like old friends; not a harsh word was spoken, and the play acting was kept up to the end. Humble as ever, Mazarin followed Condé to his coach, still attempting to save his own skin. But Condé escaped him, jumped into his coach and with a burst of laughter ordered the coachman to set off at top speed, as Mazarin was making a deep bow at the door. Nothing remained for the fallen minister but to take the road of exile towards Germany. He had taken it upon himself to carry off the crown jewels. The queen, not at all convinced of the wisdom of this strange decision, had asked for them back but he turned a deaf ear. Mazarin may have been thinking of keeping the jewels as a bargaining counter.[13]

In Paris a triumphant reception awaited the three liberated princes. The same crowd which had applauded their arrest a year before gathered on the edge of the city to cheer them on their way. First they had to thank the queen for freeing them, and to cap everything, the Duc d'Orléans took them in person to Anne's bedside. There was a distinct coolness on both sides. Condé briefly thanked the queen; her response was even briefer. Of those present, only the king showed any warmth, embracing his cousin Condé several times and paying him the most unexpected compliments. Hypocrisy, rather than sympathy, would seem the likelier explanation, and at this point the son and pupil proved stronger than the mother and teacher.

Anne had certainly been right not to free the princes without guarantees. Indeed, Condé hastened to join Gaston d'Orléans in trying to wrest from the government the little power that still remained to it, and demands and insults followed one another daily. But all this might come to an end before long for in September of that year, 1651, Louis XIV would come of age. With Anne removed from power, it would no longer be possible to trim the monarchy's power, so the princes worked towards the immediate summoning of the Estates General. They wanted the mass of deputies to be assembled in the hopes that the atmosphere of political licence would encourage the deputies to inveigh against the power of the government – especially as it was practically non-existent. According to the princes' scenario the monarchy would be asked to give an account of its stewardship; there would be a great deal of mud slinging and finally the power of the monarchy would be checked, confined, divided. Sensing what was coming, Anne of Austria held firm and refused to issue the summons.

All that the queen regent could do now was to resist, for she could no longer act. Her position, her very existence was hanging by a thread. No sooner had she decided to bring her regency to a close, as she had a right to do, than the Duc d'Orléans, in the name of his purely expedient friendship with Mazarin who shared the regency, became violently angry and swore to avenge the cardinal. Beaufort and Retz, opportunistic as ever, proposed to raise the city, arm the population and take the king from the Palais Royal. In the end, Condé, the least mad of these madmen, threw in his weight against such a plan.[14]

The effect on France as a whole, pulled this way and that by the forces of foreign powers, the monarchy and the *Fronde*, was devastating. Famine and death were everywhere. The town of Etampes, not far from Paris, was almost empty; those of its inhabitants who had not been massacred had fled. Corpses lying on the edges of the town were devoured by wolves; together with the decomposing remains of animals and manure, they befouled the atmosphere. At Saint-Quentin there were so many sick and wounded that two hundred of them were thrown out of the hospital and left to die on the highway. In Picardy someone encountered a troop of five hundred orphans under the age of seven. The peasants, their faces blackened, had nothing to eat but a few blades of oats.[15]

Exiled at Brühl, in Germany, Mazarin did not lament on the situation in which France found itself, but on his own. Abandoned by almost everyone and ignored by the rest, he was losing hope. He was even convinced that the queen, who had always supported him against everyone, had now ceased to do so. But he was moved when he received this despatch from one of his collaborators: 'I was in the little oratory yesterday and saw the king burst into tears at the mention of Your Eminence, and the queen soon did likewise.' There was nothing odd in the fact that the queen should weep when remembering her minister. But the king? Perhaps there was some affection concealed behind the child's dislike or maybe his feelings had changed in the face of the unstable situation in France. Mazarin ought to have been reassured, especially when he received this confirmation from his faithful friend, the minister Le Tellier: 'As for the king, I have twice made him burst into tears at the mere mention of your name.' Anne of Austria appears to have commented: 'Well, my son, although we have not yet been able to recall Monsieur le Cardinal, who served us so well, will you not recall him when you are of age?' But it was not enough to reassure the former prime minister, who was feverishly writing an apologia for his government, while busying himself no less feverishly with a quite different matter: his own affairs. By dint of confiscations, enforced bankruptcies, sequestrations and sales at auction, the *Fronde* had practically emptied the cardinal's coffers, but not entirely for he had had the prudence to hold a number of his possessions under assumed names.[16]

The problem was how to capitalize on what could be saved from the wreckage when he was so far from Paris. Mazarin's thoughts turned to a functionary who was particularly skilled in business affairs. Austere of mien, with sunken eyes and jet-black eyebrows, this tireless worker had proved capable and persistent. His unscrupulousness, his relentlessness, his greed for money and a touch of vanity did not displease Mazarin. His name was Colbert, a thirty-two-year-old merchant's son. Introduced by one of his uncles into the service of the minister Le Tellier, he rapidly became the link between the latter and Mazarin, who was always on the move. Through successful legal action, Colbert released the cardinal's wealth, sending part of it to Mazarin, saving whatever could be saved. Then he began to rebuild the fortune by juggling with State funds, speculating in gold and metals and dealing in letters patent. This way Colbert overcame Mazarin's mistrust and in the end obtained power of attorney from him. But he was not the only one to handle Mazarin's affairs, for the prudent cardinal divided his trust between Colbert and a detested rival. This other financial adviser, an attractive, brilliant spendthrift of thirty-six was called Nicolas Fouquet. After giving satisfaction to Mazarin in several missions of confidence he had bought the post of procurator general at the *parlement*. Thus while the monarchy lurched from one crisis to another and France was withering away with penury and suffering, the cardinal who had once been its chief minister was building up his fortune again in far-off Germany, with the help of two rival factotums who were both to enjoy an exceptional future. Meanwhile siren voices were reaching Mazarin's ears. All too aware of his talents and disgusted by the injustices that had been meted out to him, the most Catholic king of Spain begged the cardinal to enter his service: if he did so, he could name his own price. To the surprise of all, and to the amazement of the Spanish, he categorically refused. 'I replied what I had to reply, concluding that I shall end my days serving France in thought and wish, if I cannot do otherwise.'[17]

It was a pity that the princes of the blood of France could not show as much patriotism as this foreigner. Back in France, Condé was managing to irritate the *frondeurs* themselves with his impetuosity and rudeness. He had quarrelled with Retz and their respective supporters very nearly came to blows on the floor of the *parlement*; in the great hall the Duc de La Rochefoucauld, Condé's supporter, and the Duc de Brissac, Retz's cousin, could be heard calling one another *'fils de putain'* ('son of a whore'). In the midst of this sinister farce, they forgot that the date of the king's majority was drawing near. On the other hand, he was well aware of it, though he pretended not to be. Only once did he drop his disguise. Louis had taken a fancy to a certain Mlle de Frontenac. (She was not the first: Court legend had it that he had received his initiation, with or without the connivance of his mother, from Mme de Beauvais, a lame one-eyed woman, the queen's *femme de chambre* who had been expelled on Mazarin's orders for supposedly having encouraged Jarzé's ridiculous passion for Anne.) Now, Villeroi could do nothing against Mlle de Frontenac, and Anne had to intervene in person. Noticing that her son met the girl during walks that she herself had organized, she simply put an end to them. The king was furious: 'When I am master,' he declared, 'I shall go where I like – and that will be soon enough.'[18] It seemed even then that he was impatient to reign.

On the morning of 7 September 1651 the monarchy mobilized all its pomp to celebrate the king's coming of age. There were fifty helmeted guards in royal livery, a hundred of the queen's light cavalry, two hundred of the king's light cavalry in uniforms dripping with gold and silver, a hundred Swiss guards in black velvet and silver trimmings, the heralds-at-arms in red velvet tunics decorated with *fleurs-de-lys*, pages sporting blue, white and red feathers, officers of the regiment in uniforms embroidered over with gold, the Grand Provost on his horse covered with a gilded cloth, 'the Sieur Diesbach', colonel of the Swiss guards, in flame coloured satin and silver lace. The nobility followed in order of precedence; the Comte de Cléri wore a gold doublet, red and white feathers in his cap, the Chevalier Paul rode a prancing courser with a pearl-embroidered cloth; the provincial governors, the marshals of France, the great officers of the King's Household, the masters of ceremonies were all in attendance.

The king appeared in the very image of majesty, so covered with embroidery that one could not see the colour of his coat. The Prince de Conti came up to him and handed him a letter from his brother Condé, who presented his excuses at not being able to attend the ceremony. Showing neither acquiescence nor anger, just haughty contempt, without opening it Louis disdainfully handed the envelope to Villeroi and mounted his horse, a light bay Barbary, with a cloth dotted with golden *fleurs de lys*, and the procession moved off. In front of the king there was only the Master of the Horse, Comte d'Harcourt, carrying the royal sword aloft. Behind him rode his guardian, Villeroi, whose task was now officially over, and who was to be rewarded with a dukedom for making such a poor job of it; then came the pages, the equerries and the guards.

The dazzling parade moved slowly through the street, thick with people; their cries of 'Long live the king' had never echoed so loud and clear. After mass in the Sainte-Chapelle, the assembled dignitaries moved off to the great hall of the *parlement*, to hear the speeches of the Chancellor and of the queen regent as she relinquished her control. Louis replied to his mother, who then rose and walked over to him to make a deep bow. Her son raised her up and embraced her: 'I beg you to continue to give me your good advice and after me to be head of my Council.' He had just entered his fourteenth year.

CHAPTER 4

The Storm-Tossed Monarch

Anne of Austria's task was officially at an end, but she remained head of the council and effectively in control. Louis XIV did not really assume the power that had come to him legally, yet on several occasions previously he had shown impatience to reach the fateful date. For her part, Anne was equally impatient to hand over power to him, to be relieved at last of its unbearable burden. How often had she repeated to Mme de Motteville how she wished she could retire to the convent of the Val-de-Grâce.[1] Yet when the moment came, she retained the power that her son had left with her. She was aware that he was not ready to assume it, especially in such a period of instability. No one in France was surprised, no one protested; it was as if everyone knew that it would happen. Mme de Motteville approved the queen's decision on the grounds of 'the king's youth'.[2] But it was not unknown for kings to assume full power even at the youthful age of thirteen, as Louis was. In fact, everyone was aware, directly or indirectly, of the king's inadequacies, not least Louis himself. He had in any case realized that his mother was indispensable to him, acknowledging the fact, in an oblique, rather pompous way, in his *Memoirs*: 'The vigour with which this princess sustained my crown at a time when I could not act was to me a mark of her affection and virtue.' There was nothing of the possessive mother about her: 'I had nothing to fear from her ambition,' he was to write. There was, in fact, an established situation that a mere ceremony of majority could not change. 'The custom that I had formed,' he was to say later, 'of living in the same apartments and dining at the same table with her, the assiduity with which I saw her each day, was not a law that I had imposed upon myself for reasons of State, but a mark of the pleasure that I took in her company.'[3] Anne still held the power that she had not sought, and Louis' impatience to take it over would seem to have been no more than impulsiveness and whim.

On the other hand, he kept up the illusion of impatience. Emotionally neglected, Louis had observed that when he assumed the image of king he became the object of homage and flattery. He had only to enter the skin of his mythical character to feel grown up and self-assured. It would not be as a man, as a leader, as a general that he would make his mark, but as a king. From this point of view being king meant appearing to be king, assuming a majestic image, maintaining an imposing, severe air, surrounding oneself with luxury and pomp. The slightest detail had its own importance in this theatrical representation and he understood the value of ceremonial. He had excelled in the role of king from childhood, whether on the throne or on the stage. A year earlier he began appearing with his courtiers in the splendid ballets presented at Court. On these occasions Louis put on costumes that were even more extravagant than those of official ceremonies. He was dressed as a god-king and performed a long solo. He was an accomplished dancer and enjoyed the way that all eyes were only on him. On stage he could dazzle and dominate just as he had done a short time ago in the midst of his glittering Court. Was it theatre that was becoming reality or reality that was becoming theatre?

The thirteen-year-old youth was anxious, nevertheless, to show that he was not only king in processions or on stage. One night there was a ball, which the whole family attended. Louis' brother, Philippe, danced non-stop until he tripped over his partner's skirt and went sprawling across the floor. Mme de Beauvais's daughter burst out laughing, and Philippe, crimson with rage and embarrassment, gave her a resounding swipe. 'Let him be whipped,' the king ordered, outraged that his brother could so forget himself in his presence as to strike a young girl.[4] Of course it was unthinkable that the first in line to the throne should actually be whipped just for losing his temper at a ball.

Meanwhile, and more seriously, Louis' uncles and cousins, Orléans and Condés, were to 'forget themselves' still more by taking it into their heads to forbid him to name his prime minister without their approval. Condé demanded that any decision should await his return to Paris and Orléans threatened that if Condé's orders were not followed he would never set foot in the Palais Royal again. Louis ignored them and without even replying appointed the ministers of his (and his mother's) choice. Next day, the Duc d'Orléans came to pay his respects as if nothing had happened, but Condé was missing.[5] It certainly looked as though the king had succeeded where the most experienced political heads of France had failed for so many years. From his distant viewpoint in Germany, Mazarin was thrown into despair, realizing what such a victory meant for him. If the king was learning how to govern so quickly, he might no longer have any need of the cardinal, and he feared that he would never be recalled. Mazarin was unaware that at that very moment Condé's actions would indirectly lead to his hoped-for recall. The prince was caught in a dilemma. Should he return to the bosom of the government or set a new civil war alight: submit or rebel? A number of his supporters were in favour of peace, but once again it was a woman who was determined to change his mind. During a dramatic council of war, the Duchesse de Longueville, who thought of nothing but love affairs, helped her brother to make up his mind; Condé took the plunge and declared war on the king. He went to Bordeaux which at once rallied to the rebellion. As Conti and Longueville took to the road, cities and provinces, solicited by both parties, declared themselves one by one for or against the king. France, which had hardly had time to come together again after the *Fronde* of the *parlement*, found itself once more in pieces, shattered by the *Fronde* of the princes.

Anne of Austria now took things in hand; up till now she had hidden her intention to bring the cardinal back, but once the rebels had thrown off their masks, the queen could do the same: 'Now that we are in the midst of civil war there is nothing worse to be feared: I wish to bring him back.' Mazarin would not return alone, either; he would return at the head of an army which he had recruited at great expense and which he placed at the service of the king at a time when the government had most need of troops as soon as he received the royal summons.[6] The news that Mazarin was on his way sowed consternation and anger everywhere.[7] Spurred on by this, the Paris *parlement* dared more than it had ever dared: it passed a decree putting a price on his head and promising 150,000 *livres* to anyone who killed the cardinal whom the king was preparing to receive with all due solemnity. The fact that the king's council immediately overruled this decree in no way mitigated its impudence. Mazarin, for his part, still had some doubts as to the wisdom of accepting, then finally made up his mind and entered France. He rejoined the queen and her son once more on 30 January 1652 at Poitiers. He brought back with him a gift beyond price: Turenne, the former rebel general, had come to command the king's army against the former general of that same army, Condé, and the most farcical of tragedies began all over again.

The battles were rather lacking in seriousness. The royalist and rebel troops met at Bléneau near the Loire. As usual Condé got everything wrong but news of the battle was exaggerated beyond belief. The alarm was given at Giens, quite near where the Court was encamped, so trunks were packed and coaches harnessed in great haste with the intention of crossing the Loire and then blowing up the bridges. The king had mounted his horse and, followed excitedly by a number of young aristocrats, left the town, galloping in the direction of the rebel troops. 'The king is coming,' the rumour spread through the royalist army. 'Long live the king! To battle! To battle!' Mazarin had to chase after his pupil and stop him in mid-field for the king should not expose himself uselessly and risk his life at the first battle. The king agreed to turn back for there was not, in any case, going to be a battle. Condé's victory had obviously been exaggerated and, instead of exploiting his advantage, he immediately retreated.

Since Mazarin's return His Most Christian Majesty Louis XIV, who appointed and dismissed ministers, had become a small boy again. He had asked to be put at the head of his army in order to learn how to command but naturally his mother had refused. He was consulted about nothing and he had no power, even in the smallest detail. For instance, an officer. M. de Créquy, asked the king if he could replace his lieutenant who had been killed in action and the king promised to talk about it to his prime minister. Several days passed, and after a week Créquy returned. The king said nothing, shifted uneasily from one foot to the other, blushed, leaned over to the faithful La Porte and whispered in his ear: 'I talked to him about it, but it was no use.'[8] Since Mazarin's return, Louis was again no more than a figurehead. No one was to know how the boy felt before such humiliation and powerlessness for he neither confided in anyone nor betrayed what he felt.

Since he was no longer a king in fact Louis reverted to childish behaviour. Waking up one morning Louis absent-mindedly spat onto his young brother's bed. Philippe was furious; he was already showing the propensity for cleanliness that was to astonish a particularly filthy century. Louis shrugged his shoulders and laughed when Philippe shook with rage. The latter retaliated by urinating on the king's bed, whereupon Louis attacked him and the brothers had to be separated by force. Philippe quickly forgot the incident, but Louis's temper did not subside and he was still frothing with fury long afterwards.[9]

Back in Paris, each day brought new incidents that verged on anarchy. Under the pretext of demonstrating against Mazarin, the mob went on the rampage, shouting, stealing and destroying property. Mlle de Guise's coach was stopped. Maréchal d'Ornano had to flee on foot through the streets. The young Mme de Montchal got away only after being severely beaten up. There were however two happy individuals in the midst of all this anarchy. One was Paul Scarron, a brilliant poet, who, though a cripple, was also given to debauchery. At forty-two, he fell in love with a girl of seventeen who had recently arrived in Paris. Born in Martinique of a father 'who may have been a gentleman', landing at La Rochelle and taken in by a miserly old aunt, she had plumbed the depths of poverty. With no money, no family, she had felt lost on arrival at the capital, so was overjoyed at the poet's offer of marriage. He may have been deformed, but he was a good man. He did not have a great deal of money but he had enough for her never to go hungry again, and anyway, he knew everybody in Paris and would be able to introduce her into society. This disparate but happy couple were married on 4 April 1652.[10] Chubby and fresh-faced, she was the young Françoise d'Aubigné who, one day was to be called the Marquise de Maintenon.

In the rest of Paris, however, things were going from bad to worse. Soon one was to hear the unthinkable cry, rapidly reproduced in tract after tract, 'No king, no princes, long live liberty!'[11] It was the first time in the history of France that the dreaded words had been spoken openly. They were not said very loudly or for very long, but they were to remain in people's memories, to be repeated at the right moment and with more conviction: 'No king, no *parlementaires*, no bourgeois.' In

1652, it seemed like a dream. The people, driven wild by hunger and suffering, constantly pulled this way and that, manipulated, roused to revolt then defeated, crushed by different parties, suddenly became aware that it had been exploited and betrayed by everybody. But the bold writers did not know then how their ideas would, a century later, be taken up with a vengeance. In 1652, the idea of 'no king' was bad enough. But no *parlementaires*, no bourgeois? The interested parties, astonished as they might well have been, reacted swiftly. Several of the republican ringleaders were arrested and hanged, but the infernal slogan continued to echo in people's minds. If that was where the folly of princes led, then perhaps royal government was not so bad after all; at least it maintained order.

If the bourgeois had had enough, the ordinary people were at the end of their tether. The peasants sought refuge in Paris, still haunted by the vision of their devastated fields and the memory of the terrifying violence that they had witnessed. They cursed the name of Condé under their breath even though scarcely a few weeks before he had made a triumphal entry into the capital. In certain regions, which had had no real harvest for five years, men were so weak that they could no longer walk, 'crawling like lizards over the dunghills', their bodies devoured by vermin which they no longer had the strength to crush. Some had been driven so wild with hunger that they gnawed their own fists. The living wandered aimlessly among the corpses, and it was hard to tell one from the other. The stink was so great that it even reached Paris, and ladies walking near the ramparts had to hold their noses.[12] Yet all this was nothing to what was to come. A worse scourge was approaching from the east in the person of Charles IV, the Duc de Lorraine, and his soldiers, whom Condé had called to his aid. This Beast of the Apocalypse was noted for his good humour and cynicism combined with a touch of madness. An adventurer who had been deprived of his crown, he wandered through Europe at the head of a small, lawless, ruthless army of veterans. Their motto – 'Strike hard, take all and give nothing back' – proudly emblazoned on their standards, merely confirmed their reputation. Since the peasants no longer had anything to steal or loot, even after a thorough search, Charles' army went straight for the castles and abbeys. Aristocrats and prelates protested vigorously. 'Each of my soldiers is like a thing possessed and at the sight of loot becomes possessed of three devils and it is impossible to tame them,' Charles proudly explained. He left behind him a wake of unimaginable horrors, of corpses tortured and flayed in all manner of ways.[13] At Château-Thierry, one peace-loving man saw the soldiers torture a magistrate, Etienne du Bary, whom they tied to a pillar in the church of Saint-Crépin. He heard the crackling of fires, the sound of gunfire, the cries of the tortured throughout the town. This enemy of violence was a thirty-one-year-old poet, as yet unknown, named Jean de La Fontaine.[14]

The killing also helped the Duc de Lorraine to provide provisions for his army. He actually boasted that, when necessary, his soldiers ate the dead and even the wounded. He loved his soldiers, inventing games that were worthy of them, like putting a child in an oven or whipping a husband and wife with thorn branches to see which of the two would die first. After a journey rich in such entertainments, the duke arrived at the gates of Paris and struck camp. Condé had chosen his ally well; such a general and such an army would make quick work of the royalist army. But Lorraine displayed a certain levity that disturbed his allies. When a beautiful *frondeuse* wanted to discuss politics with him, he picked up a guitar and replied, 'Let us rather dance, Madame, it suits you better than talking shop.' Later Monseigneur de Retz intimated that he wished to speak to Charles. 'With priests one has to pray to God,' he said. 'Give me a rosary.'[15] This specialist in black humour had quickly understood the situation: the true strength lay with the royalist camp. Skirmishes had already taken place when a royalist emissary was despatched to the duke's camp, no less a person than Charles Stuart, king of England in exile, son of the beheaded Charles I, and Louis' first cousin. He enquired what the Duc de Lorraine was doing outside Paris; if it was his intention to attack the king, to do so would be quite absurd and serve no purpose. They sat down around a table, went through the motions of negotiating and signed an agreement. The king assured Lorraine of his good will and Lorraine returned home without making any demands.

While the corpses left by the merry Duc de Lorraine were rotting, as Paris sank into anarchy and the Court took to the road, recovering a city here, a province there, Mazarin was busily engaged in his own financial affairs. The sudden change from power and fortune to exile and ruin had marked him forever. Power might again elude him, but at least he would never be short of money. His aim was to amass an enormous amount of money as quickly as possible and Colbert was proving more indispensable than ever in this respect. Reimbursements from state revenues for the losses suffered during exile, the search for the scattered collections bought back at low price, the selling of Court posts to the highest bidder, the sale on a large scale of peerages, the formation of a maritime empire with a view to trading with the whole world, these were some of the solutions to which the faithful factotum had recourse in order to rebuild his master's fortune. He juggled with business matters with a cynicism that often bordered on dishonesty. As usual he helped himself on the way, pocketing considerable sums, or acquiring some attractive property for his family. But he was far from satisfied with his role. If he revealed his talents it was with the overriding ambition to use them one day in politics. Like master, like servant; if Mazarin depended on him for his money, he depended on Mazarin for his future.[16]

Mazarin's experiences in exile had toughened him; there seemed to be nothing he would not attempt even, if some accounts are to be believed, the utter humiliation of the king. 'At Melum, on the feast of St John of the same year 1652, the king having dined with His Eminence, and having remained with him until seven in the evening, he sent me to say that he would like to have his bath; when his bath was ready he arrived looking sad, and I knew what was troubling him without him having to tell me.'[17] It seemed, according to La Porte's account, that the king of France had just endured the ultimate outrage. But who had dared to perpetrate it? He had been dining quietly with Mazarin, together with a few handsome boys of his circle, including Paolo Mancini, his nephew, Brienne and Vivonne. La Porte did not know and was never to know. Was it Mazarin, or had Mazarin left it to one of the others? Had Paolo Mancini committed the act under the approving eye of his uncle, or had Mazarin himself, under the stress of all his responsibilities, forgotten himself sufficiently to violate the person of the healthy, vigorous fourteen-year-old boy with whom he practically lived? Had the brilliant old homosexual, who had always submitted the self-conscious youth to his will, finally in a moment of madness made him the object of his desire? Nothing was impossible between these two extraordinary beings, bound together in a relationship of hate and love, so mysterious, so misunderstood, that only a few insinuations emerge from expurgated memoirs and official correspondence. La Porte could not have invented a calumny at once so precise and so specific: 'I spent five days trying to decide whether I would tell the queen ... In the end I told her, at first she was glad that I had done so and told me that I had never rendered her so great a service. But since I did not name the author of the deed, not being entirely certain, it was the cause of my ruin.'[18] Less than a year later, La Porte was suddenly disgraced, dismissed, exiled. It was claimed that he had committed the act of which he accused the cardinal,[19] because, La Porte was to maintain, the queen had told Mazarin about the incident in all innocence and the cardinal, realizing that he had been discovered, had no alternative but to get rid of the witness.[20] Meanwhile the other version was gaining ground, whether the cardinal liked it or not. It was exacerbated by the fact that Mazarin, throwing all his weight into incriminating La Porte, seemed to point to himself as the culprit. Many years later, after the death of both Anne of Austria and Mazarin, La Porte was to be rehabilitated and even received by the king. Le Tellier brought him back: 'The way has been smoothed for you,' he told La Porte, 'but refrain from entering into any explanations with His Majesty.'[21] Louis XIV would probably never have received him again if his accusations against Mazarin had not had a grain of truth in them.

Meanwhile, in Paris the situation was deteriorating so much each day that when Mme de Motteville learnt that the queen had reached Saint-Denis, she decided to go out and meet her. One of the Grande Mademoiselle's coaches was taking her as far as Chaillot, and hardly had she passed through when the advance guard of Condé's army appeared. Little did she know at the time that a few hours later she would have fallen into the hands of her enemies. It should be said, however, that Condé's soldiers did not have too bad a reputation. She knew them well, having seen them in Paris: they shouted and threatened, but those 'sheep', as de Motteville called them, were not really dangerous. After her first night in the shelter of Saint-Denis she was woken at dawn by the roll of drums: it was the rearguard of the royal army marching on Paris to fight Condé's troops. The queen also rose early and went to the Carmelite convent to pray for their success. On her knees before the Blessed Sacrament, she rose only to go to the convent grill for news of the battle that was taking place near the Porte Saint-Antoine.[22] There were dead, a great many dead, people she knew well, both in her own and in the enemy camp. She wept over the death of the handsome Duc de Nemours, one of the most famous *frondeurs*, and over La Rochefoucauld, Longueville's evil genius, who had been practically blinded by musket fire. Condé was in a bad way; he was backed up against the walls of Paris when suddenly a volley of cannon shot cut through the front ranks of the royal army, fired from the top of the Bastille. Apparently, the Grande Mademoiselle could not resist taking part and firing on the troops of her cousin the king. This intervention saved the situation for Condé, who was able to slip into Paris, the very image of the hero, sword in hand, covered in blood, dust and sweat. But the Parisian bourgeois felt that the tide was turning, and the more moderate of them decided to seek the royal pardon. The princes, who had everything to lose from a peace, and the ordinary people, who had nothing more to lose, united against the bourgeoisie. Terror reigned in the capital, now packed with refugees. Bands of brigands, vaguely claiming allegiance to Condé, laid down the law. 'Let us boldly loosen the reins, let us pile up the carnage, respecting neither the great nor the small, neither the young nor the old, neither the males nor the females. Let us kill, loot, destroy . . . ,' one of them wrote. On the evening of 4 July 1652, a huge, drunken, hate-filled crowd gathered around the Hôtel de Ville, where burghers and municipal authorities were deliberating. The crowd consisted mainly of ordinary people, but there were soldiers there, too, who flanked the demonstrators inconspicuously, launching slogans at the right moment and directing its movements. It was difficult to say whether they were in the pay of Beaufort or Condé. In any event, Condé suddenly came out of the Hôtel de Ville and announced: 'Those people do not want to do anything for us, they are all "Mazarins".' Suddenly, from all sides, shots were being fired on the Hôtel de Ville, then the building was set alight. Asphyxiated by the smoke, coughing and spitting, presidents, councillors, rapporteurs, lawyers, and magistrates came out on to the steps, to be massacred. They were stabbed, disembowelled, hacked to pieces on the spot. One lawyer, fleeing the scene, asked the help of a richly dressed man, who replied, 'Good God! We need a bit of disorder!' He happened to have fallen on one of the ringleaders. The mob wanted to enter the building to kill all those who were still hiding there. Amidst clouds of smoke, shots were fired in the staircases and corridors. The Maréchal de L'Hôpital, the governor of Paris, one of the most sought-after victims, put on the uniform of one of his guards in order to flee undetected. The provost of merchants managed to hide in a dark corner and was trapped there for hours. Only greed distracted the crowd from satisfying their murderous instincts. The killing stopped in order to loot and several lives were spared in return for raising a ransom. President de Guénégaud was pulled this way and that by several rival gangs who wanted to tear him to pieces, but, dragged from the mêlée by the strongest band, he was forced to pay 200 *livres*. To protect this goose and its golden eggs, his attackers tore off his rich clothes, dressed him in rags and marched him away through the rival bands undetected.

When begged to invervene, the princes obstinately refused to put an end to the madness which they had acquiesced in, if not actually aroused. The first to become alarmed at the storm that he had unleashed was the weakest and most impulsive of them, Gaston d'Orléans. He begged Condé to do something, but Condé, with biting sarcasm, replied, 'I don't know the first thing about it and, anyway, I'm a great coward. Send M. de Beaufort. The people know and love him. He knows how their minds work.' Beaufort obliged, went down into the cellars of the Hôtel de Ville and brought out barrels of wine which were then rolled across the square and broken up. The crowd fell upon the wine and the carnage ended in a massive drinking party.

The news arriving at Saint-Denis was terrifying: the whole of Paris was aflame, the population bleeding to death. The Court was horrified. Next morning, Paris, too, was horrified. This time the overwhelming majority of the population had had enough, and especially they had had enough of Condé. At that point, he was offered the most generous terms for peace by none other than Mazarin. The cardinal sensed that the whole business was drawing to a close, but he underestimated Condé's stubbornness, and the prince refused any accommodation. Mazarin's next ruse was to leave the Court; the rebellion, which was cracking and leaking on all sides, maintained an appearance of cohesion only on the basis of mutual hatred of the cardinal, but if he was removed the rebellion would collapse. The most difficult person to persuade of this logic was the king himself. Oddly enough, he did not want Mazarin to leave, even for a short time, even as a trick, even if Mazarin himself argued forcefully in favour of it.[23] In the end, he agreed and the cardinal departed for the Ardennes. Thus Condé was left in a commanding position but, as Mazarin had foreseen, the exasperation he had aroused among the Parisians paralysed any initiative he still possessed. In the end he too left Paris for Flanders, where he put himself at the service of the Spanish. Mazarin was the undoubted winner of this particular game, watching and controlling everything from his Ardennes retreat. As anticipated the rebellion broke up of its own accord. The people once again protested its fidelity to the king and the king granted an amnesty, returning to his capital to make yet another triumphal entry.

In spite of the success of his plan, Mazarin was once again prey to doubts. Supposing he were not recalled, supposing it had all been arranged in advance? Supposing the king, in his absence, had escaped from his influence and no longer needed to call on his services?[24] The king's attitude merely confirmed his fears. Disdaining the Palais Royal, which was open to attack at the least riot, the king decided to move into the old fortress, the palace of his ancestors, the Louvre. He summoned the *parlement* and forbade it categorically to meddle in affairs of State. He then settled a few scores: the Grande Mademoiselle was expelled from the Tuileries; Beaufort, Broussel and others were exiled; Monseigneur de Retz, who had been made a cardinal, was the next to be dealt with. Orders were given to Capitaine Pradelle to arrest him at home, but Pradelle asked for written instructions. Louis picked up his pen: 'I have commanded Pradelle to carry out the present order on the person of Cardinal de Retz, even to arrest him dead or alive in the event of any resistance on his part.' Anne was horrified at the thought of killing a prince of the church, and persuaded Louis that it would be better to arrest him in the Louvre. It proved difficult to lure him to the fortress. They waited for weeks, but still he did not come. Christmas 1652 was approaching and Retz felt obliged to pay his respects to the royal family. setting foot inside the Louvre at last. On the stairs he met the king, coming down from visiting his mother. The king could not have been more gracious, inviting Retz to greet the queen. As he led Retz to her apartments he spoke of a new comedy that he was planning. He chattered on about this and that, laughed, greeted various persons on the way, including some pleasantry whispered in the ear of the captain of the guards, Villequier. 'And above all make sure that there is no one on the stage,' he concluded. Father Paulin, his confessor, came up to the king: it was midday, time to go to mass. Louis called Retz and directed him to the chapel. In the middle of the service Villequier appeared and interrupted the king's prayers to whisper something to him. The king turned to Father Paulin: 'Cardinal de Retz will be arrested here.'[25]

Motteville was in ecstasies over 'this judicious act of moderation'. But what was the point of pushing hypocrisy so far? There could be no question of sparing Retz – Louis had signed his death warrant – or of taking precautions. The king was master, especially in his own house. Why should he want to be so pleasant to the man he was about to arrest? This comedy, carried rather too far, was really an admission of weakness, the weakness of a young man unsure of himself, wanting to feel more cunning than the most cunning man in France by tricking him. Louis's self-justification ran: Monseigneur de Retz is not as clever as people say, because he was taken in by the king, therefore the king is cleverer that Retz because he persuaded Retz to believe him.

With the ground cleared by the disappearance of the *frondeurs* and the arrest of his worst enemy, Retz, Mazarin could now officially reappear.

Latterly he had been receiving letters from his friends urging him to come back, and at last the long awaited formal order arrived from the king. Mazarin now played hard to get, finding innumerable excuses to delay his return. When he was quite sure that desire for his presence was at its height, in February 1653 he decided to present himself at Court.

The *Fronde* was practically at an end. The queen regent had set the original example by challenging her late husband's will, and *parlementaires* and burghers followed, demanding parliamentary monarchy without actually realizing it, not out of any liberalizing spirit but in order to protect their own sordid interests. Princes and nobles entered the fray to satisfy various, often contradictory ambitions, displaying above all their selfishness. During that time, the richest of the nobles had been seen to align themselves with the most active extremists; a commander-in-chief had been abandoned by his troops when he tried to make them cross over to the enemy; the king of France's own cousin had drawn his sword in the service of the king of Spain, his traditional enemy. Above all women had been seen to play a determinant role. Royal power was vested in a woman, Anne of Austria, supported by a strong but in many respects feminine spirit, Mazarin. The opposition were women: Chevreuse, Longueville, the Grande Mademoiselle. Impetuosity had reigned supreme. In an uninterrupted succession of dramatic events and reversals, the circus of intrigues and love affairs unfolded against the appalling backcloth of double war, foreign and civil. The farce was matched by the horror. It was then that the first republican, revolutionary, anarchistic cries rose up from an abominably betrayed people, or at least from those who still had the strength to shout. Moreover, the irresponsibility of the *Fronde* was all the more sinister in that the price to be paid for it in human life, penury and suffering was so high; it was also noted for its inconstancy and an astonishing confusion of values. And yet, even though it had ruined France, even though it had put its very existence in danger, the *Fronde* was not a serious political entity. This explains why it fizzled out. The *Fronde* was certainly a reaction against Richelieu's centralizing dictatorship and a last-ditch attempt to avoid it happening again. That is why it was above all utterly anachronistic. From the outset the *Fronde* was in the rearguard of history. It was also something of a recreation for its participants: they amused themselves as they waded through blood.

The *frondeurs* were also finished and would never be rehabilitated. The Prince de Conti, after a final attempt to capture Bordeaux, retreated, requesting the hand of that former negotiating point, Mazarin's niece, Mme Martinozzi. The Duchesse de Chevreuse was to go further: later she was to marry her grandson off to Colbert's daughter. (Colbert was by that time prime minister), then end her life in the utmost humiliation. The Duchesse de Longueville, renouncing frivolity and politics at once, retired to a convent where she set about leading a more edifying life. Similarly Gaston d'Orléans shut himself up in his Château de Blois, and spent his days in prayer, perhaps to gain forgiveness for so many acts of cowardice and betrayal. Setting aside any such pious solution, Cardinal de Retz escaped from prison in Nantes and reached Rome, where he was to compose the *Memoirs* that place him among the best writers of his century. Similarly, La Rochefoucauld, now retired and nearly blind, wrote his cynical maxims – either in astonishing contrast to or as a logical conclusion of a past filled with amorous adventure and political intrigue. Beaufort, the rabble-rouser, got himself killed in Crete on an expedition against the Turks. Condé was to wait for seven years and peace with Spain before returning, solemnly, theatrically, proudly, to throw himself at the feet of his king. Once pardoned, the one-time genius of the battlefield soon realized that he no longer had a place in that changed world.

These men and women had made an atrocious mess of things, as often as not out of a criminal lack of awareness. But all were remarkable, in their gifts and talents, in the passions that drove them on to a life that was exceptional in its fierce independence. If their actions were never equal to their valour, they remained nevertheless attractive or likable because they displayed so much personality. But not one survived unchanged, for the era of personalities was drawing to an end.

CHAPTER 5

Mazarin's Revenge

It is easy to imagine the state of the French economy after five years of savage civil war. The State coffers were, of course, empty. Nothing more could be expected from taxation; the provinces were so ruined that they could pay nothing. But this was the very moment when the government had an urgent need of money to consolidate the still wavering fidelity of the governors of cities and provinces. Convinced that bribes could recreate French unity, Mazarin heroically decided to pawn his own jewellery in order to find the necessary money.

This temporary detachment did not prevent him from remaining as single-mindedly self-interested as ever. Finding himself at the head of affairs for the fourth time, he was more determined than ever to waste no time building up his fortune.[1] He had already been dealing in gold and currency. Now he was also to deal in commodities like sugar and rare spices. Not content with possessing a commercial fleet, he began to finance privateers, blurring once and for all the dividing line between the State's revenues and his own. To control the fantastic business network, extending over every branch of the economy, there was of course the indispensable Colbert.[2].

Seeing Mazarin again, Queen Anne was disagreeably surprised. She was expecting her old collaborator and companion: she found a new master. Instead of the insidious charmer she had dreamt of during his absence, she found an ill-tempered man who avoided her. Now he had a grudge against everybody, including her; he felt he had been abandoned by all in both his exiles. To his desire to reassert, if not actually revenge, himself, was added a degree of self-interest. In the past Mazarin had listened to the queen, shown consideration for her, courted her, but at that time it was she who held power. Since then the king had come of age, he was no longer a child and was becoming bolder each day; it was he who represented the power of tomorrow, and it was to him that Mazarin turned. Anne, whose feminine characteristics overrode every-thing else, refused to understand. She would employ all her womanly charms to attract the attentions of her erstwhile admirer; she reproached him tenderly; she sadly evoked happy memories of long ago. She set aside the role of queen and became simply a woman to the misogynist who now found her exasperating. He could no longer bear the flabby, indolent, dim woman, conscious at all times of her rank. He even went so far as to refer to her as a lazy, bigoted fool in front of her closest companions. Without him she would certainly have been incapable of governing France, and Mazarin now saw how right her late husband had been to distrust her. Even in public there were occasions when he could no longer contain himself: he would interrupt her, reply curtly, bully her, give her orders. And yet, to his great chagrin, he found that he still needed her. The idea of eliminating the mother in order to stay and dominate the son alone proved to be erroneous. Anne, not Mazarin, governed the king and Mazarin had to maintain power by governing her. He was forced to pay court to her despite himself, reluctantly playing along with her semi-amorous games, forever claiming that she had upset him in order to forestall her saying the same of him, endlessly protesting in order to parry her protestations. In an inimitable, involuted style, laced with allusions that were sometimes transparent, sometimes obscure, he wrote her letters overflowing with false tenderness: 'If it were permitted me to send you my heart, assuredly you would find there things that would not please you, and more at this moment that I am writing to you than ever before.' These amorous expressions were to astonish posterity, but they did not stem from passion, only from the fashion – and the exigencies – of the time.[3]

With the king, Mazarin appeared imperious and harsh. He held a grudge against the boy for making him tremble with fear during those years of exile, and keeping him on tenterhooks awaiting his recall. With subtle brutality he showed the king that he had resumed all his power. Were the king to grant the slightest favour without consulting his mentor, Mazarin would 'rebuke him as if he were a schoolboy, telling him that he understood nothing about such things and that he should leave everything to him; as a result the individual to whom the king had given it got nothing and the cardinal gave it to someone else without the king daring to complain.'[4] Arrogantly, Mazarin ignored protocol; the prime minister did not go to the king, the king came, several times a day, to the prime minister, 'to whom he paid court like a mere courtier ... [Mazarin] would receive the king in an off-hand way, scarcely rising when he entered and left and never accompanying him to the door ...'[5]

It is puzzling that Louis put up with it, and after Mazarin's death, he was to ask himself why as well. But in a situation that was still so unstable, with so many opponents narrowly defeated and rebellion always ready to break out again, it was better to keep 'so skilful, so clever a minister, who had survived so many factions, who loved me and whom I loved, and who had rendered me great services, but whose thoughts and ways were naturally very different from mine and whom, however, I could neither contradict nor discredit without perhaps stirring up against him storms that one had found so hard to calm ...'[6] The case made out by the king is valid in many ways, but there is still something unconvincing about it. Did Louis like being dominated or did he enjoy suffering by it? Either way, it was up to him to avoid this dilemma. There had always been strange, complex, obscure relations between the two individuals; as a child Louis had found it difficult to accept the yoke (to which he was to acquiesce as a youth), from a man who hurt, humiliated and violated his heart, mind and perhaps even his body. Mazarin knew that he subjugated the teenaged king when he was in front of him, but he always remained terrified lest he lose that grip when the boy was no longer there. There is something very contradictory in those bonds that only the death of the older man was to break and which many historians have presented as the natural attachment of a grateful son for an adoptive father. There was not an ounce of trust in their relationship, but there was a certain mutual, unacknowledged esteem, hatred and perhaps also an odd sort of love. There was certainly much more than mutual benefit in their momentous union, which lasted for so long.

The king was quite right to fear the instability of the situation; the *parlement* – yet again – was up to its old tricks. Thinking that they were still living in the good old days of the *Fronde*, the *parlementaires* had now taken to actually discussing edicts that Louis had brought to have registered a few days before they ratified them. This was extremely impudent: they did not represent the nation; they had not even been elected by it. They were lawyers, not deputies, but they were demanding the unthinkable innovation of a parliamentary debate just when the monarchy was busy re-establishing its absolutism. The *parlementaires* were never to be more retrogressive than when they seemed to be innovatory. The king was staying at Vincennes and was out hunting on the April morning of 1655 when he was informed that they had met to debate his edicts. Without even changing, he clapped spurs to his horse and rode to Paris, making a sensational entrance to the *parlement* in hunting clothes: a red jerkin, grey hat and knee-length boots. 'Everyone knows how much your assemblies have disturbed my State and what dangerous effects they have produced,' he stormed. 'I have learnt that you intend to continue them under pretext of deliberating on the edicts that were once read and published in my presence. I have come expressly to forbid you to continue . . .' And he departed again for Vincennes to resume hunting, leaving the *parlementaires* petrified for once. The only way they could think of to react was to lodge a pathetic complaint with Mazarin against the king's costume, as a lack of deference to their august body. Mazarin merely nodded and the *parlementaires* retired, grumbling, perhaps aware of the ridiculous inanity of their actions.[7] After all these years, it only needed a sentence spoken by an angry young man to silence the *parlement* at last. It was to remain silent for exactly sixty years. The impact of that scene was such that it passed into legend, adding a whip clasped in the king's hand and the apocryphal retort, *'L'État, c'est moi'*, ('I am the State'). Contemporaries were so astonished that they refused to believe that this submissive boy had been capable of turning himself into a thundering Zeus unaided, and suspected the king's minister of arranging this theatrical gesture.

Mazarin was neglecting the queen mother. Among other things he was not writing to her often enough and did not pay enough attention to the letters that she wrote to him. She was very displeased with him, and if this was the case, how long would it be before the king, too, became displeased. When he received a message from the king to this effect, a precursor of inevitable disgrace, Mazarin was at the front in the north of France, for the war with Spain was continuing. Fortunately, he had been warned of it in a letter by the queen mother the night before. Before writing to his prime minister the king had wanted to convince his mother that she had been ill-treated by him and she dashed to her writing table. Louis' calculation was simple enough. Like everyone else he had noticed the Italian's indifference and disdain for the woman to whom he owed everything. Louis' plan was to widen the gap and sow discord between his mother and his minister who in spite of everything, remained united in order to dominate him all the more. This way Louis hoped that he would no longer be dominated by either and would be able to do as he liked; he would be master at last. Whatever the reason, what actually happened gives the lie to the reasons that Louis was later to give to explain his submission to Mazarin.

In this episode of the comedy, the three protagonists remained entirely true to themselves. The future Sun King revealed once again an astonishing pettiness and a flagrant weakness in audacity. Instead of turning against the man who had acted so badly towards her, loyal, faithful Anne warned Mazarin of the danger and clung to their old friendship, and Mazarin reacted with all his usual speed, subtlety and opportunism. The despised woman with whom he regularly lost his temper, at once became the natural, unshakable ally, once the alarm had been sounded from the king's side. Suddenly she was no longer a lazy fool but a cherished elderly lady and a great queen on whom he would pour the treasures of his most respectful and tender attentions. Unable to leave the front, he wrote letter after letter to the queen in which gratitude, affection, deference, even servility, jostled with one another in the amorous language of the period in which the tone of unbridled passion expressed the most banal sentiments and in a secret code – mysterious signs and enigmatic nicknames – worthy of a romantic novel. He begged her to bring the king and himself together, he the most devoted, the most humble of her servants. He was determined on his return to Court to take the king in hand. He would be careful not to allow the boy out of his sight, for even though he had recently dominated the *parlement* he remained the same sly, weak boy who needed constant supervision and whom only he, Mazarin, knew how to tame.[8]

Having left the king to wallow in ignorance for years on end, Mazarin suddenly decided to make up for lost time, and the entire Court noticed this sensational innovation. To begin with the cardinal invited his sovereign to attend all the councils of ministers, at which the boy got so bored that he would get up and tiptoe out, preferring to discuss a new ballet that he was rehearsing or tune his guitar with a friend.[9] The cardinal, however, devoted several hours a day to Louis' education. Alone together in his office he revealed the world and mankind to the young king, giving him object lessons in history, politics and economics, gradually initiating him into the affairs of State. Historians sometimes express admiration for Mazarin's devoted sense of education, but this was not the view of contemporaries. They understood what Mazarin had understood, namely, that the king might one day take revenge on the man responsible for his painful ignorance up to that time.[10] Mazarin vigorously pursued his pedagogical role, staking everything on the king's laziness, which, he told himself, would always stand in the way of his learning enough to feel capable of government. Moreover, it is arguable that his 'lessons' had much practical value, for although the cardinal prime minister spent several hours alone with His Majesty, in sight and hearing of the Court, he seems to have kept prudently to general ideas and vague principles, according to the king's former tutor, the old Duc de Villeroi.[11]

Mazarin did give some specified advice, but it was dictated by his own bitter experience: reduce the power of the princes of the blood royal, keep courtiers at a distance, mistrust ministers, promise a great deal to the people, but deliver as little as possible. With dazzling cynicism, the Mazarinian style could be summed up in the words: 'Take their money, but spare their blood.' These were excellent enough maxims in general, but they were all negative, adding up not to the politics of attack, but of defence. His advice lacked its corollary, a plan of action, and if Louis did not have the vision and character to invent one, he would remain confined within Mazarin's defences.

Mazarin did have one moment of panic, when the mistrust and duplicity he was trying to inculcate in his pupil appeared to be already well established. A warning from the king's confessor, Father Paulin, did nothing to reassure him: 'Your Eminence will allow his faithful servant to tell him that he should allow only his most dependable creatures to approach His Majesty.' The suspicious Italian anxiously scrutinized the silent, solid, impenetrable boy. 'Don't give it a thought!' his friend, the Maréchal de Gramont reassured him. 'The king is weak and would never think of removing you from power.' 'Ah! Monsieur le Maréchal,' the cardinal replied in his terrible Italian accent, 'you do not know him, there is enough stuff in him to make four kings and an honest man.'

But he was wrong to be so anxious. Although Mazarin watched him anxiously, he did not register the slightest trace of irritation, neither did he expect or take part in anything to do with actual government. Apart from the cardinal's 'lessons', he spent his time at military or theatrical spectacles, thinking of little else, and in which Mazarin encouraged him

71

with all the subtle power at his disposal. The cardinal only allowed young scatterbrains near him, who were incapable of serious conversation let alone of political discussion. He still mistrusted anyone who approached the king without having first been vetted by him. The king's tutor, Mme de Motteville's brother, had not been appointed by the cardinal, and was observed with the greatest suspicion, so much so that on the advice of his own family and of the queen herself, the poor fellow thought it would be more prudent to sell his post.[12] As an additional precaution, Mazarin imported a new cargo of nephews and nieces from Italy, brought to Court by the cardinal's sisters in person. Before producing them at Court, their attentive brother put these provincial Italian women through an intensive training that was to transform them into elegant Parisians. They brought with them one of the Martinozzi girls and three Mancinis, a boy – Filippo – and two girls, one of whom was called Maria, a dark beauty with large black eyes. More would be heard of Maria Mancini in due course. In sending for her parents, Mazarin was acting not so much as a Machiavellian politician as a good Sicilian *mafioso*. *La famiglia* was sacred: it had to remain united, its members always ready to help one another. It was up to the successful uncle who had made a fortune to look after the entire tribe, without allowing personal tastes or inclinations to get in the way. In fact, he was killing two birds with one stone: this new cargo of petulant Italian girls captivated the king as much as the first had done, but this time more dangerously for now he had reached adolescence. He darted from one to the other quite incapable of deciding between them: amused, stung, seduced by each in turn. Whether or not they had been given any specific instructions while the king amused himself with them, they enabled their uncle to rule in peace.

Life at court was all masked balls, comedies and ballets, in which the king excelled. At the Louvre, there was a tendency to keep to the already classic repertoire, and one night, a troupe of newly fashionable players appeared in the guardroom before the king for the first time in *Nicomède*, a tragedy by Corneille. The actresses were certainly pretty, but Corneille's lines failed to win over an audience impatient for more entertaining spectacles. They applauded politely. The leader of the troupe, a tall, thin, gawky young man with a sardonic expression, stepped forward. He asked His Majesty if they might go on to play *Le Docteur Amoureux*, one of the farces with which they had been entertaining the provinces, and His Majesty readily agreed. *Le Docteur Amoureux* was a triumph and Louis arranged for the troupe to take over the theatre of the Petit Bourbon, where it could give free rein to its talents. The leading player bowed, almost mockingly: his name was Molière.

In the cardinal's quarters cards were considered more important than the theatre, and gambling went on all night. The king was happy to join in; on one occasion he was on particularly good form and his partner, the Chevalier de Rohan, owed him a large sum in *louis d'or*. Rohan placed on the table 800 *louis* and 200 Spanish *pistoles* to make up the sum of his debt. But the king insisted, 'They must be *louis*.' The Chevalier picked up his *pistoles* and threw them out of the window. 'Since Your Majesty does not want them,' he shouted, 'they are worthless!' Outraged, the king complained to Mazarin of the man's insolence. He got little sympathy: 'Sire, the Chevalier de Rohan has acted like a king and you like the Chevalier de Rohan.' Mazarin would not have made this contemptuous reply, however, had he known the dangerous ideas fermenting in the crazy head of that impetuous knight.

The king also liked to escape from the Court and pay incognito visits to fairs, or to walk in the gardens in the moonlight. Once, on his return from an entertainment, the royal coach outstripped the horseguards. The king was delighted. 'How wonderful it would be if we were attacked by robbers,' he remarked. The king's brother, Philippe, preferred to disguise himself as a woman in a blonde wig, attending balls in the middle of Lent. 'Did you see the Capuchin monks and nuns?' someone asked him. There was a dreadful scandal: that the king's brother should wear drag was considered quite natural, but for others to disguise themselves as monks and nuns was disgraceful. Louis and his mother were obliged to go through the motions of swearing to revenge the insult to 'Holy Mother Church'.

Though the king was quite punctilious in religious matters, he could be very slack where Court protocol was concerned. The Grande Mademoiselle was horrified by an incident at a ball given by the Maréchal de L'Hôpital that they had attended bedecked in their best finery. The king sat down at the table. 'Since this is the only place left,' he remarked, 'I shall have to sit here!' A special place had not been reserved for the head of State, and the king, passing dishes and telling people to start before him, was insulting protocol. The Grande Mademoiselle expressed her astonishment in no uncertain terms. 'He doesn't care for ceremonies,' Queen Anne replied, which caused considerable offence among the fussier members of the Court.

The young king was still flirting with one or other of the Italian nieces, and for the moment, his favourite was the Duchesse de Mercoeur, Laura Mancini. Anne gave a small private ball in honour of Queen Henrietta of England, the ruined, exiled widow of Charles I, and her daughter, also named Henrietta, a thin, precocious, untrustworthy child. As the men chose their partners, the king rushed towards Laura, but his mother leapt from her chair, snatched the Italian girl from her son's arms and ordered him in a whisper to go and invite the English princess to dance. Terribly embarrassed, the Queen of England intervened: her daughter had hurt her foot, she would not be able to dance, the king was therefore quite free to choose a different partner. Very well, retorted Anne of Austria, if the English princess cannot dance, the king shall not dance either.[13] There was no need for such a fuss, because very soon Louis dropped Mercoeur in favour of her younger sister, Olympia Mancini. This dangerous, imperious, biting and cruel intriguer of eighteen years could do nothing without causing trouble. Soon her flirtation with the king set the entire Court buzzing; the Grande Mademoiselle was long to remember the day when Olympia forced a party of courtiers to climb 'the most incommodious' rocks in Fontainebleau, 'where, I understand, not even goats have penetrated'. The king then summoned the ramblers to follow him on a different path and they were obliged to come down again at full speed – at the risk of breaking their necks. That evening, returning to the castle by torchlight, they set the forest on fire.[14]

At this point, a phenomenon arrived in Paris of which the whole of Europe was talking. Having become queen at the age of six on the death of her father, Gustavus Adolphus, at eighteen, Christina of Sweden had dismissed her regents and ruled alone. Then, after ten brilliant years she had abdicated, and had thereafter wandered around Europe: she even gave up Protestantism in order to travel more freely through the Catholic countries. Speaking eight languages, translating Greek and Latin from childhood, versed in every branch of learning, she was regarded as a great scholar. At thirty, with one shoulder higher than the other, large, round, intense eyes and dirty hands, wearing whatever came first to hand in a medley of male and female clothes, she had the reputation of being an eccentric and an inveterate debauchee. It was said that she organized orgies, with or without men. She completely disconcerted the French Court, ignoring protocol, swearing like a trooper, putting her legs up on chairs and saying whatever came into her head. She affected to despise women for their ignorance and frivolity, and the only member of her sex she was really interested in was to be Ninon de Lenclos, the most famous courtesan of the century. (It was rumoured that Ninon had among others seduced the terrible Richelieu and who, half a century later and over eighty years of age, could still charm the young Voltaire.) When musicians were sent to distract Christina's sleepless hours, she pulled open the curtain of her bed and, sticking out her gorgon's head surmounted by a napkin of doubtful cleanliness, barked 'Damnation, but they sing well!' The Italian *castrati* were struck dumb with terror and the concert had to be broken off. At social gatherings she would come out with remarks that made the hair of the prudish Anne of Austria stand on end: 'Faith, Madame, I'd fuck every day if it gave me pleasure, but I don't care for women's slime. Were I a man it would be quite different.' She did worse than that in the queen's eyes by taking delight in encouraging the flirtation between Louis and Olympia Mancini, even talking of marriage. 'If I were in your place, I'd marry someone I loved,' she told Louis. The idea of the French King marrying a Mancini was preposterous, and Christina, in spite of being ex-queen of Sweden was politely but firmly asked to leave Paris.[15]

These triflings passed and the king left the Mancini girls behind, falling in love instead with the fair-haired, gentle, gracious Mlle de La Motte d'Argencourt who had recently entered the queen mother's service. Anne's reaction was typically Spanish: she became anxious for her son's virtue. The lords of the Court reacted quite differently; as the Grande Mademoiselle noted with satisfaction, 'They hoped that this affair would continue and have a good influence on his health.' Despite past love affairs, so voluptuously described by the chroniclers, despite Mme de Beauvais, to whom legend attributes the honour of initiating him, it seemed that Louis was still not really interested in sexual activity. For his part, Mazarin had decided to put an end to the affair, preferring the king to attend to his nieces, and begged the queen to show firmness. In order to keep on good terms with him, the girl's mother, Mme de La Motte, repeated to Mazarin the confidences that the king had made to her daughter and which the girl in all innocence, had faithfully repeated to her mother. The cardinal learnt that the king had promised that if she gave in to him he would resist the opposition of the queen and Mazarin.

It needed more than the love of a girl to shake off so heavy a tutelage. By dint of exhortations, prayers and remonstrances – an offence to God, the horror of sin, fear of hell – Queen Anne won through. Her son broke off the relationship and went out to Vincennes for a change of air. His mother breathed a sigh of relief – but not for long; although the king came back to Paris full of good resolutions, during a ball who should come up to him and take him by the hand but Mlle de La Motte d'Argencourt. He turned first pale, then red; his hand trembled in the young girl's hand – and Mazarin had to come to the rescue. He took the king aside and repeated to him all the secrets that Louis had told the girl. The king trembled and turned away, without so much as a glance in the direction of Mlle de La Motte, who soon received an order to enter a convent, where, disappointed and betrayed, she was to end her days in some sort of peace.[16]

France was at war, as usual, against the Spanish. For the king, waging war was a matter of knowing the names of the officers and the numbers of soldiers in each regiment, designing their uniforms, comparing the quality of their music. He was forever talking to the Grande Mademoiselle about his musketeers and his light cavalry. 'Your grandfather did not go into battle so young,' she said, intending a compliment, 'Yet he did more than I,' Louis replied. 'So far I haven't been allowed to go as often as I would like; but in the future I hope that people will have cause to talk about me.'[17]

People very soon had cause to talk about him, but not in the way he intended, for he fell ill. Whether it arose from infections rife among the wounded or the unhealthiness of the climate, the king developed a fever and had to be taken to Calais. The doctors were aghast at the symptoms they observed: 'Extraordinary weakness . . . unbearable headaches . . . bloated body covered with red, violet and blackish spots . . . the tongue thick and black.' Bladder and sphincter were slackening and the patient was soiling his sheets,[18] but in their legendary ignorance the doctors bled and purged for all they were worth, thus aggravating his condition.

As he declined, Court intrigues grew proportionately, for if the king died, his brother Philippe would become king. In a few days Philippe became the epicentre of everyone's calculations, hopes, manoeuvres – especially those of the intriguing, gossipy women with whom he loved to spend his time. His best friend, Mme de Choisy, repeated to anyone who would listen: 'I am about to become the king's favourite.' She did not, for all that, dream of becoming the mistress of this well-known homosexual, but, because she had protected his passion for the Comte de Guiche, she had insinuated herself into his private life and become his confidant. To strengthen her hold over him she tried to detach him from the queen and cardinal by telling horrifying tales about them. Mme de Choisy went further; it was said that the unrepentant former *frondeuse*, sniffing the breeze of power with delight, leapt into the future king's bed to make doubly sure of it. Other courtiers believed it to be the surest way of turning the young homosexual against women forever. Another woman, Mme de Fienne, publicly expressed her delight at the king's imminent death in the belief that his successor would soon shower her with the money she so dearly loved. In her impatience she went to spy at the door of the dying man. 'Mme de Fienne is at the door, lying on the ground to see what is happening in here,' announced the king's nurse to his mother. 'I'll go and throw her out of the window,' threatened Anne indignantly.[19]

Taking a much more realistic approach, the cardinal prime minister laid siege to Philippe's acknowledged lover, the handsome, witty, irresistible Comte de Guiche. Never had Mazarin felt himself more in danger: if the king died, it would be all over with him, he would be submerged by the formidable wave of hate that he had raised during all those years. Knowing from experience what happened in such cases, he also despatched a messenger to Paris with orders to remove his treasure and most precious objects from his palace to safety.[20] Impervious to all this contradictory ferment, Mazarin's niece, Olympia, the king's former conquest, continued to play cards night and day as if nothing were happening, while her sister Maria could not stop crying. She was thinking of the king; and she did not want him to die.[21]

While taking precautions, her uncle was also trying to prevent the worst from happening. He re-established calm and unity among the doctors, terrified by their responsibility and powerlessness. He forbade them to quarrel or abuse one another and forced them to decide unanimously on the treatment to be implemented. Thanks to him these pompous charlatans agreed at last on administering to the dying man a potion of antimony mixed with emetic wine and a laxative herb tea. For the first time the king vomited something of 'a poisonous greenish, slightly yellow nature'. Next day, there was more vomiting: 'A quantity of yellow bile, like honey, with a great deal of rotten mucus.'[22] This took him over the crisis and all that remained was to allow him to recover his strength, sapped as much by his doctors as by his illness.

Learning of the intrigues that had centred on his brother, the king concealed his real feelings beneath cruel, contemptuous teasing: 'If you had been king,' he said to Philippe, 'you would have been in a difficult position, for Mme de Choisy and Mme de Fienne would never have got on and you wouldn't have been able to keep them both. Anyway, Mme de Choisy would have been the one.' Philippe protested vehemently and sincerely; he had never wished for the king's death. 'I really do believe you,' the king replied, adding, 'when you're in Paris, you will be in love therefore with Mme d'Olonne, for the Comte de Guiche has promised her that you will.' At the mention of his lover, Monsieur turned crimson.[23]

The king liked to dwell on what took place when it was thought that he was dying – he wanted to know who smiled, who conspired, who wept. As to the latter, he was told about the cardinal's niece, little Maria Mancini, for one, to whom he had never paid the slightest attention, too concerned as he was with her older sisters. He had always thought of her as a child and, as he told his mother, he did not like little girls. He was intrigued to hear that the girl had wept for him and he took a closer look at her.[24] He discovered that the ugly duckling whom he had hardly noticed had become, in six years, a most attractive teenage girl. She was not a classic beauty but rather a fiery, feminine, witty creature, a brunette who was the exact opposite of the plump blondes then in fashion, and thus regarded by the Court as ugly. 'Short, fat, with the looks of a tavern serving-girl, but witty,' noted that connoisseur of women, Bussy-Rabutin.[25] As such, she won Louis' heart. Soon the courtiers had the satisfaction of being able to gossip endlessly about the king's young passion; no more flirtations with alluring, but insincere creatures; no more pseudo-passions for innocent young girls. Not only was Louis in love, but he was beloved of a creature herself capable of giving love. Under Maria's influence, he came to take pride in his appearance and took particular care with his wigs, and above all, he began to read. Maria made him feel ashamed of his ignorance and under her direction he threw himself into history, philosophy, poetry. The king was so transfigured that he promised to marry her, which Maria told herself was the most natural thing in the world, believing that nothing was impossible.

Her uncle the prime minister was also thinking of the king's marriage but to someone quite different in the person of the Princesse Marguerite, daughter of Mme Christine de France, Duchesse de Savoie, and sister of Louis XIII. Mme Christine was a politician to her fingertips, intelligent, imperious and cunning, and had given a lot of trouble to her brother and Richelieu by energetically following her own interests, which had not always been those of France. Now she was delighted at the idea of seeing her daughter queen of France. The same cannot be said of Anne of Austria, who hoped for better things for her son; nevertheless Mazarin set out to overcome her resistance. Outwardly he seemed utterly determined to push through the marriage between the king and the Savoyarde, but, in secret, he was aiming at another candidate, the pearl of Europe, the most inaccessible of all: the Infanta Maria Theresa of Austria, eldest daughter of King Philip IV of Spain. Such an alliance seemed hopeless when France had been at war with Spain for twenty-three years but there were signs that both sides were tiring of the hostilities and the cunning Mazarin had not missed them. By allusion and hints he made it known in Madrid that France would not be against peace – or the Infanta. The proverbial pride, sloth and inefficiency of the Spanish, combined with a prudent policy of wait-and-see, made for a delayed response. In order to force them to make up their minds, Mazarin decided to move towards an engagement with the Savoyarde and arranged for the king and Court to go to Lyon to meet the Princesse Marguerite and her family. The Duchesse de Savoie, despite her reputation for astuteness, fell into the trap and impatiently awaited the visit.

Anne of Austria grumbled still more at this prospect, especially when she learnt that Maria Mancini would be in the party. She already disapproved of her son's obviously hopeless passion for this young lady. She had of course learnt all about the promise of marriage and Mazarin had done nothing to discourage this fantasy. A horrible suspicion was beginning to grow in Anne of Austria's mind: supposing Mazarin was mad and ambitious enough not to be resolutely opposed to a marriage between the king of France and the descendant of a Sicilian cook? She did not dare say anything either to Mazarin or to her son. She instinctively disliked Maria Mancini, but the girl was Mazarin's niece and as long as her uncle did nothing to put an end to her passion, what could the Queen Mother do? Added to this was the folly of Louis taking his avowed beloved on a journey to meet his possible betrothed. Mazarin appeared to have lost his head. What did he want, what did he hope to gain by it?

On 28 November 1658, the French Court left Lyon and travelled to meet the Savoyards. First they met the duchess's luggage, borne on innumerable mules caparisoned with black or red velvet embroidered with silver. Then they caught a glimpse of the coach preceded by a dozen pages dressed in black and surrounded by guards in black and gold cloaks. Impatient to see the Princesse Marguerite, the king spurred on his horse and galloped towards her. Seeing him the Duchesse de Savoie leapt from her coach with her daughter, curtsies were made and hands kissed at the roadside. Louis took a good look at Marguerite, then returned all breathless to his mother's coach. 'She's very agreeable,' he said. 'She's very like her portraits. She's a bit dark but she has a good figure.'

The two royal families arrived at Lyon in the same coach, the king seated beside the Princesse Marguerite. He made great efforts to please, chatting to her tirelessly about what interested him most, his soldiers – their numbers, their officers, their uniforms. Then he described Paris, and Marguerite duly described Turin, the Savoy capital, to him. They talked like two lovers, as if alone in the coach. Marguerite was so bold as to interrupt the king, which shocked the Grande Mademoiselle, a stickler for protocol, who was pretending not to be listening. Just as the magnificent cortège entered Lyon between two rows of bystanders, a man in disguise slipped out of the opposite gate of the city. Having neither passport nor papers, he was afraid of stumbling on an identity check – for he was Spanish and technically an enemy. Without a hitch he reached the house in which Mazarin was staying and there, without giving either his name or an explanation, demanded to speak to the cardinal's factotum, Colbert. Fortunately Colbert agreed to see this unknown man, and in his office, with all doors shut, he removed his disguise before the stupefied Colbert who recognized Don Antonio Pimentel, a confidant of the king of Spain. Colbert immediately warned Mazarin, who ordered that the Spaniard's presence was to be concealed and arranged to see him in secret that same evening. Don Antonio immediately offered peace – *and* the Infanta, for the Spanish fish had risen to the bait. At the announcement of the forthcoming betrothal of the king to the Savoyarde, the king of Spain had abandoned his legendary impassivity. *'Esto no puede ser y no será'*, ('This cannot be and will not be'), and had despatched Don Antonio with the utmost urgency through the enemy lines. After months of calculation, of double games, of waiting and irritation, Mazarin had finally triumphed.[26]

While Don Antonio and Mazarin were negotiating in the greatest secrecy, elsewhere in the royal apartments a violent argument had broken out. Louis had made up his mind to marry the Princesse Marguerite. Anne of Austria tried to dissuade him, for she wanted the Savoyarde less than ever. It was no use; her son would not let go, even though she refused to give up. Her son flung down the ultimate argument: who was master, she or he? She burst into tears and withdrew to her room, in her distress sending her confessor to the convents in the city to order prayers to be offered up to prevent the Savoyard marriage.[27] She must have had God's ear, for Mazarin at once came in. Finding her prostrate, eyes red with tears, he said: 'There is good news, Madame.' 'What! Is there peace at last?' 'There is more, Madame, I bring Your Majesty both peace and the Infanta.' This was news indeed; her niece, her brother's daughter, her supreme hope, the only match that she had ever wanted for her son. Drunk with joy, queen and cardinal were friends again, two accomplices who had faced the whole of France together, and they congratulated one another.

But nothing was to be said to anyone, especially to the king, for there were still innumerable points to discuss with Pimentel and until everything was settled, everyone must be put off the scent. Thus during the next few days Louis XIV was allowed to pay court to the Princesse Marguerite without interruption. Maria Mancini was of course eaten up with jealousy and poured a torrent of reproaches on the king. 'Aren't you ashamed that they are trying to give you a wife who's so ugly?' she asked him in public. 'She's not only ugly, but hunchbacked,' she added. Louis thought this was rather a joke, and next morning, under the pretext of going to greet the princess, he went into her room while she was dressing, to find out if she really was hunchbacked. From this point he showed a marked indifference to his 'betrothed'; the Duchesse de Savoie was on the verge of despair but Maria was overjoyed.[28] The king's attitude cooled towards the Princesse Marguerite and Maria took the credit for it believing that the king had come back to her. But the poor girl did not know that his mother and Mazarin had let him in on the secret negotiations that would mean that he would be able to marry the Infanta.

It was still important to keep up some kind of pretence until the ultra-secret negotiations with Pimentel were completed. The queen visited convents while the king indulged in various sports, reviewed his troops, went to the playhouse, and to a ball each evening. He danced to melodies composed *impromptu* by a musician who was beginning to make a name for himself, Jean-Baptiste Lulli. And in all these amusements, Maria Mancini was with him. He was at her side at supper and in the theatre. He took the reins of his coach and, playing the coachman, drove her round the Place Bellecourt in the moonlight. He was not alone in indulging in outlandish behaviour. At one masked ball, the Comte de Guiche pretended that he did not recognize his lover, 'Monsieur', as the Prince Philippe was known, disguised, as was his custom, in women's clothing. Dragging him off during a wild saraband, de Guiche kicked Monsieur repeatedly in the backside. 'This familiarity seemed rather excessive,' concluded the tight-lipped Grande Mademoiselle.

The moment came when the Duchesse de Savoie had to be told that she had been duped – especially as rumours were beginning to spread about the presence of Pimentel. After her earlier euphoria, the Duchesse was brought down to earth with a bump. She hurried to see Mazarin, demanding a firm answer, but taken aback, the cardinal hesitated. The Duchesse became angry, shouted, stamped her foot and even, it is said, banged her head against the wall. Then Mazarin, assisted by the queen, told her the truth: it was true what people were saying about the marriage with the Infanta. How could the king do otherwise, he explained, when the peace, the happiness of France depended on it. He appealed to her to understand as a Frenchwoman – even though she had opposed France on innumerable occasions. Anyway, he temporized, nothing had been finally decided yet. If the marriage to the Infanta did not take place, it would be her daughter and no other: the king even signed a written promise. Possessed of this dubious consolation, the Duchesse de Savoie had no alternative but to return home, stifling her rage and weeping profusely, to the great amusement of Queen Anne.[29] The only person to come out of this affair with any shred of dignity was the Princesse Marguerite, who had not been overjoyed at the thought of becoming queen of France, nor was she now downcast when another was preferred to her. She contented herself two years later with the miserable Duke of Parma.

CHAPTER 6

Love Affair and Marriage

It was a very cold January in 1659, but in the Court coaches returning to Paris the travellers certainly had something to keep their spirits up. Never had the king seemed more lighthearted and the courtiers followed his example, joking and laughing along the way. Meanwhile Mazarin was pursuing his own lucrative affairs. Colbert administered on his behalf the enormous supply contracts for the armies, managed the huge amounts of capital that he had prudently placed abroad, and facilitated the transfer of secret State funds to his master's pocket – to settle his gambling debts, for example. No profit, however small, was overlooked: the entire wealth of a gentleman from Nièvre who had committed suicide was confiscated and found its way into Mazarin's possession. When some bumpkin dared to claim this inheritance, Colbert quite simply alleged that the dead man had made him a verbal promise. Colbert's ruthless efficiency caused some anxiety to Mazarin, who demanded written acknowledgement from his factotum of all the gifts and acquisitions that passed through his hands. With such a zealot in his service, he might well fear that Colbert could turn against him. Despite Mazarin's caution in this regard, Colbert knew he had the upper hand. He even dared to ask the cardinal for 20,000 crowns to buy himself an estate that he coveted. In the end Mazarin paid up – out of the king's money – and Colbert became owner of land in Seignelay, which he soon promoted to the rank of marquisate.[1]

These activities did not interfere with the pursuit of Colbert's major task: the annihilation of his hated rival, Fouquet. The first stage in this process was implicating Fouquet in Mazarin's corrupt practices: forcing him to provide enormous sums that he could not possibly collect honestly, while leaving him in no doubt that to admit failure would be tantamount to disgrace. From time to time Fouquet tried to resist, but a stern letter from Mazarin would soon bring him to heel. The second stage consisted of keeping a close watch on Fouquet and building up a file on the malpractices which, following his superior's example, he had indulged in to his own advantage: misappropriations, bribes etc. And here Colbert outstripped Fouquet in skill. He stole just as much, but more cleverly, more subtly, more secretly. And, anyway, no one would suspect that this austere man, who spent so little, could steal, while

Fouquet, who loved to display his wealth and spent it freely, was an easy target for suspicion. The third stage consisted of a memorandum to Marazin listing in detail all Fouquet's malpractices and demanding his arrest and trial.

Fortunately, Fouquet had his own spies close to the cardinal; under no illusions about Mazarin's ruthlessness and fearing that he would be taken by surprise, he drew up a plan of action for just such a contingency: his friends and clients would be mobilized, his papers and collaborators removed to safety, public opinion aroused in all classes of the population to demand his freedom and, as a last resort, he set up several fortified places in the north and west of France. In the event, a single meeting with Mazarin was enough to save Fouquet for the time being.[2] Afterwards, Fouquet showed his friend Gourville the now useless plan of action; Gourville begged him to destroy this compromising document. Fouquet promised to burn it, but in fact merely stuck it behind a mirror in his house at Saint-Mandé.[3] Meanwhile, Mazarin wrote a long letter to Colbert refuting his accusations, using Fouquet's own arguments. Sensing that his tactics had failed on this occasion, Colbert grovelled before his master, replying with unbridled hypocrisy. All the stops were pulled out: his well-tried honesty, his indignation at Fouquet's dishonesty, his wish to advise him and to put him on the right road, his hopes of being his friend providing he return to honest ways.[4]

These upsets did not prevent the cardinal from working unremittingly for the triumph of his policies. Don Antonio Pimentel arrived in the capital to continue the Franco-Spanish negotiations. It was decided to have a solemn meeting at the frontier between Mazarin and his Spanish opposite number, Don Luis de Haros. In early May 1659 orders were sent to the armies to cease hostilities on all fronts. There was peace at last, after twenty-four years of war, and as the most precious guarantee of that peace, there was the Infanta. Her marriage to the king was now agreed: all that remained was to fix the date. Everything was going well, except, that is, for one small detail: the king had never been more in love with Maria Mancini.

The cunning little vixen had taken advantage of the return journey from Lyon to make up the ground that had been lost.[5] Travelling next to him in the coach over the icy winter roads she conducted herself with such skill that by the time they arrived in Paris the king was entirely entrapped. There could now be no question of pretence: the king publicly displayed his headlong passion for the girl. He never let her out of his sight, and she followed him everywhere, even whispering in his ear in the presence of the queen mother – the height of insolence. Anne was forced to intervene quickly and forcibly, but her son responded sharply, telling her to mind her own business.[6] Nothing, it seemed, would stand in the way of the two lovers, and there was even talk again of marriage. Never mind the Infanta, Louis would marry Maria, and an exultant Maria went to announce to her uncle Mazarin that she would become queen of France.

There, right in the middle of negotiations for the Infanta, Mazarin faltered. Was he hoping for the impossible? He went off to see Anne of Austria, squirming with embarrassment. Had she heard the latest? That foolish niece of his had got it into her head that she could become the queen of France! But, while he laughed, he was scrutinizing the queen mother's reaction. 'I do not believe, Monsieur le Cardinal,' she replied, 'that the king could be capable of such baseness. But if such a notion occurs to him, I must warn you that the whole of France would be against you and against him. I would even place myself at the head of a rebellion and take my other son with me.' Mazarin had no doubt that she meant what she said.[7]

For Anne, this was the last straw. She realized, with more bitterness than ever before, the hold Mazarin had over her son. Little by little he had completely detached Louis from her, and the young companions with whom Mazarin had surrounded him merely widened the breach. No one listened to her any more and when she lowered herself to solicit a minister or functionary for a favour, she could no longer get satisfaction.[8]

Before long the cardinal shook himself out of his equivocal attitude. A document was thoughtfully placed before him which brought him to his senses. It was a properly drawn up protest from the queen mother, registered by the *parlement,* against the validity of her son's marrying without her consent. Anne really had lost her infatuation for Mazarin or rather she had learnt to know him better. She had sensed the burgeoning, as yet unspoken hope of an unimaginable marriage and realized the weakness of her own arguments. So in great secret she had consulted the councillors of State, and had Brienne draw up a solemn protest just in case.[9] Forced to admit defeat, Maria's uncle, who for a brief moment had allowed his ambition to cloud his judgement, once again became the great minister. Had his niece dared to speak of marriage to the king when peace, in the shape of the Infanta, was within reach? There was only one radical solution. She would have to leave Paris and the Court, and be separated from the king forever. Maria wept when she heard her sentence. The king was also overcome and ran to Mazarin, fell to his knees and begged the Cardinal to let him marry his niece. The crafty Italian, usually so lacking in the stuff of bravery, raised himself for a moment to the level of a Corneille hero. He refrained from abusing the king's weakness: he would not tolerate an act so contrary to the king's glory. He would not betray the trust placed in him first by the king's father and then by his mother. He would rather kill his own niece, whose master he was.[10]

The king gave in: Maria Mancini was to leave for the small town of Le Brouage, in the Charente, with some of her sisters for company. The night before her departure, sitting with his mother in her drawing-room, Louis seemed so overwhelmed with sadness that she took him aside to console him. Nothing could be done. Since she could not bear his grief-stricken look to be seen in public, she took him away into the bathroom where they stayed closeted together for an hour. The king emerged with red, swollen eyes and his mother murmured to Mme de Motteville: 'I am sorry for the king: he is both tender-hearted and reasonable. But I have just told him that I am sure that he will thank me one day for the hurt that I have caused him.'[11] Next morning, 22 June 1659, the two lovers parted, both weeping openly. The king even went so far as to accompany Maria to her carriage, in flagrant disregard of protocol. Maria's last words, as the carriage moved off, contained a reproach expressed in a sentence that is as terse as it is famous: 'You weep and you are the master.'

With Maria out of the way it was possible to take breath at last and deal with other matters than the king's inconvenient passions. Mazarin set out for Saint Jean de Luz to meet the Spanish prime minister, and the Court – led by the king and queen – set off for Bordeaux on an extended tour of the southern provinces. On the way, the king accepted the hospitality of his uncle, Gaston d'Orléans. Night had already fallen when the royal procession entered the great torch-lit courtyard of the Château de Blois, where, from a window, the beautiful, seventeen-year-old daughter of the duke's *maître d'hôtel* watched the arrival of the enormous golden coach, drawn by six horses with red harness and manes plaited with ribbons the colour of fire. She observed the young man as he got out of the coach. Her name was Louise de La Vallière, and it was the first time that she had set eyes on the king.[12] Was it love at first sight, heralding the passion that was later to consume and almost destroy her? Louis certainly did not notice her for he was thinking only of Maria – reproaching himself each day. Le Brouage was not far from Blois and his mother understood and watched him anxiously. Eventually, he asked her if she would mind if he saw Maria briefly as they passed through but Anne prudently wrote to Mazarin to ask his opinion. The cardinal who was deeply involved in the Franco-Spanish negotiations, agreed, and a meeting was arranged at Saint-Jean-d'Angély. The king galloped off to meet Maria half way from Le Brouage.[13] No written account of their meeting has survived, but we do know that a great many more tears were shed.

Maria returned to Le Brouage and Louis resumed the journey to Bordeaux with his mother and the Court. But the affair was not quite over, for Louis and Maria managed to get permission to write to one another. Anne of Austria did not think there could be any harm in it as things stood and Mazarin again agreed. He even put Colbert in charge of conveying the letters and he in turn entrusted the mission to his cousin and protégé, Colbert du Terron. The lovers were therefore able to write to one another every day with the blessing of the queen and the cardinal. Of course, it was not long before Mazarin woke up to the consequences of what was happening. But it was already too late: Louis was more in love with Maria than ever. For once Mazarin reacted with firmness: he ordered Colbert du Terron immediately to stop acting as messenger between the lovers. Mazarin wrote the king a clear, straightforward letter, in a style very different from his usual flowery, convoluted manner: if Louis did not break off immediately with Maria, there was no point in continuing negotiations with Spain and he, Mazarin, would have no alternative but to resign. The king replied in a somewhat confused, but on the whole satisfactory way. Determined to strike while the iron was hot, Mazarin went further. He sent a second letter to the king designed to turn Louis against Maria once and for all: she was an ambitious, irascible girl, a mad creature who never knew how to control herself and who showed contempt for everyone else. Lastly, Mazarin employed what he considered to be his supreme argument: she hated her uncle Mazarin. But the king's response was icy and an astonished Mazarin could only write back: 'Your bounty has never permitted you until now to write or speak to me as you have done.' Quite simply, Louis had refused to give up Maria, and both the marriage with the Infanta and the peace with Spain were put in jeopardy. For Mazarin personally, it could mean disgrace, the end.[14] Anxiety also reigned among his tribe of nieces; not among the youngest who kept Maria company at Le Brouage and who were wallowing in this romantic drama, inflamed by their semi-reclusion and in full rebellion against their uncle, but among the older ones, those who had already found husbands and fortune. Olympia Mancini, Comtesse de Soissons, was later to relate to the Abbé de Choisy that she and her sisters had seen themselves on the edge of the precipice, ready to sink into penury and oblivion.[15]

Once they had got over the initial shock, Mazarin and the queen began to reflect on the situation. There was a mystery at the heart of the king's attitude. Never before had he dared, of his own unaided volition, to oppose them. He was far too weak, they thought. There had to be someone behind him, but they could not think who it could be since, as they thought, the correspondence with Maria had been intercepted. In fact, it had not been, and thus they soon uncovered the mystery. Colbert du Terron, ignoring the cardinal's orders in order to curry favour with the king, had continued carrying the letters between the lovers and thanks to him, Maria had been able to add fuel to the fire each day. It was now the turn of Colbert, the traitor's cousin and protector, to tremble, for Mazarin would never forgive him that error. Colbert wrote to Mazarin, throwing himself at his feet, declaring that he deserved his vengeance a thousand times over. Mazarin smiled and forgave, for at least Louis and Maria could no longer communicate with one another.[16]

After mature reflection, the cardinal wrote another letter to the king, quite different in tone from the preceding one. Instead of attacking, threatening, demanding, he grovelled: 'I could not so much as entertain the thought of disputing the least thing that proceeds from you. On the contrary, I have no difficulty in submitting to your feelings and to declare that you are right in everything ...' Mazarin's diabolical calculation was to pay off. Louis, protected from Maria's influence, was infinitely flattered to see the cardinal, who only yesterday was treating him like a child, bowing before what he believed to be his omnipotence. For the last time he gave in to reason. He declared that he had no other intention but to marry the Infanta.

The storm had passed and Mazarin, smooth-tongued and once more unruffled, could resume negotiations with the Spanish prime minister, while the Court calmly pursued its unhurried tour of the southern cities: Bordeaux, Toulouse, Aix, Toulon and on 7 November 1659, the momentous Treaty of the Pyrenees was concluded between France and Spain.

Apart from gold, the Infanta brought with her a dowry valuable in a quite different way; rights over cities, provinces and, if her half-brothers continued to die very young as they were in the habit of doing, rights over an incalculable number of crowns, over the greatest empire in the world, that of her father, the king of Spain and of the Indies. Of course, before giving herself to the king of France, she solemnly had to renounce this fabulous inheritance, but Mazarin had more than one trick up his sleeve. He entrusted the wording of the Treaty to the most Jesuitical of Jesuits in order to discover later innumerable arguments in it to prove its invalidity.[17]

Early in May 1660, the Court of France arrived at Saint-Jean-de Luz for the king's wedding. When the French learnt that the bride's father, the king of Spain, was there on the frontier, they were carried away with curiosity. They rushed to cross the Bidassoa to catch a glimpse of so curious a beast. It was said that an incurable stomach illness forced him to drink nothing but women's milk and the French could no longer contain themselves at the idea of seeing the most powerful king in the world suckling a woman. They were disappointed however. Philip IV was there, pale, impassive and staring into space, sitting alone in front of a table laid as for an ordinary meal. Nevertheless there were so many spectators that a terrible scuffle followed; the table was very nearly overturned and the king of Spain crushed.[18]

Spain had been closed off by war for so long, that everything connected with it excited the interest of the French: its mysterious, hidebound Court, the haughty Spaniards themselves, dressed from top to toe in black. Of course not a detail escaped their criticism: a wretched, ill-equipped Court, not enough pomp, not enough guards, not enough drums, not enough trumpets. The priest's ornaments were hideous. The Spanish ladies, so many black-skinned skeletons with plunging necklines, made Mme de Motteville feel quite sick. To her their dresses were ill-cut and made of ugly materials, with ugly lace, ugly ribbons, ugly sleeves; their famous farthingales were monstrous, their hair ugly and inelegant, the servants' liveries unworthy of a great king. Only the gentlemen, despite their too narrow trousers, found favour in French eyes on account of the enormous precious stones sewn into their clothes.[19] The conclusion was plain: everything that came from France was ten times better than anything that came from Spain. Such self-satisfaction, such *amour propre,* was necessary if the French were to bear the insulting indifference of the Spanish, not one of whom bothered to cross the Bidassoa to see what things were like in France, which irritated Louis enormously. Mazarin, too, was irritated, for the eternally unsatisfied and quibbling Spaniards raised innumerable points of detail at the last minute that had to be argued out at length. Several times there was talk of breaking off negotiations.

At last, on 3 June, the marriage *per procurationem* took place at Fontarabie. 'Monsieur', the king's brother, and the Grande Mademoiselle were dying to attend the ceremony, but Louis, annoyed that no Spaniard had come to visit him, forbade them to go. But the Grande Mademoiselle would not be put off: in the end she was allowed to go alone, incognito. She wore black – the mourning clothes she habitually wore after her father's death – and stuck a simple cap on her hair, which had curled in the rain. She imagined that she looked 'foreign', but forgetting her incognito, she lorded it over the few French who went with her and told them where to sit in the church. There were no more than a handful of people inside the dark church, just a few guards at the door and a few Spanish Grandees on a simple bench. The king of Spain came in first, dressed in grey and silver, with the Peregrina, the most famous pearl in the world, hanging from his hat. He went and sat in a box pew covered with cloth of gold beside the high altar. Then the Infanta appeared, alone, in white satin with silver burls. As far as the French were concerned it was a hideous dress, of course, with hideous jewellery, a hideous wig, and each outstripped the other in denigrating the Spaniards who had obviously made no effort. The ceremony was conducted quickly with the minimum of grandeur.[20] However the French took advantage of the occasion to find out about the girl who, at that moment, was becoming their queen. To Mme de Motteville, Maria Theresa appeared to be a plump blonde, with quite a good figure. She had a good complexion, fine, expressionless blue eyes, but she was too short, her lips were too thick and her breasts too big.[21]

Next day, the king of Spain and the queen mother of France, brother and sister, met for the first time for forty-five years. She wanted to throw her arms around his neck, but he recoiled quickly: kissing was not in fashion. Maria Theresa was presented and she knelt down in front of her aunt. Chairs were brought in and they sat down and chatted in Spanish like two elderly bourgeois under the attentive eyes of the two Courts. They talked of the past and of the war that had just ended: 'Alas, Madame, it was the devil that did it.' They talked, too, about the future: 'Now we shall soon have grandchildren.' Mazarin came up and spoke quietly to their Majesties: there was an unknown man at the door who wanted to come in. It was Louis who, according to protocol, did not yet have the right to meet the Spaniards, but who had come to get a glimpse of his betrothed. No one was taken in by this incognito; with furtive glances at the doorway, a grotesque dialogue began. Anne coyly asked her future daughter-in-law: 'Well, what do you think of this unknown man?' Philip was shocked: 'It's not yet time for her to say,' he objected. 'When will she be able to?' 'When she has passed through this doorway.' 'And how does the doorway seem to Your Majesty?' simpered Monsieur in Maria Theresa's ear. 'Very handsome and very nice,' she replied. As they left, there was more scuffling. The French threw themselves at Maria Theresa to get a closer view and the Spaniards, who had known Anne of Austria when she was their Infanta, almost devoured her by kissing her hand. As the royal barge glided across the Bidassoa, taking Philip IV and Maria Theresa back to Spain, on the bank a lover followed them on horseback: it was Louis, gallantly accompanying his betrothed.[22]

On Sunday 6 June, in the Pavillon des Conférences, the two kings solemnly swore to respect the Treaty of the Pyrenees. On their knees, hands outstretched on the Bible, they spoke the words of the oath, surrounded by their ministers and Courtiers. It was a meeting of two different worlds. On the one side was a handsome youth, followed by a group of dazzling men and women, gleaming with feathers and embroidery, and, on the other, an ageless old man, followed by a few austere, silent *hidalgos*; on the one hand, the future with its joyful disorder, on the other, the past, for the shadow of decline was spreading over the Spanish Empire. Even so, the Spaniards displayed immense pride. The gravity and sobriety that they affected expressed an awareness that for the moment they were still the major world power. Beside them, the French in their carnival costumes, led by Louis, looked like upstarts. They may have been in fashion – after all, they created it – but the Spaniards had style. Their monarchy had no need of pomp or ornament to be noticed, such was the unshakeable assurance on which it rested. Although it was a branch of the most ancient house of Europe, the French Bourbon dynasty, by contrast, was actually a recent one; hardly two generations old. Until quite recently, it had had to fight for survival against its challengers and very nearly lost the battle. The luxury with which it surrounded itself masked the lack of confidence that still lurked behind the re-establishment it had managed to bring about. Like the monarchy that he embodied, Louis XIV had to deck himself out with frills to feel a king, while Philip IV, in his eternal dark costume, knew instinctively that he was king.

There was, however, a moment of weakness. Just as he was leaving Maria Theresa forever, Philip lost his legendary impassivity and began to weep, and his daughter and sister followed suit. Louis and Monsieur, also in tears by this time, flung their arms around his neck. He took refuge in his carriage and, ordering the driver to take him home, threw himself on his bed: 'I have come back dead. Seeing my daughter weep – as she should – was moving enough, and my sister, too, but to have to see those two boys with their arms around my neck like children, I was so moved that I could no longer bear it.'

It was the Wedding Night, and the time to retire to bed came round at last. An impatient Louis was already undressed. Maria Theresa, in a moment of animal fear, turned to her aunt Anne, tears in her eyes: *'Es muy temprano'* [It's too early]. Then she recovered her self-control: *'Presto, presto, que el Rey me espera'* [Quick, the king is waiting for me].[23]

Right up to the last moment Anne of Austria had remained apprehensive. She had had to overcome so many obstacles to arrive at this marriage, and the wound represented by Maria Mancini had hardly healed. Her son had come to thank her sincerely for having helped him to break with the Italian girl, but the Infanta was no beauty and her severe upbringing left her with no idea how to deal with men. And yet Anne was wrong: her son showed the greatest tenderness towards his young wife, treating her like a young lover. For her part, Maria Theresa seemed to have fallen in love with him from the first moment. Their union looked like being a happy one and Anne of Austria could breathe freely at last. Utterly delighted, she sent her brother a table clock encrusted with very large diamonds as a present. In return, she received a few pairs of poor quality gloves – made in Spain.

On 26 August the new queen entered her capital. A million people thronged the streets; never had the Parisians spent so much or so freely. A ruinously expensive rivalry in clothes and decorations had arisen between the tradesmen's guilds and between the different quarters of the city. In streets hung with the finest tapestries, armed burghers formed a guard of honour. In the midst of a fairytale procession came the queen's coach, a gold and silver barouche decorated with jasmine flowers and drawn by six grey horses. Maria Theresa was wearing a black and gold dress that admirably suited her pale complexion and fair hair. It was a personal triumph for her.

Among the thronging crowds, there was one woman who did not miss a single detail of the spectacle. She noted the gold embroidered cloths and the silver bits of the horses, the feathers of the musketeers, the fiery red silks of the pages, the jewellery of the princes 'which shone magnificently in the sun'. She could not take her eyes off the king, who rode alone under a brocade canopy. He possessed 'surprising grace and majesty' and in her description she concluded lovingly: 'I did not believe that there could ever have been anything so handsome.' She envied Maria Theresa: 'The queen must have gone to bed very pleased with the husband that she has chosen.' One day, that woman was to choose that same husband herself, for she was Mme Paul Scarron, the former Françoise d'Aubigny and future Marquise de Maintenon.[24]

At the very moment that he brought his foreign policy to its peak, Mazarin got bogged down in the eternal disorder of State finances. Taxation failed to bring in the required revenue and penury was spreading. No one wanted to lend money to the king – the least solvent individual in his kingdom. No one doubted that the country was heading straight for catastrophe, and Mazarin even considered declaring bankruptcy. Then, in this overcast firmament, Fouquet's star began to glow. There was no need to go to such extreme measures, he told Mazarin. The cardinal, completely at a loss, enquired where they could obtain finance. Fouquet then laid out his plan for economic and commercial revival. It was, Mazarin noted, a remarkable piece of work, but one that would only bear fruit after several years. What was to be done in the meantime? In the meantime, Fouquet declared, we will find money. And, indeed, by conjuring tricks of extraordinary virtuosity, operations of which financial morality could not possibly approve, Fouquet managed to reopen the flood gates – at the cost of a good deal of dishonesty and the ruin of several fools. But what did it matter? Gold began to flow again and Mazarin was lost in admiration. 'I have talked about it for a long time with their Majesties and they are entirely agreed that one must set great store by such a friend,' he declared.[25] This did not please Colbert. The success of his rival merely doubled his resentment, even though he would have been quite incapable of doing the same. He remained a man of order, even in the midst of the worst disorders. Fouquet, on the other hand, was the juggler, the sorcerer that the situation demanded.

In the early months of 1661, Mazarin began to decline, as young Brienne noticed when visiting him. As Brienne was leaving, Mazarin, who was very fond of him, threw his arms around him: 'His breath overcame me and I was about to faint,' Brienne wrote. 'That foul odour made such an impression upon me that the smelling of it, preceded and followed by a very bad headache, stayed with me for three days, so heavily were my delicate nostrils assailed and so to speak inundated. What breath, good heavens! The mouth of hell could not have been more foul. He gave me a mouth pastille and took one himself. Seeing the effect that he had had on me and wishing to make up for it, he said to me kindly: "There, my friend, is man. I have fine teeth and I eat little: but my ventrical is gangrened and so I shall die soon."'[26] Mazarin was lucid about his condition, but not at all resigned to it. After a life of reversals of fortune, of comebacks, of spectacular successes, of opportunities caught on the wing, fantastic rises and dizzy falls, it was hard for him to admit the inevitable for the first time. Brienne, who advised him to distribute his money to the poor to appease his conscience, got this reply: 'Oh, Monsieur de Brienne, God forbid! It took too much trouble to amass it.' 'Does not Your Eminence believe, then, in the word of the Son of God?' 'That's all very well,' Mazarin is supposed to have replied, 'but believe me money is worth more.' Then there was the scene in which Brienne again, hidden behind a tapestry, saw him in his night-cap, naked under his fur dressing-gown, walking disconsolately up and down his art gallery with all its priceless marvels, talking to himself and repeating with heart-rending sighs: 'And to think that I must leave all this.' The cardinal stopped in front of a Correggio, then Titian's *Venus,* or Annibale Carracci's *Flood,* declaring, 'And this one too! How hard it was to acquire these things! Can I now abandon them without regret? I shall never see them again where I am going. Farewell, dear pictures, which I have loved so much and which have cost me so dear!'[27]

He recovered sufficiently, however, to carry off his role in one of those death scenes, with their solemn leavetakings, that the period loved so much. When his condition became alarming, the king and queen mother paid him one of their last visits – there were to be several to prolong the pleasure – at the Château de Vincennes to which he had retired. He displayed the most perfect detachment, speaking to them of his death as if it were the most natural thing in the world. Louis and Anne were deeply moved and left the room in tears – in full view and hearing of the Court. They were, apparently, going to miss the cardinal.[28]

Brienne tried to raise Mazarin's spirits: 'Monseigneur, no one desires your death; everyone wants you to live!' But Mazarin was not convinced. 'You don't know everything,' he told Brienne, 'there is someone who desires my death!' This 'someone' was the king – Mazarin was convinced that he was merely playacting when snivelling at his bedside.[29] His natural suspicion showed him the king's impatience to be rid of him. But he also ignored the sincerity of the king's regret, which was just as inherent in their long love–hate relationship.

An ever-faithful friend despite their disagreements, Anne of Austria came back to see Mazarin with her ladies of honour. He leapt out of bed and opened his dressing-gown to reveal his skeletal legs, covered with yellow and white spots 'like the scales of a snake.' 'Look, Madame, these are the legs of Cardinal Mazarin, that once handsome man about whom the scandal sheets spoke so much ill and published so many falsehoods.' The ladies uttered cries of horror.[30] The prospect of death had obviously driven the cardinal beyond the bounds of propriety – death combined with Anne of Austria. The woman who had always exasperated him, continued to do so, when all he wanted was for her to leave him in peace. But the queen, unaware that her usual generous attentions were not wanted, obstinately insisted on coming to see him every day, 'Ah! That woman will kill me with her importunity,' he moaned. 'Will she never leave me in peace?'[31]

However the pretence of that great friendship, which was to be passed down to a naïve posterity, had to be kept up to the end. On 5 March 1661, the king and queen mother ordered public prayers to be said in the churches of Paris for the recovery of their dear friend, an honour reserved solely to the fatal illnesses of kings. As the faithful prayed for his health, Mazarin was totally absorbed in the great matter of his will. His confessor had told him that he would go to hell if he did not restore his ill-gotten wealth. 'Alas! I have nothing but what the king gave me,' Mazarin countered. 'But you must distinguish between what the king gave you and what you gave yourself.' 'Ah! If that is the case, then it must be handed back.' Everything had to be handed back. For the dying man, this was the last blow. Never at a loss for an expedient, Colbert found a loophole. Mazarin would make a will bequeathing everything to the king: in this way he would go to heaven. The king, out of dignity and good taste, would refuse the inheritance and Mazarin would merely have to make a new will in favour of his family. The cardinal was delighted with this solution. Never mind if it meant cheating God a bit – He wouldn't be the first the cardinal had cheated in his life. So the will in favour of the king was taken to its beneficiary. But two days had passed and the king had still not sent it back, nor sent any word of his intentions. Was he thinking of accepting the bequest and keeping everything? The mere possibility of such a trick put Mazarin on the rack once more. 'Ah! My poor family! My poor family will have no bread!' he cried. Colbert tried to reassure him, but without success, until at last the king's answer arrived on 6 March: he would give everything back to Mazarin. So the cardinal gaily set about writing his true will, lovingly listing his incalculable wealth for the last time.[32]

On 7 March, extreme unction was administered and the king came to take his final leave. During this last meeting Mazarin gave Louis three pieces of advice: no prime minister, no Fouquet,[33] no Anne[34]; this advice amounted to a cynical admission of the harm that Mazarin himself had done to Louis. Mazarin advised no prime minister so that the king would not fall back under a domination like that of Mazarin himself. No Fouquet, so that the king would not continue to be shamefully robbed by the man trained and appointed by Mazarin. No Anne of Austria, for she would never manage without a man at her side and she would certainly find someone to replace the cardinal ... who – he omitted to add – would once again dominate the king at one remove. Armed with these precepts, remarkable as much for their ingratitude as for their lucidity, Louis retired and Mazarin went back to work.

The illness did not interrupt his government of the country for a moment. From his bed, he continued to watch and arrange everything. He received ministers, sent despatches to the ambassadors, handed out posts and rewards. However, he would not go on much longer and the attentive, excited courtiers wondered who would succeed him. Rumour was rife and with each hour Colbert and Fouquet grew in stature. Latterly their rivalry had increased in suppressed violence as the cardinal declined and, in that unbearable waiting period, the atmosphere of the Court became stifling. In any case everyone was sure of one thing, namely that the only man who would not take power was the only one who legitimately possessed it: the king. In the opinion of all he would be quite incapable of assuming it.[35] How could he, how could he even wish to do so, after accepting Mazarin's tutelage for so long and so completely. In that crisis time, nobody thought of getting closer to Louis, flattering him, winning him over. No one had any illusions as to his true abilities, even his friend Brienne:[36] 'I sometimes found him so lacking in intelligence that I was astonished.' The king himself wept on the bosom of the Duc de Navailles, expressing profound regret that Mazarin had not been able to last four or five years more, by which time he, the king, would have been ready to take up the reins. But now it was too soon, and Louis trembled before the responsibility that was inexorably approaching.[37]

Next day the cardinal's death agony began. He was in great pain all day, abusing his doctors for incompetence. 'They have killed me,' he repeated in their presence,[38] but since the damage had been done he was getting impatient. Would this death never come? He had no fear of it, but all the same he would prefer not to suffer much longer. At last, at three in the morning, he cried out: 'Holy Virgin, have pity on me and receive my soul,' and he died, on March 9 1661.

CHAPTER 7

Louis Asserts Himself

Next morning in the Château de Vincennes, the king woke, called the nurse and enquired with a sign whether Mazarin was dead. The nurse nodded. The king ordered complete quiet, and, that nothing be said to his wife, the young queen, who was asleep. She was pregnant and the news might distress her. The king slipped out of bed, dressed quickly, and went to his study. There he remained for two hours alone. No one would ever know the thoughts of this young man of twenty-four at the moment when the responsibility of supreme power had fallen on his shoulders. Louis xiv then summoned his three principal ministers: Le Tellier (War) Lionne (Foreign Affairs) and Fouquet (Finance). He gave his first orders: from then on everything would go through him and no orders would be issued without his approval.[1]

Next day a full council of ministers was called. At four o'clock the king came in, raised his hat, greeted his advisers, replaced his hat and, standing in front of his chair, turned to the chancellor, old Séguier, and said, 'Monsieur, I have summoned you with my ministers and secretaries of State to tell you that, hitherto, I have been willing to leave the government of my affairs in the hands of the late Monsieur le Cardinal. It is now time that I should take on government myself. You will assist me with your advice when I request it ... And you, my secretaries of State, I forbid you to sign anything, even so much as a safe conduct or a passport, without orders from me ... And, Minister of Finance, I have explained my wishes to you. I would ask you to make use of Colbert, whom the late Monsieur le Cardinal recommended to me.' Fouquet bowed stiffly; his rival had not yet joined the council, but even so he had been granted an official place. The king concluded: 'The scene has changed: I shall follow other principles in the government of my State, in the administration of my finances and in negotiations abroad, than those of the late Monsieur le Cardinal. You know my wishes. It is now up to you, gentlemen, to carry them out.' 'I thought he would be ungrateful and try to act the great politician,' commented the queen mother, who had not been invited to attend.[2]

It could not be clearer: the king was no longer a figurehead manipulated by Mazarin. Mazarin himself had gone, and people had already stopped regretting his passing: he was now scarcely given a thought. That evening, the queen mother and the king both apparently bore on their faces, 'expressions of satisfaction'. This, according to Mme de Motteville who had always hated the cardinal, was because 'the horrible defects of the dead man now appeared to them in all their clarity'.[3] However, the pretence of friendship had to be kept up even beyond death. The king and queen mother went into mourning, followed by the entire Court, an unheard-of honour usually reserved only for the death of another sovereign.

Mourning or not, the king worked unremittingly. He awoke at eight, even when he had gone to bed late, slipped from the marriage bed, went into his own room, dressed quickly and read reports and files – alone. No one was to disturb him. Between ten and midday was the council. Only the king was seated, though the chancellor was allowed to lean on the bedrail if he was tired. All the ministers were those appointed by Mazarin. However, there was one newcomer, the twenty-year-old Michel Le Tellier, Marquis de Louvois, who had succeeded his father. Colbert waited in the corridor. He did not belong to the council, but the king worked alone with him. The dark genius who had been nurtured by Mazarin had been able to win over his new master with a fabulous gift of 40,000,000 *livres* belonging to the cardinal's estate, which only Colbert knew about and which, instead of handing on to Mazarin's heirs, he had taken to the king. After the council, Louis devoted some time to God – mass every day – and to his family. After lunch he went back to work with his ministers, then he gave audiences during the rest of the afternoon.

He watched over and decided everything. No one had expected that. After a childhood spent in total ignorance, during which, moreover, he had shown an evident distaste for study, after an adolescence devoted to 'games and pleasure', during which he had not had the slightest share in government, so sudden and so total a transformation astonished everyone – his intimates, his collaborators, his courtiers and the whole of Europe.[4] Regarded unanimously to be lacking in intelligence and will-power, he now revealed a capacity for work, real ability and authority. 'He suddenly appeared,' remarked an astonished Motteville, 'a politician in affairs of State, a theologian in Church affairs, and a skilled financier; where once he could scarcely express himself, now he was articulating himself perfectly always taking the right side in the councils, sensitive to the interests of individuals, but an enemy to intrigue and flattery.'[5]

Not everyone, however, was equally surprised. Even as Mazarin was declining, the king had begun to make his presence felt, in spite of his protestations of fear. Four days before the cardinal's death, he had said quite categorically to Le Tellier: 'I wish to govern myself, attend the council regularly, talk with the ministers one by one; and I am determined not to miss a single day, though I foresee that in the long term it will become tiresome.' An astonished Le Tellier went and repeated everything to Anne of Austria, who burst out laughing. 'Do you really believe him, Monsieur Le Tellier?' she asked. However, on reflection, she confided to her friend Motteville that her son would probably enjoy ruling and that she was very glad of it.[6]

He had planned his *coup* perfectly and the rigour with which he carried it off made it something of a masterpiece. The effect was felt right across Europe. Yet it remains a complete mystery: how did this young man pass in one night from ignorance and laziness to omniscience and intense activity, from the most utter dependence to the most total independence? It is important to realize what he had undergone up till that moment. Forty years later, one of the spiritual and literary glories of his reign, Archbishop Fénelon of Cambrai was to write: 'I remembered his upbringing, lacking in all instruction, the flattery that obsessed him, the traps that were set to excite in his youth every passion, the profane advice that he was given, lastly the peril of greatness and so many delicate matters; I admit that taking all these things into account, notwithstanding the great respect that is due to him, I felt much compassion for so exposed a soul.'[7]

His heart, marked forever by his childhood, was now closed against any appeal. Never having received affection, he was to give none. He was never to emerge from the solitude in which he had been left, but out of that wound he forged a weapon. He was then and he remained a man alone, distant, inaccessible. 'He betrayed no eagerness for anything whatsoever,' the ambassador of Savoy noted, 'and did not abandon his gravity, even in his entertainments and pleasures.'

He knew that people believed him to be weak and easily influenced. He had already responded by closing himself up forever. He turned it into a system of government: first, keep silent; then take your time; lastly, conceal the plans you have laid for as long as possible in order to surprise your opponents all the more. He actually wrote out this simple advice for the use of his son, who was born that same year. Behind it all one can detect, never expressed directly, a profound desire for revenge. For perhaps from this distance it is not so surprising to see the change in Louis after Mazarin's death: for although he may have seemed weak, ill-educated, indecisive, in fact he had had the example of Mazarin himself to observe, learn from and react against. The cardinal was in truth the king's greatest tutor – years of silent watchfulness had taught Louis everything he needed to grasp the reins of power when the time came.

Louis xiv believed that the 'wise monarch', should appear like an omniscient Phoenix to his collaborators. Sometimes he showers graces upon them, 'sometimes he keeps them at a distance . . . showing them that there is no darkness so malign that it is proof against the light of the knowledge that he himself possesses and which he constantly receives from all sides'.[8] Observe, spy on people, keep them on tenterhooks by an alternation of smiles and frowns, perpetually disconcert them . . . in these precepts there is something of the 'lessons' that a bitter, contemptuous Mazarin had given him in his youth.

Similarly, by reacting against Mazarin, he merely took as his inspiration the last advice that the cardinal had given him. No Anne of Austria: from the first day of his personal rule, he had excluded her from the council and when he learnt that she had given some order to a Secretary of State, he lost his composure and cried out, 'Madame, do not do such a thing again, without speaking to me first.'[9] No Fouquet: this was to follow later, but he lost nothing by waiting. No prime minister, the dying cardinal had whispered to him, and Louis obediently wrote out: 'I was determined not to have a prime minister and not to allow anyone else to assume the functions of king as long as I possessed that title.'[10]

He escaped the practice of having a prime minister quite simply, by not appointing one. Drunk with power as he now was, he found it all the easier to do without. He even believed himself to be cleverer than most other kings of his time. 'I would not claim to advise all those who wear crowns to expose themselves to this test without previously ascertaining that they are capable of carrying it off.'[11] Having examined his conscience, and having reached a favourable conclusion about himself, he could then speak of 'the miserable condition of princes who commit their people and their dignity to the conduct of a Prime Minister'.[12] And to avoid any memory of that 'miserable condition', which had been his for so long, he was never again to take on an ecclesiastic as his collaborator. Many years later, he refused to appoint Cardinal Janson, for whom he had rightly shown esteem, to the council of ministers. One of his ministers expressed surprise at his decision. 'Monsieur,' the king replied, 'I made it a rule for myself, on the death of Cardinal Mazarin, and which I have kept until now and will not change, of putting no ecclesiastic in my council, and a cardinal still less.'[13]

Yet he knew that he lacked training to rule entirely alone, so he chose his ministers carefully: 'A king who, though endowed by nature with intelligence and vigour [like himself], is lacking in experience, would no doubt do better to divide his trust among a number of skilful men.' If one is not to be disappointed, one must prevent the 'skilful men' from agreeing among themselves, that is to say, behind one's back: 'But above all beware, on this last point, of independence, know that you will never truly be sovereign if you do not so arrange matters that all those who have any necessary relations with you do not depend upon one another at all.' One should even maintain a spirit of competition between them: 'Jealousy of one often serves as a brake to the ambitions of another.'[14] What precautions, what ramparts, what defences! Thus armed against all weakness, Louis XIV could finally undertake his political programme.

First of all, there were to be no princes. They had placed themselves at the head of the opposition, even going so far as to call the nation's enemies to their aid, and the old ghosts had not yet been entirely laid.

No nobility, either. Mazarin had hated a nobility 'that had mocked and despised him'. Instead of decapitating it as his predecessor, Richelieu, had done, he more subtly corrupted and degraded it. He undermined it, overthrew traditions, encouraged all kinds of usurpations and diluted blue blood with that of commoners. In the provinces, registers had been opened and anyone, for hard cash, could design his own coat-of-arms and thus enter this exclusive class.[15] As a result, Louis despised it. 'The least defect in the order of nobility was to allow itself to mingle with an infinite number of usurpers.' On the other hand, 'the tyranny that it exercised in certain of my provinces over my vassals and over my neighbours, could no longer be tolerated'.[16] Those troublemakers, always ready to rise up in arms, and to line their pockets with their exactions, must be brought to heel and above all have no access to power: his ministers, like Mazarin's, were to be all chosen from *parlementaires* and bourgeois.

No more excessively brilliant financiers who got scandalously rich – now it was dangerous for Fouquet. 'The finances were entirely exhausted,' but 'the politicians seemed plentifully endowed, on the one hand concealing their malversations with all manner of artifices and, on the other, displaying them in insolent, audacious luxury.'[17]

No more power for the *parlementaires*. 'They had to be brought down, not so much for the evil that they had done as for that which they might be able to do in the future.'

No more separatism, for in the provinces 'one should have no governor that one cannot govern oneself'.

A glance at the France that he wished to take in hand led Louis to these very negative conclusions. Beneath each word of the instructions that he wrote out for his son was hidden the wounding memory of his own youth. The party was over for those individuals, those social classes, those corporations of State that had risen up against his crown, challenged it and fought it. They would soon see what authority was. Bring everything down, nibble away at everything, level it all: this was the king's policy. It was too bad if certain values and abilities would have to be sacrificed, certain initiatives stifled, the vital strength of the nation sapped.

In place of those age-old constructions, now dismantled and destroyed, there would be a single focus of power, the king. From the start, Louis was thoroughly imbued with the notion of his birthright. Those who regard 'their birth as the principal cause of their greatness, whatever fortune gives them or deprives them of does not seem sufficient to change either their countenance or their sentiments'.[18] Though often confronted with more intelligent men superior in intelligence to himself who had been imposed upon him, Louis had sought refuge in the knowledge of belonging to a great dynasty. He was better than they because better born – a notion that had rather lapsed among the kings of France, who had based their self-assurance rather on their strength, on popular or military support, or on the law. Louis got his dynastic pride, if not vanity, from the Habsburgs on his mother's side who were always convinced that they were the first family in the world.

He also derived much of his view of monarchy from the Habsburgs. He had to account only to the Most High. 'Kings and princes who are born to possess everything and to command everything must be subject only to God.' In return, God guaranteed him the submission of his subjects. 'It is His will that whoever is born a subject should obey without question ... There is no other maxim more established by Christianity than this humble submission of subjects towards those set over them.'[19] They should not, therefore, bother their heads with questions. Louis almost envied them; they did not even have to concern themselves with their property since 'kings are absolute lords and naturally they may dispose fully and freely of all wealth, secular as well as ecclesiastic'.[20] In fact, subjects were intended to remain like grown-up children who would be taken care of as required, providing they behaved themselves. Kings alone had the responsibilities of adults, since God had chosen them for that purpose.

It was a singularly practical theory. If accepted, there would be no more challengers to authority, no more rebellions. It was not only the king who forbade them, but God Himself. Of course, the king remained in God's debt, but it was easier to account to the Most High than to inferiors as particular as the French. This notion of the monarchy had long been current in France. Each reign had tended to reinforce it. Inheriting this tendency, Louis had been brought up in it from childhood: 'Homage is due to kings, they do as they please,' his tutor had made him write a hundred times. But it was from his mother that he derived the unshakeable conviction of its divine rightness. Imbued with the vague mystique of the imperial crown of the Holy Roman Empire, the Habsburgs quite naturally derived their power directly from God and not from the nation. They had been so buffetted from one throne to another that they would have had difficulty in choosing one of them on which to pin their power. The kings of France by contrast had tended to base their power on a vision of France as an entity with which they had identified themselves from the outset. Now, in choosing God rather than France, Louis was again siding with his maternal ancestors.

Another novelty in his political philosophy was the idea of the total submission required of all Frenchmen. This had always been required of the ordinary people, but, from now on, princes, ministers, aristocrats and *parlementaires* were to be submitted to the same régime, and there was to be protocol to remind them of this constantly. The French court, even in periods when its luxury and refinement were carried to extreme, had always been accessible. Everyone could see, approach or even speak to the king, who remained a human being. But when the 'father of the people' became God's lieutenant on earth, ceremonial took on a quite new importance. 'Those who imagine that pretentions of this kind are merely matters of ceremony are very mistaken ... Peoples ... usually base their judgement on what they see from the outside and it is usually on pomp and circumstance that they measure their respect and obedience.' Nor should the head of State be deprived of 'the slightest marks of superiority that distinguish him from other men'.[21] The easy familiarity of the past had gone forever. The palace, once open to all comers, became a sanctuary in which the monarchical liturgy was performed. Every moment of the king's day was to be regulated by protocol – an inhuman protocol that the Habsburgs, again, had elaborated and which they had made the trademark of their monarchy.

Proud of the 'greatness' of his birth, strengthened by his view of the absolute monarchy by divine right, soon to be protected by ceremonial, the myth-king concealed the weakness of the man and could appear, overnight, transformed by assurance and authority. The apprehensions that he had felt at the approach of this moment, 'which I had both desired and feared for so long,' were overcome. Overcome, too, were the stammerings of earlier days; 'That initial timidity that had caused me so much pain, especially when I had to talk for long in public, was swept aside in a moment.'[22] Thus Louis xiv, drunk with pride, could embody the image that he himself drew of the ideal king and which constituted his programme: 'All eyes were riveted on him alone; it was to him that all wishes were addressed, he alone received respect, he alone was the object of all hopes; nothing was proposed, nothing expected, nothing done, except by him alone . . .; everything else was mean, everything else was powerless, everything else was sterile and one might even say that the brilliance with which he endowed his own States, passed as if by communication into the foreign provinces. The brilliant image of greatness to which he had raised himself was carried to every corner of the world on the wings of fame. Just as he was the admiration of his subjects, he soon became the astonishment of neighbouring nations.'[23]

The omnipotent king, who had appeared overnight and astonished the world, kept within the recesses of his heart, however, a burning sense of his own ignorance: 'One rightly feels great pain at not knowing things that everyone else knows.' He decided to make up for lost time, despite the handicap. How did he find time to study when he had just taken over the government of a kingdom? 'I decided to take from my leisure the hours necessary for this work.' He studied history, the art of war, literature; but at the same time the self-taught student was ashamed of being one at his age and in his position. He studied in the greatest secrecy, alone in his bedchamber. When he was thought to be busy digesting his files, he was in fact plunged, fascinated, in his handbooks. 'I had heard tell that all the heroes whose fame had reached as far as us were perfectly instructed in letters and that they owed their qualities in part to the reflections that study had brought them.'[24] At the rate he was going, he would soon be the equal of those 'heroes'. The humiliations, the weaknesses, the sense of inferiority were forgotten. He could now declare triumphantly, 'It seemed to me that I was born a king and born to be one.'[25]

★

On 1 April 1661, the king's brother, Philippe of France, Duc d'Orléans, married his first cousin, Henrietta Stuart, princess of England, at the Palais Royal. A lot had happened since this skinny, sickly child had lived with her mother in impecunious exile in the Louvre, humiliated by the young king who had refused to dance with 'a little girl'. Cromwell was now dead and her brother Charles II had recovered his throne; she brought with her as a dowry the prestige of an English alliance. This did not make Louis any more enthusiastic about the marriage, declaring that he hated the English. Certainly, he had no liking for Henrietta. His antipathy for the girl dated from childhood and he mocked her skinny figure: 'Brother, you are going to marry all the bones in the *Saints Innocents* [a Paris cemetery].'[26] And yet, as the Grande Mademoiselle declared, it was easy to forget that she was 'like a skeleton' and, on top of that, 'crookbacked'. It was not so much her complexion 'like rose and jasmine', her dark eyes 'gentle and brilliant', her 'vermilion' lips that made her attractive, as her determination to attract. Graceful and seductive, always perfectly dressed, forever in search of entertainment, pleasure and success, she devoured life as if she knew her deficient health put it constantly in danger.

The wedding ceremony was somewhat hasty – perhaps an expression of the king's disapproval – but the new Madame, as she came to be known, was accorded an important honorary title suitable to her rank as the king's sister-in-law. Monsieur's life-long friend Mme de Choisy had one of her own protégées, Louise de la Vallière, appointed one of Henrietta's ladies of honour.

The embryonic royal dictatorship did not prevent the king and his Court from amusing themselves, often childishly, in that hot summer of 1661 at Fontainebleu. They went bathing every day and in the cool of the evening, came back on horseback, the men gambolling around the splendidly attired women. After dinner, they were driven around the canal, the light barouches flitting across the lawns to the sound of violins. They often did not return until two or three in the morning. The new Duchesse d'Orléans was, of course, the best dressed, the most animated and entertaining of all the women. After a few weeks, the courtiers had to admit what was apparent to everyone: the king had fallen for his sister-in-law! 'It seemed that pleasure would soon have to corrupt a virtue that had been so admired.'[27] What a revenge for 'all the bones in the *Saints Innocents*'! What a reversal of fortune after the childhood years spent in poverty, oblivion and humiliation. At seventeen, Henrietta reigned over the Court – and she reigned over the king's heart as well, supplanting the true queen, for the insignificant Maria Theresa was no match for her. A good-natured, pious soul, but credulous and unbelievably stupid, Maria Theresa did nothing but play cards, nibble all day long and grow fat. She stuffed herself with garlic and drank cup after cup of chocolate – a memory of Spain – which, in the courtiers' opinion, blackened her teeth. Louis demanded positively oriental submission from her. Much later, he was to give advice to his grandson, the king of Spain, on the occasion of his marriage: 'The queen is your first subject, as such and as your wife she must obey you . . . Make the queen happy, in spite of herself, if necessary. Force her to it at first.'[28]

However, Maria-Theresa gibbed at being 'forced' to allow her husband to flirt outrageously with his sister-in-law. She wept on the shoulder of her aunt and mother-in-law, Anne of Austria, who sent the faithful Motteville to teach Madame a lesson. Madame was asked to be a little more careful and behave discreetly. Above all it was those wretched walks in the middle of the night that made people talk, and she was advised to cut them out. Madame sent her mother-in-law's emissary packing,[29] so taking the bull by the horns, Anne took Madame off on an official visit to the Duchesse de Chevreuse at the Château de Dampierre.

On their return to Fontainebleau, the scandalous 'walks' were resumed, but, at this point, the cuckolded husband came on the scene. Monsieur, who had originally seemed quite unconcerned about his wife's flirtation with his brother, began to complain violently to his mother, who summoned the English ambassador. Perhaps King Charles II could make Madame, his sister, see reason and succeed where others had failed. By now the two lovers realized that things were taking a serious turn, so Henrietta worked out a new stratagem: the king would appear to be in love with some other girl in the Court. Louis thought this a brilliant idea, and delightedly, the lovers began to carry out their plans. They went through the names of all the ladies in the Court to find the ideal candidate and came up with a shortlist of three. Without wasting any time Louis opened fire on the first, Mlle de Pons, but her terrified family immediately sent her to the provinces on some false pretext. The second, Mlle de Chemerault, was quite willing to surrender to the king, but since it was just a ruse, the king dragged things out. There remained the third, Louise de La Vallière. Henrietta was particularly amused by the choice of one of her most foolish, shy, withdrawn maids of honour who, on top of everything, was lame. The trick would be all the more successful, for courtiers could be made to believe anything, and the king, while continuing to lay siege in a half-hearted manner to Mlle de Chemerault, began to make eyes at Louise.[30]

The royal lovers had foreseen everything except one: namely, that Louise had already been in love with Louis for a year, perhaps even from that night when, leaning out of the window at the Château de Blois, she had seen him for the first time. Now the master had stopped in front of her and talked to her kindly, almost amorously, and love transformed her. The previously unremarkable girl, rather too thin and slightly lame, became truly beautiful. Her clear, frank brown eyes and her ash-blonde hair went well with her gentle nature. In all innocence she declared her love for the young man who claimed in turn to love her, and there was so much spirit, so much sincerity, so much purity in her avowal that Louis believed her. He realized that she loved him completely, without limitation, without calculation, without dissimulation, without ambition, and that she loved him for himself alone. For her part Henrietta was delighted as her strategem was succeeding admirably. The comedy was working better than expected; the king, wonderful actor that he was, really seemed to be in love with La Vallière,[31] and to Henrietta's intense satisfaction, the courtiers noticed and began to talk. She told herself that soon the king would be entirely hers.

But the king was never to belong to the clever Henrietta again. Emotion had replaced passion: he was in love with Louise. Instinctively, however, he felt that this love had something so precious, so rare about it that he had to hide it, protect it. Instead of the outrageous affair expected by Henrietta he would only meet Louise in secret. One famous, perhaps apocryphal, story describes Louis and Louise, caught unexpectedly in a storm in the forest. They were alone and took shelter under a tree, where he placed his own hat on her head and she was still wearing it when they arrived back at the castle, making a sensational entrance, dripping wet, with their hair plastered down by the rain. The truth was just as romantic. On one warm summer night, the Court barouches were driven up and down the park at Fontainebleau; the king was in Madame's carriage. Savouring her triumph, Henrietta was at her most brilliant, but Louis remained silent and preoccupied. On some pretext he got out of the carriage, wandered off alone towards another carriage hidden among the trees, and there, in the darkness, hidden from all eyes, he talked at length and alone with Louise.[32]

No one guessed at first, so discreet and secret were their meetings. Even the best-informed man of the court thought he could make a play for Louise without realizing what was happening at first. This was Nicolas Fouquet, the minister of finance, a noted ladies' man who had picked out the girl so manifestly transformed by love. He made advances to her but she remained quite unmoved. Convinced that no woman could resist him, he was quite taken aback, and began asking questions and observing her to fathom the mystery. It wasn't long before he guessed and understood. Changing tactics, he managed to get Louise alone in Madame's antechamber where he poured out a torrent of compliments about the king: how the girl who was loved by him was lucky indeed, and how he, Fouquet, would like to protect and serve such a love. Louise still said nothing. Fouquet refused to give up. He sent Mme du Plessis Bellière, his mistress, friend, adviser and bawd, to see her. The lady in question explained that the minister would like to give Louise a small present – 20,000 *pistoles* – as a token of friendship. 'Twenty million would not make me take a wrong step,' the girl replied, to the lady's amazement.[33] This proved that Louise was not like the others, for almost the entire entourage of Louis xiv received just such 'small' tokens of friendship from Fouquet: secretaries, confessors, courtiers, like de Guiche, Monsieur's male lover or Olympia Mancini, were all paid by the minister to spy on the king. Fouquet even got round Anne of Austria herself. He had offered to pay off some of her enormous debts and, guessing her bitterness at her brusque removal from power, he hinted to her that she would reign fully again if he himself became prime minister. Without quite responding to his overtures, Anne of Austria did not actually reject them.[34] It was inconceivable that the queen mother of France could be tempted by Fouquet's offers but the foolish La Vallière girl reject them. It was enough to overturn Fouquet's entire ethical system. He also did not know that Louise went and told everything to Louis, who nearly choked with fury. How could that man have the temerity to try and compete with the king in love, and then corrupt the object of that love? Louis swore he would be revenged.

No Fouquet, Mazarin had told him. After the cardinal's death, the king had nevertheless talked at great length alone with Fouquet. He had told him quite clearly that he wanted to be informed of everything, and that he would keep him only if he concealed nothing from him. Fouquet poured out protests and promises, but he had failed to heed the warning. Convinced of the king's incompetence and laziness, he believed that his initial desire to work would melt like snow in the sun.[35] As a result Fouquet assumed an air of superiority with other ministers, and would shut himself up in his study while courtiers and petitioners waited in his antechamber, leaving by a secret staircase to join some highly paid 'nymph' in the garden. He continued to pour millions into his Château de Vaux which he had had built as a palace to end all palaces, and of which the whole of Paris was talking. Living from day to day, and especially at night, carefree and negligent, he had continued provocatively to spend money like water at the risk of exciting Louis' jealousy. Anne of Austria guessed this at once: 'The king likes to be rich and does not care for those who are richer than he, since they can do things that he cannot do himself.' Furthermore, Fouquet had humiliated the king by treating him too obviously like a fool. Every day he put in an account of the State finances, exaggerating the expenditure, reducing the revenues and each night Colbert took these falsifications to pieces, one by one, for the edification of his master.[36] Now, to cap it all, Fouquet had tried to seduce Louise de la Vallière, thus deciding his own ruin.

Unfortunately he was still procurator general of the *parlement*, and could only be tried by the *parlementaires* themselves. There could be no question of offering those troublemakers such an opportunity, so Fouquet had to be persuaded to sell his post. Colbert had an idea, which was immediately accepted by his master. Colbert made a point of plying the astonished Fouquet with compliments, but Colbert reassured him by explaining he wanted to be on good terms with the most capable of all ministers, the one who enjoyed the king's favour. Fouquet had in fact noticed that for some time the king had shown him a marked preference over the other ministers and asked his advice about everything, sending for him at all hours and lavishing favours upon him. 'I would give my life for the king,' Fouquet declared, 'I, too,' Colbert retorted, 'but what is the point of all these fine words? There isn't a *sou* in the coffers.' 'I would willingly sell everything I have in the world to give the king money ... even, and why not, my post as procurator general?' Colbert reinforced the hoped-for offer with flattering remarks: the king would be infinitely touched by Fouquet's devotion. Fouquet would be able to receive in exchange the coveted Order of the Holy Ghost, a decoration that he had long desired. Delightedly, he did as he had promised and hurried to announce his decision to the king, who graciously accepted the sum derived from the post, thanking him effusively. Equally delighted the king told Colbert that very evening, 'Everything is going well, he is destroying himself. He came to tell me that he would give the State all the money raised from selling his post.'[37]

It would be a risky business arresting Fouquet in Paris, which was full of his supporters, clients and colleagues, especially the *parlementaires*. On the other hand, it would be pleasing to arrest him in the country, at home, in the midst of his ill-gotten wealth. With this in mind, the king suggested that Superintendent Fouquet give a small entertainment for him at the Château de Vaux. Fouquet could hardly believe the honour being paid him: the king, the queen mother, the princes, the entire Court coming to his house. He wanted the occasion to be unique, dazzling, unforgettable, something that people would talk about for years. He could think of nothing else, and all his time was now spent arranging it. He constantly harassed the artists that he had chosen to contribute to his triumph. Though delighted at receiving his first commission, Molière, who liked to take his time, grumbled at having to finish *Les Fâcheux* in a few days: 'Never was an undertaking so rushed as this one; and it is something quite new that a comedy should be conceived, written, learnt and performed in two weeks!'

On the afternoon of 17 August 1661, the Court coaches set out from Fontainebleau for the Château de Vaux. Louis announced to his mother that he wanted to have the master of the house arrested in the middle of the party. Anne was shocked: 'Ah, my, son, this action will hardly do you honour: that poor man has ruined himself to entertain you and you intend to have him arrested and made prisoner in his own house!'[38] The king agreed to postpone the arrest and made an effort to put a good face on ill fortune, smiling graciously at Fouquet who received him with a deep bow at the castle gates. The romantic spectacle began as the visitors were taken round the park. Suddenly, on all sides, a thousand fountains began to play, and tall stems of water rose up into the golden evening sky. Cascades rippled and marine monsters spat. The dazzled courtiers were then shown the castle itself. Pictures by Le Brun, rare marbles, gilded panelling, inlaid parquet floors combined luxury with the most refined taste. This décor formed a fitting background to the collections of pictures, statues, furniture and *objêts d'art*. Mazarin had set an example for his creature, Fouquet, who followed it faithfully with a profusion of works, signed by the most famous painters and sculptors. The supper had been prepared by Vatel, the century's most famous chef and was served on thirty-six dozen gold plates and five hundred dozen silver plates. When the meal was finished the guests moved out to the open air theatre in the *Allée des Sapins*. The glory of the stage, Molière's mistress, the charming Béjart, appeared as a nymph in a flattering prologue addressed to Louis himself. Fauns, satyrs and dryads emerged from the shrubbery behind the trees, dancing a ballet to music by Lulli, then Molière presented *Les Fâcheux* in person. A fantastic fireworks display filled the starry sky before the ball began, at which six thousand guests were to dance until three in the morning. At the end of the entertainment Louis got into his coach and turned for the last time. At that very moment, the dome surmounting the château seemed to catch fire and let fly a thousand coloured rockets.

Needless to say, news of the entertainment spread far and wide. Those fortunate enough to have been invited were unanimous in praising its splendours, variety and novelty. Professional letter writers, like the Marquise de Sévigné, sent off enthusiastic accounts to the four corners of France and everyone felt that something quite exceptional had taken place. The sheer splendour of the Château de Vaux on that beautiful summer night, a unique assembly of artists, unfettered imagination served by unlimited funds, the contradictory rumours that began to circulate about Fouquet's forthcoming disgrace, the feverish atmosphere of the crowd helped to make this the high point in the career of this dazzling bourgeois, who, for one night, was able to believe that he was greater than the king of France. But in the next few days his life tumbled around him like a house of cards. Fouquet had already received a note from the faithful Mme du Plessis Bellière in the midst of the festivities, warning him that the king had planned to arrest him that evening but that the queen mother had prevented it.[39] Distracted by the symphony of glittering waters and violins, intoxicated by the admiring cries of the crowd and the explosion of the fireworks, Fouquet threw away the note. But no sooner had he rejoined the Court of Fontainebleau than his friend Gourville met him with an alarming rumour: during the visit to his Ali Baba's cave, the king had murmured to the queen mother, 'we shall make all these people regurgitate what they have taken'.[40] Fouquet decided to play for high stakes and to speak frankly to the king. It was true that, in the exercise of his functions, he had done things that were not always honest, but it was Mazarin who respected neither the law of God nor of man who had forced him to commit such fraudulent actions. It was true that he had spent a great deal on his own account; he was guilty of many of the things that he was accused of. He admitted everything and put himself in the king's hands. The king appeared to be reassured and pardoned him, and Fouquet left the room, smiling, self-confident, certain that frankness had paid off, that he was absolved, and that he was still as powerful as ever.[41]

A few days later, at the council of ministers, the king quietly proposed to abolish the orders for payment. This was a money order which the finance minister could normally sign without any supervision to pay the secret expenses of the State. It was a direct snub to Fouquet, who exploded: 'So I am nothing any more.' Minister Le Tellier nudged his colleague, Brienne. Fouquet bit his lip; his anger had betrayed him.[42]

Not long afterwards, the entire government had to leave for Nantes. Quite recently, the king had decided to visit Nantes under the official pretext of going in person to preside over the States of Brittany. Fouquet, of course, was in the party – which had been organized with him in mind. The night before the departure, sick and feverish, he received young Brienne in his bedchamber: 'What does this visit of the king's mean? What are people saying?' he asked. Brienne was evasive, but Fouquet was insistent. He knew that the Duchesse de Chevreuse was spreading faslehoods about him. He had seen that the queen mother was being distant towards him. 'I am no longer procurator general and I shall not be finance minister for much longer. I am being lured by a decoration that I may in fact never be given and here I am, lost without resources. . . . Why is the king going to Brittany and why particularly to Nantes? . . . Shall I flee? It would probably be quite easy for me to do so. Should I hide? But where?'[43]

Next day, the government took to the Loire on its way to Nantes. From his boat, young Brienne watched the two magnificent barges with fifteen oarsmen each glide slowly before him, with the ministers, including Fouquet, on board. 'One of those barges will be shipwrecked at Nantes,' murmured a clerk, standing beside him. Brienne, astonished by the remark, asked him what he meant, but the clerk refused to say more. On arriving at Nantes, Fouquet, who was sicker than ever, retired to bed and the king sent Brienne to enquire after his condition. He found Fouquet in bed, sitting up against a pile of green cushions. 'What are they saying at the castle and in Court?' Fouquet asked. 'That you are going to be arrested,' Brienne replied. 'It's Colbert, not I, who will be arrested.' 'Are you sure?' 'One could not be more sure than I am. I have myself given orders to have him taken to the Château d'Angers.'

Next day, Brienne woke at five in the morning and at six was at Fouquet's door. He found it guarded by six musketeers, and an officer approached him, demanding to know what he wanted. Brienne explained that he had come on the king's behalf to fetch the minister, but was told, 'He is no longer here. He has gone to the castle, but M. Boucherat is here, making an inventory of his papers.' Overcome with emotion, pity and fear, Brienne ordered his coachman to ride at full speed to the castle. He arrived at the gates at seven o'clock and passed an armoured carriage, with barred windows: Fouquet was inside with the officer who had just arrested him, a certain Charles d'Artagnan, a captain in the musketeers.[44]

Louis described the arrest to his mother in person, for she had remained at Fontainebleau. 'This morning the finance minister came to work with me as usual. I talked to him sometimes in one manner, sometimes in another, and pretended to look for papers until out of my study window, I noticed Artagnan in the castle courtyard and then I let the minister go. He disappeared as Artagnan was greeting the Sieur Le

Tellier, so that poor Artagnan thought that he had missed him, and sent me word by Maupertuis that he suspected that someone had told him to escape: but he caught up with him on the Place de la Grande Eglise, and arrested him on my behalf ... I had indicated that I wanted to go hunting that morning and under this pretext I had had my coaches ready and my musketeers on horseback ...'[45]

Why did the king feel he had to resort to all these underhand manoeuvres, honeyed assurances, false pardons and lies? Why did he wait so long to arrest Fouquet after deciding to get rid of him? As the disgraced minister's prison carriage, escorted by no less than a hundred musketeers, proceeded to the castle at Angers, which was to be his prison, Louis tried to explain his hesitation to his mother: 'You know that I have had it in mind for a long time; but it was impossible for me to do it earlier, because I wanted him to pay first 30,999 crowns for the navy and a number of matters had to be settled that could not be done in a day.'[46] These are unnecessary, frankly unsatisfactory explanations; he was to find others when he had leisure to write his memoirs. 'As for Fouquet, it might be found strange that I should wish to go on using him when his thefts were already well known to me; but I knew that he was intelligent and had a great knowledge of the workings of the State: this led me to imagine that providing that he admitted his past mistakes and promised to correct them he might still give me good service.'[47] After the festivities at Vaux, Fouquet had admitted his errors quite openly and promised to correct them, but this man, so brilliant, so self-assured, could not help showing his contempt for the king and reopened old wounds. With him, Louis XIV once again felt the bitter taste of humiliation that he had undergone at Mazarin's hands: the trauma of his adolescence had been such that it could not be cured. While he failed to match Fouquet in intelligence, he decided to out-class him in cunning. He took great delight in lulling his adversary's fears, describing to his mother his manoeuvres to trick those around him with a mixture of self-satisfaction and childish Machiavellianism. He boasted that he would not replace Fouquet himself: 'I declared to them [the ministers] that I no longer wanted a finance minister but wished myself to administer the finances with certain faithful retainers ... You will have no difficulty believing that certain individuals have been looking rather foolish, but I am satisfied that they now see that I am not so easily taken in as they imagined; and that the best course is to remain loyal to me.'[48]

The surprise so lovingly arranged by the king did have the desired effect. The ministers and courtiers who had once been close, too close, to Fouquet, were brought down. Lionne, pale as death, remained prostrate for so long that the king gave himself the satisfaction of comforting him. The Duc de Gesvres, an intimate of Fouquet's, who as captain of the guards should have been the one to arrest him, yelled out his disappointment with all the required baseness. 'I would have arrested my father, let alone my best friend. Does the king suspect my fidelity?' As for M. de la Feuillade, 'he seemed like a thing possessed,' Brienne tells us. Before long everyone was talking about the compromising documents found by the authorities at Fouquet's home. Above all there was his famous casket, a veritable Pandora's box filled with ministers' indiscretions, requests for money from the richest of courtiers, love letters, bills from prostitutes, reports from highly placed spies, dubious business contracts – which spread panic in Court and city.[49] It turned out that some of the most eminent people in the kingdom had been bought off and that reputedly virtuous women were far from being so. The public devoured these letters, which were hastily copied out and circulated everywhere. Often distorted, sometimes entirely invented, they caused enormous scandals from which no one could feel safe. The hundreds of great names who had been compromised by them were joined by hundreds of other innocent individuals whose reputations were stained by calumny.

One October evening in 1661, the king was dining at his mother's. It was after eleven when the Secretary of State for Foreign Affairs came in. 'What news is there, Brienne?' Louis exclaimed. An extraordinary courier had just arrived from London with despatches from the French ambassador. 'I shall inform Your Majesty of the affair when he has finished supper,' said Brienne, but the king caught him by the arm and told him to tell him at once. Brienne did so: some days before in London, the Spanish ambassador, Baron de Watteville, disputed precedence with the French ambassador, the Comte d'Estrades during a ceremony. De Watteville's servants, Thames boatmen and 'innumerable riff-raff' attacked the Frenchman's coach, tore it to pieces, cut off its horses' legs and wounded members of the French embassy including the ambassador's own son. Then the Spaniard went on his way, his coach obviously having no difficulty passing first. The king rose from the table so angry that he almost overturned it and pulled Brienne by the arm towards his room. Anne of Austria, alarmed by his expression, followed him: 'At least finish your supper!' 'I have had enough, Madame. I shall have satisfaction for this affair or I shall declare war on the king of Spain.' Anne of Austria burst into tears: 'Do not break the peace that has caused me so many tears. Remember that the king of Spain is my brother.' 'Leave me, I beg you Madame . . . Go back to the table and tell them to save just a little fruit for me.'[50]

Next day, an extraordinary council of ministers was held. The French ambassadors in Madrid and London were recalled, and the Spanish ambassador in Paris was expelled. Explanations and compensation were demanded from the king of Spain. But which, in fact, did have precedence, France or Spain? For over a century no one had been able to settle the question. Watteville, the Spanish ambassador, had not previously tried to do so, and, in any case, the riot he had triggered off was not intended to upset the ambassador of France, but to embarrass the British government, which had just concluded an alliance with

Portugal, Spain's enemy. Mortified, Philip IV wrote a letter to his daughter Maria Theresa that was intended to be shown to his son-in-law; he praised Louis to the heavens and declared that he loved him as a son, but this was not enough for Louis, who disdainfully rejected the letter. Louis would never accept what Mazarin had accepted at the Treaty of the Pyrenees. His father-in-law would have to go through the supreme humiliation of sending an extraordinary ambassador, the Marqués de Las Fuentes. He was received by the king in the drawing-room of his apartment in the Louvre, in the presence of all the ambassadors accredited to Paris. He presented his master's official apologies and declared that 'Spanish ministers would no longer compete with those of France'. Spanish pride had definitely taken a blow. The old king, whose kingdom was, admittedly, now weak and ruined, preferred to renounce a victory of protocol rather than trigger off a new war, while the young king, his nephew and son-in-law, won a triumph out of pure vanity.

Encouraged by his success, Louis was not slow to repeat the offence. The haughty Duc de Créqui, French ambassador to the Vatican, was heartily detested in Rome for his pretensions and the contempt he showed for Italians. Following his example, his servants behaved as if they were in a conquered land. One day they took it into their heads to charge some of the pope's Corsican guards, swords in hand. Southern blood and the discreet encouragement of the pope's brother, Don Mario Chigi, who hated Créqui, were enough to trigger off an anti-French riot, and the entire Corsican guard laid siege to the French embassy. Against a background of continual shouting, windows were broken and shots were fired on the coach of the ambassador's wife, who unfortunately arrived home at that very moment. Servants were wounded; one actually died. The Duc de Créqui left Rome telling everyone that the pope himself had wanted to have him assassinated. The Holy Father expelled the governor from the city and had one or two Corsicans hanged for appearance's sake but did nothing more, convinced that it was enough to play for time with the French and that in a few months it would all be over and forgotten. It came as a terrible shock when he learnt in rapid succession that Louis XIV was threatening to lay siege to Rome, that a French army had entered Italy for this purpose, that his city of Avignon had been occupied and that the *parlement* of Provence had cited him in person for spreading accusations levied against him. The pope's immediate response was to excommunicate the French, beginning with the king, but unfortunately, that particular weapon was too rusty. He then thought of calling the Catholic sovereigns to his aid, but they were otherwise engaged. When no one answered the summons, the pope was forced to accept the king's demands. He exiled his own brother, Don Mario Chigi, dissolved his Corsican guard, sent his nephew, Cardinal Chigi, to Paris to present his apologies – the first papal legate ever to be sent on such a mission – and had erected in Rome itself an explanatory pyramid, recalling the villainy of the people involved and the apologies that the French had demanded.[51]

Louis XIV had twice bluffed – and his manoeuvres had paid off both times. He was a success on the international stage, but he was also a success in France itself. At last the nation had a king who would not let himself be pushed around, who did not allow foreign villains to make fun of France and who had managed to make the whole of Europe afraid of him. The popularity of the king was to grow still further for at last France had a king who ruled alone, without favourites or prime ministers. In order to remain master, he had carefully chosen his collaborators. There were no more highly-coloured, flamboyant, provocative personalities; the *Fronde* had shown where that could lead. Instead there were efficient men, providing, of course, that their capacities did not put the young king in the shade. 'And to tell the truth,' he naïvely admitted in his memoirs, 'I saw that it was not in my interest to look for men of outstanding quality, a precaution that was all the more necessary in that such men had for so long prevented the world from knowing me better.'[52] He chose instead honest functionaries as ministers, men of humble origin, hardworking, serious, discreet, self-effacing, whose sole concern was to retain the good will of the master. They contrasted strongly with the flamboyant ministers of the past, like Richelieu and Mazarin. The rebarbative, austere Colbert, with his sullen expression and thick frowning eyebrows, had slipped discreetly into the royal cabinet, clutching a simple black bag containing his files. He still preferred to work alone with the king rather than preside over the council of ministers to which the fall of Fouquet had at last given him access. He looked like an ordinary accountant, and an accountant he wanted to be – on national level. Michel Le Tellier was still there, with his ample figure, his ingratiating smile and smooth tongue, as attractive physically as Colbert was offputting. Without vanity or affectation he maintained the simplicity of a good bourgeois, obliging and moderate in all things. Hugues de Lionne, unfortunately for him, had a penchant for gambling, which was constantly getting him into debt. But he was disinterested and indefatigable: he spent his days and even his nights if necessary working alone, without the assistance of a secretary, writing up the despatches by hand, as if he was some clerk rather than the *de facto* Minister of Foreign Affairs. These three men had one great advantage in common. They had worked with Mazarin for a long time, who had chosen them and set them on their careers. They had watched the late cardinal working with the youthful Louis and knew the king as no one else did, recognizing all his weaknesses and knowing exactly how to deal with him.

In order not to dissipate their energies competing with one another, at first they formed a discreet alliance among themselves, being careful not to arouse the master's anxiety – he was all too afraid of such understandings. The king was a man who, beneath his imposing air, was constantly afraid, an irrepressible fear of being ruled by others, inherited from his past. His ministers began by reassuring him, and in this their behaviour, the expression on their faces, the way they dressed, the way they lived, all played a part. These modest bourgeois were scarcely the kind of people who wanted to rule in the king's place; repeating to him every day that he was the master, the sole authority, that everything went through him, everything depended on him.[53] As Louis wanted to see and do everything, they hid nothing from him, bogging him down in detail, while subtly reversing the relative importance of things. They brought small matters to the forefront, endlessly discussing them with the king and respectfully carrying out his orders. Intoxicated by the exercise of his authority, Louis then let them pass quickly over more important matters, which they had kept for themselves.

The king signed, examined and ordered everything and thus his three ministers acted almost as they liked. But, they were not fully reassured, for the nobility, the courtiers, and ambassadors still had direct access to the king by virtue of their position or birth and they might open his eyes. The three ministers attempted to cloister Louis, persuading him that to allow anyone to approach and speak to him was an affront to his greatness and to the respect due to the Crown. Anyway, people who knew nothing might make mistakes or commit indiscretions that would disturb the repose so precious to the king. Timid by nature, terrified of being at a loss and not knowing what to reply, Louis clung to their arguments and henceforth an uncrossable barrier rose up around him. Everyone was moved aside, good and bad, intriguers and faithful servants alike. It was no longer possible to approach the king, except in public when there was no possibility of talking to him intimately; everyone had to pass through the faithful trio who watched over everything with such vigilance.[54] The ambassador of Savoy complained to his master: 'The king never says a word to foreigners; as for the ambassadors, he no longer talks to them during audiences.' Yet he ought not to have been surprised by this attitude, since he had seen through the ministers' game: 'Whatever may be said about the king's behaviour, he allows himself to be ruled absolutely by his ministers; they agree among themselves and do nothing for anybody except their own families.'[55]

Mistrust was so rooted in Louis that it did not entirely disappear even with the help of his ministers. He invented a game, which a smiling Le Tellier was later to confide to an astonished friend. Out of twenty matters for which each minister asked his approval in private consultation, he would agree to nineteen and reject one, purely at random, and without the minister being able to guess at the outset which it would be.[56] It was the king's way of showing that he was not easily led, even by his ministers, that he could refuse whatever he liked. This unexpected, unpredictable 'no', this puerile negative after nineteen assents, was the only mark of his authority. It was also an unconscious admission that he sometimes doubted that he possessed that authority.

His anxiety assuaged by this stratagem, Louis could feel once more that he was the king whom the whole of France obeyed and who subjugated Europe. To crown this resounding entrance onto the political stage, his son and heir was born on 1 November 1661. It was a long and difficult childbirth for Maria Theresa; the pains were so terrible that there were fears at one time for her life. At her bedside, her husband suffered as much as she did. At five in the morning, unable to bear it any longer, he took refuge in the chapel, confessed, took communion and prayed for a long time. Then he went back to hold his wife's hand, until the Dauphin was finally born at five minutes to noon. In gratitude his father made a solemn pilgrimage to Chartres for the edification of France; an hour after his return to Paris, he was back in the arms of Mlle de La Vallière.

Louis' love for Louise had grown during those last few weeks. He found that he did not see enough of her so he asked her to pretend that she was ill so that he could go and visit her in peace, in her small bedchamber under the Tuileries roof, close to Monsieur and Madame whose favourite she still was. But now Henrietta was furious. The stratagem which she had taken such delight in elaborating had brought her nothing but humiliation. The king escaped her only to fall in love with the simpleton that she herself had chosen. It was impossible for her to revenge herself, or to get rid of La Vallière because the king wished Louise to stay. But in her looks, in the tone of her voice, Henrietta could not hide her hatred for her so very unworthy rival. Louise suffered in silence.[57]

Louise was forced to share her room with another maid of honour, Mlle de Montalais, a scandal-monger of the worst kind, who was now in an enviable position to follow closely any intrigue that might be taking place inside the Tuileries palace itself. Monsieur, with an impudence bordering on boorishness, wanted to impose his lover, the Comte de Guiche, on his wife, insisting that she be pleasant to him and receive him in her apartment. He was so successful that the handsome de Guiche made a play for Madame, who fell into his arms. At first, Louis encouraged the affair, for if she had now fallen for someone else, Henrietta might now forget her disappointment and accept Louise. But the king had already been annoyed that his brother's affability, easy manner and vitality made him more popular at the Court and in Paris than himself, which led to the irresistible and petty temptation to support the wife against the husband.[58]

The lovers' indiscretions grew with each day, giving the affair disquieting proportions. Madame, sick and confined to bed, had de Guiche brought to her room disguised as a woman fortune-teller. He even went as far as predicting the future of her ladies of honour who did not recognize him. When Madame used a visit to Mme de Saint-Chamont as a pretext for meeting Guiche, Launois, the *valet de chambre*, rushed into the room and declared 'Monsieur is coming down the stairs!' With all retreat cut off, all flight impossible, the lovers panicked, but Launois took the situation in hand. 'Stand here behind the door,' he ordered de Guiche. When Monsieur came in, Launois made a pretence of bumping into him which was so forceful that Monsieur had a nosebleed. Madame and Mme de Saint-Chamont rushed up to him with towels, dabbing him, wiping him, blinding him, while the lover slipped out through the door and disappeared. But in the end everyone came to know about this farce. Monsieur, beside himself at the idea that both his lover and his wife were deceiving him, chose his wife, of course, as the object of his anger and complained to his mother.

Hugely enjoying her position in the middle of this intrigue, every evening in their small room Mlle de Montalais told La Vallière all the confidences she had collected from both parties. She begged Louise not to repeat anything, and the naïve girl promised to keep the secret that the entire Court already knew. The king, for his part, was becoming irritated by the scandal. He knew that Montalais knew and he guessed that she told everything to Louise, so he questioned her about it to find out more. But she had sworn not to say anything, and in spite of his angry insistence, she held firm. Louis flew into a towering rage, damning Henrietta, de Guiche, Montalais and even Louise to hell and left her, slamming the door. All night, Louise waited for a sign from him. Had they not promised never to sleep on a tiff? But no word came. In the morning, Louise thought that their affair was all over. Unable to bear it any longer, she went out of the Tuileries and began to walk, without knowing where she was going, along the river Seine. She reached the village of Chaillot; continuing her walk, she came to a convent, but the nuns refused to allow her into the enclosure and left her in the parlour. Exhausted, shivering, desperate, she fell to the floor, almost prostrate.[59]

'La Vallière has left. La Vallière has disappeared. La Vallière has entered a convent.' The news was whispered from one excited courtier to the next in the drawing-rooms of the Louvre, where the Spanish ambassador was taking his leave of the king. 'What is it? Tell me,' said the king, astonished at the excitement among the courtiers. 'La Vallière has taken vows at Chaillot,' he was told. Fortunately the ambassador had just left, otherwise he would have seen the king, who a few moments before had been thundering against Philip IV, suddenly pull on a coat, then leap on a horse and set off alone at a gallop. In the chapel, a preacher who was waiting for His Majesty in order to begin his Lenten sermon, could not do so. Louis, meanwhile spurred on his horse till he reached Chaillot where he found Louise still lying on the floor of the convent parlour, disfigured by tears, haggard, coughing. Louis raised her to her feet. They talked and wept in each other's arms, and then she repeated to him everything that Montalais had confided in her.[60]

Louis left at once and rode back to the Tuileries. He summoned Madame to his small study, commanding her to take Louise back into her service immediately. Henrietta replied that there was no question of that; the girl had left of her own accord: she would not be coming back. The king repeated to her all that he had learnt about her affairs, but

Henrietta remained proudly stubborn. The king wept, pleaded and in the end Henrietta gave in. Louise went back to her little room under the eaves, and soon it was being whispered at Court that the prudish girl had sacrificed her virtue to Louis and given into his desires.[61] He may have been an absolute monarch, ruling alone and unaided, intimidating everybody with his imposing airs but he could still do all the silly things that a young man in love usually does.

CHAPTER 8

Mythical King
and Mythical State

A series of disastrous harvests brought the country to a state of almost general famine. Contemporary accounts are in tragic agreement. 'The dearth is so great,' recounts a physician at Blois, 'that the peasants, for want of bread, seize on carrion.' 'There are peasants,' someone writes from Le Cotentin, 'who no longer eat anything but cabbage roots, which sends them into a kind of languor that lasts with them until they die.' The parish priest of Chambon declared that he had buried fifteen children and thirteen adults who had died of hunger, 'not counting infants at the breast, not one of which escaped'; another priest 'recently buried five children aged between eight and ten years of age, all of whom died of hunger and who were found in the straw, holding in their hands pieces of carcass filled with worms.' The powerless authorities presided over a massive exodus of the peasants towards the cities. The municipalities were soon incapable of coping with the numbers and the almshouses were filled to bursting point. Le Mans had 12,000 destitute persons. Caen could no longer feed the sick in its hospitals. 500 persons died of starvation at Valençay. In Paris, the poor sent a petition to the king declaring that 'the parish charities could no longer help them,' the hospitals refused to admit them. Local steps were taken to assist the most needy, but what could they do against the dizzy rise in prices? The government authorized the importation of corn – an incredible measure for an agricultural, cereal-producing country – but transport being what it was, the grain arrived far too late.

The State, as usual, had no money. Its total revenue amounted to the ridiculous sum of 89 million francs, more than half of which went to pay interest on the national debt – an accumulation of loans that had never been repaid taken out by the monarchy over the last hundred years. How could it extract more from the ruined provinces, when the raising of taxes was already meeting such growing resistance? When peace returned with the conclusion of the Franco-Spanish treaty, the French people expected a lightening of the tax burden which, of course, never came. Disappointed, driven to the limits of endurance by poverty and starvation, they rose in rebellion in various parts of the country. At Orléans, the rioters looted the granaries and a woman was hanged as an example. In the Boulonnais the so-called Lustucru war broke out as groups of armed peasants attacked the detachments of troops that had come to enforce back payment of taxes. As a result, 3,000 prisoners were taken, 400 of whom were sent to the galleys and the ringleaders hanged. The Landes, rebelling against an increase in the tax on the transport of goods, had a gentleman-adventurer, Bernard d'Audipus, at their head who took them into hiding. It took two years to dislodge them, and the king did not dare to hang the popular hero who enjoyed the support of all classes, but made him a colonel in the army. Meanwhile, the provincial *Intendant* was sending prisoners to the galleys or hanging them by the dozen.[1]

France was learning what the king's new justice was like. In the past, punishment was meted out harshly but more or less at random, according to circumstances, sometimes quickly and brutally, sometimes leniently, with pardons and suspensions of penalty. From now on, illegality was to be put down swiftly, thoroughly and efficiently; punishment had to make an impression on people. It all bore the mark of Colbert. The reports piled up on his desk, giving him daily information about rebel movements and military operations. He got the information, then gave his orders with all the meticulousness of a clerk. Suppressing the slightest revolt, sending out the constabulary, or better still the army wherever disaffection raised its head, he achieved a miracle: taxes began to be paid and, because expenditure had been considerably reduced since the end of the hostilities, the finances of the State began to pick up.

After carrying out the Herculean task of unravelling the intricacies of French finances, Colbert turned his attention to the administration, knowing that the health of the first depended on the second. Sweeping away the prerogatives and particularisms that gave the kingdom of France its originality and variety, he set up in their place the State. A State without colour, without passion, inhuman and pitiless – a State in his own image. A mythical State that served as a complement to the mythical king invented by his patron. It was the embryo of the modern State, a levelling, centralizing empire, and France, exhausted by the *Fronde* and its disorders, did not oppose it.

Encouraged by success, he attacked trade. In order to limit imports, he decided to create manufactures that would compete with foreign products, but here he lacked the required skill, 'always magnificent in ideas and almost always unfortunate in execution'. He began by seeking advice from those whom he believed best qualified to give it: 'He talked to merchants,' the Abbé de Choisy recounts, 'and asked them as a minister the secrets of their trade, which, old merchants that they were, they were careful to hide from him.' Thus he created industries which, according to his contemporary enemies, brought in less than they had cost to set up.[2]

The companies of the Indies that he launched were entrusted in particular with the slave trade. The king had made it clear that their trading should consist of horses, salt meat and negroes, for slaves had to be bought to fill the galleys increasingly required by war and commerce. The first director of the East India Company was instructed to supply at least two to three hundred slaves a year. If he failed to do so, application would be made to the Grand Master of Malta to buy 'Moors' and 'Turks'. Since this particular merchandise had become rare, the pope was asked if the 'Schismatic Greeks', (in other words, members of the Greek Orthodox church), might also be considered as sub-humans, and the accommodating pope gave his consent. So Christians – 'schismatics' – were to join 'pagans' in the galleys. However, since some people were not entirely happy to take part in this trafficking with which the Church in its time had reproached Islam, the justification was given that human cattle bought on the eastern and western markets to be thrown into the galleys ought to regard such an improvement in its lot with satisfaction; better a galley slave than just slave!

Either the slaves refused to be convinced or the merchants did not know their job, for there was still a shortage of merchandise, and Colbert was in ever greater need of galley slaves. He then appealed to the French legal system, ordering the courts to condemn as many criminals as possible to the galleys. The *parlements* were strongly urged to commute death sentences to life sentences in the galleys. A judge at Poitiers, who had done his duty by supplying thirty prisoners, was congratulated and an advocate general of the *parlement* at Toulouse was criticized for failing to come up with more. Complaints were made about officers who freed galley slaves who had completed their sentence without first asking permission from their superiors. Guards who damaged the merchandise by their ill treatment were severely reprimanded. Strict instructions were given that merchandise that left port alive should arrive at its destination in the same condition. And since the life of a prisoner was no worse than any other, the administration even suggested sending to the galleys 'all the beggars and idlers of the kingdom'.[3]

One person Colbert would dearly have loved to see in the galleys, or, preferably, on the scaffold was Fouquet. Colbert and Louis competed zealously to have him condemned. The former superintendent's trial had opened some months before, for which the government had appointed a court made up of hand-picked *parlementaires*. Fouquet rejected the validity of this court and declared that he would recognize as judge only the Paris *parlement*. This plea was ignored and it was decided to try the accused as a deaf mute, the charges being conveyed to him in his cell in writing and his answers presented in the same manner.

The king chose as prosecutors Olivier d'Ormesson and Le Cormier de Sainte-Hélène; Fouquet's family suspected them of partiality and rejected them. Again, the king ignored the objection. Similarly, he found the president of the court, Lamoignon, lacking in rigour and replaced him by the Chancellor Séguier. For his part, Fouquet rejected the procurator general, Omer Talon, the clerk of the court and two of the judges, including one of Colbert's relations. Again the objections were ignored. He demanded to see all the evidence in order to prepare his defence. The request was rejected. Faced with such blatant partiality, some of the government appointees began to change sides; in particular d'Ormesson showed during his investigation that the so-called documents seized at Fouquet's house and which were being used as exhibits in the case were false. The government then decided to hit back. Colbert deprived d'Ormesson of the Intendance of Picardy and went in person to the prosecutor's father to show him where his son's interest lay, but nothing came of it.[4]

All the government's manoeuvres, its indecent display of arbitrary power had a very bad effect on the public. To make matters worse, despite all the measures taken by the police, documents in the case and Fouquet's own defence were reprinted by the underground presses and were circulating everywhere. Fouquet's friends, following Olivier d'Ormesson, refused to be intimidated. They wrote innumerable letters of complaint, or, like La Fontaine, wrote verses. Countless songs and satires appeared against the 'hyenas' who were tearing the superintendent to pieces, and influenced by this vast movement of opinion, the court hardened in its attitude against the government's intimidation.[5] It was removed forthwith from the pernicious atmosphere of Paris to Fontainebleau, close to the king's current residence. Fouquet himself, after changing prison four times, was finally locked up in the Château de Moret. He was deprived of the right to see his lawyers more than twice a week, and then only in the presence of Captain d'Artagnan who, after arresting him at Nantes, had remained his jailer.

To all this pressure, Fouquet responded with denials, requests and protests, and, using his long experience of the *parlement,* he won every time. In this game the subtlety of the mouse was able to laugh at the brutality of the cat. All the prevaricating enraged Chancellor Séguier, who could not wait to have the defendant hanged. Beside himself with rage at seeing himself outmatched, on one occasion he tore up and threw into the fire a hundred and seventy-two decrees that had been brought to him for signature.[6]

It was two years before Fouquet finally appeared before the court in Paris, in November 1664. Despite all the doctoring and falsification of the evidence, the charge was a good deal less serious than the actions of the government would have led one to believe. Fouquet was accused of misappropriation and maladministration, but he had no difficulty in showing that most of it derived from the system imposed by Mazarin. So he was accused of conspiracy against the State; this was more serious. Fouquet was even shown to have written in his own hand a detailed plan to seize power, which was found hidden behind a mirror in his house at Saint-Mandé. This was none other than the rather shaky, vague plan, long forgotten, which he had jotted down when he was about to be arrested by Mazarin at Colbert's instigation and which he then omitted to burn, against Gourville's advice. 'A rough draft of no consequence' was how Mme de Motteville described the principal exhibit.[7] But

Richelieu had always maintained, 'Give me four lines in a man's hand and I shall prosecute him.' Four pages in Fouquet's hand were enough for Colbert to send him to the scaffold. He was guilty of nothing less than 'a crime against the State', Séguier screamed at him. Fouquet turned to his judges: 'I would beg these gentlemen to be so kind as to allow me to explain what a crime against the State is: it is when one occupies one of the principal posts of the land, when one has the confidence of the Prince and when, suddenly, one goes over to the side of one's enemies, engages one's whole family in the same interests, uses one's son-in-law to leave the ways open for a foreign army to enter the kingdom.' In other words, Fouquet outlined point by point what Chancellor Séguier had done during the *Fronde*. The entire court burst out laughing.[8]

From then on things were rushed through, and on December 1664, thirteen judges voted for banishment for life and only nine for the death penalty; Fouquet had saved his skin. An explosion of joy shook Paris, not only the Paris of the *parlementaires* and friends of the former superintendent, but also the ordinary people. Olivier d'Ormesson had to bar his door to escape the crowd that had come to congratulate him. Even d'Artagnan, won over by his prisoner, flung his arms around the neck of the upright judge. Louis was in Louise de La Vallière's bedchamber when informed of the sentence: 'If he had been condemned to death, I would have let him die,' he commented.[9] His disappointment was to lay heavily on Fouquet's fate: he altered the sentence from banishment to detention for life in the sinister fortress at Pignerol. He exiled Fouquet's wife and mother to Montluçon, and it was with great difficulty that the latter, at the age of seventy-two, was allowed to keep with her Fouquet's youngest son. Meanwhile the judges were to learn that they would suffer for their display of integrity.

Councillor Roquesaute, who supported d'Ormesson's conclusions, was exiled to Quimper on a false charge. The advocate-general Bailly was also exiled for threatening one of the judges with dishonour if he obeyed the government. President Ponchartrain, who resisted Séguier's pressure, was never to be able to hand over his post to his son to whom all advancement was refused for eighteen years. As for Olivier d'Ormesson, the most 'guilty' of all, he obtained neither the post of State councillor that had been promised to him on the death of his father, nor any other, and was condemned to an early retirement. It cost dearly to oppose royal 'justice'.

In the whole of this affair, the king and Colbert wallowed together in iniquity, linked together henceforth in the eyes of public opinion in the crime of injustice. For Colbert Fouquet had represented the contrary image to the myth-State that he was trying to impose – and he had set out to destroy a rival whom he had always hated with a rancour that had built up over many years. He may perhaps also have had an intention to compromise the king, in order to bind him to himself all the more. As for the king, there were no limits to his desire for revenge against Mazarin's creature who had ignored and humiliated him and who had refused to fall on his knees before the image of the myth-king. Louis must have felt incredibly inferior to this brilliant man to pursue him with such determination. The idea of making an example of the dishonest minister was in fact actuated by personal hate. Public opinion understood this very well and, though at first it demanded severe treatment against the dissipator of national resources, it ended by siding with him against the shameful conduct of the State. 'Thus,' concluded d'Ormesson, 'Monsieur Fouquet, who was an object of horror during his imprisonment and whom the whole of Paris could not wait to see executed after his trial had begun, had become the subject of public concern and consideration through the hatred that everyone has in his heart against the present government.'[10] Through his partiality, pettiness, duplicity and cruelty, Louis made a martyr out of Fouquet who seemed at first so ill-suited to the role.

While Louis XIV was busy destroying Fouquet, others were seeking to destroy his mistress Louise de La Vallière. One day, a letter was brought to Mme Molina, Maria Theresa's Spanish *femme de chambre,* addressed to her mistress. She recognized on the envelope the writing of the Queen of Spain, but was surprised to see that the letter was crumpled and badly folded. Because she feared it might contain bad news of Philip IV who was sick, and because she wished to spare her mistress an emotional upheaval, she opened the letter and read it. In a writing quite different from that of the envelope, in bad Spanish mixed with French, the writer revealed to the queen the affair between her husband and Louise. Refraining of course from taking the letter to her mistress, Molina, on Anne of Austria's advice, went and showed it to the king, who blushed deeply on reading it. Who was this anonymous letter from? Who could wish so much ill to Louise as to betray her to his wife?[11]

The king felt the circle of gossip and intrigue tightening dangerously around Louise and himself. However, he was determined to preserve the mystery, if not the secret, of his affair. One may well wonder how he imagined that he could manage to do so when protocol and the curiosity of courtiers placed him under constant surveillance, and when his juvenile love for Louise had already made him commit some incredible gaffes. Even so, somehow he did manage to do so, more or less. The memoirs and letters of the time all mention the famous affair, but Court and city generally were quite unaware of its extent for several years. The king's entourage who had certainly noticed Louis' liking for Louise, obviously hesitated to attribute it to a passing love affair. Lastly, those who were paid to find out all they could, such as Henrietta, Duchesse d'Orléans, maintained a curious silence about it. This affair, of which every detail is known to history, gave rise for the moment only to vague, unsubstantiated rumours, and most observers were on the wrong scent. The most surprising thing about it is the manner in which Louis maintained its secrecy. When he set out for battle against the Duke of Lorraine he decided to use Colbert as an intermediary between himself and Louise, for Colbert was the only man he could really trust. It was, therefore, the nation's austere accountant who was to transmit the letters of the master, 'on which there is no address' to 'the person I mentioned on leaving. You know who I mean.' The unfeeling iceberg had become the messenger of love.[12]

It was Colbert, too, who was given the task of setting up the favourite in her own quarters, for after two years of love, the king had realized that she was badly lodged under the Tuileries roof. So he bought a house for her, not a palace, but a modest, two-storey house in the Palais Royal gardens. Colbert found the servants and bought the linen, for Louise de La Valliére was pregnant and everything had to be ready for the birth. On 18 December 1663, Doctor Boucher warned that the birth pains had begun. Louis was at Louise's bedside, but he had to leave her: he had to attend a hunting expedition. At half-past three, next morning, Boucher scribbled a note to Colbert: 'We have a boy. He is very strong. Mother and child are doing well, thank God. I await further orders.' The orders came: the child was to be immediately taken away from his mother to avoid gossip. He was to be taken to the country and handed over to the Beauchamps. Inevitably, they were former servants of Colbert's.[13]

'Four friends whose acquaintance began with Parnassus formed a sort of society that I would call an Academy if they had been greater in number and if they had paid as much regard to the Muses as to pleasure.' The four friends referred to were so inseparable that one of them rented a room in the Rue du Vieux-Colombier so that they might meet more often, in more convenient circumstances. And indeed their pleasure consisted above all in talking about pleasure. Each of them delighted in recounting his amorous exploits, discussing gastronomy, exchanging addresses of good restaurants, talking about women, mistresses, good fortunes, and when they went off to the theatre, it was also to go backstage to get a closer look at the actresses. In short, they enjoyed themselves quite shamelessly. 'If, after talking at length of their pleasures,' one of them was to write, 'the conversation happened to turn to some point concerning science or letters, it was not ignored.' For writing was their domain, their kingdom, of which they would one day be the kings not only in their own century but in the whole of French literature. The organizer of their meetings, the most authoritarian of the four, was a young man of twenty-eight, loyal and frank, curt and sometimes cutting, who talked loudly and at length. Some satires of his had already circulated in the salons; his name was Boileau. The Benjamin of the four, at twenty-five, was more discreet, but he was also better looking and nobler of manner. He smiled gently but his humour could be caustic. His name was Racine: he had written as yet only two tragedies, one of which had not been published. The oldest of the four was forty-three. He caught fire if the conversation interested him but he could also sink to the deepest fits of absentmindedness. His absences alternating with his unexpected appearances and his probably calculated naïveties, were a great joy to the others. People were talking about the tales that he had published, but La Fontaine had not yet attained fame. The best known of the four was Molière, famous at forty-two. He was also the least talkative: he listened to the others, smiling sadly. He was the best possible friend.

On that particular day, Molière was reading to them his latest comedy, *L'Hypocrite,* an extremely funny and incisive attack on the inquisitorial, dictatorial and stifling hypocrisy of certain churchmen. The others, delighted at seeing the bigots denounced at last, applauded noisily. Molière was expecting to launch this firebrand at the latest entertainment the king was planning. What would the priests say? What would the queen mother, their protector, say? Would the king authorize such a satire against the clergy? Molière reassured them: the king not only approved, he had actively encouraged it. So much the worse for the others; the king had decided to amuse himself.

This extraordinary entertainment, which was already on everyone's lips, was in fact a present from the king to his beloved, Louise de La Vallière. It was not described as such openly, but it was clear enough for those who had eyes to see. It was to take place at Versailles, which was already making problems for Colbert. For some time the king had become uselessly, ridiculously infatuated with his father's small castle there. Not content with staying for long periods, he wanted to transform it, to enlarge it. With surly frankness, an expression of the zeal with which he watched over his master's interests, Colbert scolded him for this whim. What was the point of building in that God-forsaken place, in the middle of all those marshes? He was convinced that it would lead nowhere: 'That house is fitted more for Your Majesty's pleasure and entertainment than for his glory ... However, if Your Majesty were to seek in Versailles the one hundred and fifty thousand crowns that have been spent in it over the last two years, he would certainly have difficulty finding them ...'[14]

It would need several thousand crowns to pay for the entertainment that the king was presenting at Versailles and at which La Vallière would appear for the first time since she had become his favourite. There would be six hundred guests and it would last for one week, with each evening bringing new entertainments. There was a tourney in the old style, in the park lit by lamps hung from the trees. The king, wearing silver armour encrusted with diamonds, his helmet supporting flame-coloured feathers, personified Roger, the hero in love with the beautiful Angélique. When the spectacle was over, Lulli came forward at the head of a vast company of musicians playing his compositions. The supper at which Louis took his place at the royal table was illuminated by a profusion of green and silver candelabra held at arms' length by masked figures wearing make-up and disguise. Next day, Molière gave his

Princesse d'Elide, an occasional piece, which he stuffed with more or less direct allusions to the king's love.

Was it possible that the modest Louise, for whom the king was spending all this money under the pretext of amusing himself, was still resisting him? Certainly, she resisted this ostentatious pomp, this fantastic indirect publicity. She had given in to the king's desire, but she loved Louis too much to resist this impossible love. Her conscience still hated the adultery that she inevitably committed with Louis. The secret heroine of the entertainment was in fact its victim.

The third evening was given up to sorcery, with the appearance of the enchantress Alcina, borne by a sea monster. Nymphs perched on whales recited verse, there was a ballet of giants 'of prodigious size', then, in the midst of thunder, Alcina's palace was engulfed in a fantastic fireworks display reflected in the still water of the pools. Officially the entertainment was over but the king extended it for several days longer. Molière gave the first three acts of *L'Hypocrite,* which was soon to be called *Tartuffe.* 'The Pleasures of the Enchanted Island', as the marvellous entertainment was aptly named, evoked irresistibly the spectacle given by Fouquet at Vaux, 'The Pleasure of the Drunken Parvenu'. It had proved fatal to him, but it had set a trend for the jealous.

Anne of Austria rejected certain aspects of this entertainment. She was far from amused by the fun that her son had poked at her by allowing the performance of *Tartuffe,* about which the religious party she protected besieged her with criticism. One priest from Paris called down divine vengeance from his pulpit on the 'devil clad in flesh and dressed as a man and the most notorious sinner and libertine that the centuries have ever seen'. Anne insisted that the archbishop of Paris go in person to protest to Louis and *Tartuffe* was suddenly forbidden. Was it a condemnation? Far from it; Louis carefully weighed the words that were to appear in the *Gazette:* 'He defended it in public, however, and deprived himself of that pleasure so that others, less capable of making a just judgement of it, might not be abused.' Every cloud has a silver lining, for Molière, revolted by the victory of the religious party, was to take his revenge by writing his purest, strangest masterpiece – *Don Juan* – a veritable challenge to the conventions.

The religious party was reassured: the king may fornicate as he wishes, but he should not interfere with the clergy. Queen Anne did not, however, see it in this way. She begged her son once again to abandon the scandal of his liaison with Louise, which he had just brought out into the open. 'So, Madame, must one believe everything that one hears? I would have thought that you, less than anyone, would preach such a gospel: however, since I have never interfered with the affairs of others, it seems to me that I should be treated in the same way.' His mother was dumbstruck, for Louis had just thrown back at her all the rumours that had been circulating about her love for the handsome Duke of Buckingham and about her passion for Mazarin. He had wanted to insult his mother and had well and truly succeeded. Weeping,

Anne complained bitterly of her misfortunes to her women. '*Ai Molina!*
Estos niños', she repeated all day long to her daughter-in-law's Spanish
femme de chambre. An attempt at reconciliation by Monsieur and
Madame had no result. Emerging from a laboriously arranged meeting
in which the king had not said a word, Anne went to complain to her
younger son about his brother's conduct: 'You see how he treats me.'
And she threatened to retire once and for all to the convent of the Val-
de-Grâce.[15] Then the king gave in. His mother irritated him, because, in
his opinion, she continued to treat the sovereign who was imposing his
will on France and on Europe as a small boy.

Even so, he had great affection for her; it was deep and it was mutual.
But they both found it difficult to express their feelings: she from lack of
depth, he from clumsiness. He had no wish for a long estrangement,
especially if it were to become public and lead to the queen mother's
departure from Court. But it was she who made the first move – he was
too proud to do so. She asked to speak to him, fearing the new
humiliation of a snub, but he accepted gladly and fell into her arms. He
even went down on his knees to beg forgiveness. He wept, he pleaded,
and she finally acceded. She promised not to retire to the Val-de-Grâce
and to remain with him always. She took advantage of the situation to
tell him what she thought of him: he was too vain, too rancorous and
too flighty. For his part, he indicated that he was only too well aware of
his passion for women, as it had brought him enough suffering. He was
ashamed of it; he had done everything he could to restrain it, but his
desire was so obviously stronger than his reason that he could no longer
resist it. Recognizing one's errors is better than nothing, she reassured
him; God had not entirely abandoned him.

The meeting however, left her less than satisfied. She was reconciled
with her son; he had beaten his breast, but he had not given in on any
point or renounced any of his errors. He wanted to keep his mother
with him without having to pay the price that she demanded for his
comfort. Hardly had he made it up with her than he began to flaunt his
mistress ever more openly. He went walking with her every day. He
took her for a short stay at his brother's Château de Villers-Cotterêts.
He even dared to introduce his mistress at the Château de Vincennes
when the Court was in residence there and play cards with her in his
mother's apartment when the queen mother was sick and confined to
her bedchamber.

By a piece of luck that Louis had been banking on, Maria Theresa,
who was pregnant, also kept to her room that day, but it did not prevent
her from learning before long of the presence in the palace of that
'*putana*' (whore), as she called her. To cap it all, her husband had asked
her through her lady of honour, Mme de Montansier, to be so kind as to
receive the '*putana*'. Maria Theresa gibbed at such tactlessness. 'May I
dare to tell Your Majesty', the messenger added, 'that if you show
understanding towards the king, he will no doubt be moved, but if you
refuse him, he will only become more embittered: in any case, Madame,

if the king loves this girl, your coldness will not cure him of it.' 'But, Madame,' said the unhappy queen in self-defence, 'how can I see that girl! I love the king and the king loves only her!' At this point the king, who had been listening at the door, burst in so suddenly that his wife's nose began to bleed.[16]

Her anger and sorrow affected her badly, and she went into premature labour. Exhaustion and pain brought her close to death and she was given extreme unction. At her bedside, her husband wailed and sobbed, tearing at his hair, beside himself with grief: 'It is a great misfortune to lose a child, but I shall console myself provided God leaves me the queen and my child can be baptized.' God proved indulgent towards the sinner, for the queen survived and the child – a girl – was baptized, before dying shortly after birth, on 16 November 1644. It was perhaps fortunate that this baby disappeared so quickly, for horrifying descriptions of it were circulating: it was a monster, black and covered in hair.[17] The gossip knew no bounds. How could the pious and holy Maria Theresa bring such a malformation of nature into the world? Perhaps, it was said, she had looked at a negro too long, which had had such an effect on her that it gave her nightmares. The baby was soon hidden away in its tiny grave, and the conjecture subsided.

Thirty-one years later, however, a young black woman was to take the veil at the convent of the Benedictine nuns at Moret. The nuns were surprised not so much by the colour of her skin as by the extraordinary attention the girl was to receive from the Court; the Dauphin and his children were to visit her several times. The nuns could not believe their ears when, one day, hearing the hunting horns of the Dauphin's party in the forest nearby, the young woman cried out: 'There's my brother out hunting!' Her Christian names, which were later discovered in a register, may be significant: she was called Louise-Maria-Thérèse.[18]

Did the king have a bastard daughter by a black woman or did the queen, the very pious Maria Theresa, sleep with a black man? She had earlier been given a negro page of between ten and twelve years old, called 'Nabo', in whose company she had had her portrait painted. The boy, who had grown up in the meantime, disappeared one day 'very suddenly' when it was officially announced that the queen was pregnant. Throughout her pregnancy, the queen was in the grip of 'black' forebodings, which were amply justified by her painful confinement. One can imagine the stupefaction of the doctors forced to write in their accounts that the queen gave birth that day to 'a small girl, black as ink, from head to toe'.[19]

Two months after the public birth of the highly mysterious 'Moorish' girl came the very discreet birth of the not at all mysterious second bastard child of Louise de La Vallière. Every precaution had been taken, once again by Colbert, who was awaiting the happy event in person at a concealed door to the favourite's apartment. The physician brought the new-born child to the all-powerful prime minister, who took her away into the January night.[20]

126

Colbert did not employ too much of his usual meticulousness to protect the favourite from rumours for, around her, invisible and ever present, had gathered his enemies: the Comtesse de Soissons, the infernal Olympia and her lover the perfidious Vardes, that hothead the Comte de Guiche and his mistress, the impetuous Henrietta. Louise, however, was to be left alone for a while, for these palace wolves, wrapped up in their intrigues and blinded by their jealousy, were soon to destroy one another. Vardes was to express doubts in public about Madame's virtue. Informed of this, Madame went immediately to the king to demand justice and Vardes was despatched at once to the Bastille to meditate on his insolence. A furious Olympia spat her venom in every direction. She let it be known that the famous false letter from the queen of Spain warning Maria Theresa of the liaison between the king and Mlle de La Vallière had been written by Guiche with Madame's complicity. In any case, she added, Madame was a spy in the service of England. Madame, informed of these kindnesses, got out her big guns and, rushing back to the king, admitted everything to him from the beginning in a torrent of passionate, hate-filled words: yes, she had known of the existence of that false letter, but it had been written by Olympia and Vardes, Guiche merely wrote it out in bad Spanish. Then she poured out one by one a list of Olympia's intrigues, calumnies and dubious advice. Poor Guiche! It was no longer a time for lies. Convinced and edified, Louis took immediate action. Guiche was exiled to Holland and Olympia expelled from Court;[21] it would not be long before she planned revenge.

Bonne-Nouvelle, the quarter of Paris built on former fortifications, had a very bad reputation. There, in the middle of wasteland, was an enclosure with a sort of rustic grotto. In this lair lived a rather vulgar twenty-nine year old woman, ample of figure, with small, bright, cunning eyes. She was called Catherine Montvoisin, or 'La Voisin' for short. She had been a fortune-teller from childhood and people accused her of witchcraft. She was also an unqualified midwife doubling as an abortionist, who buried the compromising little corpses in her garden. She had installed a cooking stove in the grotto, on which she concocted potions. One day three Court ladies appeared. One of them held out her hand to be read. 'You have been beloved of a great prince,' said the fortune-teller. 'Will I be again?' 'No, that cannot be.' 'It must be.' 'It will be very difficult.' Olympia – for it was she – rose, furious. 'I shall find the means,' she declared and left.[22]

It was already late when Louise de La Vallière, alone in her apartment, felt sleep overtaking her. Suddenly her pet dog began to bark and Louise listened attentively. She heard a noise in the next room, as if someone were trying to break in at the window. She leapt out of bed and ran screaming to her maid's room. The alarm was raised, but it was too late. No one was there, but hooks and a rope ladder were found against the wall. The king ordered a watch to be set on his beloved's house by discreet guards and he expressly ordered her food to be tasted first by someone else, for Louis knew his friend Olympia and her weakness for poisons too well.[23]

Anne of Austria no longer had a place in the Court where so much offended her. She felt superseded, of no further use to her elder son, who increasingly did as he liked. On several occasions she talked of retiring to the Val-de-Grâce, not as before in the heat of argument, but after a careful examination of her situation. Each time she was begged not to do so by her friends and by the king himself. Where her resolution failed her, death was to triumph for in that spring of 1665, she was stricken by an incurable cancer, the first signs of which had appeared towards the end of the previous year. At the approach of this inevitable death, Mme de Motteville felt that the great moment of her life had come. She sat at the bedside of her mistress and long-time friend, describing in detail the progress of the illness, recording every word spoken by the heroic patient and the attitudes of her family and entourage.

The curtain rose, of course, with a dispute over the inheritance. Anne of Austria wanted to make her will and to give more to her younger son, who was less well provided for than the elder. The king gibbed at this: he wanted the large pearls that his mother was expecting to leave to Monsieur, while Maria Theresa, in order to annoy Madame, supported Madame's husband. In the end, a solution was found: the king would have the pearls, but he would pay Monsieur for them.

A tumour soon appeared under the patient's arm. The surgeons came in and, armed with their knives, cut into it – without anaesthetic, of course. 'Ah, Lord! I offer up this pain to you: receive it as satisfaction for my sins,' repeated the patient during this intolerable ordeal. After the evacuation of a great deal of blood and pus, she remained very weak, pale and covered with a cold sweat. The royal family gathered once more round her bed, with much weeping and gnashing of teeth. The pain increased and the wound would not heal, so the physicians decided to take her to Paris, 'no doubt because they believed that the king wished it'. The queen was wrapped in a cloak of grey taffeta and placed in a litter of black velvet. On the way, she stopped off at her dear Val-de-Grâce: 'I am now content. Let God dispose of me as He will,' and she lay down exhausted by the journey, feverish, and suffering from the early stages of gangrene. It was not long before the king and his family, courtiers and physicians grew tired of having to go to the distant Val-de-Grâce every day; the doctors gave orders that the queen mother be brought to the Louvre, and without being asked her opinion, she was removed forever from the one place where she would most have liked to live or at least to die. As a welcoming present at the Louvre, limewater was placed on the wound under her arm to disinfect it but it aggravated the pain beyond endurance. Incapable of sleep Anne felt that she was going mad with the agony. To make her torture worse the surgeons set about every morning and evening slashing the wound with razors and taking away whole slices of gangrened flesh. All this was done in the presence of the family and attending courtiers, to the queen mother's great shame, forced as she was to expose part of her body to them.

At the end of September a courier arrived from Madrid with news of the death of King Philip IV. Maria Theresa fainted in her husband's arms, but Anne of Austria commented sadly on the news: 'I shall soon follow him.' The dead man's daughter and sister wept so much that their husband and son was also forced to produce a few tears. In fact he was already gloating over his prospects as a result of his father-in-law's death, according to calculations secretly drawn up by the late Mazarin.

Anne continued to suffer and weaken, but she held out and her children got used to the presence of their dying mother. Despite the approach of the fatal outcome, despite the mourning for the king of Spain, they could not resist the entertainments arranged to mark the New Year of 1666. On 5 January, Monsieur gave a magnificent ball in which he and his guests, led by the king, amused themselves quite openly. Maria Theresa refused to accompany her husband, but she chose his costume: violet cloth to recall the mourning for her father-in-law, but covered with enormous pearls and diamonds. Two days later, the festivities resumed for the marriage of Mlle d'Artigny, a friend of Louise de La Vallière, to the Comte de Roulle. While both queens deplored the entertainments held indirectly in honour of the favourite, the king and his brother went to the monstrous ball given by the Duc de Créqui and then on to a theatrical show in honour of the wedding. On their return, Maria Theresa informed them that the patient's fever had increased and her pulse weakened. The gangrened wound on her arm was giving off an unbearable odour: and this was perhaps the most painful suffering for a woman so punctilious in matters of cleanliness and so sensitive to smells. 'It was such a stench that one could hardly sup when one came from seeing it dressed,' the Grande Mademoiselle noted. Anne's body was dreadfully swollen, and further eruptions appeared with tumours and abscesses on her shoulders. Her head was so enlarged that she could not hold it up, while her arms and hands were so heavy that she no longer had the strength to lift them. Observing her limbs, which had once been her pride, she sighed: 'My hand is swollen! It is time to go!'

It was time to receive extreme unction, as the great bell of Notre Dame began to ring. The dying woman received the host with all due piety, but as the holy oils were placed on the different parts of her body, she had a last reflex of coquetry: 'Make sure you lift my cap, lest this oil gets on it, or it will smell bad ...' Then she made her farewells to her kneeling family, in tears around her bed. However, Mme de Motteville noted that the royal tears were less abundant than she would have thought possible.

From the depths of her torpor, the dying woman heard the voice of her elder son. Suddenly her eyes, already covered with the whiteness of death, opened wide, still bright: 'Ah! There's the king,' she said with much joy and tenderness. She had truly loved her child, however inadequately, and she knew him, too. 'Go, my son,' she said. 'Go and have your supper.'

The night was so bad that the family did not leave the room, and the king leant against a solid silver table. Suddenly, the dying woman's head slumped. 'The queen is dead!' someone said; hearing the cries, she woke and opened her eyes. The king, on the other hand, was nearly fainting; his legs began to give way, he was supported on either side and led out forcibly to the bathroom where cold water was sprinkled on his face. His attendants prevented him from going back into his mother's room, for fear of the emotional shock it would have on him, and he obeyed. Philippe, however, did not leave his mother's bedside, in spite of Louis telling him twice not to stay. Monsieur refused to leave. He observed with horror the deformed, purulent, stinking, rotting, yet still living body of a once elegant, coquettish woman. 'Ah, Mme de Motteville!' he asked, 'Is this the queen, my mother?' Suddenly he cried out. The king heard him from the bathroom. 'Is she dead, then?' he asked the physician who had just come in. 'Yes, Sire,' he was told and he burst into tears. It was nearly five in the morning on Wednesday 20 January 1666.

That same morning, Monsieur took refuge in his country house at Saint-Cloud in order to hide his distress. The king called him back to Paris for the opening of the will, but Monsieur begged to be left alone. It was only after the formality of reading the will that the king gave free course to his own distress, weeping all night in his room. 'This tragedy,' he explained, 'though the outcome of a long illness, did not fail to move me so terribly that for several days I was incapable of thinking about anything else but the loss that I had sustained.' He apologized for this proof of humanity, 'for although I have constantly told you that a prince must sacrifice all private considerations to the well-being of his empire, there are circumstances when this maxim cannot be practised at first'.[24] Only a few days of distress were allowed a great king for his mother's death.

CHAPTER 9

Of Wars and Women

The day after the queen mother's death, the corporations of State went to Saint-Germain to present their condolences to the king. At the mass in the castle chapel, the astounded *parlementaires* were able to observe next to Queen Maria Theresa no less a person than Mlle de La Vallière. Anne of Austria was no sooner buried than her son, freed of all constraints, showed that he was determined to impose his mistress on the world. Only three months later the king was showing the healthiest good spirits, as he led the Court in the Oise for three days of military manoeuvres. He spent almost the entire journey in his coach singing at the top of his voice. In between all the marching, there was entertainment for all – though in mourning, of course – and everyone amused themselves more than ever.[1]

In Paris, however, a certain lady had ample reason to mourn the queen mother's death. A widow for several years and reduced to poverty, she had obtained from Anne of Austria a pension that allowed her to subsist, but the pension ceased with the death of the queen. Despite her humble circumstances this lady had been able to make friends in high places who interceded so forcefully in her favour with the king that Louis, beside himself with irritation, cried: 'Shall I always have to hear about Widow Scarron?' She was Françoise d'Aubigné, widow of the poet Paul Scarron. The courtiers, imitating their master, made fun of her, and a contemporary phrase referring to a bore went 'he's as importunate as the widow Scarron'. However, one person at Court remained a particularly faithful friend of the unfortunate widow: she did not give in. She was called Françoise Athénaïs de Rochechouart de Mortemart, Marquise de Montespan. Despite the rebuffs already administered by others, she went to see the king and demanded the pension due to her protégée. 'Am I to hear once again of the widow Scarron? . . .' the king wailed. Undeterred Mme de Montespan held on and won through; in the end, the king gave in out of sheer exhaustion.[2]

This dazzling twenty-five year old was beginning to make a name for herself at Court. Like Louise de La Vallière, Athénaïs de Mortemart was fair-haired, but she was plump, while the other was thin; she was brilliant, whereas the favourite was sweet-natured. Louise came from the lowest ranks of nobility; Athénaïs possessed an aristocratic pride that made her regard her family the equal if not the superior of the House of France. She also possessed a biting wit that bordered on cruelty. La Vallière was generally regarded as stupid; Montespan made a whole salon laugh with her sallies. The first seemed to be turned inwards to the internal light that shone in her heart; the second constantly dazzled with all the brilliance of a coquette. This attractive woman first caught the attention of Monsieur, of all the men in the court the least sexually interested in women, but who loved to spend hours chatting in their company. She made him laugh so much that she became indispensable. Her husband, Monsieur de Montespan, was not at all pleased. He was a brave, determined, slightly mad individual, as morose as his wife was brilliant. Jealous of the success that she had had with Monsieur (though it could hardly be regarded as compromising), he declared that he would take her off to the country. Monsieur had to employ all his charm and authority to persuade him not to do so: 'M de Montespan, I have a favour to ask of you, but you must grant it to me, otherwise I have to admit that I shall be extremely put out: you must leave your wife in Paris all this winter until May.' The jealous husband had no alternative but to give in. His wife met with less success with the king, who did not care for people whose wit drew attention to his own mental slowness; when he saw this proud, bantering, petulant woman his immediate reaction was to run for cover. He criticized his younger brother for consorting with her too much. 'She's witty. She amuses me,' Monsieur declared in her defence, unaware that this was exactly what his elder brother reproached her with.

To prevent his new friend being taken from Court, Monsieur had her appointed palace lady to the queen. Mme de Montespan immediately won the heart of Maria Theresa by her good humour: the queen often needed someone to cheer her up. In the evening, while she waited for the king to return to the marriage bed, the queen was entertained so well that she quite forgot the monotony of those sad hours. Moreover, Maria Theresa knew that she could trust her: Montespan was an 'honest woman', a religious woman who criticized the Court revellers, and who loved her husband as much as the queen loved hers.[3] By a sense of balance worthy of her ingenuity, Montespan also became friendly with Louise de La Vallière. The two women got on well, probably because they were so different, and soon became inseparable. But the target of these operations was the king, whose attention the beautiful young woman would have dearly liked to have attracted. He could hardly move a step without finding her there, at his brother's, at his wife's, at his mistress's. The more attractive she made herself, the more refractory he became to this ballet of seduction. 'She can do what she likes, but I don't want her,' he told his brother. Yet he was beginning to get used to her presence – no small matter where this shy man who hated surprises and new faces was concerned. Athénaïs had chosen the right moment to cast her net, for in that spring of 1666 observers were unanimous in concluding that the king was beginning to tire of La Vallière. The prospect of the favourite's disgrace caused a stir in the Court and aroused the hopes of a good many ladies.[4]

In her smoky grotto, in the middle of the wastelands of Bonne-Nouvelle, Catherine Montvoisin had never been so busy. Society men and women, more or less incognito, were queueing at her door for predictions about the future, horoscopes, love potions, pacts with the devil. La Voisin did not know which way to turn and soon had to be joined by competent collaborators: the Abbé Guibourg, a debauched, cross-eyed sorcerer, and François Mariette, another lapsed priest. Mmes de La Motte, de Grammont and de Polignac ventured out to the sordid suburb to find means of supplanting the favourite in the king's heart and of getting rid, while they were about it, of both an encumbrance and a tiring lover. The Comtesse de Roulle, Mlle d'Artigny, whose marriage the king had attended a few days before his mother's death, actually demanded the death of her friend and protectress, La Vallière. In the end, Mme de Montespan herself arrived for consultation in order to gain 'the king's friendship'.[5]

La Voisin's incantations may have been effective since Louise de La Vallière did undergo a terrible experience. Pregnant once again, she felt the first pains while in the midst of the Court, at the Château de la Vincennes, before she had time to return to her own quarters. She was in a chamber leading to the chapel, bent double with pain, when Madame came in on her way to mass. She stopped, astonished to see the young woman groaning, pale, and covered in sweat. Louise, who wanted at all costs to hide the truth, found strength enough to whisper: 'Madame! I'm dying of stomach ache.' As soon as Madame had gone, Louise called the doctor: 'Hurry, I want it all to be over before she comes back.' When Madame came back, she found the favourite lying on her bed, fully dressed, made up and surrounded by sweet-smelling flowers, though at the time their scent was regarded as fatal to women in childbirth. That same evening, Louise put on her great Court robes in order to receive guests as usual. She watched the courtiers play cards, supped with them and stood until dawn, constantly on the verge of fainting.[6] The baby had already been smuggled out and was on his way to join his brother and sister, now in the hands of Mme Colbert.[7] The king was not there: he had left that very morning for Versailles. His favourite's births no longer amused him – nor, in fact, did the favourite, for he now had eyes only for Mme de Montespan.

She was aware of this and suddenly panicked. She was not particularly given to eroticism, and, proud of her wit, she hoped to win the king over not only by her beauty but also by her intelligence. She hoped that she would be able to rule him by holding out the vague hope that she would give in to him one day, without actually sacrificing her virtue.[8] But the gleam that she found in the king's eyes had nothing to do with any admiration he might feel for her intelligence. Not hesitating to go into reverse but fearful that it might be too late, she went to her husband and admitted that the king was in love with her. M de Montespan shrugged his shoulders, but his wife swore that there was no doubt about it and begged him to take her as quickly as possible to the country and far from the Court, to wait for the king's caprice to pass. M de Montespan refused. Always unpredictable, he had been jealous of the homosexual Monsieur, but refused to be so of the philandering king. Thus Mme de Montespan remained at the king's mercy.[9]

Louis gave a dazzling present to La Vallière; without warning her, he bought an enormous estate for herself and their daughter, and made her Duchesse de Vaujours. Handing the decree to the first president of the *parlement* to be registered, Louis asked him, 'Did you not do silly things when you were young?' 'There are few of us who have not done so,' the austere judge retorted, somewhat surprised. 'I am doing one now; I must go through with it but I won't do it again'.[10] If the king was somewhat embarrassed, what can the woman have felt who was thus so royally dismissed? Her condition as mistress of a married man and unmarried mother displayed for all to see was made even more shameful and ridiculous by a title intended to reward the greatest services rendered to the country.[11] Actually in committing this indiscretion, the king was thinking not so much of La Vallière as of the sole survivor of the illegitimate children they had had: 'I thought it just to ensure that this child enjoyed the honour of its birth.'[12] Thus everything that affected His Majesty remained automatically beyond shame and scandal. A child sired by him was no longer a bastard produced by adultery, but a demi-god conveying the most glorious blood in the world. Everyone including Louise, understood that the distinction it had pleased him to dishonour her with was merely a mark of his indifference to her. He made a public declaration of the liaison that he had for so long maintained in secret because he was now ready to break it off, and rumours had it that La Vallière would now marry and retire from Court.

The biggest talking point was now whether war would break out. What was at stake was important: Flanders, the Brabant and Franche-Comté, but the pretext was very slim indeed. According to the so-called Law of Devolution, exhumed by Louis XIV, those rich provinces that had belonged to King Philip IV of Spain should now revert to the children of his first marriage, that is to say, to Queen Maria Theresa, and therefore to France. In any case, Louis added as a further argument, it was only natural that he should take them for himself since his wife's dowry had never been paid. Here the king was merely reviving one of Mazarin's ideas, dating from 1648, when the cardinal had insisted on the need to seize the Netherlands in order to establish a bulwark for the north of France. He had already got his constitutional lawyers to study the causes of invalidity in the renunciation of the paternal inheritance that Queen Maria Theresa had solemnly signed.[13] There was also the desire to do battle. It was all very well presiding over councils of ministers and studying files, but that was not how to acquire glory and make a mark in the world.

Sensing his master's impatience, one young minister used all his strength to urge him in that direction. Louvois had entered the council by the back door, obtaining the inherited post from his father, Le Tellier. At twenty-five this thick-set, violent, choleric and ambitious man had decided to get rid of Colbert, who was generally opposed to war because it cost too much and upset his beloved commerce. Under Louvois' influence, the king threw himself into adventure. He laid his plans carefully, taking great pleasure in pulling the wool over the public's eyes: 'To amuse everyone I announced that I was going on a journey to Brest . . . I deceived the Spaniards by offering them a new trade treaty.'[14] His lawyers, however, worked without interruption, and in May 1966, he notified Spain of his arguments for retaking the disputed territory. Without waiting for a response, he sent his army into the Netherlands. The moment was well chosen, for an incapable queen regent was governing the Spanish empire in a state of utter confusion and penniless ineptitude during the minority of her perpetually sick son, King Charles II.

In Europe, Louis' arguments were regarded as being based on patent bad faith and it was thought neither decent nor honest to violate the Peace of the Pyrenees, which he had solemnly sworn to, in order to attack a child.[15] In France, however, there was overwhelming support for the king. Never mind the widow and orphan – they were foreigners anyway. Right up to the last moment, the Marqués de Fuentes, Spanish ambassador in France, tried to believe that there would be no war, but in Brussels, the Marqués de Castel de Rodrigo, governor of the Netherlands, had no illusions concerning either Louis XIV's intentions or the aid that he could expect from Spain. His appeals for help went unanswered. Without troops, without defences, amid general pessimism, what could he hope for?

Louis had still not declared war, but he was at the frontier, leading his army like a scarecrow from town to town. The Court was at Compiègne when, at five o'clock one morning, the Grande Mademoiselle was dragged from her sleep by noise above her. Furious at having been woken, she sent her servants to have the noise stopped. The answer came back: it was the queen having her baggage packed as a message had come from the king summoning the Court to the theatre of operations. In the most utter confusion, everyone packed feverishly and rushed out to the awaiting coaches.[16] Only Louise de La Vallière did not share in this joyful excitement, for she was not in the party: the king had ordered her to go back to Paris and await his good pleasure there.[17]

On its way to the north, the Court stopped for one evening at La Ferté. Suddenly, the Grande Mademoiselle noticed odd comings and goings. 'What's happening?' she asked. 'Mme de La Vallière arrives this evening,' she was told. 'What!' responded the astounded princess, 'Without being called?' In the queen's coach, the ladies started to chatter about the favourite's incredible insolence. Loudest in her criticism was Mme de Montespan. The others echoed her. The queen wept. 'Heaven preserve me from being the king's mistress!' La Montespan concluded, 'But if I were, I would certainly be ashamed in the queen's presence.'[18] Montespan was not being as hypocritical as might be thought. She still wanted an ambiguous friendship that would allow her to dominate the king, as Olympia Mancini, Comtesse de Soissons, had done, but she baulked at becoming the king's mistress! 'If I were so unfortunate that such a thing happened to me, I would hide myself away for the rest of my life.'[19] She did not make this avowal in front of the queen, but to her confidante and friend, the widow Scarron, who was the least likely of her contemporaries to have tried to whitewash her reputation. Louise, who was travelling in her own coach, guessed the virtuous indignation of these ladies. She felt alone, sad, discouraged, exhausted. She was pregnant once again and overcome by the heat.

Next morning, as the long line of coaches reached a certain height, the travellers could suddenly see the army across the plain. That was where the king was, and Louise's heart began to tremble. Suddenly a coach was seen to leave the procession and drive, at top speed, across the fields towards the troops, towards the king. 'Stop her!' yelled Maria Theresa, who had recognized the favourite's coach. But there was no way of stopping excited horses galloping across fields on a sunny morning. When at last the coach, covered in dust, stopped in front of the king, and when that familiar face disfigured by fatigue, emotion and sweat, leaned out of the window, the king welcomed her with a curt, 'What, Madame! In front of the queen?'[20]

And yet, that evening at Avesnes, where the Court struck camp, the king was in her coach in the sight and hearing of all. Next day, she climbed into the queen's coach and lunched at the royal table – her new title of duchess gave her the right to do so and no one thought to protest. She was, after all, the favourite. The king was with La Vallière, the king was flaunting La Vallière – everything was as it should be. But the Grande Mademoiselle, the most perspicacious of the observers thought differently. She had noticed certain bizarre details. The guards who had been placed between the king's bedchamber and Montespan's had been dismissed without explanation. The king was in his bed-chamber, but La Montespan was not with the queen. At lunch, the queen complained of her husband: 'The king came to bed at four o'clock, it was daylight. I don't know what he could have been doing all that time.' The king suppressed a smile, and the Grande Mademoiselle did not dare to look up for fear of catching her cousin's eye.[21] Louise also kept her eyes cast down. The king had not been with her until four in the morning. She understood, as did the Grande Mademoiselle: Mme de Montespan had given in at last.[22]

Unable to send troops and shells against the French army – where would he find the money to pay for them? – the Marqués de Castel Rodrigo, governor of the Netherlands, bombarded it with tracts against the king: 'A soft, effeminate man who always takes a mistress with him and always in the same coach as the queen.'[23] This innovation in the science of war was admittedly rather surprising. What were those women doing, summoned to the camp by the king, all excited by adventure and constantly chattering about the dangers of battle? What need had the king to have those immense tents lined with damask and lit by carved wooden chandeliers, painted in gold, from which the wounded and dying were kept at a respectful distance? Why did officers need to travel in glass coaches instead of on horseback as before? Why were they ruining themselves, with equipages, silver table services and banquets? It was all on the master's orders.[24] War must only be a source of pleasure, punctuated by victorious *Te Deums*: powder to be thrown in everyone's eyes. Grandeur and power were to be measured, according to Louis XIV, in gold, silver, silk, feathers. Even at war, the Court had to dance the ballet of illusion before the entranced soldiers.

Military operations, too, were rather like a ballet; not so much a battle, as a military parade. Lacking troops, munitions and money, the Spaniards retreated almost without resistance, almost without firing a single shot, and the cities of the North fell one after another like ripe fruit into the hands of the French. On the other hand, the journalists of the gazettes, poets and letter writers spoke pompously of the king's brilliant conquests. Indeed, this way of waging war suited the king perfectly. Regiments marching off in perfect order, a siege conducted according to all the rules of the art that could be learned in handbooks – that was what appealed to the king. This war was merely the reproduction or the extension of the military manoeuvres of which he never tired, and which had fascinated him from childhood.[25] There was something of the regimental sergeant-major about Louis XIV. The Spanish had understood; there was nothing left for them but to laugh; they made endless fun of the 'king of military reviews'.[26] Louis, doing what he liked best, took no notice. He assumed a martial air: his face was thin and tanned, his hair rolled up, and he had started to grow a small moustache. 'He sometimes spent half-an-hour in front of his looking-glass arranging it with wax', the ambassador of Savoy noted.[27]

And the towns continued to fall one by one into his lap. If the desperate Flemish begged Heaven to stop Louis XIV's advance, the French soldiers were furious for exactly the opposite reason. They regarded the campaign as being conducted in the face of common sense and a delighted ambassador of Savoy faithfully repeated to his master the rumours of disaffection that he heard in the camp. The commander-in-chief, Turenne, was gaga and the other generals no better. The Maréchal d'Humières was 'an ignoramus', Pradel just a 'simple, good-natured fellow', Duras was hardly good enough 'to post guard' and the camp marshals were 'mere children'. As for the king, he was certainly no soldier. He did not know how to fight and he lacked courage: 'It is said that His Majesty is afraid and has always been frightened to death of violence; the life he leads with his mistresses goes some way to explain the hatred that people have for him.' Without him, they could advance further, more quickly: 'The army is furious that more could have been

137

won.' Why did they not take Cambrai, Namur, Mons, Valenciennes and so many other towns that would have opened their gates to them?[28]

With half the accessible towns already conquered and general exasperation at its height, the king suddenly broke off the campaign in early autumn and returned to his Court to receive their applause. Entertainments, concerts, comedies and balls followed one another at Saint-Germain, Versailles and the Tuileries. La Vallière took little part in these celebrations, and the king wanted to visit her at Saint-Germain. Alone at last with his erstwhile love, deformed by pregnancy, tenderness and desire seized him. He flung his arms around her, embraced her, caressed her. Suddenly she was seized with a violent spasm. The waters had already broken, drenching Louis' coat, embroidered with pearls and diamonds. Terrified, he ran to the window and called for help, then he ran back to hold Louise in his arms. She was shaking with terrible convulsions. 'She's dead,' cried Mme de Choisy, which was an exaggeration. Louis burst into tears. 'In God's name, give her back to me and take everything I have.' During the birth, he remained on his knees at the foot of the bed, weeping and sobbing, so pitiful a sight that even the doctors burst into tears. At last Louise gave birth to a boy, who was to be the Comte de Vermandois.[29] Despite this touching scene of which he was quite unaware, the ambassador of Savoy declared: 'The king loves Montespan. She does not detest him, but she is holding firm.'[30]

In fact, Montespan had already been the king's mistress for several months. It is still a mystery how they managed to isolate themselves so discreetly under the constant gaze of the entire Court. One woman, at least, was in the know: La Voisin. For some time, Montespan had been going to her for aphrodisiacs consisting of a base of toads, moles' teeth and a powder made from human material, to which was added decoctions of cantharides (Spanish fly).[31]

At the beginning of 1668, observers were taking an interest in important troop movements in eastern France. Where was Louis XIV going to strike now?[32]

Louis himself was delighted by these suppositions and revealed nothing about his intentions: 'I found a way of gathering 18,000 men together without them being able to perceive my purpose.'[33] On 1 February, he announced that he was setting out for Burgundy and, next day, in appalling weather, he left Saint-Germain for the Spanish province of Franche-Comté which he had set his heart on. Twelve days after his departure he entered Dol, which had held out for only four days, for the province was even less well defended than the Netherlands. As the winter was proving particularly harsh, the benevolent king showed concern – not for his soldiers, but for the courtiers who followed him: 'I tried to soften the rigours of the weather for people of quality, by the good cheer that I offered them.'[34] In three weeks, Franche-Comté was conquered, with an ease that made someone remark to the loser himself, the Spanish governor: 'The king of France could have sent his lackeys to take possession of this country instead of coming in person.' Europe grit its teeth at the success, and everywhere it was thought that Louis XIV had gone too far. The powers protested; the king of France was made to understand that it would be in his own interest to stay where he was if he did not want half of Europe on his back. And Louis XIV, satiated and docile, concluded the Treaty of Aix-la-Chapelle, proving perfectly willing to give up Franche-Comté, but retaining Flanders.[35]

In honour of his recent victory, the king gave the most dazzling entertainment of his entire reign at Versailles, the details of which were arranged with the same meticulousness as his military reviews. On that July evening 1668, the food was laid out in five enormous buffets, with mountains of cold meats, a palace made of marzipan and trees bearing preserved fruit. A temporary theatre for three thousand spectators had been set up in the grounds – the exterior in foliage, the interior hung with royal tapestries. Molière gave his *Georges Dandin,* interspersed with concerts and ballets: a hundred courtiers danced the triumph of Bacchus. The supper took place in another 'salon' in the park, decorated with vases of flowers, crystal balls and garlands suspended from silver-spangled gauze sashes. The king sat in front of a rock from which sprang a thousand cascades. The meal was served on five services of fifty-six dishes each. After this feast the guests went off to dance in another hall, made of marble and porphyry, lit by a hundred crystal chandeliers. Then they proceeded through darkened avenues to the terrace from which suddenly one could see the entire castle alight in an apocalyptic fireworks display. From the roofs, the fountains, the trees, on every side, thousands of flaming egrets appeared; when these had gone out, the light of day had already replaced the flames of illusion.

Louise de La Vallière was present and received the honours due a duchess and the consideration accorded the favourite, but the entertainment was really a homage to another woman – the king could not take his eyes off Mme de Montespan.[36] He did not care if this excessive display was seen as a provocation. 'A stage-manager king', 'tyrant', 'whore-monger', were some of the curses thrown at him by a poorly dressed woman as he passed by in his coach. 'Is it to me that you speak?' the astonished king enquired. 'Yes, tyrant, yes, a whore-monger', the woman replied. When the king had recovered from the shock, he acted swiftly: the woman was arrested, thrown into prison and publicly whipped 'most soundly, though she did not let a word of complaint pass her lips, enduring it all like a martyrdom and for the love of God'. This commentary by Olivier d'Ormesson was proof of which side public opinion was on. Perhaps he knew that the woman had lost her son in an accident during the building of the Château de Versailles.[37]

Peace having been concluded between France and Spain, the troops were demobilized. One officer, with his discharge signed by the king in his pocket, came back to Paris where his wife was waiting for him. He was not in a hurry, and took the journey in short stages. When he reached the capital, there was only one topic of conversation – the fabulous entertainment that had just been given at Versailles in honour of the king's new mistress, Mme de Montespan. The man shuddered, for he was her husband.[38]

In her apartment in the Château de Saint-Germain, Mme de Montansier was receiving a crowd of visitors who had come to compliment her on her husband's appointment as the Dauphin's guardian, when M de Montespan appeared: 'So it was you who assisted the king's affair with my wife during the Court's visit to Flanders. You dirty bawd!' And he left, slamming the door on the petrified spectators. The king was informed and gave orders to arrest the madman, but he had already disappeared.

Terrified by the idea that her husband might try to kill her, Mme de Montespan sought refuge with her friend Mme de Montansier. But the door of the apartment smashed open and there was M de Montespan, who had managed to force his way in. La Montespan ran screaming into La Montansier's arms as her husband threw insult after insult at her. When he had at last exhausted his stock of abuse, Montespan raised his stick and rushed at her. The women started shouting and screaming, and menservants dashed in, bound up the madman, dragged him away, still screaming abuse, and threw him out.[39]

He disappeared once again, but this time the police made a better job of finding him and he was arrested and imprisoned. After a few weeks, the king relented, Montespan was exiled to a distant part of the country and forbidden to leave without express permission. There the rejected husband erased his wife from his existence in the most theatrical manner. He ordered the entire province to celebrate her 'death': her 'funeral' took place with great pomp and he went into 'mourning'. This man, who had the audacity not to approve of Louis sleeping with his wife, combined the sublime with the ridiculous in a spine-chilling parody.

These incidents led the king to take greater steps to protect his intimacy with Athénaïs: he would not make her his official mistress, the one who attracted most of the observation and slander of the envious, but kept that role for Louise de La Vallière. Louis set up his two mistresses side by side: the official and the unofficial, the one he loved and the one who loved him. In the Château de Saint-Germain they were lodged together in what was poetically called 'the ladies' apartment', and when the king went to visit Montespan, he had to go through La Vallière's bedchamber.[40] Desperate at the rejection of the man she still loved, Louise was condemned to see him pay homage every day to the woman who claimed to be her friend and who had replaced her in his affections. It was too much and one day she could no longer hold back her complaints. The king calmly withstood the storm: 'I am too honest to conceal the truth from you further. It is true that I love Mme de

Montespan, but that does not prevent me from loving you as I should. You must be content with whatever I do for you without desiring more, because I do not like being constrained.' Louise refused to understand, breaking into sobs and resuming her catalogue of complaints. The king grew angry: 'If you want me to go on loving you, you must demand nothing of me. It is my wish that you should live with Mme de Montespan as you have done in the past. If you slight that lady in any way, you will force me to take other steps.'[41] He was very fond of Louise and believed he had proved it to her by making sure that she was given the respect due to the favourite, and by making her a duchess and a millionaire. Women are always the same, he must have thought – never satisfied: 'They are eloquent in their utterances, pressing in their prayers, stubborn in their feelings and all this is often based on nothing more than an aversion they may have for this person, a wish to advance that person, or some promise that they have made unthinkingly. No secret is safe with them: if they are lacking in intelligence, they may reveal out of simplicity what should most have been hidden; and if they are intelligent, they never lack for intrigues and secret liaisons.'[42] For Louis xiv, women were little birds, treacherous, stubborn and indiscreet: objects to be used. Louise was to have her use as well, as a screen for his love.

This screen proved all the more useful when Louis made Mme de Montespan become pregnant for the first time. Since it was important to maintain a minimum of discretion where bastards born of a double adultery were concerned, Athénaïs gave birth in secret, as had Louise; no mean feat in the Château de Saint-Germain, in the middle of the Court which was resident there in March 1671. For this Athénaïs required the services of her dear friend, the irresistible Lauzun. Scarcely had the baby been born than it was wrapped in a sheet and handed over to him, without even the time being taken to swaddle it properly. Lauzun, forced to cross the queen's apartments, was afraid lest the parcel under his arm would suddenly start screaming but he finally reached a small gate in the park without mishap. There a coach was waiting, and a woman descended, holding out her arms to take the baby. It was the widow Scarron.[43] Mme de Montespan had regarded her as a friend for years, appreciating her intelligence, efficiency and good nature, so it was natural that she should have thought of her to look after the children that she would have by the king. It was also a way of obtaining for her friend extra income that she needed so badly. Playing nursemaid to the royal bastards was not exactly what the widow Scarron had in mind, however, and at first, she had refused. Then she changed her mind, saying that she would agree on condition that the king asked her to do so in person, which he condescended to do so.[44] One day Mme Scarron would be called Mme de Maintenon and the baby she was furtively taking away with her would become the Duc du Maine.

CHAPTER 10

Upsets in the Royal Family

Just as the courtiers were surprised to see that La Vallière was still at Court, so too were they hasty in imagining that Colbert was disgraced. Louvois, however, was. Believing that he could take decisions without reference to anybody and that there was no longer any need for him to restrain his temper, he now appeared as he really was, impolite, short-tempered, crude and violent. He had fallen out with everybody. Officers complained of his manners. This was all that was needed for the Court to regard his disgrace as imminent and, consequently, to believe that Colbert's power was more assured and more extensive than ever. The icy, unapproachable minister had never been popular, but with his omnipotence restored his unpopularity increased. He was accused of a lust for power, outrageous favouritism towards his family and corruption.

In order to demonstrate the importance he accorded these rumours and to silence the gossip-mongers, Louis XIV paid a solemn visit to his minister. He was no more renouncing Colbert than he was rejecting Louise de La Vallière. He could not detach himself so easily from a past that had become a habit. There was something reassuring about the old guard that even the most attractive of newcomers did not possess. The courtiers fell obediently into step. When Colbert was appointed Secretary of State, a new favour, Court and city hastened to congratulate him. When his son had defended a thesis at the Collège de Clermont, princes, cardinals, ministers and nobles insisted on attending with such unanimity that the king's palace was emptied. Louis was not entirely pleased. He had intended marking the favour in which he held his minister, but not to the point of being abandoned for him. People had better not get it into their heads that they should honour a minister more than a king.[1]

Louis believed firmly that no one should appear more important than the king, even for a moment. No minister, no prince, not even his only brother, poor Philippe. Over and over again their dying mother had recommended him to the king, and a tearful Louis had promised to do everything she wished. But as soon as Philippe began to make demands, Louis gibbed. Philippe had begun by suggesting that Henrietta, his wife, should have the right to sit on a backed chair when attending the queen and not on a mere stool. 'What I was able to do,' the king explained, 'was to make him see that I did not think that I could grant him anything that seemed to bring him closer to me, if only by virtue of the respect that I owed my rank.' When Philippe asked for the governorship of Languedoc, left vacant by the death of a prince of the royal blood, Louis commented: 'My brother had made a claim on this governorship, but although I was kindly disposed towards him, I did not think that I should give it to him. I knew, from my own experience, how dangerous it was to place the governorships in the hands of a prince of the blood royal and especially the king's brother.'[2] Louis was content to shrug his shoulders: 'But, in the end, my brother adopted towards me a certain behaviour that would have led me to fear something troublesome, if I had not known the quality of his heart and mind.'[3]

He had nothing but contempt for his frivolous younger brother, so lacking in consistency and seriousness. If he had so little 'quality' why did he systematically refuse him any promotion, even of an honorary kind. It was as if the slightest elevation might constitute a threat to the elder brother, and to the State. The principle of maintaining the royal princes in a subordinate rank was based on unfortunate experiences in the past, but applying it to an only brother who had always declared and proved his loyalty seemed to stem rather from a certain unconscious jealousy. Proof of this was the satisfaction with which Louis XIV regarded Philippe's faults and vices, which he confused with lack of backbone. Did he himself not write with a sort of naïve cynicism: 'It could be to the advantage of the ruler to see all those who are closest to him by birth, far removed from him by their conduct. This great gap that his virtue puts between them and him places him in a better light in the eyes of all the world.' He was determined to stress the infinite distance that separated the image that he wished to portray of the imposing, grave, hard-working king and that of the bejewelled, pleasure-loving, lazy prince.

Indirectly he encouraged Monsieur's descent into the hell of homosexuality, which he himself held in horror. Far from disapproving, he smiled ironically at the account of a ball at the Palais Royal. Monsieur, who had always loved dressing up, had disguised himself as a woman, spent hours in front of the mirror making himself up, sticking on beauty spots, fixing his earrings, then, after a final, self-satisfied look in the mirror, put on his mask and entered the ballroom. He went and sat down among the women, chatted with them, agreed to take off his mask after coyly refusing, but in fact delighted at the opportunity of displaying his beauty.[4] Then he went to dance a minuet with his new lover, the Chevalier de Lorraine. This magnificent gigolo, a breathtakingly handsome bastard of the House of Guise, had a treacherous, ruthless mind. He had completely captivated Monsieur; and at first the king had protected the liaison, delighted by the new scandal, especially when Lorraine skilfully calmed his perpetual fears about his younger brother's caprices. 'Sire, Monsieur is a good man; he loves Your

Majesty; believe me, he would never do anything to displease you,' he declared. 'Will you stand surety for him?' the king asked. 'I will, Sire.' 'I am very glad of it.'[5]

Then the king began to worry about the influence that an intelligent man like Lorraine might have on the weak-willed Monsieur. Why did Philippe demand the governorship of Languedoc with such insistence? Why was Philippe so unpleasant to his wife when the king had a particular job for her? Louis was planning in the greatest secrecy to send Henrietta to England to negotiate a treaty of alliance with her brother, Charles II. Was he unaware that he was rubbing salt into his younger brother's wounds precisely by offering his wife a job that Philippe would dearly have loved himself? Or was he trying to humiliate the husband at the risk of sowing discord between husband and wife?

Monsieur suspected something without knowing exactly what, and grew more and more irritated. He was always seeing his wife in secret conversations with the king. It only took a few days for the Chevalier de Lorraine to get to the bottom of it. When Monsieur was informed, he exploded. His wife was to be sent without him as ambassador extraordinary, whereas he was never sent anywhere. He dashed into the king, determined to have a showdown but Louis held firm, then started an investigation which led back to the Chevalier de Lorraine.

At this point, the Bishop of Langres died. He had held two wealthy abbeys in the gift of Monsieur, which Monsieur now told the king that he had given to Lorraine. There can be no question of it, the king replied. Monsieur returned and announced to everyone's astonishment that he was leaving the Court.

Shortly afterwards, Le Tellier called on Monsieur, who was furiously discussing the king's decision with his lover. The minister had an unpleasant message from Louis: the Chevalier de Lorraine was invited to leave or Le Tellier would be forced to have him arrested in the Duc d'Orléans' own room. Monsieur threw his arms around his lover's neck, hugged him, embraced him, wept. Lorraine, very calm and haughty, left and went down into the castle courtyard, where he was arrested in the correct manner and despatched to Montpellier. In his room, Monsieur sobbed, wept, shrieked and, finally, fainted. He threw himself at his brother's feet to ask pardon for his lover, but in vain; Monsieur's mood passed from pain to anger. He grabbed Henrietta, whom he accused of being the cause of all his misfortunes, forced her into his coach and left the castle to sulk on his estate at Villers-Cotterêts.[6]

'I beg you to say to the king,' he wrote to Colbert, 'that I have come here in the extremist pain, forced to remove myself from his sight, or remain ashamed in his Court. That I beg him to consider what people would say in society if they saw me merry and unconcerned in the midst of the Carnival, while an innocent prince [Lorraine], the best friend I have in the world and who holds me most dear languishes for love of me in a wretched prison.' Then, growing firmer, he went on: 'The manner in which he was seized was for me the most tangible affront that could be offered me.' Finally, he gave vent to resentment: 'Moreover the king has asked my wife whose side she was on, which clearly suggests that he wanted to give her permission not to do her duty in my regard by fleeing with me.'[7] Henrietta had to pay for her trouble-making by performing her marital duties. In his rage, the confirmed homosexual found the strength to make love to her several times a day in the hope of making her pregnant and preventing her departure for England.[8] Eventually sensing the absurdity of his position, Monsieur agreed to reappear at Saint-Germain after a few weeks where he was received with delight. His anger had not subsided, however, and he unburdened himself to his cousin, the Grande Mademoiselle: he hated his wife, for it was she who was responsible for the whole affair. Next day it was Henrietta's turn to come and weep on the shoulder of the sympathetic cousin: 'If, when I did anything wrong, he had strangled me, he would have done me a service; but he forgave me and still comes to torment me for nothing ...'[9]

With harmony apparently restored in the royal family and Mme de Montespan having recovered from her recent childbirth, the Court was able to set out in April 1670 for a tour of Flanders, which had recently been conquered and where the situation was still precarious. There was some concern as to the wisdom of the king's latest whim. 'Some say that it is simply a pleasure jaunt,' the ambassador of Savoy reported, 'others a child's eagerness and others boasting, since the king cares neither for war nor for danger.'[10] Louis had a fine new glass coach built, in which he rode with the queen, Mme de La Vallière and Mme de Montespan. Although it was peacetime he was flanked by an army corps. The weather was frightful; it rained incessantly and the coaches got bogged down in the poor roads. Baggage fell off into the mud and the horses had to be beaten before they would move. It was nearly ten o'clock at night, on a road lit only by a few torches, as the royal cortège approached Landrecies, when the governor's son came to announce that the rain had so swollen the river that it could scarcely be forded. They turned back, but where would they stay the night? There was a small house in the middle of a field nearby so they got down out of the carriages to explore it. Mme de Béthune brandished a candle before the queen to light her way. The Grande Mademoiselle was holding up her train when Maria Theresa fell into a hole full of mud. 'Cousin, pull me out,' sobbed the queen. 'Madame, I'm stuck in a hole, wait until I pull myself out.'

The Court party managed to have an improvised dinner sent to them from Landrecies. The soup – so cold that it seemed ready to freeze – had such an 'ill appearance' that the queen refused to touch it. The others, that is to say, the king, Monsieur, Madame, the Grande Mademoiselle, the king's two mistresses and the queen's ladies of honour, despatched it in no time at all. Seeing them devour the soup the queen felt hungrier than ever but not a drop was left. She stamped her foot, and the others repressed their giggles. Then a plate of meat arrived so hard that the Grande Mademoiselle needed all her strength to pull a wing from a chicken.

In the only bedroom, a fire had been lit and the only bed had been prepared for the queen. Three mattresses were brought for the others. 'What! Everyone sleep together?' the queen expostulated. 'Where's the harm in everyone being on mattresses, fully dressed?' the king asked innocently. 'I don't see what's wrong with it. Ask my cousin, and we'll do as she says.' The Grande Mademoiselle had already unlaced her corset and put on a dressing-gown over her travelling clothes. The king and his brother followed suit, then put on their nightcaps and everyone slept side by side on the mattresses, Monsieur at one end, then, in order: Henrietta, the king, the Grande Mademoiselle, La Vallière, Montespan, the Duchesse de Créqui, La Vallière's sister-in-law and, lastly, one of the queen's maids of honour.

Even under these conditions the exhausted travellers might have slept, but all night they were subjected to mooing and braying from the animals in the stable next door, disturbed by the unusual commotion. Then there were the great officers of the Crown who, coming for orders, rushed in and very nearly walked over the royal bedfellows. One of them got his spur caught in La Vallière's bonnet jumping over the mattress, which made everyone laugh. Finally, at four in the morning, Louvois turned up. 'The bridge is ready,' he announced, 'and day is breaking.'

They continued their tour of the towns that had been taken from Spain. On the other side of the frontier, the Spaniards observed these movements and bandied courtesies to them. They fired off a few salvos in the king's honour and the governor of divided Flanders sent his son to convey his respects. The Court moved slowly towards Dunkirk where Madame was to embark for England. Henrietta became sad at the approach of this departure, which ought to have delighted her. For hours on end she remained downcast, silent, avoiding company as much as she could. She ate little and lost weight, all because Monsieur, at the prospect of his wife's triumph, behaved more and more odiously towards her. 'It was predicted to me,' he said one day in front of Henrietta and the other ladies, 'that I shall have several wives and indeed I think I will; for judging by Madame's condition one may be forgiven for believing that she will not live for much longer, indeed that she will die very soon.'[11]

Madame arrived back from England in June and in triumph. Her brother Charles II had received her with affection and honour, the English lords had outdone one another in gallantry and the people cheered her. Moreover, she had succeeded in her mission since she came back with the Treaty of Dover in her pocket. She was soon brought down to earth however, for, as was only too predictable, her success merely exasperated her husband. The sulks, the attacks, the unkind words began all over again and the king's congratulations aroused them all the more. Her beautiful eyes frequently filled with tears. she no longer had the strength to fight. Her health was deteriorating and when she went to visit the queen at Versailles, it was said that she looked like 'a dressed corpse to which a little rouge had been applied'.

On the Sunday afternoon of 29 June 1670, the Grande Mademoiselle left her room in Versailles and bumped into the Comte d'Agen, who passed by shouting 'Madame is dying!' She ran to the queen, who had already heard the news. 'Madame is dying and do you know what she's saying? She thinks she is being poisoned. She was perfectly well in the drawing-room at Saint-Cloud; she drank a glass of chicory water that her apothecary had brought her; a quarter of an hour later she began to shout out that she felt as if there was a fire in her stomach. She couldn't bear it any longer ...' The king, the queen and the Grande Mademoiselle hurried to Saint-Cloud. On arrival at the castle, the Grande Mademoiselle felt reassured on seeing the untroubled faces around her and on hearing Monsieur express surprise at their visit. She was still more surprised when she found Henrietta lying on a small improvised bed, dishevelled, unbuttoned and deathly pale, as thin as a rake and calling out in pain. The queen burst into tears, as did the Grande Mademoiselle. But others displayed hateful indifference. 'Vomit, Madame,' her husband repeated to her, 'or that bile will snuff you out.' The physicians looked at one another and said nothing.

Meanwhile the courtiers went to and fro in the room and chatted as if nothing at all were amiss; the Grande Mademoiselle even heard some people laughing. Always able to rise to the occasion she took Monsieur to one side and said, 'They don't seem to realize that she is dying; someone should talk to her about God.' 'You're quite right, it's quite shameful,' Monsieur replied. 'Who shall we send for now who would look well in the Gazette? Ah! I know – the Abbé Bossuet, who was recently appointed to the bishopric of Condom.' While Bossuet was sent for, the king, tears flowing, took his farewell of Madame and went back to Versailles; Henrietta of England died at three in the morning. After lunch on the same day the king summoned the Grande Mademoiselle and came straight to the point: 'There is a place vacant, cousin. Would you like to fill it?' Mademoiselle paled: 'You are the master, and I shall never have any other desire but yours.' 'I shall do what I can and keep you informed,' the king concluded. Henrietta's body was barely cold but Louis was already thinking of replacing her by giving the richest heiress in France to his brother.[12]

Public opinion was in less of a hurry and was still preoccupied with Madame's death. At the Court, in France and in the whole of Europe the cry went up: Madame had been poisoned. The exile of the sinister Lorraine, her husband's hatred for her, her sudden pains, her rapid death and her own accusations concerning the glass of chicory water did not fail to arouse suspicion; the English were so indignant that in London,

Charles II had to beg the French ambassador not to go out for fear of being attacked. Rumours spread so widely that the king felt obliged to order an autopsy of Madame, which was carried out in the presence of the English ambassador; no trace of poison was found in the body.[13]

Many years later, the Marquis d'Effiat, a leading member of Monsieur's homosexual circle, an intimate and accomplice of the Chevalier de Lorraine and an altogether unsavoury character, told the following story to a friend: Lorraine had realized that as long as Henrietta was alive he had no chance of coming back to Court. Moreover, he had sent a highly recommended poison to d'Effiat from Italy where he was travelling. After careful planning, on 29 June 1670, d'Effiat took advantage of the fact that he was alone for a moment in Madame's antechamber to open a cupboard and pour poison into the bottle of chicory water. Surprised at this point by the *valet de chambre* he got out of it by explaining that he had been dying of thirst and was looking for water to drink. After Madame's death next day, the *valet de chambre* told what had happened. D'Effiat was seized during the night by six guards and brought before the king, who assumed his most terrifying demeanour. 'Listen to me carefully, my friend,' he said. 'If you admit everything to me, whatever you may have done, I shall forgive you ... But be careful not to hide anything, for if you do, you will be dead before leaving here. Was Madame poisoned?' 'Yes, Sire,' came the reply. 'Who poisoned her and how?' D'Effiat then told the whole story in detail. The king hesitated for a moment, then, staring at d'Effiat, asked: 'And does my brother know anything about it?' 'No, Sire, none of us were stupid enough to tell him. He can't keep a secret.' 'Ah!' said the king, visibly relieved. 'That is all I wanted to know ...'[14] Did d'Effiat tell the truth or was he simply trying to play up his own importance by accusing himself of a crime? No one knows, and it is conceivable that Henrietta, who was always in poor health, may anyway have been suffering from a fatal illness, whose course could have been accelerated by poison.

As the rumours of Madame's poisoning continued to circulate despite the autopsy results, Bossuet, the bishop selected at random by Monsieur because he 'will look well in the Gazette', was appointed to speak her funeral oration and to coin his famous phrase: *'Madame se meurt; Madame est morte.'* ('Madame is dying; Madame is dead.')

Louise de La Vallière nearly suffered the same fate as Madame. She suddenly fell ill and in a few days seemed to be on her deathbed. Delirious with fever, dripping with sweat, writhing on her bed surrounded by her doctors and priests, she already saw herself, the sinner in hell. When she recovered, she turned to God: 'May I never forget the spectacle of my death agony and of your justice ...' Now it was her duty, nay, her dearest wish, to expiate her courtesan's life. But she would not renounce the trappings of luxury or leave the Court. On the contrary, she would remain there, clinging to it in the knowledge that she could not suffer more anywhere else. She wanted to undergo the torture of seeing the man she still loved, loved by another woman. As if to help her expiate her sins Mme de Montespan changed her attitude to Louise and set out deliberately to humiliate her. She used her former rival as a *femme de chambre,* having herself dressed and her hair done by Louise before receiving the king, and boasting of her friend's talent as a hairdresser and maid. She made fun of Louise, needling her in a thousand witty and cruelly different ways.

Enthralled by Athénaïs, the king followed suit and was pleased to wound the woman he had once so loved, less treacherously than his mistress, but more crudely. Returning from the hunt, he sat down in Louise's apartment to take off his boots, comb his hair and adjust his clothes before going into Montespan's room. As he left, he threw at the castoff mistress his little spaniel, Malice. 'There, Madame,' he snapped, 'this is all you need for company.'[15] Why did the lovers treat Louise so badly when she had done nothing to them? That, of course, was why they were so determined to hurt her. Athénaïs possessed the cruelty of an intelligent woman, just as Louis possessed the cruelty of a weak man with a willing victim. Louise's apparently boundless submission merely exasperated her former lover and ex-friend. They wanted to drive her to the limit, cause a reaction, an explosion, a revolt. They would then have something to reproach her with, something that would extinguish the vague remorse that Louise's attitude continued to feed. But since her aim was to endure everything, Louise refused them this satisfaction. Were the lovers aware that they were offering their victim the hoped-for possibility of enduring martyrdom? 'Do I not see them every day?' she scribbled to her confessor. 'Do my eyes not follow their eyes? Am I not sitting beside my rival while he is also beside her, but far from me? Ah! Father, may God punish me if I blaspheme, I know what hell is, but I cannot imagine a hell more terrible than that which is in my heart.'[16]

If Louis could not bear Louise's submission, he found the lack of it in his subjects more unbearable. There was rebellion in Vivarais, in south-eastern France. A bad winter was followed by rumours about new taxes on childbirths and on new clothes. No one knew who had invented these absurdities, perhaps an *agent provocateur,* but their dire poverty helped the peasants to swallow this nonsense. A minor riot at Aubenas on 30 April 1670 triggered off a series of riots in which the peasants rose up with the cry: 'No more taxes. Death to the bloodsuckers of the people.'

The alarm bells rang and looting followed its usual course. The bourgeois dug themselves in at home, but a few landed aristocrats with enlightened ideas listened. One of them, a former officer named Antoine de Rourre, dreamed of a better society with a fairer tax and legal system, and became a popular leader in the provinces. When begged by the peasants to lead them in their fight, he accepted, a revolutionary before his time, and found himself at the head of 2,000 undisciplined men, armed with staves and sickles.

Attempts at conciliation by well-meaning aristocrats failed in the face of the government's stubbornness and lack of understanding. The rebels took Aubenas with considerable slaughter, carrying the mutilated limbs of their victims across the town, despite the contrary orders of Antoine de Rourre who had lost control of events. The provincial governor asked to negotiate with Rourre, only with a view to giving reinforcements time to arrive on the scene – 6,000 soldiers were advancing by forced march in the direction of Vivarais. On 25 July 1670, the two forces met in the evening. Fewer in number, badly armed, badly commanded and badly trained, the peasants were crushed and a pitiless repression struck the province. A number of rebels were hanged or put on the wheel alive. Six hundred others were sent to the galleys. Women were tortured, all the inhabitants of Rourre's village were executed, while soldiers ransomed, killed or raped as they wished.

Crazed with terror the villagers fled on to the roads, leaving everything behind them. Louis, evidently ignorant of what was happening in Vivarais, naïvely concluded: 'I was instilling so strict a discipline in my troops ... that they never gave the slightest reason for complaint.'[17] Arrested and brought back to Aubenas, Antoine de Rourre was put on the wheel alive in the public square, his head and limbs exposed to the four corners of the town. His house was razed to the ground, his wife and children banished from France. None of this would have happened if any attempt had been made to crush the absurd rumours about new iniquitous taxes and to calm with a few concessions peasants who were in no way opposed either to the monarchy or to law and order.[18]

As 1670 drew to a close, the Court was preoccupied less with the troublemakers of Vivarais crushed by the soldiery than with a fantastic love affair. The Grande Mademoiselle had already drawn up an impressive list of potential husbands, including the kings of France, Spain, Portugal, England, the German emperor, the Duke of Savoy and Monsieur himself. But then the most eligible spinster in Europe fell in love with Lauzun, who was a mere count, six years her junior, short and none too clean in his habits, but a witty rogue. This swaggering, impudent, ladies' man, extraordinarily gifted in bed, was in no way a suitable husband for Her Royal Highness, first cousin of Louis XIV and the richest heiress in France, perhaps in Europe, But Love had spoken to this formidable matron who at the age of forty-three had retained the heart of a young girl. She did not know how to declare her love and kept buzzing around Lauzun who, cunning as he was, refused to take the hint. One day she took her courage in both hands: 'I am resolved to marry a French lord. What do you think Monsieur?' she asked him. 'Ah, Mademoiselle! Would Your Royal Highness stoop so low?' he countered. In the days that followed he appeared not to notice the allusions, the tender looks, the approaching steps of the middle-aged maiden. One

Friday evening, she showed him a sealed letter, saying, 'His name is inside, but I don't have the strength to give it to you. I am too ashamed. Friday is an unlucky day, but I shall give it to you on Saturday.' 'Give it to me now,' Lauzun replied, 'and I promise I shall put it under my pillow and not open it until midnight has struck.' In this letter there were only three words, disarming in their naïvety; 'It is you.'

The following Sunday, she saw him again in public at the Court. He said nothing, showed no trace of emotion. She on the other hand was trembling with passion. At last she managed to corner him in the queen's bedchamber. 'I'm not simple enough to believe you,' he replied. 'You're making fun of me.' And the cunning Lauzun pretended to avoid her. Several days passed before he gave her any encouragement whatsoever: 'There are moments when I think it is not an illusion. I allow myself to feel joy; then I retreat into myself and decide that it is not.' The Grande Mademoiselle decided to speak directly to the king. 'I cannot approve such a marriage,' Louis told her, 'but you are forty years old and I cannot stop you.' But, he explained to his cousin, he did not want to have anything to do with her decision; Lauzun was a friend of his, but he had made many enemies for himself. The king did not wish to appear to be favouring him. And he recommended the greatest discretion: 'Let no no one know of it.' The prospective betrothed was so 'discreet' in her joy that soon the entire aristocracy rushed to congratulate the royal princess who had, paid it the unparalleled honour of deigning to marry one of its members. But her family did not see it like that – particularly the queen. It was outrageous that Lauzun should become a cousin through marriage of a Habsburg. She went and berated the king on the matter. Monsieur was the next to make a terrible scene before his brother. Then the Prince de Condé and the Duc de Bourbon besieged the sovereign. Quite oblivious to all these dynastic concerns, the betrothed was lovingly preparing her future husband's room in the Palais de Luxembourg and showing it to admiring visitors: 'Don't you think a younger brother of Gascogne would be comfortable here?' It was the night before the long expected day; they were to be married the following noon, by the parish priest in the church of Charenton.

Lauzun left the Luxembourg and went to sleep for the last time in his bachelor apartment. The Grande Mademoiselle remained alone with Mme de Nogent, her beloved's sister, her future sister-in-law. It was eight in the evening when a messenger from the Louvre was announced: 'The king has commanded me to tell you to come to him at once.' Anticipating bad news, the Grande Mademoiselle went trembling to the Palace where she was shown into the king's room. She found him alone, sad and embarrassed. 'I am in despair at what I have to say to you,' he began. 'I am told that people are saying in the world that I sacrificed you to make M de Lauzun's fortune; that would do me harm abroad and I cannot allow this affair to go forward.' The bride-to-be understood. She burst into tears. She pleaded with him: 'Sire, it would be better to kill me than to place me in such a situation.' 'You are right to complain, strike me if you will,' he said and, taking the best line of defence, he fell to his own knees before his kneeling cousin and wept in her arms.[19]

At the Luxembourg the Grande Mademoiselle's friends, warned of the king's summons, waited in her room for the results of the audience. Suddenly shouting was heard. Two valets ran in, saying, 'Leave quickly by the stairs.' They dashed for the doors, but the Abbé de Choisy, more curious than the others, hung back. What he saw was a dishevelled, vociferous fury, her arms held up to heaven, cursing the king, the princes, the whole world, smashing furniture as she passed, overturning knick-knacks, throwing vases to the floor – between the Louvre and the Luxembourg, she had smashed all the windows in her coach. She threw herself on her bed and remained prostrate, without moving or speaking all that night and the following day and then she burst into torrents of tears. She refused to get up and received visits of condolence from her friends in Court. In front of them, she beat her fists on the pillow next to hers, 'He would have been there! He would have been there!'

Feeling somewhat guilty about this grotesque affair in which his intervention had transformed a spinster's infatuation into a human tragedy, the king himself then behaved in a quite ridiculous manner. He sent out a circular signed in his own hand to all his ambassadors abroad, recounting the affair and ordering them to explain it to the governments to which they were accredited, a procedure which made the whole of Europe laugh. It was in fact Mme de Montespan who had changed Louis xiv's mind. She had been accused by the royal family of having arranged this misalliance as she was an intimate friend of Lauzun. She won her way back into favour by siding with the queen, Monsieur and the princes who were outraged by the marriage. She spoke tenderly to her lover and so convinced him that he himself believed that he wanted to prevent the marriage. He never knew why he had given his consent and he knew even less why he had withdrawn it.

In his circular, Louis xiv had praised Lauzun's attitude after he had been told in person of the king's intention to prevent the marriage. By way of reward, Lauzun was promised the post of Grand Master of the Artillery, but time passed and Lauzun saw no such promotion coming his way. He went to Montespan. He was not aware of the role of his 'friend' in the affair of his marriage, but he knew it was in his interest not to reproach her with it and, on the contrary, to derive the maximum possible benefit from the debt that she now had with him. He asked her to speak to the king in order to obtain a promise of the post. Montespan swore that she would do all in her power to help him. But Lauzun, who knew his friend only too well, took the precaution of becoming her *femme de chambre*'s lover in order to keep a closer watch on her. He persuaded the accommodating servant woman to let him hide under her mistress's bed when the king would be paying her a visit. So, as Louis and Athénaïs were chatting side by side on the bed, Lauzun was beneath, holding his breath. 'No!' the king expostulated. 'Lauzun would not have the artillery,' and Montespan warmly approved of his decision, betraying her friend even more. When the king went to dress for the evening and Montespan went into her dressing-room to change, Lauzun slipped from under the bed and went off.

When she came out of her apartment to join the Court, she bumped into Lauzun, who held out his hand to her and smiled at her respectfully, asking if she had been kind enough to speak about him to the king. She assured him that she had warmly recommended her dear friend, that she had even told the king that no one would be better qualified than he for the artillery. There was, she said, nothing she would not do to help her friend. Then, still smiling and in the same tone of voice, Lauzun murmured: 'Liar, bitch, whore.' And he repeated word for word her conversation with her lover, bowed respectfully and left her. Montespan entered the drawing-room, made a few steps and fainted.[20]

Some days later the Grande Mademoiselle's ex-betrothed was being driven towards the sinister fortress of Pignerol in Savoy, the price he had to pay for the luxury of insulting a royal favourite. Hardly had he arrived at Pignerol than he began to set the dungeon on fire. Then he dug holes through the walls and entertained himself by going from cell to cell, talking with the various inmates. One day, he found himself in front of Fouquet, who had been there for seven years. The ex-superintendent, delighted by this unexpected distraction and avid for news, asked question after question, but he soon became serious again. He must be talking to a madman. Little Lauzun, whom he had left as the lowest of courtiers, appeared to have become Colonel-General of the Dragoons, a friend of the king, Duc de Montpensier and the betrothed of a Royal Highness. Moreover, Lauzun appeared to have called the king's mistress a whore. Fouquet was now really afraid, but not knowing what else to do, he resigned himself to listening to this nonsense to the end.

The Shrove Tuesday ball of 1671 at the Palais des Tuileries was not a particularly joyful occasion. Instead of dancing, the courtiers preferred to whisper in corners. Several times the entertainment had come close to being cancelled. The Duchesse de La Vallière did not appear nor did the Marquise de Montespan. Something was happening, but what? In fact, Louise de La Vallière had quite simply had enough. The daily suffering had proved more than she could bear, so she had decided to leave the Court and had announced her decision to the king. Next day, Ash Wednesday, in the early hours of the morning, she left the palace. She was wearing a poor grey linen dress and had not wanted to take anything with her. She drove towards Chaillot, as she had already done once before and sought refuge at St Mary's Convent.

The king was informed, but he altered nothing in his programme. At the expected hour he got into his coach with Montespan and the Grande Mademoiselle and rode off to Versailles. But there, in the coach, he began to weep. His mistress thought that she ought to imitate him and his cousin joined in the tears, not on the favourite's behalf, but because of her imprisoned betrothed. When they arrived at Versailles, the king asked to be left alone with Montespan and informed her that he intended to bring Louise back, but several messengers came back empty handed. The king appealed to Colbert, the eternal jack of all trades. Colbert acted firmly, so firmly that he considered drawing up a summons if Louise did not follow him. Torn between king and God, weakened by suffering and tension, Louise gave in. She agreed to resume her place with the poor proviso 'that the king would allow her to retire if she could not go on'. At six in the evening, she left St Mary's Convent with Colbert.

Louis welcomed her back to Versailles with visible emotion. La Vallière was once more in favour, and La Vallière seemed to be more powerful than ever.[21] People wondered who was to be the more powerful, La Vallière or Montespan? If La Vallière, why keep Montespan? If Montespan, why bring La Vallière back? The courtiers exchanged their impressions. 'I don't understand what the king is doing at all,' admitted Bussy-Rabutin,[22] the gallant priest who had been exiled for years but who never missed an item of court gossip. With La Vallière back and the lovers at pains to please her, the trio began to function as before. Athénaïs could once more rule the roost at Court, launching fashions and inventing hairstyles which were soon imitated by all the women, including the queen, and showering members of her family with favours.

The Church was becoming disturbed by the somewhat exotic conception of marriage that the king seemed to have adopted. His confessor, Father Annat, who did not know which way to turn with the succession of royal but illegitimate births, threatened to retire. Louis gaily accepted his resignation and urged him to choose a more accommodating successor. He seemed quite unmoved when preachers in the pulpit compared him with King David coveting his neighbour's goods.

'If the respect I have for you, Sire, only allows me to tell the truth in a roundabout way, you must have more penetration than I have boldness. But if, after all my care and consideration, the truth does not please you, be warned that it will be taken from you and that Jesus Christ will avenge the contempt in which His words are held,' one cleric declared. The indignant courtiers wondered how he dared insult the king. 'The preacher has done his duty. It is up to us to do ours,' said the king, putting an end to any further comment.[23]

In order to do his 'duty' the king took his two mistresses and his wife on a new tour of Flanders in April 1671. The news that his delightful three-year-old son, the Duc d'Anjou was dying came as a terrible warning. One morning, the queen's dwarf, Bricmini, came into the Grande Mademoiselle's bedchamber and woke her with the cry: 'You will die, you, too, you grown-ups; your nephew is dead.'[24] What upset

Louis most was learning that people interpreted this sad event as just punishment for his scandalous conduct.[25]

As 1671 drew to an end, he consoled himself by receiving the new wife that he had found for Monsieur. Princesse Elizabeth Charlotte of Bavaria, nicknamed Liselotte, but known later as 'the Palatine', was a nineteen-year-old orphan, rather short of money but endowed with rights of inheritance over the Palatinate which interested Louis enormously. She formed a vivid contrast with the dead Henrietta. She herself was under no illusions about her lack of beauty: 'I have always been ugly and I have become even more so as a result of the smallpox; I am short and monstrously fat, rather cube-shaped; my skin is red, with yellow spots; my nose is speckled with the smallpox, as are my two cheeks; I have a big mouth and bad teeth and that's all there is to say about my pretty face.'[26]

Convinced of the pre-eminence of everything German – from the antiquity of the families to gastronomy – she arrived determined not to be impressed by France and the Court that were so talked about abroad. Her hearty, affectionate manner, her outspokenness, her habit of going on unexpected outings, her love of fresh air and her stamina on horseback gave great pleasure to her brother-in-law. On the other hand, there was some anxiety as to how this enormous Teuton, devoid of the most elementary elegance, utterly ignorant of any refinement, would attract her tiny husband, smothered in ribbons, jewellery and perfumes. However, they both showed willing. When retiring for his wedding night, Philippe armed himself with a huge rosary, jangling with relics and medals. Hearing a metallic tinkling under the sheets, Liselotte asked: 'God forgive me, Monsieur, but it seems to me that you have brought your relics and images of the Virgin into a country that is quite unknown to them.' Philippe burst out laughing: 'You have been a Huguenot, you don't know what power relics and images of the Holy Virgin have. They protect from all evil whatever parts one rubs with them.' 'You're not going to tell me that the Virgin is honoured by rubbing her image on the parts intended to destroy virginity?'[27] The recipe must have been effective, however, for all the royal families of Europe would one day descend from the union of this effeminate man and this manly woman.

To complete the marriage the king presented his brother with a magnificent gift: he gave him back his lover, the Chevalier de Lorraine, who was still in exile. 'I wish to give you this present ... I am giving him back to you and I want you to be under this obligation to me all your life and to love him for love of me.' Happiness coupled with surprise threw Monsieur at the king's feet: 'My brother, this is not how brothers should embrace,' said Louis.[28] With a brotherly hug of reconciliation, the new husband set about loving his lover out of love for the king.

CHAPTER 11

The French Goliath against the Dutch David

Conrad van Beunigen, councillor of the city of Amsterdam, leaned over the medal that the engraver had just struck. He saw his own features standing out against a sun, and he read the motto: '*In conspecto meo, stetit sol*' ('On seeing me, the sun stood still'). Then he looked at the medal that he had just received from Paris: the king of France had had his emblem, the sun, engraved upon it with the motto: '*Nec pluribus impar.*' ('Unlike all others.')[1] He laughed to himself as he imagined Louis xiv's fury when the Dutch burgher's reply to the humourless vanity of the pompous sovereign appeared before him. True or false, the anecdote is merely one episode in the war of the medals. Scarcely had the French government brought out its medals to praise the master than their doubles appeared in Holland, in which mottoes and emblems, so dear to Louis xiv, appeared mutilated and shortened. To this was added the war of the gazettes. Newspapers and pamphlets printed in Holland, carried throughout France and Europe the juiciest gossip about Louis' love life, revealing every scandal and every liaison. Louis was furious. The Dutch did not care – they were the richest, most dynamic country in Europe and their war fleet sheltered them from any attack . . . by sea.

How good it seemed to live in Holland in the 1660s. Prosperity reigned in that small country, which had snatched its independence from the Spanish barely a century before. The population's love of hard work and efficiency had paid off. Towns built of pink brick were expanding in a countryside as calm as a landscape by Ruysdael or Hobbema. Everything in this clean, neat Holland was comfortable and above all at peace. There was no war on the horizon. France remained the great ally and England, the traditional enemy, had also become a 'friend'. As a guarantee of peace the Dutch had given her New Amsterdam, the city that they had founded in America and which the English had renamed New York in honour of their king's brother, the Duke of York.

The future seemed so prosperous for the Dutch that recently they had even abolished their last remnants of hereditary monarchy, the Stadholderate held by the House of Orange. The Grand Pensionary, Jan de Witt, assisted by his brother Cornelius, presided over a republic, democratic certainly, but also immensely rich. Flooding the markets with its products, trading with the entire world, sending its merchant fleets into all the seas which it dominated, opening companies almost everywhere, improving its banking system, Holland had become the leading world economic power.

This was all very unfortunate for Colbert, who was doing his best to raise the French economy to a level at which it could compete. He could doctor the reports he received and blacken whole pages of instructions, but it was no use: the companies that he had set up had not managed to compete with the Dutch. The customs war that he had embarked on turned against him, the economic espionage in which he had indulged and the bribes that his ambassador at The Hague distributed to corrupt the Dutch proved useless. He grumbled, he threatened, but the Dutch took no notice.[2]

'You speak to me very loudly, Monsieur l'Ambassadeur. A less moderate king than myself would have had you thrown out of the windows of the Louvre,' snapped Louis, unable to contain himself before the calm boldness of the Dutch ambassador. It was the same van Beunigen featured on the medal who, refusing to be intimidated and keeping his hat on his head, replied tit for tat. 'That brewer is certainly insolent,' the king said to Brienne after retiring with dignity. 'Yes, no doubt, Sire, I wanted to throw his hat at your feet.' 'You would have been quite wrong to do so,' the king replied, 'but he will pay for it sooner or later, and his masters, too.'[3]

The greatest army of the century, with the most formidable artillery and commanded by the most famous generals, had concentrated in northern France. The perplexed Dutch wondered what these disturbing preparations were for. Would the French dare to attack on land? To do so, the French would have to pass through the Spanish Netherlands which would trigger off a new war with Spain or through the states of the Archbishop of Cologne and of the Bishop of Münster. That was the problem: these prelates had smiled on Louis and had allowed themselves to be bought. England at any case would not drop its ally. 'My hope is that Charles II will not abandon us and that he will keep his promise to the States,' wrote his nephew, William of Orange. But that, too, was the problem: Louis seemed to have bought off Charles II as well. What were the secret terms of that Treaty of Dover that Henrietta, Duchesse d'Orléans had negotiated with her brother shortly before her death? Had not the British government become, in recent months, singularly cold and distant towards Holland? At least the Dutch still had gunpowder and shot to defend themselves if need be. But who, in fact, was continually buying munitions from these same Dutch to such a degree that they had almost emptied their reserves, if not the French government? And Jan de Witt, after several carefree years and false hopes, suddenly woke and found himself on the edge of the abyss.

'We are ready to do everything in our power to persuade Your Majesty of the perfect inclination we have to pay him the honour and deference due to his person and to his high dignity:' thus the States of

Holland anxiously wrote to Louis in January 1672. How had they offended? What reparations did he demand? Were his military preparations directed at them? The answer came back: 'I shall make such use of my troops as my dignity demands and I need account to no one.' Now it was little use the Dutch smashing the die of the criminal medals that had offended him. The answer of the king of France was clear: wounded vanity can only be washed away in blood.[4]

There was not even a declaration of war. On 22 March 1672, near the Isle of Wight, an English squadron attacked a Dutch fleet on its way back from Smyrna, even though the two governments were officially allies. Some days later, the bourgeois of Paris learnt from a herald-at-arms that their master had gone to war because he had not been given adequate satisfaction by the States General.

Right up to the last moment Goliath concealed the fact that he had decided to crush David. With all his military might the most powerful king in Europe was getting ready to pounce on the little people that had dared to make fun of him and which, over-confident as it was, had neglected to prepare its defences. It was his way of maintaining his glory. The nobility, traditionally impatient to fight, noisily approved. Finance and trade were delighted to annihilate a dangerous competitor and the clergy could not wait to confound those heretical protestants.

'It seemed to me so important to the reputation of my arms to begin my campaign with some brilliant stroke and I did not regard an attack on Maestricht as sufficient for that ... I considered it more advantageous to my purpose and less common for glory to attack at one and the same time four places on the Rhine ... With this in mind, I chose Rhinsberg, Wesel, Burick and Orsoi ...'[5] Louis threw himself into the assault on glory and the chosen towns fell one after another into his hands, either because they were not defended, or because of the incompetence of their officers, or because of the panic of their citizens.

Now he was on the Rhine behind which the amazing reserves of the Dutch were amassed: four to five hundred cavalry and two miserable regiments of foot soldiers without cannon ... against twenty-five thousand men and powerful artillery. Once pounded by French cannon, the Dutch did not ask for more and threw down their arms. 'Spare us our lives!' they cried on their knees. 'Give no quarter to this rabble,' yelled young Longueville, son of the heroine of the *Fronde*. He was blind drunk and didn't know what he was doing. He fired into the mass of Dutch soldiers, but the 'rabble' replied and shot him dead before fleeing in every direction.[6] Thus the French army pulled off 'that famous crossing of the Rhine, an action unique in its audacity and almost foolhardy', as the future Maréchal de Villars described it.[7] Huge compositions painted by such artists as Lebrun and Van der Meulen, Gobelins tapestries, poets' odes, dithyrambic articles in the gazettes and, of course, medals sang its praises; propaganda was doing a good job.

And the towns continued to fall. 'The king receives all the news of his good fortune with great moderation, he is the first to laugh and cannot keep a straight face before all those deputies from towns and officers of war who come and prostrate themselves at his feet, but one can also notice that he lives in a great interior joy,' said the ambassador of Savoy, who noticed everything.[8] What a joy, indeed, to devour those little Dutch who caused him no difficulty and hardly resisted at all. They had neither leader, nor soldiers, nor munitions, nor allies. The worse it was for them, the more glory came to Louis. He was impatient for it: 'He would very much like this affair to be ended so that he could enjoy the glory of having defeated his enemies in a short time.'[9] But this point of view was not shared by his officers. This was not war – it was more like yet another military parade. Where was the danger, where was the suspense? Not to mention the fact that the way things were going, the campaign would soon be over, before they had earned enough to pay off the debts incurred buying equipment. They were already at Utrecht, which had just capitulated.

To mark this great deed, Louis made a triumphal entry into the town. The Dutch might have tried to put a good face on defeat, had they not seen Catholic priests behind the conqueror, just like the time of the Spanish Inquisition. What was the point of fighting for independence if it was to see that symbol of oppression once more? Cardinal de Bouillon solemnly reconsecrated the old cathedral, soiled by the Reformation, to the True Religion after having burnt the furniture that had served the Calvinist religion 'for heresy'. And the governor of the town followed, to the horror of his fellow citizens, behind the Holy Sacrament in the Corpus Christi procession that had been abolished for a hundred years.[10]

Amsterdam was about to fall, and after Amsterdam, there would be no more Holland. Already Gourville, the prince de Condé's factotum, had received a deputation of the city's Jews; two million francs would be donated to him if, when he took the city he spared their quarter.[11] The municipal council deliberated as to how they would send the city keys to the conqueror. 'At least wait·until they ask for them,' interrupted the burgomaster. The rich had already taken the necessary steps. They would leave the country and settle in Indonesia, their distant colony. Many families had already taken the road to Germany in order to flee the French advance and Hamburg and Vienna were full of refugees.

Meanwhile, what remained of their country sank into anarchy. Schools were shut, factories closed down and the authorities could not cope. As the burghers buried their treasure, bands of looters formed, joined by armed peasants and deserters. 'Treason is so widespread that one can no longer trust anyone,' one refugee complained. Espionage and corruption, systematized by the French, had worked miracles. What was left of the army and navy had sunk into demoralization and mutiny. A whole people, left to itself, betrayed, furious and desperate, tore its country to pieces.[12] And Holland, now on its knees, asked for pardon. Four deputies from the States General went to the French camp to ask for peace, and there was hardly anything they would not offer.

Louvois made them wait for a whole week and then received them with a carefully calculated curtness that was shocking for the period. If they wanted peace, they had to give up the Dutch territory beyond the Rhine; repeal every trading law that was unfavourable to France, without reciprocity; pay twenty million francs; re-establish Catholicism everywhere, give satisfaction to France's English and German allies and . . . strike a gold medal each year that declared that they owed their liberty to His Majesty.[13]

The Dutch deputies rose, left in silence and returned to Amsterdam. Louis also went home to his Court. 'Nothing has been lacking in my undertakings and in the course of this war, I can boast that I have shown what France can do alone . . . And I find myself able to put fear into my enemies, to astonish my neighbours and to confound the envious . . . In short, France has shown what a difference there is between other nations and that which she has produced.'[14] Louis had conquered Holland; he left it to his generals to finish off the job, dropping his troops in the middle of a war to return to see his mistress who had just given him a new son, as indeed had his wife. Perhaps one cannot blame the happy father who went into raptures over his legitimate and illegitimate offspring which had arrived so conveniently together.

The barouche was travelling at a dizzy speed on the Fontainebleau road. Several travellers had piled into the light carriage which had only been made for one person. The coachmen, who saw an accident at every bump, were furious, but they could do nothing. The travelling coach had overturned and one had to take what one found, when there was no time to look very far: the constabulary were waiting at the Roanne bridge to prevent anyone from crossing and the travellers had had to take a roundabout way along the smaller lanes to avoid them. The postmaster, who had been ordered not to provide fresh horses, had been persuaded to do so with a hefty bribe. They had to hurry, for the constabulary, seeing that they had been given the slip, were searching the area and, having found the tracks of the barouche, were galloping in its pursuit. In spite of the danger, the occupants of the carriage were in high good humour. The woman who seemed to be the mistress – the others were obviously *femmes de chambre* – was laughing heartily. She was in her early thirties but her features had suffered from excessive thinness and nervousness. Her huge, dark, flashing eyes dominated her face. She was covered with magnificent jewellery, as if for a Court ball, but her linen, which she had not changed for several days, was rather soiled. The Principessa Colonna, formerly Maria Mancini, was fleeing her husband and Italy, and had landed in Provence on her way to Paris. An order endorsed by the king enjoined her not to continue, but she took no notice, for she believed herself to be the only woman the king had ever loved, for whom he had been ready to sacrifice his crown.

She did not care if the queen fulminated, if the entire Court condemned her extravagant escapade, if her sister Hortensia, who had come with her, had abandoned her. She did not care if her other sisters, Olympia, Comtesse de Soissons, and the Duchesse de Bouillon inveighed more loudly than anyone else against her crazy behaviour. The king would be moved, and would receive her. In fact, the king rejected her. Furious, she wrote to him a torrent of reproaches as in the good old days of their passionate affair. Then she asked him for forgiveness. The only reply was a very cold, very sharp note from Colbert. She wrote back: 'The beginning of your letter gave me great pleasure, Monseigneur, seeing that the king had kindly accepted my apologies and was willing to grant me his protection as before; but what followed led me to believe that he would be glad to see me far from his kingdom ... Anyhow, I do not know the map well enough to choose a convent in a town sixty kilometres from Paris. He has only to say where he would like me to go and I will go there ... Just tell the king that I would like to speak to him one day before I go away, and that it will be for the last time in my life. Grant me this grace, I beg you, Monseigneur, and then, I promise him that I shall go even further than he wishes ...'

But the impulsive, passionate young man she had known no longer existed except in her memory. The invincible conqueror, whose wife and mistress had just provided him with children, had no intention of allowing a past that he had erased from his memory to be resuscitated. He refused this final interview. 'I would never have believed what I have seen,' the unfortunate woman said to Colbert. 'I shall not say more about it because I am not able to control myself as well as you; it is better to end it all ...' The king added insult to injury by sending her a thousand pistoles, with the understanding that the payment would be repeated every six months on condition that she behaved herself and did not come near Paris.[15]

Amsterdam was not be taken by the French, for Amsterdam had become an island. The magistrates of the city had taken the terrible decision to pierce the dykes that isolated the region from the sea. The water carried everything away, villages, cattle, trees, country houses. Leyden and Delft, with their palaces, their exotic hot houses and their treasures were now no more than a marsh. In this way Amsterdam had been transformed into a marine fortress around which the Dutch fleet cruised. Whole provinces, many fortresses, the control of the seas, Holland and the Spanish Netherlands at his mercy – that was what Louis would have got if he had accepted the propositions of the Dutch deputies but it was not Louis who decided, but Louvois – and Louvois wanted more.

'Adversity is imputed only to one man,' Jan de Witt remarked bitterly. The Dutch, driven wild by suffering and humiliation, held him responsible for the inconceivable disaster. They began by taking it out on his brother Cornelius who was less highly placed. He was arrested for treason and corruption, stripped of his offices, tortured and condemned to banishment for life. Jan, who meanwhile had resigned, went to visit him in his cell. The furious crowd besieged the prison at The Hague and demanded both brothers. It broke down the gates and spread, shouting and screaming, through the staircases and corridors. Jan and Cornelius de Witt were bludgeoned, stabbed and hacked to pieces on the spot, their bloody corpses dragged to the scaffold and hanged by their feet. Those whom Spinoza called 'the last of the barbarians' seized the corpses, emasculated them and cut them into pieces. 'For two sous and a jug of beer I bought a finger from Jan de Witt's hand,' one witness was to recount.[16]

Europe had not yet recovered from the speed with which Holland had collapsed. But, suddenly, she began to stir again. The Elector of Brandenburg sent 25,000 men to the assistance of the Dutch. The governor of the Spanish Netherlands secretly supplied them with 12,000 soldiers. In England public opinion demanded that its king should take no further part in this iniquity. The emperor Leopold I himself, after taking communion, brandished a crucifix, took God as witness of the justice of his cause and sent 25,000 men to join up with the Dutch army which, being unable to fight in its own country – half of it being occupied, the other half flooded – went into Germany to try to cut off the communications of the French army.

Who, then, had been able to gather an army together in this ghost-like country? Who had pulled the strings of their passivity and found himself behind their manoeuvres? He was a short, puny young man of twenty-two, whose feeble body was constantly shaken by an asthmatic cough. Gloomy, quiet and austere, he did not gamble or drink and went to bed early. He hated society and avoided the company of women, preferring to be with a few friends, who, on occasion, were his favourites. His aquiline nose, his flashing eyes and his mouth, almost devoid of lips, betrayed an unparalleled intelligence and will power. This quiet, phlegmatic boy had been well educated and was extraordinarily gifted in languages for his period and his rank. For he was a prince, the head of the House of Orange and the grandson of William the Silent, whose Christian name he bore. Almost from birth, William had had a grudge against Louis XIV. He was ten years old when his cousin the king of France, taking advantage of the confusion among his guardians, occupied his city of Orange in Provence, demolished its fortifications and pocketed its revenues. He had heard the coarse laughter of the Court of France when it was known that the States General, on the evening of the invasion of Holland, had appointed this inexperienced boy as commander-in-chief of the Dutch troops.

He knew that Louis referred to him sarcastically as 'the little lord of Breda' and sensed all the contempt of the absolute king for the unimportant prince who did not even have the rank of sovereign – he was the hereditary *statholder,* that is to say, governor of Holland – and who had allowed this semblance of power to be taken from him during his minority. When, to limit the damage, he had sent his personal representative with the deputation from the States General to the royal camp to ask for peace, Louvois refused to receive him. William never forgave this insult.

What could he have done, with the French forces four times superior, the treason and corruption surrounding him and the States, whose contradictory instructions he was supposed to obey, hopelessly divided? What could he do against the obstacles erected by the instinctive mistrust of the republican Jan de Witt? But the Republic, of which Jan de Witt had been the moving spirit, had sunk into what looked like irrecoverable national catastrophe, so the office of Statholder was revived.

His position of power was now unchallenged, but he also had to face the collapse of his country alone. He was able to restore the unity of his country by making himself champion of a Protestantism that the French had themselves reinforced by bringing the abhorred Catholicism back with them. But he still had to find troops. It was then that Louis himself graciously sent an army to his cousin William. Instead of keeping the 25,000 Dutch prisoners of war, Louis, at Louvois' instigation, decided to hand them back for ransom: ten crowns per cavalry soldier, five per foot soldier. William paid and his soldiers returned, and he was soon in a position to take the offensive and attack Charleroi.[17]

The Maréchal de Luxembourg was ill with a very bad cold. His French troops were not in the best condition: they found it difficult to exercise on narrow dykes and were hungry, sick, exhausted. However, plans were carefully laid. The winter of 1672 arrived, turning their own weapon – water – against the Dutch themselves. The sea which acted as a protective cover for their country had turned into ice, making them once more vulnerable. The Maréchal de Luxembourg only had to put iron studs on his soldiers' boots for them to set out on the ice and to take the undefended capital. At the last moment, however, there was a sudden thaw, the ice gave in and the soldiers found themselves in the water, half frozen and paralysed by their heavy armour. Many drowned, while others were able to reach the dyke and return to their base at Utrecht, exhausted and demoralized. They had been promised that they would be able to loot The Hague.[18]

The army of occupation had been taking it easy. They requisitioned as much as they could in a country that had been bled by war, floods and winter. Whenever the mood took them, they entered private houses and, the occupants having been ordered to leave their doors unlocked at all times, helped themselves. They did not hesitate to raise ever more burdensome taxes. 'I have received the state of the contributions, the sum total has exceeded my expectations,' Louvois reassured an intendant, who apologized 'for all the cruelties that he had committed to extract so little money.' 'I beg you not to attenuate your harshness and to pursue these matters with all imaginable rigour,' Louvois concluded.[19]

The soldiers of the Maréchal de Luxembourg, deprived of their looting, were certainly in a mood to resort to 'harshness'. On their way they fell on Bodegrave and Savmmerdame, two small towns which, left without defence, opened their gates to them. And Bodegrave and Savmmerdame were to pay for The Hague ... with Luxembourg's permission. Seized by a sudden frenzy, the French soldiers dashed upon the inhabitants, spearing them, butchering them, torturing them, raping the women, then, after having looted or smashed everything, set fire to the two towns.[20] The French army had acquired a taste for this new sport. The Maréchal de Luxembourg had more refined excitements up his sleeve: 'I admit that I took pleasure in seeing with my own eyes the house of the prince of Orange and that of his favourite the Rhingrave, two of the prettiest castles imaginable, go up in flames.'[21] This was too bad for the Dutch! They didn't deserve any better: for they were not men, but, according to Louvois, beasts, who allow themselves to be led by people who think only of their own interests.[22] But the beasts had memories and forty years later, Voltaire, passing through Holland, was to see schoolchildren learning to read from books that recounted the French atrocities.

As the Dutch wept on that 17 February 1673, an audience of good Parisians was laughing its fill at one of the first performances of Molière's *Le Malade Imaginaire* at the theatre of the Palais Royal. The Court theatre had not wanted to take the play. For some time now, it had been Lulli and his musical and choreographic entertainments that had enjoyed the king's preference. Molière was not put out: he preferred his faithful Parisian public. Never had he been more confident in his acting than on that winter's afternoon, never had his virtuosity been more dazzling. And yet three hours before he had arrived at the theatre half dead. For some time his chest illness had been worsening at an alarming rate. The actors and his pretty wife, Armande Béjart who was appearing with him, all had been shocked by his appearance and begged him not to act that day. 'What can I do? There are fifty workers who have only their day's pay to live on. What will they do if we don't play? I would reproach myself for not giving them bread a single day, if it was within my power to do so.' Extremely weak, he dressed and made up his hollow eyes, his pinched nose and his pale cheeks. As he came on the stage, the miracle took place: the dying man became once more the incomparable actor. The final scene came to an end in roars of laughter. On stage, the imaginary invalid writhed in pain. Suddenly, the actor convulsed again and the public laughed still louder. Molière felt the blood rising into his mouth. He turned away for a moment. No one had seen. The applause brought the house down. He was dragged off the stage and taken home, coughing, choking, spitting blood into his handkerchief. He asked for a priest, and his valet ran to the nearby church of Saint-Eustache to fetch one. Two priests on duty refused:

'What! Extreme unction for that heretic! Never!' Those 'Tartuffes' had waited a long time to take their revenge on the man who had exposed them on the stage. After knocking on innumerable doors the valet found a good-hearted priest who was willing to come. It was too late: Molière died at ten in the evening.

'No religious burial: Molière died without the sacraments of the Church,' declared the parish priest of Saint-Eustache whose fault it was he had not. Molière's widow, Armande Béjart, threw herself at the king's feet. 'It's the concern of my lord Archbishop of Paris,' the king replied, but nevertheless he supported the request with a favourable recommendation. The archbishop allowed the ceremony, provided that it was carried out as discreetly as possible. The burial took place at night in the light of torches held by all the dead man's friends. A simple wooden coffin was followed by a thousand poor people in tears. 'What will have been the greatest achievement of my reign?' an elderly Louis was later to ask Boileau. 'There can be no doubt, Sire: Molière.' The astonished king said nothing at first, then, almost to himself, he murmured: 'Really, that buffoon? I wouldn't have believed it.' The king paused again, turned to Boileau and said: 'But you know more about these things than I, you are no doubt right.'

The queen of France was ill. She was staying at Tournai in a large house with the ladies of the Court. After several days, her 'vapours' had still not left her and physicians were sent for from Paris. They examined her, argued among themselves, raised their arms in despair and admitted defeat. Had they looked, they might have found the cause in the Tournai citadel. The Grande Mademoiselle had friends among the officers of the garrison who informed her that Mme de Montespan resided behind the fortress walls, well hidden from view. It was little use setting a fashion for full, flowing dresses, she could still not conceal the fact that she was pregnant once more, so she had to remain cloistered, in the company of the faithful and indispensable widow Scarron, who was soon to have had enough of that prisoner's life and curse 'the boring fortress'.[23] There could be no question of Montespan staying behind and giving birth in peace and quiet; the king needed her there. It was too bad if she was in the ninth month of pregnancy. Women were not allowed to be delicate when they were expecting a child; they should put up with the cold, the heat, the hunger, the thirst, bumpy rides in coaches and the dust raised by the horses of the escort, the harsh conditions of the temporary encampments. This was *Lex Ludovica* – Louis' law. The Grande Mademoiselle was immediately informed when, on 1 June 1673, up in the citadel, Mme de Montespan gave birth to a beautiful baby girl, just before the city of Maestricht surrendered.[24]

Louis had reserved the siege of the city for himself. He liked sieges more than anything – much more than battles, his soldiers often remarked. But he had shown a quite special affection for this siege and had found a new collaborator, Sebastien de Vauban, who understood that passion and shared it. A poor, forty-year-old member of the gentry, de Vauban had once fought in the armies of the *Fronde,* but had become a faithful servant of the monarchy. This incorruptible, sincere man had only one interest in his life: fortifications. There, before Maestricht, he would endlessly discuss trenches, parallel lines, open mines, covered ways, demilunes and horn-works with the king. However, despite their carefully drawn-up plans, the besieged forces defended themselves with great determination. Among the French victims was Captain d'Artagnan, Fouquet's former jailer. The Grande Mademoiselle was grieved: d'Artagnan was practically the only person who could talk to the king about liberating dear Lauzun, who was still under lock and key. The Grande Mademoiselle had lost a friend and the novel had gained a hero. D'Artagnan died before Maestricht, only to be reborn, two hundred years later, under the pen of Alexandre Dumas and was to know, thanks to *The Three Musketeers,* an immortality more assured than any number of years of good and loyal service to Louis XIV would have brought him.

Maestricht could no longer resist Louis XIV and fell. M de Vauban was desolate. The siege was over so quickly that he had not had time to dig enough mines and to display all the resources of his art. Seven thousand besieged against 30,000 besiegers and the incessant fire of fifty huge cannon did not allow a city to maintain a long siege. In the midst of the triumphant sounds of *Te Deums* there rose the sour notes of discontent. They were discreet murmurs, it is true. 'They are great victories,' wrote Bussy-Rabutin from his eternal exile, 'but in truth, they cost private citizens dearly.' 'For Paris, everyone has ruined himself,' the Comtesse de Scudéry replied, 'the entire Court is in the army ... One would rather die than find a thousand *pistoles* there ... The courtiers have found no money this year except as security against their campaigns.' And Bussy-Rabutin retorted: 'Since you find Paris as beggarly as you say, you can imagine how the provinces are for money, for here there is nothing to live on. I think that commodities will now be the only currency; wine will be bought with wheat and wheat with wine.'[25]

Maria Theresa was just as dissatisfied. The king paid her the greatest honours and took his meals publicly with her, but, despite his icy politeness, he still flaunted his mistresses. The king got into the marriage bed every night – often, unfortunately, at dawn. He made love to her less and less, and that was something for which she had acquired a very definite taste. To fill her empty days she had only her devotions and cards. To fill her empty apartments, she had only her dogs and her hideous dwarfs, like those that Velásquez had painted with her sister in *Las Meninas.* She loved her dwarfs, calling them 'my heart', 'my boy', 'my son', but it was not enough. The frustration and humiliation had embittered her. La Molina, her Spanish *femme de chambre,* 'the ugliest creature ever seen', prepared the chocolate with which she stuffed herself in secret and each evening made her prune juice laxative. Only La Molina knew how to concoct those oily Spanish dishes, that black soup that smelled of dishwater, made of cabbage, pepper and spices, which the Grande Mademoiselle found quite inedible. The embittered old servant was the seed of discord who stirred up wifely jealousy and turned her against her husband. He finally decided to get rid of La Molina. Maria Theresa danced with rage, screamed, tore out her hair, but there was nothing to be done, except to approach the king through his mistress. Montespan, delighted at the prospect of doing the queen a good turn, went to the king and asked him to allow La Molina to stay, and the king, of course, gave in. La Molina remained, complaining as always. A delighted Maria Theresa was duly grateful to her rival and Montespan gloated, an ironic smile on her lips.[26]

Mme Scarron was not happy either. She felt genuine love for the royal bastards who had been put in her care. They needed a balanced diet, regular hours and a lot of sleep. But their mother Mme de Montespan, capricious as ever and the proud possessor of an iron constitution, did not understand such solicitude and was constantly altering the programme laid down; she spoilt the little darlings, stuffed them with sweetmeats and kept them up late. The governess protested: 'My advice is listened to: sometimes she is grateful for it, sometimes she gets angry at it, she never follows it and she is always sorry in the end.' It was the eternal conflict between the preoccupied mother and the alien 'nanny'. The nanny could not go on. She did everything, worked herself to death and never got a word of thanks. On the other hand, she had to endure Montespan's moods, her bouts of anger and her persistent wheedling; she had to listen to her confidences, which she could well do without. On top of all that, the master did not like her and did not hide the fact. 'The king did not care for me,' she was to say much later, 'and for quite a long time he even had an aversion towards me. He feared me for my wit, imagining that I was a difficult person who cared only for sublime things.' Louis hated cultivated, sophisticated wits: they reminded him of his own ignorance, especially when they were women, whom he despised. Louis also distrusted the widow Scarron because he felt that she disapproved of his conduct in matters of love. One day, despite her prudence and discretion, she was bold enough to say what she thought. Sitting beside the master at one of his military reviews, she remarked: 'What would you do, Sire, if you were told that one of those young men was living openly with another's wife as if she were his own?' That a preacher should speak in this way from the pulpit was bad enough, it was after all his job, but it was hard to take from a nursemaid ...[27]

'For two days now the rumour of my retirement has become so widespread that all my friends and acquaintances have talked to me about it and commiserated with me; I don't know why people are talking about it, for I have done nothing that could have been remarked upon.' In a Court in which everything was known at once, naïve Louise de La Vallière imagined that she could keep the secret of her irrevocable decision to enter a convent. She had never ceased thinking about it from the day she had sought refuge with the sisters of St Mary and the king had ordered her to come back. This time she had chosen the strictest order, the Carmelites. With La Vallière in a convent, the lovers would no longer have a screen, even if it had become an increasingly fictitious one. Fiction or not, there had to be a screen: the favourite had still not managed to get a separation from her husband and the children that she had had by the king could legally be claimed by M de Montespan. No, La Vallière would not join the Carmelites, or at least not yet. Bossuet, who took charge of Louise's soul, was forced to observe that things were not always so easy and advised delay.

These excuses and temporizings took their toll on the nerves of the unfortunate woman and Louis decided to take decisive steps through the zealous Bossuet. The most powerful preacher in France, the scourge of sin, the mouthpiece of God, went to persuade the king's present mistress to allow his former mistress to enter a convent. The response was even more extravagant. Mme de Montespan sent Mme Scarron to reason with La Vallière. Were not the Carmelites rather too severe for a woman used to the comforts of palace life? Would it not be better to wait, to find a compromise solution? 'That would not be a penance,' Louise interrupted. 'Such a life would be too pleasant. That is not what I am looking for.' 'But think about it,' Mme Scarron insisted, 'There you are, gleaming with gold, and in two days you'll be covered with sackcloth!'[28]

One winter morning in 1673 the parish priest of Saint-Germain saw three persons enter his church to have a baby baptized. The godfather was a three-year-old boy; the godmother a beautiful, very grand lady with a slight limp. After the ceremony the priest opened the parish register. 'On the eighteenth day of December Louise Françoise, born on the first day of June of the previous year, was baptized ... The godfather, Louis Auguste ...; the godmother, the lady Louise Francoise de La Baume au Blanc, Duchesse de La Vallière.' There was nothing else in the register – no father, mother, nor godfather's surname. On the other hand, the surname of the godmother shone like a beacon in all this obscurity. Louise must have been forced to act as godmother, because Louis and Montespan wanted to settle their affairs before allowing her to enter a convent. First they realized that they had forgotten to baptize their latest born – whose birth in the citadel of Tournai had given Maria Theresa the vapours. They had asked Louise to be the godmother, for the unknown father was the king of France, the unknown mother, the Marquise de Montespan and the godfather with no surname, was their son, the future Duc du Maine. So the former favourite held her rival's bastard over the baptismal font ... She might even have been the child's mother, for Montespan had thought at one point of having her bastards declared legal by making La Vallière adopt them, but the gentle Louise had turned down any such suggestion.[29]

Once Athénaïs' separation was legitimized, Louise's presence was no longer indispensable to the lovers, but she had still not solved her own problems. She had to arrange her financial situation, pay her debts, make provision for her mother and children, leave pensions for her sisters, reward her servants, settle everything in fact before leaving the outside world. At last, after months and months of postponements and pressure, the great moment arrived. 'We have wept a great deal,' Monsieur whispered to his cousin, the Grande Mademoiselle, who was observing the king's red eyes during mass. La Vallière went to take her leave of him forever. He burst into tears. She simply curtseyed and walked off. She was also determined to ask Maria Theresa for her forgiveness for having offended her for so long and so publicly. Exercise a little discretion, the Maréchal de La Motte advised her. 'Since my crimes have been public, so too should be the penance.' So Louise went and threw herself at Maria Theresa's feet. The good queen raised her up, pressed her to her bosom, and assured her of her complete forgiveness. Montespan, however, became more and more irritated by these moving scenes. La Vallière had occupied the centre of the stage for some days now and what a performance she had been putting on. To break the spell, Athénaïs demanded that Louise dine with her during her last evening at Court.

Next day, Louise put on her most beautiful dress, as befitted a duchess. Perhaps it was in the dress with flared sleeves, white and pink silk embroidered with gold, set off with rubies, which she wears in the portrait that she had had made as a souvenir for her children. She attended mass with the Court in the Chapel at Versailles, then, followed by her family, she mounted her coach, as the king smothered his sobs in a large handkerchief. When she had passed the castle gates, people appeared on either side of the road. In Paris, in the Faubourg Saint-Jacques, everyone appeared at the windows. Many women were crying. The coach stopped in front of the Carmelite convent. Louise got out, kissed her children goodbye, then, without turning round, crossed the threshold. The heavy gates shut behind her forever.[30]

'She's not the first sinner to be converted,' concluded the Grande Mademoiselle, by way of lightening the gloom. For in the coach which the very next day took the ladies to Franche-Comté, the talk was only of La Vallière. Never had Louise been so present in the carriage as when her place was empty. In her corner, La Montespan remained silent, absorbed in her own thoughts. And then the conversation turned elsewhere, and La Vallière was forgotten. 'We were soon consoled,' noted the Grande Mademoiselle, who had never really liked her.[31]

'At the moment, Sire,' wrote Colbert, 'that we were anxiously awaiting the outcome of the attack on the citadel of Besançon, we received the happy and most welcome news that it was taken. Caesar took the city and boasted of it in his works. The power of the entire House of Austria has been applied for seven years to making it impregnable and Your Majesty takes this citadel in twenty-four hours. We must fall silent, Sire, in admiration, thanking God every day for bringing us to birth under the reign of such a king as Your Majesty.' Colbert never wasted an opportunity of flattering his master.[32]

At the camp of Chavan the Grande Mademoiselle was at her window when she saw a musketeer running past, shouting: 'Dol is capitulating.' Louis had conquered Franche-Comté. It was about time. Not so long ago he had been faced by nothing but defenceless Dutchmen; this time he was faced by a European coalition of powers alarmed by his ambitions. Since then, his armies had partly re-established the situation, but it had been a close thing.

Delighted by the fall of Dol, he took the ladies out to see his new possession. He gave them a lesson in strategy *in situ*, explaining the siege to them in great detail. However fascinating his account may have been, the Grande Mademoiselle was horrified by what she saw around her: officers and soldiers covered with bloody bandages, dragging themselves along, crying out in pain, the walls bespattered with blood, mines still smoking and others lying about that had still not gone off. War certainly had a price and the Grande Mademoiselle was not the only one to realize it. Not one of the noble families was without a death to mourn. The generals complained that recruits came in fewer and fewer numbers and ever diminishing quality, while the people cried that the taxes continued to rise.[33]

CHAPTER 12

The Mistress and the Governess

At the age of thirty-four, Cauzé de Nazelles, an officer from the gentry, found himself back at school. Maimed for life by his war wounds, no longer of any use in the army, he decided to learn Latin with a view to entering the Church, and joined the classes given by Affinius Van der Enden, a Fleming reputed to be the best Latin teacher in Paris. As well as Latin, the old scholar, who had known Spinoza, taught philosophy, poetry, medicine, surgery, civil law, canon law, Hebrew and Greek. To make it easier to attend his classes, Cauzé de Nazelles took a room at his teacher's house where several other students were lodgers. One spring night, unable to sleep, he was at his window when he noticed a young man quietly entering a secret door in the garden and walk without a sound towards the house, where Van der Enden welcomed him with open arms. What perplexed Cauzé de Nazelles most was that he recognized the visitor. He was an officer like himself, named Gilles de La Treaumont. He was only about twenty years old, but he had already earned himself a bad reputation: deep in debt, capable of anything 'dishonourable,' 'a dangerous spirit'. What was the dubious La Treaumont doing at the house of the wise old Van der Enden? Intrigued, Cauzé de Nazelles set up a discreet surveillance of the nocturnal comings and goings, which became frequent. One night, La Treaumont brought with him another individual whom Cauzé de Nazelles recognized at once by his justly renowned appearance and good looks: the Chevalier de Rohan. What could a member of one of the greatest families of France, a childhood friend of the king, a former Master of the Royal Hunt, be doing with a bad lot like La Treaumont?

Cauzé de Nazelles decided to find out more. For some time now he had been showing a mild interest in Marianne Van der Enden, the daughter of the house, so it was an easy matter to persuade her to let him hide in the room where these gentlemen met nightly. Rohan, La Treaumont and Van der Enden argued excitedly. The moment had come, the country could take no more, this war was costing too much. Brittany, Guyenne and above all Normandy were disaffected. The city of Rouen had just been taxed with a new exceptional contribution and the Normans, crushed by taxes, were on the verge of rebellion. Everything was ready. The Count of Monterey, governor of the

Spanish Netherlands, had promised his aid, and Holland was waiting for the right moment to go into action. The five hundred guards' uniforms were almost ready, their friends had been warned and were only awaiting a signal. As for weapons, they would be distributed when required. All that remained was to discover what day the Dauphin would go wolf hunting in the Normandy woods. Ten disguised guards would be enough to seize him – he would be alone with his groom – and take him to the coast, where barges would be waiting to transfer him to a Dutch boat, left cruising off the Normandy coast. With ten other guards they would take Honfleur. And from there . . .

The gentlemen were leaving when Cauzé de Nazelles returned to his room, trembling, unable to believe his ears. He would not hesitate for a moment to denounce that good-for-nothing La Treaumont, but how could he denounce Van der Enden for whom he had nothing but esteem and gratitude, or a great lord like Rohan? Who would believe him?

On 4 July 1674 festivities began in the Château de Versailles to celebrate the king's conquest of Franche-Comté. The Court assembled in a grove which had been decorated by Mme de Montespan for a banquet. There were festoons of flowers and orange-trees; pyramids of fruit rose from the grassy paths. Then Lulli's opera *Alceste* was given in the castle courtyard.

Supper was served at midnight in the marble courtyard around a column bearing six hundred candles. Then the Court rushed out to the terrace to admire the fireworks display over the Grand Canal. Le Brun had erected, to the glory of the king, a huge obelisk surrounded by images of the famous and surmounted by a sun that caught light and disappeared in multicoloured sparks into the starry sky.[1]

From the dungeon of his castle at Mannheim, the Elector Palatine was attending another fireworks display: the two cities and twenty-five villages that Turenne's army had just set alight. The Elector Palatine was frantic with anger and horror; he was not even at war with France! Turenne had crossed his territory to fight the troops of the emperor. Yes, retorted Turenne, but peasants in the Palatinate had killed several stragglers belonging to the French army and cut up their corpses into small pieces, so how could he prevent the soldiers avenging their comrades? Turenne had already seized Alsace and Lorraine, which, in order to prevent the enemy from finding food there, he had ravaged to such an extent that the French intendant had begged him to moderate his actions. 'I shall do so when ordered to do so,' he replied. And it was on 'orders' that he set fire to the rich, peaceful Palatinate. In his powerlessness, the Elector Palatine found the only response worthy of a gentleman: He challenged Turenne to a duel. Turenne replied: 'I am not free to accept it' – Louis had forbidden it – 'being unable to dispose freely of my person, but I shall appear at the head of the army that I command against the army that His Highness will care to send against me.'[2] But as His Highness was at peace, he had no army to fight.

★

'Why have you taken so long to inform me? Everything you have told me is of the greatest importance; you should have realized this and warned me immediately.' Louvois stared angrily at Cauzé de Nazelles after listening to him attentively, without interrupting him. The thirty-four-year-old student, involved in spite of himself in a plot against the security of State, had at last made up his mind to tell everything he had heard at his master's house and had chosen one evening when Louvois was in Paris. He had gone to ask for an audience, 'for an affair of great importance to the king and of the utmost urgency' and had been received at once.

Meanwhile at Versailles, the final entertainment of the series was, of course, the most fantastic. The king and the Court embarked on the Grand Canal. A doll's fleet awaited them, gondolas with their gondoliers, graciously sent by the Republic of Venice, gilded ships with silk riggings, supporting multicoloured brocade tents. Pyramids of water and light bordered the banks. At the end of the canal, the designers had created the illusion of a huge palace, all light and colour. The silence of the night was interrupted only by music coming from the barge following the royal barge. The sound of the violins seemed to animate the transparent giants which, in the distance, represented the gods of Olympus. Gold-embroidered standards and flags on the ships' masts fluttered gently in the night breeze. The oars dug silver furrows in the water, where the glittering decorations were reflected, and slowly the gilded gondolas glided through a dream world.[3]

Meanwhile, La Treaumont was not particularly surprised when the Sieur de Brissac, captain of the guards, came into his room – they had long been friends. It was only when he saw the guards behind Brissac that he understood that he was being arrested. He asked permission to take some clean linen with him; his old friend agreed. Le Treaumont fumbled in a drawer, then turned round, a pistol in each hand. He pointed the gun at Brissac, fired and killed one of the guards. Brissac looked him straight in the eye and cried: 'Shoot! Shoot!' The guards, mistaking this for an order, fired off their weapons at La Treaumont. Bleeding from ten wounds, he whispered dying: 'I have nothing to tell you and I have not said that I was a criminal, but neither fear, which has never taken me by surprise, nor your threats will ever get anything out of me . . .' The Chevalier de Rohan had already been arrested by Brissac, on 11 September 1674 as he was leaving mass at the Château de Versailles, and he had been taken to the Bastille.

But where was Van der Enden hiding? When the authorities arrived to pick him up at his home, they drew a blank. Louvois ordered Cauzé de Nazelles himself to trail Mme Van der Enden. He followed her through the streets of Paris to the Quai des Grands Augustins, where she hired a cab. Fortunately, Cauzé de Nazelles was able to find another one. At the gates of Paris, he just had time to take three guards from the checkpoint on with him. Mme Van der Enden led them to Le Bourget where she stopped in front of a modest inn. Cauzé de Nazelles followed her up the stairs to the top floor and burst into the room where she had entered a few minutes before. She was alone with Van der Enden, disguised as a poor old man, dressed in rags, with long hair and beard. Seeing the guards around Cauzé de Nazelles he thought they had arrested de Nazelles as his accomplice and swore that he was innocent, which made Cauzé de Nazelles' position even more embarrassing.

Rohan and his accomplices had wanted to found an invincible popular State that would flourish and progress through the unified efforts of all towards general prosperity and liberty. All official posts would be suspended until 'the people and nobility had elected leaders who would govern them according to the laws drawn up by them, the people and nobility, and which they could alter as they thought fit'.[4] According to plans found by the police the unfortunate conspirators wanted to establish a democratic republic in France. No more monarchy, no more Louis XIV, but the nobles reserved to themselves the right to elect the officers of the army from among their number. As for the soldiers, far from waging war, they would concern themselves 'with poor widows and orphans, families in need, public health ... tasks useful in a Republic.' Lastly 'no distinction would be made between Catholics and Protestants'. Religious liberty? That would not please the Jesuits, who dominated the king.[5]

The Chevalier de Rohan was sure that he would escape death. Even if he had wanted to overthrow the régime, unleash civil war and call on the enemy to help him they would not execute a Rohan. That is certainly what Mme de Montespan thought – she had once known him and had even had a light-hearted flirtation with him. But she dared not say anything to the king. Louis himself was very tempted to grant such a pardon. But Louvois intervened: 'You must make an example of him.' And Louis gave in.

'If you had shown less strength of mind, or more fear of death,' his mistress wrote to the Chevalier de Rohan, 'I would take great care to prepare you gradually for it and to teach you how little hope you should have in life, but since you never feared anything I do not think that you will be afraid of losing a life for which you have so often shown contempt ...'

She was wrong, however, for Rohan did not want to die. Father Bourdaloue, the famous preacher, tried six days in succession to exhort the condemned man to resign himself to death, but in vain. Theology having failed, he went and asked Captain Megalotti of the Bastille guard for inspiration. He spoke a language that the condemned man knew: 'Monsieur le Chevalier, should a man of your profession be afraid of death? Lord! Imagine that you are at the head of a trench with cannon balls exploding all around you. Imagine that you are mounting an attack.' And the Chevalier de Rohan allowed his head to be cut off with his accomplices on 27 November 1674. Van der Enden, after being subjected to torture, was hanged.

★

Since Montespan's bastards had been legitimized, 'Nanny Scarron' had been officially installed with them in the royal palaces, and her troubles grew accordingly. Previously hidden in a discreet retreat, she had only seen the children's mother and father occasionally. Now she had them continually on her back. For his part, Louis would have preferred spending quiet evenings alone with his mistress, but Athénaïs thought only of amusing herself and playing cards. Louis bored her to death. She was not at all dazzled by her situation, even if she took advantage of it. In this all-powerful king whom she had wanted to dominate by her wit and who had forced her to dominate him by the senses, she saw only a dull, timid, inhibited man. So rather than remain alone with him listening to him and yawning, she brought along the widow Scarron as company. This, however, did not prevent her from proving capricious, domineering and generally unpleasant towards her lover. When subjected to such treatment, Louis looked foolish and at a loss. So, when he had had enough, who could he confide in? The only person to whom he dared say what he had to say, the only witness of the treatment that Athénaïs subjected him to, was the widow Scarron, the clever woman whom he had so mistrusted. He was grateful to her, but it irritated him that she was always there when he was with his mistress. Suspicious as he was, he even went so far as to be jealous of her for the friendship, the complicity, that bound her to Athénaïs. What did they say to one another when he left his mistress's room and the two women stayed behind, chatting often late into the night? What did they say about him? At last, he asked his mistress as a favour not to talk to the widow Scarron in the evening any more. Athénaïs promised. The widow Scarron guessed the origin of her friend's sudden silence: 'I understand, you have been asked not to speak to me. I should turn this sacrifice to the benefit of my sleep.'

This docility did not prevent Athénaïs from upbraiding her more and more frequently about the children. As a mother she was furious when they turned out to be more fond of their governess than of her. She accused Mme Scarron of trying to steal them from her, especially young Louis-Auguste, the Duc du Maine, his father's favourite. The widow Scarron adored this precocious, lively child. She resented the fact that Montespan could be so unmotherly towards him and she did not hesitate to give him all the tenderness he lacked. She set about educating him, which his father noticed and gave her all credit for it. This further enraged Mme de Montespan and she tried to discredit Mme Scarron to the king. One day, Louis arrived in the middle of a particularly violent argument and innocently asked what was happening: 'If Your Majesty would be so kind as to go next door I shall have the honour of telling him.' His Majesty went next door and the widow Scarron, leaving Montespan behind, unburdened herself to him. She recounted everything: Athénaïs's harshness, unfairness, cruelty, vulgarity. The king, of course, was only too well aware of this, having been at the receiving end of it often enough. However, he felt obliged to defend his mistress:

'Haven't you ever noticed how her beautiful eyes fill with tears when she is told of some generous or touching act?'

Beautiful eyes or not, 'Nanny' Scarron had had enough. Despite her love for the children, she was waiting for the first opportunity to leave. But, before doing so, she wanted to find a small place of her own, a country house to retire to. She found exactly what she was looking for, the Château de Maintenon, which was for sale, and Montespan, unpredictable as ever, promised to extract the money out of the king to pay for it. The widow Scarron rubbed her hands with glee. She would have a place of her own. The only trouble was, the castle was in a delapidated state and the gardens wild. Where would she find the money to restore it all? 'Leave it to me,' Montespan interrupted, cooperative for once. She attacked while her lover was attending her toilette. He turned a deaf ear; she insisted; he refused. Was he being asked to fork out money again for the 'fine wit' whom he so mistrusted, for that woman whose intimacy with his mistress irritated him so much? Having started, however, Montespan was not going to give up. Tempers flared. The only witness of the scene, the Maréchal de Lorges, then captain of the guards, did not know where to put himself. Louis exploded: 'I have already done too much for that creature. I cannot understand this whim of yours concerning her, nor your stubbornness in keeping her when I have asked you so many times to get rid of her. I admit that I myself find her unbearable, so, providing I am promised that I shall never see her again or speak to her again, I shall give still more, though, in truth, I have already given too much to a creature of that kind.'[6] For once, Montespan kept her mouth shut. Thus the governess became lady of a castle even if it was delapidated; indeed, she took on its name. The widow Scarron disappeared and re-emerged as Madame de Maintenon.[7]

After the demands of the governess, the king now had to listen to the complaints of the generals. Turenne had had to dash off in the middle of winter to stop the armies of the emperor that had crossed the Rhine and were threatening Alsace. He had managed to repulse them, but this was with no thanks to 'the Court'. He had been forced to submit his campaign plans in advance and they were sent back to him completely altered. 'I was ordered to cover both the upper and the lower Rhine. The king wanted to decide everything, command everything from a distance, without attending the campaign. This, again, was the fault of Louvois, who had put the idea into Louis' head so that he might himself become commander-in-chief and issue orders in the king's name. Individuals who deserve the title of valet rather than captain are promoted, without consulting us, of course. The king cleverly decided to take all the glory for the victories and to leave to the generals the shame of the defeats.' The man behind all of this was, of course, Louvois. Turenne, at his wits' end, demanded that his reports should no longer pass through the censorship of the minister and that the king should reply to them in person. The king gave in. Turenne, much relieved, began to write directly to the king, but Louvois read his letters and dictated to the master the answers that he was supposed to be ignorant of.[8] Thus everyone was happy.

Lent came round once more, triggering off a powerful offensive from the clergy. Things were not going well for the French armies in the first months of 1675, they had suffered notable reverses. Had these reverses anything to do with the fact that His Majesty was living in sin? The finest orators of the century repeated to him endlessly that to avoid God's punishment, it would be better if His Majesty put an end to the scandal of his liaison with Montespan. Bossuet had already succeeded in getting La Vallière into a convent. He now felt it was the right moment to despatch Montespan as well. The clergy were in their element. God's punishment and eternal damnation were phrases that had haunted Louis from childhood. He could not resist women, he told himself, and he was sincere, but that did not mean that he was self-satisfied, so he listened to these sirens of holy water. And it was with redoubled piety and assiduity that he followed the Lenten services, in the company of . . . Mme de Montespan. She, too, was sincerely pious.

Bossuet decided to strike while the iron was hot. One evening, he discreetly threw a grey cloak over his head in order not to be recognized, went to the favourite and delivered a sermon at her. But he had met his match. He dared to talk of pride, she rounded on him, when it was he, Bossuet, who was eaten up with pride. She accused him of wanting to get rid of her because he wanted to dominate the king. She suggested striking a bargain. How much did he want? An archbishopric, a cardinal's hat, a minister's portfolio? Bossuet stood firm, but it did not help his cause.

Montespan's anger did not subside. It was obvious they were trying to get rid of her. Someone else gave secret approval to this fine plan, who was supporting the priests behind the scenes; who talked endlessly of God, who, even without saying anything, stood as a reproach between Athénaïs and the king. It was, of course, that church mouse Maintenon. And, for the first time, the king seemed to find her presence less disagreeable . . . The king spoke to her more and more often . . . The king listened to her talk about religion. La Montespan thought it was time all that stopped. 'Sire, if you love me, look ill upon the governess.' Meekly, Louis tried to treat Mme de Maintenon coldly, but, since he felt rather guilty about it, he still invited her that evening to dinner and gave her a few friendly signs.

Louis was very irritated. He did not know how to establish harmony between the two women. One of them made scenes as soon as he so much as smiled at the other and the other, who was so good with the children, threatened to leave at every end and turn. Louis explained the situation to Louvois and asked him to find a solution. Delighted at being thought indispensable, the minister talked at length to La Maintenon, or rather he listened to her as she poured forth a torrent of recriminations. He agreed with her points: yes, she had been abominably treated; yes, La Montespan was a monster, but could she not be a little more patient?

The king was so pleased with what she had done for the children. Louvois' solution was to arrange for the two women to have a 'frank and loyal' exchange of views at which Montespan was all sugar and honey. She promised to behave better and to be kind to Maintenon. But Maintenon knew how much she could depend on her friend's constancy. She would leave, she had made up her mind, and no honeyed promises would make her go back on her decision, but she could not abandon her little darling, the Duc du Maine, at present. He had a large boil on his backside, and was running a temperature, so she would stay until he was better. But then she swore she would leave, before the end of the year.[9]

On Maundy Thursday, 10 April 1675, the Abbé Lecuyer, vicar of the parish of Versailles, had his work cut out to hear the confessions of the crowd wanting to perform their Easter duties. Suddenly his heart missed a beat. Through the wooden grille he recognized the woman kneeling in front of him, asking for absolution. 'Is that the Mme de Montespan who scandalized the whole of France?' he admonished her. 'Come, come, Madame, cease your scandals and then you may come and throw yourself at the feet of Jesus Christ's ministers.' Mme de Montespan was furious. 'A confessor is obliged to receive any penitent. He has no right to refuse absolution,' she screamed at the king, demanding that the vicar be punished. 'Let us ask Bossuet's opinion,' the king suggested. And Bossuet, delighted at the opportunity, enthusiastically approved the vicar's decision.[10]

'Care should be taken in the execution of the edicts, since the greed of those who carry them out leads to acts of violence and injustices that may in turn be a cause of violence,' wrote the Duc de Chaulnes, governor of Brittany, to Colbert. He was on leave in Paris, but he was disturbed. He knew that the new taxes decreed by Colbert to pay for the war – the establishment of stamped paper, a tobacco monopoly, a government stamp on tin ware – were straws that would break the camel's back as far as the Bretons were concerned. He did not know that at Rennes, at the very moment he was writing, two thousand of those good Bretons were already laying waste to the city. The governor of Rennes was also away. So it was his son, the young Coetlogon, who was left with the task of re-establishing order. He did not have a single soldier to hand as Rennes had the privilege of being exempt from a garrison. He needed an order from the governor to summon the local militia. What then, should he do? Coetlogon called the nobility to arms and they responded to a man. At the head of the gentlemen, sword in hand, he charged the demonstrators who fell back and dispersed. The death toll rose to thirty.

The Duc de Chaulnes decided to return home. Scarcely had he entered a pacified Rennes than he was told of disturbances at Nantes. Mme Veillonne, a confectioner's wife, and Mme Lejeune, a joiner's wife, were leading a huge procession of demonstrators. Mme Veillonne was captured and imprisoned, while the Bishop of Nantes, Monseigneur de La Baume, went to harangue the demonstrators. They threw themselves on him, led him off, shut him up in the chapel of Saint-Yves and sent a messenger to the governor of Nantes, M de Molac, that they would hang the bishop if Molac had Mme Veillonne hanged. Molac handed over the lady, the demonstrators handed back the prelate and everything settled down. Molac congratulated himself on having avoided bloodshed. 'It is in blood that riot should be drowned,' Louvois replied in the name of Louis XIV, outraged at Molac's weakness. Molac was sacked at once. The Duc de Chaulnes could breathe at last as calm returned to Brittany.[11]

The Court was astounded when the news broke that La Montespan had left. The priests had turned out to be strongest, for Louis had sworn never to see her again. Athénaïs had thought it prudent to make the first move and, with a heavy heart, set herself up in Paris: 'The poor child tells me that her mistress has been throwing indescribable fits of rage. She has seen no one for two days. She writes from morning to night and when she goes to bed tears it all up. Her state makes me pity her. No one feels sorry for her, although she has done good to many people.' Despite the edifying end of the paragraph, Mme de Maintenon's jubilation is clear enough. With what delight she read the reports from the servant-girl appointed by her to spy on her friend. 'Her state makes me pity her,' she repeated to the king, to whom the separation came as a terrible blow and who had no one else to talk to about the absent woman other than the 'friend', the 'fine wit', sometimes repulsed, sometimes sought after, the gentle woman who knew how to listen, understand and console. And La Maintenon made splendid use of her advantage, expressing pity for the absent woman while confirming the king in his heroic decision. 'I saw the king yesterday, do not fear: it seems to me that I spoke to him as a Christian and as a true friend of Mme de Montespan.' Athénaïs was not wrong to mistrust her 'true friend'.

When Louis XIV was preparing to go to war, Mme de Maintenon was anxious. 'We shall see whether the king leaves for Flanders without saying goodbye,' she remarked. For Louis was dying to see his mistress again before leaving. Just once more, he begged. Out of the question replied Bossuet, 'nothing is more contrary to the laws of the Church'. Laws of the Church or not, Louis could contain himself no longer and, before leaving, made a discreet stop-off at Clagny, the estate quite near to Versailles that he had given to Athénaïs for her retirement. No one will know, he told himself, especially not the priests. 'Father, you should be pleased with me, Mme de Montespan is at Clagny,' he said hypocritically to Father Bourdaloue. 'Yes, Sire, but God would be better pleased if Clagny were forty leagues from Versailles!' Priests had eyes and ears everywhere.[12]

★

179

'Fat pig,' yelled the huge, angry, hate-filled mob at the Duc de Chaulnes, governor of Brittany, who, from the steps of his house, tried to speak to them on 9 June 1675. 'Kill him, kill him,' yelled the crowd and two hundred rifles were aimed at the duke, who did not bat an eyelid. The crowd were protesting because he had brought a hundred and fifty soldiers into Rennes in case they were needed to maintain order. 'Give the order to fire on the demonstrators,' begged the gentlemen who surrounded Chaulnes. 'Drown the riot in blood,' ordered Louvois from Paris. 'Let us talk,' the duke replied. He promised to have the provocative soldiers removed from the city and, as if by magic, the storm subsided. 'Popular emotions have been appeased by the prudence and firm conduct of M le Duc de Chaulnes,' Coetlogon reported to Louvois, who was rather disappointed at not having a few corpses among the demonstrators.

It was then that Sébastien Le Balp thought that the moment of his revenge had come. A former notary who had once been deprived of his office and imprisoned for embezzlement, he now found himself general-in-chief of an enormous troop of Breton peasants, whom he led to the support of the rioters at Châteaulin. He at last had the fight that he had dreamt about so much. He threw himself into the mêlée enthusiastic-ally. The same day, a group of peasants sacked the Château de la Boüexière and set fire to it. With this first castle in flames, the looters moved in. There were soon twenty thousand armed peasants who, led by Balp, sacked the castles of Lower Brittany. It was no longer taxes that they were attacking, but the nobility. The lucid Duc de Chaulnes himself agreed that they had a case. 'It is certain that the nobility has treated the peasants very badly; they are now taking their revenge . . .'

Having taken control, their first act of revenge was a thorough revision of the law: abolition of seignorial rights ('as a violation of Armorican liberty'), abolition of ecclesiastical taxes, abolition of stamped paper (which 'will be held in execration by them and their descendants'), abolition of the salt tax ('you are enjoined to fire upon it as upon a mad dog'). Furthermore, the upper crust would no longer have a monopoly of justice, which 'will be carried out by capable persons chosen by the noble inhabitants'. Further, 'Money deriving from ancient forage will be used to buy tobacco, which will be distributed with the blessed bread at parish masses for the satisfaction of the parishioners.' Lastly, to mark the abolition of class barriers, 'there will be marriages' between the peasants, now referred to as 'the noble inhabitants', and the gentry. The brave Bretons, loyal subjects of the Sun King, showed themselves to be bolder than the revolutionaries of 1789.

'You will judge of their brutality,' complained the Duc de Chaulnes, 'by the fact that the word revolt is not regarded as a criminal term in their language.' Thus legalized, revolt spread. Castles and tax offices continued to be burnt down, nobles and tax collectors killed, together with members of the clergy, for the rich abbeys were also looted. The lower clergy, which had made common cause with the rebels, also found an opportunity of revenging itself on its superiors. The small towns were soon attacked. Two thousand peasants attacked Pontivy at midday and killed fifteen people. Certain aristocrats resisted, like the Duchesse de Rohan threatened in her Château de Josselin, firing on the demonstrators. Others, like the Marquise de Trévigny, gave in; before a notary, she signed a document drawn up in advance, denouncing her seignorial rights. It is worth remembering that Sébastien Le Balp was the leader of the rebellion, was also a notary. But the actions of the rebels also imply forethought – the continuation of a traditional hostility to the central power whose roots are buried in history.

The Duc de Chaulnes did not have enough troops to recapture an entire province. Even Rennes, to which he was confined, was not safe. Anything could happen to turn an everyday incident into a massacre. The friends of the Duchesse de Chaulnes trembled for her, knowing that she was practically a prisoner in the city. She courageously refused to change her daily routine. One day, in her coach, she passed through the area of the Rue Haute. Emerging from nowhere, a crowd surrounded the coach and stopped it. 'We have come, Madame la Duchesse, to ask you for a favour; we've come to ask you if you would be so kind as to give a name to a child that is to be baptized.' 'I would be most happy to, my good people,' the duchess replied. 'There, you ugly old hunchback, there's the child we'd like you to name.' And the stinking carcass of a cat landed on the duchess's knees.

All this discord was sweet music to a Europe now united against Louis XIV. French spies working in Germany reported 'great hopes on the rebellions in France' and a Dutch fleet was cruising along the Breton coasts, just in case.[13] Louis, irritated by the agitation, decided to put himself at the head of the reinforcements that were setting out for Brittany. He had just come back from the front. Before setting out for the West, he went and had lunch at Clagny, alone with his mistress, having decided this was really not the moment to listen to priests. But, as they say, there is no peace for the wicked. During the meal, a messenger brought urgent news, which Louis read and went white: in Germany, Turenne had been killed at the battle of Saalsbach.

Grave and pale the king returned to Versailles and entered the drawing-room where the Court were waiting to attend his dinner: 'We have lost the father of the nation,' he announced. Consternation was everywhere, and the whole of France went into mourning.[14] The hero was buried at the camp at Saalsbach. Drums draped in black crêpe beat slowly, soldiers formed a guard of honour. Many wept. But it was from the enemy camp that the finest homage was paid to Turenne. At the announcement of his death, cries of joy mingled with the joyful sound of trumpets and cymbals, and the commander-in-chief of the imperial troops, old Montecuculli, could not conceal his delight.[15]

If Turenne was dead, the priests declared, it was because God had punished the king for seeing his mistress again. It was God's punishment if the Maréchal de Créqui, through his own fault, saw his army torn to pieces at Consarbruch and if Captain Bois Jourdan treacherously handed over the town of Trier to the enemy. It was God's punishment if the city of Bordeaux, where 'the spirit of sedition and rebellion' reigned, had risen up against the new taxes, if in Poitou 'the spirits of the people were overheated', if the population of Boulogne was on the verge of rebellion, if disorders were breaking out at Saint-Jean-de-Luz, if shots were being fired at Pau.[16] It was God's punishment if Sébastien Le Balp continued to rampage with impunity throughout Brittany at the head of his army. Louis had to give up going there to re-establish order himself as he was needed urgently, to replace Turenne and contain the foreign enemy's advance. There only remained old Condé, crippled with gout, and even he was sceptical about his chances in Brittany.[17] What would God do when he saw that La Montespan had returned to her apartment at Versailles? Was she not one of the queen's ladies of honour and should she not live under the same roof as her mistress in order to carry out her duties? Nevertheless, the bigots frowned. 'We have done enough to annoy the priests – and everyone else,' Mme de Sévigné remarked.[18]

Dig in and hold firm was the tactic adopted by Mme de Maintenon. La Montespan, back in her old position, was operating a prudent retreat, owing to the precarious health of the darling Duc du Maine. It was decided that the best thing for him would be to take the waters at Barèges in the Pyrenees. Mme de Maintenon left the Court with her beloved ward. With the field temporarily clear, Montespan launched an attack to regain lost ground. First, she threw in all her charm against her lover: 'For this she used the means that had always served her best. She tried to enliven the king, thinking up endless occasions for his entertainment.' Then she launched her attack on Maintenon. Wrapping up her treachery in humour, she discharged all her poison against the absent woman. But she had to admit that her weapons were rusty: the king 'no longer responded to her propositions and urgings with the same pleasure or the same ardour that he once had done'. So Montespan, who had never been able to contain her emotions, vented such venom on the governess that knowledge of the quarrel entered the public domain: 'That fine friendship between Mme de Montespan and her friend, who is now away travelling, has become a veritable aversion for the past two years,' remarked Sévigné.

In September 1675 battle raged around the Château de Tymur, in Lower Brittany. But Sébastien La Balp's peasants were no longer dealing with frightened lords or inexperienced militias. They were faced by a regular army, the reinforcements so long awaited by the Duc de Chaulnes. Le Balp fought like a lion, but 'he was torn to pieces by the lords of that castle; and after Balp's death, the rebels took flight and dispersed'.[19] The collapse was everywhere, as Mme de Sévigné reported: 'Our poor Lower Bretons march in forties and fifties across the fields and as soon as they see soldiers, they fall to their knees and say *mea culpa* . . .'[20]

'*Mea culpa*', cried the Breton peasants. 'We have hanged and put to the wheel a good quantity of them,' one aristocratic lady replied with satisfaction. Carhaix was Sébastien La Balp's headquarters, and it was there that the Duc de Chaulnes began his campaign. Well supported by the reinforcements that had arrived from Germany, he could carry out Louvois' orders and pass over into repression, helped by the rich, who were determined to make the lower orders pay for the fright that they had been given. Throughout the region, denunciations were followed by mass arrests and summary executions. The Duc de Chaulnes remarked that 'the trees are beginning to lean over on the highways around Quimperlé with the weight that has been put on them': Then he entered Rennes at the head of the reinforcements, marching in battle order, with guns loaded. They would see what was coming to them, those Rennais who had called him 'a fat pig': military occupation of the city, exile of the Breton *parlement,* disarmament of the bourgeois militias, confiscation of the city's artillery and, finally, destruction of the suburbs, in particular the Rue Haute where a dead cat had been thrown at that 'ugly hunchback', the Duchesse de Chaulnes. Of course the hundred thousand soldiers that had come as reinforcements lived among the inhabitants, at their expense. The States of Brittany met and demanded that they be sent away. By way of reply they were required to pay three million francs as a 'gift', and instead of sending away the reinforcements, new ones were brought in. Three regiments were now turned on the province, spreading violence and terror. They stole, looted, massacred, the rather belated response from the Louis-Louvois tandem to peasants who, at the beginning of the revolt, had sent a petition to Versailles which read: 'The entire people, sorely pressed by poverty and need, beg His Majesty to turn a compassionate eye upon them and to relieve their suffering.' His Majesty's method of relieving suffering reached such proportions that even the Duc de Chaulnes took his courage in both hands and wrote to Louvois: 'I cannot express to you, Monseigneur, what ravages the troops commit on their way ... This province is being treated like an enemy country.'[21]

The door of the king's bedchamber opened, and who should come in but Mme de Maintenon, holding the Duc du Maine's hand. It was a happy surprise as he was not expecting them so early. Louis embraced the child and congratulated the governess on how well he looked. Barèges had really done him good, but how they had both missed him. For Maintenon, the king's welcome was tantamount to permission to stay, but in fact she still wanted to leave at the end of the year. Life at Court, with its gossip, intrigues, agitation, and on top of everything else Montespan's scenes, was no life for her. She longed for the peace and tranquillity of her home at Maintenon. She sought the approval of her confessor, but was surprised by his reaction. 'There can be no question of leaving,' said the Abbé Gobelin, 'be indifferent to what may contradict your wishes, forget whatever troubles your repose, seek God in everything you do, but, in God's name, do not leave under any pretext. Hold fast!' Maintenon was perplexed: 'You will remember, no doubt, that it was you who wanted me to remain at Court and I left it as soon as you advised me to . . .'[22]

'I want to show that I know how to embarrass my enemies simply by my presence, for I know that they wish for nothing more than my return to France.'[23] As if to prove Louis right, the cities of Flanders that he was besieging in the first months of 1676 surrendered one by one, impressed perhaps by the august apparition. So much so that William of Orange experienced a temporary depression: the French army was ravaging the region of Nijmegen, his Spanish allies were sending him no help, he had no more money to pay his troops and, on top of that, he had to go and help to save the city of Condé besieged by Louis. He met the French army at Heurtebise. He bravely braced himself for battle for he knew that Louis was going to attack him. Who could miss such an opportunity? There were 48,000 French and he, William, had only 35,000 men. Suddenly he heard cannon fire. Was it the French attacking? But they were merely firing off a salvo in honour of the Duc d'Orléans, who had just taken the town of Bouchain. William knew that he would lose nothing by waiting.[24]

'Gentlemen, what should we do?' Louis asked. With him were the indispensable Louvois, four marshals of France, senior officers and courtiers – all on horseback. Around them was the French army, impatient to join battle, certain of victory. But Louvois did not know his master well enough. 'No battle,' he snapped. The marshals looked at one another. D'Hummières, an intimate friend of Louvois, supported him, as did Schomberg. La Feuillade, 'after some words of doubtful sense', supported them. Only Lorges, Turenne's nephew, came out firmly in favour of battle. Less senior officers 'merely stammered'. Louis regretted their opinions as he would very much have liked to go into battle, but he had to give in to the majority and 'sacrificed his wishes to the advantage of the State'. And, thereupon, he rode off. There was no doubt that the great conqueror preferred sieges to battles.

On the other hand, he sent a herald to William of Orange to ask for a safe conduct for a servant who had been sent to fetch wine for his table. Courteously, William granted his safe conduct, but thoroughly questioned the herald. Where was the French army? Why had it not attacked? And the herald related in detail what had been said at the council of war. William smiled triumphantly. 'You will tell the Maréchal de Lorges that he was right to want battle. I could not have avoided it if I had been attacked and I would certainly have been beaten.'[25]

CHAPTER 13

Montespan's Golden Crown

Conscious of their responsibilities, the matrons of the court were on tenterhooks. They were not to lose sight of the king and Mme de Montespan for a moment. Those were the conditions of the compromise worked out by Athénaïs now that the king was coming back from the front. He was to be condemned to see his former favourite in front of the entire Court. She would have preferred an earlier, more discreet meeting, but Bossuet declared there could be no question of them being alone together. She protested that they would not be alone: it would just be a brief visit by the king to Mme de Montespan in the presence of 'the most respectable and gravest ladies of the Court.' Bossuet gave in: anything so long as it avoided starting up those pernicious flames once again. With craning necks, eyes fixed upon him, the matrons saw the king enter Athénaïs' apartment and come up to her. They strained their ears to catch everything that was said. Suddenly they frowned: the couple had imperceptibly moved beyond the agreed distance. The matrons could no longer hear, but they could see the former lovers, in a corner, whispering and weeping. But what was happening? Louis and Athénaïs, hand in hand, came back to the matrons, made a deep bow, then quickly fled into the next room and banged the door. And the matrons, utterly taken aback, had to wait a long time in silence, imagining in horror what could be taking place on the other side of the door. The most furious of all was Mme de Maintenon: 'I did tell you that the Bishop of Meaux [Bossuet] would be taken in by this whole business. He is a very intelligent man, but he does not understand the Court: he wanted to convert them, but for all his zeal he has only succeeded in bringing them together.' Love had triumphed. Love – or was it simply desire? Bussy-Rabutin was not wrong about Louis' feelings for La Vallière and for Montespan: 'His Majesty loved neither of them. What he felt for them was not passion, but lust and I believe it became a habit with him. Those ladies are not strictly speaking mistresses; they are the sort of women with whom the master sleeps.'[1]

Whether she was that sort of woman or not, it was a triumphant creature, more beautiful than ever, who resumed her position as official favourite, 'She no longer had either restraint or human respect,' Mlle d'Aumale, a very young friend of Maintenon's, complained. 'Convincing herself that everything was her due and that she owed nothing to anybody, she wanted everything to bend before her: she no longer showed respect either for rank or dignity.' For Mme de Maintenon, in particular, she showed less respect than ever. It was above all on her that the full vent of the glorious Athénaïs' pride, caprice and temper were unleashed. This time, contrary to all expectations, Maintenon held firm, for Athénaïs could no longer undermine the king's 'esteem and consideration' for her. In her triumph, Athénaïs did not take very much notice.[2]

A new twenty-two room apartment on the first floor had been reserved for Athénaïs in the Château de Versailles, whereas even the queen had to be content with eleven rooms on the second floor. In the palace, which was moving towards completion, the king was already distributing accommodation and showing off the new appointments to his justly dazzled Court. Everything had to be ready on time. To make sure, 22,000 labourers were at work in the buildings and gardens of this palace to end all palaces.

It was just unfortunate if the unhealthy climate of the area made many of them ill. It was just unfortunate if there were a lot of accidents at work. Whole cartloads of corpses were carried out each night so as not to alarm the survivors. Despite this precaution, they began to find out what sinister reward awaited them and rebelled against their working conditions to such an extent that the constabulary had to intervene. The ringleaders were thrown into prison. No one would be allowed to disturb the exquisite existence described by an ecstatic Sévigné: 'At three o'clock ... what is called the Court of France is to be found in the fine apartments that you know so well. Everything is divinely furnished, everything is quite splendid ... One moves from one place to another without encountering the slightest congestion anywhere. This agreeable confusion without confusion of the choicest of everything lasts until six o'clock. At six, we get into barouches ... You know how those barouches are constructed; you don't sit opposite one another, but everyone faces the same way. We go out on the canal, in gondolas, and there is music; we come back at ten o'clock for the comedy; when midnight strikes, we go into the banquet ...'[3]

While they were banqueting at Versailles, at the Flanders front, Louvois spoke for the master: 'It is the king's intention that ...' And everybody, from the general down to the privates carried out the orders, for the master saw everything, knew everything, foresaw everything and was an oracle in all matters. There was no quality that a perspicacious and perfidious observer like Primi Visconti did not attribute to him at this time: 'a perfect knowledge of affairs', 'extraordinary memory', 'a marvellous ability to throw light on what neither ministers, nor their servants have been able to sort out', an ability to maintain secrecy about his plans and to get the best out of those who carried them out. Here, at least, was one king who knew how to rule. So the ministers went into the council chamber 'trembling', knowing that each time they were being subjected to the most meticulous of examinations. They constantly feared being caught out. A mere gesture, a look from the master, was enough either to overwhelm them with pleasure or to annihilate them. It was above all this 'foxy' look that hypnotized ministers, courtiers and generals alike. Louis was perfectly aware of this power: 'At a mere glance, whether in a room, in the chapel, or on a campaign, I see everyone.' But if his self-control gave him such power, what need was there to pretend, to play the role attributed to him by Primi Visconti: 'When a door opens, the king immediately arranges his attitude and takes on another facial expression as if he were about to appear on the stage; in short he is in every respect very good at playing the king.'[4] He played the king, but was he really one? Certainly not in the army, where the king was actually Louvois.

In order to achieve this Louvois had only to follow the tactics developed by his father, Michel Le Tellier, with Colbert and Lionne at the time of Louis xiv's coup d'état: he only had to tease his thirst for glory and authority, persuade Louis to command his armies in person from his office, but draw up all the plans of campaign himself under the pretext of 'sparing' the master from the crushing labour involved – and get him to approve them as if they were his own. Then Louvois had only to send them to headquarters with instructions to follow them to the letter. Taking into account neither tactical planning, nor the opinion of experts, the armies advanced or retreated according to the plans that Louis imagined he had drawn up. It was a system of blinding absurdity. Fortunately for Louvois, the terrain lent itself to Louvois' omnipotence: an enemy cannon-ball had killed Turenne and gout had put Condé out of action – and they were the only generals who might have resisted the minister. Their successors, Humières, Créqui and even Luxembourg, were under his heel. 'It is the king's intention that . . .' In order to consolidate his authority, Louvois got hold of the promotion list and promoted only his own 'yes men'.[5] The result of this tight control exercised over the army was that the generals neglected their duties and thought only of pleasing the minister who had become, one of his enemies declared, 'The general of all the armies and the master of all those who commanded them.'[6]

However, Louvois did make mistakes. One day, the king received a request from a young British officer who wanted to command an English regiment in the service of France. He was a man of dubious character and was being kept by the mistress of the king of England, the imperious Barbara Castlemain. He refused to marry the immensely rich heiress intended for him by his father, because he was in love with a devilish woman called Sarah Jennings, so he decided to emigrate. But Louvois, warned of his past, rejected him: 'Monsieur de Churchill is too given over to his pleasure to be able to carry out his duties adequately.'[7] 'Monsieur de Churchill' was to keep a grudge against France and, years later, Louis was to be confronted by that same Churchill, now the Duke of Marlborough. As for Sarah Jennings, with whom Churchill was infatuated, a great many things were to depend on her.

With her peace of mind restored by the withdrawal of the beautiful, ambitious Soubise, who had for a short time captivated the king's attention, La Montespan triumphed once more: 'They tell me that the beautiful Madame has reappeared in the fine apartment as before,' Sévigné reported. Athénaïs then sported the uniform of her profession, that famous dress that Sévigné described for later centuries: 'Gold upon gold, re-embroidered with gold, hemmed with gold and on gold thread, re-embroidered with one gold mixed with another to produce the most divine material that has ever been imagined.' The sensual sorceress in her fairy costume held her lover safely in thrall: 'The two friends were together yesterday. Joy has returned at last and all the jealous laughter has disappeared.' Soon a new pregnancy was to crown this 'returned' joy. Everything would have been perfect in Athénaïs' paradise if there had been no Maintenon, ever modest, ever present, ever in the king's good books.

Sometimes a volcano in eruption, sometimes a mosquito loaded with poison, Athénaïs lashed out, needled, attacked her former friend, who would only weep on her confessor's bosom: 'I cannot continue for long the life that I lead. I take too much upon myself for the body or the mind and perhaps both not to succumb. Let God do with me as He will.'[8]

Not only did Athénaïs have to struggle against her rival for the king's mind, but she also had to fight off other competitors in the king's bed, Louis seemed indeed to be in the grip of a sexual hunger that his sister-in-law, the Palatine, described with detachment: 'Everything was grist to his mill, provided it was female: peasant girls, gardeners' daughters, chamber-maids, ladies of quality, provided that they pretended that they were in love with him.'[9] And Athénaïs had to put her imagination to the test to scuttle the beauties one by one to whom he had thrown his handkerchief . . . Mlle de Grancey: 'But, Sire, she has already had a bastard by the Duc de Lorraine.' The Princesse de Wurtemburg: 'But, Sire, she is the mistress of an alchemist.' Mme de Saint-Martin: 'There is nothing to be said about her, for Your Majesty would not stoop to the wife of a mere intendant!' Mme des Oeillets: 'Your Majesty may sleep with her as long as he likes and even have a daughter that he will refuse to recognize. She's my *femme de chambre* and I keep an eye on her.' On the other hand, Athénaïs must have been worried by the other side of Louis whom Mme des Oeillets sometimes found sitting by the fireside for hours on end, silent, thoughtful, sighing deeply and quite obviously bored.[10]

At the beginning of 1677, Louis returned to the war in Flanders and forgot his women and his boredom as he set about the sieges so dear to his heart. That year, he took his brother with him, who in turn brought along his lover, the Chevalier de Lorraine, and went off on his elder brother's orders, to lay siege to Saint-Omer. Suddenly the scouts announced that William of Orange was approaching on a forced march, at the head of a powerful army, double that of Monsieur's. Monsieur dropped the siege and dashed off to meet him, on the plain of Cassel, while his second-in-command, the Maréchal d'Humières, terrified, asked for urgent assistance. The Maréchal de Luxembourg set out at the head of eight battalions, arrived during the night at Monsieur's camp, woke him up and the two reviewed their troops. They presented a curious picture, those two dwarfs side by side on horseback: the prince in ribbons and make-up, simpering and pot-bellied, waving his tiny, beringed hands about, and the old soldier, hunchbacked, bright-eyed, a cynical grin on his face, like a dangerously evil imp. At dawn on 10 April 1677, battle was joined. Soon William of Orange's right wing retreated. William then had the audacity to change strategy in mid-battle. He depleted his centre and his left wing and secretly sent his soldiers behind the hedges and hollows of the ground to the help of his right wing. None of the French generals, though highly experienced, suspected the manoeuvre. Suddenly, in a flash of genius, Monsieur guessed what was happening and charged at the head of his musketeers at William's positions, which none of the French suspected were depleted. In an instant, the big-bellied homosexual was transformed into a magnificent warrior, plunging headlong into danger, fighting like a lion, sword in hand, reforming squadrons that had given way. Around him the musketeers fell in whole ranks, twenty of his aides-de-camp were struck, his lover, the Chevalier de Lorraine, was wounded in the temple, he himself had his shield pierced by two bullets and his horse was wounded. He went on fighting, drunk with joy, in a cloud of dust and smoke, and in a final charge broke through the Dutch lines. A furious William of Orange could not prevent a rout of his troops and marked the face of a runaway as he passed, shouting: 'There, wretch, I shall at least mark you before having you hanged.' But he was carried off by the flood of his fleeing compatriots. Luxembourg had already reached his camp and was making free with his gold table service, but Monsieur soon caught up with the aquisitive marshal and forbade him or his troops from looting. A prince was no ordinary soldier. 'Monsieur has won one of the most complete battles that we have ever seen in our time,' Luxembourg reported, disappointed, but impartial.[11]

For Louis, the news came like an unprecedented slap in the face. That frivolous younger brother, that effeminate, who wore high heels and set out with the army made up as if for a ball, that brainless epicure, had won a brilliant victory at the point of his sword, whereas, he, the king, had never been able and would never be able to do anything but sieges. The disappointment was so acute that the king, usually so self-controlled, could not conceal it. 'It is almost as if', Primi Visconti recounted, 'the king would have willingly given ten million francs to have lost the battle of Cassel.'[12] His mortification was just beginning. He had to reply with delight to the letters of congratulation that flooded in. But his fury peeped through the hypocrisy and the dryness of his reply to old Condé: 'Cousin, you are right to congratulate me on the battle of Cassel. If I had won it in person, I could not have been more

189

touched, either by the extent of the victory, or by the achievement in winning it above all for my brother's honour.'[13] On the return journey, he had to smile back at the cheering crowd that came out to welcome the two brothers. 'Long live the king and Monsieur who won the battle!' Lastly, he had to show pleasure when the Parisian crowd, still devoted to his brother, exploded with joy on seeing them again. In a moment, the character that he had built up as the absolute master of his subjects, the sultan in the midst of his harem, the conqueror feared and admired by the whole of Europe, had disappeared. And he was left face to face with his torturing limitations. Limitations in his role as leader – he could not lead his troops – and limitations even in his social class – he could not fight as a gentleman should. The fact that he never again gave any military command to his brother and sent him back forever to idleness and the company of his favourites did little to help: the mark would remain indelible.

There was a single optimistic note in this period: he learnt that on 4 May his mistress had given him a fine daughter, Françoise-Marie. Athénaïs had retired discreetly for the birth to the home of her good friend, Mme de Maintenon, at the Château de Maintenon. The apple of discord, the king, being absent, the two ladies could calmly resume the course of their strange friendship: 'Let us not be taken in by this affair,' Montespan observed, 'let us talk as if we have nothing to quarrel about; it is of course understood that we shall resume our quarrels on our return.' However, the good friend was not to look after the baby as she had done previously. Her standing now forbade her assuming the role of nanny. The baby would soon be taken away by Louvois in person, and entrusted to Mme de Jussac, chosen in concert by the two friends – Montespan because she was old and Maintenon because she was respectable.

The favourite was leading a dog's life. No sooner had Athénaïs recovered from the birth than she had to go back to keeping her lover on the straight and narrow of extra-conjugal fidelity. Some months before, a look had been enough for the ravishing Mlle de Ludres to become the king's mistress. So Athénaïs had attacked according to her well-tried method. Mlle de Ludres: 'But, Sire, she has herpes.' Unfortunately, Louis had already noted *de visu et de tatu* ('by sight and touch') that the beautiful Ludres did not have herpes. 'Get out you wretch,' yelled Athénaïs, when Ludres dared to enter her apartment and she threw herself on the poor girl with the evident intention of strangling her. But Ludres was stupid: she strutted about, assumed airs, let everyone know that she was the master's mistress, and would soon be his favourite. But the master always had a horror of these displays, especially if he had not ordered them himself. So away with the beautiful Ludres, with or without herpes! But she must not be allowed to go just anywhere, Athénaïs insisted with all her customary rancour. Not only must she leave the Court, she must enter a convent. And so Mlle de Ludres was ordered to join the Daughters of St Mary in the Faubourg Saint-Germain.[14]

Covered with enormous diamonds, Montespan lorded it in her armchair, like the queen offering mere stools to the duchesses. She never travelled without a bodyguard. She spent the fabulous sum of 800,000 *livres* a year; to this one can add monthly payments running into hundreds of thousands of *livres* for her clothes, her gambling and the support of her bastards. She intended to proclaim her victory in the face of the world, so that such observers as La Sévigné should sing her praises: 'What a triumph at Versailles! What redoubled pride! What resumption of possession . . . All constraints are banished so that she may seem to have her way and persuade everybody that never was domination more firmly established . . . The attachment seems greater than ever; you should see how they look at one another; never has love revived as that one did.' Bussy-Rabutin, unlike his cousin Sévigné, was not taken in: 'I have noticed that although the king loves her dearly, he loves himself even more.'[15]

It was certainly not love that pushed William of Orange to the lady of his choice. Crushed at Cassel, he felt a strong need for external supports. He remembered that a year earlier a secret emissary from the Court of England had come to The Hague to explore the possibility of a marriage with the king's niece, Princess Mary. Nothing came of it, though it was not turned down. On the other hand, he had indignantly rejected the proposition made to him about the same time by the ambassador of France: as a pledge of friendship, Louis was willing to give him the daughter that he had had by La Vallière. 'The Princes of Orange are accustomed to marry the legitimate daughters of great kings and not their bastards,' William replied. Louis, for his part, was extremely put out that anyone should refuse his bastard daughter.

Now William was thinking again of the English proposition and he sent young Bentinck to London to resume negotiations.[16] He could not have arrived at a more opportune moment. A protestant prince, an enemy of France, a protestant marriage, that was what was needed, Charles II said to himself. He knew how angry his subjects were with France, which subsidized him, directed his policies and meddled in everything, including his private life. So before long, William of Orange brought a wife back with him to Holland: Princess Mary, a sixteen-year-old girl, quite pretty, fairly intelligent, somewhat simple and ignorant, but well meaning. He ignored her from the beginning, remaining cold and distant with her. He was unfaithful to her with women *and* men – but she had made up her mind to prove to be a devoted and obedient wife. However, she soon began to notice that her husband felt a kind of embarrassment, almost a feeling of inferiority, in her presence. She unburdened herself to a leading protestant divine, Gilbert Burnet, who was visiting Holland. Burnet offered one explanation for her husband's attitude: 'It's because one day you will be queen of England,' he replied. Charles II would certainly never have a legitimate child and his brother and heir, the Duke of York, Mary's father, did not yet have a son. It was therefore Mary, in all probability, who would one day be heir to the English throne. 'Well, when I am queen, my husband will be king,' she concluded. 'Things are not so simple,' Burnet cautioned. 'According to the English constitution, the queen's husband does not automatically become king. The solution lies in Your Highness' hands.' 'I have no need of time or reflection. If I am the queen, he shall be king.'[17]

Louis became very alarmed at the prospect: William was now a nephew by marriage of the king of England. William was allied to England by the treaty that had just been signed. Above all, William might one day be king of England. In public, Louis made light of it: 'Those beggars are well matched.' All the more furious that he had intended Princess Mary for his own son, the Dauphin, privately he swore that it would never happen.[18]

In the snow, rain and mud, the long procession of coaches flanked by guards on horseback moved towards Flanders in that January 1678. The king was taking the queen and the ladies to visit the northern provinces once more. Gallantly, he had his troops reviewed by Montespan. The sight of this superb woman so excited the German soldiers that they began to cry out: 'Königs Hure, Königs Hure!' (The king's whore! The king's whore.) 'How was the review, Madame?' the king asked her at dinner. 'Splendid,' she replied, 'except that I find the Germans too naïve in calling everything by its proper name.'[19]

Leaving the ladies that he had brought with him in order to allay the enemy's suspicions, Louis suddenly rode post-haste to Ghent, at the head of his army and took that city, as well as Ypres, threatened Antwerp and, passing through Luxembourg, laid siege to Mons. This was his response to the marriage of William of Orange. It was from the height of these victories that he offered peace to the European coalition: he took Franche-Comté and several towns in the Netherlands from Spain and, from the emperor, he won Alsace and control of Lorraine. On the other hand, he was willing to hand back a number of towns in the Netherlands, including Ghent, which he had just taken, in order to please the Dutch and to provide them with a protective barrier. The price was so high that the neutral English, the only ones not contributing to its payment, talked of going to war to put an end to this imperialism. The Dutch were less than enthusiastic: they got more than they had hoped for and wanted peace. This ran counter to the wishes of their leader, Stadtholder William of Orange, who was determined to continue the war at all costs. However, his opinion was ignored and the Dutch sat down at the conference table at Nijmegen.[20] Louis told them they had until 10 May to reply, and he set off for Saint-Germain where he arrived just in time to see La Montespan give birth to another bastard, her last, the future Comte de Toulouse.

Meanwhile, at Nijmegen, the plenipotentiaries of the various powers were giving birth to peace. The treaty was signed on 10 August 1678 according to the conditions laid down by Louis. William went back to Holland to sulk. He was already thinking of reforming the coalition against Louis that peace had just dissolved. Louis should have heeded the judgement of the preacher Massillon on 'the little lord of Breda': 'A long-sighted prince; skilled in forming alliances and bringing minds together; happier causing wars than fighting them, more to be feared in the secrecy of the cabinet than at the head of armies; an enemy whom hatred of the French had made capable of imagining great things and carrying them out: one of those geniuses who seem born to move sovereign peoples according to their will.'[21]

'Banco', cried La Montespan. The financier Bonju, who was banker, turned up a card. The bank had won. Montespan had lost four hundred thousand *pistoles*. 'Let us stop now, Madame,' said Bonju. 'Not at all,' she replied, 'I intend winning back what I have lost.' And so each night she returned to the gambling table. Even on Christmas night of 1678, Athénaïs lost 700,000 *livres*, which she won back in one stroke by betting 50,000 *pistoles* on three cards. One evening she lost three million *livres* at a stroke, but Louis graciously went on paying her debts. The courtiers remarked that Athénaïs had him more than ever in her grip. 'His favour increases every day,' they repeated. What other lover would allow his mistress to lose a million *livres* on a single card. Anyway, he liked his Court to spend. He himself had always been a gambler, and once lost several million in a game that lasted all night. It was dawn when he left the gambling table, leaving Montespan to win back what she could. 'Am I still king?' he asked, on waking several hours later,[22] wondering if the royal function was compatible with his losses. Primi Visconti, more perspicacious than the regular courtiers, remarked that the king was beginning to be irritated and embarrassed by Athénaïs' excesses.[23] It certainly seemed that she had lost all sense of proportion, at both the gambling and the dining table. She ate constantly and excessively: she had become quite enormous. Primi Visconti, who watched her get out of her coach, caught a glimpse of one of her legs: it was as wide as his own body.[24]

'That whore will be the death of me,' wept Queen Maria Theresa, speaking of La Montespan, who openly made fun of her. Where was the sweet, modest La Vallière? Why had she given way to this mocking viper? One day, Maria Theresa got a fright: her coach got stuck in the mud and the rain had so filled it with water that it began to flounder. When the accident was described to the king, 'the whore' burst out laughing and cried, 'The queen has been drinking again.' Even the king was shocked: 'Remember, Madame, she is your mistress.'[25] But La Montespan reigned without rival and wanted everyone to know it. She had her own court, which was at the centre of the other Court. It was to this 'court' that courtiers, ministers and generals hastened, for she was the source of favours and advancement. She reigned with her own weapons: an indomitable, headstrong character, a fierce pride, but one devoid of all pettiness, and, above all, a dazzling wit, 'a wit of so peculiar a kind, so delicate, so subtle but always so natural and so agreeable that it stood out as quite unique'.[26] That wit enabled her to crush all her rivals, but Maintenon was still there, a crack in her triumph, a shadow in her sunny present. 'You love the king and you are trying to seduce him,' Athénaïs complained. 'It ill behoves you to reproach me for something for which you yourself set the example,' her friend retorted, calmly. 'Your favour will last only as long as mine.' snapped Athénaïs. 'If I had intended what you ascribe to me, would I have asked you so often to get me permission to retire?' replied Mme de Maintenon. 'And what is keeping you here?' came the retort. 'The will of the king, my duty, my gratitude and the interests of those close to me,' was the self-confident answer.[27]

Confronted by this new assurance, Athénaïs hit well below the belt, exhuming a past that Maintenon preferred to be dead and buried, in particular the crippled poet, Paul Scarron. 'I understand that your late husband told his friends that you wanted to put into your marriage contract that you would have to stay with him only during the day, but that from ten o'clock in the evening onwards you would be your own mistress,' Mme de Montespan said accusingly. Maintenon, for once icy and haughty, replied: 'And do you happen to know, Madame, which notary drew up this contract?'[28]

The Palatine summed up the general feeling: 'La Montespan was the devil incarnate.'[29] What a difference between her and her beloved and well named lady of honour, Marie-Angélique de Fontanges. 'Beautiful as an angel', people said of the girl. 'Stupid as a mule,' rumour added.[30] But she was so romantic and so trustful. She recounted to the Palatine a strange dream that she had had: 'I was climbing a mountain. When I got to the top, I was dazzled by a shining cloud, then, immediately, I found myself again in threatening darkness. Then I woke up in a cold sweat, quite terrified.' The Palatine could not interpret dreams, but Marie-Angélique's confessor could: 'Be careful; that mountain is the Court, where you will attain a brilliant position; but it will not last for long ...'[31]

CHAPTER 14

Poison in the Air

What was the king doing riding incognito at night on the Paris road, accompanied only by a few guards? Why was he not asleep in the Château de Saint-Germain, where the Court was residing in March 1679? His coach pulled up in front of the Palais Royal. Was he paying a visit to his brother and sister-in-law? No, for he was careful to conceal his identity. He went up a secret staircase quickly and silently, and knocked on a door. One of the Palatine's maids of honour, Mlle des Adrets, let him in and took him to a room, then withdrew. For the moment 'the dazzling cloud' surrounded Marie-Angélique de Fontanges, for it was she that the king had come to see. She was not surprised, she had been waiting for months, for years. She knew that she was radiantly beautiful: everyone had been telling her for so long, and at home in her Auvergne manor house where she had lived until the previous year, she had subsisted on a diet of chivalric romances. She would one day be the heroine who captured the heart of Prince Charming, she told herself, and now that day had come. Prince Charming was standing there before her; Renaud had seen Angélique and had fallen head over heels in love.[1] Without hesitating, she gave herself to the king, who returned to Saint-Germain before dawn. But he was to return.

During one of his nocturnal journeys, he had been recognized – he had even been followed. So he installed Marie-Angélique in an isolated apartment in the Château de Saint-Germain. In public, she was neither seen nor recognized. He never so much as looked at her, let alone greeted her. He pretended that he was completely ignorant of her existence. The innocent believed that he had kept his secret, but the Court radar had already recorded his affair. La Montespan caused a scene. They were alone, but Athénaïs shouted her abuse so loudly that the courtiers, craning their ears at the door, heard everything. 'People fuss too much and I'm sick of it,' the king interrupted. This warning did not stop Athénaïs, who returned to the fray with a second scene even more violent than the first.[2]

'Madame de Montespan suddenly left Saint-Germain on Wednesday the fifteenth of this month for Paris. It is said that there is some coolness between the couple and it derives from her jealousy of one of Madame's girls called Fontanges ...' And Mme de Scudéry concludes philosophi-cally: 'Providing she can go without love, she will have the king's consideration. That is all an honest man who no longer loves can do ...'³ But 'going without' was not Athénaïs' strong point.

The problem facing Nicolas de La Reynie, first lieutenant of police for Paris had nothing to do with La Fontanges or La Montespan. What he had just told the king was much more serious. It had all begun two years before. In a confessional of the Jesuit church in the Rue Saint-Antoine an anonymous note had been found concerning the existence of a plot to poison the king. A routine interrogation of the priests was carried out, in which they made no bones about the fact that a number of their penitents, especially women, accused themselves of having poisoned someone. This gave Lieutenant La Reynie, who was in charge of the investigation, pause for thought. He arrested an alchemist and his mistress, a tailor's wife, a fortune-teller. Their statements astonished him. It appeared that poisoning was practised on a large scale at every social level. 'A man's life is practically for sale,' he concluded. 'It is almost the only remedy used when there are unwanted children.' Every trail that La Reynie followed up led to La Voisin, that highly successful sorceress in the suburb of Bonne-Nouvelle. So, on 12 March 1679, he had her arrested, together with her faithful collaborator, Le Sage. She did not need much persuading to reveal all; she talked and talked. What crimes, but above all what names, poured out! La Reynie trembled with fear. It was no longer the bourgeoisie, but the nobility, and the upper echelons of the nobility, that were swallowing miracle 'cures' and love potions, poisoning parents and friends, carrying out abortions, invok-ing the devil and practising magic that was certainly more black than white.

La Reynie decided to inform the king. The simple-minded, innocent Louis was horrified and indignant. 'Let light be thrown on the whole matter and let justice punish all the guilty, whoever they may be,' he declared. He immediately appointed a special commission, the *Chambre Ardente*, to judge the affair, presided over by La Reynie. Armed with this *carte blanche*, La Reynie arrested large numbers of suspects and soon the Court was rife with rumours. The prisons of Vincennes and the Bastille were full. Lists of suspects were circulating. There was sometimes, however, a comic side to the affair. The Duchesse de Foix was compromised because a note in her hand had been found at La Voisin's that read: 'The more I rub, the more they grow.' The king himself took the trouble to question the duchess on the strange meaning of this sentence. Acutely embarrassed, the duchess finally admitted that she had asked La Voisin for a cream to enlarge her breasts ... People laughed, but they were also afraid, for arrests were being made on the merest suspicion, on the least substantiated denunciation. The *Chambre Ardente* was no respecter of persons, rank or sex. It was like being back in the old days of the Inquisition.⁴

Meanwhile, the secret that Louis hoped to keep about his affair was leaked everywhere. The first person to betray him was the girl herself, beautiful, stupid Fontanges, delighted at seeing her dream realized at last; she did and said so much, that even those who were rather out of touch could no longer ignore her success. Maintenon raised her hands to the heavens and poured out her anxieties to her confessor: 'I beg you to pray, and to get others to pray, for the king, who is on the edge of a great precipice.' Ignored in favour of this ravishing precipice,[5] Montespan, to everyone's surprise, took it all much more philosophically: 'It is much better to see one another seldom on good terms, than often with embarrassment.' And so Athénaïs turned to religion. She spent a lot of time talking to priests, and she followed all the Lenten offices.[6] Could it be that she was testing the efficacy of Maintenon's recipe? In any case, this exemplary conduct brought her back into the good graces of the queen and enabled her to expatiate on 'the great sin committed by the king', the sin of sleeping with Fontanges rather than with her.

The devil having turned into a hermit against all expectations, it was only right that she should be rewarded. The title of duchess was the usual price given for this kind of service, but this was impossible, for M. de Montespan would have to be made a duke at the same time. That troublemaker was already on the rampage at the very idea, ready to trigger off a new scandal. So Jack-of-all-trades Colbert obediently jotted down the following: 'Since the king wishes to give particular expression to the consideration and esteem that he has for the person of Mme de Montespan by giving her a rank that distinguishes her from the other ladies of the Court, it is His Majesty's wish that she should enjoy for the rest of her life the same honours, ranks, prerogatives, precedences and other advantages enjoyed by duchesses . . .'[7]

Montespan became a duchess without a title and Louis was naïve enough to think that he could buy his peace in this way. The devil did not slumber for long, especially if condemned to attending La Fontanges' triumph. It began in the usual way, by mockery: 'Would His Majesty be inclining towards the rustic style?' Indeed, Fontanges' provinciality stood out a mile. 'It is also said that she had quite a reputation at home. It must be amusing for the king to follow where so many peasants have been.' Then the eruption occurred in Maintenon's presence. A flood of reproaches and abuses was thrown at the king, who stood his ground. But human patience has its limits. 'I have already told you, Madame, I do not wish to be bothered with all this.' Thereupon he left. 'What is to be done?' the startled Montespan asked Maintenon. 'God, Madame.' 'What God? You were one of the king's accomplices, just as his confessor, that Father La Chaise, was. Why does he not demand that the king break with La Fontanges as he did with me?' 'Mlle de Fontanges is not married. She's not committing adultery . . .' 'Your Father La Chaise is a mere night-stool!'

But what was the point of the row? No good could come of it. So the diabolical Montespan, having become a hermit once more, smiled at Fontanges, gave her advice on her clothes, even dressed her with her own fair hands one evening for a ball. And Fontanges, taken in by this apparent change of heart, lavished magnificent presents on Montespan, paid for from the royal coffers. In short, harmony reigned, as Primi Visconti observed, attending mass in the chapel of the Château de Saint-Germain. The queen, as was right and proper, was in the middle; Montespan was in the left-hand gallery, surrounded by the bastards that she had given the king, and Fontanges, in the right-hand gallery, like a 'divinity', as Sévigné remarked. She had not listened to Montespan's advice and had dressed with a lack of discretion bordering on bad taste: an over-abundance of jewellery, silk of the same colour as the one worn by the king and ribbons that seemed to imitate the great sash of the Order of the Holy Ghost. She piously followed the service in her missal, said her rosary and raised her eyes to heaven in a fine religious upsurge that she shared with Montespan.[8]

Who at this time would have dared to criticize the idol who represented absolute monarchy in all its splendour? 'Grand air', 'majestic mien', 'presence', were the terms used to describe him by the dazzled spectators. 'In public,' Primi Visconti adds, 'he remains silent and serious for he has all the gravity of a theatrical king.' 'Theatrical'? Was Primi Visconti aware of the gravity of what he was saying? Maybe Louis was theatrical, but he was attentive to the morality of his Court. Just because he publicly maintained two mistresses did not mean he tolerated such departures from the moral code in others. What was naturally permitted to gods could never be so to mere humans. He strongly disapproved of passionate affairs, whose consequent disorder impaired the dignity of his Court.[9] Gallantry must not have free rein in the new order that he had created.[10]

Everything had to conform to this order. His niece, Marie-Louise, daughter of Monsieur and the dead Henrietta, was ordered to marry the king of Spain. This amounted to exiling the unfortunate girl to the middle of a xenophobic country in a stuffy, funereal court, riven by intrigues, and handing her over to a pathetically hideous degenerate. The unfortunate girl could not face such a prospect: she wept and pleaded. Her uncle's compliments fell like a death blow: 'I could not do better for my own daughter.' 'You could do something better for your niece,' she replied. And, in summer 1679, Marie-Louise d'Orléans set out sobbing towards her sad fate.[11] *Rex dixit*. (The king had spoken.)

Rex dixit, and, in November 1679, the Minister of Foreign Affairs, the faithful Pomponne, was suddenly dismissed and disgraced. It was actually 'Louvois and Colbert have spoken', but, of course, Louis did not know this. Pomponne was assuming too much importance, so, for once, the two villains worked together. The opportunity arose when the coded despatches concerning the conclusion of an important negotiation reached the ministry while Pomponne was at home in the country, and the official who dealt with codes was at the opera. Louvois dashed to the king and innocently handed him his own copy of the despatches. But Pomponne should have informed him! Pomponne was resting at home, instead of serving His Majesty. Then Colbert turned up and added a little oil to the fire lit by Louvois. When Pomponne calmly returned from the country, he found an order to submit his resignation and to return to the home that he seemed to care more about than his work.

But the king wondered if his hand had not been just a little forced; Pomponne was really not so bad. But a great king does not recognize weakness or error in himself: he does not have them. However ... the disgraced man was summoned in the greatest secrecy to the king's office. 'Ah, Monsieur de Pomponne, how I shall miss you! I felt such distress at dismissing you. Now then, let us talk about my affairs. Perhaps you would give me the benefit of your advice.' 'I am Your Majesty's humble servant,' Pomponne replied. And as he dismissed him, the king was kind enough to add: 'I would like to recall you, but I cannot do so at the moment. I ask you to promise to come to my council without refusing when I ask you to do so and, in the meantime, to maintain an absolute secrecy about this meeting.'[12] For posterity, Louis felt obliged to hide this fantastic admission of weakness, so in his Memoirs he hid behind pompous verbiage and covered with sacrosanct reasons of State the iniquity that he later discovered: 'I had to order him to retire because everything he touched lost the greatness and strength that one should have when executing the orders of a king of France who is not unfortunate.[13] *Rex dixit* ... He believed it himself ... but sometimes with a touch of doubt.

Rex dixit, and on his orders Nicolas de La Reynie, first criminal lieutenant and president of the *Chambre Ardente*, continued to incriminate suspects from all walks of life in the Poisons Affair: the latest were Mme de Dreux and Mme Le Féron, accused of trying to poison their respective husbands, a *rapporteur* at the Council of State and a president of the *parlement* – small fry beside the famous name that was on everyone's lips in that autumn of 1679. According to La Voisin's statement, Racine, the illustrious Racine, the greatest tragic writer of the reign, had poisoned out of jealousy the mistress that he had secretly married, that same Du Parc whom he had pinched from Molière's company. No one would be spared, *Rex dixit*, and Louvois wrote to the judges, 'the necessary orders for the arrest of M. Racine will be sent as soon as you request it.' But, wisely, the judges did not accept La Voisin's statement.

On the other hand, they greedily arrested other bearers of some of the most illustrious names of the nobility, which Court and Town hastened to repeat: Mme de Polignac, the Marquis de Cessac, Master of the Robes, Mme de Rourre, La Vallière's former friend, accused of trying to poison her, the Maréchale de La Ferté, the Marquise d'Alluye, accused of getting rid of her brother-in-law, the Princesse de Tingry, lastly, the Duchesse de Bouillon, Mazarin's niece, the sister of the Comtesse de Soissons and Maria Mancini and wife of a sovereign prince. According to some she was accused of poisoning a manservant who knew too much about her illicit affairs, according to others of trying to get rid of her own husband in order to marry a younger lover . . . who was none other than her sister's son.[14] The ravishing duchess made her entrance in court with one hand in that of her supposedly encumbering husband and the other in that of the young nephew-lover. Not for a moment did she lose her composure during the proceedings. On the contrary, when asked by one of the judges if she had ever seen the devil, she replied: 'Yes, and I see him now and he looks like a judge.' When she left the court parents and friends of the irresistible defendant turned her exit into a triumph.[15]

The arrests continued to escalate. On the morning of 24 January 1680, the Maréchal de Luxembourg, victor of a hundred battles and friend of the all-powerful Louvois, came to pay court to the king as usual and as usual was given the most gracious welcome. That same afternoon Luxembourg was warned that he was about to be arrested for taking part in the Poisons Affair. Profoundly shocked, he dashed off to the king, only to be told: 'If you're innocent, all you have to do is go to prison of your own accord. I've appointed the best judges to examine these cases and I'm leaving them to conduct them.' After such a refusal, Luxembourg had no alternative but to do as he was told and turn up at the Bastille in person. In view of his rank, he was put into 'quite a fine room'. One hour later, an order arrived to transfer him to one of those tiny barred cells 'from which one can hardly see the sky'. Luxembourg was distraught: he may have sinned by carelessness, in loving too many women other than his wife, but to be accused of dabbling in sorcery! He was, of course, innocent, but he was never to recover from the shame. 'Whatever Your Majesty has heard against M de Luxembourg is nothing compared with the declaration contained in that examination in which M de Luxembourg is accused of having sought the deaths of his own wife and that of M le Maréchal de Crequi, the marriage of his daughter with my son, in order to enter the Duchy of Montmorency.' In fact, it was Louvois who was responsible for bringing all these charges against the marshal.[16] Luxembourg had too much personality, too much weight, too much success and too much popularity to be a mere protégé, so he had to go. The Poisons Affair provided a convenient pretext. Louvois slipped in between a Louis obsessed by the idea of equal justice for all and La Reynie, to whom the statements of La Voisin and her accomplices became ever more staggering. Louvois had realized that the king suspected that the law was protecting the well off and that he had a deep-seated terror of poison. He had also noticed that his enemy Colbert disapproved of the publicity given to the affair. So, seizing upon the slightest piece of extravagant 'evidence' provided by the defendants and making a great show of zeal in order to impress the master, he took advantage of the situation to settle his own scores: 'It gave full rein to Louvois, a cunning and resentful man, to ruin anyone he wished,' a contemporary explained.[17]

★

One Wednesday evening in January 1680, Olympia Mancini, the Comtesse de Soissons, was at home playing cards with a few friends, when her brother-in-law, the Duc de Bouillon, arrived. He took her aside in a small drawing-room. He had come from the king. Mme de Soissons was seriously implicated in the Poisons Affair. In the name of their old friendship, His Majesty was willing to allow her the choice between the Bastille if she was innocent or immediate exile if she was guilty. Olympia did not hesitate: 'M. Louvois is my mortal enemy because I refused to allow my daughter to marry his son. He has influence enough to have me accused. He has false witnesses. Since he has gone so far as to have a charge laid against a person such as me, he will complete the crime and have me mount the scaffold or at least hold me in prison for the rest of my days. I would rather run away.' In the drawing-room, the guests were getting impatient: dinner time had long passed. Mme La Comtesse had gone out, they were told, Mme La Comtesse was dining in town. The guests left, with a good deal of comment and speculation on their part. Meanwhile, Olympia hurriedly packed all her jewellery and other valuables, and all the money she could lay her hands on, got into her coach with the Marquise d'Alluyre, who was also implicated in the affair, and, at three in the morning, left Paris in the direction of Belgium.[18]

One person to whom this departure gave great pleasure was Mme de Montespan, for Olympia was superintendant of the Queen's Household and, of course, had to resign the post. Why should I not take her place? Athénaïs asked herself. She mentioned it to Colbert, who spoke about it to the king, whereupon two hundred thousand crowns were paid to Olympia to buy the post from her and give it to Athénaïs. Athénaïs was, of course, delighted: with this post secured, there could be no question of having her sent away from Court when her presence was no longer desired.

Her pleasure was short-lived, for the king made La Fontanges a duchess in order to balance things out. Athénaïs resented that this daughter of a nobody, her provincial rival, an idiot, was raised to the same rank as herself. The news triggered off the usual scenario: torrents of tears, stifled rage, cries, curses, a hail of abuse, with, this time, an additional borrowing from Greek tragedy in the form of a threat to kill her children, like the sorceress Medea. The king remained impassive; the courtiers giggled.[19]

It would have been easier had there been merely the new duchess, but the old rival, Mme de Maintenon, was still there, too. That modest, discreet woman disturbed her, forever practising her devotions, but so strong-willed. Athénaïs had known her for so long, but still did not understand her: she never exposed a weak flank, she faced up to Athénaïs without ever losing her calm, she obviously had the king in her sights, but she did not seem to want to jump into bed with him. What did she want? What was she planning? 'You are trying to become the king's mistress,' Athénaïs would accuse her. 'Then there would be three of us! I in name, that girl [Fontanges] in fact and you in spirit.' Mme de Maintenon replied, 'You pay too much attention to your resentments.'[20] Athénaïs, sensing that she was no longer up to the task, formed an anti-Maintenon pressure group. She approached Louvois, hitherto her deadly enemy. Their common interests – the elimination of any strong influence over the king – brought them together. They engaged the services of the Duc de La Rochefoucauld, son of the author of the *Maxims*, a simpleton who, for that very reason, was a great friend of the king's. By calumnies, criticisms and insinuations, favourite, minister and companion made a concerted attack on the king to persuade him to disgrace Maintenon. However, these efforts came to nothing and their authors soon bit the dust.[21] Maintenon observed Montespan with detachment: 'It is a strange thing that we can neither live together nor apart. I love her and I cannot convince myself that she hates me.'[22]

The mountain built up by the Poisons Affair brought forth a mouse. After arresting great lords, wives of *parlementaires*, fortune-tellers and necromancers seemingly at random, after filling volumes with examinations and statements, it was realized that at most the fashionable 'criminals' had behaved very foolishly and that there had been a great deal of charlatanism among the 'sorcerers'. The charges amounted to two minor cases of poisoning and seven or eight abortions and sacrileges. Public opinion remained deeply dissatisfied and indignant. What was the point of creating such a state of suspense involving the whole of France, what was the point of sullying the reputations of so many honest families, compromising so many great names, locking up princesses and marshals for so little? 'That Chamber has no excuse for the most imprudent conduct in the world, of arresting individuals so lightly,' concluded Bussy-Rabutin. The Maréchal de Luxembourg was soon to leave prison. Since the accusation of poisoning had not been substantiated an attempt had been made to implicate him an affair of corruption and counterfeit coinage, but with no more success. Many of the illustrious suspects whose names had been mentioned had not even been arrested. People did not hesitate to accuse Louvois and his thirst for vengeance, or La Reynie and his ambition. Public opinion believed that the two men had artificially blown up with poison gas a huge terrifying balloon that had finally burst.[23]

On the other hand, the extraordinary publicity given to the affair left certain regrettable ideas in a number of heads: wives lumbered with an elderly husband or families patiently awaiting the death of a rich uncle discovered that by putting certain powders in the soup it was possible to hasten matters in the desired direction. Side by side with this, a veritable psychosis of poison grew up, and the slightest stomach ache was the pretext for arresting all the kitchen staff and servants.[24]

Still at her post, Mme de Sévigné happened to be with a few friends at the window of the Hôtel de Sully, in the Rue Saint-Antoine, on the Wednesday of 22 February 1680. The sensitive letter-writer who was so fond of executions, was waiting to watch the procession taking La

Voisin to the Place de Grève, where she was to be burnt alive. Warned of her condemnation the evening before, she had immediately invited her guard to sup with her. They ate well, drank enormous quantities of wine and sang song after song. (The condemned woman was particularly noted for her repertoire of lewd songs.) Then she slept for eight hours and woke up just in time to be tortured according to the custom. Sévigné craned her neck, trying to catch a glimpse of her in her cart, dressed entirely in white and crimson with fury. Profoundly shocked, the Marquise noticed that the woman violently pushed away her confessor and the crucifix that he was holding out to her. With La Voisin reduced to ashes, the courtiers could breathe once again: the affair was closed. Nevertheless her daughter and several of her accomplices were kept in custody until further information had been obtained.[25]

The pestilential vapours of the Poisons Affair had been dissipated and in that spring of 1680 the main topic of concern was the marriage of the Dauphin, the King's sole legitimate son and heir. This blockhead, now nineteen, had always been crushed by his father and had sought refuge in silent, self-satisfied idleness. He had always been regarded as a simpleton, though the Palatine maintained that he was not as stupid as people thought. The political imperatives of his father gave him as his betrothed the reputedly ugly daughter of the Elector of Bavaria, Maria Anne. Queen Maria Theresa sent Livry, her first maître d'hôtel, to judge the girl's physical appearance. A sceptical Livry came back with this report: 'At first sight she is not beautiful.' Soon the betrothed's coach approached. It stopped and Maria Anne got out and threw herself at her future mother-in-law's feet. Alas, Livry had not been mistaken: there was something disproportionate about the excessively long face and the excessively large nose. With her white brocade dress, matching ribbons and her dark, frizzy hair, she looked like a fly that had fallen into milk. The cold had made her cheeks red. To cap it all, she did not look very healthy.[26] The king had brought a quantity of jewels arranged with exquisite taste by Montespan. Ecstatic cries greeted the present: 'Mine was not so beautiful, though I was a greater lady,' complained Maria Theresa, for whom nothing was ever right.

No one took any notice of the queen's ill humour, just as no one had asked her opinion about the establishment of the new Dauphine's household. Who was to be appointed to what posts? The courtiers busied themselves furiously and intrigue was rife. Names were mentioned: the Mistress of the Robes would be the Maréchale de Rochefort, an eminently respectable lady – no surprise there. The second Mistress of the Robes – but there had never been a second Mistress of the Robes – was to be the Marquise de Maintenon.[27] The entire Court was dumbstruck. Of course, everyone knew about the king's friendship for her and talked about it constantly. But a quasi-clandestine link, whose progress was followed by a small number of initiates was one thing; the unprecedented favour accorded the ex-governess of the royal bastards, a semi-servant born into the lowest rank of the nobility, the widow of a disreputable, dissolute poet, was a very different matter.[28]

Athénaïs hastened to the king and flung her supreme weapon at the new Mistress of the Robes. She informed him that the pious, pure, virtuous Mme de Maintenon was nothing of the kind when she was a mere widow Scarron. She had enjoyed her widowhood and enjoyed the company of a great many men. That paragon of all the virtues was no more than a 'public woman'. Athénaïs was no doubt exaggerating, but what she said contained more than a grain of truth. Long before Mme de Maintenon, the secular nun who was one day to turn Versailles into a convent, there had been Françoise d'Aubigné, a pretty young widow, charming and attractive, highly sought after in the Paris salons and as flirtatious as the great ladies who ignored her. But Athénaïs let fly this poisoned arrow too late. Well aware of her rancour, Louis regarded her revelations as calumny. He did not wish to believe them and so he did not believe them.[29]

However, the most blinded of the courtiers had had their eyes opened and the more hesitant hesitated no longer. Despite Montespan, despite Fontanges, the new star was La Maintenon. But what sort of star? 'The entire Court was astonished ... No one knew what to believe,' observed Primi Visconti. The king's mistress? She was too old, though there are men who love old women, some remarked. The king's confidante? More like his bawd, others retorted. 'One did not know with whom one was dealing,' Primi Visconti concludes. It was made all the more difficult by the fact that this star, unlike the others, did everything to conceal its brightness.[30] She was to be depicted for posterity piously dressed all in black. She had great reserve and restraint, but a frankness, a simplicity, almost an ordinariness that made her even more enigmatic. In any case, there was no longer any question of her retiring from the Court. 'I cannot envisage any likelihood of my early retirement; I must therefore work for my salvation here ...'[31]

The courtiers discussed at length the attentions lavished by the king on the Dauphine, his new daughter-in-law. It was truly extraordinary. He found time to go and see her every day. At first it was a matter of daily visits lasting two hours, then two visits a day, then whole evenings, from six to ten o'clock. Did she, perhaps, have the good fortune of having the Sun King to herself? The truth came out in the end; Louis regularly went up in the direction of his daughter-in-law's apartment, but he stopped on the way at the apartment next door ... that of the second Mistress of the Robes: it was Maintenon whom he went to see. And while the courtiers patiently counted the hours that these visits lasted, the two of them sat there next to one another, chatting quietly for hours on end.

The heart had its reasons when Louis talked alone with Maintenon, but the flesh also had its reasons when he slept with Fontanges. The foolish, romantic Angélique did not realize that it was only her body that her lover was interested in. She was already seeing herself in the life of the great favourites of history: she was a duchess, pensions were showered upon her and she was expecting the king's child. She went about in her coach and eight, convinced, like the courtiers, that her position had never been more secure, which irritated both La Montespan and La Maintenon. Fontanges' exasperating vanity brought them together and made them allies. Duly instructed by Montespan, Maintenon called on Fontanges and tried to persuade her to give up Satan of her own free will and to leave the king. The nobility of her mission so animated her that she herself was to describe the scene. From Maintenon's first words, Fontanges stumbled and slumped into a chair, trying feebly to defend herself: 'But, Madame, you talk to me about giving up a passion as if it were a matter of taking off a dress.'

The 'dress' which she refused to take off was soon to be snatched from her. In the long term, the most beautiful body in the world cannot make up for stupidity and vanity. The summer of 1680 arrived and the Court radars detected a certain slackening in the king's passion for Angélique. The unfortunate girl clung to him in the most clumsy way. She wanted to leave Fontainebleau the same day as her lover, despite her advanced pregnancy, but she had a violent haemmorrhage and had to be put to bed. She felt deathly weak: she had a fever. The Court had already left and the king with it. The weeks passed, Angélique did not recover. Her beauty, her only capital, disappeared. Where were the roses in that sickly paleness? Where were the exquisite features in that swelling and puffiness? Very shortly, she retired to the abbey of Maubuisson. She no longer wanted to live: what was the point of being a duchess and covered in gold when what she wanted was the king's heart and she would never have it again. For a time, the courtiers felt sorry for her, for the way in which the king had treated her, like a servant girl. They acknowledged her as the 'martyr of the king's pleasures' – and could not wait to forget her. Maintenon breathed more freely and Montespan smiled triumphantly.[32]

The Palatine, too, was pleased, for at last she had found a little boy to play with her son Philippe. Louis de Rouvroy was five years old and the son of a favourite – probably a lover – of the late King Louis XIII. He was studying German – which was the best possible passport in the eyes of the Palatine, so she arranged for him to learn this indispensable language with her son. Louis was brought to the Palais Royal, and was given a guided tour by the young Philippe d'Orleans, a year older than him. As they strolled through the galleries and salons stuffed with masterpieces, a friendship was born between the two boys that was to be interrupted only by death. No one could have suspected that in bringing young Louis de Rouvroy into the Palais Royal the wolf was being let into the fold of the Court, for one day, as the Duc de Saint-

Simon, he would chronicle its actions with the most astonishing ferocity.

Pale and trembling, Nicolas de La Reynie entered the king's office and, after some hesitation, handed him a report. They were the statements of Marguerite Voisin, daughter of the sorceress burnt at the stake, of the sorcerer Le Sage, and of the two unfrocked priests who assisted La Voisin, the Abbés Marielle and Guibourg. They had been questioned by the *Chambre Ardente*, which had continued to function with diminished activity. From the first lines, the king started and blushed violently. The name constantly on the sorceress's lips was Mme de Montespan. In order to keep the king's love, the report alleged she had called up the devil and she had had love powders made that consisted of the most repugnant ingredients. Then she had tried to kill the king, she had offered La Voisin 100,000 *livres* for a poisoned foot-stool, contact with which would bring certain death. She had tried to assassinate La Fontanges with poisoned gloves that would have sent her into a decline. Lastly, she had had several black masses said in the course of which, her naked body serving as the altar, the Abbé Guibourg had disembowelled a young child over her and collected the blood in a chalice.

The king shut the file and looked up at La Reynie. The criminal lieutenant trembled. In a toneless voice, the king gave his orders: absolute secrecy on the Montespan file; absolutely no one must see it. All examinations and investigations must stop, and the *Chambre Ardente* was suspended *sine die*.[33]

CHAPTER 15

Out-and-Out Imperialism

'Confront me with those who accuse me. Not one of them knows me. I answer on my life that not one of them will say who I am.' So spoke Mlle des Oeillets, Montespan's *femme de chambre*, with whom the king in earlier days had had a passing affair that resulted in a bastard daughter whom he refused to acknowledge. La Voisin's daughter and her accomplices had all implicated her in the accusations that they had levied against her mistress.

The *Chambre Ardente* was suspended, but the investigation continued in the greatest secrecy, for Louis was still in the grip of terrible suspicion. Was Montespan guilty? He wanted to know the truth, but he was also afraid of knowing it. As a sop to his conscience, he appointed Louvois to question Mlle des Oeillets in person and to confront her with the accused. If they recognized her Louis would know the truth. He argued with himself, he hesitated, then finally made up his mind. There would be a confrontation, but it must be carried out with the utmost precautions, in complete secrecy.

In the gloomy dawn of that November morning, Louvois and La Reynie rehearsed Des Oeillets in her role as they travelled in her sealed carriage to the dungeon of Vincennes. It was La Reynie who interrogated Le Sage, La Voisin's factotum. At a discreet sign Des Oeillets appeared. Le Sage gave a start: 'Why! It's Mme de Montespan's *femme de chambre*! She often came to fetch black powders and white powders for her mistress.'

It was now the Abbé Guibourg's turn. Des Oeillets was brought in again: 'But it's Mme de Montespan's *femme de chambre*! I've said black masses over her naked body, just as I did with her mistress.'

Finally, they confronted her with La Voisin's daughter: 'Ah, Mlle des Oeillets! I often saw her at my mother's.' It seemed that Montespan *was* guilty.

'They're all lying, they've never seen me,' swore Mlle des Oeillets persistently. And indeed, none of La Voisin's other accomplices with whom the same scenario was repeated had in fact recognized her, and there was no examination and cross-examination. It was no longer so certain that Montespan was guilty, but doubts remained.

At this point, Colbert intervened, calling a halt to these absurdities.

There had been enough of these unproven accusations and obsessive suspicions. He told the king it was all Louvois' fault, that he had fabricated the whole thing. To allay the king's fears he suggested handing over the file to a lawyer who would examine it, take it to pieces, weigh up the pros and cons and come to a conclusion once and for all. Maître Duplessis, a renowned lawyer, was given the task of drawing up the memorandum that would bring the king relief – or grief.

If Montespan had wanted to poison the king and had got La Voisin to give her a stool that would kill on contact, how could the sorceress have got into the palace and approached the king? If there was poison to be administered, why did not La Montespan, who saw the king night and day, do it herself? And why would Montespan want to rid herself of her lover, of the source of her power? Any attempt on her part to poison the king would indicate an incredible stupidity of which Montespan was certainly exempt. And why would Montespan poison La Fontanges? Fontanges was certainly beautiful, but hardly dangerous in the long term. Why not poison Maintenon as well?

It was said that Montespan had had black masses said over her naked body in the course of which children had been sacrificed. Montespan had always been sincerely pious, rendering to the king what was the king's, that is to say, her body, and to God what was God's. With the perfect serenity of a woman and an aristocrat, she alternated adultery and the strict practices of her religion. Would she ever have consented to such sacrilegious abomination? Could such a great lady, so proud of her rank, have lowered herself to such degrading practices?

Anyway even under torture La Voisin, who had given the most illustrious names, never mentioned hers. For her, Montespan was merely one of the more ordinary customers, content simply to ask for some aphrodisiac, but certainly innocent. With their belated and sensational revelations, La Voisin's accomplices must have been trying to protect their own lives by compromising the favourite. These were the conclusions of Maître Duplessis, for whom the accusations did not stand up.

Thus the *Chambre Ardente* was finally closed. Another of La Voisin's accomplices, La Filastre, was burnt at the stake, but the others, those who had pronounced the sacred name of Montespan, disappeared. They did not appear before judges, they were not executed in a public place – they might have talked before the Court or from the scaffold. So no judgement was passed, except one *in pace* in some sombre provincial fortress where they were to finish their days, it was hoped, in silence.[1]

All's well that ends well ... for Montespan, but not for Louis. The accusation against his mistress had come like a bombshell and had suddenly thrown him back into the insecurity, shyness, fear, weakness that had dogged him since childhood. There, in the gilded serenity of his harem, those terrifying words – crime, sacrilege, poison – words that still haunted him, had come like a bolt from the blue and had profoundly shaken him. And what if the accusation had been proved?

That woman who, for so many years, had shared his intimate life, who he had held so often in his arms, offering her naked body to a blasphemy made doubly horrible by human sacrifice. The image continued to haunt the king. He had been too shaken to be able to rid himself of it, too vulnerable to demand the truth from the outset, whatever it may have been, and he was still too weak to remove all suspicion even when its absurdity had been demonstrated to him.

He avoided Athénaïs, he avoided her eyes, he avoided any private meeting with her. He could not make up his mind whether to break with her or make it up. Rarely the imposing mask of the king had so ill concealed the man's fears and weaknesses. Finally, after weeks of evasion on his part and slow, tortuous manoeuvres on the part of the Montespan lobby – led by Colbert – the lovers met in secret. How did he admit to her what oppressed him? No one would ever know. But we know Athénaïs' reaction: it was worthy of her character and suited the absurdity of the accusations. She got upon her high horse. From defendant she became prosecution. Who had dared to suspect her? Who were these back-stairs spies who imagined that they could compromise her? And what kind of a king was he to have believed them for an instant? Was it worthy of him so much as to listen to such filthy nonsense? Remorse immediately swamped suspicion. Confronted by this haughty, proud and wounded woman, Louis was once more a small boy. Athénaïs soon had him back under her thumb and it was with head held high that she left the meeting.[2]

More confident than ever of her power, she then decided to play her trump card. She had noticed that the Grande Mademoiselle often seemed preoccupied. Those sudden silences, those dreaming eyes, those deep sighs had a name: Lauzun, who was still in prison at Pignerol. For ten years, his beloved thought about him, hoped and despaired. Would the king pardon him one day? Would he free him? 'Try to be agreeable to the king and he may give you your heart's desire,' Montespan remarked, by way of an opening move. The Grande Mademoiselle looked at her wide-eyed. What could she do to please the king? She racked her brains, but she could think of nothing. A mutual friend then took it upon himself to enlighten her: 'Suppose you gave him hope that you might make M du Maine your heir.' For Montespan had her eyes on the Grande Mademoiselle's fortune, the largest in France, if not in Europe, for her son: Lauzun in exchange for the fabulous fortune. The Grande Mademoiselle leapt at the bait; if Lauzun were freed and she allowed to marry him, all her money, all her property would one day go to the young bastard.

Next day, Louis summoned his cousin: 'Mme de Montespan informed me, yesterday evening, of your good intentions with regard to the Duc de Maine. I am touched by it, as I should be, since it is out of friendship for me that you do it . . . For my part, I assure you that at every opportunity I shall recognize the marks that you have given me of your friendship.' That was all. Not a word about Lauzun, either that day or during the following days. The Grande Mademoiselle went back to Athénaïs. 'You must be patient,' she was told. Patience was all very well but time was passing and there was no Lauzun on the horizon. Montespan then made another move: 'You must make a gift to the Duc du Maine of your principality of Dombes and of your Comté d'Eu.' 'But he will get it in my will,' the Grande Mademoiselle countered. 'There is no need to repeat it. It reminds me of my death, which I have no desire to see.' 'One does not play lightly with the king. When one has promised, one must stick to it.' 'And what if afterwards, when I have given it, I'm tricked and he is not set free.' They talked and talked, but got nowhere. At last Montespan came out with the supreme argument: it was either a gift at once or the Bastille for Lauzun. And the poor love-sick woman gave in, giving the Duc du Maine the principality of Dombes and the Comté d'Eu.

Having done this, there was still no Lauzun. 'You must be patient.' And so the Grande Mademoiselle, more impatient than ever, was condemned to wait. At last she was summoned by Montespan. With beating heart, she dashed to the favourite's apartment: 'The king has asked me to tell you that he will have M. Lauzun removed from Pignerol and taken to Bourbon.' 'What! He isn't coming straight here after all I've done?' 'I don't know enough about it; he leaves the choice to you as to who will guard him; for he wants it still to look like a prison.' The Grande Mademoiselle burst into tears and Montespan snapped, 'You're very difficult to please; when you have one thing you want another.'

But the *coup de grâce* for the Grande Mademoiselle was yet to come. It was delivered that same evening during a walk with the favourite in the park at Saint-Germain: 'The king has asked me to tell you that he wants you to give up any idea of marrying M de Lauzun.' The unfortunate woman gave vent to a deluge of tears, recriminations, reminders of the terms of their agreement. Montespan calmly replied: 'I never promised you anything.' There was to be no Lauzun to share her life at the Court, no possibility of joining him in his new enforced rustication, no marriage in the future. And the Duc du Maine was Prince de Dombes and Comte d'Eu. His mother rejoiced at having thus assured his material future and his father took great delight in all this scheming, making fun of his cousin, while pursuing his revenge upon a gentleman who, long ago, had dared to defy him. I've been tricked, the Grande Mademoiselle said to herself, I've been tricked.

Lauzun, on the other hand, was delighted. At Pignerol, he no longer had time to dig tunnels in the wall in order to surprise Fouquet who had died several months before after being shut up for nineteen years in the same prison. From his various forced residences, Lauzun wrote to his 'betrothed', begging her to intervene on his behalf, complaining of the slow death to which he was being subjected. But visitors brought back a quite different picture; Lauzun was enjoying himself immensely at Amboise and paying court to all the women.

As justice would have it, it was at La Montespan's that the Grande Mademoiselle finally saw her 'betrothed' for the first time after eleven years of separation. The irresistible lady's man came in, wearing clothes, according to his beloved, that were completely out of fashion, 'dating from long before his imprisonment, too short, and torn here and there' and 'a filthy wig'. Montespan had the tact to withdraw. 'You will feel more at ease talking alone.'

Lauzun threw himself at his princess's feet, thanked her profusely for his liberation, covered her with tears. The Grande Mademoiselle remained open-mouthed, as if frozen. She had hoped for this moment for too long to feel the intense happiness that she had expected of it. There was a sort of unacknowledged disappointment in the dryness with which she describes the scene. And, anyway, the dashing lover had clearly aged. 'Don't you find that he has changed?' she asked everyone. 'Don't you think that he has changed?' she even asked Maintenon, who replied, sourly, 'He has not paid me the honour of visiting me.'

'Although I have long awaited the news that you have given me, it still leaves me surprised and angry.' The king was angry on learning of the death of the Duchesse de Fontanges who had never recovered from her miscarriage. She had reappeared in Court, but only briefly, hardly able to stand up. She then dragged on for a few weeks, moving from convent to convent, before dying on 28 June 1681 at Port-Royal in the presence of a single friend. The king was also surprised by the death at the age of twenty-one of the young woman so brimming with health until her mysterious illness. Courtiers, considerably less surprised, were unanimous in accusing Montespan of poisoning her rival. The Palatine even provided the details. Montespan had bribed one of Fontanges' lackeys to pour poison into her milk and to poison, at random, two of her manservants. With her pride and her wit, Athénaïs had made too many enemies and the Poisons Affair was still fresh in everyone's mind. So the foul insinuation spread once again through the palace corridors and even reached the bed in which the king was frolicking with his plump mistress. In an instant the terrible suspicion, which Athénaïs thought had been buried forever, had returned. The king cold-shouldered her. In order to remove all doubt, La Reynie, practical as ever, proposed an autopsy of the dead woman. But Louis hesitated to open a door on the truth, gripped once more by his fear of confronting it.

Yet the autopsy was carried out. Poison there, poison here, poison everywhere was found in Fontanges' body, repeated those who wished to seem well informed. The physicians remained more circumspect in their convoluted language: 'The cause of the lady's death must be attributed solely to the total corruption of the right lobes on the lung which occurred as a result of the alteration between hot and dry disorders in her liver which, having produced a large quantity of bilious and acrid blood, appears to have caused the losses that had occurred previously.' In short, they concluded that the woman had died a natural death. The king could breathe once more and brought back his favourite for the umpteenth time. But it was never to be the same again between them. The doubt and fear that had assailed him had left their mark on this weak man.[3]

The Triumph of Love was the – symbolic – title of the formidable spectacle given at the Château de Saint-Germain, a mythological-allusive ballet-opera-revue that marked the high point of the carnival of 1681. The king had given up performing on a stage himself: his family appeared instead. His son, the Dauphin, replaced him, but since this blockhead lacked his father's grace, he had only a minor part, that of an 'Indian' follower of Bacchus. His wife, the Dauphine, played Flora, the Comte de Vermandois, bastard son of the king and of La Vallière, played the travesty role of Love and the seven-year-old Mlle de Nantes, bastard daughter of the king and of Montespan, played Youth. The principal roles were wisely left to professional ballerinas who danced and leapt among the bedecked princes and princesses.[4]

'Everybody is at the ballet; and I am alone in my room, where for several days now I have spent a large part of my time resting, which I find most agreeable.'[5] Obviously, Eros was not Maintenon's God – she preferred to abstain from appearing at these entertainments, where, she knew, she had no place. To all appearances, she spurned these depraved activities ... awaiting her hour. Montespan, at the height of her triumph, could afford to show some magnanimity to the friend-enemy who was so careful not to take her at face value: 'Mme de Montespan and I took a walk together today, arm in arm, laughing much; we are no better for it.' A monumental masked ball closed the dazzling carnival given in Montespan's honour.[6]

The following day, Lent began. 'Sinners, repent,' cried the priests. 'Sinner, repent,' Maintenon repeated *sotto voce*. As if to prove her right, God's sword came down. On 6 February 1681, Mlle de Tours, illegitimate daughter of the king and Montespan, died not long before her eighth birthday. 'The king was touched,' Maintenon continued, then, more circumspectly: 'and I shall tell you later what I know of the sorrow of Mme de Montespan.'[7]

However the death of Mlle de Tours tolled the knell for the mother, who wrote to her son, the Duc du Maine: 'I shall say nothing of my sorrow; you are too good-hearted not to have felt it yourself; as for Mlle de Nantes, everyone admired her; but I confess that I paid too dearly for the praise to have felt it; every spot here – where I saw the poor little one – so affects me that I am quite willing to undertake a journey which, in itself, is the most disagreeable in the world, in the hope that the dissipation will diminish somewhat the vapours that have not left me since our loss.'[8]

The sorrow, whose sincerity Maintenon seemed to doubt, over-whelmed Montespan. Suddenly she felt exhausted and, for the first time in her life, no longer had any desire to struggle. Let Maintenon have first place, she seemed to be saying, since Maintenon has won.[9]

Colbert had reason to feel pleased with himself: he had married off his three daughters to three dukes – Chevreuse, Beauvillière and Mortemart – had his brother, Croissy, appointed Minister of Foreign Affairs, his eldest son, Seignelay, Minister of Commerce and of the Navy, his other sons superintendent of buildings and co-adjutor to the Archbishop of Rouen. Unfortunately for Colbert, however, another dynasty was rising in opposition to his own. The brother was Archbishop of Reims, the sister Duchesse d'Aumont, the daughter Duchesse de La Roche-Guyon, a son was Minister of War, another son, Master of the Robes, and a cousin Captain of the *'Cent Suisses'*, the Swiss Guards. This dynasty bore the name of Louvois.[10]

None of this pleased Louis. He had wanted bourgeois ministers in order to avoid the difficulties his predecessors had had with the aristocracy, yet he had allowed his ministers' sons to acquire some dubious titles, let his dukes marry their daughters and swallow the enormous dowries built up by their successful fathers. He had wanted to surround himself with obscure men who would have neither support nor followers, isolated from one another, depending solely on his good graces and yet, almost without realizing it, out of fear of new faces, and because he let them lead him by the nose, he had gradually allowed them to occupy the highest posts in the land. Now he could rid himself neither of Colbert nor of Louvois, for it was no longer one but ten Colberts, ten Louvois, that he would have to get rid of – an unthinkable operation. He had believed that he had cleverly maintained a rivalry that held them in check, but it was this very rivalry that swamped him in the end. He had believed that he could play one off against the other, whereas he was in reality no more than a balloon tossed from one minister to the next.

'Monsieur Colbert, I have just seen the finest and best arranged fortifications in the world; but, what surprised me about them, was how inexpensive they were. How is it that here, at Versailles, we are spending frightful sums and we see almost nothing done?'[11] The king did not seem to understand that fortifications were built on the same model by soldiers who are paid practically nothing, whereas Versailles required thousands of skilled, highly paid workers.

'Monsieur Colbert, I need sixty million for the extraordinary expenses of war!' 'Alas, Sire! I fear . . .' 'Think about it, there is someone else who would do what is required, if you do not wish to do it yourself.' Louvois again – and that was not all. 'M Colbert, I am told that there have been abuses concerning supplies to the arsenals at Toulon and Marseille.' Colbert could not explain to the king that when one is responsible for the entire French economy, one cannot have one's eye on everything, still less on everyone.

'M Colbert, there is knavery in the accounts that you have submitted to me for the works at Versailles.' 'Sire. I think I can flatter myself at least that such a word does not apply to me.' 'No! But you should have paid more attention to it.'

Did the king hesitate a moment before uttering that 'No'? As he listened to Louis making accusations against him that he knew came from his rival Louvois, did Colbert give a thought to the files that he had once so lovingly prepared one night to ruin Fouquet? Twenty years of power had worn him out and the master's suspicions undermined him. Like Montespan he had lost all pleasure in action and the strength to defend himself. 'Before,' one of his clerks recounts, 'one saw him set to work rubbing his hands; now, when he works, he bears a pained expression, even, sometimes, sighing. From being easy-going, he has become difficult to please and much less work gets done than during the early years of his administration.'[12] Colbert's star was fading and Louvois had won. Drums beat, trumpets snarled, and out and out imperialism was set loose.

Since the Treaty of Nijmegen, the cannon had been silent throughout Europe. This did not please Louis, who was thoroughly bored by this silence, since he could no longer find anything to satisfy his lust for glory. 'Peace tormented him,' said Saint-Simon. 'So he sought to awake war once more.'[13] But first he sent an army of lawyers to fight in Lorraine, Alsace, Franche-Comté and Flanders. Their task was to go through the archives and find lands that had once depended on the present possessions of France and to annex them.

Next it was Spain's turn to join the firing line. Louis would, indeed, evacuate the town of Coutrai in the Netherlands, as he had agreed to do in the Treaty of Nijmegen, but first Spain would have to pay a heavy indemnity. The town of Alost and its surroundings, on the other hand, would go back to France. By what right, an indignant Spain demanded. The same treaty had 'forgotten' to mention it. But above all it was the city of Luxembourg that Louis wanted and was claiming from Spain. Better to lose everything than give up Luxembourg, replied the Spanish government, losing all patience. So the French troops blockaded Luxembourg.

At this point, a veritable *coup de théâtre* occurred. The king of France, aware of the new danger from the Ottoman Turks in central Europe and wishing to assist Christendom in opposing them, showed his magnanimity by dropping his claims over Luxembourg and withdrawing his troops. Louis was really waiting for the emperor, harassed by the Turks, to call on his troops from Luxembourg to the rescue, thus giving Louis a golden pretext to meddle in his affairs.

In Mantua, the Duke was in a cruel dilemma. The income from his tiny State was so insignificant compared with the means required to give him the luxury and comfort he required. Then suddenly he was presented with Tantalus, in the form of two individuals disguised as theatrical peasants, Messieurs de Catinat and d'Asfeld, extraordinary and most secret ambassadors of the king of France. They had come to offer him an enormous sum of money for his fortress at Casal. The Duke of Mantua was delighted; he was quite ready to sign at once and pocket the money. But counsellor Ercole Mattioli, advised caution: 'What would Spain and the emperor say if Your Grace ceded to France the fortress that commands the entire Po Valley?' Would they not invade his States, dethrone him, and ruin him? Had they not already got wind of the negotiations? But the French had an answer to everything: His Most Christian Majesty deigned to take His Highness of Mantua and his States under his protection and to guarantee him against any 'accident'. His mind at rest, the fat duke signed the sale of Casal. But, he wondered, who the devil could have warned the Spanish of these intrigues? The much better equipped French secret service knew, however. It was Mattioli himself who, while negotiating with France, had informed Spain. Would the traitor go unpunished? One day Mattioli disappeared. It was all so carefully planned that he was never to be seen again and no one was ever to know what became of him. The minister of a sovereign prince, seized on foreign territory and thrown into the deepest dungeon – such a flagrant violation of international law had to be covered up forever. The prisoner had to be prevented from communicating with anybody at all, his name had to be omitted from the registers of his various prisons and hidden from all eyes, even from his gaolers. He would have to wear a velvet mask to his dying day. Perhaps it was from this same little piece of stuff that Voltaire was to fashion an iron mask; for the little Italian double agent was to become a prototype for the Iron Mask, probably the dullest and least romantic, but the most plausible of this prestigious gallery. With Mattioli out of the way and the Duke of Mantua replete with gold, the French troops were able to take possession of Casal on 30 September 1681.

The same day other French troops entered Strasbourg. For a time Louis had cast a greedy eye on 'the mistress of the Rhine', so vast, so highly populous, so rich, so well armed that, according to Voltaire, it formed an entire Republic on its own.[14] The French began in the usual way by setting lawyers on to the affair. But in the case of Strasbourg, despite sleepless nights spent pouring over old charters, they found nothing to back up the king's claims.

Strasbourg unquestionably belonged to the Empire, with so many liberties and privileges that it was practically an independent city, delighted to be so and determined to remain so. Lawyers having failed, money was tried. Jupiter-Louvois showered gold on the magistrates. The French then resorted to psychological warfare. Suddenly French troops, led by the terrible Louvois in person, appeared, carried off the men defending the Rhine and surrounded the city.

The terrified inhabitants were desperate. They knew that their attachment to France would mean the complete loss of their freedoms. 'Let us surrender without resistance or we shall be destroyed,' murmured their corrupted magistrates. In their terror, the people gave in. They opened their gates and Louvois, entering at the head of his troops, looked for all the world like a Roman emperor.[15]

'So your master is aiming at being the universal monarch,' William of Orange spat out at Gourville, France's representative. With Strasbourg occupied 'without any legal formalities',[16] this time, Europe, which had previously been content to grumble at each of Louis XIV's dubious annexations, was up in arms. The Empire, Sweden and Holland hastened to sign a treaty of association. England made threats. Spain spoke of war.

But Spain was too 'weak and languishing'[17] to constitute a real threat. The king of England, all too dependent on subsidies from the king of France, was too clever not to divert the war-like intentions of his parliament. Sweden found herself opposed by her hereditary enemy, Denmark, with whom France had hastily signed a treaty of alliance. The emperor had Hungarian rebels on his hands, and the Turks were spreading across his states and at whom the representatives of the king of France were making encouraging smiles.[18]

As for Holland, she was not as her Stadtholder, William of Orange, would have liked; he was forced to admit his inability to set up an anti-Louis XIV coalition: 'I am highly despised in your country,' he snapped at Gourville. 'Actually we do you more honour, for we hate you dearly,' Gourville replied, flatteringly.[19] As evidence of his hatred Louis once again occupied the principality of Orange. 'My only hope is to live long enough to avenge this affront,' cried William.[20]

The pope was the next to protest when Louis laid into *his* rights. Trouble had been brewing for a long time. An insignificant affair was to serve as the trigger for a measure that was to have grave consequences. Eight years before, Louis XIV had decided that he would take over the income from vacant bishoprics. A declaration of 1673 gave this right, known as the Régale, to the Crown, and it was ratified by a general assembly of the French clergy. But two old friends, the Bishops of Alet and of Pamier, refused to accede and quite simply excommunicated the beneficiaries of these celebrated revenues. When a simple decision of the Council of State annulled their ex-communication, they appealed to the pope. The king, as usual, turned to his lawyers. A rapporteur at the Council of State drew up a 'Treaty on the authority of the king concerning the administration of the Church', which was a declaration of legal war on the Vatican. The pope responded with a brief contradicting the king's views. The king threw in his face 'the indefeasible right of the Crown of France'. The pope fired off briefs at the king and annulled his decisions. The *parlement* intervened, without anyone asking, and for once, on the side of the Crown, condemning the papal 'abuses'. The pope threatened the king with sanctions. The king convened a new assembly of the clergy. He threw in the heavy artillery of the prelates who supported him and the Régale was of course confirmed, which was nothing compared with the four articles that followed: independence of the king from the pope in temporal matters, superiority of the church councils over the pope, limitation of the religious powers of the pope, non-recognition of the personal infallibility of the pope.

It had needed the miserable affair of the Régale, allowed to become poisoned with long-standing resentments, to set off the enormous challenge to papal authority constituted by the 'liberties of the Gallic Church'. French bishops delighted at the prospect of limiting Vatican imperialism, a *parlement* ever ready to get on its high horse, the confused but still active groundswell of a thinking, liberal bourgeoisie, irritated by the supra-nationality of the papacy, a king trembling before the Church but ready to do anything as soon as he imagined his authority threatened, these were the various tendencies that came together to challenge the pope. Never mind if the celebrated articles were not within the competence of a mere assembly of clergy. Never mind if a number of bishops did not agree. Never mind if universities, respectful of law, expressed reservations. The pope was left the last word, but what last word? One more brief in which, of course, he protested. He denounced the blow that had been given him, but refrained from returning it.[21]

CHAPTER 16

Decor for a Theatrical King

Preceded by a double row of galloping musketeers, surrounded by a swarm of armed cavalrymen and drawn by six bay horses, the king's red coach was driving at full speed. The queen's coach, drawn by six white horses, followed him, preceding the sinuous comet of the Court carriages. The procession reached the square that led to the forecourt of the palace of Versailles, and passed between two rows of French and Swiss guards presenting arms. The fifes sounded, the drums beat, the standards flapped in the wind. Massed between the coaches which had already arrived, the Versailles crowd, mingling with servants and lackeys, acclaimed the sovereign at length. On that morning of 6 May 1682 Louis had wanted to surround his arrival in the palace with some solemnity, to indicate that it was there that he would henceforth reside.[1] After flouting Europe and putting the pope in his place, he had decided to settle into his new home.

In fact, he had been thinking of making Versailles his private capital and the centre of his government for thirteen years, but the scepticism of his courtiers and Colbert's open hostility to the project had made him act surreptitiously. Bit by bit he had extended his father's small hunting castle. From year to year, he had spent more and more time there. One idea, however, had dominated the somewhat irregular building of this enormous complex: 'Let it be done to accord with our greatness,' the king had ordered his architects.

Nothing was ready, however, when he did move in. The winter, which had been particularly cold, had held up work; the workmen had refused to finish the outer wall, the trenches of the new aqueduct were still exposed, abandoned sites dotted the path here and there. Inside, masons, carpenters, painters and decorators continued to fill the palace with dust, noise and smells. Louvois asked the king to forgive him. 'Although the work has been held up,' the master replied, 'I shall leave in any case on Wednesday morning, in order to be at Versailles at five o'clock. Take more care with my bedchamber than with the rest.'[2] In the name of greatness the courtiers were not supposed to see or hear the hundreds of workmen, sawing, hammering, planing and plastering under their noses.

It was just unfortunate if foul-smelling draughts blew through the drawing-room and galleries, unfortunate if the sauces froze in the exquisitely carved dishes or if the wine carafes were full of ice. People were asphyxiated by the new paint. Either they shivered or they were smoked like hams – for the chimneys worked badly. When fires were lit, the fog became so dense in the sumptuous drawing-rooms that it was only possible to make out vague shadows as one breathed in the acrid smell of soot.[3]

Louis treated such details as unworthy of his attention and the courtiers were asked to do likewise. Similarly, they were not to complain about being packed together in small rooms, with excessively low ceilings, airless and highly uncomfortable. Despite the 282 lodgings, the 1,252 rooms with fireplaces and the 800 rooms without fireplaces, dukes, princes and dignitaries were reduced to sleeping on top of one another. Given the conditions in which lords and ladies had to endure, no one bothered to find out how the 7,000 servants, 4,000 infantry and 4,000 cavalry belonging to the royal guard lived.[4] Living close to the sun does not allow for questions.

The courtiers refrained from criticizing the climate, the environment or the architecture of their luxury concentration camp. For Primi Visconti, who was homesick for his native Italy, 'the countryside was disagreeable', nothing but sand and unhealthy marshes, putrid water and bad air which, at the height of summer, made everyone in the Court sick, except the king and himself.

As for the architecture, it lacked order and overall design.[5] This criticism was taken up in detail by Saint-Simon: 'Wings that took off without holding on to anything', a chapel that was a sad representation of an immense catafalque which crushed the whole design, drawing-rooms 'piled one on top of another', quite unsuitable apartments for the king and queen, with rooms that had 'the darkest, the most closed in, the most unpleasant views'. From a distance, it was like looking at 'a palace that had been burnt down, of which the top floor and roof were still missing'. All this was the fault of the architect, Mansart, an unpleasant flatterer who had convinced the king that he was a master architect when in fact he knew nothing: 'He was clever enough to bring to the king plans that he had deliberately left unfinished, leaving it to the king, with some discreetly offered help from himself, to see either the fault to be corrected or some better way of doing it. Mansart would then express surprise at how right the king was and declare that he was a mere schoolboy compared to him . . .' Poor Louis XIV, even taken in by his tradesmen! The gardens, an example of 'bad taste' of which even 'a short visit is enough to fill one with horror', were no better. 'One reached cool shade only by passing through a vast torrid zone, at the end of which there is nothing to be done but walk up and down.' The celebrated waters were 'green, thick, muddy . . . spreading unhealthy, noticeable humidity and a smell that was even more so'.

'There is no end to the monstrous defects of this huge palace,' Saint-Simon concluded, before delivering the final blow against 'this masterpiece, so ruinous and in such bad taste'.[6] Primi Visconti had already expressed astonishment at the insensate expense incurred by Versailles. These gentlemen had their own way of avenging their condemnation to this over-gilded prison.

On the other hand, they were expected to admire the results. A dazzling, multi-coloured iridescence of marble and a delicate tracery of gilded woodwork overladen with trophies and emblems served as a background for the most extraordinary creations of the decorative arts: marquetry furniture inlaid with gilded bronze, armchairs covered with golden velvet, cabinets with innumerable secret drawers set with hard stones. Countless knick-knacks in oriental porcelain, silver or vermeil were displayed on the commodes, on the console-tables and even on the ground. Chandeliers dripping with crystal were reflected in the mirrors. On the inlaid parquet floors glowed the floral designs of enormous carpets made at the Savonnerie, while the ceilings swarmed with an allegorical Olympus. On the walls, the painters reigned: Poussin, Lebrun and Mignard tried to compete with their great Italian predecessors, Veronese, Correggio, Raphael, Mantegna, Giorgione, Leonardo. Did the courtiers pause in the small drawing-room that followed the Salon Ovale to observe the Gioconda's smile? They preferred to examine in detail the rooms of 'curiosities or rarities' in which the king had lovingly arranged his most precious objects in marquetry cabinets or on leather topped tables: antique marble, gold or silver statuettes, vases made of agate, cornelian, heliotrope, amethyst and emerald root, grotesque figures in pearls or rubies. What struck the visitors most, on entering, was on the mantlepiece: the *Nef du Roi*, an enormous object vaguely reminiscent of the form of a vase and containing several kilos of solid gold, chiselled on every seam and dotted with precious stones. They were then amused to recognize, among the profusion of antique cameos and engraved stones, the famous agate known as 'the apotheosis of Germanicus'. They lingered before the huge jaspar basin in which the emperor Charles v had been baptized.[7] Urged on by their taste and a genuine artistic sense, the Valois, who had married into the Medicis, had been enlightened patrons. Louis had more the meticulousness, the greed, the collector's passion of his Habsburg ancestors, combined with a wish to create an entirely original decor in which new forms would carry magnificence and grandeur to a level never before envisaged. 'Let it be done to accord with our greatness!' And gold served as the common denominator of all these disparate elements. Walls, furniture, hangings, objects were painted gold, covered with gold, inlaid with gold, embroidered with gold. Gold bespattered Versailles. Gold was the hallmark of that complex, which still has no rival, though it is now no more than an empty shell.

Gold was the colour of the sun. The sun was the emblem of the king, reproduced endlessly throughout the Château de Versailles. Louis xiv justified his choice by drawing a portrait of the day star that was, in all modesty, an obvious self-portrait: 'We chose as body the sun, which is the most noble of all, and which, by its unique quality, by the brightness that surrounds it, by the light that it communicates to the other stars . . . which form for it a kind of court, by the good that it does in all places, constantly producing, on all sides, life, joy and action, by its constant movement, in which it seems nevertheless always at peace, by that constant, invariable course, from which it never departs or deflects, is certainly the most vivid and finest image of a great monarch. Those who saw me govern with such facility and without being in the least incommoded by any of the innumerable cares demanded of kingship, persuaded me to add the earth's globe and for its soul *"Nec Pluribus impar"*: by which it is to be understood that being sufficient unto myself for so many things, I would no doubt be sufficient to govern still other empires, as the sun illuminates other worlds.'[8]

It needed a good dose of Germanic heaviness, in both style and content, to be so fulsomely self-flattering. Louis had found the sun emblem back in the ballets of his youth in which he had played Apollo, God of the sun. 'It was there,' he confided, 'that I began to assume the emblem that I have kept ever since.'[9] Versailles was in truth the concrete transposition of a theatrical decor, the only setting in which he could really be at ease.

In his childhood and in youth, Louis had only been a king on stage, when, during magnificent ballets and pantomimes, he appeared with plumed helmet and studded with precious stones. Naturally enough, he had wanted to build himself a stage that would replace the temporary, shifting stages on which he had only played occasionally. He had stuck his decor down in an unfrequented, isolated place, in the middle of wild, unattractive countryside; there he summoned up a palace-capital, which he surrounded by an entirely artificial environment. Versailles was a theatre in which he could shut himself up and play the role of king without interruption. Thus the illusion of his youth was realized. In order to avoid any return to reality, he was practically never to leave Versailles.

His great-grandfather, Philip II of Spain, had built the prodigious Escorial, in order to shut himself up to converse with his only superior in the universe, God. This immeasurable pride was equalled only by the immeasurable vanity of Louis XIV who, in his Olympus on the edge of Paris, *was* God.

In his small, austere apartments in the Escorial, with a simple chair as a throne, Philip II was king, he knew he was king and could not conceive that anyone on earth could doubt it. Louis, on the other hand, needed to surround himself with exaggeratedly gilded decor and seat himself on the immense throne of chiselled vermeil, surmounted by a gleaming canopy, to believe that he was king and to make others believe it. Louis inherited this *noveau riche* taste from two *nouveaux riches* mentors, Mazarin and Fouquet, of whom he had been jealous to the point of imitation. In time, Versailles became the height of good taste and was imitated everywhere. Where the great baroque style had once flourished in Italy, Germany and even in England, it was now the Louis XIV style in its Versailles apotheosis that was to be copied. No European sovereign was spared this epidemic. From the Czarina of all the Russias to the least German princeling, everyone had to have his Versailles, and a good many of them ruined themselves in the attempt. Even the Sultan of Morocco, Mulay Idriss, and the emperor of China, Kien Long, ordered their own little Versailles, one at Meknes, the other at Yuan Min Yuan.

This fashion was to spread to posterity: Ludwig II, King of Bavaria, the possessor of deplorable taste, copied half a Versailles of plaster in the middle of the nineteenth century and at the beginning of the next century several maharajas built imitations in the middle of the red sands of Rajasthan. Versailles, the monument to the vanity of one man, aroused the vanity of all.

'This is a veritable brothel,' whispered the Duke of Palestrima to Primi Visconti, observing with amazement the mixed, noisy crowd circulating, without any sense of decorum, through the galleries of Versailles. The palace was certainly an Olympus, but entrance was free and the morals no less so.[10] The drunkenness and heterosexual debauchery were bad enough, but the homosexuals, organized into a Confraternity with entrance examinations, oaths, statutes, etc, were really too much!

The parish priest of Versailles talked at length about this deplorable situation with Mme de Maintenon and begged her to mention it to the king, 'I have done so already,' she replied. 'And one day when I was urging him to put some order in these matters, he replied that one would have to begin with his brother.'[11] It was impossible to take Monsieur to task. But then to the fury of the Palatine, Monsieur's favourite, the Chevalier de Lorraine, took a great liking to the Comte de Vermandois, illegitimate son of Louis and La Vallière. Since his mother had disappeared into a convent, the boy – now fifteen, charming, vivacious, of excellent manners – had been placed under the protection of the Palatine, but this did not prevent Lorraine from introducing the boy into the Confraternity.[12] Then the inevitable happened. Vermandois was summoned by the king, his father. Jupiter, thundering with haughty anger, ordered him to name his accomplices. Vermandois, trembling with fear, cited names, more names, ever more names. It was now Jupiter's turn to be downcast. The vice, which he had held in horror since his childhood, had contaminated the royal family, the most illustrious noble family and the immediate entourage of the heir to the throne, the Dauphin. Then Jupiter struck. The Prince de La Roche-sur-Yon, son of the Prince de Conti, was exiled to Chantilly; others were expelled from the Court, including the Prince de Turenne, one of the Maréchal de Créqui's sons, the Chevalier de Saint-Maure, one of Louvois' cousins whom the king himself had placed in the Dauphin's entourage, a childhood friend of the same Dauphin and one of his former pages still in service. In vain did the king's friend, the Duc de La Rochefoucauld, beg him to spare the shame of his family and not to dismiss his relations, the Comte de Roucy and the Vidame de Laon. In vain did the Master of the Horse, Lorraine's brother, intervene to spare his other brother, the Comte de Marsan.[13] It is extraordinary in the circumstances that Louis XIV allowed Monsieur to consider giving one of the most inveterate reprobates, the sinister Marquis d'Effiat, as a tutor to his son, thus unleashing a howl of vehement protest from the Palatine.[14]

The expulsions were a display of ostentatious severity, when discretion would have been more effective. They also revealed incomprehensible tolerance; Louis, in the grip of suddenly revived fears from long ago, acted incoherently. As often in such cases, the only real victim was the most innocent. Vermandois, forcibly separated from his father, treated as a leper by the Court, was taken off desperate to Normandy. After a certain lapse of time, the Palatine asked the king to forgive him, but in vain. 'The poor boy is so repentant about his misdeeds,' she began. 'I am not yet disposed to see him; I am still too angry with him,' the king replied.[15] In order to get back into favour, Vermandois was to go to war the following year and fight with such enthusiasm and lack of concern for his own life, that he fell ill at the siege of Courtrai, and died before his seventeenth birthday.

Bossuet went to the Carmelite convent to announce the terrible news to the boy's mother. The ex-Duchesse de La Vallière burst into tears, then, remembering the state of sin in which she had lived and which had brought Vermandois into the world, she uttered these terrifying words of abnegation: 'It is too much to weep for the death of a son for whose birth I have not wept enough.'[16]

'Mme la Dauphine has given birth to a boy.' On the threshold of the antechamber, Louis XIV in person announced the birth of the future Duc de Bourgogne to the assembled courtiers on that July day in 1682. He was radiant. The noisome clouds of scandal had lifted, all anxieties had vanished. In spite of his entourage, the Dauphin, who had remained healthy in body and mind, had a son. The courtiers, encouraged by the Master's joy, rushed up to him, and trampling protocol underfoot jostled him, kissed him and bore him in triumph to his apartments. In the courtyards, 'the low people seemed to have lost their senses'. Bonfires were lit with anything that was found lying about – gilded sedan chairs, panelling and parquet flooring intended for the palace. A furious *valet de chambre* went to inform the king of this sacrilege, but Louis burst out laughing: 'Let them be. We shall have other flooring.'[17] He was happy.

Even if the furnishings at Versailles were marked by a scandal and a number of material problems, Louis could be happy; the order that he had desired reigned, that new order that so much astonished Primi Visconti: princes of the blood royal whose position was reduced to distinctions of protocol, princesses 'more slaves than the women of a harem', foreign princes reduced to the rank 'of mere knights', aristocrats who 'were afraid of the king as schoolboys of their master and who, in fact, now live under the king like so many novices under a father director', as a servile and fearful Court.[18] Louis XIV 'wants only humble people with no hidden intentions'. This rather untalented man, this dupe, so open to this or that influence, had succeeded where his predecessors, considerably more gifted than he, had failed: he had managed to tame those princes and great nobles who had once been so powerful and so turbulent.

He had drawn up his programme sixteen years earlier in describing the ideal relationship between king and subjects: 'He alone receives all respect, he alone is the object of all hopes; nothing is carried out, nothing is expected, nothing is done except by him alone ... *All the rest is servile, all the rest is powerless, all the rest is sterile.*'[19] It was a long-term labour, conceived in his youth and methodically pursued since Mazarin's death; it consisted above all of a skilful erosion of the nobility, of its pride, its antiquity, its authenticity, the purity of its blood. The idea came from Mazarin, a commoner by birth, who, to make fun of the aristocrats while providing some additional income, had opened up throughout France an 'Armorial de France', in which anyone who had the money could have his own coat of arms designed. 'Genealogists' began to flourish, producing, at will and for a very fat fee, prodigious family trees.[20]

The Palatine who, as a good German, knew her Gotha by heart and spent her time climbing genealogical trees, was furious: 'Nobility is easily acquired in France ... I cannot get used to such a thing.'[21] This nobility, so punctilious where its precedents were concerned, so fascinated by complicated protocol, might therefore be thought particular about names and titles and closed to those who did not have *la pura sangre*. It was in fact wide open to every usurper, stuffed with false titles bristling with false genealogies. Undermining their pride, Louis replaced it with vanity, leaving the false to mingle with the true and lending hope to all pretentions.

Similarly, he dangled the prospect of gold before the nobility that had once been richer and therefore more detached than the king. To subject it all the more, he put it under his financial dependence. Fouquet had had the idea of filling the Court and government with these creatures, then catching them on the three-pronged fork of gambling (which he encouraged), debts (which he settled) and pensions (which he granted).[22] It was a programme scrupulously continued by Louis. Attracted by the brilliance of the Court, forced to appear there constantly, caught up in a whirlwind of entertainment that left them no respite, the nobles no longer had any time to concern themselves with their own lands and fortune, while their money disappeared in the ruinous costumes required by a fashionable existence.

Louis drew tirelessly on the State coffers to fill the gaps. He paid off the debts of the Duc de La Rochefoucauld (and at what a price!). 'Never did a servant act with such sedulousness, baseness and, it has to be said, such slavishness.' Saint-Simon may have been jealous, but he was right in describing the king's friend in this way. La Rochefoucauld could only absent himself three or four times a year to dine in Paris. If he went once to his estate at Verteuil, in Poitou, of which he was so fond, a note recalled him to Versailles after a few days. Even old age and sickness did not bring an interruption to his 'slavery'. Weakened, almost blind, he still had to drag himself out hunting with the king. But, as he could no longer see, he stuck the bleeding foot of the dead deer in the king's eye or ear when making the traditional presentation. Louis suggested that he take a little rest; he was 'heartbroken'.[23] Was he no longer the king's friend? Being the king's friend was a dog's life.

To avoid arousing jealousy, the king also gave 40,000 crowns to his other friend, the Master of the Horse, and 20,000 crowns so as not to be accused of favouritism to his other friend's brother, the Chevalier de Lorraine.[24] Everyone was happy as Louis constantly extended his circle of 'clients'. Similarly he encouraged marriages between great names and great fortunes, thus killing two birds with one stone. Saint-Simon inveighed against these misalliances. He could not bear to see the Comte d'Evreaux, nephew of the Cardinal de Bouillon, better endowed with ancestors than income, marry the daughter of Crozat, 'who, far from being a mere clerk, then a small financier, ended up as treasurer of the clergy' and the Croesus of Paris. He grumbled, but to no avail; he still had to make visits to congratulate Crozat's 'numerous and grotesque relations'; the Duchesse de Bouillon, the betrothed man's mother, rubbed her hands no less vigorously, calling her future daughter-in-law 'my little gold ingot'.[25]

Against the running sore of gambling, the king, *parlement* and police were united. The gambling dens were closed, games of chance forbidden; imprisonment and fines were handed out to those who contravened the new regulations. But as the *parlement* was fulminating against '*hoca*', a sort of lotto–roulette, at Versailles courtiers were losing extravagant sums of money. 'The *hoca* is forbidden under pain of death and it is played in the king's own household,' La Sévigné declared, with some surprise. 'Five thousand *pistoles* before dinner is nothing; the palace is a veritable gambling den.'[26] Louis, morally shocked at the sight of his people ruining themselves around the gaming table, allowed his courtiers to transform his Olympus into a gambling den far more pernicious than the secret casinos that he had shut. 'Gamblers are like madmen, one shouts, the other bangs the table so heavily with his fist that the whole room shakes, the third blasphemes in such a way as to make one's hair stand on end; all seem beside themselves and are terrible to see.'[27] The Palatine was horrified to discover this gambling hell in the royal sanctuary, but Louis made light of it. The more the nobles spent the better.

The poor courtiers had to find some artificial stimulant to compensate for the service constantly required at Court. For Louis had elevated absence to the status of crime. For those who persisted in this sacrilege the axe fell in the form of a contemptuous remark from the royal lips: 'I have never seen that man', or 'I do not know him.'[28] 'He was someone of little consequence, for he did not come to Court,' declared the king about the Marquis de Châteaumorant, who had just been murdered by a soldier. After such a condemnation of the victim, the murderer had no difficulty saving his head.[29]

Even when sick or troubled, the unconditionally assiduous did not have the right to miss a single service of the royal liturgy: lunch, dinner, entertainment. Grief-stricken and with eyes red with tears, the Duchesse de Saint-Simon had to go dancing for three hours after learning of the death of her best friend, the Comtesse de La Marck.[30]

It is hardly surprising, then, if these entertainments on order were unbearably tense. 'Everything there was more concentrated, more reserved, more constrained, and also less free, less open, less joyful than the ordinary genius of the nation would dictate,' declared the envoy from Brandenburg, who had not expected to find this heavy atmosphere in France.[31] Apart from the exceptional entertainments, regularly three times a week, the members of the Court had to attend special evenings known as '*Appartement*' evenings. A thousand courtiers, in full ceremonial dress, circulated in the Great Apartments. Refreshment was taken in the Salon de Venus – mountains of cakes, pyramids of fruit. Drinks were served in the Salon Abondance – wines and liquers, fruit juices and coffee. Billiards were played in the Salon de Diane and music given in the Salon de Mars. Cards were played in the Salon de Mercure. There was dancing in the Salon d'Apollon.[32] 'The *Appartement* is a quite unbearable thing,' complained the Palatine, who hated these chores.

The courtiers were so many 'Capuchins' whom it pleased their 'Superior' to tyrannize. One had to stuff oneself when one was not hungry, for the king liked hearty eaters and bitterly criticized delicate stomachs. One had to be comfortable when one was shivering with cold, for the king never felt the cold and despised those who suffered from it. When travelling, there was no question of stopping for a moment to satisfy the need of nature: the king had a bladder that could stand anything and expected the bladders of all his courtiers to be in tune with his.[33] There was no question of taking snuff or chewing tobacco in his presence for the king could not stand tobacco.

After so many kings of France who were lively, spontaneous, accessible, lacking in pride and stiffness, so full of natural good spirits, Louis, that icy, haughty, inaccessible automaton in his sanctuary, was much more like a Habsburg. An almost superhuman self-control enabled him to play the king without faltering, every day, at every moment. The production ran as smoothly as those of the ballets of his youth. Every gesture, every movement, even the most trivial action of everyday life was codified. The spectacle was repeated according to the hour, the day, or the season, without the slightest alteration. Louis xiv willingly submitted his own existence to clock-work regularity, following the rules of Etiquette to the very 'T'. One sensed that the slightest hitch would bring disarray, if not collapse. But who would think of putting a single speck of dust into the workings of the king of France? And it was that inhuman, obsessive, smooth-running ballet that enabled him to impose his image on his century as he was to leave his mark on posterity.

Despite this constraint, the unexpected did sometimes upset the established order. Etiquette may regulate everything, foresee everything, but sometimes the courtiers, with the king at their head, abandoned themselves to childish behaviour that contrasted with the pomp of Versailles. At table, the imposing Sun King did not hesitate to throw pellets of bread at the ladies, and allow them to respond likewise. On feast-days, he even went so far as to throw apples and oranges. One evening, Mlle de Viantais, having aimed a particularly hard plum at the royal head, a hurt and furious Louis XIV threw 'an entire dressed salad' in her face.[31]

Mischief had its place in the dazzling convent where the new order reigned. The princes amused themselves by lighting crackers under the chair of the Princesse d'Harcourt, the Court butt, 'a big, fat, bustling creature, the colour of milky soup, with thick, ugly lips and tow-like hair'. After this portrait, Saint-Simon bravely recounts how, one winter's night, the princesses and their ladies of honour secretly got into the Princesse d'Harcourt's apartment, suddenly drew back the curtains of her bed and bombarded her with snowballs. 'That dirty creature, lying in her bed, suddenly awoke from her sleep, crumpled and drowned with snow on the pillows and everywhere, disshevelled, shouting her head off and wriggling like an eel, without knowing where to put herself, was a spectacle that diverted them for a good deal longer than half an hour, so that the nymph swam in her bed, from which water dripped on all sides, drowning the whole room'.

When the princesses had grown tired of playing pranks on the Princesse d'Harcourt, they turned to Mme Panache, 'a poor wretch with blubber lips and red-rimmed eyes, who had been introduced into the Court as a kind of fool'. They took great pleasure in filling her pockets with meats and stews, 'the sauce from which trickled down her skirts'.[35]

People were terribly dirty at Versailles. Glittering courtiers and women dripping with jewels spat, vomited, urinated, defecated in the corridors and staircases;[36] it was the fashion of the time. The Palatine did not take offence at having to walk through turds at Versailles. On the other hand, she could not bear to see women take snuff with dirty noses 'as if they had plunged it in filth ... I admit that I find that very disgusting'.[37] One evening, at the king's gaming party, Boysseulh, the commanding officer of the Household Cavalry, noticed that someone who was winning a large amount of money held extra cards up his sleeve. He took him suddenly by the arm and shook him like a plum tree; the guilty cards fell like petals. The cheat got up and went out quietly. It was a simple, everyday incident that bothered no one.[38]

Just as they cheated, people stole for fun. Mme Bouillon, looking over Monsieur's collection of bezoars, pinched a couple and discreetly disappeared. But Monsieur, who had seen her, ran after her, and tried to snatch the objects from the thief. So the king's brother and the duchess fought it out there and then, watched by rather surprised courtiers. The victory went, rather immorally, to the duchess, who stalked off triumphantly bearing her bezoars.[39] Theft was a daily occurrence at Versailles: during a ball the king handed back an officer's wallet; on another occasion, one of the Dauphin's diamond earrings went missing.[40] The royal horses' silver-decorated harness disappeared without anyone expressing surprise.[41]

One evening, the king was dining as usual in the first antechamber. Sitting with his back to the chimney breast in his red velvet armchair, before a table laden with gold plate, he was devouring one dish after another. The room was full of standing courtiers, respectfully observing the royal glutton. Suddenly a parcel thrown by an unknown man in the crowd flew over people's heads and landed on the royal table with remarkable precision. The king, remaining quite impassive, remarked: 'I think they are my fringes.' Some days before, thieves had dared to cut off the gold fringes on the door hangings of the Great Antechamber and of the king's own bedchamber, taking a piece of bedspread with them as a souvenir. The first *valet de chambre*, Bontemps, had been in despair. The artistically thrown parcel was opened, the fringes were there, with an anonymous note: 'Here are your fringes, Bontemps, they weren't worth the trouble. My respects to the king.' 'That was very insolent,' the king commented indifferently and plunged his fingers greedily into his food.[42]

The Hispano-Habsburg mentality was never to have free rein in France. Somewhere the French spirit rebelled against this new constraint. Never would the dignity, the discipline, the discretion of an Escorial reign at Versailles. Never would Louis xiv have a Court stand in line like the trees in avenues designed by his gardener, Le Nôtre. Flaunting his mistresses, bringing up his bastard children, Louis xiv himself contradicted the imposing image that he wished to give his Court. Too bad, the master must have said to himself. The important thing was the etiquette that surrounded him should be respected and that the liturgy that made him a daily idol should be performed without hitch. Anything else was a mere trifle.

One problem remained however that was not a trifle. It was a thorn in the idol's foot, or rather two million thorns in the form of two million protestants. It was the dying wish of his mother, Anne of Austria, that he should exterminate heresy.[43] Indeed, his glory required it. The most powerful monarch could not decently accept among his subjects troublemakers whose very practice of another religion other than his own turned them into opponents. The conqueror now had time to reconquer those lost souls that flourished in his Empire. Indeed it was his duty, insisted the priests, who reminded him of the heavy debt that 'the disorders of his past life' had put him into in relation to God. They were banking on the sincere, but utterly ignorant and unconsidered piety of their illustrious penitent who listened to them blindly.[44] What the priests ordered, the people clamoured for. Protestants were the rich, and the rich of the most hated kind, financiers, arms manufacturers, great merchants who aroused the jealousy of peasants, workers, craftsmen; protestants were aliens.[45]

Protestants were English, the hereditary enemy, but above all Dutch, the new, universally hated enemy. They were a 'fifth column', enemies of France, foreign spies, agents of subversion, instruments of the devil. To the French, William of Orange was the epitome of a protestant.[46] 'Protestants go home,' they yelled, delirious with chauvinism. Urged on by his priests, borne up, not to say carried away, by a virulently anti-protestant public opinion, Louis decided to have done with them once and for all.

Would he suddenly order their expulsion, as his maternal ancestors, the Catholic kings had done with the Moors and the Jews? Or, worse, was he going to perpetrate a new, more general Massacre of St Bartholomew's Eve, as so many of his good Catholic subjects hoped? No, he was to act gradually, or rather he was to continue the policy that he had initiated long ago, but in an intensified form. The protestants were gradually to see themselves oppressed by a series of restrictive or vexatious measures. The practice of their religion underwent ever more extended limitations. At the same time, they were restricted in their professional activities: public offices, consulates, municipal posts, the postal services and legal offices were closed to protestants. They were expelled from professions that brought them into direct contact with the population. In certain towns, they were refused access to mastership in the trades. Each day brought new discriminatory measures.[47]

It was at this stage that Louvois had the brilliant idea of killing two birds with one stone, namely the '*dragonnades*' – the forcible billeting of troops on protestant families. The armies maintained by His Majesty would be housed, fed and laundered at the expense of the recalcitrants and the soldiers would know how to conduct themselves in such a way that protestants would lose adherents.[48] The effect of the *dragonnades* was massive and instantaneous. Exposed to a sudden unleashing of violence and exactions, the protestants, terrorized and ruined, had no alternative but flight . . . or conversion. And already Holland was opening its doors to an impressive number of refugees.[49]

Colbert, for whom tolerance had always been synonymous with prosperity, and who was determined to protect a hard-working, industrious community that was essential to the French economy, intervened. The *dragonnades* were suspended – but not for long. Louvois won a decisive victory over his old adversary and on 4 July 1681 declared that 'It was a mistake to believe that the king protected the protestants'.[50]

There were general measures against protestants, but it was preferred to give full freedom to the anti-protestant zeal of the bishops, intendants, judges and lords. The administrative correspondence of the years 1680–82 is filled with examples in which the State intervened indirectly rather than directly, concerning itself with the least particular case, right down to the smallest detail. The king was to support the *parlement* of Guyenne in its decree forbidding protestant judges on the lands of lord high justices. He advised reducing the number of protestant goldsmiths in Tours to the advantage of Catholic goldsmiths. He expressed his satisfaction to the lord high justices who excluded protestant judges from their lands, and he intervened in person ... to order a protestant gardener at the Château de Blois to sell his post. When the opportunity presented itself, he could satisfy old resentments: the town of Orange was threatened with an interruption of its trade with France if it continued to accept children from French protestant families. It was a long way from the stakes of the Inquisition on which Philip II, convinced of his divine right, burnt his own heretics. Now the repression was more discreet, and therefore weaker. There was weakness, too, in the order to encourage the conversion of protestants: 'Reward those who change at the expense of those who do not change.'[51] And the administrative correspondence continues the story. The king would reward M Nointel if he converted his father. The king forced a protestant who had thrown his converted son out of the house to supply his needs. The king would drop legal action against a protestant in order to get his conversion and that of his family. Mild sentences in court, tax advantages, financial help, pensions, everything came the way of the new convert. 'Corruption will obviate the use of violence,' it was repeated sanctimoniously.[52]

If the protestants were entering a bad period, the involuntary champion of Catholicism, the daughter of the Catholic kings, Queen Maria Theresa of France, could not believe her luck. Her husband, who she had never ceased to love as he had never ceased to betray her, came closer to her. He smiled on her, he often came to see her, he tried to entertain her. Better still, whereas he had been in the habit of dropping her as soon as dinner was over in order to join one of his odious mistresses, he now stayed with her. She had her Louis to herself for whole evenings. However, since she did not believe in miracles, naïve as she was, Maria Theresa soon realized that she owed this extraordinary transformation to Mme de Maintenon. It was she who urged the king into the arms of his eternally grateful wife. What a contrast with the treachery of La Montespan, the arrogance of the ephemeral mistresses or even the devouring passion of the gentle La Vallière!

So Maria Theresa would not listen to those who tried to warn her against Maintenon's favour: 'The king has never treated me with so much tenderness since he listened to her.' And Maria Theresa gave her portrait to Maintenon for her feast-day, and Maintenon received it with all due humility. Maria Theresa publicly gave signs of favour to this new 'Sainte Françoise': 'God has raised up Mme de Maintenon in order to give me back the king's heart.'[53] Maria Theresa was overcome with happiness . . . 'Sainte Françoise' could at last feel that her position was safe. With a heart or a temperament as inflammable as that of the king, one was never safe from a new fall. A new favourite would be damnation for the king and danger for Sainte Françoise. With Maria Theresa, there would be no sin for the first and no rivalry for the second. One could hardly be too grateful for so valuable a friend. So the king had Mme de Maintenon brought down from the second floor and set up in a fine, four-roomed apartment on the same floor as his own. Who would be surprised at that? Who would protest? Certainly not the only other person concerned, the queen.

Maria Theresa was to know happiness just at the moment she fell ill. It was nothing very much, just an abscess in her armpit that had given her a slight fever. After three days the fever increased a little. It was nothing serious, the fever was caused by the pain, declared the Medical Faculty. Next morning, Fagon, her physician, decided to bleed the patient. The queen's surgeon, Gervais, objected: if she was bled, the abscess would burst from the inside. Fagon persisted and ordered Gervais to proceed with the bleeding. 'Monsieur, do you know what you are saying? It will kill my mistress.' 'Do as I order, Gervais'. Gervais burst into tears: 'Do you want to kill the queen, my mistress?' The bleeding was to be carried out at eleven in the morning.[54] Fagon administered a laxative to the queen, which further weakened the body already poisoned by the puss from the abscess that had burst internally, as Gervais had predicted. Maria Theresa knew that she would not survive much longer. All that she had suffered suddenly came back to her. 'In all my life, from the day I became queen, I have not had a single day of true content'.[55] She died at three o'clock in the afternoon on 30 July 1683.

'It is the first pain that she has ever caused me,' her widower remarked for the gallery and for posterity. He displayed a proper sorrow, but not enough as to convince a sceptic of the Maintenon clan, who thought that he was 'touched rather than grieved'. In any case, his feelings soon changed when he caught sight of Mme de Maintenon, with red eyes, a sad air, draped in mourning veils. The king found this quite unexpected display of hypocrisy extremely humorous and teased her mercilessly about it.[56] They were still laughing in the coaches full of courtiers that took the dead queen to Saint-Denis, her last resting place. The musketeers of the escort thought nothing of leaving the procession to go and hunt a few rabbits in the plain. The same informality welcomed the Grande Mademoiselle, who hurried back to Court from which she had been absent at the time of Maria Theresa's death. Monsieur, her cousin, launched into a detailed description of the funeral ceremony. 'So that is how grieving people express themselves,' remarked Mme de Montespan, who was present.[57]

She had at least shed plenty of genuine tears on the death of the queen whom she had treated abominably. Crocodile tears, the Maintenon clan adjudged them. They were tears for herself, in actual fact, since the queen's death removed Athénaïs's post as superintendent of her household, and she was wondering what would become of her position at Court. Could she simply stay there when her favour had gone up in smoke or would she be forced to resume married life with her terrifying husband?[58]

CHAPTER 17

La Maintenon, the Reluctant Bride

Mme de Montespan knew that Louis could not remain long without a woman in his bed. She had realized that the priests had brought the era of the mistresses to an end, so why should he not take a second wife? 'He should think of remarrying as soon as possible; otherwise, if I know him, he will make a bad marriage, rather than make none at all,' she declared, to which her friend, the Maréchale de Noailles added: 'He may marry the first laundry girl that he takes a fancy to.'[1] Mme de Maintenon, aware of the same problems, called for God's intervention. 'Do not let up praying for him,' she asked her friend Mme de Brinon, 'he has more need of grace than ever to bear a state so contrary to his inclinations and habits.'[2]

Did she fear that the king would take a new mistress, or did her anxiety betray something more important, some formidable element that was being played out in the greatest secrecy? Five days before urging Mme de Brinon to pray God for her august friend she had written to her turbulent brother, who was thinking of giving up his retirement at Vichy to return to Paris and be near her. It was on 7 August, 1683, a week before the Queen's death. 'I do not pretend to constrain you by preventing you from coming to Paris' she wrote, 'but it seems to me that it will be more disagreeable being near without seeing me than being far away and communicating with me.' She was determined to keep her indiscreet brother at a distance; if he insisted and came to Paris, she would not be able to see him. What could lie behind such isolationism? 'The reason that prevents you seeing me is so useful and so glorious that you should only be delighted by it: it does not suit me to have any commerce ...'[3]

What mysteries and what prospects? Beneath the calm tone one can detect nervousness, not to say anxiety, and a sort of triumphant joy ready to burst forth. What could the king have said? What was he thinking about now, with his wife scarcely buried? Maintenon said nothing. On the other hand, she looked very displeased when someone suggested that her august friend had a new mistress. 'The news that you bring me is false,' she announced to Mme de Villette, 'the king has no such inclination; you can say so without appearing ill-informed.'[4]

At this point, the pope entered the fray by sending a present to 'Sainte

Françoise', who was rather embarrassed by this ostentatious mark of favour: 'With all my heart I would have liked to conceal the present that I have received from Rome.' The service that she was rendering the Church must have been considerable indeed for the pope himself to send such a token of satisfaction, gratitude and encouragement. If the pope had been informed of the situation, it must have been because the priests had been meddling in it. But what was this information? Despite the impenetrable secrecy, there was the habitual talk at Court and with very little solid information to go on. However the names of the king and Mme de Maintenon began to be linked together. This led to a haughty denial: 'There is nothing to reply to on the subject of Louis and Françoise, it is sheer folly,'[5] Maintenon swore to Mme de Brinon.

Undoubtedly, the clergy was behind the alchemy now working in the mysterious conscience of the king; their influence was all too evident in the new measures against the protestants. One by one the professions had been closed to them: midwife, notary, procurator, court usher, merchant, surgeon, apothecary, wine merchant, surveyor, etc. Suddenly control over the education of their children was taken from them; sons and daughters were authorized, from the age of seven, to be converted to the True Religion. Bastards were declared *ipso facto* Catholic. No more than ten persons could attend a protestant burial. The backs of chapel pews had to be removed to make them more uncomfortable. Protestants no longer had the right to employ Catholic servants, and before long any servants at all.[6] Soon all that would remain would be to order the protestants to wear the yellow star . . .

'So many people have become converted, as I told Your Majesty, at the mere sight of the troops,' Louvois repeated to Louis every day. And the king rubbed his hands thanking the faithful minister for having had the brilliant idea of billeting the army on protestant citizens. The system must have been effective since Marillac boasted of having brought back, in a single year, 38,000 lost sheep into the bosom of the Catholic Church.

The king was not aware that his soldiers converted the protestants by looting them, molesting them and torturing them. And so the inevitable happened. As the Holy Sacrament was being solemnly carried through the streets of Saint-Hyppolite, in Languedoc, the priest noticed that there was a man in the crowd who did not bow low enough – a protestant, of course. The priest leapt at him and struck him. The inhabitants took advantage of the situation to raze the town chapel to the ground and 4,000 protestants remained without their pastor. They immediately armed themselves. Throughout Languedoc, their co-religionists followed their lead. The spark ran along the fuse. Incidents took place in Dauphiné, in the Vivarais and in the Cévennes. This was just what Louvois had been waiting for. He ordered his troops to lay waste wherever there was trouble. The Duc de Noailles, governor of Languedoc, who until then had tried to contain the fanaticism of the clergy, realized that his career was at stake. If they wanted devastation, they would get it. To begin with, the protestants of Saint-Hyppolite were fined 150,000 *livres*. Dragoons were despatched to various parts of the region. Pastors were hanged, chapels demolished, massacres carried out here and there. There had been disturbances at Nîmes: the dragoons re-established order so well there that the city was converted in twenty-four hours. A new intendant, Basville, arrived to assist Noailles. He began by congratulating a captain who had killed sixty protestants at La Combe du Coutel, but regretted that the captain 'did not cut off the noses of all the women'. At his instigation, the persecutions took on a new momentum.

Of this devoted functionary, his own son said: 'His zeal in the service of the king always went beyond what the king himself must have expected.' And the Duc du Noailles could write to Versailles that there had been some disorders, but not on a serious scale, and that everything had returned to 'wisdom and discipline'.[7]

There was no longer anyone in the council of ministers to demand that this 'wisdom and discipline' be made the object of an investigation. Colbert, the only individual who would have dared to do so, was dying. The courtiers were in no doubt that a single criticism from the king had been enough to bring him to the verge of death. For those conditioned creatures, a word, a look from the master carried life or death. The cause of Colbert's present illness was a newly built wall at Versailles, finished quickly and cheaply, which had collapsed and Colbert, as Superintendent of Buildings, was blamed. The master uttered a reproach. Colbert upbraided the Parisian contractors so vehemently that he fell ill. The king wrote to him from Fontainebleau, instructing him to take care of his health, but he was already so ill that he could not make out the letter himself. It was read to him. He said nothing. 'Don't you want to answer the king?' his wife enquired. 'It is too late for that!' he murmured. 'It is the King of Kings that I must now think of answering.'

He died on 6 September 1683. The courtiers were disappointed: the king did not display the grief that they rightly expected.[8] The people, on the other hand, did not hide their feelings against the author of so many new-fangled taxes, and guards had to be sent to protect the funeral procession against their vengeful fury.

Nothing stopped the vulture Louvois from swooping on his rival's succession, however. The dead man's son, Seignelay, was prevented from succeeding his father as Minister of State. The Ministry of Finances was given to Le Pelletier, Louvois' relation and creature. Louvois himself took over the post of Superintendent of Buildings, to prevent it passing to another of Colbert's sons, Ormoy. As things were going, the court could see that nothing would remain of Colbert's dynasty, until recently so powerful. But, to everyone's surprise, Seignelay did keep the Ministry of the Navy; Colbert's brother, Croissy, kept Foreign Affairs; and one day they would see the son-in-law, Beauvilliers, head of the Council of Finance and guardian of the heir to the throne, the Duc de Bourgogne.

Louvois knew very well who was responsible for this sudden brake on his vengeful lust for power. Mme de Maintenon had always mistrusted Louvois and had not forgotten that he had been involved in innumerable intrigues set up by Montespan to discredit her. So she persuaded her august friend that it would be better to continue his policy of balancing power between the ministers.[9] Nor was the Court unaware of who was responsible and saw it as a new manifestation of the ever-increasing favour shown her. Observers, convinced of Maintenon's omnipotence, had little idea of the strange anxieties that possessed her at this time and which she shared with her director of conscience, the Abbé Gobelin, in one of the few letters of this period to escape destruction: 'I feel great regret about the last visit you paid me. Our time was ill employed and allowed you to sense something of what was disturbing me; however, it is now over, at least it appears to be, and I have achieved a peace of mind that it would give me greater pleasure to share with you than the troubles that I have communicated to you. . . . Farewell, Monsieur; do not forget me before God, for I have great need of strength to make good use of my happiness.'[10] Thus the storm passed, the black clouds of doubt were dissipated and gave place to a radiant dawn. But what could that happiness be that required so much strength? It could not be the simple fact of seeing her august friend back on the straight and narrow path. What was it, then? The mystery was as impenetrable as ever.

'We, Mehmet, by grace of heaven, glorious and most powerful emperor of Babylon and Judea, of East and of West, king of all the kings of earth and heaven, great king of Holy Arabia and of Mauritania, king of Jerusalem by birth and glory, lord and master of the sepulchre of the crucified God denied by the infidels, we give unto thee, Roman emperor, and to thee, king of Poland, and to all the supporters of both, Our Most Holy Word as follows: We are preparing to bring war into thy wretched country . . . With neither pity nor mercy shall we trample your miserable little country beneath our horses' hooves and We shall bring iron and fire. Above all, We order thee to await us before thy capital city of Vienna, so that We may sever thy head from thy body. And thou, too, kinglet of Poland, do likewise. We shall exterminate thee, thee and thy followers, and We shall remove from the face of the earth, even to the last remnants those lowliest creatures of divine creation, the infidels . . .'

On receiving this epistle, the Emperor Leopold I and his ally John Sobieski, the king of Poland, could only conclude that the Sultan Mehmet IV would soon follow word with deed. Three thousand Turks, led by the Grand Vizier Kara Mustapha, swept across the Balkan plains and moved northwards, destroying everything as they passed. Despite the danger, Vienna stayed calm: the Turks, disdaining the capital, plunged towards Hungary. The Imperial Court had not moved, and in the fields the peasants quietly went about their harvests ... When a messenger arrived with all haste to announce that the Turks, after a wrong manoeuvre, were in fact moving straight on Vienna, it was already too late: the Turks were at the city walls Panic soon spread everywhere. There was no time to take either money or jewellery; emperor, empress, archdukes and courtiers rushed in unimaginable disorder for the Danube bridge which was still free.

They rode all day, stopping only at nightfall in a forest to sleep under the stars. Only a little straw was found for the Empress Eleonore, six months pregnant, to rest on. Then they reached Linz, but it was thought that they were still too close to danger and they did not stop until they reached Passau, on the Bavarian frontier.[11] In Vienna, encircled by the Turkish hordes and deserted by its sovereign, terror followed confusion. The whole of Europe waited hour by hour for the fall of the city, reputedly so ill-fortified and defended only by a handful of soldiers.

At Versailles, Louis rubbed his hands with glee. His emissaries had worked well by cleverly urging the sultan to invade the territories of the emperor, whose alliance with the king of Poland would not prevent the inevitable. At the right moment, Louis made a noble gesture: he solemnly declared that he would not attack the Netherlands, would refrain from taking advantage of the circumstances and, as a sign of good faith, he lifted the siege of the city of Luxembourg, which his troops were blockading. He knew what would happen next: the emperor would appeal to him for help. He kept his armies under pressure, ready to fly to the help of his good brother Leopold ... with the firm intention of thus becoming the protector of the Empire and of having the Dauphin elected king of the Romans, in other words heir of the empire. His agents repeated throughout the courts of Europe that Leopold I was a nonentity and that only he, Louis XIV, offered any guarantee against the Turks.[12]

But the appeal from the emperor never arrived. At the beginning of September 1683, Louis XIV removed his mask and sent his troops, commanded by the Maréchal d'Humières, against the Netherlands. '... It is possible,' he wrote to Humières, 'that some of the Spanish troops might enter villages under my domination to carry out executions or to take prisoners; I wish you to do twenty times as much in the lands under the Spanish obedience, so that the subjects of the Catholic king suffer twenty times more harm than mine will have received.'

Armed with these instructions, the French soldiers conscientiously ravaged Flanders, burning and looting as they went. Fleeing the countryside, the refugees filled the towns, so the streets of Brussels soon looked like encampments.[13]

Louis made light of the Turkish threat as being so much the worse for Vienna. But Vienna, against all expectations, had just been delivered. King Sobieski of Poland had at last joined up with the small imperial forces and had attacked the Turks at the head of his troops. On 12 September 1683, at seven in the evening, the proud armies of Allah, destined to reduce the infidels to dust, were completely routed and the Grand Vizier was unable to stop their mad flight. He himself had to abandon his camp so precipitously that he left prodigious treasures behind, and the marvelling victors threw themselves on the piles of bejewelled weapons, precious objects, brocades gleaming with gold and costly carpets.

Victorious but shamed, Emperor Leopold returned to his capital. Ingratitude being the best antidote against humiliation, he sheltered behind protocol in order to avoid expressing his gratitude to the king of Poland, who was already being acclaimed throughout Europe as the saviour of Christendom. Mounted on his superb stallion, Sobieski came forward, a giant with shaved head, drooping moustache, an enormous pearl hanging from his plumed hat. In front of him, wretchedly dressed, perched on a mere pony, Leopold looked a sorry, pitiable sight. He hardly raised his hat and, instead of emotional thanks, muttered a few words on the protection that emperors had always extended to the Poles. 'Brother, I am glad to have rendered you this service,' retorted the victor, in ringing tones. The Palatines rushed to kiss the imperial boot, but Sobieski stopped them: 'Do not stoop so low.' The emperor stooped even lower: on his orders, Sobieski was made to pay – and dearly – for all the supplies his army needed for the return journey and the Polish wounded were turned out from the Viennese hospitals.

Outraged by this unexpected reversal of fortune, Louis XIV abandoned what little restraint remained to him. The French troops, led by Maréchal d'Humières and Maréchal de Boufflers, continued to move through Flanders without meeting much resistance, leaving death and destruction in their wake. Even the suburbs of Brussels were devastated and the Bruxellois, shut in behind their ramparts, could do nothing about it. The city of Luxembourg was bombarded once again. Courtrai and Dixmude were seized. Trier was conquered and its fortifications razed to the ground. French lawyers maintained, without batting an eyelid, that none of this contravened the spirit of the Nijmegen peace treaty.[14]

In October 1683, Mme de Maintenon fell ill: she suffered from migraines caused by over-strain and a slight attack of depression brought on by the tension of recent weeks. 'Do not be concerned about me, I beg you: I have only a few aches and pains, which are quite normal with me, as you know, but when one is on stage, everything is known and exaggerated.'[15] It was not easy to keep the secret that made her so happy when one was on view to the entire Court. In any case, she managed to keep her secret in her correspondence over the next few months – or those parts of it that have not been destroyed – and which is an extraordinary tissue of banalities.

On the other hand, the king was less discreet. One day, he asked Louvois, point blank and as if out of the blue: 'What would you say if I married Mme de Maintenon?' Louvois stood rooted to the spot with stupefaction: 'Oh Sire, is Your Majesty really thinking what he is saying? The greatest king in the world marry the widow Scarron? Do you wish to dishonour yourself?' Louvois was beside himself, he wept, he threw himself at the king's feet: 'Remove me from my posts, put me into prison, but I shall never see such an indignity.' The king was as embarrassed as he was furious: 'Get up! Are you mad! Have you taken leave of your senses?' Exit Louvois.[16]

It was past midnight on a certain day in autumn 1683. Everyone was asleep, or rather, everyone was supposed to be asleep in the Château de Versailles. Yet the light was still on in one of the rooms in the king's apartments. Present there were Louis XIV, Mme de Maintenon, the Archbishop of Paris, Harlay, the Marquis de Montchevreuil, and Maintenon's life-long friend, the king's first *valet de chambre*, Bontemps – and Louvois. Father La Chaise, the king's confessor, was saying mass on a portable altar. Then the archbishop came up: 'Louis, will you take Françoise as your lawful wedded wife?' 'Françoise, will you take Louis as your lawful wedded husband?' The ceremony was already over. The Sun King had married the former goose girl. The prediction of the Duchesse de Noailles had almost come true: he had not married a 'laundress' but he might as well have done so.

Louis XIV married 'the sickly widow of that famous cripple Scarron', as Saint-Simon later described it. 'For the proudest of kings, the most profound, the most public, the most durable, the most unprecedented humiliation, one that posterity will not wish to believe, was reserved by Fortune, or, if one may presume to say so, Providence.[17]

Louis could not do without the presence and the body of a woman. The fear of hell now forbade him to seek one outside the legitimate bonds of marriage. Maintenon was still appetizing enough and knew how to satisfy a demanding desire even in late middle age. At fifty, there was no danger of her having children, which would have inextricably complicated the situation, nor was there any danger of stormy passion, sudden changes of mood, dramas, scenes, no danger of continual demands, requests for favours or money. No danger of seeing a great family clinging to the skirts of the latest favourite. Maintenon had proved herself. Above all she knew how to please – that was her art. 'Pleasing, ingratiating, easy-going', she always tried to please everyone, a need to be liked that Saint-Simon attributes to 'the abjection and distress' of her past. For years she had offered Louis a loving, devoted and practical friendship, which had sustained him in crisis, in times of weakness and loneliness and which, in the end, had snatched him from the eternal damnation to which he was rushing and put him back on the path of salvation. She retained that extreme discretion that Louis insisted on so much. She betrayed no confidence. She refrained from putting herself forward, content to remain in the shade, showing herself as little as possible, keeping her family at a distance – her brother Aubigné was paid to know this. She knew how to merge discreetly into the familiar landscape of the king's entourage, essential for this shy man who hated the unexpected and found a new face disturbing. Lastly, she never manifested the slightest desire to 'rule' this man who had so often been in the grip of a powerless determination not to allow himself to be manipulated. Even if she had wanted to, she would no doubt have been incapable of 'ruling' him. For, in fact, she was incapable of logical thought and beneath her apparent dignity, seriousness and reserve, she was in fact frivolous, muddle-headed and changeable, incapable of deep reflection, of thinking on a large scale, of drawing up long-term plans, of following any other line but the rigid, extraordinarily narrow line of her conscience.

This woman, who was to have one of the most exceptional destinies in history, had done practically nothing to achieve it. It was Montespan who had chosen her to look after her bastard children. It was Montespan who pushed her towards the king, despite his very strong reluctance, as an unthreatening substitute for herself when the king got too bored with her. It was Louis, forgetting his first impression, who approached her for advice, help, company. It was Louis who turned her into a friend, at first a privileged, then an exclusive friend, as the favourites declined. It was Louis who kept her when she wanted to leave the Court and find her own peace – Louis and the priests, for it was the priests who imposed on Maintenon the duty to remain where she was when she felt she could no longer do so. It was the priests who inspired in her that mission for drawing the king away from sin.

It was the priests who certainly overcame her hesitations when she was presented with the inconceivable proposition of marrying the king of France, for, once again, she was tormented by doubts. Her letters make this clear enough. But she gave in – mainly out of inertia. Laziness and pride were her principal faults, she admitted. Already her laziness had sustained a severe shock when she was merely the king's friend. To remain available day and night, to keep company for hours on end the most powerful and therefore the most difficult man in Europe, to be confronted point blank with the most complex situations, the most difficult problems, to provide advice and help whenever it was required, to follow, despite her shyness and reserve, the hectic life lived by the king and by the Court, how often she must have had enough of it all! The marriage made official the task that she regarded as well nigh unbearable, while depriving her of any means of escape.

She thought of refusing the responsibility which she had not sought. In the end, she proved to be the slave of her destiny, the instrument of the priests, the king's victim, and accepted it. 'My God, give me the grace of the state to which you have called me, that I may bear its sorrows as a true Christian, that I may sanctify its pleasures, that I may seek Your glory in all things, that I may bear it before the princes among whom You have placed me, that I may serve in the king's salvation . . . You who hold in Your hands the hearts of kings, open that of the king, so that I may pour into it the good that You desire . . . Grant that I may save myself with him, that I may love him in You and for You that he may love me likewise.'[18] Where was love to be found in this missionary's prayer? No, Maintenon did not love Louis XIV, and what he took for love was merely zeal in her mission. A mission which, despite awareness of her weakness, exalted her. Had she given voice to her pride? Certainly, but she cleverly offered it up to God. She would have been angry with herself if she had been proud of marrying a king, especially the most illustrious of his century. She was proud, she persuaded herself, of being able to contribute to his salvation. In this way she could conceal the feeling of revenge that could not have failed to assail her. How often she must have remembered past poverty and humiliation when she found herself in the place of the queen of France!

The fact remains that never for a moment did she lose her head. She accepted her destiny as she had always, almost naturally, accepted what had happened to her, but she also had a great deal of bourgeois common sense. A duchess or a princess might have been drunk with pride: Maintenon was born too low in the aristocratic scale not to have borrowed a great deal from the class immediately below hers, the bourgeoisie, with which in fact she had spent much of her life. As the wife of the king of France, she retained her reserve, her bourgeois stolidity. She was not humble in the face of her unimaginable husband. But she had immense pride in remaining humble before the position to which God had called her.

Anyway, Louis made no attempt to turn her into one of those dazzling stars that turned around the sun. It was he who descended to Maintenon's rank. Because of her he was already becoming a little bourgeois himself. In deciding to act out the role that he had written for himself, he had rather exaggerated his own abilities: he would not give up performing his 'one man show' before his Court, before France, before the world, but, from now on, he needed several hours of relaxation every day. And he found that relaxation in the woman who represented the other side of the role that he acted out on stage: evenings spent by the fireside, chatting quietly with a woman devoid of pretensions, a private, comfortable existence. There, at last, with no one to observe him, he could take off the mask that oppressed him. Maintenon was the 'cosy corner' without which the Sun King, in his palace of gold and mirrors, could no longer live. Maintenon gave Louis a devotion, the real basis of which he was unaware, but which he had found in no other woman. She attracted him physically and he could make love to her without sinning. She was leading him to his salvation and thus keeping back the fear of hell. She broke the loneliness that he had always felt and to which his position, his existence and his character had condemned him; thus Louis XIV loved Mme de Maintenon.

In principle this marriage was to remain secret; this, at least was the assurance given to Louvois. For her part, Maintenon was the first to keep it – naturally enough. Several months were to pass before she referred to her new situation – and then in the most veiled terms: 'Our conditions are different,' she wrote to her brother in June 1684, 'mine is dazzling, yours quiet, and perhaps only people of good sense would find it as good. God has put me where I am; I shall have to manage as best I can; He knows that I have not sought it; I shall never raise myself higher and I am already too high!'[19] She did not want the marriage, she admitted, but, having obeyed the orders of providence, she would try to make the best of it. She was to take care to destroy her private correspondence with her directors of conscience and with the king. Once, much later, Maintenon, having become a widow and retired from the world at Saint Cyr, did let drop a semi-confidence. Her friend, Mme du Pérou, was comparing the situation of the king's favourites with her own, when Maintenon interrupted her and said that as far as she was concerned, they were 'secret bonds'.[20] No more was said.

During the first months of her marriage, Maintenon concerned herself exclusively with her favourite plaything, the educational establishment for poor girls run by her friend, Mme de Brinon, and to which the king had given the Château de Noisy, near Versailles.

It was a way for her of escaping the king, the Court and the interminable ceremonies at Versailles, under the unassailable pretext of devoting herself to a useful task. At the slightest opportunity Maintenon fled from the exhausting existence that she did not want and went to Noisy to teach the catechism or to tend the sick. In that tiny world, so far from that of the Court but so close to that which had been hers for so many years, she found the relaxation that allowed her to breathe.

'She believes herself to be the universal abbess ... she thinks she's a Mother of the Church,' mocked Saint-Simon, who had detected her lack of discernment and broadness of mind. '... Hence a sea of frivolous occupations: illusory, painful, always deceptive, letters and answers to the infinite, directions of chosen souls and all sorts of nonsense that usually amounted to nothing.'[21]

The tone was nothing if not devotional. Not only had the king never been more assiduous in his attendence at church services, but he let it be understood loudly and clearly that he noticed those who did not perform their Easter duties and that he would appreciate it if people observed their religious obligations. Immediately, there was a rush to the churches, and the religious-minded Maintenon set smiled as they watched battle-scarred coquettes like La Montespan, La Soubise, La Gramont, the Duchesse de Lude, fall before the altar.[22]

The Palatine, who was highly placed enough to keep her common sense, was exasperated by all this religiosity: 'Before the old slut reigned here, religion in France was a reasonable matter; but she has spoilt everything ... and when people wish to be reasonable, the old woman and the confessor have them thrown into prison or exiled.'[23] This was rather unfair to Maintenon, but certainly expressed the Palatine's repulsion for the growing bigotry and for the woman whose power was measured by that bigotry. For the Palatine had understood that there was a new authority in France.

Yet, to all appearances, nothing had changed. There was singular pride in the affectation with which La Maintenon refrained from exceeding her very modest official position. In the Court as a whole she was lost among the other ladies, with nothing to distinguish her from them. Saint-Simon was to see her in the drawing-rooms of Fontaine-bleau, giving place to all the titled women and even to women 'of distinguished quality', claiming nothing, polite with everybody, talking to everybody.[24] But more often Maintenon stayed closeted in her apartment. It was there that she was queen and that the king was hers.

In public, Louis did not depart an inch from protocol for her, except in one small detail. He called her 'Madame', not 'Madame de Mainte-non' or 'Madame la Marquise', just 'Madame.' She was the only woman he referred to in this way. Such an innovation gave rise to interminable commentaries at Court,[25] and as always, the king was quite unaware of it. Out of habit, as if as a 'screen', he even kept his acknowledged mistress, La Montespan, in her position, if not in his favour. He continued to visit her twice a day because he had been in the habit of doing so for so long. But now he had to go down to the ground floor, for he had moved the favourite from her magnificent apartment on the first floor.[26]

Montespan realized quite clearly that she had lost the battle forever and that Maintenon was now more than the king's friend. She was not the only one. The courtiers, too, recorded the invisible, but enormous change. Maintenon had at last become the king's mistress; the rumour spread quickly ... and was not long in reaching the interested party. The poor devout woman was horror-stricken, and ran to her husband. She was accused of being his mistress, and could not bear it. What was to be done? Let us declare the marriage, announced the king. Despite his promise, despite the decision to keep this most secret of secrets, it caused Louis not the slightest embarrassment to admit that he was married to the widow Scarron. Nothing could tarnish the brightness of the Sun. The response exploded without hesitation. Maintenon's character, her past conduct, everything prepared her for an unequivocal rejection. She knew only too well that she had won the king's esteem by successive negatives that prefigured this supreme 'no'.

If the marriage was not declared, what would be done to silence the defamatory rumours? They asked the priests' opinion; after all, it was they who had cooked up the whole affair. So confessors and directors of conscience were summoned to an extraordinary council, and the solution found was certainly worthy of the ingenious spirit of the good Fathers. If there were no declaration of marriage, what harm would there be in letting it be understood that there would be one before long, that is to say, launch a campaign of rumour to persuade public opinion that the marriage was on the point of being made public? Since it would be nothing but rumour, there would be no need either to confirm or to deny it and, at the same time, the gossip about the marriage would kill the gossip about the affair.[27]

Maintenon's enemies, alerted by the deliberately planted rumours, would swear that she had forced the king's hand in order to get this monstrous union proclaimed and that she would pursue with all her enmity those advisers who had tried to stop Louis from going down that fateful slope.[28] It seemed to them to be equally unthinkable that the king would have thought of admitting such a shameful fact and that Maintenon should have refused such a triumph.

'I have been very well since I have been at Versailles and the certainty that we are at peace with the Dutch gives me great joy.'[29] The satisfaction of the peace-loving Maintenon found a counterpart, in June 1684, in the impotent rage of the war-loving William of Orange: 'It is heaven's curse that our people are so ill disposed or so ignorant as not to see that the French are playing with us.'[30] For, by a war of stealth, Louis was still nibbling away at the Spanish Netherlands, without anyone, least of all the Dutch themselves, doing anything about it. Sowing terror throughout the Netherlands, winning battles even in Spain itself, intimidating the great powers, refusing any compromise proposed by William, Louis achieved his ends: to keep Luxembourg and its province at a cost of a twenty-year truce that the Spanish and Dutch would be all too happy to accept.[31]

On Tuesday 15 May 1685 an important visitor was expected at Versailles. From eleven in the morning, the king had been in the throne room to ensure that the courtiers were there in full strength. The state rooms were already filled. In his armoured coach, the awaited visitor was thinking once again of the evil fate which, on that day of humiliation, was taking him, Francesco Imperiali Lescaro, doge of the Republic of Genoa, to Versailles. If only there had not been those cursed ships. The naval dockyards at Genoa had built and armed four fine ships for Spain, warships for the enemy of France. Already irritated by the fierce independence of the tiny state, and egged on by his envoy at Genoa, François de Saint-Olon, an excitable and arrogant individual, Louis was not slow to respond. In the May of 1684, fifty French warships came and blockaded the Genoese port. The senate of the city sent a delegation to compliment the French Navy Minister, Seignelay, one of Colbert's sons, who happened to be on board. Seignelay replied to these courtesies with a shower of criticisms culminating in a twenty-four hour ultimatum. The delay had not expired when, suddenly, the French cannons began to fire. Gothic churches and baroque palaces, the pride of the city, collapsed in flames under 14,000 cannonballs. The bombardment lasted continually for twenty-four hours. Then Seignelay sent the French consul to the doge with a new ultimatum.

'Our Republic is not accustomed to receiving propositions in the form of cannonballs; it puts its trust entirely in the justice of its cause and in the fearlessness of its citizens who, in the midst of fire and flame, would rather perish than consent to so shameful a treaty.' If the doge replied so proudly, it was because he was expecting 2,000 Spaniards sent as urgent reinforcements by the governor of Milan. But the Spanish soldiers could do nothing against the ravages of the French cannonballs which began to fall once more.

Genoa, which had been called 'La Superba', Genoa the Proud lay in ruins. In order to avoid total destruction, the doge was forced to accept the conditions of the king of France.[32] At the pope's request, Louis XIV agreed to grant a month's delay, one short month . . . with an enormous fine for each week's delay. 'I wish to take neither the city of Genoa, nor any part of their state, lest I disturb the peace that I have given Europe,'[33] he concluded, with the evidence of 14,000 graves as proof of his 'sincerity'.

And now, a year later, the doge, accompanied by four senators, was nearing the moment when his State would be humiliated. His coach crossed the outer gates of Versailles. Once again he was being conditioned by a clever architectural and decorative mise-en-scène. Successively buildings and courtyards formed a subtle gradation leading to the castle itself, which rose on the highest ground. As he advanced, the decoration became progressively richer until, in the final courtyard, it burst in a symphony of white, blue, red and gold. The gilding gleamed on railings, balconies and roofs and gradually led the eye towards the centre of the perspective, the king's room. Everywhere, statues, singly and in groups, by a clever use of ancient mythology and history, exalted the power of the king. The doge's eye paused for a moment on the opulent female forms in stone that personified Justice, Prudence, Renown, Strength, Generosity, all those royal virtues of which the Republic of Genoa had had such a striking demonstration.

Inhabitants of distant lands, Indians, Greeks, Persians, Turks, etc. leaned over the balustrades to watch the doge pass. These trompe-l'oeil figures suggested the impatience of all people to come and honour the greatest king on earth. From the windows of the first floor, the doge discovered the park. Arbours and lines of statues had the same function as the columns and porticos of the architecture, as the string of drawing-rooms, each leading to the next, that of giving the illusion of infinite space. By the play of mirrors, the walls did not stop the eye and the painted perspectives on the ceilings doubled the height of the rooms. Each detail, by illusion or allusion, served the royal propaganda, of which the whole castle was a formidable instrument. Each of the rooms of the great apartment through which the doge walked had as its theme one of the planets that moved around the sun, the last being devoted to Apollo, God of the Sun, a transparent reference to the Sun King.[34] Lastly, the doge crossed the threshold of the Hall of Mirrors, which had only been completed the year before. There, gold gave way to silver; the tables that supported the porphyry and alabaster vases, the stools, the containers of the still green orange trees, the eight-branched candelabra, were all of delicately worked solid silver.[35]

Le Brun had not finished painting the ceiling, already swarming with mythological divinities, moving around the king of the gods – a Zeus of distinctively Bourbon features, complete with periwig – for, letting hyperbole rip, the deification of Louis was carried to its logical conclusion. Not only were the king's victories depicted over and over again, but there were also pictures representing the defeats of his enemies, the Empire, Holland, Spain.[36]

Advancing with the slowness appropriate to his dignity, the doge, in a robe and cap of red velvet, and his four senators, in robes and caps of black velvet, crossed the two huge Savonnerie carpets, beneath nineteen crystal and silver chandeliers hanging from cords in the form of entwined flowers. On arriving before the throne at the end of the gallery, the doge officially presented the Republic's apologies. He did not seem embarrassed, the courtiers observed, astonished that a stranger could seem so unmoved before the majesty of their lord and master. The king replied briefly and each of the senators made a short speech.

By taking Genoa, Louis had sought no diplomatic, commercial or territorial advantage, but a pretext to display his power and to terrorize Europe a little more – a somewhat superfluous exercise, one might say. Thousands of dead and one of the most beautiful cities in Italy ruined was the price that Louis XIV had made them pay for the fleeting satisfaction of seeing a doge come to him and be humiliated. Having got his satisfaction, he became once again amiable, and, his vanity satiated, he became doubly affable towards the doge.

'The king's graces did not make me forget the disgrace suffered by my country,' this man of spirit remarked. From being an impudent recalcitrant who had dared to challenge his Majesty's authority, the doge had become, in an instant, a guest of honour, regaled with everything that Versailles could offer in terms of entertainment. After such lavish treatment, the doge was sent back to his ruined capital, laden with presents: snuff-boxes glittering with diamonds, Gobelins tapestries, portraits of the king intended no doubt to be revered by the Genoese.[37]

The good doge, observing the Sun King enthroned 'in majesty', did not suspect that, out in the corridors, this same king was a man crippled with the most humiliating illnesses. For a long time now the king had suffered from gout and could hardly walk. Since 'a worm, half a foot long, alive' had been found in his stools, it was realized that he had tapeworms which condemned him to the constant torment of hunger. He crammed himself with food and had to swallow purgative after purgative in order 'to carry away, by their use, the matters that had provided the vapours from which he had been attacked'. His ten daily stools carried 'much bile, mucus and bloody glairs', often, too, 'much raw and indigestible matter and, among other things, many truffles that had hardly been digested'. In fact, he no longer had enough teeth to chew his food; the last of them had been taken out so well that the dentist had smashed his upper jaw and removed part of the palate. Before long, pus and an 'almost corpse-like' smell emerged from the hole. Worse still, food and drink got into it, only to re-emerge through his nose. In order to remedy this inconvenience, the butcher-surgeons

246

applied a red–hot cauterizing iron to the perforated jaw ten times over without anaesthetic, of course, and without the heroic patient blenching. However, it is well known that toothache is a cause of ill-temper and two million Frenchmen were soon to have to bear their sovereign's ill-temper.[38]

CHAPTER 18

General Exasperation

The protestants refused to understand that they were caught in a trap. It was with amazement and horror that they learnt, on Friday 19 October 1685, that the Edict of Nantes, which had been the very basis of their existence in France for over a century, had been revoked.

Since any action by the Sun King could not fail to be a brilliant success, he commemorated the event by having a medal struck in which, crowned by victory, he was depicted trampling heresy underfoot. The protestants had to live through the tragic reverse side of that medal. Two million of them, caught in a gigantic net by the simple expedient of closing the frontiers, suddenly found themselves confronted by the threat that had hung over them for years.

'The king wants you to deal harshly with the last ones who persist in displeasing him,' Louvois wrote to the Duc de Noailles. So it was the soldiers who 'dealt' with the protestants, using the slogan 'kill, kill, or Catholic'. But, before killing them, they used them as playthings: they were whipped to death, buckets of ice-cold water were thrown on them in mid-winter, burning hot candle-grease was poured on their heads drop by drop, their nails were pulled out, they were blown up with a bellows until they burst, they were set fire to in straw like chickens, they were made to sit on burning coals, a husband would be tortured in front of his wife or a daughter raped in front of her parents. And Intendant Basville, the torturers' model, could proudly write: 'There is not a single parish that has not been well cleaned out.'[1]

The law took over from the exhausted imagination of the soldiery. In December 1685 appeared what was perhaps the most pitiless decree in the history of France: 'Every child between the ages of five and sixteen will be removed in eight days' time' from its protestant parents and transplanted into a Catholic family, a convent, or an approved school.[2]

Parents could no longer resist brute force; children did so in their place. Two orphaned girls, eight and ten years old, surnamed Mirat, were taken from their grandmother at Meaux. As the archers took them away in a coach, they smashed the windows, cut themselves and tried to throw themselves out on to the road. They were given to a Catholic family – and they ran away. They were found and locked up in a convent at Charonne – and they climbed over the walls. Judge

Lamoignon, who had had them taken away, put them under lock and key in his own house. They screamed so loudly that the king himself heard them and ordered them to be given back to their families. But the Bishop of Meaux, the great Bossuet himself, intervened, and they were put into prison.[3]

Children's mothers were put into convents, prisons or, when these were full, hospitals, which were merely antechambers of death, like that at Valence, which was infamous throughout France. The children who were in the same hospital died like flies or 'disappeared', having been sold by the director. One starving 'patient' was found to have eaten two of his own fingers before dying. In order to empty the prisons, women and old men were sent to the American colonies. The most obstinate women, those caught escaping disguised as men, were thrown into houses for reformed prostitutes.

The men were sent to the galleys and, in order to accelerate recruitment to His Majesty's navy, the intendant Basville did not hesitate to count as men young protestants of fifteen years old and one of twelve was condemned to the oars for life for accompanying his father to chapel.

One December day, a chain gang set off for Charonne, but since the captain in charge did not want to be encumbered with sick men, they had hardly arrived than he had the prisoners stripped naked in the freezing cold under the pretext of examining their personal belongings and left them in that state for two hours. Eighteen prisoners died and the chain gang could at last set out again, lighter than before. Those who survived long enough to reach Marseille or Toulon were chained to their galley seats and packed in tight for years on end, if not for the rest of their lives. They were whipped, ate, digested, slept, fell ill without ever, for a single day, or for a single hour, being able to move. 'Those men,' Michelet was to say, 'are no longer men, but element: they have become sea, they are no more than algae and shell-fish.'

'It was the doing not of the king, but of La Maintenon, that old sacristy sorceress, whom the Jesuits put into the good king's bed to deceive him.' Rolland, one of the future leaders of the protestant rebellion, declared this conviction which was shared by La Maintenon's own sister-in-law, the Palatine: 'The old woman and the Jesuits have persuaded the king that if he persecuted the protestants, he would thus efface before God and the world the scandal that resulted from the double adultery in which he lived with La Montespan: he is being deceived.' 'I shall no doubt be taxed with too blind and too simple a good faith,' retorted Mlle d'Aumale, a faithful follower of the 'Old Woman', 'if I dare to swear that Mme de Maintenon had nothing to do with what then happened; I expect it but, whatever one may say or think, I am determined to tell the truth and I dare to affirm that she had no part in what was done and knew no more about it than the king.'

Ezechiel Spanheim, minister for Brandenburg in France, maintained that if it was not La Maintenon, then it was Father La Chaise, the king's confessor, who had deceived his penitent. Father La Chaise was guilty only of weakness, replied the memorialist Duclos. Always afraid of losing his place, he had not dared to stop the torrent that he had not started; he was merely a 'timid priest who trembled before whomever he saw at his feet'.[4]

Who, then, was responsible for it? Louvois, of course. Contemporaries were at one in accusing him of unleashing the persecution of the protestants; Louvois needed some great success in order to keep his exclusive credit with the king; Louvois had thought up the *dragonnades*; Louvois prevented anyone approaching the king and telling him the truth; Louvois deceived the king, fed him with illusions, concealed the facts from him, falsified the reports, exaggerated the statistics.

It was the general opinion that the king could not possibly have known and approved the horrors committed in his name. Even a protestant like Rolland, who was to rebel against the state, was convinced of this: 'The king had no part in the atrocious beating meted out on the backs of the Huguenots; he was ignorant of the unbelievable evils that afflicted his good province of Languedoc and we had to implore God continually that he should at last open the king's mind and reveal to him the barbaric actions of his ministers.'[5]

The French excused Louis XIV by seeing him as the very thing that he was most anxious not to be, a weak man. But was that weakness so deep-rooted that he really saw nothing, or was it that he did not want to see anything? The fact remains that Louis approved the decrees which, for several years, gradually tightened the yoke around the protestants' necks. He personally signed the revocation of the Edict of Nantes, thus violating the promise given by his grandfather, Henri IV. The priests were able to take advantage of his ignorance and weakness to persuade him that he was earning his way to heaven; it was nevertheless the case that he regarded those protestants who refused to bow to his will as rebels – rebels not against the Catholic Church, but rebels against his royal authority. And he treated them accordingly. He authorized all the repressive measures meted against the protestants with his haughty signature – 'Louis'. The 'skilled politician' discussed with his collaborators behind closed doors means of eliminating the protestants and with bureaucratic efficiency he settled for the most radical means. This 'sensitive' man, who would shed a tear over a mere trifle, was interested only in the final solution of the protestant problem.

The tortures inflicted by the soldiery, the massacres, all the horrors to which the protestants were subjected obviously did not appear on the generals' and intendants' reports that he read, but did he believe, could he have believed, in these thousands of spontaneous conversions? If so, why the need for all those measures concerning the new converts? They were prohibited from sending their children abroad; those who frequented protestant embassies were arrested; they were supervised in the carrying out of their new religious duties with a view to catching them out; they were not accepted for municipal posts if they did not produce a certificate from their parish priests; spies were sent to their assemblies, but spies 'who were capable and had their ear'.[6] If Louis was so doubtful of the sincerity of the conversions, it was because he must have known that they had not been obtained by gentle persuasion.

Had he wanted to let the blame fall on Louvois? His vanity would not have allowed him to contemplate the idea that he had been deceived. 'I want them converted. Use whatever means you think fit. I don't wish to know what they are.' That, more or less, was what he told Louvois and his collaborators. And Louvois, who thought he was being clever, deliberately deceived him without realizing that the king was willingly allowing himself to be deceived about the details. His life-long fear, his refusal to tolerate in his kingdom any independent body, drove Louis to undermine the protestant community as soon as he saw it as a divisive element. Then, when his vanity was outraged by their stubbornness he made up his mind to have done with them once and for all.

There was also in his attitude a complacent hypocrisy and an unconscious harshness. Above all one suspects a narrowness of mind and a lack of depth in his analysis of reality, defects that he did his best to conceal, but which did not escape the fine observation of Spanheim: 'Although he has sufficient ability to understand world affairs, it may be said that he does not concern himself enough with them to digest them and to consider them in all their implications.'[7] In fact, the decision to revoke the Edict of Nantes is evidence of the superficiality of his analysis.

The almost unanimous applause of good French Catholics confirmed him in his course. The lower classes and petty-bourgeoisie welcomed the revocation 'with the greatest joy', while, from the height of the pulpit, Bossuet's great voice lent justification to the persecutions and delighted the entire Court.[8] Rumours as to the abominable excesses finally filtered through. The parish priest of Versailles light-heartedly attributed these inevitable excesses to 'a lack of moderation on the part of military men' and the courtiers accepted 'this rather new way of converting people, but one that had its good effects',[9] and the litany of tortures, massacres, rapes and other horrors was dismissed as 'a small evil for a great good'.[10]

The protestants had no other solution than flight – but flight with the frontiers sealed, whole armies in pursuit, and a mass of Catholics transformed into stool pigeons. Nevertheless, many did try to flee. They clambered into simple rowing boats to cross the sea. They hid in the holds of ships about to embark, at the bottom of empty barrels or under heaps of coal, only to wait two more weeks in that state for a favourable wind or to fall into the hands of pirates and be sold as slaves. Enormous sums were paid out to frontier runners who, on the way, killed them and took all their possessions. Decrees tried to stop the outflow of protestants: 'Anyone denouncing someone fleeing the galleys will have half his goods in perpetuity.' 'Anyone aiding or guiding the fugitive will be himself condemned to the galleys in perpetuity.'[11]

Despite threats and difficulties, thousands of protestants managed to emigrate. Geneva, the citadel of Calvinism, welcomed them with open arms and in the end was feeding four thousand of them. Genoa, the very Catholic Italian republic, which knew what it cost to offend the Sun King, not only welcomed the French protestants, but réfused to extradite them, as Louis demanded. The Elector of Brandenburg published the Edict of Potsdam, which officially welcomed the protestant refugees to his States.[12]

'I hear he stinks alive and his cankers will stink worse when he is dead, and so will his memory to all eternity ...'[13] This violent declaration from an Englishman about Louis certainly expresses the indignation of the whole of England at the time. In taverns and villages, a great flowering of satires and songs expressed this feeling while, in the churches, collections were publicly made for the protestants.

It was obviously in Holland that the reaction was sharpest. At the news of the revocation, the States decreed a day of national mourning and a general fast. The refugees flooded towards that 'great ark of the fugitives' to the extent of 55,000 in 1686. An annual credit was voted for them, rented accommodation was allocated to them from secret funds, but, above all, they were put where there was room for them and Frenchmen swelled the ranks of Holland's army and enriched its commerce, its industries, its manufactures, its universities. They brought not only their hatred of the Bourbon, but horrifying tales about the sufferings that they had endured, which the press reproduced every day.

Even the city council of Amsterdam, bombarded with petitions, besieged with weeping families, abandoned its notoriously pro-French attitude. Suddenly indignation cemented a union between William of Orange and his recalcitrant subjects. The flight of capital from France assumed alarming proportions. Louis XIV decreed that the goods of fleeing protestants should be seized, but to little effect: twenty million *livres* found its way into Holland and the outflow of capital continued to rise.

There were cries of horror in the protestant world, but there was also a rumbling of criticism in the Catholic world. Far from making common cause with the 'armed missionaries' of the king of France, the most Catholic Spain, especially adept at burning heretics, and even the head of the Catholic Church, Pope Innocent XI, condemned the persecutions.[14]

'During the whole of his life Louis XIV was the curse and pest of Europe. No worse enemy of human freedom has ever appeared in the trappings of polite civilization. Insatiable appetite, cold, calculating ruthlessness, monumental conceit, presented themselves armed with fire and sword. The veneer of culture and good manners, of brilliant ceremonies and elaborate etiquette, only adds a heightening effect to the villainy of his life's story. Better the barbarian conquerors of antiquity, primordial figures of the abyss, than this high-heeled, beperiwigged dandy, strutting amid the bows and scrapes of his mistresses and confessors to the torment of his age.'[15] This vitriolic portrait by Sir Winston Churchill on the subject of the revocation of the Edict of Nantes sums up perfectly the reaction of Europe at the time.

A treaty of defensive alliance was signed at Augsburg in July 1686 between the emperor, the princes of the Holy Roman Empire, Spain and Sweden. The contracting powers declared that they would no longer tolerate the contraventions of civil rights, and that if necessary they would lend each other mutual assistance. William of Orange did not sign the treaty; he had no need to. It was he who had arranged this grenade for later use. It was he who had brought together irreconcilable adversaries against Louis, protestants and Catholics, enemies and allies of France alike.[16]

Learning the news, Louis shrugged his shoulders. He had something better to do at that moment, for, on 1 September 1689, he was preparing to receive an embassy from the other end of the world. The originator of the whole affair was a Greek called Konstantine Phalquon, son of a poor tavern-keeper in Cephalonia, who had become, after a series of incredible adventures, Grand Vizier of the King of Siam and the most powerful man in the kingdom. Needing support, Konstantine let it be known that he would welcome a French presence in Siam, and that his exotic king would not only protect the Christians, but even suggested that he might become a Christian himself. He then sent off a delegation to Versailles.

Sensing that there was a great deal to be gained, Louis received these ambassadors from the east with all the brilliance at his command. The Siamese threw themselves on all fours in front of the silver throne of the great king and remained there long enough for a Court painter, the press photographer of the period, to be able to immortalize the scene. Then one of them delivered a long speech, 'which in no sense betrayed his barbarian origins', and they withdrew backwards, leaving a mass of gifts in front of the throne.

Louis sent a large French mission to Siam that contained a rather special volunteer, the Abbé de Choisy. In his childhood the Abbé had been dressed as a little girl by his mother to play dolls with Monsieur and later, had led an extravagant double life as a priest in Paris and as a beautiful woman in the provinces. The French found that Konstantine had been indulging in wish-fulfilment. His Buddhist Majesty had no intention of embracing Catholicism and the prospect of a French presence in Siam remained particularly slim. Moreover, a *coup d'état* put an end to their last chances. The privileged colonists were killed or expelled. Konstantine was the first to meet his death and his widow, having been practically queen of Siam, was condemned to work in the kitchens, 'a task for which she was born', Voltaire adds. 'That was what the success of that fine establishment and those fine embassies amounted to,' commented Geoffroy Saint-Hilaire. It was unfortunate that the ingenious Greek had fed the king of France with illusions, but the

253

reception of the ambassadors from Siam enabled Louis nonetheless to produce an excellent publicity sequence on his theatre of illusions. Nothing remained of the Siamese but their gifts, gold vases, Chinese lacquer-work, screens, porcelain. Surveying these riches the ignorant Louvois asked: 'And how much is all this worth? One thousand five hundred *pistoles*?'[17]

What cost considerably more – 2,400,000 *livres* to be precise – was the present that the king gave his beloved. Not some incredible pension, dazzling jewel, or fairy palace for Maintenon, but an educational establishment for two hundred and fifty poor daughters of the nobility. It was a homage that Maintenon had paid to her own past: she remembered how, as a girl, she had known hunger and humiliation, even though she had been born into the aristocracy. The house at Noisy was too temporary and too close to the Babylon of Versailles. Maintenon wanted to build something more durable, larger, more beautiful. The king put at her disposal a treasury and the talents of his reign. Louvois was appointed to find the site, Mansard to build the buildings, Racine and Boileau to correct the statutes drawn up by the Bishop of Chartres, which were full of spelling mistakes. Before long, Louis had become as enthusiastic about the project as his wife and concerned himself with the smallest details. 'The king is very busy with Saint-Cyr; he has corrected the choir in several more places'; 'the king does not want the superior to have a ring; he considers that a cross is enough'; 'the king takes exception to cows in a garden; don't expect us to put up with any at Saint-Cyr', his wife wrote proudly. Louis and Françoise amused themselves for hours on end building their little house for 250 dolls. Of course, Louis had a medal struck to mark the laying of the foundation stone; he designed the coat-of-arms for the foundation himself; he berated the foremen. 'The king wants to have Saint-Cyr finished.' The works were completed in two years and Maintenon could write triumphantly to the superior at Noisy: 'Departure ordered from Noisy to Saint-Cyr'. 'The regal splendour of the buildings', 'the finest establishment that has been built in France for a hundred years', the courtiers proclaimed before this strange present given to the strange favourite. What munificence to surround poverty! What splendour in humility! What pride in piety! It certainly bore Maintenon's mark.[18]

'The king was operated on this morning.' The news broke like a bombshell on that Monday, 18 November 1686, and spread rapidly from one dismayed courtier to another. 'The large intestine that communicates with the fundament was found to be rotten.'[19] In other words, he had a fistula, a long, suppurating ulcer in part of his intestinal canal. Other remedies having failed to work, it was decided to operate in the greatest secrecy. Apart from the surgeon and physician, no one was told except his wife, Father La Chaise and Louvois. Félix, the surgeon, had even tried out a new surgical knife of his own invention on the fistulas of dead persons, according to some – and on the fistulas of living people, kindly provided by Louvois, declared others. Several human guinea pigs had even died and must have been buried in secret. Nevertheless, the experiments having proved positive, Félix successfully set about the king with his knife that morning at seven o'clock. Messengers were despatched to bring the news to the dispersed members of the royal family. Abandoning the hunt, the fat Dauphin rode at full speed to Versailles and threw himself, weeping, at his father's bedside. 'All is going well, my son, and please God I shall have no pain.'

The ambassadors who had come to congratulate him, found him very lively. He sang in his bed. He demanded food more substantial than the broths to which he had been condemned. He got up to shave. He received his mistress as usual. He did too much. Soon he was in such pain that he was running with sweat. He had to be operated on again. Several incisions were made on one occasion, then on another, then again.[20]

'Is it done, gentlemen?' he asked the surgeons, as they cut him about. 'Finish your task and do not treat me as a king; I want to be treated as if I were a peasant.'[21] Fine words: for these ignorant butchers there was neither king nor peasant. The last operation was the most painful, but he came round at last. 'A large operation has been performed upon the king', it was announced. 'How they have hurt him!' repeated the ordinary people in the Paris streets, visibly moved. A chair-porter wept. 'They cut him twenty times and the poor man never complained.'[22]

Spontaneously, Parisians rushed into the churches to pray for the king's recovery, and when God granted them their wish, an explosion of Te Deums, public concerts, illuminations took place in all the towns of France. The French were delighted to celebrate the recovery of a king 'who, after raising the name of France above all others, was on the point of overwhelming with happiness a nation that he had already overwhelmed with glory'.[23]

Louis XIV enjoyed extraordinary popularity but, as always at such times, there was someone who went too far. The Maréchal de La Feuillade, who had quarrelled with the ministers, feared their revenge. So he bought a site in Paris and in the middle of the square that he had built – the present Place des Victoires – erected a fine statue of the king. That, in itself was enough. But, on the pedestal, there were the inevitable bas reliefs recalling his great actions. At the four corners bound slaves represented the four great European powers which, perhaps saturated with insults, did not protest. The four lanterns placed on the columns that were to remain lit all night, like so many sanctuary lamps before the Blessed Scarament, brought a smile to people's lips. The inscription on the pedestal, 'Viro Immortalis', ('To the Immortal Man'), made people snigger. At the dedication ceremony the Maréchal led the slow procession before princes and courtiers on compulsory duty. There was a guards regiment, officers of the constabulary, the

Duc de Gesvres, governor of Paris, the city archers, the provost of the merchants 'and the whole corporation of the city'. The statue was uncovered. Then the procession proceeded round it three times to the deafening accompaniment of trumpets, drums, cymbals, gunshot salutes and cries of 'Long live the King!' The officers saluted in military fashion and the civilians made deep bows; the only thing lacking was incense.

Suddenly, the common sense of the French recovered and people giggled openly at this pomp and circumstance worthy of the emperors of a declining Roman empire. Each morning, mocking verses were found scribbled on the pedestal and, in the end, the statue had to be railed in and guarded.[24] Was the king embarrassed by this excessive adulation? Not at all, for he had himself ordered the municipality to take part in the dedication ceremony.[25] Vanity had finally turned the king's head. He drowned his feelings of inferiority in the certainty that he was the greatest king, the greatest head of government, the greatest general, the greatest builder of his time; he would have around him only men low enough to confirm him constantly in that opinion. 'Flexibility, baseness, an admiring, dependent, grovelling manner, and above all a generally nondescript air, were the only ways to please him,' Saint-Simon declared angrily.

The pope, on the other hand, considered that Louis, instead of being a respectable, elder son of the church, was acting as if he were its father. Innocent XI, as a good Milanese, could be very determined. Never having been able to tolerate the principles of the Gallican Church, he refused investiture to the bishops who had subscribed to it. He had bitterly criticized Louis XIV for having secretly assisted the Turks, whereas he, Innocent XI, had taken money out of his own pocket to help the emperor and the king of Poland. He also condemned just as sharply the anti-protestant persecutions: 'Men must be led to the temple, not dragged into it,' he remarked.

Innocent took it into his head to put an end to the freedoms enjoyed by the foreign embassies in Rome, much-abused privileges which, among other things, placed thieves and murderers outside the reach of the Roman police in the diplomatic quarters. One by one, the European sovereigns gave in with good grace. Freedoms there are, freedoms there shall be, thundered Louis. But, pleaded the Papal Nuncio, all the potentates have accepted their abolition. 'I have never regulated myself according to others; it is I who serve as an example,' he was heard to reply. And Louis XIV despatched a new ambassador to Rome with instructions to defy the pope. He chose the Marquis de Lavardin and promised him the Order of the Holy Ghost, which the Marquis had coveted for years, if he succeeded in his mission of enraging His Holiness. In November 1687, Lavardin advanced not towards Rome but on Rome, surrounded by a thousand soldiers, with a view to having the abolished freedoms respected. Lavardin's guards knocked down the pope's customs officers who wanted to inspect the ambassador's baggage and the ambassador himself made a triumphal entry into Rome, throwing silver coins to the people who cried, 'Long live the king of France and his ambassador!' Thereupon, he settled quietly into the Palazzo Farnese, guarded by his army.

The king had a debate opened at the *Parlement* of Paris, which was only too delighted at an opportunity of displaying its anti-clericalism. Talon, the advocate general, called Innocent a propagator of heresy and an old fool who was in his second childhood. And so Innocent, who, in La Fontaine's words was 'neither holy nor a father', had no alternative but to throw himself into the arms of France's enemies. The opportunity was not slow in coming. In June 1688, the Archbishop-Elector of Cologne had just died and his co-adjutor, Cardinal von Fürstemberg, was making the necessary arrangements to have himself elected his successor. Fürstemberg was Louis XIV's creature, and it was tantamount to electing Louis himself. The emperor immediately rang the alarm bell. There was great commotion in Vienna, in Amsterdam, in Rome. Another candidate, Prince Clement of Bavaria, was hastily proposed. However, it appeared that he was not of the required age – he was scarcely seventeen. The objection was brushed aside. Innocent, only too happy to thwart Louis, produced a brief declaring the young Bavarian eligible.[26]

Then the two parties set about trying to buy the votes of the canon electors. William of Orange and Louis raised the stakes each day, but it seemed that Fürstemberg would win. Unfortunately, he had a mistress, the Comtesse de La Marck, who tightened the cords of the purse so generously opened by the king of France, and he was unable to achieve the required majority: he was two votes short. Each party proclaimed his candidate the winner; when asked to settle the dispute, the pope was only too delighted to confirm the election of the prince of Bavaria, the minor with a minority of votes. Louis replied by occupying Avignon, a possession of the Holy See, and by taking the Nuncio as a hostage. By exasperating everyone in this rather sordid affair, Louis had managed to bring together the head of the Catholic Church and the champion of protestantism, William of Orange.[27]

However, on 10 June 1688, he received some good news: at St James' Palace a son had been born to his dear cousin, James II who had succeeded his brother Charles II at his death in 1658. London celebrated with bonfires, but these were soon to be put out by a sudden rain of lampoons and broadsheets. 'The Prince of Wales is not the king's son!' 'The Prince of Wales shall not reign!' These were some of the things the happy father had to read on the gates of his own palace. But it was the king of England himself, together with the king of France, who was responsible for this outbreak of hatred.

By his example and advice, Louis was driving his cousin James, whose reign could have been untroubled, to the abyss. The English had two phobias, absolute monarchy and Catholicism: and James II, with a blindness verging on ignorance, was trying to use the first in order to establish the second. He received Jesuits, Capuchins and even a papal nuncio at his Court; he abolished the privileges of the cities; he publicly urged his troops to become converted; he imprisoned in the Tower of London those bishops who protested; he deposed the Bishop of London. If he wanted his subjects to revolt, he could not have set about it better. In Rome, even the cardinals sneered: 'That man has people excommunicated and he will lose the little Catholicism that remains in England.' Throughout the country, this provocation, without rhyme nor reason, was creating an unprecedented outcry. To cap it all, the king's second wife, an Italian princess, chose that moment to give birth to a male Catholic heir. whereas hitherto the heiress had been the eldest daughter of the first marriage, Princess Mary, a good Anglican married to William of Orange.

The Palatine had kept some friends among the French protestants who had taken refuge in Holland. One of them wrote to her that William was secretly preparing to land in England, and she passed the information on to her brother-in-law Louis. That same evening he accosted her, laughing: 'My ministers are of the opinion that you are ill-informed and that there is not a word of truth in what you have been told.' 'Time will tell who is better informed, Your Majesty's ministers or my correspondent,' she retorted angrily.[28] D'Avaux, the French ambassador in Holland, soon confirmed the information: William was planning an invasion of England. Chimeras, replied Barillon, the French ambassador in England. Chimeras, repeated King James II.

However, Louis was becoming alarmed and offered his cousin a fleet and an army of 30,000 men. 'If you accept them, Sire,' his faithful minister, Sunderland, said to King James, 'all your subjects will rise up against you.' And, swollen by a sudden patriotic pride, James refused. Wishing to defend his cousin in spite of himself, Louis XIV sent an ultimatum to Holland on 2 September 1688: he would declare war at the slightest attempt on England, to which he was bound by a treaty of alliance. The Dutch States General were furious at the revelation of this secret pact. King James was profoundly embarrassed and publicly denied the alliance with France.

This led Louis to suspect James of connivance with Holland, while Holland was more than ever convinced of his close alliance with the French king.[29] The most terrifying rumours shook England: the Irish Catholics were coming to the king's rescue; no, they were Frenchmen. The papists were preparing a massacre of all protestants; King James had sold his kingdom to Louis XIV. No one was sure of anything or anybody. For his part, William repeated to anyone who would listen that England had to be delivered from popery and servitude, but that there was no question of harming his beloved father-in-law, King James. He set out quietly, on the evening of 11 November. In the middle of the Channel, he met the forty large warships sent by James to stop him. The English fleet let him by, with strong encouragements to carry on.

William was in England. King James immediately dropped everything, abolished all the absolutist and pro-Catholic measures, 'destroying in a flick of the wrist everything that he had done since his accession to the throne'. But it was too late. Members of parliament, regiments, great lords rushed to put themselves under William's banner. The faithful minister Sunderland did not have to change sides: for months he had been in on the plot, betraying his master and broadcasting all his errors. But King James was even more affected by the defection of his favourite, the lieutenant-general of his armies and brother of his beloved mistress, the same John Churchill whose services Louis, through Louvois, had haughtily rejected long ago. Lastly, the king's own daughter, Anne, abandoned him. James did not even have time to think of resisting: everyone had already deserted him.

On that evening of 19 December 1688, London underwent an attack of feverish violence: any stranger was suspected of being a Jesuit in disguise and risked his skin, while in Whitehall, almost deserted, King James and Queen Mary, surrounded by traitors and spies, retired to bed as usual. Everyone was asleep in the palace when the king surreptitiously rose and called his valet: 'You will find a man at the antechamber door. Bring him here.' The man appeared. It was Lauzun, the Grande Mademoiselle's 'betrothed' who had been banished from the Court and who, unable to bear provincial life, had asked his king for permission to travel. During his stay in England he had won the confidence of King James. 'I entrust you with my queen and my son. You must do all you can to take them to France.' Lauzun offered his hand to the queen, a chambermaid carried the infant Prince of Wales and, through secret staircases, they reached the Thames quayside. The journey to Lambeth in an open barge, in pouring rain and a driving wind, was particularly uncomfortable. At Lambeth, they did not find the carriage that was supposed to be waiting for them. Lauzun set off in search of it. The queen, left alone with the two chambermaids and the baby, not daring to knock on anyone's door for fear of being recognized, took refuge against the storm in a churchtower, trembling lest she be seen by a night watchman. At last Lauzun came back with the carriage. They reached Gravesend without mishap and embarked on the ship that was waiting for them. The queen of England had reached a safe asylum and Lauzun had won his return and pardon.

Knowing that his wife and son were safe, James decided to flee, but missed his embarkation, was caught by the populace and agreed to return to London where he made his entry to the cheers of the crowd. He was back as king in his palace at Whitehall. But William was approaching the capital and sent him an emissary: the respectful and faithful son-in-law had no thought of harming his father-in-law, but, in view of the general animosity of the English, it would be better if the father-in-law retired, temporarily of course, to Rochester. The father-in-law understood the situation, especially as his last faithful guards had just been replaced by William's. He set out at once for Rochester and there, quite happy to trick William's guards, managed to embark secretly for France, unaware that his faithful son-in-law had given orders to let him escape.[30] Relieved to have escaped intact, James, his wife and son were received by Louis XIV with all the honours due to reigning sovereigns. 'This is your home,' said their host, having taken them to the Château de Saint-Germain.[31] However the courtiers were less concerned with them than with *Esther*. What, after all, was England after *Esther*?

In order to entertain her pupils at Saint-Cyr in some useful way, Mme de Maintenon had the brilliant idea of getting them to act plays. Racine's *Andromaque* had been made part of their repertoire and the ladies surpassed themselves, acting love to perfection. This did not altogether please their patron. 'Our little girls' – apparently, they were not so little – 'have just played your *Andromaque* and have played it so well that they will never act in any of your plays again,' she wrote to the confused author, as if accusing him of writing obscenity. To set matters straight, Racine was ordered to compose some moral or historical poem, devoid of any sulphurous love interest, which the young ladies would be able to recite without danger.

Racine consulted Boileau. His friend advised him to give it up, writing plays was not his line. But, after a good deal of research, Racine hit upon the biblical story of *Esther*, the virtuous Jewess who became wife of the King of Babylon. He worked flat out at the play and soon, with trembling hands, was able to take the completed manuscript to Maintenon. What would she find to complain of this time? But Maintenon approved. For the story of Esther, as rewritten by the skilful Racine, involved some significant resemblances. 'The haughty Vasthi', the wife repudiated by King Assuerus for Esther, was Montespan. The imperious Amman, the minister who flattered himself that he ruled his master, was Louvois, while Esther, who sacrificed herself in the name of religion to marry the glorious king, was, of course, 'St Françoise' herself.

So *Esther* was given the thumbs up. Rehearsals began under Racine's direction. The wise virgins soon became stage-struck and the good ladies of Saint-Cyr soon lost control of the situation. The excitement reached its peak when it was announced that the king would attend the first night. Suddenly, the entire Court was interested. *Esther* was the only topic of conversation; people would stoop to anything to get invited to the first night. The priests intervened, of course, and outdid one another in denouncing the wave of frivolity and indecency that was sweeping through the house of God. 'Things have gone too far,' repeated the parish priest of Versailles, who had perfidiously gone to Maintenon to suggest that if so many gentlemen of the Court were so anxious to attend the performance, it was not so much for Racine's fine verses, as for the beauty of the budding actresses. Maintenon now bitterly regretted her involvement in the whole enterprise. 'It has quite worn me out and I have resolved, though I have not yet said so, not to have it performed in public. The king will come and after that our actresses will be sick ...' She longed for peace and quiet.[32] But where were peace and quiet to be found when one was the wife of the king of France?

At last, on 26 January 1689, at three o'clock in the afternoon, the first performance took place. The king arrived, accompanied by a small but select entourage consisting of the Dauphin, the Prince de Condé, Bossuet, and others.

Stage fright made Mlle de Maisonfort perpetrate some amusing slips of the tongue: instead of saying *'Et le Persan superbe,'* she said, *'Et le serpent superbe'*. There were hysterical tears backstage. 'Well, that's the end of my play,' lamented Racine. But everything went off well. That evening, at dinner, the king talked of nothing else, and suddenly *Esther* was a triumph.[33] The play was performed several times; princes and princesses of the blood royal attended the fourth performance, together with the exiled James II and Queen Mary, much to the fury of the Palatine: 'The old slut [Maintenon] passed herself off before the king of England as so pious and so humble that the queen took her for a saint.'[34] Every courtier was dying to see *Esther*. Maintenon, completely at her wits' end, dropped her opposition and the play went on being performed.

CHAPTER 19

The First Troubles

The very day that James II fled his kingdom William moved into St James' Palace. Sixty-eight members of the British parliament had gathered to offer him the provisional government; William asked for three days to think it over. When the three days were up, he was met by 240 MPs urging him to accept and he agreed at last. To general rejoicing, he expelled the papal nuncio and the French ambassador from England. Then his supporters raised a new question in the House of Commons: was the throne vacant or not? Yes, came the answer. Then to whom should it be offered? This new question was debated, and it was agreed to declare William and his wife Mary, king and queen of England. William who had been waiting for this moment for months, accepted with all due restraint, then ordered that his coronation should proceed without delay and with all the pomp of the Anglican Church. 'Have you seen the farce of the coronation? What do you think of those idiotic old papist ceremonies?' he asked as he left.[1]

The tenacious William had long realized that Holland was no longer a sufficient springboard to face up to his deadly enemy. He had long had his eye on England. He had been helped beyond his wildest dreams by the incredible stupidity of his father-in-law and by the exasperating policies of Louis XIV. The gloomy, taciturn 'little lord of Breda' had hoisted himself by his prodigious will-power on to the throne of England and become a redoubtable enemy for the proud king who had once so despised him. He abandoned his beloved Holland, where he appointed his friend Heinsius Grand Pensionary. This former enemy of the House of Orange had rallied to William as soon as he realized that he was the only force capable of stopping Louis XIV. And he had had personal experience of Louis XIV. Sent officially to France by the Dutch States to protest against territorial annexation in peacetime, he had been threatened with the Bastille by Louvois.[2] Heinsius was yet another man of substance whom the brutality and insensitivity of French policies had turned into a prime enemy.

Worms was burning, Speyer was burning, Mannheim was burning, Kreuznach was burning, Openheim was burning, Heidelberg was burning. The rich, ancient cities of the Palatinate were being systematically reduced to ashes, together with their venerable monuments, their

Gothic churches and their baroque castles. Orders were orders. Louvois had persuaded Louis XIV that it was indispensable to destroy everything between the French frontiers and the enemy armies in order to prevent the latter from subsisting. The idea was to transform the German provinces into a desert and the brave imperial soldier would be reduced to hunger, all for the salvation of the State. So the order was signed to destroy everything.

As it turned out, they destroyed quite a few human beings, too, and to the massacres of stone were added massacres of flesh. Women of all ages, from young girls to old women, were stripped, raped and tortured. Crops, forests, vineyards were torn up, cut down, with the express order not to re-establish them. Four hundred thousand refugees crowded the roads in search of an improbable shelter or hid themselves in the forests, 'preferring the wolves to the French'. In short, Attila had returned. Even his lieutenants complained. The Maréchal de Duras, who 'was busy burning everything and burning it again', had the courage to write to Louvois: 'Distress at destroying such considerable cities as Worms and Speyer has forced me to represent to His Majesty the ill effects that such desolation might have in the world on His reputation and on His glory: such a course is most harmful and cannot but antagonize the whole of Europe.'[3]

'But, Madame, it is to defend your own interests that we act,' Louvois had the impudence to reply to the Palatine who, repressing her despair, her rage and her hatred of the minister, went to ask him to spare her country.[4] So saying, he went off to work with the king in Maintenon's apartment. As he left them, he remarked: 'I have the strong impression, Sire, that scruple is the only reason that holds you back from consenting to so necessary a thing as the burning of Trier. I thought to do you service by delivering you of it and taking charge of it myself; with this in view, without wishing to speak to you again about it, I have despatched a messenger with the order to burn Trier as soon as they receive it.' Louis leapt up, beside himself with fury, picked up the firetongs and dashed at Louvois. Maintenon threw herself between them: 'Sire! What are you going to do?' But Louvois had already got to the door. Louis called him back, his eyes mad with rage. 'Send a messenger at once with a counter-order and make sure that he gets there in time; and know that your head will answer if a single house is burnt.' Drawn and trembling, Louvois rushed to his office and waited . . . for the messenger to come in the first place, for he had lied: he had not intended sending an order to burn Trier without first speaking to the king about it. As Saint-Simon said: 'All he had to do was alter his despatches and tell his messenger to take off his boots.'[5]

Who was really ruling France? Louis kept himself informed, he read his generals' reports. It was he who signed the orders. Voltaire even accused him of wanting to sack the Palatinate in order to revenge himself on the Elector Palatine. But Louis was in Louvois' hands as he was in the hands of all his ministers. With age, his lack of feeling, combined with cruelty, had convinced him that it was necessary to destroy the Palatinate. Had he recoiled when this strategy, so fine on paper, had become an appalling reality in the reports that he read? Had he repented of his decision, when faced with the disapproval of his own generals? In which case, had he not jumped at the first opportunity to use Louvois' excessive zeal as an excuse to rectify it? Again, who was deceiving whom?

'Scourge of God', 'mad werewolf', 'dangerous madman', such were some of the terms used by the Germans to describe Louis in the lampoons of the time.[6] As for the French, they were incendiarists, blasphemers, murderers, who had thrown themselves on a defenceless people. The memory of these horrors, carefully maintained and exaggerated, was to last until our own time and be made use of with each new Franco-German war. Before this inconceivable barbarity, this systematic and useless cruelty, horror and anger swept through Europe. In England there was a 'storm of protest', and William hastened to take advantage of his new subjects' good will to declare war on France and to bring together within the Grand Alliance Holland, of course, the Empire and Spain, later to be joined by the Duke of Savoy.[7]

The result was not slow in coming. The Allies recaptured Bonn from the French and the Maréchal de Boufflers, in retaliation against this defeat, put 600 German soldiers taken prisoner at Kochem to the sword. The Spanish repulsed Noailles, who had invaded Catalonia, and threw him back to the other side of the Pyrenees. The Maréchal d'Huxelles inexplicably capitulated in a besieged Mainz just as help was arriving. In the Netherlands, the Maréchal d'Humières was defeated out of sheer stupidity at Warcourt. Obviously, the officers murmured, d'Huxelles and d'Humières are creatures of Louvois, chosen for their docility rather than their military ability.[8]

'France must wake up and feel the weight of the terrible tyranny under which it groans and consider the happy liberty enjoyed by neighbouring states ... France alone, the most beautiful country in Europe, the most noble part of the world, is subjected to cruel, tyrannical domination and to power that knows no bounds ... Today, all liberty is lost, even that of speaking and complaining.'[9] Liberty, tyranny ... We are not in 1789, but exactly a century earlier, in 1689. The clouds of incense raised to the statue of the Sun King in the Place des Victoires have cleared. The European nations, bound to the pedestal of the statue, had all said 'Enough' to Louis XIV. 'Enough', replied the slaves inside, bound perhaps, but their mouths unsewn, repeating the blasphemous words of liberty and tyranny in all the innumerable lampoons that spread to every part of the kingdom. Not unnaturally, the author of the most famous of them, *The Sighs of an Enslaved France,* was a protestant.

Louis may have 'seized' the protestants' property but it did not do him much good. The war had exhausted his resources just at the point when it had become impossible to stop it. To refill the state coffers, he took the proud, but financially negligible and artistically criminal, decision of melting down his gold and silver work. Tables, pedestals, coffers, stools, torches, chandeliers, mirrors, basins, buckets, plates, orange-tree containers, railings, everything with silver or vermeil on it, in all 2,500 marvels of goldsmith's work, vanished into the melting pot. They fetched two and a half million *livres,* nothing compared to what they might have realized had they remained exquisitely sculptured *objets d'art.* 'We have seen the entire artistic achievements of a reign destroyed,' Pierre de Nolhac wrote. Louis had wanted to make a spectacular and demagogic gesture, but it was a flop, for his contemporaries Primi Visconti and Saint-Simon denounced the stupidity and barbarity of that holocaust.[10]

Louis sacrificed his 'silver' and Louvois was forced to sacrifice his creature, the Maréchal d'Humières, who was too obviously an irremediable nonentity. The king himself chose his successor, the Maréchal de Luxembourg, but Luxembourg was the reverse of a nonentity and committed the unpardonable crime of not being docile. Moreover, everybody knew that Louvois hated him. 'I promise you', the king was forced to write to him, 'that I shall take care that Louvois acts correctly towards you. I shall force him to sacrifice to the good of my service the hate that he has for you; you will write only to me, your letters will not go through him.'[11] The king had spoken and Louvois had to bend his knee. So Louis was not as blind as people thought. Why, then, did he often let Louvois have his way?' 'You will write only to me.' If Louis distrusted his minister so much, why did he keep him on? Where was his renowned absolutism?

Luxembourg opened his campaign in Flanders and on 30 June 1690 won the victory of Fleurus. Louvois could not stop the whole of France lauding him to the skies,[12] so Louvois took it out on the Duke of Savoy. The wise Victor Amadeus wanted only one thing: to maintain his neutrality. He was even willing, for a consideration, to allow the French troops to cross his territory. But Louvois had had a grudge against him ever since the Piedmontese customs-officers had confiscated goods that he was having sent from Italy, so he had sent such contradictory orders to Catinat, who was negotiating with Victor Amadeus, that neither of them knew what was happening. Victor Amadeus decided to write directly to Louis, but there was no reply. Not only had Louvois intercepted the letter, but he had taken advantage of it to add insolence to the already exorbitant demands that he was making. At this point, the Duke of Savoy went to the carnival at Venice, where he met his first cousin, the Duke of Bavaria, an active member of the anti-French league. If Louvois was doing everything to force Victor Amadeus to join the war against France, the allies could not wait to have him in their camp. The Bavarian cousin had no difficulty in getting him to join the coalition against France. Louvois had given himself a lot of trouble in turning this neutral sovereign, son-in-law of Monsieur and grandson of a Frenchwoman, into an enemy of France.[13]

Catinat came back to Savoy unexpectedly with 20,000 soldiers as an argument to prevent the duke from joining the coalition. But it was too late; he could only open hostilities and, faithful to Louvois' style, began by butchering the garrison of the small town of Cabours, which he had just taken. The duke cried for help, but his new allies had other fish to fry. Nevertheless, the duke had an ardent advocate at the emperor's Court in the person of a distant cousin. Son of Maurice de Savoie Carignan, Comte de Soissons, and of Olympia Mancini, Eugène had first been intended for the church and as a result had received two abbeys. Louis had nicknamed him ironically 'le petit abbé', but he cared more about fighting than saying mass. Since his father was dead and his mother Olympia exiled, he had no support, but had nevertheless begged Louis to give him a regiment. Louis had teased the frail young man with his trumpet nose, his ugly mouth, his greasy hair, and, with all the haughtiness at his command, refused his services. Deeply hurt, Eugène had gone off and offered his sword to the emperor. 'Don't you think that is a great loss to me?' Louis asked his courtiers sarcastically. In fact, Eugène fought so well against the Turks that he was made a lieutenant-general at the age of twenty-five.

He worked so hard on behalf of the Duke of Savoy that he persuaded the emperor to send 7,000 troops. What interested him was not so much helping his cousin as fighting the French. He desperately wanted to thrust down Louis XIV's throat the contempt that he had showered on him;[14] in this the 'little priest' was curiously like the 'little lord of Breda'. By his blind contempt, Louis had aroused in Eugène the same hatred as in William and their fantastic destinies were to be inspired by, if not built on, a desire for revenge. One had already become king of England and the other, as Prince Eugène, was to be the greatest general of his time.

One July morning in 1690, in Paris, the Chevalier de Quincy, coming down from his room in Paris, was astonished to find the innkeeper busy making an effigy out of straw and old clothes. To this he attached a fine notice on which Quincy read: 'Behold the infamous usurper.' The innkeeper took it out into the courtyard, followed by Quincy, hoisted it up on to a pile of faggots and set light to them. As the effigy burned, the innkeeper took out an old musket and merrily fired at it. Quincy wondered whether the innkeeper had gone mad. But no! Did he not know, he was asked, that William III was dead, killed in battle in Ireland? The whole of Paris repeated the wonderful news and spontaneous expressions of joy erupted everywhere. The burghers shut up shop and went to celebrate in the streets. The wine flowed and bonfires were lit at the crossroads. The bells rang out and the Bastille cannon was fired. Was it possible that the king of France would order salvos for the death of his enemy? No, it was merely a show of excessive zeal on the commandant's part.[15] La Fontaine rejoiced as much as every good

Frenchman, but he met a sceptic, the Abbé de Choisy, who had come back from Siam without having converted the king. 'Let us wait until the news of William's death has been confirmed,' the prudent priest advised him. 'Let us bet on it,' La Fontaine persisted. Choisy agreed, but soon La Fontaine was to write sadly, 'And the rumour of his death cost me a fine *louis*.'[16] For William, far from being dead, was delivering a sound defeat to his dear father-in-law!

Louis had sent James II to recapture his kingdoms. They decided to begin with the most Catholic of them, Ireland. The situation could not have been better for the dethroned king – he had 30,000 soldiers with him. They were commanded by the indispensable Lauzun, with the support of an overwhelming majority of the Irish. The Scots, who had not recovered from William's usurpation, were ready to follow him. Admiral de Tourville had just annihilated the Anglo-Dutch fleet and the English coasts were now open for a landing, and William was far away, held up in London. So everything had been thought of . . . except the stupidity of James, who, for four months, stubbornly persisted with the siege of the small city of Londonderry, thus giving William plenty of time to get the necessary reinforcements to Ireland.

Though begun in a way that was not favourable to him, the battle soon turned to William's advantage. The Irish dispersed first and the French found it difficult to hold out. In the most utter confusion, that fine army collapsed. King James had not even deigned to appear on the battlefield. Learning of the disaster, he threw in the sponge, left Ireland and his supporters to their fate and set off for France as quickly as possible.[17] He got there just in time to hear the news of his son-in-law's 'death'. Serious people were shocked by the indecent joy of the French on that occasion. However, the senior clergy, led by Bossuet and Fénelon, called on Providence to help them in the fight against him. The writers Boileau and La Bruyère poured insults upon him. The gentle Sévigné called him 'the Attila of our time' and serenely approved of the necessity of his death.[18] To the people, he was 'the infamous usurper'. In fact, to the French in general, he was the cur who had the impudence to bark continuously against the glory of France. They were all behind their king, who knew how to strike the cur's muzzle.

Meanwhile, William quietly completed his success in Ireland, before returning to his capital where he was given a triumphant welcome. Similar scenes to those that had occurred in Paris were repeated in London. The bells rang out, the people danced around bonfires and burned effigies – of Louis.[19] But, this time, it was not an illusion. For the first time, protestantism had defeated catholicism, and William had beaten Louis.

'Has the sun ever seen anything more proud and more bold than the siege of Mons, while all the enemy powers conspire out of base jealousy against a domination which, by a truly Christian moderation, has merely kept them in peace and rest?' Nationalism had certainly turned Frenchmen's heads, for this extravagant encomium of Louis' utterly revolting and quite unjustified imperialism was the work of a cultured, intelligent man, and, what is worse, a man of God. He was, in fact, the Abbé Gobelin, writing to Maintenon to console her for the absence of her husband at the war in Flanders. Full of attentiveness, Louis wrote from the front to assure her of 'a truth that pleases me too much for me not to share it with you; for I cherish you always and I consider you to a degree that I cannot express; and, indeed, whatever friendship you have for me, I have still more for you, being with all my heart entirely yours.'[20] This was one of the few personal messages to escape Maintenon's later auto-da-fé of her papers.

The king's heart may have been with her at Versailles, but this did not prevent him from indulging in his favourite military pastime, inspection. One morning, finding a platoon of cavalry badly positioned, he put it elsewhere. Passing again after lunch, he found the platoon back in the same place. 'Who placed you here, captain?' he demanded. 'Monsieur de Louvois,' came the reply. 'But did you not tell him that it was I who placed you?' 'Yes, Sire.' The king went back to his headquarters in high dudgeon: 'Monsieur de Louvois believes himself to be a great man of war and that he knows everything.'[21] Despite this significant hitch, Mons was not to hold out much longer. Mons was to fall. The news exploded like a bomb at the delightful Loo Castle, where William was resting. William dashed to The Hague, gathered together 50,000 soldiers and marched straight on Mons, arriving just in time to attend the surrender of the city. While Louis returned in triumph to Versailles, there was nothing more for William to do but to return crestfallen to England, where he found a furious opposition awaiting him.[22] A victorious usurper was one thing, but a defeated one was quite another matter.

Louis XIV had taken Mons, but he had not defeated Louvois. This time, it was in the presence of ministers meeting in council that the argument began. Once again, Louvois had sent instructions without referring to the king. Louis exploded: 'You shall pay for those orders with your head.' The ministers, their noses stuck in their papers, dared not move. Louvois, crimson with fury, got up, threw his papers on to the table and declared: 'If that's how it is to be, I no longer wish to concern myself with your affairs,' and left, slamming the door behind him.[23]

This time he realized that he had gone too far and that the king was rapidly losing patience. 'I do not know,' he said to his friend Beringhen, first equerry to the king, 'whether he will stop at relieving me of my offices or whether he will put me in prison; I really do not care, since I shall no longer be master.' During the days that followed, Louvois tried to reassure himself, remembering his long experience of the king's weakness. He went to relax at Meudon and, after lunch, went for a drive with the Maréchale de Rochefort and her daughter. He was absent-minded, preoccupied. The ladies tried to be as inconspicuous as possible as he began to think aloud: 'Will he do it? Will they make him do it? No; and yet . . . No, he wouldn't dare.' His grip had loosened on the reins and the horses went straight into a lake, followed by the carriage. Mme de Rochefort cried out, snatched the reins from Louvois' hands and pulled on them as best she could. Louvois woke up: 'Yes, I was dreaming and forgot completely about the carriage.'[24]

However, nothing changed in the routine and on the afternoon of 16 July 1691, Louvois went to work as usual with the king in Mme de Maintenon's apartment. He looked so ill that at four o'clock the king interrupted the session and sent him home to rest. In Versailles, the latest news was transmitted minute by minute. Louvois was sick; Louvois had been bled; Louvois felt more and more oppressed; Louvois wanted to be bled again; Louvois had sent for his son; Louvois was dead. In Mme de Châteauneuf's apartment a short, thin, nervous, bony-faced young man with a high-pitched voice, an arrogant expression and piercing eyes, was bubbling with excitement: it was Saint-Simon. For some time he had been frequenting the Court, observing everything, recording everything, but he had not yet had anything unusual to get his teeth into, no event worthy of the man who was to become the most pitiless observer of the century. But today was the great day. Louvois was dead. What an event for a fifteen-year-old youth to witness. He dashed up the stairs to see how the king was taking it during his walk. He did not take his eyes off him as the king strode up and down the terrace. He noted that he often looked up to the windows of the apartment where Louvois had just died. 'He appeared to me with his usual majesty, but with a new lightness of step, as if a burden had been taken from him.'[25] The joy that Louis displayed 'with unparalleled good faith'[26] and the suddenness and convenience of a death that had occurred when everyone knew that things between Louvois and the king were going badly, naturally made many people suspect poison; it was the obsession of the period. No, the king was too good to poison anyone, concluded the Abbé de Choisy. It isn't the king, but La Maintenon, declared the Palatine.[27] However, the autopsy showed quite clearly that Louvois had died from an apoplectic fit.

Monsieur dashed from Saint-Cloud to commiserate with his brother: 'I congratulate you, Sire, on the great loss that you have sustained.' 'I, not at all . . . If Louvois had not died promptly, you would have seen him in the Bastille before two days were up.'[28]

'This year has been a happy one for me,' the king announced one day at dinner. 'I have been relieved of three men whom I could no longer bear, M de Louvois, Seignelay and La Feuillade.' The Palatine then put her foot in it: 'Ah, but, Monsieur, aren't you coming apart?'[29] Louis blushed and looked down. The Palatine could not understand the king's weakness. Louvois had certainly grasped that weakness, used and abused it, but he hadn't known when to stop. Yet he had had to pull very hard on the strings to make Louis react. What proofs of Louvois' authoritarianism and duplicity Louis needed before jumping from one extreme to another. He put up with anything for years, then, one day, it was the end: prison, a trial – which he had been secretly planning. The dazzling punishment that he had been preparing for Louvois was intended to efface the humiliation of having put up with him for so long: in fact, it was a perfect admission of his weakness, and by condemning Louvois he was condemning himself.

'I was overjoyed, Madame, to receive some tokens of remembrance from Mme de Montespan. I feared I was out of favour with her. God knows if I have done anything to deserve it and how my heart goes out to her. I would be curious to learn what she thought about the horrible death of that man [Louvois].'[30] There is considerable venom in this letter from Maintenon to the Abbesse de Fontevrault, Montespan's sister. Louvois, her enemy, was dead. Her relief was matched only by the vexation she imagined to be Montespan's, for Louvois had been Montespan's friend and ally. With Louvois gone, Athénaïs was defeated at last, excluded from the Court from which she had been suddenly forced to retire, though she still had her apartment at Versailles. But Mme de Maintenon found a way. In May 1691, Montespan learnt that she had been deprived of the care of her eleven-year-old daughter, Mlle de Blois, who had been entrusted to Mme de Montchevreuil, a close friend of Maintenon's. Montespan immediately summoned Bossuet: if that was how it was, she was leaving; he was to tell the king that she asked permission to retire to Paris, to the convent of St Joseph. Louis was delighted. She may retire, he told Bossuet, but she must give up her apartment at Versailles, as he happened to need it. 'Madame, the king orders you to give up your apartment at once.' Montespan's own son, the Duc du Maine was given the task of conveying this cruel order to her. He was Maintenon's favourite and had long ago chosen his victorious governess in preference to his defeated mother. Montespan, who was more angry than hurt, vacated the premises. Her apartment was, of course, given to the Duc du Maine.[31]

The false innocence of Maintenon's letter to the Abbesse de Fontrevault, which she fired like a Parthian shot, ill became the holy 'St Françoise'. . . The sweet-natured La Vallière and the plodding Colbert were the major influences of Louis' youth; the proud Montespan and the imperious Louvois symbolized his triumphant forties. But from now on, Maintenon, alone and without rival, would represent his old age.

'I am no more a great lady now than I was in the Rue des Tournelles when you did not spare me the truth about myself,' she explained to her confessor, the Abbé Gobelin.[32] Having won all along the line, she became even more discreet. She dressed tastefully, but without gold or embroidery, 'very modestly, and so in an older style than her age required'. The monthly presents from her husband, the income from her estate at Maintenon and her long-standing pensions hardly amounted to 100,000 *livres* a year, a sum that Montespan used to throw away in a single night at the gambling table. Moreover, she spent little, did not keep open house, maintained quite a small number of servants and her equipages were reduced to a minimum. She rose early, and if she did not go at once to Saint-Cyr, she took the opportunity of giving 'obscure audiences pertaining to acts of charity or spiritual guidance'. Her day was spent reading, writing, praying, receiving some minister or great person – but as little as possible. She lunched and dined at home with at most a small group of old, female, friends. Within that palace, thronged with bustling courtiers, ceaselessly echoing to the sounds of festivities, she managed to lead a quiet, regular, even bourgeois existence. She never visited the king except when he was ill, but, of course, she was always at home at the appointed hour for the king's daily visits. They each had an armchair separated by a table, in front of which was a stool for the minister who had come to work with the king. While the two men discussed the country's affairs, she continued with her needlework. At nine o'clock, two women undressed her, she had a light supper and retired to bed, while the king and the minister went on working. At ten o'clock, the king left her to join the Court at supper, the curtains were drawn around her bed and she went to sleep.[33]

Saint-Simon has meticulously analysed her manner of ruling her husband, that is to say, France. According to him, as the king was working with his ministers in front of her, she did not so much as bat an eyelid, to all appearances entirely absorbed in her needlework. When asked her opinion, she replied briefly, prudently, or pretended that she knew nothing about the matter in question. In fact, everything had been settled in advance between her and the minister and, imperceptibly, they brought the king round to the desired position. If the king persisted in the contrary point of view, they diverted his attention, blurred the issue, only to return to the charge at the right moment. If an opinion were too plainly, too readily offered, if the minister had made a proposal too obviously in line with her wishes, the king would greet it with blank rejection, or even with one of his 'terrible exits'. She would then lie low and wait for the storm to pass. Imperceptibly, she had managed to acquire control over every appointment and every favour, and she meddled more and more in foreign and military affairs, her preferred spheres of activity.[34]

Saint-Simon observed, as did the entire Court, the exceptional favour that the king lavished upon her, and that everything was decided in her apartment. But Saint-Simon never actually went there. Mlle d'Aumale, on the other hand, was a frequent visitor and therefore a much more credible witness. 'I can and dare testify that the king was adamant that she take not the slightest part in the affairs of state, he never asked her opinion and she never gave it; as for the councils that sometimes took place in her bedchamber, I can also testify that all the rumours concerning them are false: whenever the king and minister were working in Mme de Maintenon's bedchamber, she would retire to some distance, take no part in what was said, neither the king nor the ministers ever consulted her and, when the business in hand had been concluded, and she was allowed to rejoin the king, she knew nothing at all of what had been said.' Ever scrupulous, Mlle d'Aumale added a note to her manuscript: 'It is true that when the council had ended and he was free to come closer to her, it was then that the king sometimes confided to her what had been said or arranged, and then he would ask her for her opinion, and she in fact told him what she thought about it ... I may add moreover that very seldom, if ever, or at the very most almost never, did the opinion that she then expressed alter in any way the arrangements that had been made.'[35]

Mme de Maintenon had no power, despite appearances to the contrary and the unanimous view of the Court. To alter Louis' opinions, whose misogyny would not have left the least particle of power to a woman, one would have to have been a Machiavelli in skirts endowed with prodigious cunning and energy. Maintenon was certainly not such a person.

She wondered what she was doing at Versailles. She did not seek power, but she wished to accomplish her mission of converting the king, the Court, France. She did not feel fitted for the role which the priests had intended for her. What she wanted above all was to live in peace and quiet, far from the Court and to concern herself solely with her beloved Saint-Cyr. But did she have the right to abandon her post? She unburdened herself to her directors of conscience and her anxiety may be measured by their answers, which have alone survived. 'I understand your worries, your cares, your impatience,' the Abbé des Marais assured her.

In fact, Mme de Maintenon was content enough in herself – she had always been – but, the precise opposite of her husband, very uncomfortable in her role. This woman, carried to the heights of glory, remained alone, without support, without power, somewhat at a loss. So all her solicitude was lavished on the bastard children. Maintenon showed indulgence only to them, for their very birth was a source of reassurance to her. Her false position as a secret wife reproached her with their false position as illegitimate children, while there was undoubted embarrassment between her and the legitimate family. The king understood and shared that embarrassment. His unpleasant memories of his uncles and cousins during the *Fronde* had left him with a determination to reduce the influence of his family, just as his weakness made him instinctively dominate those closest to him. Since his remarriage, fear of criticism or disapproval had reinforced these tendencies. His sole legitimate son presented no problem, but the same could not be said of his brother and sister-in-law. However Monsieur may be 'smitten by deplorable tastes' and 'sinking into debauchery', however much his brother the king may have formally reduced him to the status of a servant and kept him financially in tow by paying the debts incurred by his lovers, Louis knew that Monsieur would never swallow the misalliance with La Maintenon.[36] As for the Palatine: 'The old slut knows perfectly well that I am a German woman and cannot abide a misalliance, and she imagined that it was because of me that the king did not wish to make his marriage public; that is why she hates me so much.'[37]

In January 1692, imagine then the dismay of the Palatine when she learnt that the king wanted to marry off Mlle de Blois, the last illegitimate daughter that he had had by Montespan, to her only son, Philippe d'Orléans, Duc de Chartres. A bastard for her son? The Palatine was furious. Bastardy was to her as bad as misalliance. The 'old slut' had struck again, and a double blow at that. She had mortally humiliated the Palatine and hoisted those accursed bastards still higher. That two of them should already have been married to Condés and Contis belonging to a very junior branch of the royal family was bad enough, but to give the youngest of them to the king's only nephew, fifth in line to the throne, the heir to the fabulous fortune of the Orléans, was really too much.

The Palatine summoned her son. Philippe d'Orléans was a strapping fellow of eighteen, a great lover of women and wine, remarkably intelligent, curious about everything, exceedingly good-natured but lazy and weak. Affected by his mother's anger, he promised to do whatever she wished. Never, never would he marry the bastard. Some days later, entering the king's study, to which she had been summoned unexpectedly after lunch, the Palatine found her husband and son, both with downcast eyes, looking extremely embarrassed. Before she had time to express surprise, the king turned to her and said: 'I hope, Madame, that you will not oppose an affair that Monsieur so much desires and to which your son consents: I refer to his marriage to Mlle de Blois. I confess that I desire it with all my heart.' The Palatine was dumbfounded. She stared furiously at the two guilty men, husband and son, then managed to mutter: 'If that is what they want, I have nothing to say.'

The king had laid his plans with care. Knowing his brother to be intransigent where bad marriages and bastardies were concerned, he confided in Monsieur's long-standing lover, the Chevalier de Lorraine, and his brother the Master of the Horse. Very well, they said, they would try to bring Monsieur round, but for their part, they each demanded the Order of the Holy Ghost and precedence before dukes. Louis conceded with ill grace. When Monsieur had finally been convinced, Louis XIV summoned the young Philippe d'Orléans in the presence of his father: 'I cannot give you a better token of my affection than to offer you my daughter's hand. But I have no wish to force you to take it and I shall leave you quite free to act as you think fit.' This was spoken, 'with that terrifying majesty that came so naturally to the king'. Philippe stammered: 'You are the master, Sire, but my wishes depend on those of my father and mother.' 'If you consent to the marriage, your father and mother will not oppose it, is that not so, brother?' he concluded, turning to Monsieur. Thereupon he summoned the Princess Palatine, and the three Orléans, father, mother and son, were caught in the trap.

The Palatine's anger did not subside, however. She would pace up and down the Hall of Mirrors, gesticulating, weeping, 'looking for all the world like Ceres, after the rape of her daugher Proserpina'. The next morning, Saint-Simon saw her arrive in the Hall of Mirrors, as angry as ever. Her son came up to kiss her hand. There and then she exploded in front of the entire Court. By way of greeting she delivered him a mighty blow, which 'filled the innumerable onlookers, of which I was one, with amazement'.[38] As for the betrothed girl, the beautiful but languid Mlle de Blois, she remained quite indifferent to all this commotion. All she wanted was one day to be Duchesse d'Orléans, for at fifteen she was already possessed of that insensate pride that was to earn her from her husband the nickname 'Madame Lucifer'. A good friend came and hinted that her betrothed was in fact in love with her sister, the Duchesse de Bourbon: 'I am not concerned that he should love me. I am only concerned that he should marry me.' He did.[39]

No sooner had Mlle de Blois, the bastard born of a double adultery, entered the House of Orléans, than the illustrious family benefited, as if by chance, from the first of those juicy legacies which were to make it the richest family in France. On 5 April 1693, the Grande Mademoiselle died at the age of sixty-three. To the end, she had refused to see Lauzun again. Although rumours of a secret marriage between them have persisted to our own time, relations between them continued to worsen since the return to Court of the lively betrothed. The truth was, Lauzun was bored to distraction by the naïve and spirited old maid. She was extremely jealous and treated him alternately with studied charm and coarse insults. The more exasperated she became, the more indifferent he grew – until she finally got rid of him.[40] Nevertheless, at her death, Lauzun acted out the role of the bereaved husband and appeared in mourning cloak before the king, who did not find the spectacle to his taste.[41] This display of grief did not prevent Lauzun, at the age of sixty-two, from marrying a ravishing young virgin soon afterwards.

Even in death, Mademoiselle was not to be left undisturbed. The vigil over her body took place with all the customary pomp, attended by princesses, ladies-in-waiting, monks, heralds-at-arms, gentlemen of her service. Suddenly the silence and tranquillity were broken by a violent explosion, followed by a quite unbearable stench. Horror and terror swept through the assembled mourners. Ladies fainted, others sought to flee. The doorways were congested as monks and noblemen trampled each other underfoot. The crowd, all dressed in ceremonial black, ran out into the gardens. Only there was a semblance of calm restored. But what had happened? The dead woman's entrails, badly embalmed and sealed up in an urn left on a table, had quite simply fermented and the gas given off had burst the vessel asunder. As the fear subsided, people began to laugh quite openly;[42] it had always been said that this romantic princess, whose amorous adventures had aroused so much comment, would have to end with a bang.

As for the fortune of 'the richest princess in Europe', it passed to

Monsieur, to whom she had left everything. 'But,' Saint-Simon adds, 'the largest morsels had escaped,' that is, her fabulous gifts to the Duc du Maine, extracted from Mademoiselle in an attempt to get Lauzun back.

With his only nephew relegated by a marriage to a bastard, and his beloved bastard son immensely rich, Louis could be content. Nevertheless, he was still worried about his son the Dauphin. For some time now, he had felt that something underhand was going on in that quarter. He knew that the good-tempered, obedient young fellow was quite incapable of plotting, but dangerous intriguers might well use the heir to the throne as a focus of opposition: what was an important coterie today might be a powerful party tomorrow. Louis' instinctive mistrust was aroused at once, increased tenfold in that it concerned his inoffensive successor.

The entire affair was centred on Mlle Choin. However, this young lady was a source rather of mirth than of fear, and the entire Court made fun of her appearance. 'A short, fat, ugly, dark-skinned, snub-nosed girl' (Saint-Simon); 'she looks like a pug'; 'a big mouth full of rotten teeth that stank so much that one could smell them at the other end of the room'; 'a horribly thick neck' (the Palatine); 'a backstairs wit' (Mme de Caylus); to which others added 'a nose pointing up to the sky', 'a complexion the colour of tanned leather' and 'the deportment of a barrel'. To cap it all, her middle name was Joly (pretty), Emilie Joly de Choin. But this monster was the confidante of the Princesse de Conti, the Dauphin's bastard half-sister, in whose quarter Monseigneur spent his days and who had a great influence over him; furthermore, the Princesse de Conti had a lover, a handsome officer, M de Clermont-Chate, an intimate of the Maréchal de Luxembourg. What, then, was being cooked up between the most popular commanding officer in the army and the heir to the throne? Louis, keeping a close watch on the situation, learnt that everything was being planned in letters between Clermont-Chate, then on active service, and Mlle Choin. A word from him and the secret service would intercept the compromising letters, open them and hand them over to him. They were certainly compromising, but not in the way he imagined ... One evening, the Princesse de Conti was summoned to the king, her father. 'Do you recognize the writing?' he asked, handing several documents to her. She certainly did recognize it, for the documents were written in her own hand and that of Clermont-Chate; they were love letters. The young princess thought she would faint with shame. The king scolded her as expected; then handed her some other letters, from Mlle Choin and Clermont-Chate. From the very first words, the poor princess was dumbfounded: Choin and Clermont-Chate were also lovers; her confidante and her lover were having an affair behind her back. 'Come now, my daughter, compose yourself,' said the king, in an attempt at paternal consolation, 'read on.' The princess had already run her eyes over the terrible, searing words. 'Read aloud,' her father suddenly ordered her, in a commanding tone, and the unhappy woman had to read out, loud and clear, the contemptuous mockery that her lover and her friend poured upon her in their private correspondence. The king did not spare her a single line. Her eyes flooded with tears, and she could hardly bring herself to speak, choking with rage, shame and despair. Each word acted as balm upon the king. At that precise moment, he remembered the mocking words that the Princesse de Conti had written, not so long ago, to her husband and to her beloved brother-in-law, on the subject of the king and La Maintenon. It was sweet, if cruel vengeance of a father on his daughter. He had planned it and he savoured it to the full before showing that he could be understanding, for she had thrown herself on her knees to demand the punishment of the guilty pair. The unfaithful lover was ordered to resign his command and to retire to Dauphiné. The treacherous friend was expelled from the Court the following day and retired to Paris. However, it was not thought prudent to deal too severely with her for the indiscreet correspondence contained an incredible revelation: La Choin was also the mistress ... of the Dauphin.[43] The heir to the throne's penchant for her was common enough knowledge. The Palatine had remarked that Monseigneur was so 'entranced' by her enormous breasts that he would beat upon them 'as one might upon a pair of kettledrums'.[44] But this was not at all the same thing as the discovery that this girl, the ugliest in the Court, should be the future king's favourite. Monseigneur's tastes would never fail to take the courtiers by surprise and upset their calculations.

'I was rather astonished that you should speak to me of my wife; this surprised me at first and quite took my breath away.'[45] Monseigneur wrote those lines to La Maintenon, but by that time his Bavarian Dauphine was dead.[46] Did the reference to 'my wife' mean the widower secretly married Emilie? They had to get rid of the monster at the time, but she was still treated with consideration.

It was understandable that the Princesse de Conti looked rather sorry for herself at the small supper given by the king at Marly. On the other hand, her father was in the best of moods. His behaviour even verged on childishness, as he amused himself by throwing olives at his other bastards, the Duchesse de Bourbon and the Duchesse de Chartres. These ladies, in the heat of battle, drank more than was good for them, a particular weakness for which they were well noted, and as they got up from the table, they were swaying slightly. The king, still laughing, walked past the Princesse de Conti, who stood there as stern as a judge, and remarked drily: 'Your gravity suits ill the drunkenness of your sisters.' At which Conti whispered into a friend's ear, just loud enough to be heard: 'I'd rather be grave than a sponge.' To which the Duchesse de Chartres replied, in the faintest of voices: 'I'd rather be a sponge than a rag-bag;' 'rags' being M de Clermont-Chate and other officers of the Princesse de Conti's bodyguard.[47]

CHAPTER 20

'France is one great hospital'

The war of words between the royal bastards coincided with real war in
Flanders, Germany, Italy, Spain and at sea; from 1691 to 1695 war
continued on every front. Mme de Maintenon did not refrain from
grumbling. Her husband had taken her with him to battle – which she
hated – and while he lay siege to Namur, she was left to her own devices
at Dinant: a 'filthy town', awful houses in which 'one can't see a thing',
dominated by 'frightful rocks', cobblestones so pointed that one trips up
on them, streets so bad that 'the coaches bump enough to break the
springs'. She certainly agreed with Suzon, her maid, who wondered
why the king persisted in taking 'such towns' and did not leave them to
his enemies. The water was undrinkable and one could not find bread,
which was reserved for the army. Everything was exorbitantly expensive. 'Unplucked chickens cost 30 *sous,* meat 8 *sous* a pound, and
very bad it is.'[1] The bourgeoise had awakened in her: she did her sums
and raised her hands to heaven.

Meanwhile, Luxembourg, at the head of 80,000 men, stopped
William coming to the help of Namur, which the king's artillery was
bombarding night and day. One could hear the cannon fire at Dinant,
which scarcely improved Maintenon's mood. To cap it all, it never
stopped raining; the church might at least have attenuated her misfortunes: but the music there was terrible, and, to make it even more
unpleasant, the priests burnt so much incense that one was smoked like a
ham.[2]

However, 'the siege of Namur is going very well, advances are being
made and so far very few people had been killed'. She only hoped that it
would be over soon, for Maintenon could no longer bear 'smelling only
tobacco, hearing only drums, eating only cheese, seeing only bastions,
demilunes, counter-scarps'. She would certainly change all the glory in
the world for a little comfort. 'I am just a little woman and I would
willingly change places with my dear ladies doing their needlework; I
hope I shall have that pleasure soon and that Namur would prefer to
surrender than be entirely ruined.'[3] God heard her prayer, Namur
surrendered in June 1692 and she was able at last to see Versailles again,
accompanied by her husband.

★

In his camp, William was champing at the bit and waiting for the first opportunity to attack Luxembourg's army. But the cunning Luxembourg had taken precautions. He had sent a spy to the enemy, a musician called – appropriately enough – Millevoix. As he charmed William's ears, Millevoix recorded everything that was being planned and, each day, sent his report through the lines to Luxembourg. It won't be tomorrow, concluded Luxembourg, reading Millevoix's report, which had just been brought to him. Tomorrow, wrote the faithful spy, the enemy troops are going to advance, but don't worry, don't move, they will simply be looking for fodder. So Luxembourg went to sleep with a quiet mind.

It was eight o'clock next morning, 3 August 1692, when one of his officers sent out on reconnaissance, came breathlessly back with terrible news. William III's entire army was advancing on the French camp, not looking for fodder, but to attack: a French brigade had been put to flight and Luxembourg's right wing had already been breached. Luxembourg was to learn later that Millevoix had been uncovered and that William had forced him to write a false report in order to surprise him all the more.

It had come as a complete surprise and the situation was almost desperate. Luxembourg had only a short time to choose a favourable terrain, draw up a plan of battle and reform his right flank. However he succeeded in doing so, then led the charge in person. Three times he rallied his retreating troops and three times brought them back into the fight. There were to be 6,000 dead in each camp, but the victory of Steinkirk was to go to France.[4]

'All these victories give me all the more pleasure in that they do not change the king's heart as to his good intentions for peace ... We can only hope that God will enlighten our enemies as to their insane assurance that they will defeat France. We shall fight them everywhere for it is the cause of God that the king is defending.'[5] Thus Maintenon herself wrote, in the grip of the nationalist virus.

The following spring, the Maréchal de Lorge and the Dauphin once again successfully invaded the Palatinate. Louvois was dead and this time no order was given for the systematic destruction of the countryside. Unfortunately, the soldiers, remembering the entertainments of 1689 – lootings, rapes, massacres – refused to admit that times had changed. The inhabitants of Heidelberg, seeing the French at their gates, had realized what was coming to them. The effects of the bombardment and burning of their city, which had been destroyed three years earlier, were sufficient indication of the invaders' conduct. The governor lost his head, abandoned the city and shut himself up in the castle. Women and children took refuge in the churches. In one such church, the doors were suddenly blown open and French soldiers appeared on the threshold, sword in hand. They paused, then ran on the women, tearing off their clothes, raping them on the flagstones, on the altars, in front of the children. This orgy of the living was followed by an orgy of the dead. Tombs were opened and the corpses of the electors scattered around. The corpse of the Palatine's own father was given very special treatment: the head was cut off and kicked around the church. Then, as a fitting conclusion to the evening, the four corners of the city were set on fire. The governor surrendered and soon 15,000 civilians were on the streets, fleeing in all directions, by the light of their burning city. Naturally enough, a medal was struck to commemorate this great victory.[6]

Maintenon was not pleased either. The king had dragged her off to war again and the litany of complaints resumed: 'rather uncomfortable journey', 'bad weather', 'even worse roads', 'fairly uncomfortable accommodation', 'rheumatism'. She was dead with fatigue, but in her pitching and jolting coach, she persisted in embroidering church ornaments for Saint-Cyr. Fortunately, her husband turned out to be in the mood for devotion. 'Every evening the king ends the day with Benediction: God is everywhere and honoured everywhere: it is a great consolation.' Soon she was jumping for joy. Heidelberg had been taken, which meant that the king would desert the army and go home with her.[7] 'Sire, you cannot leave the army at this moment,' begged the Maréchal de Luxembourg. 'The Prince of Orange is close by, driven back into his entrenched camp at Park, with a smaller army than ours. Let us attack him, and the Netherlands will be ours.' The king would not listen even when Luxembourg got down on his knees to beg him to change his mind. There was consternation and anger throughout the army. Even the ordinary soldiers criticized the king. It was all Maintenon's fault. She hated being at war; she wanted to go home and was making the king follow her.[8]

When William heard the news from one of his spies, he would not believe it at first. He knew that he was in an indefensible position, at the mercy of a French attack. 'Only a miracle can save me,' he repeated to his friend, the Prince de Vaudemont. So great was his anxiety that he rejected the wild hope of seeing Louis miss such a fine an opportunity. The spy's second message confirmed the news. William was exultant: his army and his country were saved thanks to Mme de Maintenon, for he too believed that it was she who had inspired this tactical error.[9] The war of the medals continued in the absence of battles. He had the most impertinent medal struck: a Louis XIV, drawn in his chariot by furies dressed like the young ladies of Saint-Cyr, bearing the motto 'Venit, vidit et non vicit'.[10]

Despite Louis' absence, Luxembourg drove William out of Neerwinden, on 29 July 1693. For Saint-Simon, with the third squadron of the Royal Roussillon regiment, it has his first great battle. Wearing his blue and gold uniform, he had been on his horse, 'an excellent dock-tailed brown bay', from four in the morning. The attack began at first light, and Saint-Simon charged three times in succession. When his horse showed signs of tiring, he had his *valet-de-chambre* get another and Saint-Simon charged twice more. When the battle was over, he scribbled a note to his mother to reassure her.[11]

At the same time the Maréchal de Luxembourg also wrote to his master: 'Your enemies have worked wonders, your troops even better. For me, Sire, I have no other merit than to have carried out your orders. You told me to attack a city and join battle: I have taken the first and won the second!'[12] Saint-Simon, for his part, went on a tour of inspection of the battlefield. The number of corpses surprised him: 'The victory so disputed, cost dear.' In fact, there were 20,000 dead, a record for the period.[13]

Luxembourg's officers wanted to pursue their advantage, but the generals could not agree: they had no orders from the king. What would His Majesty say? What would he think of them? Louvois was dead, but his fatal system had outlasted him: operations were decided on at Versailles and carried out by generals lacking in initiative. And once more they did not budge.

Having carried out his orders – to win victories – Luxembourg could now devote himself to his other passion – women. On his return from the front, the sixty-year-old general still had the temperament of a young man. Since his age and physique set the great fortunes out of reach, he was reduced to paying for his ever more numerous creatures. He indulged himself so much at Versailles that he fell ill and found himself, in a few days, at death's door. Before the general emotion, Louis, who in fact did not like the general, felt obliged to send for news of his condition every day.[14] Despite this solicitude, Luxembourg died on 4 January 1695.

For the next campaign, Louis sent his childhood friend, Villeroi, into Flanders, to counter William's dark designs. For weeks on end, the two armies played at hide-and-seek. Suddenly Villeroi learned that William had removed his mask and was moving rapidly on Namur, his secret objective. William had only left the army commanded by the Prince de Vaudemont to keep the French amused. Villeroi pursued him relentlessly. He knew that if he caught up with him, the Netherlands would be his. On the evening of 13 July 1695, Villeroi managed to corner Vaudemont and next morning he launched a general attack. Certain of victory, he gave orders to his left flank, which was nearer to Vaudemont, to charge first and sat back contentedly to observe the spectacle. Nobody moved. Villeroi sent orders to the Duc du Maine, commander of the left flank, to hurry. The Duc de Maine was at confession. Villeroi was furious. Out on the field, his officers were weeping, begging the Duc du Maine to order the charge. The Duc du Maine stammered excuses and did nothing. Vaudemont had already gone. The army blushed. Villeroi was more liable to anger than anyone, but he remained a courtier and sent his reports off to the king. 'The diligence that M de Vaudemont employed in his retreat has saved it from my hopes, which I had thought certain.' At Marly, the king remained puzzled by this ambiguous report. Had not Villeroi written the night before that Vaudemont was at his mercy? He noted the silence of his courtiers, their embarrassed faces. Who could he trust? Who could he ask? He decided to question his *valet-de-chambre*, Lavienne. Lavienne, who did not have the presence of mind to invent a lie, looked terribly embarrassed and said nothing. The king insisted, bombarding him with questions. In the end Lavienne blurted out the truth: Vaudemont was allowed to escape only because of the Duc du Maine's cowardice.[15] The king was thunderstruck – his son, his favourite son, a coward! He could still hear the unanimous praise heaped on the courage of the others, after Steinkirk and Neerwinden, on his nephews, the legitimate ones, Conti, Bourbon, and, above all, Philippe d'Orléans, the fat boy who had turned out to be a hero in battle. And now he found that the eldest in his heart, the only one in whom he had placed his hopes of countering the success of the others, was a coward. During luncheon, in front of his courtiers, he struggled to conceal his true feelings, but his expression spoke volumes. As he rose from the table, he noticed a valet slipping a biscuit into his pocket. It was the last straw: he pushed aside his courtiers, rushed at the valet, cane raised and, yelling insults, struck him several times. The valet fled. The king remained there, 'with the look of a man no longer in possession of himself', red-faced, the stump of his cane in his hand, continuing to abuse the valet, then he ran off to La Maintenon's apartment. Terror had transformed the courtiers into pillars of salt. Never before had the superlative actor, always so much in control of himself, allowed his feelings to break through his Olympian calm – and then to make such a scene over such a trifle[16] Later, they were to draw their own conclusions, make some connection between an unfortunate valet found pinching a biscuit and the favourite son of the king of France who had lost a victory.

When troubles come they come not single spies, but in battalions. Louis learnt that Namur had fallen. In his rage, he ordered Villeroi to go and bombard the city of Brussels. 3,000 bombs and 1,200 rounds of shot were fired off. 'Such misery has not been seen for centuries,' a Dutch witness recounted, 'the suffering is indescribable. The inhabitants of the lower city have taken their possessions up on to the hill, but the fire is sweeping through the city, driven by the wind, not only the market place, but from Bergshaat onwards everything is in ashes, the churches, the monasteries, the fishmarket.' M de Vigny, commanding the French artillery observed his work: 'We can see most of the houses of the city of Brussels burning ... I have never seen so great a fire, nor so much desolation as there is in this city.' And, very pleased with himself, he concludes: 'I believe that the king's intentions will be well carried out and that he will be pleased with my work.'[17] Catinat may have won yet another brilliant victory over the Duke of Savoy at La Marsale, in October 1693, but he could not prevent the duke from invading the Dauphiné and recapturing the key fortress of Casal. Similarly, in Catalonia, the Duc de Noailles, although he had defeated the Spanish and taken Girone, was forced once again to retreat to the other side of the Pyrenees. The French were beginning to wonder seriously what purpose was being served by these fine victories.[18] In the good old days, Louis XIV would simply walk into his neighbours' lands and, after great battles whose names every schoolboy had to learn, devour whole provinces. Now, despite all the *Te Deums*, the enemy was constantly being reborn from its ashes and taking back whatever the French had taken from it. France was victorious and exhausted. The allies were inexhaustible and no longer lost anything. Of that series of brilliant victories, there remained only a costly and useless prize. 'I am sick of this endless war and would give anything for peace.' Here Maintenon expressed the general feeling of the French, including her husband. Meanwhile, 'God will be for him against all: he is pious and the others sacrifice religion to their own passions'.[19] She was not condemned to know the reality of war, like the unfortunate Racine who, appointed the king's historian, had to follow all the campaigns closely and supped full of horrors. 'I wish all these poor people were at home in their cottages with their wives and children and I in my study,' he wrote.[20]

He did not know that 'these poor people' would have nothing to eat when they got back to their cottages. The cost of Louis' imperialist policy, the cost of war, which the State tried to pay for with a host of new taxes introduced at random since Colbert's death, the interruption to trade, the resulting economic disaster and the elimination of industrious protestants, had emptied the State coffers and the cottage larders. To this was added a series of catastrophic harvests, unusually harsh winters, floods and frosts. It was Paris that suffered the worst famine. The drained provinces could no longer feed the capital and the few wheat convoys to make their way there were stopped by bands of furious peasants. The price of cereals rose dizzily; speculation made matters worse. Riots broke out and bakeries were attacked.[21]

'As for the penury, we know nothing of it here and we would dearly like to assuage it, but one is pressed on every side,' admitted Maintenon. With a European war on one's hands, the entire country in ferment, the capital starving, the sharks of finance avid for gain and not a *sou* in the coffers, there was little that 'one' could do. Furthermore, 'one' had health problems. Maintenon wanted to replace the king's first physician, Daquin, by her own protégé Fagon. Daquin had had the misfortune to have been Montespan's creature, whereas Fagon had the advantage of being the physician of the beloved royal bastards.

Fagon, of course, declared in favour of a diagnosis contrary to that of his predecessor. The king was not of a bilious but of a lymphatic temperament, he declared. It was the champagne recommended by Daquin that was the cause of his melancholic humours. So no more champagne, but instead stimulating, cheering burgundy. Reims was outraged that its sparkling wine was deemed less good than the coarse red wine next door and the two provinces were soon on the verge of open war. However, despite this crucial change of drink, despite Fagon's genius, the king was suffering from a whole range of ills; colds complicated 'by humours which, ceasing to flow through the nose, were taking a more harmful course', causing as a result 'an abundant discharge of serosities through the nose, thus blocking the head', a 'fluxion' that swelled the right cheek, a boil that was soon to stretch from one ear to the other 'like a piece of roasted flesh, all suppurating', frequent attacks of indigestion that forced the Sun King to defecate up to eighteen times a day and which filled the basins 'with excrement and froth serosities', sometimes 'with matter like cow excrement', sometimes 'oily and very burning serosities with a prodigious quantity of green peas' – still the same inability to chew; lastly, the attacks of gout that confined him to his chair – he had to be carried from room to room – and forced him to spend whole nights without sleep, 'with the vapours and much discomfort'.[22] The Palatine suddenly saw an old man in place of the radiant prince that she had tenderly loved. 'He is sinking, he seems fat and old, it's as if His Majesty had grown smaller, his face has changed and is hardly recognizable; each day brings new wrinkles.'[23]

His health and the innumerable cares that besieged him made him subject to sudden changes of mood. 'What are you reading there, Madame?' he asked, suddenly entering La Maintenon's room. She did not have time to hide the document. As soon as he spoke, he frowned. It was a terrible report on the misery of the kingdom and its causes. 'Who wrote that?' demanded the king. 'I am sworn to secrecy, Sire.' Louis cared nothing for secrecy. Who had written this indirect criticism of his government? Maintenon was forced to admit it: 'It's by Racine'. 'Because he has a perfect command of verse, does he think he knows everything?' asked the king. 'And because he is a poet does he wish to be a minister?' Maintenon did not dare to admit that it was at her insistence that Racine had committed his sad reflections to paper,[24] poor Racine, who, like so many Frenchmen, could no longer make ends meet, especially with the new taxes. He wrote a fine pamphlet begging the king to be exempted from them. 'That cannot be,' replied the master.[25] Racine was able to pay because he was able to write insolent reports.

It was a sad fate. 'I am deprived of the honour of seeing you,' he wrote to Maintenon. 'I hardly dare to count on your protection.' Despite this pathetic appeal, Maintenon did not in fact see him. She was afraid, for the king was angry with Racine. The king no longer wanted to see Racine.[26] And Racine, seeing the king in the park, had to dash into a thicket lest the Master's furious gaze alight upon him.[27] When he died, in 1699, the king appeared suitably moved.[28] It was the least he could do for the greatest playwright of his century.

Louis had already been irritated by Racine's pessimistic reflections on the situation. When L'Ombre de M Scarron, ('M Scarron's Shadow'), appeared he was frankly furious. First because the pamphlet enjoyed an enormous success, secondly because, among other pleasantries, it referred openly to his secret marriage.[29] Maintenon had also read it and was appalled. Why all these lampoons against her? Why this hatred? She did not understand,[30] but she sighed and said nothing. Her husband did not see things in the same way. On his orders, those responsible for the publication of *L'Ombre de M Scarron*, the compositor, the apprentice binder and the apprentice bookseller were arrested, tortured and the first two hanged in the Place de Grève.[31] Woe betide anyone else who cast aspersions on 'St Françoise', but this repression did not stop either the pamphlets or the indirect cause of their revival: penury.

A bourgeois in Basse-Auvergne scrupulously noted the ravages of the famine. In the villages, he observed, mortality had risen sevenfold. Every day at Clermont, he saw about thirty fresh corpses in the streets and on the dunghills. The municipality, fearing an epidemic, expelled all the poor from the city. Three months later, with the situation still worse, they were allowed to come back. The bourgeois saw them, lying down sick before the gates, awaiting death. He learned that in the village of Saint-Bonnet, parents disinterred their baby, buried the day before, and ate it.[32]

At Versailles, they used statistics: in the course of the winter of 1693-4, only 96,000 deaths from hunger were recorded. 'Your people, who You should love as Your children and who until now have been such passionate supporters of Your Cause, are dying of hunger ... You have destroyed half the real forces within Your State in order to carry out and to defend vain conquests outside it. The whole of France is nothing but one great hospital, without equipment or provisions ... While Your people lack bread, You do not wish to see the extremity to which You are reduced ... You fear to open Your eyes. You fear that others will open them for You. You fear being reduced to losing some part of Your glory. That glory that hardens Your heart is dearer to You than justice, than Your own repose, than the preservation of Your peoples who perish each day from sicknesses caused by famine, even than Your eternal salvation ...'

The king was condemned to read whole pages of such criticism. Everything was grist to the mill: his false love of God, his piety, which consisted 'only in superstition and in superficial practices', his custom of receiving 'praise extravagant to the point of idolatry'; the unjust wars, the illegal acquisitions, the treaties that he had forced the defeated to sign 'with a knife at their throats', with the result that 'your odious name and the whole of the French nation are hated by our neighbours'; the ministers who trampled over laws and traditions on their path to dictatorial power, corrupt magistrates, the ruined, bankrupt nobility. As a result, 'the people itself – it has to be said – who have loved You so much, who have had such trust in You, are beginning to lose those feelings of friendship, trust and even respect.' Then came the parting shot: 'Your council has neither strength nor vigour for good. At least Mme de Maintenon and M le Duc de Beauvilliers [a minister] ought to enjoy Your trust sufficiently to disabuse You. But their weakness and their timidity dishonour them and scandalize everybody.'[33]

Who wrote this appalling indictment that spared the king nothing: neither his policies, nor his collaborators, nor his intimates, nor his wife, nor his pride, nor his conscience? Who had dared to go further than his bitterest enemy, his most extreme opponent, would have dreamt of? The letter was anonymous, but Louis had no difficulty in recognizing the style of that most gentle of priests, François de Salignac de La Mothe Fénelon, Archbishop of Cambrai, tutor to His Majesty's grandson. He was a tall, thin, pale man, the essence of sweetness and seriousness, who combined the learning of a doctor of the Church, the style of a great lord and the charitable solicitude of a pastor, but who, nevertheless, was eaten up by a devouring secret ambition.

Would the Sun King disgrace the madman who dared to attack him? Would he strip him of his offices and lock him up in the Bastille? No, the Sun King did not react: he submitted himself to the man of God, he was paralysed before such an avalanche of reproaches, intimidated by this unprecedented challenge. Such incredible tolerance is an indication of the man's deepest contradictions. But he was to take his revenge on Fénelon over the grotesque affair of 'quietism'.

It all began with a pretty young widow, Mme Guyon, who became so taken up with mysticism that she dreamt of becoming the French Teresa of Avila. She adopted the teaching of a young Spanish Jesuit on the absolute quietism of the soul in a state of perfect contemplation. When she arrived in Paris, she set about proselytizing her beliefs from her home. News of her reached Fénelon and he went to see her and was not put off by what Voltaire called her 'mumbo-jumbo'. Voltaire claimed that the unfortunate woman was unable to wear corsets for the influx of grace suffocated her; furthermore, by a system of 'communicating vessels', her excess of grace regularly passed into the person she was talking to. In a moment of ecstasy she had 'married Jesus Christ,' no less, and had since refused to pray to the saints; 'The mistress of the house does not address servants,' she commented.

Fénelon liked her as she was – Saint-Simon refers to their 'sublime amalgam'. He then introduced Mme Guyon to his friends, the Ducs de Chevreuse and de Beauvilliers, who presided over a powerful pressure group in the service of virtue and good. He then took a further step and introduced Guyon to Maintenon, an intimate of this group. At their first meeting, Maintenon frowned at the sight of Guyon's rather too plunging neckline, but the lady's modesty, piety and, let us say, her acute sense of flattery, carried the day. Maintenon invited Guyon several times to her table. In view of this success, Fénelon, on the best possible terms with Maintenon, urged her to introduce Guyon to Saint-Cyr, in order to ruin his rival, Bishop Jodet of Chartres, who had jurisdiction over Saint-Cyr. The ignorance and stupidity of the country bumpkin were to serve as a perfect foil to Guyon's perfumed learning and haughty manner. Before long the whole of Saint-Cyr had turned 'quietist'.

The 'bumpkin' Bishop of Chartres learned of this. He was shrewder than Fénelon had given him credit for. He appointed two ladies of Saint-Cyr to inform him of Guyon's activities and teachings, while pretending to be sympathetic to them. The two spies provided an accurate account to Jodet, who piled up evidence against Guyon. When his file was complete, he went to Maintenon. Mme Guyon's doctrines were contrary to the teachings of the Church: Saint-Cyr was infected with heresy.

Dumbfounded and frightened, Maintenon dropped Guyon at once and excluded her from Saint-Cyr. Guyon pathetically asked for justice to be done, but Maintenon turned a deaf ear. She no longer knew Guyon. For what Maintenon feared above everything else had happened. The priests had aroused the king's suspicions and presented Guyon to him as the devil incarnate. Maintenon was terrified of being compromised. She was furious with Fénelon for getting her involved in such an imprudent course. But Fénelon was more courageous than she and, instead of dropping Guyon, cleverly advised her to take her case to Bossuet. By entrusting her faith to him, she stopped any possible thunderbolts. The Archbishop of Paris, de Harlay, who was hated by both Fénelon and Maintenon, took great pleasure in ostentatiously condemning Guyon's doctrine and, as expected, Bossuet was content to make her promise to give up teaching it. Thereupon, Fénelon was given the archbishopric of Cambrai and, at his express request, he obtained permission to be consecrated by Bossuet . . . at Saint-Cyr. He thus killed two birds with one stone: he put himself on good terms with a powerful opponent by flattering him and humiliated the Bishop of Chartres, who, normally, would have been given the task of consecrating him since Saint-Cyr was in his diocese.[34]

Thereupon, the Archbishop of Paris, the 'scandalous, false, cunning, crafty enemy of all virtue' de Harlay, died. Immediately Maintenon saw an opportunity of putting a reliable friend into this eminent position, the Bishop of Châlons, M de Noailles, whose relations were members of her intimate circle. In order to get him to Paris, Maintenon emerged from her fearful passivity and prudence to deploy quite unusual energy, tenacity and cunning. She overcame her hesitations, bombarding him with letters full of what was intended to be maternal tenderness, but which were shot through with complicity, not to say a deeper, unconscious feeling. She had deliberately used trickery with the king and, unusually for her, admitted to him who her candidate was: 'One sometimes has to trick the king in order to serve him.' She dared to administer a slap in the face to his rival, Father La Chaise, the king's confessor, who, as a good Jesuit, wanted a friend of the Jesuits as archbishop. So Noailles was duly appointed.

What could be happening in that small, dark house, the inhabitants of the Faubourg Saint-Antoine asked themselves. The door only opened when someone knocked on it according to an agreed code; as soon as night had fallen, people came and went in a most mysterious fashion and the owners were never seen. It is all very suspicious, repeated the good trades-people, who went and warned the police. Perhaps that was where Mme Guyon is hiding, it was immediately suggested in high places, for the beautiful prophetess, fallen from favour and ordered to leave Paris, had disappeared, giving the slip to the 'shadows' who had been told to follow her. Immediately the police sleuth hounds were sent to observe the house. One day, without her noticing, they followed a maid, who was coming back from the market, to the mystery door and, after she had knocked according to the code, they managed to get into the house. It was indeed Mme Guyon who, despite her promises, was continuing to teach to a circle of faithful disciples.[35] Mme Guyon was sent to the Bastille, 'with orders to be well treated, but with the strictest orders not to allow her to see, write to or receive news from anybody'.[36] Why such strict orders?

Guyon herself was certainly little more than a nonentity, but that gentle crank, who had been content to babble on for a few society ladies in quest of the sublime, had been used as a Trojan Horse by rival prelates secretly and ferociously fighting to win the minds of the king and Maintenon. They pulled the couple this way and that and, taking advantage of the husband's lack of knowledge and the wife's lack of judgement, got them to swallow almost anything. Fénelon built Guyon up into a prophetess, while the Bishop of Chartres and the late Archbishop of Paris, saw her as a terrible danger for the Church. Influenced by the latters' advice, the king came to see the harmless crank as a heretical firebrand and struck accordingly.

To console herself for having been taken in by Guyon, Maintenon threw herself into the spiritual arms of the new Archbishop of Paris, dear Noailles. She adopted a freedom of expression with him that she neither had nor ever was to have with anyone else. She let him know all the sorrows that she had had to endure in trying to convert so difficult and stubborn a man as King Louis. To Noailles she did what she had done for no one else; she passed judgement on her husband. 'He replied to me that he was not a consistent man in anything ... One has to get him used to things and not surprise him ... He fears the new in everything ... I do not believe that he is a liar.' The judgments are infrequent, brief and watered down. Yet anyone who knows Maintenon can detect a certain contempt for Louis XIV in them.

It was 1696 and the war was continuing on all fronts. In northern Italy, Prince Eugène was urging his cousin and ally, the Duke of Savoy, to pursue their advantage and to go and take the key fortress of Pignerol from the French. Victor Amadeus agreed enthusiastically, but curiously postponed the expedition. Eventually Prince Eugène, who knew his cousin well, began to be suspicious. Was the duke thinking of doing a deal with the French? The idea surprised him, however: the spies that he had prudently placed in Victor Amadeus's entourage had reported back nothing suspicious. On his return to Vienna, he shared his suspicions with the emperor and, to find out where the duke stood, forced him to renew the alliance. Victor Amadeus expressed perfect willingness to do so and promised whatever was wanted of him.

Thereupon, Victor Amadeus went on a pilgrimage to the shrine of Our Lady of Loretto. Prince Eugène was again taken aback for, as one commentator put it, 'devotion was not a defect that could be attributed to this prince'. The campaign opened as expected and a French army entered Piedmont, with the declared intention of laying siege to Turin. But, curiously enough, it remained inactive for a good month at the camp of La Rivolte, while the Duke of Savoy methodically withdrew the allied troops from his fortified positions and replaced them by his good Piedmontese. Suddenly, on 12 July 1696, a truce of one month was announced between France and Savoy. Prince Eugène's eyes were opened at last. The duke had been negotiating in secret with the French for months; with the same tenacity that Louvois had used to get him into the war, Louis XIV was trying to get him out of it. But how could negotiations be carried out when one was surrounded by Prince Eugène's spies? His method was to choose the pious screen of the pilgrimage to Loretto.[37]

All hope being lost of getting the duke back, the emperor's troops began operations against the Franco-Savoyard troops commanded by the Duke of Savoy himself, who thus won the peculiar distinction of having been, in the space of two months, commander-in-chief of both camps. The fighting continued, but the negotiations went on in secret just as furiously. The allies were beginning to understand that they had lost the battle and, on 8 October 1696, signed the treaty by which Italy was declared neutral.[38]

The Bishop of Constance, a faithful vassal of the emperor's, and the emperor's ambassador in Switzerland were getting worried. Their spies had informed them that in a discreet inn in the township of Stechborn mysterious individuals had been having even more mysterious meetings. Two of these individuals were no less than Count von Velos and Herr von Seilern, both members of the Imperial Court. But who were the other two, named as Monsieurs de Boursière and du Breuil?

The Bishop of Constance, determined to get to the bottom of it, sent his spies to stay at the same inn. It did not take long to recognize the two Frenchmen, the Comte de Crécy and the Abbé Morel, members of the French Court. But why those assumed names? Why those long daily meetings behind closed doors? Had the king of France sent emissaries to parley with the traitors and to cook up some action against the emperor? The bishop was horrified. The poor man was unaware that it was the emperor himself who had sent Velos and Seilern to meet Louis' emissaries in such total secrecy that he had wanted to warn neither his ambassador in Switzerland nor the faithful bishop.

For several months, Louis had been thinking of bringing the ruinous war to an end; it was serving no purpose and was dragging on interminably. There was no question of coming to an agreement with England and Holland: William III would see to that. Spain, determined to recover what she had lost, was not interested. On the other hand, the emperor, threatened by the Turks who were once again looming on his horizon, seemed ready to listen. So a meeting was arranged, as discreetly as possible, at Stechborn.

The Bishop of Constance, still in ignorance and increasingly anxious, decided to surround the suspect inn with his constabulary. Seeing armed men prowling around, it was the negotiators' turn to be worried. It was imperative that they should not be arrested or the secret negotiations would be discovered. The first to make off were, by an irony of fate, the emperor's representatives, swiftly followed by the Frenchmen.

Eventually everyone seemed ready to negotiate.. The English were increasingly unwilling to vote credits for the war. The Dutch were complaining of the considerable losses that their trade was sustaining as a result of the war. The emperor had the Turks on his hands. Only Spain persisted, but a new, brilliant campaign by the French soon brought them round. So, before long, everyone was around the negotiating table at Ryswick Castle in Holland.

Louis XIV had weighty arguments to speak of peace: 80,000 troops in Flanders, 40,000 on the Rhine, 40,000 in Piedmont and another army in Catalonia.[39] He talked as if he had won the war but, on 20 September 1697, he signed the treaty of Ryswick as if he had lost it. He handed back to the empire and to Spain almost everything he had taken from them in Catalonia, Flanders and Alsace. He even handed back Lorraine to its duke who, though the emperor's general, had been dispossessed of it. Lastly, he recognized William as king of England and promised to lend no more assistance to his enemies.

The courtiers praised the Master's 'moderation', but an indignant public opinion unrestrainedly lampooned this shameful display of weakness.[40] France was exhausted, famine was rampant and the coffers of the State were empty. Louis wanted to put an end to the expense incurred by war, for the machine for fabricating his glory was no longer producing anything. He seized the first sign of war-weariness in Europe to treat with his enemies, then dropped everything without appearing to give in. However, such very good reasons do not entirely explain his incomprehensible generosity. Did he, one wonders, have some longer-term intention?

In the short term, protestant hopes were raised. Louis had recognized the champion of protestantism as king of England, he had handed back his principality of Orange and protestant practices had been re-established. Was toleration looming on the horizon? Officially, the king was content to publish, on the clergy's advice, a declaration calculated to improve the situation of the new converts. Unofficially, however, he sent out secret instructions forbidding any violence against the prot-estants. But this Jesuitical solution was not going to put a sudden end to the fanaticism of the intendants and priests that had been freely unleashed for years. The king's instructions were interpreted in a sense exactly contrary to their intention. The king forbade sending protestant children to catechism classes, so it was concluded that the girls should be shut up in convents. The king forbade acts of violence, so more cases were brought against protestants and more prosecutions handed out. The Intendant Basville, convinced that 'the effect of the Inquisition was a happy one, since heresy was stamped out', made sure that 'the king's will' was respected, despite the king and his will. And a protestant describes 'fat Basville, like some monster set loose in the circus, judging, condemning, dragooning, deporting and hanging with all his might'.

Yet Basville was surprised: the more he condemned, the more protestants there were to condemn. 'Prophets' sprang up everywhere, miracles were on the increase and there were more and more reports of 'desert assemblies', in which thousands of protestants gathered together in deserted places. They soon developed into collective hysteria, with ecstatic prophets and believers being thrown to the ground. 'It was a great shaking of convulsionaries, it was the divine Sabbath.' The protestants came back from them ready for martyrdom, sometimes even yearning for it. Above all the young learned to suffer for their faith. Women 'seized by that sacred fury' got themselves hanged 'in batches'. The protestants had 'radiant visions of the heavens opened up' as their blood ran in floods. The fanaticism of their persecutors had given birth to the fanaticism of the persecuted. Basville and 'all the hell-hounds of the impious beast' (Louis XIV) were unconsciously manufacturing a bomb the power of which they were quite incapable of imagining.

CHAPTER 21

Battles of Will

It was not bombs that exploded at the Court of France, but the finest fireworks in honour of the Duc de Bourgogne's marriage. In accordance with the clauses agreed upon with the Duke of Savoy when getting him to change camp, his daughter, Adelaide, arrived in France to marry the eldest of Louis XIV's grandsons. The grandfather, who went to meet the girl at Montargis, wrote an enthusiastic description of her to Maintenon, who had remained at Fontainebleau. He gave a detailed account of her face, her eyes, her eyelids, her complexion, her mouth, her hair, her teeth, her hands, her figure, her walk. He brought a torch close to her face to examine her all the better and went to see her undressed in order to find out what kind of a body she had. Everything about her pleased him except the way she curtseyed – he repeated this twice – which was altogether too Italian.[1] He saw her as the most ravishing automaton and, in fact, Adelaide was to be a doll for Louis XIV and Maintenon to play with.

'Maman has asked me to send you her very best wishes and to ask you to give me yours; teach me, I pray you, whatever I need to know to please the king.'[2] Even though Adelaide had been thoroughly initiated by her cunning mother, she nevertheless possessed a prodigious skill in courtly matters for a child of twelve. With a flick of the wrist, she had won over the king and Maintenon. Indirectly, too, she confirmed Maintenon in her position as virtual queen of France. Already her mother, preoccupied with her training, had written to Maintenon asking her to look after her daughter. Maintenon's schoolmistress heart could not resist such an appeal. She took young Adelaide in charge, trained her, and turned her into her masterpiece, a superior pupil of Saint-Cyr. But to do that she had to emerge from the shadows. After all, how could she concern herself with the heiress to the throne and remain in the background. For more than ten years, the wife of the king of France had kept to the chiaroscuro of her apartment, wrapped in a sort of semi-mystery, with the result that she was regarded by France and the whole of Europe as a formidable tutelary power. Then a shrewd child came, took her by the hand, led her out into the light and pushed her on to the great stage of the century. The king had fixed the marriage festivities for December 1697. He had made it plain that he was expecting his courtiers to renew their wardrobes for the occasion. So immediately there was a rush on all the luxury tailors and dressmakers. With the full weight of royal authority behind them, the ladies gleefully set about ruining their husbands with fripperies, so much so indeed that the king himself found some bills excessive, but once the floodgates were open, he found it impossible to stop the torrent. Saint-Simon gibbed at having to pay out 20,000 *livres* for clothes, but the excitement that reigned in society drowned his bitterness.[3]

For the wedding ceremony, the king wore a costume of gold and the young bridegroom black, pink and gold, with diamond buttons.[4] The enormous ball on 11 December marked the climax of these festivities. In the Hall of Mirrors lit *a giorno* an immense crowd rustled with satin, brocade and precious stones. 'It was, therefore, a crowd and the disorder overwhelmed even the king. Monsieur was beaten and trodden on by the throng ... There was no room, and it could not have been otherwise; people pushed their way through as best they could.'[5] All those festivities, all that expense, all that extravagance ... for a white wedding. The bridal couple were laid out in the nuptial bed where the king showed them to the ambassador of Savoy, but once the officials had retired, the Duc de Bourgogne was taken away and conducted to his apartment. The couple of the year were too young, at fifteen and twelve, to give themselves up to the joys of love. 'I would have stayed in the bed,' commented the bridegroom's young brother, the Duc du Berry, then aged eleven.[6]

Spring 1698: excitement at Court was renewed on account of a curiosity: the personal envoy of the king of England, William of Orange. Louis' mortal enemy had decided to send him a magnificent embassy, the first after so many years of war. It was headed by his long-standing favourite, Bentinck, now Earl of Portland, which redoubled the curiosity of the courtiers. 'Dazzling', 'the air of a gentleman and courtier', magnificent courtesy, almost haughty dignity, numerous splendidly-attired attendants, everything combined to make Portland an instant success.[7]

To honour Louis, William sent him what was dearest to him, but mischiefmakers insinuated that in fact William had wanted to get his former lover out of the way just as a new star was appearing in his firmament in the person of the young Dutchman Keppel. Saint-Simon refused to attribute his mission to such frivolous motives and, wishing to appear well-informed at all times, maintained that Portland had been sent to demand the expulsion of the other king of England, James II, whose presence in France, with all the honours that were paid him, remained a thorn in William's flesh. Louis would not be bargained with. He would no longer aid his cousin James – he had promised that – but he refused to expel him or to deprive him of his empty title.[8] Was it to get his refusal accepted that he covered Portland with such incredible honours? One evening, he accorded him the honour of holding the sacrosanct *bougeoir*, a sort of flat candlestick; he received him after taking a purge; he even allowed him inside the balustrade around his bed.[9] Saint-Simon lost himself in conjecture, but he did not guess that Portland's mission might have a quite different, wider and more secret purpose.

Somewhere in Europe there lived a man dressed all in black around whom a most affecting drama was being played out. He was almost born an old man, for degeneration had affected his body even to the bone. Never had a face, even in the most flattering portraits, borne such cruel marks. His father and his mother, his four grandparents, six of his eight great-grandparents belonged to the same family and were closely related. He was paying for this consanguinity, which had reached preposterous proportions, with a somewhat deranged mind, weakness of character and continual illnesses of all kinds. Torn between his inadequacies and his responsibilities, this man preserved a sense of dignity and honour that lent him a certain greatness in his misery. He was only thirty-seven years old, he had married twice but it was obvious that this deferred corpse was incapable of having children. This would not have mattered if his fortune was not one of the most fabulous in history. For the Habsburg Charles II of Spain possessed, apart from the Netherlands, half of Italy and the whole of Latin America, from California to Terra del Fuego, and other colonies around the world. His empire might be in decline, but this pathetic creature was nevertheless the greatest king on earth. Everyone was beginning to wonder with growing disquiet who would inherit this incredible collection of crowns. There were three possible candidates: the Dauphin of France (or one of his sons) as the only son of Charles II's older sister, Queen Maria Theresa, but King Louis had ratified his wife's solemn renunciation of that inheritance; Prince Joseph Ferdinand of Bavaria – aged six – as the only grandson of Charles' younger sister, the Infanta Margaret Theresa, but the link was regarded as rather too tenuous; and one of the sons of the Emperor Leopold I, widower of that same Margaret Theresa – they were, in fact, children of the emperor's second marriage, but they belonged to the same family as Charles II, the Habsburgs, and Vienna and Madrid had always intermarried.

Whenever a new illness brought Charles II down, the vultures crowded in around his bed: his mother, his second wife, the ambassadors of interested powers, courtiers in the pay of possible heirs and the Spaniards themselves, anxious for the fate of their country, intrigued as best they could and pulled the unfortunate man this way and that. Conscious as much as anyone of the fearsome problem, Charles had long understood, like everyone else, that the greatest affair of his life would be his death. His mothers, Maria Anna of Austria, who hated her family, had made him draw up a first will in favour of the Bavarian candidates, then she died. His second wife, Maria Anna of Bavaria, who also detested her family, made him draw up a second will in favour of the Austrian candidate.[10] But Europe knew nothing of these arrangements when Charles II had a sudden relapse and it was not thought that he would live much longer. In her usual way, the Palatine announced loud and clear what everyone else was thinking to themselves: 'One does not have to be a prophet to guess that if the king of Spain dies without a child, it will give rise to a terrible war; all the powers are claiming the succession; none of them will wish to give in to any other and it will only be decided by war.'[11]

William III had understood this too. He had no right or claim to the succession: he could therefore appear as a disinterested arbiter. Furthermore, under no circumstances did he want the Spanish empire to pass in its entirety either to Louis XIV or to the Emperor Leopold, realizing the danger of such concentration of power. There was only one solution in his eyes: partition. He knew very well that Charles II would never accept such a dismemberment. It would have to be done despite him and the spoils carved up while he was still alive. The Emperor Leopold, who regarded the Spanish empire as a family possession, would not hear of it. But what about Louis XIV? Louis XIV, who had just demonstrated such strange moderation in the Treaty of Ryswick in order to improve his deplorable image as an imperialist ogre, might also prove that he was not necessarily motivated by greed in the matter of the Spanish succession. William knew how to catch the ball in flight and discreet conversations, while the Ryswick negotiations were going on, took place between his representatives and those of Louis XIV with a view to studying the possible grounds of agreement. William then sent Portland to Versailles, not to get an old lover out of the way, nor to demand the expulsion of his father-in-law, James II, but in fact to forward the affair. Hence the extraordinary and ostentatious honours showered on Portland by Louis who had made up his mind to prove accommodating. Indeed, he proved so accommodating that after a few months of negotiations the partition treaty had been worked out: the Bavarian would have Spain and the colonies; the Dauphin, Naples, Sicily and a Spanish province; the emperor's second son would have Milan.

Charles' indignation when he learnt the terms of this fine agreement knew no bounds. Those hyenas were tearing him apart while he was still alive and, worse, were handing round the pieces. He announced with much sound and fury that he would never allow the partition of his empire and followed the announcement with a final will. It was a catastrophe, the accomplices murmured to one another: he was so (legitimately) furious that he would, of course, leave everything to the emperor. In fact, it was to the Bavarian that the king of Spain bequeathed his entire inheritance. In spite of his indignation, he had understood, in the light of the partition treaty, that the powers would never allow the reunification of the empire of the Habsburgs. William was jubilant. Neither the emperor nor Louis would get the cake. Louis did his best to put a good face on it; he would get nothing, but neither would the emperor. The emperor was obliged to bow before the will of his cousin: the Bavarian was a more direct heir than he. The spectre of a European conflict retreated and everyone breathed a sigh of relief.[12]

In late August 1698, outside Compiègne, 60,000 men and an entire headquarters were awaiting His Majesty's pleasure. Was Louis xiv planning for a new war while peace had hardly been signed? No, this formidable deployment of forces was intended merely as a spectacle, the spectacle of the century. Ostensibly, it was a series of military manoeuvres intended to complete the military training of the heir presumptive, the Duc de Bourgogne, but the real purpose was to show Europe that France, exhausted by war, starved by bad harvests, divided by the protestant question, was still a military power.

'Do not touch,' Louis seemed to be saying, perhaps with an eye on the Spanish succession: everything had been settled in that quarter, but who knows? What was at issue was too enormous not to pursue a secret life in the minds of the interested parties. Since there was to be a spectacle at Compiègne there would also be spectators. The king took almost the entire royal family, the melancholy ex-king and queen of England, foreign ambassadors – for whom the operation had really been put on – ministers, dukes and courtiers. Left out of it at first, the ladies expressed a desire to go too; the king 'relented' and allowed all those who wanted to go to do so. Of course, almost all of them were only too delighted. However, it was not they, but the officers who indulged in the greater coquetry. The king had let it be known that he wanted no expense spared, so they all indulged in new uniforms, new gold braid, new horses and got themselves up to their ears in debt.

Although splendidly furnished wooden houses and enormous tents had been set up to accommodate the guests, the villages and farms for four leagues around were packed with visitors. Dukes had to be put up in pairs by the local inhabitants and Saint-Simon shared the house of the Sieur Chambandon with the Duc de Rohan. The Maréchal du Boufflers, commanding this luxury army and realizing where his duty lay, brought with him seventy-two cooks and 342 servants. Night and day, there were 'all sorts of hot and cold drinks', wines from France and abroad, game, venison from every province in the land, fish brought from river and sea by special courier. There were marches, counter-marches, assaults, simulated battles and, of course, sieges of cities: the programme changed every day. Never had Louis xiv more deserved the nickname 'king of reviews'.[13]

This prodigious entertainment, under a vaguely military pretext, was intended only to throw the dust in people's eyes and, in this, it excelled. It did not matter if entire regiments were to be in debt for years. It did not matter if this great spectacle did not impress the king. Through all the illusions that he had been offering the world for the past forty years, he was the only person he was really trying to take in. But if the unforgettable entertainments of 'The Pleasures of the Enchanted Island' had been a homage to La Vallière, if Montespan had presided over a series of extravagantly splendid carnivals, all the warlike luxury of the camp at Compiègne seemed to be dedicated to the true queen of the entertainment, to a woman who hated war and the army more than anyone, Mme de Maintenon:

'Compiègne, 3 September 1698 ... The king hardly leaves my apartment; you know, Monseigneur, what I think about that. Pray for me; but think less about my health than about my real needs. Patience is one of the most urgently required.'

Compiègne, 9 September 1698. 'No, Monseigneur, I have no respite here. The king comes into my room three times a day and in doing so interrupts whatever I am doing. I acknowledge that God has given me the grace to be insensitive to the honours that surround me and to feel only the subjection and constraint that they bring, *amour-propre* is dead on that point, but Monseigneur, my love of rest, freedom and my own way is still very much alive.' Maintenon could not have expressed more clearly to her dear Archbishop of Paris that she had had enough.[14] The whole of Europe envied her for being where she was and she dreamt only of leaving it. Indeed, during the last few months her cup of bitterness and disgust had overflowed. And it was Fénelon who was really behind it all.

With Mme Guyon in prison, Fénelon had not lost his head and, with a fine display of courage, had published 'The explanation of the maxims of the saints on the interior life' in order to defend Guyon in the guise of an apologia of quietism. Bossuet threw himself at the king's feet: 'Pardon, Sire, pardon for not warning earlier of the fatal heresy of M de Cambrai'. In fact, Bossuet had at last realized that he had been taken in by Fénelon, whose actions had had no other aim but to neutralize him, in order to allow Fénelon quietly to advance his pawns. Having suddenly woken up to the reality of the situation, Bossuet had only to pronounce the magic word 'heresy' to turn the king against the Bishop of Cambrai. This came all the more easily in that the king had not forgotten the cruelly pertinent criticism that Fénelon had made of him. For him, Fénelon was still 'the finest and most chimerical mind in my kingdom'. But a fine mind was exactly what he hated and feared.

Determined to crush the beast, Bossuet published 'The Facts about Quietism', in which he annihilated Guyon, Fénelon and other quietists. This was all the king needed: he let fly his thunderbolt. Priests and gentlemen in the entourage of the Duc de Bourgogne, Fénelon's ward, were expelled from Court. M de Cambrai's brother was dismissed from the army and his friends, the 'dukes of virtue' were on the verge of disgrace. It was left to the pope to condemn M de Cambrai himself.[15] The storm did not even spare Maintenon, even though she had done her best to minimize the affair from the beginning, guessing what it might cost her.[16]

How she cursed the false friends who had put her into such an embarrassing situation. Maintenon set aside, Maintenon in disgrace –

the priests who had put her where she was shuddered. Surely they could not allow all their work to go to waste! It was the Bishop of Chartres, so ill-treated by Fénelon, who took it upon himself to write directly to the king to plead Maintenon's cause. 'I shall willingly go surety, Sire, that no one could love you more tenderly or more respectfully than she loves you. She will never betray you, though she has betrayed herself . . . It seems clear enough, Sire, that God wanted to give you a help-mate like yourself, in the midst of that troop of self-interested and deceitful men that pay court to you, granting you a woman who is like the strong woman of Scripture, concerned only with the glory and salvation of her spouse and with all kinds of good works . . .'[17] These lines could not express more clearly the priests' determination to maintain in her post their most valuable agent, nor provide more striking proof that it was they who were behind Louis xiv's second marriage.

Alas! It was not enough to overcome the mistrust that had been aroused in her husband. They had also to raise his wife's morale, now at its lowest ebb. The Bishop of Chartres went back to his desk: 'Offer to God all your sorrows and offer them for the king and for the State. Add to patience sweetness, humility and the spirit of penitence.'[18] As regards patience, Maintenon felt the blade of disgrace come so near her that she fell ill. Moved by her plight, the king had a change of heart: 'Come now, Madame, do We have to see you die for that affair?'[19]

The new pope, Innocent iii, was highly embarrassed. Apart from a few mystical excesses, he found nothing to condemn in Fénelon's work. But, in letter after letter, Louis urged him to exert pitiless 'impartiality' against M de Cambrai. Innocent was willing to go so far as a subtle criticism, but Louis demanded an outright condemnation. Thus the pope wrote a pontifical brief condemning Bossuet's victim unremittingly.[20]

Fénelon learnt of his condemnation just as he was about to go into the pulpit in Cambrai cathedral. He seemed not in the least put out and, in place of the sermon that he had planned, he improvised another on the spur of the moment. Taking as his theme submission to the Church, he delivered one of his most powerful, moving sermons. He had the courage to end by publicly announcing his condemnation, his retraction of the opinions that he may have advanced and his full and entire submission to the judgment of the head of the Church, forbidding anyone to defend him. This noble self-criticism, this theatrical submission, in fact gave him the last word. He had so perfectly and rapidly presented his defeat that he transformed it into a triumph over the colleagues who had attacked him. Rid of the heretical vipers that he had harboured in his breast, Louis could relax. He had not understood, any more than Maintenon had, they had both been puppets manipulated by the prelates, in their ruthless struggle for ecclesiastic power.

The worst of the storm had passed, but the black clouds did not clear for Maintenon. Her husband took delight in contradicting her on everything, in not following her advice and showing that he had no confidence in her judgment. As he moved away from her, the king came closer to the accursed Jesuits. If she so much as moved, the Jesuits uttered the dreadful name of Fénelon the heretic with whom she had become so imprudently linked. Worse, the king took advantage of the situation to neglect his religious duties, which Maintenon took so much trouble to force upon him: 'One seems to me to be less devout: one did not want vespers yesterday.' 'One came here with the intention of forgetting everything in order to think only of entertaining oneself. That, Monseigneur, was our catechism.' 'One rehearsed dances in my study and I have more desire to weep than to divert myself.'[21] Louis xiv had closed himself off from Maintenon, but habit, selfishness and perhaps an unconsciously sadistic pleasure made him seek out her company with the same assiduity, which made her sense of power-lessness all the more acute. 'I would be too well paid for the slavery in which I find myself if I could do some good; but, Monseigneur, I can only shudder at the way things are turning out.' And she let out this cry of distress: 'I am never out of the king's sight!'[22]

Fortunately, Maintenon had her dear archbishop to pour her heart out to. But did it not look as if that monument of security, too, was becoming suspect?

M de Noailles appeared to be protecting the Jansenists . . . Could it be that M de Noailles was himself a Jansenist? The terrible word was out, but it was only because he had warmly recommended in one of his pastoral letters as Bishop of Chartres a work by a certain Father Quesnel of the Oratory, which was regarded as the height of Jansenism.[23] Noailles recognized the attack on him as the work of the Jesuits and went at once to demand – and to be granted – justice from the king.[24] Maintenon had got off with a fright, but this new shock had not improved her morale. Her existence was 'a veritable martyrdom that only God could have exposed me to'. In her complaints she began openly to criticize the author of her ills more and more, the king, her husband: 'One wants everything in relation to oneself and I see with pain that a taste for good is not coming'; 'it is a result of birth and upbringing that always hides oneself from the truth and thinks that things are hidden when no one is talking about them'; 'intentions are fine, but one does not care enough for work'; 'he is implacable towards the faults of others and is delighted to provide himself with a reason for not consulting good people because they are too credulous'.[25] Stubborn, frivolous, spendthrift, deceitful, lazy, hard and selfish – that was how the Sun King really appeared to his wife.

Mme Barin, the widow of the palace printer, was beginning to read the manuscript that her visitor had left with her. From the first few pages, she realized that the romantic, poetic story of Ulysses' son, stuffed with edifying maxims, was a remarkable piece of writing. The man who had brought it to her was certainly not its author, who, as was the fashion, wished no doubt to preserve his anonymity. Mme Barin bought the manuscript from the man without hesitation and went, according to custom, to ask for the king's privilege to print it. The censors, seeing nothing contrary to religion or good morals in this work of pure literature, granted the privilege without difficulty. So Mme Barin set about printing *The Third Book of the Odyssey or the Adventures of Telemachus, son of Ulysses*, with the privilege of the king dated 6 April 1699. The printer had reached page 280 of the first volume when the police burst in and seized the manuscript and all the already printed pages. Mme Barin protested: 'And what about the privilege of the king?' 'It is an affair of State and silence must be kept about the whole business, or else . . .'

Mme Barin would have been less surprised if she had known that the anonymous author was none other than Fénelon. Several years earlier, M de Cambrai had written this work with no other intention than to evoke the ancient history of which he was so fond and to wrap up his reflections in a poetic fantasy. He had written it at one go. Voltaire, who saw the original manuscript, assures us that there were less than ten corrections. Exiled in his diocese, Fénelon had brought the work out and given it to one of his servants to copy. The literate servant immediately realizing the value of what he was copying and urged on by greed, had sold the manuscript to Mme Barin.

The police raid, far from frightening Mme Barin, made her bolder than ever. She realized that she was sitting on a goldmine and, as she had prudently kept back one or two copies of the work from the police, she set about selling them at a very high price indeed. The king had wanted to kill *Telemachus* at birth; instead, he launched it on the wings of fame. Despite the active police investigation and the cases brought against printers and booksellers, thousands of incomplete copies of *Telemachus* spread like wildfire through Paris and the provinces. Adrianus Moetgens, a bookseller at The Hague, bought one of the complete copies from Mme Barin and, in July, brought out in haste the first foreign edition. It had an immediate, extraordinary success. The *Telemachus* epidemic spread like lightning. It was translated into every European language and, since each new edition was sold as soon as it was printed, the book went on being published at an incredible pace in every country. This Idomeneus, king of Crete, spendthrift, haughty, the scourge of all his neighbours, had to be Louis xiv! No one doubted that the greatest disgraced celebrity in France had wanted to make a veiled, but all the more effective criticism of his persecutor. Fénelon may have written the book before his disgrace, he may have assured his friend the Duc de Beauvilliers of his most sincere and devoted feelings for the king, but Europe was only too delighted to see the Sun King so splendidly ridiculed at last. Fénelon himself was too proud and too noble to lower himself to deny the rumours. He was responsible neither for the appearance nor for the success of *Telemachus*. That should be enough: it was certainly enough to exasperate the king who, as usual, doubting everything, everybody and above all himself, lunged once more towards the side of public opinion and saw in *Telemachus* what its author had not put there.[26]

However, he had other fish to fry at this time for, on 6 February 1699, young Joseph Ferdinand of Bavaria, the child to whom Charles II of Spain had left his entire empire, died in Brussels. It was immediately suspected that the emperor was responsible for sending to heaven the only obstacle that still separated him from the Spanish succession. These unjust suspicions were justified by the bitterness of the politicians. The young Bavarian had been the best, if not the only, solution to the problem; now everything had to begin over again. The seraglios of Madrid, Vienna, Versailles, The Hague and Rome began to rustle with intrigue. William III, who had turned into the angel of Peace, went bravely back to work. He made a new approach to Louis XIV, carried out new negotiations and reached a new agreement.

The emperor's second son, the Archduke Charles, was to receive what Joseph Ferdinand would have received in the first partition treaty: Spain, the Netherlands and the colonial empire, providing these territories did not become part of the empire. Likewise the Dauphin would get Naples, Sicily and part of Spain. Milan and its territories went to the Duke of Lorraine, who would re-assign his province to France. The extravagant juggling of provinces and crowns, the indecent waltz of wills, treaties and heirs led to this messy, but given the circumstances, practical agreement. England, Holland and France signed the second partition treaty. The emperor and Charles II could be tackled later and, anyway, the treaty had to remain for the moment ultra-secret. William could breathe a sigh of relief: 'We only signed this partition treaty to preserve peace in Europe.'[27]

Thursday 14 January 1700: Ball at the Duchesse de Noailles', which lasted until three in the morning.

Saturday 16 January: performance of the opera *Alceste*, played by the Duc de Bourgogne and the Princesse de Conti, followed by a ball at the Duchesse du Maine's.

Thursday 21 January: masked ball at Marly, the Duchesse de Bourgogne disguised as Flora. Entry of the queen of the Amazons, 'trapeze artists and fencers'. Ballets. Dancing until two in the morning.

Friday 22 January: masked ball at Marly, with a country wedding as theme. Entry of Savoyards, Harlequins and Punches.

Wednesday 27 February: ball in the king's state apartment at Versailles. The Duchesse de Bourgogne dances until four in the morning.[28]

A frenzy of socializing had seized the Court. People ruined themselves to buy clothes and disguises. 'So you are dressing yourself in rags,' someone remarked to a woman unfortunate enough to wear the same dress twice. The king himself led the festivities. He had given orders that people should amuse themselves and the docile courtiers obeyed.[29] The year 1699 had just come to an end and with it the seventeenth century. France and Europe were at peace and there was no cloud on the horizon. Louis was still the greatest king in the world and he was determined to show it in the only way that suited him, display.

Around this time a sovereign from a far-off land, the Emperor Moulay Ismail of Morocco, had just sent him an embassy to ask him for the hand of his bastard daughter, Marie-Anne, widow of the Prince de Conti. Everyone roared with laughter at the ridiculous impudence of the swarthy princeling for, of course, no one knew that Moulay Ismail was one of the greatest kings of that country, about which they knew almost nothing, even where it was to be found. The king took refuge behind the difference of religion and refused with the most polished contempt.[30] Louis had avoided the potentate of the sands just as he had refused, some months earlier, to receive the potentate of the snows, who had also come from the confines of Europe, the Tsar of Muscovy, Peter Alexeyvich,[31] who was visiting Europe, acquiring the skills that would enable him to initiate a radical transformation of his country. His dearest wish was to see France and its king.

'Too much trouble', Louis replied and, anyway, the Muscovite was not as important as the Duke of Lorraine, whom he had just received with great magnificence.[32] The ageing Apollo of Versailles was certainly a man of the century that was drawing to a close. He showed not the slightest interest in the two individuals who were to become the greatest stars of the eighteenth century: one a twenty-eight year old half-savage man with a throne dripping in blood who was to invent modern Russia, and the eighteen-year-old hero, a madman of genius who was to cross history like a meteor, Charles XII of Sweden.

Thursday 4 February 1700: Masked ball at Marly. Entry in the Spanish style led by the Duchesse de Bourgogne. The Duchesses de Chartres and de Bourbon dressed as American women. Monseigneur le Dauphin as a baby (which must have pleased him). Ballets by the company of the Paris opera.

Friday 5 February: Masked ball at Versailles. The Duchesse de Bourgogne as a witch. Masquerade on the theme of Don Quixote, with Monseigneur as Sancho Panza (he certainly knew how to choose his disguises).

Monday 8 February: Ball given by the Chancellor of France and his wife for the Duchesse de Bourgogne. A short comedy, fine music, a magnificent entertainment but too many masques from Paris.

Saturday 13 February: Ballet danced by the Duchesse de Bourgogne.

Monday 15 February: the Duchesse de Bourgogne goes to the ball given by the Duchesse d'Antin at the Hôtel de Soissons.

Tuesday 16 February: the Duchesse de Bourgogne goes to the ball at the Duchesse du Maine's.[33]

Young Adelaide was definitely the queen of the festivities and it was for her that the king triggered off this whirlwind of socializing. He certainly knew how to amuse the young. It had been only during the last three months that the newly-weds had been allowed to let their hair down. On their wedding night, the master of ceremonies, Baron de Breteuil, had led the Duc de Bourgogne, in a magnificent déshabillé in the most solemn way possible 'to the gates of the field of battle' ... However the 'battle' had taken place secretly some time before. One night, the Duchesse de Lude, Adelaide's lady of honour, who slept in the same bedroom as her mistress, had woken at a most inopportune moment to find the Duc de Bourgogne in his future wife's bed. She had chased him away and reported the incident to the king. 'I have learnt, Monsieur,' the grandfather scolded, 'that certain things have taken place that might harm your health. I will ask you that this will not happen again.' 'Sire, I am in excellent health', his grandson retorted insolently. He was madly in love with his wife. He had eyes only for her, he thought only of sleeping with her. On one particular evening, he was happy as Adelaide, instead of running off to some ball, told him that she wanted to go to bed early. Philippe ran to undress and rushed to Adelaide's bedroom. 'Where is Madame?' 'Here,' replied a voice from under the sheets. Philippe tore off his dressing-gown and leapt into bed. But whom did he suddenly see, standing beside the bed, in full Court dress but Adelaide. 'What is this, Monsieur? You who pretend to be so devout. I find you between the sheets with one of the prettiest women in the country.' 'But ... but ...' 'Look, Monsieur, who is in bed beside you.' It was Mme de La Vrillière, a willing party to Adelaide's joke. 'Filthy, impudent wretch,' yelled Philippe, running after La Vrillière, slippers in hand, to beat her, but the woman ran off barefoot and everyone collapsed with laughter.[34]

Thursday 18 February: Masquerade at Monseigneur's on the theme of the Grand Turk and the animals of his menagerie.

Friday 19 February: Masked ball at Marly on the theme of playing-cards.

Sunday, Monday: balls and masquerades one after another ...

Shrove Tuesday 23 February: Grand masked ball given by the king that lasted until one in the morning. Then the Duc and Duchesse de Bourgogne go to a ball given by the Master of the Horse. The Duchesse de Bourgogne stays there until five in the morning then goes directly to church to receive the ashes – it was already Ash Wednesday – before returning home at seven in the morning.[35]

Sunday 28 February: The king has a sumptuary edict drawn up: a limitation on gold and silver material. No more gilding in houses and coaches, no more gold or silver on servants' liveries.[36] The carnival was over, everybody was ruined and it was time to observe Lent.

'Religion is little known at Court: one wishes to accommodate it to oneself and not to accommodate oneself to it; one wishes to practise all the externals and not the spirit ... One understands very well here that one must properly perform the fasts, almsgivings, stations of the cross and the rest; but it is not at all expected that one should be converted ...

One does not wish to be damned; but there is no way of loving God and changing one's life . . .; but ignorance is extreme and the heart is not yet touched . . .'[37] Obviously for Mme de Maintenon, the devil himself had triumphed with this debauch of entertainments; the king, who had amused himself hugely, took advantage of the occasion to listen to her less. But there was nothing like a little jubilee like the one she was preparing with her dear Archbishop of Paris to bring the wandering sheep back once more to the fold.[38]

This project was greeted by a general outcry. Influential individuals, under the most varied pretexts, besieged the king to persuade him to withdraw or at least to limit the jubilee, and the king's ears, still echoing with the music of the ball, did not care for this celestial music. Nevertheless, Maintenon won the day. 'The king orders me to tell you, Monseigneur, that you are to do in this jubilee whatever you like,' she wrote triumphantly to her dear archbishop, who, on top of everything, was given a cardinal's hat.[39] With a liberal sprinkling of holy water, France could enter the eighteenth century.

CHAPTER 22

Europe Accedes – Then Fights Back

Another mirror shattered. Like a fury, Marie-Anne of Bavaria-Neuburg, queen of Spain and of the Indies, kicked the furniture, broke mirrors, smashed vases, but she was careful to choose only those precious objects imported from France.

The secret of the treaty signed by France, England and Holland, partitioning the Spanish empire, was out and there was general indignation in Madrid. The unfortunate Charles II cried out as if stabbed, which was more or less what had happened. He retired to the monastery of the Escorial, went down among the gloomy marbles of the family vault and had the coffins of his father, his mother, his first wife, the gentle Marie-Louise d'Orléans, opened. He threw himself weeping on Marie-Louise's half putrefied corpse. 'A clamour of protest' fell on the Marquis d'Harcourt, the French ambassador in Spain, who, at his wits' end, decided to leave with no other thought but 'to go rabbit shooting with his servant' and await events. In London, the Spanish ambassador protested against the partition treaty in such insulting terms that William gave him four days to leave England.

It was by four lines written in his own hand that Charles II informed the emperor, his cousin, of his absolute opposition to the partition.[1] In Vienna, the French ambassador Villars and the ambassador of England and Holland, Jacob Hop, were on tenterhooks. For months, they had been trying, unsuccessfully, to get Emperor Leopold I to accept the partition. 'It is incredible and against all natural right to partition a succession before it is open,' the emperor had replied. However the imperial government had not closed the door on negotiations, alternately giving the Englishman the impression that he was ready to make a deal with the Frenchman and the Frenchman that he might come to an agreement with the Englishman.

July 1700: a new Spanish ambassador, the Duke of Moles, arrived in Vienna. Villars and Hop repeated to themselves, despairingly, that he was bringing a testament from Charles II in favour of the emperor's second son, the Archduke Charles. Villars and Hop pressed the emperor more urgently to accept the partition: 'I am the king of Spain's closest relation and I cannot, during his life, enter into any treaty concerning his succession,' Leopold repeated. Anyway, he added, the king of Spain is perfectly well and may yet have children. But everyone knew that Charles II was dying. This does not mean, however, concluded the emperor's minister, that we might not one day come to an agreement . . . Whereupon Charles II asked the emperor to send his troops to make sure of his States in Italy, to be countered by threats from Louis and William, that if a single imperial soldier entered Italy, French and English troops would go in to oppose him.

September 1700: Villars and Hop were panic-stricken. A messenger had just brought news that Charles II had already been given extreme unction. At Versailles, the Spanish ambassador, the Marquis of Castel dos Rios, was given a quite unprecedented long private audience with the king, with no ministers present.

5 October 1700: Louis XIV ordered a partial mobilization.

6 October 1700: Louis XIV wrote to Villars that Charles II would not last much longer and that he must force the emperor to accept partition. French troops massed on the Pyrenees. A messenger, who left France on 17 October, informed Villars that the king of Spain was dead. Villars requested an urgent audience with the emperor, as a new messenger arrived from France: the king of Spain was not dead. Another messenger from Madrid: the king of Spain was dead. The next messenger again denied the news. The imperial ministers held out a ray of hope for Villars: 'If you go back to France and the king of Spain dies, come back here: the more important matters may sometimes be completed in a short space of time.'[2]

2 November 1700: A huge, excited, impatient crowd filled the drawing-rooms of the royal palace in Madrid. The entire Court was there, together with the clergy, innumerable officials, all that the capital understood as the 'Grandees of Spain' and all the foreign ambassadors. All eyes were directed impatiently on the door behind which, for several hours, the Council of State of Spain has been in session.

Charles II had finally died the day before, at three o'clock in the afternoon, and the council had met to open the will. No one wanted to miss this extraordinary moment of history when an empire 'on which the sun never sets' was to change hands without anyone knowing into whose hands it would fall. Everyone there was eaten up with curiosity to know who the heir would be – they already knew that there would only be one. The emperor's ambassador, Count Harrach, certain that his master's hour of triumph was approaching, assumed grand airs, while the representative of France, Blécourt – the official ambassador, d'Harcourt, was at the frontier at the head of troops ready to invade Spain – was trying to appear as unconcerned as possible.

The door of the council chamber opened at last. The Duke of Abrantes came out and the door shut behind him. Abrantes scanned the silent crowd, caught sight of Blécourt, scrutinized him, then looked away. He saw Count Harrach, put his arms around his neck and cried in Spanish: 'Sir, it is with extreme joy . . .' He kissed him again. 'Yes, sir, it is with extreme joy that for all my life . . .' He interrupted himself again to kiss the ambassador once more, then resumed, 'And with the greatest consent that I leave you and take leave of the most august House of Austria.' And, leaving Harrach transfixed, he ran out of the palace pursued by a yelling crowd demanding to know the name of the heir. Blécourt was to know soon enough. He had already understood. He ran to send a messenger to Louis XIV: France, Louis XIV, had won. The second son of the Dauphin, Philippe, Duc d'Anjou, was now the master of the Spanish empire.[3]

On the morning of 9 November 1700, Louis received the news at Fontainebleau. He cancelled his hunt, lunched as usual maintaining an inscrutable face, announced the death of the king of Spain, his cousin and brother-in-law, and decreed a period of Court mourning.[4] Then he summoned the Dauphin and his ministers in Mme de Maintenon's rooms. The council lasted for four hours. Never had Louis been confronted by so dramatic a dilemma. Charles II's will left everything to the Duc d'Anjou and, failing him, to the Archduke Charles. To accept would be to raise against France the whole of Europe, which would never allow its power to extend beyond the Pyrenees. To refuse would be to allow the Habsburgs to encircle France and double their power. Suddenly, the Dauphin woke up: 'Swimming in grease and apathy as he was, he seemed another man.' There was no question of refusing the will, no question of refusing his son Anjou what was rightfully his. 'And you, Madame, what do you say about all this?' the king demanded. Maintenon looked bashful and did not want to answer, but Louis insisted. 'Monseigneur is right,' she said at last. 'You must accept the will.' The king dissolved the council without reaching a decision.[5]

On Tuesday 16 November, in the morning, the Spanish ambassador entered the king's study. Louis, pointing to the Duc D'Anjou, said: 'You may salute him as your king.' Castel dos Rios threw himself on his knees before Philip V, King of Spain and of the Indies. The double doors of the room were flung open and the Court came in: 'Gentlemen, this is the king of Spain . . .' After the appropriate embraces and congratulations, they all went off to mass. In the chapel gallery there was a single cushion for the king of France. Louis XIV picked it up and handed it to his grandson, who had now become a king. Philip refused it and both kings heard mass without a cushion.[6]

It was only on 18 November that Emperor Leopold learned of the death of his cousin Charles II. In fact, Louis had given orders to the post masters not to provide horses for several days to anyone, especially messengers, until he had made up his mind about the will. Leopold's first reaction was to send 30,000 troops into Italy and place 20,000 on the Rhine: there could be no question of recognizing Philip V. On the other hand, Holland, Portugal, England and the European states recognized the new king of Spain one after another. The Italian states, relieved at not having to put up with the presence of the emperor in Italy, were the keenest on the new arrangement. For Savoy, there was a price to be paid: 60,000 crowns a month for the duke and the hand of his second daughter for Philip. England and Holland who, for two years, had done everything they could for a partition, accepted an undivided Spain and the emperor, who had for so long taken refuge behind Charles II's wishes, refused to accept his will. Contradictions aside, the situation could not have been better for Louis and Philip and yet . . .

'I never relied much on engagements with France: but must confess that I did not think they would, in the face of the whole world, break a solemn treaty before it was well accomplished . . . We must admit that we are dupes.' All William III's rancour burst forth in this letter to Heinsius, the Grand Pensionary of Holland. The suspicions that he had felt on learning the terms of Charles II's will while dining at Hampton Court, had turned into bitter certainty. While Louis XIV was eagerly sharing his views on the partition, negotiating with him, signing treaties, he had been intriguing in Madrid to get Charles II to sign a will in favour of his grandson. Many people in Europe thought as William did and denounced this duplicity.[7] In France, on the other hand, people maintained that the outcome of the will had come as a complete surprise to Louis: Saint-Simon swore as much; Voltaire, and a succession of historians after him, were to do likewise.

It was obvious by their reaction after the first partition treaty that neither Charles II nor the Spanish, would ever accept under any pretext or under whatever pressure, the dissolution of the Spanish empire. It had become obvious, ever since the death of young Joseph Ferdinand, that there could only be two candidates for the inheritance: the Archduke Charles and the Duc d'Anjou. Everything concurred to make Charles II favour the first: they belonged to the same family; Vienna and Madrid had been linked for over a hundred years; Louis had done everything to alienate Charles II with his constant acts of aggression and above all by deciding on his succession while he was still alive and over his head. So, quite naturally, Charles II had written to his cousin Leopold that he would leave his empire to his son Charles.

Among the Grandees of Spain, who were unanimously opposed to partition, there were a number however who were hostile to the Austrians. 'Leopold's ministers have minds like the goats' horns of my country, small, hard and twisted,' the Bishop of Lerida had written. Encouraged, it is said, by French gold,[8] the pro-French hidalgos decided to go into action, but realized that they would not be able to do anything without the prime minister, Cardinal Portocarrero, 'a tall, pale man,' corpulent and majestic, not especially cunning but stubborn and proud,[9] who, despite his pro-Austrian sympathies, allowed himself to be convinced by the hidalgos . . . and by French gold, Louis' adversaries maintained. 'It will be the Duc d'Anjou and none other, on the word of Portocarrero,' he soon declared.

And yet the fortress in front of him seemed impregnable. The queen, the emperor's sister-in-law, was pro-Austrian. The Countess of Berlizt, her favourite, who dominated her completely, was pro-Austrian. The king's confessor, Father Diaz, placed there by the queen, was pro-Austrian. But nothing deterred Portocarrero, who began his assault. He began by denouncing the thefts of La Berlizt who, knowing that she was hated, did not wait a moment longer and fled to Germany with her treasure. The German regiment in Madrid was dismissed and the Prince of Hesse-Darmstadt was politely, but firmly thanked for his services. The pope's support was obtained to get rid of Diaz without delay and to replace him by another priest, devoted to Portocarrero. There remained the queen, but the queen was now isolated, without support.[10] She was neutralized with big promises, among others, it is said, that she would marry the Dauphin of France on the death of Charles II.[11] Nothing now protected Charles from his assailants. Weak, dying, and tormented he may have been, but he still could think of nothing but the Habsburgs in general and the Archduke Charles in particular.

Portocarrero and the new confessor now attacked him. His life ebbing away and tortured by doubt, hesitating and delaying, Charles refused to give in. Time was running out for he was sinking rapidly. So Portocarrero returned relentlessly to the fray. 'The Duc d'Anjou cannot inherit because of the renunciation of his grandmother, my sister Maria Theresa,' the poor man objected. 'Write to the pope to ask his advice,' suggested Portocarrero. Charles did so and felt immediately relieved: the highest spiritual authority in Christendom would decide for him.[12] On receiving the secret letter, the pope appointed a commission of theologians to examine the case: 'Theology and avarice,' said one historian, 'are not so foreign from one another that they cannot often be brought together in a single man, especially in Italians. Louis was not unaware of this: he showered gold on the Sacred Congregation and the minds of the learned doctors were suddenly illuminated : the renunciation in question was null and void.'[13] And on 16 July 1700, the pope replied in his finest handwriting to Charles II that 'the children of the Dauphin were the true, sole, legitimate heirs of his monarchy and they excluded all others'.[14]

In the greatest secrecy, insisted on by Portocarrero in order to deceive the Austrian spies, Charles ordered his secretary, Ubilla, to draw up a new will, the fourth. On 2 October 1700, he threw the will in favour of the archduke into the fire and signed the document bequeathing his crowns to the Duc d'Anjou. Portocarrero terrorized the Council members sufficiently to make them accept the king's decision and to swear to the most absolute secrecy. Charles had nothing left to do but to die, which he did less than a month later, and Louis had merely pretended to be surprised when he was told the terms of the will. And his days of suspense, in which he hesitated before accepting it, were play acting. For there can be no question that he knew the contents of the will through the Spanish ambassador, Castel dos Rios, according to Saint-Simon, and through Cardinal Jason, to whom the pope had spoken, according to Voltaire. A significant detail is that, on 17 September 1700,

Louis made his ambassador in Spain, the Marquis d'Harcourt, a duke. The antiquity of the marquis's family, his post and his apparent services are not enough to explain such an honour, for which, some signal service would be required ... such as, for example, being His Most Christian Majesty's supplier of funds to His Catholic Majesty's hidalgos and ministers. But why had Louis deceived William about the partition? He had done so both to deceive his own people as to his real intentions, to play the cunning William at his own game, and also to arrange an alternative solution in case his intrigues did not come off. If the archduke had been declared the heir, Louis would certainly have insisted on partition. In short, the king of France bet on both alternatives.

If the whole of Europe apart from the emperor recognized Philip v, it was because Louis xiv had used his favourite method, intimidation. He had threatened to send his troops into Italy if the emperor massed his there at Charles ii's request. He had concentrated his troops on the Pyrenees at the approach of Charles's death. Lastly, under the pretext of protecting the Spanish Netherlands which now belonged to his grandson, he had occupied them militarily and made sure that he had the frontier fortresses under control. Having turned his cannon on Holland, he had demanded why that power was taking so long to recognize Philip. The Grand Pensionary Heinsius, seeing his country threatened by invasion as at the time of the Dutch wars, called on William for help. But, to send arms and troops, the king of England had to get a vote through Parliament. As it happened, his Commons had just completed the disarmament of England and seemed quite unaware of European realities. With no help forthcoming from William, Heinsius was forced to recognize Philip v just before William himself did the same.[15]

After summoning the German princes around him, the emperor had sent Count Wratislav to sound out the English and Dutch. William had assured him that he would act at the first opportunity and that this opportunity was rapidly approaching. The Commons had already realized that a Frenchman on the Spanish throne meant that the Mediterranean was becoming a French lake and that the freedom of British trade was greatly at risk there. They listened to William's war-like propositions. In short, scarcely had Philip v been recognized than preparations were already being made to oppose French domination of the Spanish empire.

'We behave at Marly like people who have nothing to do. The king of France dances and the king of Spain hunts during the day and plays at *cligne-musette* in the evening in his room. I wish he had already left and, if I had a voice in the chapter, he would have gone off at once to take possession of so fine a succession.'[16] In fact, Maintenon had been given a voice in the chapter. Saint-Simon had already expressed surprise that the dramatic councils in which the acceptance of the will had been discussed should have taken place in her apartment. Scarcely had Philip left for his new kingdom, after tearful farewells, according to the fashion of the times, than Maintenon set about following him step by step with correspondence. To the Duc d'Harcourt, who had remained ambassador in Spain and who was to be the grandfather's voice at the grandson's court, she explained how to handle Philip v and gave detailed and frequent instructions on how the grandson should behave towards the grandfather.[17] Certainly she was not meddling in politics; she was merely concerning herself at a distance with an inexperienced young man, now isolated in his new country, rather like a grandmother *in partibus*. Was she not already playing that role with the Duchesse de Bourgogne? Hitherto she had confined herself to the bastards, but now she was extending her power to the legitimate children of the young generation. This role remained a family affair, but where Philip v was concerned, family affairs automatically had international repercussions.

Before long Philip was given a much appreciated present in the form of the Princess of Savoy, whom the king had chosen for him as his wife. She was a young, dark girl, vivacious and attractive, quite as pretty as her sister, the Duchesse de Bourgogne. Of course, Maintenon had had a hand in making up the entourage of the future Queen of Spain and chose individuals most suited to training the innocent girl. It was above all the choice of the '*camarera mayor*', intended to be a *de facto* governess for the young queen, that had caused her most trouble. At last she was able to write to Harcourt, 'I propose Mme de Bracciano . . . She is a woman of wit, gentleness, politeness, knowledge of foreigners and is liked everywhere.'[18] Under the title of Duchesse de Bracciano was concealed the celebrated Anne-Marie de La Trémoille, Princesse des Ursins. She was a tall, dark, woman in her fifties, 'pleasing, insinuating, gentle', with a rather crazed look about her, and a superb bosom, which she liked to show off in clothes that were much too young for her.[19] This penniless widow, excellent in every respect, concealed a stubbornness, a pride, an ambition and a sense of intrigue that were also quite limitless.

At Albaredo, in Piedmont, about twenty French and Spanish troops were ferrying across the Adige when rifle fire sounded from the bank, wounding or killing some of them. The gunfire had come from the emperor's soldiers. Without waiting for possible allies or declaring war, Leopold I had hastily sent his troops into northern Italy under the command of Prince Eugène, who could not wait to pit himself against the French.[20] The Albaredo incident was the first act of hostility in a European war that was to last for twelve years. However, there was no talk of war for the moment since negotiations were still under way. 'In the state in which you find me, it is easy for you to judge whether or not I want war,' pleaded William to d'Avaux, France's long-standing ambassador at The Hague. He may be sincere, the French said to themselves. The demon commander was now seriously ill, almost paralysed in both legs, and could no longer head his troops. 'But,' William added, 'if the king starts a war for me, I shall use the little life that remains to me to defend my subjects and my allies.' It was, then, up to Louis to decide whether he wanted war or peace.[21] Louis' only reply was to mobilize his armies one by one and to appoint their commanders. There was to be a command for everyone ... except for the Duc de Chartres, his nephew, Philippe d'Orléans. Louis did not trust him, and quite rightly: no sooner did the Orléans go to war than they became heroes, thus providing a cruel contrast with others. They knew how to fight all too well, therefore they would not fight. Grumbling with indignation and urged on by the Palatine, Monsieur put in a plea: Chartres is a brainless idiot, thundered the king, he knows about nothing but chasing girls and acting the fool. And whose fault is that? Monsieur retorted. This boy is condemned to idleness, while his cousins are given commands. If he had something better to do than 'polishing the floors of Versailles, he would not act the fool'.

Some days later, the altercation resumed again. 'My daughter is very annoyed; her husband, your son, is being openly unfaithful to her with Mlle Lery.' 'Some fathers have led lives that give them little authority to criticize their children.' 'My daughter is too patient with your son.' 'Did not the queen have to be patient when you took her travelling with your mistresses?' Suddenly the two brothers started to shout at one another. An usher put his head through the door to warn them that they would be heard in the drawing-rooms. They lowered their voices somewhat, but the argument was violent as ever and not a single sentence escaped Saint-Simon, who was listening in the room next door. 'In marrying off my son, you promised him the sun and the moon and you have done nothing. This marriage has brought him nothing but dishonour and shame, and no advantage.' 'The war will soon force me to make several economies and since you are proving so unhelpful, I shall begin to economize on your pensions before my own.' A whole life of humiliation, bitterness and powerlessness had suddenly erupted in Monsieur. Against this torrent of resentment from his profoundly wounded younger brother, the elder responded with nothing better than meanness and waved the miserable weapon with which he thought to cow everybody – money.

At this point, luncheon was announced. Monsieur went out, his face 'bright red, his eyes ablaze with anger'. At table, he gorged himself. In the afternoon he went home to Saint-Cloud and continued to stuff himself with fruit, pastries and jams. He had dinner with a small group of friends. At the dessert, he was pouring out a liqueur for the Duchesse de Bouillon when, suddenly, he began to stammer, then leant heavily on the shoulder of his son Chartres. He was having a fit of apoplexy. Everyone cried out, bustled about and shouted for help. Monsieur was taken to his room, 'he was shaken, walked about and bled a great deal', and stuffed with laxatives. Chartres sent a messenger to Marly to inform the king, who had not yet gone to bed. Louis went to awaken Maintenon, ordered his coaches to stand ready, but did not move: after that morning's scene, he suspected that his brother was putting on an act. In the middle of the night a messenger woke him up. The remedies

were not working and Monsieur was in a coma. The king leapt out of
bed, dressed hastily and jumped into his coach, followed by the court in
indescribable disorder. Ladies and gentlemen piled into the first
available coaches. Louis arrived at his brother's bedside at three in the
morning; Monsieur was still in a coma. The king wept a great deal and
at eight o'clock, observing that there was no hope, returned to Marly,
followed by the docile courtiers. Saint-Cloud, a moment before
crowded out with people, was deserted. Monsieur was abandoned by
everyone even before he was dead. He died on a day bed, surrounded by
'servants and junior officers', who had plucked up courage to enter his
study out of curiosity.

At eleven in the morning, Louis sent for his physician Fagon and
ordered him to go to Monsieur. Fagon's face told its own story. 'What!
Has my brother died?' 'Yes, Sire, no remedy worked.' Louis burst into
tears. Mme de Maintenon begged him to stay and have lunch with her,
but no, protocol had to be respected, he would lunch before his Court,
weeping as abundantly as ever. That stay at Marly would end gloomily,
the courtiers thought to themselves. Next morning, the ladies put on
the appropriate faces to call on Maintenon and nearly collapsed with
surprise on hearing the king singing opera prologues in the next room.
'Would you care for a game of cards?' the Duc de Bourgogne asked the
Duc de Monfort after lunch. 'Cards, how can you think of such a thing
with Monsieur's body still warm?' 'Excuse me, I am well aware of the
fact, but the king does not want us to be bored at Marly, and has
ordered me to get everyone to play and in case nobody dares to be the
first to do so, I have to set an example.'[22]

In that summer of 1701, the Maréchal de Catinat, still billetted in
northern Italy, had a lot to worry about. For months, his troops had
faced the Imperial army commanded by Prince Eugène. But Louis xiv
had given the peculiar order not to oppose the enemy's advance. War
had not been declared and Louis did not want to be accused of starting
it. What, then, was to be done, if not to continue to retreat? 'Retreat,
when our army is the stronger?' the king asked in astonishment. The
generals, who wanted to replace him blamed Catinat. So Louis placed
the Maréchal de Villeroi over Catinat. His childhood friend was a
pompous fool, who made up for his inadequacies by the favour he
enjoyed with the king. Villeroi swore to revive the honour of France
and, once in Italy, explained to Catinat how battles were won and
treated the Duke of Savoy, a sovereign prince allied to France and
officially commander-in-chief, as a petty general in his pay. 'We must
attack Prince Eugène at the post of Chiari where he has retrenched,'
declared Villeroi. His defences were impregnable and the post had no
strategic importance, everyone objected unanimously. 'My orders are
orders,' concluded Villeroi. So they attacked Chiari. After leaving time
for a few thousand French soldiers to get themselves killed, Villeroi

ordered a retreat, then ran to Versailles to proffer his own explanations.[23]

The first battle had been fought, the first defeat sustained, but a war had still not been declared. 'You may know as much of peace and war as we do here, for the whole depends on the French, for if they will not give a reasonable satisfaction to the Emperor, you know what the consequence of that will be.' It was in this mood that William III's envoy arrived at The Hague to negotiate with d'Avaux. For this mission, William chose John Churchill, who had won his trust by betraying James II at the right moment. He demanded the withdrawal of the French troops from the Netherlands and as 'a reasonable satisfaction' to the emperor, who had been ignored by Charles II's will, some compensation in Italy or the Netherlands, for example.

Louis' sharp unanswerable '*niet*' to these reasonable propositions was marked by d'Avaux's departure on 5 August 1701. As a result, William's firmest opponents, the English Tories and the burghers of Amsterdam, gave him *carte blanche*. At The Hague, Churchill hastily went about changing his batteries and negotiating with the emperor's representatives. On 7 September, he signed in the name of England an alliance with Holland and the Empire: through negotiation or arms, they would get Louis XIV to agree that he would never link the crowns of France and Spain and that he would grant the emperor the oft-repeated 'reasonable satisfaction'.[24] But still war had not broken out.

Louis heard the advice and decided that on the approaching death of James II, he would not recognize James's son as king of England. It was useless to inflict gratuitous insult on William, especially after recognizing him as king of England in the Treaty of Ryswick. On 13 September Louis went to Saint-Germain to take a last farewell of his cousin. The dying man opened his eyes for a moment, just long enough for Louis to tell him that he would solemnly and publicly recognize his son, James, as sole legitimate king of England, Scotland and Ireland, for in the intervening weeks James II's wife, Mary of Modena, had come to plead with Louis, Maintenon had shared her grief and the king had changed his mind . . .[25]

William learnt that Louis had recognized 'James III' despite treaties, wisdom or mere prudence. First he put on violet mourning dress for his uncle and father-in-law whom he had dethroned, then he recalled the ambassador in France and expelled the French ambassador from London.[26] In England, universal indignation gave rise to violent demonstrations everywhere. The whole country was clamouring for war. Parliament immediately passed a bill declaring the Pretender James Stuart guilty of high treason and condemning him to death *in absentia*. They would have no 'French' king. They preferred the Dutch king, whom they had never liked, whose policies they constantly opposed and whom they had nearly torn to pieces for allowing himself to be taken in by the partition treaty. The whole of England let William know that the country was behind him.[27] By his chivalrous, but unconsidered and stupid error, Louis had unleashed British public opinion against himself and brought William unhoped-for support from his political opponents and from his entire people. But still war had not broken out.

Perhaps it never would, for its artisan William, the gloomy, sickly genius who pulled the strings of the anti-French coalition, was declining rapidly. Nevertheless he had managed to extract from his Parliament all the money he needed, raised troops, engaged foreign mercenaries and armed his ships. He himself felt utterly exhausted. Then, with the greatest calm, he put his affairs in order. Between two terrible attacks of vomiting, he received his ministers and councillors and gave them his instructions. He had a very long interview with the woman who would one day soon succeed him: Princess Anne of England, his late wife's sister and James II's other protestant daughter. She was a rather characterless, well-meaning but masochistic woman.[28] William employed his remaining strength to persuade her to continue his policies.

The next day, 19 March 1702, about ten o'clock in the morning, he died, after drinking a cup of chocolate. William was not to see the fulfillment of all he had worked for during the previous two years: the official declaration of war by England, Holland, the Emperor and the princes of Europe on France, which was ratified some weeks later. He had lost a race against death, but he had triggered off the mechanism that was almost to crush France. At the announcement of his death, Louis was content to declare that he would not wear mourning and forbade three French dukes, close cousins of the dead king, to wear it.[29] It was the difference between determination and meanness.

The fact that Louis lost no time in taking official possession of the principality of Orange[30] – the ultimate revenge on William – did not improve his situation. He could only set weakened armies against the European coalition set up by William. The disastrous system installed by Louvois still survived, which meant that even the smallest details of the military operations had to come from Versailles: hence the hesitations, delays, inadequate commands and above all disorder. Very young, inexperienced men were allowed to buy regiments. The promotion of the poorest depended on the favour of a minister or an influential courtier. During the campaigns, horses and servants impeded movement and added to the mouths to feed. Supplies were inadequate, often inefficiently administered and, thanks to widespread corruption, military units often existed only on paper. Finally, discipline had become increasingly lax. It was with this war machine that Louis XIV was to oppose the whole of Europe.[31]

'Sometimes he spends a whole day in his study doing accounts; I often see him racking his brains, pouring over the figures, beginning all over again several times and not leaving them until he has finished; he will not delegate work to his ministers. He depends on no one for the command of his armies ... He holds several councils a day in which very serious, often tiresome affairs like wars, famines and other afflictions are discussed. He has, at present, a government of two great kingdoms for nothing is decided on in Spain except on his orders . . .'[32] Maintenon almost pitied her husband: the Spanish empire and a hostile European coalition on his hands, on top of France itself. Louis was cruelly lacking in collaborators at this difficult moment. At Mazarin's death, he had declared that he would be his own prime minister. From now on, whether he wanted it or not, he was his own council of ministers.

'Tell me, Catinat, what is really happening in Italy? Why have you not informed me of the facts?' 'I have held nothing back, I have always given Your Majesty and Monsieur Chamillart a detailed account of the facts to which Your Majesty refers today.' Somewhat ruffled, the king summoned Chamillart, his Minister of War and Finance, and repeated Catinat's assertions. Chamillart lowered his head: 'I accept that everything he says is true.' 'Are you aware, Chamillart, that by your silence you have caused me, unjustly, to be displeased with M Catinat?' 'Sire, you are right, but it is not my fault.' 'And whose is it then? Mine?' 'No Sire, but I dare to tell you with the utmost truth that it is not mine either.' The king, more and more astonished, insisted that he get to the bottom of it. 'I have the letters from M Catinat to Mme de Maintenon and, as their contents would have caused much pain and embarrassment to Your Majesty, she never wanted them to reach you.' The royal face lit up with the most intense satisfaction: 'The poor woman! She loses her head as soon as anything concerns me.' It was amazing that she loved him so much that she did everything to spare him worry. The king's manly pride swelled at the prospect of the naïve devotion and unlimited love of which he was the object.[33]

What her husband took for the tender feelings of a wife was simply fidelity to her mission as the king's spiritual nurse. However, with time, her domain had imperceptibly extended. She had taken it upon herself to set up a *cordon sanitaire* around her husband to spare him worries that she regarded as useless.[34] This was easy enough since ministers, generals and ambassadors had got into the habit of writing to her and going through her. Already ministers had set up a barrier around Louis to protect their power. From now on she did as much to preserve her husband's peace . . . and her own, by the same token.

Since dear Villeroi had stupidly allowed himself to be made prisoner by Prince Eugène at Cremona, the king thought of 'trying out' the Duc de Vendôme by giving him the important command of his armies in Italy. An illegitimate grandson of Henry IV, Vendôme had inherited his grandfather's courage, boldness and military genius, but not his tastes. He flaunted his homosexuality and scandalized the Court by public orgies with his servants and officers. Excessively insolent and proud, but a skilful courtier, he was also an unrestrained glutton, lazy and dirty, and was in the habit of spending the morning on his commode, writing, receiving guests, giving orders and eating while defecating.[35]

For several months Vendôme and Eugène amused themselves with one another, setting off in pursuit, moving their armies around, engaging in minor, but bloody fights, and when they met in an important battle at Luzara, on 15 August 1702, the result was a draw, each side withdrawing behind his retrenchments and each celebrating his brilliant victory with a *Te Deum*. The Chevalier de Quincy, sheltering with Vendôme's army behind his retrenchment, was lulled to sleep, not by triumphant choruses, but by the death agonies of the wounded. For him dawn broke on a Dantesque spectacle of dead and dying, a swarm of arms and legs moving feebly. Those who had the strength called for help, but the soldiers who ventured out to bring it were shot down by the artillery of the opposite camp. The rotten corpses set off an epidemic that caused new deaths. 'The two generals ought to have declared a truce in order to get the corpses buried; neither of them thought of doing so.'[36]

In Flanders, John Churchill, who had in the meantime been made Earl (and later Duke) of Marlborough, a title that he was to make known throughout the world, had been appointed commander-in-chief and demonstrated the good lessons that he had learnt long ago from Turenne, under whom he had served as a volunteer. He gained ground, leaving Boufflers, who had inadequate troops, no alternative but to retreat as cleverly as possible.

Similarly, Catinat, in command at Strasbourg, had to let the imperial troops of Prince Louis of Baden take Landau and advance unchecked. One of Catinat's lieutenant-generals, the same Villars who had been negotiating in Vienna two years before, could stand it no longer. With colossal cheek, 'this child of fortune'[37] dared – with the consent of Versailles – to do what Catinat could not. He attacked the imperial forces with far fewer troops at his command, at Friedlingen on 14 October 1702, and won a total victory, which he then hastened to take to Versailles and lay at the king's feet.

'It is usually about ten in the evening,' Louis replied, 'that Chamillart comes to work with me and, in over three months, he has brought me nothing but disagreeable things. As the time for his arrival approached my blood would curdle. You have pulled me out of that state. You may depend upon my gratitude.' By way of reward Villars was given the much coveted marshal's baton.[38]

Philip v, too, could afford to be pleased. He had been informed that a cargo containing an enormous quantity of gold, silver and precious stones from the Latin American colonies, which had been expected for two years, had safely arrived. The great galleons were entering the Bay of Vigo in north-west Spain. The first chests were being unloaded when, at the entrance to the bay, there suddenly appeared a fleet flying the British flag. The British sailors landed, took the fortresses that protected the harbour and cut the chain that blocked the entrance. The unloaded chests were hastily put on to 'an endless number of oxen and mules', which were driven through the passes behind Vigo, but most of the treasure remained on board the fifteen encircled galleons. Rather than allow the fabulous cargo to fall into the enemy's hands, their commanding officers ordered the ships to be set on fire and, slowly, the vessels sank, taking with them untold wealth to the bottom of the sea.[39] Right up to our own day, the treasure of the 'galleons of Vigo' have excited the imagination of generations and given rise, even quite recently, to innumerable attempts to recover it.

CHAPTER 23

Fire on All Fronts

The roads were no longer safe. Castles had been taken, churches burnt, parishes abandoned, villages deserted, fairs emptied, priests murdered, hostages executed in reprisals. All Catholics feared for their lives. In that winter of 1702-3 the protestant terror reigned in the Cévennes and Languedoc. What Basville had believed were isolated incidents were the rumblings of a serious rebellion, and the Camisard movement was born. The Camisards were all peasants, said to fight in dirty shirts – hence their nickname. There were no nobles or bourgeois for, even if they were sympathetic, the rich feared for their wealth: the rebels, like the instrument of repression, put property in danger. On the other hand, they did have leaders: Pierre Laporte, known as Rolland and nicknamed by his men 'the Chevalier Rolland', 'visited by God' at the age of twenty-two, an incomparable orator, a prestigious leader, an idealist, fanatical but wise, a legendary hero, 'handsome, noble and generous' and Jean Cavalier, twenty-one years old, a short, stocky man with a large head, and a mass of fair hair, a baker by trade, but possessing some education, who tamed crowds by his gifts of preaching and prophecy, a cunning and brave tactician. As a surprised M de Saint-Hilaire remarked; 'They elected leaders from among themselves who were in truth of lowly birth, but who made up for this defect by much courage and ability.'

The Camisards were well organized. Mountain caves served them as supply stations, weapon foundries, improvised mills. Their tactic was constant mobility, their general youth enabling them to climb ravines and mountains; they did not indulge in formal battles, but ambushes, set up with the complicity of the whole population; they were fiercely disciplined: no looting, no debauchery, no useless or hasty cruelty: Cavalier had the four murderers of the beautiful Mme de Miramon hanged. Lastly, the Camisards had a cause: 'Freedom of worship and freedom of conscience.' They were fighting not against authority, but against those who abused it: 'Ah! If only the king knew!' Fanaticism urged them on: fanaticism and women, or rather the fanaticism of the women. In combat, the women were the keener, more audacious. The prophetesses fought to the death. 'Kill! Kill! Long live the sword of the eternal!' yelled Lucrèce Guigon, known as 'La Vivaraise', as

318

she seized a dragoon's sabre in order to kill off wounded soldiers.

At first Basville responded with his usual method: repression. The terrorized priests sent 'crowds' of protestants to the courts, which condemned them to the galleys or to death. Twelve thousand protestants were condemned, including 5,000 to the galleys, and floggings of 150 lashes were revived. But repression was no longer enough, for the Camisards were using the same method: two villages would be burnt down for every village burnt by the 'enemy', the numbers of protestants 'murdered' would be met by a similar number of Catholics 'executed'. The Camisards were everywhere: they attacked where and when they were least expected. Cavalier sent men disguised as soldiers of the king into the enemy camp. He walked around Nîmes dressed as a merchant, under the very noses of the officers whose men were looking for him in the mountains. Basville and his acolytes were completely at a loss and his reports, which were more and more alarming, were evidence of his inability to cope, though he never admitted it.

Since he was not capable of striking any harder, a fierce old reactionary – the Maréchal de Montrevel – was sent with 20,000 soldiers. Montrevel arrived in January 1703 and immediately launched a fierce campaign of repression: for every murder, whole communities would burn. Villages would be set alight for a mere trifle. Montrevel managed to beat Rolland at Pompignan in a raid that cost him 200 deaths. Another, on 29 April, brought 300 deaths. But his speciality was reprisals and here he went well beyond Basville, who still clung to a semblance of legality. For Montrevel there was no law but his own! Montrevel himself, while paying court in a gallant but senile manner to the ladies, boasted of having run through with his sword '300 of the best men you could see'. Another day, attending the mass execution of young protestants, he observed bitterly that 'they let themselves be executed with extraordinary ferocity'.

But his masterstroke was the mill on the Ajour, near Nîmes. It was Palm Sunday; he was at table, already slightly drunk, when he was informed that 300 protestants, men, women, and children, had risked everything to be at the mill on the Ajour to celebrate the great Christian festival in secret. Montrevel ordered the mill to be surrounded and set on fire. Those who tried to escape landed on a wall of bayonets. There was only one survivor, a very young girl, whom Montrevel wanted to have hanged. A cry of horror rose throughout Languedoc. Bishop Fléchier approved of 'this necessary example to stop the pride of these people'. Montrevel razed the mill ruins to the ground, and the nickname of 'the butcher of the Ajour mill' stayed with him.[1]

There was war in Languedoc between the Maréchal de Montrevel and Jean Cavalier. There was war in Madrid between Cardinal d'Estrées and the Princesse des Ursins. Another illegitimate grandson of Henry IV, he was the French ambassador appointed to assist the grandson in the name of the grandfather, that is to say, to rule Spain in Louis XIV's name. She was the lady, excellent in every respect, chosen by Maintenon to train the young Marie-Louise, Philip v's wife. The ambassador spoke to the husband with all the authority of the grandfather. The princess dominated the wife who developed a veritable passion for her. Marie-Louise, for her part, dominated her husband, who was so madly in love with her that he could not do without her. No sooner was he at war, separated from her, than abstinence caused 'prodigious swellings and considerable vapours'. The Princesse des Ursins, realizing that to rule the queen of Spain was not a sufficiently secure base, had arranged much more substantial support for herself. She had begun to write regularly to Maintenon, informing her, soliciting her, flattering her, in short, amiably suggesting to her the equation by which Maintenon ruled Ursins, who ruled the queen, who ruled the king – whereas in fact it was she, the princess, who manipulated all three. Once this situation was established, the cardinal and the princess, two old friends of long-standing, declared war on one another. The cardinal bombarded Louis XIV and his ministers with denunciations of the princess for wanting to undermine French influence and to expel the French from Spain. The princess complained bitterly to the queen, who complained bitterly to the king against the cardinal. As a result, Philip v expelled the cardinal from his council of ministers.[2] A furious letter arrived from the grandfather: 'I chose d'Estrées as the man most accomplished in affairs ... and at a time when you have most need of his talents, when it is most necessary to take prompt resolutions for your safety and that of your kingdom, you show in yourself an unfortunate facility to believe that, suddenly, you are able to rule alone a monarchy that the most skilful of your predecessors would have had difficulty in bringing to the state in which it is now ...'

From anger, Philip's grandfather passed to threats. 'I love you too tenderly to resolve to abandon you. You will reduce me to this unfortunate extremity however if I am no longer informed of what is happening in your councils. It is not right that my subjects should be absolutely ruined to sustain Spain in spite of herself.'[3]

In response to this message, Philip v quite simply asked for the recall of the cardinal. And his grandfather complied without batting an eyelid. 'I know why you asked me to recall Cardinal d'Estrées: I give my consent to it ...'[4] Was Louis XIV afraid of losing the king of Spain over whom he exerted full authority? Or was Maintenon behind it all? In effect, the king's ambassador was sacrificed to Maintenon's ambassador. It was beyond the cardinal's comprehension. He left, blazing with anger and making the gloomiest prophecies. He left behind him a time bomb in the person of his nephew, the Abbé d'Estrées. The princess triumphed and the episode was brought to a close.[5]

Once again the Duke of Savoy began to needle his cousin and ally, the king of France, in the most disagreeable manner. The emperor discreetly offered Montferrat, Mantua, Valencia, Alexandria, the entire region between the Po and Tanaro to the duke, plus a pension in excess of that paid him by Louis XIV. The duke was finding the siren voice from Vienna more and more pleasant to the ear. He may have one daughter who was heir to the throne of France and another queen of Spain, but he would not refuse to wage war on them to extend his territory. He may use the discretion that was usual in his transactions, but French spies got wind of it.[6] On 10 August 1703, the duke learnt that Vendôme had suddenly disarmed his 5,000 troops and received the following letter from the king of France: 'Cousin, since religion, honour, interest, alliances and your signature count for nothing between us, I am sending my cousin the Duc de Vendôme at the head of my armies to explain my intentions to you; he will give you only twenty-four hours to make up your mind.'[7] Twenty-four hours was more than the duke needed, without arms – Vendôme had taken them – or equipment, to pass over to the enemy camp.

To the east, relations were strained between the Maréchal de Villars and the Elector of Bavaria, France's ally, since they had combined their armies, both victorious in Germany. Villars wanted to advance on Vienna. The Elector wanted to seize the Tyrol, which he did, only to be forced out of it and to come back, rather shamefaced, with an exhausted army. Villars was furious: 'We must prevent the two imperial armies from joining up. Let us attack together.' 'I shall confer with my generals and ministers.' 'I am your general and your minister,' yelled Villars. 'I must protect my states, which are in danger,' the Elector replied. 'Well, if Your Electoral Highness does not wish to seize the opportunity with his Bavarians, I shall fight with the French.' And Villars gave the order to attack, on 20 September 1703, in the plain of Hochstadt. The Elector, swallowing his rage, was forced to follow him and fight despite his better judgment. From the first exchange of fire, the two enemy armies were seized with panic and retreated in opposite directions. In a moment, Villars found himself almost alone on the battlefield. He caught up with his troops, brought them back and won a victory. The Elector, mortified, seized the city of Augsburg. The road to Vienna was open.[8]

In Languedoc, there was great dissatisfaction among the troops. The Camisards, who could not be pinned down, were paralyzing an entire province, wiping out whole regiments, raising taxes, meting out justice. Basville then worked out a marvellous plan, which he sent to Versailles for approval. Let us demolish all the houses of the villages, deport their inhabitants and the Camisards, deprived of their source of supplies, will be forced to go down into the plain where we shall have the pleasure of exterminating them: 'Good', Louis scribbled in the margin of the plan, in September 1703. So they set about what Michelet called 'the St Bartholomew's Day Massacre of the houses'. But their troubles were not over. The troops found deserted villages and houses made of granite too hard to demolish. Could they burn them down? asked Basville.

'Good,' the king replied once more. And an immense fire was lit over hundreds of kilometres. From the woods where they had taken refuge the inhabitants watched their houses go up in smoke: as a result, the numbers flocking to the Camisards were incalculable. Basville's plan had failed.

Then Montrevel had his 'great idea': destroy all the ovens and mills and starve out the 'fanatics'. This fine tactic was no more successful than the previous one and Basville took pleasure in writing the most treacherous reports for Chamillart. He then polished up his new plan: the parishes would be visited one by one, and all suspects removed. The visits were certainly effective. After 'visiting' the Borque valley and the Valleragne area, Brigadier Plaque left 600 corpses behind him. The same figure was achieved during a visit by Lieutenant-General Lalande at the beginning of 1704. A jealous Montrevel came out with his new plan: the formation of Catholic commando units, the 'Cadets of the Cross', which received the blessing of the bishops; in their path, they left torture, rape and massacre, with pontifical indulgence. They discovered a new speciality: placing powder flasks between the thighs of raped girls, then lighting them. The wave of reprisals from the Camisards left the province horror-stricken. Throughout the south-west total anarchy reigned; at Versailles, exasperation. Montrevel was declared an incompetent and recalled.

Despite their common success, the Maréchal de Villars could no longer bear the Elector of Bavaria and asked to be recalled from Germany. For his part, the Elector of Bavaria could not bear the Maréchal de Villars, and asked that he be recalled.[9] Louis received Villars on his return. 'More considerable wars to be waged would suit you better, but you will do me a very important service if you can stop a revolt that may become very dangerous . . .' Louis had decided to send Villars to replace Montrevel against the Camisards. Villars suggested dealing with them rather differently from his predecessors, to wave the carrot rather than the stick, 'which is not only useless, but totally contrary'. 'I put myself in your hands,' the king replied, 'and believe me I prefer to keep my peoples than to lose them, which I believe to be certain if this unfortunate revolt continues.'[10]

Villars arrived in the south-west in April 1704. Soon a general amnesty was declared; passports were offered to those 'fanatics' who wanted to leave the kingdom and an understanding was worked out with the protestant nobles and bourgeois. Tours of pacification, supported by speeches by Villars were carried out with a view to bringing the stray sheep back to their senses. Discipline was re-established. Basville and his henchmen were muzzled and the 'Cadets of the Cross', the commando units invented by Montrevel, were disarmed. Villars offered an olive branch to the protestant fanatics and silenced the Catholics. Then he offered to meet Cavalier, who agreed. On 14 May 1704, Villars awaited him in the garden of the Franciscan priory at Nîmes, with Montrevel and Basville at his side and fifty armed dragoons behind him. Cavalier arrived, escorted by fifty cavalry, whom he ranged opposite the marshal's dragoons. He moved forward. Villars was momentarily taken aback. Could this plump, short youth, 'with the face of a sixteen-year-old schoolboy', really be the 'Prince of the Cévennes', who had kept the king's armies busy for two years? The marshal offered his 'kindest regards'. Cavalier replied, perfectly at ease. Then they discussed the conditions for a surrender of the Camisards. 'Fat Basville', who had been stifling his rage from the outset, suddenly burst out, fulminating and threatening. Villars ordered him to be quiet. 'And you, Monsieur Cavalier, would you not like to serve the king?' 'I shall serve him with all my heart, Monsieur le Maréchal, if my demands are met.' Cavalier saluted, got back into the saddle and went off for a drink at the inn. He kept his word and surrendered with a thousand Camisards.[11]

Who was the peasant whom Chamillart was accompanying up the secret staircase that led to the king's study on 15 July 1704? His rough homespun coat, his woollen stockings and his heavy shoes stood out among the gold, mirrors and marble of Versailles. It was Jean Cavalier, who was determined 'to talk things over with His Majesty' and Villars had had to agree. His Majesty was at mass. Chamillart and Cavalier waited. Suddenly, there was a commotion and the double doors were flung open. The king stood there, haughty, proud, imposing. 'Sire, this is Cavalier, leader of the rebels, who has come to implore Your Majesty's clemency.' Cavalier was dumbstruck. He stood there, fiddling with his hat. 'What have you to tell me and why did you take up arms against me?' Suddenly, Cavalier emerged from his paralysis and began to recount everything: the women and children taken away and imprisoned, the *dragonnades*, Basville's and Montrevel's exactions, the lootings, the rapes, the tortures, the massacres. The king listened in silence; he seemed visibly moved. 'And the dragoons murdered every one of the women and children.' The king suddenly turned to Chamillart. 'Yes, Sire, a band of vagabonds, punished on Montrevel's orders.' 'No, Sire! I will answer with my head that everything I am telling you is true.' And Cavalier continued.

Was Louis really ignorant of all this?[12] The Camisards had a point when they wailed, 'Oh! If only the king knew!' But what about the royal 'Good' written in the margin of Basville's plan to destroy the village houses and deport the 'fanatics'? Had he not read, then, the reports on the massacres, the statistics on the dead, the accounts of the battles fought with the rebels and of the 'mopping up' operations against the brigands? Louis knew the situation, but only on paper. The reports made no mention of 'excesses', and it was these excesses that made this chapter of his reign so abominable and which were the cause of such formidable resistance. This he did not understand and would never understand. He was moved because he was confronted for a moment with a reality that horrified him, but he did not act upon it and soon recovered. This is proved by the final blunder of his interview with

Cavalier. 'Will you become a good Catholic, Monsieur Cavalier?' he asked. 'Sire, my life is in Your Majesty's hands and I am ready to give it in his service, but where my religion is concerned I have resolved not to change it for all the kingdoms in the world.' 'Very well, but behave yourself in future.'[13] Louis had not understood, could not understand. 'Behave yourself in future.' He was dry, preoccupied, already thinking of this next appointment.

'Cavalier is a traitor. No surrender.' The unanimous cry went up among the Camisards. One by one, the leaders broke off negotiations with Villars, just when foreign enemies were intervening, promising them money, arms and troops.[14] No one listened any more to Cavalier's final appeal for reason, while from his side Villars was getting nothing but bad news. The English had taken Gibraltar; Marlborough and Prince Eugène were rushing to the help of Austria.

Villeroi, freed from his prison, went off in pursuit of Marlborough, but he lost track of him on the way. He swerved towards the Palatinate, in order to join up with the army of the Maréchal de Tallard. As usual, Villeroi began to assume airs and to hand out orders to his cousin and protégé. But Tallard, who had become his equal in rank gibbed and, between two reviews, the two marshals had a violent argument. What was to be done, they asked one another, after these preliminaries, which had lasted for two weeks. Without an order, we cannot move. So they drew up a fine plan of campaign, sent it off to Versailles and patiently awaited the answer. Meanwhile, Marlborough defeated the Elector of Bavaria's 8,000 troops, crossed the Danube and joined up with Eugène.

The god of war, seated in his chariot, surrounded by nymphs and warriors, passed slowly before the Sun King, followed by the Thames, the Rhine, the Meuse and the Danube which, represented by the most graceful dancers from the *corps de ballet*, had just made their submission to the Seine. To the sound of drums, trumpets and oboes an immense triumphal arch lit up at the end of the park at Marly: the words 'For Adelaide' appeared in letters of fire, for the entertainment was being given in honour of the Duc and Duchesse de Bourgogne. A son had been born to them two months before and, with four generations still alive, the future of the House of France was assured. So the entire Court had gathered, together with a crowd of people from Paris who had been allowed to come into the park to share the spectacle. At nine o'clock, the first rockets were let off in a fantastic fireworks display that transformed the warm summer night of 12 August 1704 into day.[15]

The next morning, at Höchstädt in Germany, Tallard, Marsin and the Elector of Bavaria, at the head of their 60,000 troops, met the 52,000 men commanded by Marlborough and Eugène. It was the first time that the tall, pink-faced, cold-mannered Englishman, with his mocking smile, always calm and affable, and the dark, olive-skinned Eugène, half-Italian and half-French, with his skull of a head, theatrical and excitable, had combined their very different talents. At half-past twelve, battle was joined. Almost immediately, Marlborough broke through Tallard's right flank. Tallard dashed from one place to another, giving orders, bringing up his reserves, rallying his retreating cavalry. He galloped towards one of his fleeing squadrons. He was unlucky: it was an enemy squadron, but Tallard, who was extremely short-sighted, had failed to recognize the uniform, and he was taken prisoner. A rout followed: officers and soldiers ran like madmen to throw themselves into the Danube. No one thought of bringing up the 11,000 reserves encamped in the village of Blenheim. The Marquis de Clérambault, who was in command of them, went off to get news, met the flood of fleeing troops, learnt that Tallard had been taken prisoner, lost his head, fled with the others, leapt into the Danube and was drowned. His army surrendered without firing a single shot.[16]

12,000 dead, 14,000 soldiers and 1,200 officers taken prisoner, plus Tallard, the whole of the artillery and equipment in the hands of the enemy: thus at the end of the day, stood the account of the crushing defeat at Höchstädt. The French army was practically annihilated, Bavaria was in the hands of the imperial forces and the Elector had to take refuge in Brussels. Gallantly, Prince Eugène invited the French prisoners to an opera in which he had five prologues sung to the glory of Louis XIV, commenting, 'You see how I like to listen to the praises of your Master.'[17] Then, in private, with another Frenchman who had passed over to the enemy, he confided: 'The French are finished . . . They let themselves be beaten and taken like sheep. What generals! What pitiful conduct! . . . On my honour, a child would have beaten them. Tallard allowed himself to be taken like a fool. I said to Marlborough that he should be sent back to fight again.'[18]

'I do not doubt that you are deeply touched by the general loss and by the particular losses,' Maintenon wrote to Noailles. 'God be praised for everything and may His anger, which we have so amply deserved, be appeased. Alas, we suffer from great evils and we deserve still greater ones. I have always feared the punishment of sensuality and ambition . . .'[19] The sensuality and ambition of whom, if not of Louis XIV? It was all his fault and God was merely punishing him. 'We have so amply deserved His anger.' Maintenon had the charity to say 'we' rather than 'he'. But the criticism is there, in all its virulence. She seems much more muted in her description of royal indifference: 'I had not seen him for a moment in a mood.' Public opinion rose up against the generals. Their foolish incompetence was denounced and everyone argued as to which of them should be given the prize for stupidity.[20] Saint-Simon could not get over 'those prodigies of error, blindness, stupidity, piled one upon another, so gross and unbelievable.'[21]

Villars! Everyone agreed that only Villars could re-establish the situation. But Villars was down in the Cévennes. The Camisard leaders had broken off negotiations and taken up arms once more, so he had no alternative but to resume Montrevel's old method: burnings and massacres. But scarcely had one cut off the head of one Camisard then ten sprang up. Government troops had managed to prevent the English fleet from landing its reinforcements, but at the last moment they had to go off and stop attempted rebellions in the Dauphiné and Rouergue financed by the enemy.

On the evening of 13 August 1704, a spy named Malorte arrived post haste at Uzès. He knew that he was at last going to win the prize of 100 *louis d'or*, for he had discovered that Rolland and his friend, the handsome Maillet, a twenty-six year old tanner, were at the Château de Castelnau, with their sweethearts the Cornelli sisters. A battalion was immediately sent off and it had no difficulty overcoming Rolland's small troop. He himself managed to escape, but he was recaptured in a ditch; he gave himself up to the officer, and a dragoon killed him with a rifle shot. Maillet and four of his lieutenants were arrested. Basville turned up to condemn them to be drawn alive in a public square in Nîmes. Then, just at that moment, a conspiracy was discovered extending throughout Languedoc, organized by the Camisard leader Ravenel. Three hundred and fifty Camisards were executed. Finally, on 2 January 1705, the last Camisard leader, Salles, surrendered with his troops. 'Your Majesty may consider the revolt at an end,' Villars wrote, 'and the last roots have been severed.' 'Monsieur le Maréchal,' Louis replied, 'I am very pleased with you and, so that you may be in no doubt about it, I am making you a duke.' And he sent him off at once to the eastern front.[22]

King Louis was reading one of the reports that he regularly received from the Abbé d'Estrées, left as ambassador in Spain by his uncle the cardinal. As usual, it consisted of a stream of venomous accusations against the Princesse des Ursins. She ruled alone, she held the king and queen completely in her power, she had got rid of all those who opposed her, but she saw to it that everything went through her two creatures, the corrupt Orry and his equerry d'Aubigny. Moreover, she had secretly married the latter. Suddenly Louis XIV gave a start. What did he see, written in the margin, beside the accusation of a secret marriage? 'Married? No!' In the Princesse des Ursins' own hand. Did she dare to have the correspondence of the ambassador of France to the king interrupted by her secret services *and* have the unparalleled effrontery to add a remark of her own? It was the last straw!

Louis gave orders by return to the Abbé d'Estrées to expel the Princesse des Ursins. But before doing so, he added, the Abbé should get the king out of Madrid, for 'the queen's tears might prevent him from deferring to my counsels'. The Abbé succeeded in sending Philip V to the front without his wife and an emissary from Louis XIV had only to present himself at the royal palace in Madrid with four hundred guards in case of resistance and a brief letter from Louis ordered 'his cousin', the Princesse des Ursins, to leave. Haughty and proud, the princess complied without protest, and retired for a few days to Alcala, near Madrid, where the queen, mad with despair, ran to join her. Then, after heart-rending farewells, the princess reluctantly took the road to France. To save the Abbé d'Estrées from 'any disagreeable repercussions' from the affair Louis recalled him and replaced him by the Duc de Gramont. Then he wrote a long, sugary letter to the Spanish queen. The princess had wanted power only for herself, she had given nothing but bad advice to the queen, she had shown neither devotion, nor true affection to her benefactress. 'You wish, at fifteen years of age, to rule a great, unstable monarchy, without advice.' After putting her in her place, he delivered his compliments: 'I know that your mind is well in advance of your years. I am delighted that you are taking part in affairs. I approve that the king entrusts everything to you.' Lastly, she could in future ask for anything she liked from her dear grandfather: 'For I desire nothing more than to give you pleasure and to express my tender feelings towards you in the smallest as in the greatest things.' After that, the young Savoyarde could not refuse to accept the *fait accompli*.[23]

The Maréchal de Tessé then arrived in Madrid to direct operations against the enemy armies that had landed in Portugal. He arrived in the middle of the dramatic affair and wanted to be informed. 'I think I have worn out my lungs in the secret conversations I have had with their lordships the Grandees, the most important of whom I was beginning to become acquainted with, by dint of seeing them in the evening in private talks, without ceremony, nightcap on my head and cup of chocolate in my hand.' He soon got used to the idea that there was only one solution when 'there was an indecisive king who could not take and would never take it upon himself to say "I wish it" and who is head over heels in love with his wife, who spares nothing to win his love': it was to recall the Princesse des Ursins. First of all, he set about calming the fears of the queen of Spain: all would go well, providing she was patient. Then he turned not to Louis XIV or to his ministers, but to Maintenon, knowing that he was knocking at the right door. Maintenon, who was very attached to her protégée, was delighted with what Tessé told her. Ignoring his parallel manoeuvres, the French ambassador, Gramont, lost his head, harassed Philip V and so frightened him that the Spanish king wrote a letter asking that the princess should not come back and, the following day, wrote another, dictated by his wife, to beg her to return. Under Maintenon's influence, Louis XIV decided to receive the princess at last.[24] On Sunday 12 January 1705, wearing a formal court dress, she crossed the apartments of Versailles, filled with curious onlookers, and entered the study where Louis XIV and Maintenon awaited her. She stayed there for three hours. 'There are still many things that we have not talked about with Madame des Ursins,' commented the king during dinner. The next day, a second interview took place, almost as long as the first.[25] 'Cousin, since I have spoken with the Princesse des Ursins, I have come to the conclusion that she must be sent back to Spain.' Gramont grimaced as he read his master's letter: to rub it in, it was he who would announce the news to Marie Louise. 'She remained in ecstasy, as they say, in a swoon, and very nearly flung her arms around my neck in the presence of the king.' It needed the stubbornness of a young queen of fifteen, the pragmatism of a marshal, the skill and self-control of the cunning princess and Maintenon's extraordinary malleability to make Louis change a decision that had been urged upon him by the wisdom of his ministers and the exasperation of the Spaniards. By way of justice, the return of the disgraced woman was a triumph. Followed by courtiers, ambassadors and, of course, Tessé, Philip v and Maria Louisa went as far as Cavillas to meet her. Maria Louisa leapt out of her coach and threw herself into the princess's arms, 'as a daughter separated from her mother by unjust persecutors might do'. Philip v invited her into his coach, but no, it was alone in her own coach, as *camarera mayor*, that the princess made her entry into Madrid.[26]

For his part, Villars did what was expected of him: he contained the enemy in the east. Money had been scraped together, the garrisons had been emptied and an army had been conjured up for him. As a result, he was able to make the enemy retreat without joining battle.

In Italy, Vendôme had been so successful in capturing the Duke of Savoy's towns and fortresses that the duke was almost on the point of losing all his States and seeing his capital Turin taken over. Sensing which way the wind was blowing, the Italian princes sent a stream of emissaries to Vendôme. The Duke of Parma, a prudent man and an ally of France, sent his bishop, who arrived at the French camp surrounded by the whole of his chapter. Entering the tent, the prelate was somewhat taken aback when Vendôme, as was his custom, received him on his privy. He did his best to take no notice and set about trying to please the commander-in-chief. Noticing Vendôme's spotty face, he remarked: 'It seems to me sir, that you are overheated. The air of this country can't be good.' 'It's much worse for my body than for my face. Look!' And, getting up, Vendôme showed the bishop his spotty backside. 'I see, sir, that I am not the proper person to deal with you. Your manners and your rank sort ill together,' retorted the bishop, who left in as dignified a fashion as he could. He told the Duke of Parma that he would not be returning.

The Duke of Parma had a sort of court jester, his gardener's son Alberoni, who put on a priest's soutane one day thinking that the dog-collar would prove a better passport than a peasant's smock. The duke sent this comic character to Vendôme in place of the bishop. Vendôme received him, sitting as usual on his commode, whereupon Alberoni made him roar with laughter with his bawdy jokes. In the middle of the interview Vendôme suddenly stood up and lovingly 'wiped his arse', watching Alberoni all the time to see how he would pass the test. '*O culo di angelo,'* ('Angelic arse!') cried Alberoni ecstatically, then rushed up to kiss the marvel. Vendôme was astonished and delighted, and invited Alberoni to come again. Alberoni realized where his luck lay and returned later, preparing soups for Vendôme with cheese and 'other foreign sauces', of which the commander-in-chief was particularly fond. Alberoni allowed himself to be initiated into homosexuality, and before long Vendôme could not do without him. With his own *'culo di angelo'* the Parmesan gardener's son climbed the first step of the ladder that was to make him a cardinal, prime minister, absolute master of Spain for several years and very nearly pope.

'As for war, in Spain it is the most abject and most despised of all professions. We are trying to bring it back into honour; but troops . . . *nada*; money, *nada* . . .; order . . . *nada*. If we are made to work, we shall work, the recruits tell us, but shooting a rifle or cleaning one, *nada* . . .'[27] This was the material that the Marèchal de Tessé, commanding operations in the Iberian peninsula, had to work with to oppose the Imperial English and Portuguese forces, who were trying to invade Spain by both land and sea. The Prince of Darmstadt managed to land near Barcelona and the Catalans, as ever delighted at an opportunity to be different, welcomed them with open arms, cheering the usurping archduke Charles II. It was decided to lay siege to Barcelona, beginning with the fortress of Montjuich, which defended the city. The Prince of Darmstadt, who had bribed the commandant of the fortress, moved confidently towards its walls. He was very surprised to be met by a volley of cannon balls – so astonished in fact that he fell dead under artillery fire. The viceroy of Catalonia, having had wind of the commandant's betrayal had had him hanged secretly and replaced by a faithful officer, but a small bomb which had fallen in the fortress rolled into the powder magazine and everything was blown up. First Catalonia, then the province of Valencia declared in favour of the archduke, in October 1705.[28] 'I admit that I find things are not going too well in that quarter and that something should be done about it,' the Duc du Bourgogne commented naïvely to Philip V.[29]

What was done was an exceptional levy of 25,000 men. Going to Sunday mass at Marly, Louis saw a contingent of these troops pass by, full of enthusiasm at the prospect of going off and getting themselves killed for him. Ah! What good fellows they were: the king did not stint in his praise for the enthusiasm of the recruits. But Saint-Simon sighed, for he, like so many others, was aware of the harsh realities. He had seen recruitment carried out on his own properties: desperate men wept crying that they were being sent to their deaths, and mutilated themselves in order to be declared unsuitable for service. But how could the king be told that the few recruits whose loyalty he had witnessed had been paid by ministers and put there to deceive him? How could his eyes be opened?

CHAPTER 24

Defeats, Intrigues and Miseries

France was stronger than ever; her armies were on the point of conquering Europe and the defeats of 1705, which was now drawing to a close, were mere trifles. That, at least, was what Louis implicitly declared when he let it be known that he wanted celebrations and festivities for the carnival of 1706. He amused himself watching the young people skating on the frozen lakes and himself joined in a sleigh expedition. He gave a great masked ball at Marly where, on his orders, even the elderly had to be disguised. He threw a gauze domino over his coat and stayed up late observing his courtiers whirl about him.[1]

The Palatine was bored to death. She had never cared for great entertainments and, apart from balls, the Court was little better than a convent. At the king's dinner, it was like being 'in a nuns' refectory' – monastic silence, whispering in corners, a general atmosphere of gloom. The bad news depressed people, despite the forced smiles. Everyone distrusted everyone else, intrigue was rife in the corridors and a rush of lampoons violently criticized the king and his ministers. 'The Court is all sadness, boredom and mistrust.' In fact there was scarcely a Court at all. Where were the evening parties where the crowd of courtiers splendidly-attired used to meet every day in the state apartments around the gambling and refreshment tables? Apart from at balls, people only met in small groups at Mme de Maintenon's apartments or at the Duchesse de Bourgogne's. Under the pretext of being at home in an informal situation, protocol was neglected to the horror of both the Palatine and Saint-Simon. At Adelaide's, Mme de Maintenon alone sat in an armchair while the king himself was content with a folding chair. In her apartment, Maintenon had herself served by Adelaide and the other young princesses as if it were a game; they passed the dishes to her, changing her plates and pouring her wine. Few courtiers had the temerity to advise the Palatine to do likewise. 'I was not brought up to lower myself and I am too old to give myself over to childish games.'[2]

Maintenon, too, was bored to death. She had spent a few days at the Trianon and had come back 'as dazed' as she had been before. There was nothing but spiteful jealousy between the women and stupid quibbling between the men. The king was furious because the Duchesse de Rohan had come to dinner without being invited. The Duchesse de La Ferté had made herself look ridiculous by exhibiting a pair of breasts 'blacker than a chimney'. Mme de Bourgogne, 'who always wants what she does not have and neglects what she has', had been insufferable. And then there was the king. He parked himself in her apartment for hours on end to work and write, so no one could talk for fear of disturbing him. 'I never used to be bored, but I have certainly known boredom of late and I think that I would not be able to stay here if I did not think that it was here that God wanted me. Ah well! If you had to be in my room, without saying a word, you would burst, would you not?'[3]

If it had only been a question of that silence, that boredom, Maintenon might have endured it, but she also had to subject herself to the king's carnal appetites, for the sixty-seven year old man still had a demanding temperament. One day, beside herself, she asked the Bishop of Chartres, point blank if she could refuse to give herself to her husband. The prelate's reply was a masterpiece of ecclesiastical hypocrisy and was already a foreshadowing of the bourgeois frustration of the nineteenth century. 'It betokens a great purity on your part to preserve him who has been entrusted to you from the impurities and scandals in which he might otherwise fall and it is at the same time an act of patience, of submission, of justice and of charity ... You must serve as an asylum for that weak man, who would otherwise be lost ... What grace is to be found in being the instrument of the counsels of God and of doing out of pure virtue what so many other women do without merit or out of passion. A pure soul becomes ever more purified in those states that God has sanctified, so that it will soon be like the angels in heaven.'[4] Copulation was no longer a pleasure, but an apostolate. Resigned to her fate, Maintenon went back to the conjugal bed, like any pious bourgeoise of the following century.

The Duc de Bourgogne was also dejected. He was so cold that he could hardly write. He complained of his younger brother, the Duc de Berry, who gambled for too high stakes and was continually drunk. In fact, Bourgogne's married life was not happy. He adored his wife and he was deeply upset that she did not reciprocate his feelings. If he was at war, she did not write to him as often as she had promised to. In fact, Adelaide did not have the time. She was the only person to amuse herself in the midst of that collection of wet blankets, and did so with a vengeance. She had completely subjugated the king and Maintenon, whom she called 'aunt'. She took fantastic liberties with them, such as having an enema administered in their presence in the middle of the drawing-room,[5] or making remarks full of allusions of doubtful taste. 'One has to admit, aunt, that in England queens govern better than kings, for under kings it is women who rule and under queens men.' But the old couple burst out laughing:[6] they found her irresistibly amusing! One day Adelaide came skipping into Maintenon's room, rummaged among her papers, picked up a letter, began to read it but suddenly stopped and blushed. 'What's the matter, my sweet?' Maintenon asked. A deadly silence ensued. Maintenon walked over to the girl and glanced at the letter: 'Well! It's a letter from Mme d'Espinoy. Now that's what comes of being so inquisitive; one sometimes finds out what one does not want to know. Since you have read it, read it to the end, and if you have any sense, learn from it.' So Adelaide had to read a complete account, hour by hour, of her activities over the past few days: nocturnal rides, games with the valets, meetings with certain young men . . . The message was clear: she could do as she liked, but shouldn't forget that her 'aunt' knew everything.[7] In fact Maintenon spoiled the girl: 'She is charming and even her faults are likeable, she is loved more than she should be. One senses this, but cannot help it.'[8]

The Maréchal de Villeroi had never been so happy there in Flanders with his 80,000 men opposite Marlborough's army. At last he had revenge within his grasp. He had been advised to wait for the Maréchal de Marcin's reinforcements: but he intended to crush Marlborough alone. He lovingly disposed his corps. He placed his left flank behind the marshes. An objection might have been that it wouldn't be able to cross the marshes to attack Marlborough's right flank, but if made, Villeroi disregarded it. Seeing their position, Marlborough withdrew his right flank and concentrated his forces on his centre and left, near the village of Ramillies. Lieutenant-general de Bassion begged Villeroi to do the same, to reduce the numbers on his left and to concentrate his forces against the bulk of Marlborough's. But he would not hear of it. He had made his plans and that was that.

The Elector of Bavaria arrived post haste from Brussels. He offered advice, but it was too late; the order to attack had been given. Battle was joined at two in the afternoon, on 23 May 1706. Half-an-hour later, the French army was in complete disarray. Its left flank, hemmed in by the marshes, could do nothing. Villeroi lost 20,000 men, but he also lost his head, horrified by the disaster for which he alone was responsible. He refused to defend Ghent, as the Elector of Bavaria begged him to do, and had no other thought than to retreat without stopping.[9] Above all, he refused to inform the king of his defeat. After five days he brought himself to scribble an obfuscating note announcing defeat. What defeat? Where? asked an anxious Louis. What were the losses? Where was the army? He waited for further messengers, but none arrived. He demanded news: nothing, nobody knew anything. Unable to bear it any longer, he sent Chamillart in person to Flanders to get on-the-spot information. Learning the truth in all its gory detail from his minister's mouth, Louis publicly commiserated with Villeroi and warmly defended him against the unanimous criticism to which he suspected Villeroi was being subjected.

'For myself, I was astonished, overwhelmed, outraged, petrified at once,' Maintenon admitted. 'The outburst has reached such proportions in the army and in Paris that I do not think the king can go on supporting the Maréchal de Villeroi . . .' So Louis wrote as a friend in his own hand, letting him down as lightly as possible, advising him to resign. Villeroi replied that he saw no reason for doing so. Twice, three times, four times, the king wrote to him in the same vein. In the end it was Villeroi who became angry: the king could relieve him of his command, but he would not resign. On retiring to bed, the king announced that Villeroi had so insistently requested to be relieved of his command that he had been unable to refuse him. Villeroi rejected this last attempt to save him. 'Monsieur le Maréchal, one is not happy at our age,' Louis remarked gently to his old friend, who had at last been recalled from the front. After the 'unfortunate battle', Marlborough had gone on to take Antwerp, Brussels, Ostend, Ghent, the Brabant, then Flanders, which immediately recognized the Archduke Charles as its sovereign.

For its part, the Portuguese army was advancing to Estremadura, then into Castille, without much difficulty. The Duke of Berwick, the bastard whom Marlborough's sister Arabella Churchill had given James II of England, had been sent by the French against them with inadequate and badly trained troops. He had not been able to do much, especially as he had a skilled campaigner opposite him in 'Milord' Galloway; under this very English name hid a French turncoat, the Comte de Ruvigny. Thus an Englishman, Marlborough's nephew, commanded the French troops and a Frenchman commanded the Anglo-Portuguese troops. Madrid was in panic.[10] In the early morning, a coach with its green curtains lowered went through the gates of the city and took the road for the north; the queen and the Princesse des Ursins were secretly fleeing. The king left to join Berwick, the Grandees deserted the capital and retired to the provinces, and the Portuguese entered Madrid.[11]

At Versailles Louis and Maintenon opened a casket and sadly observed the glittering stones. They were the crown jewels of Spain brought by a trusted valet so that they would not fall into the enemy's hands. With tears in her eyes Maintenon toyed with the most beautiful pearl in the world, La Peregrina,[12] which had decorated Philip II's hat and which is still worn by the present queen of Spain.

Despite her sorrow at knowing that her sister had been chased out of her capital, the Duchesse de Bourgogne continued to surround Louis and Maintenon with her atmosphere of childish gaiety. She was often there, alone with them in their study. She jumped up and down, sat on their knees, embraced them, pulled their chins, tickled them, caressed them, patted them. The old couple were won over by her gaiety. She flew around the room, opened drawers, rummaged among their things, opened letters. One day she picked up a document and as she began to read it her pretty little face suddenly changed expression. Tears came into her eyes. 'So Turin is going to be taken, my dear aunt,' she cried. She had just read the order to step up the siege and to take her own father's capital, and burst into uncontrollable tears. Maintenon tried to console her and murmured: 'Don't worry, Turin will never be taken.' 'Don't push my father too far,' the little duchess entreated.[13] This pathetic appeal must have reached the ears of the Duc de La Feuillade, who was commanding the operations for the siege of Turin, for the 140 cannon, 110,000 cannonballs, 21,000 bombs and 27,100 grenades that he had at his disposal to crush the city could not prevail against his stupidity. He had not even thought of encircling Turin, so people came and went from the 'besieged' city with ease. Even the Duke of Savoy himself was able to leave. At the news of his departure La Feuillade dropped his siege and set off in pursuit with all his cavalry. The duke, who knew his own country backwards, made him lose still more precious time by forcing him to pursue him from valley to valley.

Meanwhile, Prince Eugène, sent to help Turin, joined up with the Duke of Savoy and marched in the direction of the French army. The council of war met under the chairmanship of the Duc d'Orléans, son of the late Monsieur, who had been appointed commander-in-chief. 'Our lines of defence are too stretched,' explained the duke, 'Prince Eugène will have no difficulty in breaching them. Let us concentrate our forces and attack him. Anyway, the French soldier is better in attack than in defence.' 'Let's not move,' replied La Feuillade. But the lieutenant-generals were unanimously in favour of attack. The Maréchal de Marcin, the eye of Versailles, took a piece of paper from his pocket: it was the king's orders to stay where they were. The Duc d'Orléans had the double mortification of realizing that they were going into certain defeat and that he commanded only in name.

In the night of 6–7 September 1706, he was woken by one of his spies. Eugène was attacking the castle of Pianneze, with the intention of crossing the Doire. Orléans woke Marcin and begged him to march at once towards the enemy with a view to stopping his manoeuvre. But the king's orders were not to move, replied Marcin. Thus Eugène quietly crossed the Doire and moved his troops right up to the French lines. The Duc d'Orléans sent for forty-six battalions uselessly posted on a nearby height to reinforce the first lines that would meet Eugène's attack, but they would not move, on La Feuillade's orders. The Duc d'Orléans sent for other reserve battalions and ordered them to cross a small bridge. La Feuillade posted himself in person on the bridge to stop them. At ten in the morning, Eugène attacked and sliced through the French lines as through butter. La Feuillade ran in every direction, tore at his hair, and was quite incapable of giving further orders. The Duc d'Orléans, however, did give orders but he was not obeyed. He was wounded in the hip, then in the wrist. He held up, rallied the retreating soldiers and led squadrons in a charge, but pain and loss of blood forced him to give up. Marcin was seriously wounded in the thigh and taken prisoner. The French were utterly routed: 'What followed was nothing but trouble, confusion, retreat, flight, discomfiture.' Shortly afterwards Milan, Mantua, Piedmont and the kingdom of Naples fell into the hands of the enemy allies.[14]

Having lost Bavaria at Höchstädt, Flanders at Ramillies and Italy at Turin, towards the end of 1706 Louis decided that it might be judicious to negotiate. England and Holland contemptuously rejected his request and the war continued.

But there was no money to pay for it. 'The State finances are so exhausted that nothing can be promised for the future, not even being able to pay the troops for the rest of the campaign; huge sums are owed them. The income for the year 1708 has already been used up, credit is exhausted . . .'[15] So began a report to the king drawn up by Chamillart, Minister of Finance and War in 1707, but it was a prematurely aged Chamillart, yellow complexioned, weak in his legs, who no longer ate, no longer slept and no longer knew what was to be done.[16]

Then the Maréchal de Vauban took his courage in both hands. A thickset man, with a hard peasant-like face, but in fact noted for his kindness and gentleness, Vauban was reputedly the most honest, virtuous man in the country. He had long been concerned at the fate of the people. For forty years, wars and the building of his famous fortifications had sent him throughout France and enabled him to see what others refused to see: the poverty of the people. He had studied the problem, he had asked people questions, he had secretly sent his assistants to build up his files. His conclusions were that 10 per cent of the French had been reduced to begging; 50 per cent just about managed to survive; 30 per cent were in financial difficulties or in debt. There remained the rich 10 per cent, the old and the new nobility, the magistrature, the Church and the upper bourgeoisie. Vauban then proposed scrapping the jungle of existing taxes and replacing them by a single tax on income proportional to wealth, that is to say, the abolition of fiscal privileges, including those of the royal family, and the abolition of tax-farmers, sub-farmers and agents, who sucked dry both people and State and who multiplied in proportion to the taxes. However, prudent as he was, he had his *Project for a Royal Tithe* published clandestinely.

The explosion of hatred that its appearance gave rise to overwhelmed Vauban himself. Each class threatened by the project 'blushed for its own interest'. Vauban had only one possible supporter left: the king. He went and presented the work to Louis himself. But Louis had his head filled with the outrage of ministers, courtiers, prelates and *parlementaires* and gave Vauban a good dressing down. Vauban left the royal study a finished man. On 14 February 1707, the *Project for a Royal Tithe* was forbidden. The police was ordered to find the anonymous author whose identity everybody knew. Threatened with a house search and imprisonment, and suffering from bronchitis, Vauban retired to his bed for the last time.[17] 'I have lost a man who had great affection for my person and for the State,' Louis remarked[18] on learning of his death, with perhaps a touch of remorse that Vauban may have been right in spite of his naïvety. For one had to be naïve to propose such a simple solution, unrealizable unless some outrageous genius could get it adopted.

'For heaven's sake, Madame, no melancholy.' From her exile at Burgos, the queen of Spain was writing to Maintenon. The cry of 'Long live the king' went up from the massed crowd on the square and forced her to interrupt her letter. She appeared on the balcony with Philip v. 'Long live the fidelity of the Castillians,' she replied. 'Long live the king and long live the queen,' yelled the kneeling crowd. 'Long live Philip,' replied the Madrid crowd when Milord Galloway proclaimed the Archduke Charles king. The echo of that 'Long live Philip' reached as far as Toledo, Valencia, and all the towns conquered by the allies. Even at Barcelona, people were beginning to complain about the Austrians. It had needed the arrival of the detested Portuguese, then the Germans and English, to awaken Spain from her slumbers, and by an irony of fate that other stranger catapulted to Madrid by his French grandfather, the traditional enemy of Spain, became the national emblem around which the Spanish gathered. The Maréchal de Tessé no longer heard *'nada'*, but *'todo'*. As a result Berwick recaptured Segovia, expelled the allies from Madrid and pushed them back to the frontiers. In late September 1706, Philip v and Marie Louise had returned to Madrid and to a frantically cheering crowd. *'Mueran los traidores'* ('Death to the traitors'), cried the populace, lighting bonfires with furniture belonging to the few Grandees who had collaborated with the Austrians.

It was now with the help of the Spanish that Berwick crushed the allied troops at Almanza, near Valencia, on 25 April 1707. Six thousand corpses lay on the battlefield. Neither of the two candidates – Philip v and the archduke – was present at the memorable event. 'We are very foolish to get ourselves killed for those two simpletons,'[19] commented the outspoken Lord Peterborough. On the other hand, the Duc d'Orléans, recently appointed commander-in-chief of the Franco-Spanish troops, was furious at arriving after the battle. He went off and took Saragossa while Berwick captured Valencia, then they joined up to lay siege to the formidable fortress of Lerida.

The new-found enthusiasm of the Spanish was not enough. They needed a proper commissariat to get rid of the allies. But the commissariat was the Spanish government and the Spanish government was the Princesse des Ursins. With each act of negligence, each error, each problem, the Duc d'Orléans, tracing the chain of responsibility, came to the princess, more powerful than ever and whole-heartedly supported by Maintenon. The two women's interference in politics and warfare and the resulting inefficiency exasperated the Duc d'Orléans. He consoled himself by getting drunk with his officers: 'Gentlemen, let us drink to the health of our *con*-captain and *con*-lieutenant.' This coarse allusion to the two women was received with a burst of thunderous laughter. The Princesse des Ursins was immediately informed and hastened to repeat it to Mme de Maintenon. From that moment, both were to harbour deep hatred for the Duc d'Orléans.[20]

Two hundred thousand *livres* from Wurtemberg, 330,000 *livres* from Baden, 220,000 *livres* from the Margravate of Dourlach, 300,000 *livres* from Swabia and the same from Franconia – the Maréchal de Villars certainly put his back into raising contributions wherever he went. He was a past master in the art of becoming a millionaire in a short space of time. He also knew how to win at a time when this quality had become dangerously rare among French generals. He broke through the barrage of enemy lines that blocked eastern France and spread out through southern Germany. However, anxious that King Louis might take exception to the sudden, excessive increase in his fortune, he took the precaution of writing to inform him that he had levied some contributions in the German provinces that he had taken, but money was sent to pay and maintain his army so that it would not cost His Majesty anything. And His Majesty, who was plunged in the worst financial straits, praised the excellent intentions of his faithful marshal. Villars knew that the imperial forces were hard pressed and wanted to advance further into Germany, as far as Vienna. But Louis held him back and in order to ensure his obedience, he deprived him of his best troops and sent them to Toulon.[21]

Could Toulon, in the heart of Provence, in France itself, be in danger? This was Prince Eugène's idea. Instead of dashing into Germany to stop Villars, he had decided to imitate him and to advance right into enemy territory. His target was Toulon, followed by Marseille. The frontiers were badly defended here – no one expected an invasion of France from the Mediterranean. In addition to his own army, Eugène had that of the Duke of Savoy at his disposal – and the English fleet cruising along the Provençal coasts. Toulon could not be defended against such formidable forces. The Maréchal de Tessé, leaving Dauphiné, set off by forced marches, but it was not certain that he would arrive in time. There was a strong risk that Toulon would fall and Marseille would not be able to hold out much longer. Next on the list would be the Cévennes and Languedoc, where the protestants were always ready to break out in revolt.[22]

Fear reigned at Versailles. The king 'suffered a fluxion', 'for one is not used either to suffer or to be defeated', Maintenon noted. The allies continued to advance, meeting practically no resistance. The Duke of Savoy stopped at Nice to visit the English fleet and claim the £1,000,000 in gold promised by London for his campaign. But the English were rather short of money. Could His Highness wait a little? No million, no movement, he replied; they would wait at Nice as long as necessary. The English and the Savoyards argued all day. In the end, the English were forced to hand over their million and the Savoyards set out. But, meanwhile, Tessé had arrived at Toulon, and had had time to build up an impregnable line of defence on the St Catherine Heights. Without capturing the Heights, there would be no Toulon. The Duke of Savoy summoned a council of war and proposed raising the siege at once and returning the way they had come. It might have seemed like defeat, but in fact Eugène's idea had been excellent. It would be sometime yet before they would know how to benefit from the effect of surprise and psychological shock on the French at the spectacle of their country suddenly being invaded, so the allies withdrew on 22 August 1701.[23]

Nevertheless the enemy had penetrated right into France, almost without resistance. Some months before, a strange event had already proved that this was less incredible than people liked to believe. One evening in March, the king's first equerry, Beringhen, was returning from Versailles to Paris in a royal coach bearing the *fleur de lys* on its doors. He was crossing the plain just before the Pont de Sèvres when, suddenly, about thirty men sprung up out of the darkness and stopped the coach. 'Would Monseigneur please get out?' one of them asked. Monseigneur? What Monseigneur? In fact the brigands, seeing the torches, the lackeys and the *fleur de lys* thought that the occupant was the Dauphin, whose coach was to pass five minutes later. Despite their error, they put Beringhen on a horse and took him off, treating him with great politeness. The leader presented himself: Guetem, former violinist of the Elector of Bavaria, who had become a colonel in the Dutch army. He had recruited some thirty French Huguenot émigrés in Holland with a view to kidnapping an important Frenchman. They had crossed France, disguised as merchants and, awaiting a suitable opportunity, some had even been so bold as to go and see the king dining at Versailles. As they took their prisoner to the northern frontier, the police and army were put on alert. They had already crossed the Somme when they were arrested near Ham. The stable staff at Versailles had wanted to celebrate the deliverance of their much loved superior, but Louis, jealous of the publicity given to his first equerry, decreed that there would be no rejoicing, no bonfires. Beringhen, who had turned from prisoner to jailor, wanted to treat Guetem with the same courtesy that Guetem had shown him. He brought him back himself to Versailles and presented him to the king, where Guetem declared himself to be so surprised that he was unable to speak. With a gracious smile, Louis xiv sent him back to Beringhen, who entertained him for ten days or so, showed him Paris and exhibited him everywhere, before sending him back to Holland.[24]

Maintenon suffered great distress at the death of Mme de Montespan. Since her departure from the Court, Athénaïs had cut herself off from everything that she had once loved. Her table, once so refined, had become extremely frugal; she wore coarse linen and was only left with the melancholy pleasure of opening her wardrobe and gazing at the marvellous silk and brocade dresses. Her body, which she had taken such delight in maintaining, had lately been bruised with bracelets, garters and an iron-studded belt. On the other hand, she had abandoned the sharp edge of her much feared wit and an uncharitable remark never passed her lips. She had sent back to the king the fantastic pearl necklace that he had given her and distributed her fortune to the poor. She had even been reconciled with her husband and had decently gone into mourning at his death. She spent her days praying and making clothes for the poor. She was left only with her beauty, her pride and her fear of death. However, when she was taken seriously ill at Bourbon, even this fear had suddenly left her. 'Father, exhort me as simply as you can, I am an ignorant woman,' she had said to the Capuchin who had come to administer extreme unction. After a public confession of her scandalous life, she died peacefully in the night of 27 May 1707. Louis learnt the news when he was about to go out hunting. He did not postpone his trip and never again spoke of the woman to whom he had been attached for so long. 'When I dismissed Mme de Montespan, I never expected to see her again, so she was already dead for me', the king wrote. But Mme de Maintenon was the most affected of all. Her life had been bound up with Montespan's so closely for so long, she had loved and hated her so much, she had struggled so hard against her, she was bound to be moved by her death. But she did not have the right to give free rein to her sorrow and had to hide in her closet to weep in peace. And the Duchesse de Bourgogne, who had followed her, was left speechless by the sight of this woman weeping for a former rival whom she had so meticulously removed.[25]

Maintenon also suffered from the way the king treated Adelaide. The girl had already lost one baby, the young Duc de Bretagne, and was pregnant again, yet the king insisted on taking her to Marly every Sunday. Maintenon and Fagon had tried to point out to him discreetly the danger that this presented to a young woman in her state, but without success. The king could not do without Adelaide's presence. One morning, he was walking beside the carp pond at Versailles, surrounded by his courtiers, when the Duchesse de Lude ran up, a horrified look on her face. The Duchesse de Bourgogne had had a miscarriage. A chorus of lamentation rose up from the courtiers. The king exploded: 'Thank God! I shall no longer be thwarted in my travels and in whatever I want to do by the representations of doctors and the reasonings of matrons. I shall come and go as I please and I shall be left in peace.' This incredible declaration was followed by 'a silence in which one could hear a pin drop'; the courtiers were paralysed with embarrassment. The king leaned over the balustrade, observed the water in the pond and made some remark about one of the carp which was met by silence. The king said no more and walked off, at which the courtiers' tongues were loosened and a great deal was said about this incredibly selfish display.[26]

Indeed everything seemed to conspire against Maintenon. Her director of conscience, the Bishop of Chartres, had quarrelled with her favourite confidant, the Archbishop of Paris, neither of the prelates being able to bear the influence of the other on the 'matron'. Thereupon, the Jesuits, also jealous of Noailles' influence, opened an offensive against him by bringing out the old accusation of Jansenism. Noailles defended himself furiously. Caught between all these contradictory opinions, Maintenon admitted that she understood little of it, but begged Noailles to be conciliatory. Why kill one another over words? Why not make a short, clear declaration condemning Jansenism without qualification? Noailles refused ever to give in to the enemy. Faced with such stubbornness, Maintenon was not far from believing the Jesuits and suspecting the archbishop of being a Jansenist.

The Jesuits suddenly stopped their attack. 'The Jesuits want peace and they promise to punish those of the Society who write against you', she announced triumphantly to Noailles. The king smiled on her again: 'You have never been so good. I feel my attachment for you growing.' Her relief was not to last long. The Jesuits launched into an attack once more, but this time indirectly. They attacked not Noailles, but the nuns of Port-Royal des Champs, who were suspected of Jansenism. Sanctions were taken against them – expulsion, dispersal, incarceration – and they demanded that Noailles approve them. Disgusted by this unjust severity, Noailles refused, but asked Maintenon's advice. Should he act against his conscience in order to please her and calm the king? Maintenon would not be drawn and referred him to God for advice, but did not hide the fact that his attitude had aroused her suspicions.[27]

France was supposed to be exhausted, but still supplied 100,000 men to defeat the 80,000 men of Marlborough and Eugène in Flanders. To command this formidable force, Louis appointed no less a person than the heir presumptive to the throne, the Duc de Bourgogne, with the Duc de Vendôme as second-in-command. Scarcely had this army begun its march than the gates of the cities of Flanders opened as if by magic. The Duc de Bourgogne entered Ghent, Ypres, Bruges and the States of the Province laid their respects at his feet. One day the Austrians, the French the next; the Flemish, prudent as ever, took the wise course of giving a triumphant welcome to each new arrival.[28]

'I have seen the towns taken and retaken so many times that I see nothing stable anymore,'[29] Maintenon commented, somewhat pessimistically. For already friction could be heard in the high command. Bourgogne, young and serious, idealistic and pacific, moved by sincere piety and a profound sense of duty, could not get on with a cynical old debauch like Vendôme, who, moreover, had no desire to collect laurels for Bourgogne and be blamed for his errors. Having decided to go and lay siege to Audenarde, which he expected to take easily, he wasted two days in marches and countermarches. On 11 July 1708, Lieutenant-General de Biron received orders to advance on Escaut and met head on with the entire allied army. The messenger that he sent found Vendôme at dinner. 'The enemy already there? Impossible, Biron is making it up!' Vendôme expostulated, irritated at being wrong in his predictions. A second messenger arrived in the middle of an argument among superior officers. The third at last forced Vendôme to leave the table. The order was for Biron to attack the entire enemy, while Vendôme would come to his aid as soon as possible. Biron thought Vendôme had gone mad. But orders were orders, and when the Maréchal de Matignon then ordered him not to move, Biron dismounted.

Vendôme suddenly decided to attack; he had missed his siege so now he would have his battle. But there was no real plan and no precise instructions were given. The engagement turned in utter confusion as everyone fought for himself, in an instinctive, unco-ordinated way. The regiments no longer recognized each other. Four thousand French soldiers, marching without knowing where they were going, found themselves several kilometres from the field of battle and were taken prisoner without a fight. The disorder was such that it even affected the enemy, and night fell after that crazy day leaving neither victors nor vanquished.

Vendôme decreed that the fight would resume the following day. In the circumstances, the Duc de Bourgogne favoured a retreat. 'Remember that you have come to the army only on condition that you obey me,' Vendôme snapped. Messengers arrived on all sides announcing that the confusion was increasing minute by minute. The disorder was such that the enemy sent their drummers to beat a retreat in the French style and the French regiments retreated. Once the movement had been started, it was impossible to stop it.[30] Eugène rubbed his hands with glee: 'One is not sorry sometimes to make the king repent of his contempt,'[31] he remarked to Biron, who had been taken a prisoner. Old grudges were not quickly forgotten and when genius is put in their service, they become dangerous.

The mass of French soldiers that marched past Ghent, Ypres, Tournai, no longer looked like an army, abandoning all the ground won some weeks before. The Duc de Bourgogne commented to Mme de Maintenon: 'You were only too right when I saw you tremble at the sight of our affairs being put into the hands of the Duc du Vendôme . . . He was in no sense a general, he made no provisions, no arrangements, he did not even take the trouble to obtain news of the enemy, whom he always despised.' There followed a list of Vendôme's negligences. 'Lastly, Madame, the king is quite deceived to have so great an opinion of him. I am not the only one to say so; the entire army says as much. He has never had the confidence of the officers and he has lost the confidence of the men . . .'[32]

'Oh God! When will this horrible bloodshed cease?' sighed Queen Anne of England, when she learnt, at Windsor, of the heavy losses at the battle of Audenarde. On the other hand, the mordant, fiery, malicious and perverse Sarah Jennings, Marlborough's wife, who for years had dominated and humiliated the queen, turning her into her servant and holding her under her thumb, exulted at the news. Once again, her husband, her adored Marlborough, had conquered at Audenarde, so they must have a *Te Deum* to celebrate the victory. The queen must appear resplendent in all her jewels before the nation and the representatives of the whole of Europe. And, as her office dictated, she would take from their caskets the marvellous Crown jewels. However, on the appointed day, just as they were about to set out for St Paul's Cathedral, Queen Anne appeared wearing not a single jewel and Sarah went red with rage. This is Abigail Hill's doing, she thought instantly.

Several years before, Sarah had placed her poverty-stricken relation as a companion-spy in the queen's service. Abigail was as gentle as Sarah was imperious, but no less astute. She would play the harpsichord for hours on end for Anne who loved music and tend her during her frequent illnesses. Gradually, she had become a sort of nurse to the queen – a nurse for her body, but also for her heart. She comforted her patient after each scene caused by Sarah. And the queen, after having known the bitter satisfactions of masochism for so long, discovered the consolation of tenderness. When Sarah threw a fit of jealousy against Abigail, it was too late. Anne now depended as much on the servant as on her mistress. Little by little, Abigail had begun to slip political remarks into her talks with the queen and to encourage her secret Tory sympathies, whereas Sarah, the unchallenged queen of the Whigs, defended and promoted her friends with all the passion at her command. One day, during the previous year, Sarah had learnt that Abigail had married without asking her permission and that the queen had attended the wedding without asking her for her opinion. Unable to control her temper and secure in her long-standing knowledge of the queen, she inflicted on her one of those mad scenes of which Anne had once been so fond and which used to leave her panting at Sarah's feet. But for the first time Anne had resisted and had warmly defended Abigail. Sarah had left in a furious temper, but she had been unable to regain lost ground. Ever since things had not been the same between Morley and Freeman, as these ladies nicknamed one another in their private correspondence. Sarah-Freeman was seeing Anne-Morley slip from her grasp.

And now, on that day of glory for her husband, Sarah drove in the royal coach, sitting beside the queen who was wearing no jewellery. No one knows what the two women said to one another, as the procession drove slowly through the streets of London, but the queen was visibly upset and angry as she descended from the coach in front of St Paul's. She began to climb the steps, then suddenly turned round to Sarah and there, in front of the assembled courtiers and officials, began to upbraid her vehemently. 'Be quiet, not here,' Sarah ordered her.[33] Two days later, all the Courts of Europe were informed of the incident and Versailles was buzzing with rumours: if Sarah was disgraced, it meant the disgrace of Marlborough and the Whigs, the party of out-and-out war, it meant a complete reversal of the situation and the possibility of negotiating peace. But was it really the beginning of Sarah's disgrace or a passing crisis?

Meanwhile Prince Eugène, disdaining to take the cities of Flanders abandoned by the French yet again, made an audacious breakthrough in the direction of Lille. The French army, still superior in numbers, set off once again to attack him. At Versailles, from day to day, from hour to hour, they awaited news of the battle. The Duchesse de Bourgogne and the ladies spent the night in the chapel praying for their husbands. The courtiers' lackeys besieged Chamillart's ante-chamber. The king, impatiently pacing up and down, demanded if there was any news yet. As soon as horses' hoofs were heard in the street everyone gave a start: was it the messenger who had been so long expected? But there was no messenger, and there was no battle either. Days passed and there was still no battle.[34]

All this was the fault of the Duc de Bourgogne: he had wanted to withdraw to Audenarde and did not want to attack. The rumour broke in Paris, at Versailles, in the provinces. It spread through the drawing-rooms, into the streets, into the cafés, into the taverns, it produced a flowering of lampoons and scurrilous songs attacking Bourgogne's cowardice. The Vendôme party had done its work well. Even at Court the côterie benefited from two major advantages: Chamillart and the Duc du Maine, a natural ally of Vendôme on account of his illegitimacy, according to Saint-Simon, but actually jealous of the favour accorded Bourgogne and Adelaide by the king and Maintenon. The campaign of rumours was so well orchestrated that it affected everyone, even Bourgogne's own father, the Dauphin, and, eventually, even the king himself, before whom no one dared any longer to say anything in favour of his grandson. Only Maintenon resisted the general trend. The treacherous remarks made to her by her beloved Maine did not make her change her opinion of Bourgogne. This was because Adelaide had already got a secure foothold and Adelaide was quite willing to say anything against Vendôme to anyone who would listen to her. But neither Adelaide, imprudent and inexperienced as she was, nor the timid Maintenon, could change the king's mind or public opinion.[35]

If there had been no battle, it was simply because the general staff never managed to agree on the place and hour of the attack, because Vendôme, as usual, spent too much time on plans that were too risky to be accepted.[36] Lacking in self-confidence, and pulled between contradictory opinions, Bourgogne failed to impose any authority or arrive at any decision. With bitter lucidity, he lamented his weakness and prayed to God with pathetic fervour.[37] Meanwhile, Eugène was quietly laying siege to Lille, and the city fell on 26 October 1708. The French army watched the siege without intervening, while the high command bickered among themselves with increasing bitterness. 'That's what comes of never going to mass: now you see how we are rewarded,' a courtier belonging to the pious Bourgogne's party remarked to Vendôme. 'Do you imagine that Marlborough goes to mass more often than me?' Vendôme retorted.[38] And so the French army lost, with the same indifference, Ghent, Bruges, etc, and the deputies of the States came once again to pay their respects to Prince Eugène.

Louis was working as usual with Ponchartrain in Mme de Maintenon's room. He was frowning. He was making a great but unsuccessful effort to concentrate, but he was preoccupied. Ponchartrain made himself as unobtrusive as possible, observing the emotions that were to be read on the king's face and maintaining a serious air. Sitting in her armchair, which she had draped with red damask to keep out draughts, Maintenon did not open her mouth. She, too, seemed elsewhere. Adelaide, more excited than ever and quite incapable of keeping still, darted from one door to the other. Any minute her husband, who was on his way back from the front, would enter the room. What welcome would the king give his grandson, the prince everyone called a coward? Time went by. The silences became longer and heavier. Suddenly, the footmen opened the double doors, and there stood the Duc de Bourgogne. Everyone froze. Bourgogne took a few steps forward and stopped, paralysed with shyness. Louis got up at last and made two steps towards him. He opened his arms; he hugged his grandson to him, then pointing to Adelaide said, 'Have you nothing to say?' Bourgogne turned to her, looking at her tenderly, but was incapable of moving, taking her in his arms, or speaking to her. He took control of himself and went over to greet Maintenon. They exchanged a few banal remarks, then the king said: 'It is not right to delay any longer your pleasure at finding one another again. Off you go, children.' Louis de Bourgogne and Adelaide left the room. Thus the king gave his pardon, making it known that he knew his grandson was not a coward.[39] One evening shortly afterwards, Saint-Simon was walking in a corridor, preceded by a footman holding a torch, when he saw two men coming towards him, alone, without servants or torches. By the light of his torch, Saint-Simon recognized the Duc de Vendôme and Alberoni. As they passed one another, the two dukes bowed politely to one another. Saint-Simon had time to notice Vendôme's 'sad look'. The king had given him a wonderful welcome on his arrival, but had refused to speak of public affairs with him. The Dauphin had been excessively pleasant, but had not wished to go with him to Anet. Vendôme had taken his accomplice, the Duc du Maine, to greet the Duchesse de Bourgogne. She was at the hairdresser's, surrounded by her courtiers. She glanced at them, then adjusted her mirror, without moving, without saying a word. No one spoke to them. Vendôme and Maine stood there for a quarter of an hour, stuck in the middle of the room, stared at by the onlookers, in total silence. What were they supposed to do? They stole out, but Vendôme had understood that he had lost. The truth had emerged at last; he was in disgrace and retired to his Château d'Anet.[40]

The king's confessor, Father La Chaise, was dying. At eighty, he was much diminished in body and in mind, but Louis, who was used to Father La Chaise, did not wish to lose him on any pretext. The illness worsened, and his legs became ulcerated. 'His memory dimmed, his judgment enfeebled, his knowledge blurred,' his mind had gone, but Louis continued to confess to the old dotard, right to the end. It was only when the priest was at death's door that he let him go, regretfully. Father La Chaise still found the strength to write to his penitent, begging him to choose his successor from his Society, before dying on 20 January 1709.[41]

At Maintenon's instigation, a council met to choose his successor. Her director of conscience, the Bishop of Chartres, was present, as were the Ducs de La Vertu, Beauvilliers and Chevreuse, who had come back into favour after the fall of their friend, Fénelon. After a month of deliberations, their choice alighted on an unknown from among five candidates proposed by La Chaise: Father Le Tellier, provincial of the Jesuits in Paris, a solitary, austere man, without relations or friends, an indefatigable worker and an erudite theologian. 'Are you related to Messieurs Le Tellier [Louvois and his father]?' the king asked him politely, the first time they met. 'I, Sire! Far from it; I'm a poor peasant from Lower Normandy, where my father was a farmer.' This rustic frankness charmed the king.[42] Le Tellier was obviously not one of those unctuous prelates who tangled one up in their subtleties. Louis did not know that he was introducing a 'Torquemada' into his private circle, for Le Tellier was the embodiment of religious fanaticism, violence, terror and the implacable will to destroy anything that remotely resembled heresy.

CHAPTER 25

Louis' 'Great Winter'

On 5 January 1709, the Chevalier de Quincy was on his way back from supper about two in the morning when he noticed that the Parisian air had become excessively cold. After a fairly bad November, the weather had recently improved and Quincy had thought that the worst of the winter had passed. But during the next few days, the temperature continued to fall and the cold increased in intensity. The Great Winter had struck the whole of Europe, and was to last for four bitter months.[1] The canals of Venice, French rivers, the English Channel and even the Tagus had frozen over; ports were blocked and communications interrupted. In Provence, Italy and Spain, fruit trees, vines, olive trees and vegetables froze in the ground. Cattle and game were dying of cold. On 25 January, snow began to fall and went on falling for ten days without interruption. On 6 March, a new wave of cold hit Europe, more extreme even than the previous one, so whatever had survived until then now perished. Gardens, orchards and even forests were wiped out. Wolves came out of their lairs and attacked peasants and travellers. There was no longer a single grain of wheat; it had frozen in the ground and the entire harvest was lost. Famine took the kingdom of France by the throat. The rest of Europe, which had also been attacked by the cold, had shown more foresight and had filled its barns with wheat, but in France lack of foresight, waste and speculation had eaten up the reserves from the previous autumn.

Louis decided to import grain. Never mind the fact that the coffers were empty and that the English fleet were intercepting convoys coming from Africa and the Levant. Speculators shared out what the enemy allowed to get through. The grain disappeared and the price of bread rose dizzily. Substitutes appeared: wheat mixed with couch grass, bread made of fern or of asphodel, or boiled roots. 'We saw men and women, children great and small, with soiled faces and hands,' observed the parish priest of Vincelles in the Yonne, 'scraping the earth with their fingernails, looking for certain small roots, which they devoured when they had found them. Others, less industrious, munched grass with the animals; others, completely exhausted, lay beside the lanes waiting for death.' *'Fame Petiit'*, (died of hunger'), the parish priests of the entire kingdom wrote in their parish registers every day. They no longer had

346

time to identify the corpses – there were too many of them along the roadside – and proceeded to anonymous, collective burials. In Paris, Councillor Menin did not have time to eat his bread before it was already frozen. 'I have seen,' he wrote 'two young Savoyards found dead, frozen in a doorway where they had stuck themselves, arms around one another to keep warm.'[2]

'If you knew my misery, you would not want to take this bread from me', replied a woman who had just been arrested for theft in a bakery. The police inspector ordered her to take him to her house. There he found three small children 'wrapped up' in rags, squeezed into a corner, trembling with cold. 'Where is your father?' he asked the eldest. 'Behind the door,' came the reply. The inspector opened the door and recoiled with horror: their father was hanging there, having killed himself out of desperation.[3]

From despair to revolt is but a step, quickly taken. In the towns, bakeries and markets were looted. On the roads, convoys of wheat had to be escorted by soldiers in order to avoid attack. Troops of beggars, deserters from the army, women and skeleton-like children, wandered throughout the countryside, attacking convents and castles suspected of hoarding reserves of wheat. Workers went on strike at Rouen and troops had to intervene to re-establish order. Eight hundred men attacked the Intendant of the Bourbonnais, who narrowly escaped being killed. 'No one will be safe any more, either in the towns or the country', concluded the provost of the merchants in Lyon.[4]

'Our Father who art at Marly, your name is no longer glorious, thy will is done neither on land nor on sea; give us this day our daily bread because we are dying of hunger; forgive your enemies who have fought against you, but do not forgive your generals and lead us not into the temptation of changing master, but deliver us from La Maintenon. Amen.'[5] This irreverent Pater Noster could be read on the walls of Paris, which were covered with seditious notices, accompanied by a great new flowering of lampoons and satirical songs. The king was the object of violent attack. Assisted by hunger, insolence turned into challenge. 'Such insults deserve only contempt,' the Lieutenant of Police d'Argenson repeated, carefully burning the seditious writings that piled up on his desk, to prevent them reaching the master.[6] 'Bread', yelled the women who stopped the coach of Monseigneur le Dauphin, who had come to Paris to attend a performance at the Opera. Green with fear – the guards dared not repulse the furies for fear of being massacred – Monseigneur escaped by throwing some coins out of the window and promising the earth. But he swore that he would not be caught again and refrained from setting foot in the capital.[7]

'Bread, bread,' shouted the women in rags, clinging to the gilded railings of Versailles. They had come in a crowd on foot from Paris, but the guards pushed them away, hoping that His Majesty would not hear their shouts.[8] In the palace, the courtiers' faces grew longer, not because of this intrusion from below, but because they were suffering as much as the people from cold, if not from hunger. Bottles of wine and spirits burst on the side-boards and Saint-Simon, dining in the Duc de Villeroi's small ante-chamber looked sadly at the pieces of ice that dropped into his glass.[9] Imperturbable as ever, Louis did not notice the layer of ice that covered his wine and even the sauce in his plate. Despite the killing temperature he continued his daily walks in the park; eventually, however, he noticed the sore noses and streaming eyes of the courtiers and guards who heroically accompanied him and, with a sigh, decided to give up his outings.[10] Influenza and pneumonia even decimated his Court – the cold attacked anyone of a weak disposition.

Famine was merely one more problem. Whatever happened, the machine kept going and the king faced up to it. At The Hague a certain Petkum, vaguely representing a German prince who was allied to the Dutch, was approached by the Elector of Bavaria, an ally of France, with a view to initiating possible negotiations. At Versailles Chamillart let it be known very discreetly in the right quarters that the French government might not persist in keeping Philip v on the throne of Spain, providing some spoils from the Spanish empire came its way. Suddenly, Petkum came to Paris as discreetly as possible to sound out French intentions, while, with the same discretion, Louis sent Judge Rouille as ambassador to Antwerp, in order to meet Bruys and Vanderdussen, two magistrates from the city of Amsterdam. He was purposely taken to one of the villages in which his master's troops had burnt down the houses and murdered the inhabitants. There the two Dutch burghers adopted the same tone that, twenty years before, Louis had adopted with the hard-pressed representatives of Holland. What did defeated France have to offer her victors? Rouille bravely followed his instructions: France might cease supporting Philip v on the throne of Spain, providing she was given sufficient compensation. The reply was staggering: to begin with, the king of France himself would have to force his grandson to abandon Spain, and without compensation. As for the rest, they would see later. If these conditions were not met, it would be out-and-out war. Rouille made no reply to the affrontery of the two Dutch burghers. He probably guessed that the two magistrates, the States General that they represented and even Holland as a whole were not the real parties to such a deal and that, in fact, it was Marlborough and Prince Eugène who pulled the strings of the negotiations.[11] In any case, the tone of his despatches became more and more desperate. What was to be done?

That morning, in the drawing-rooms at Marly, Lauzun wore his most honeyed smile, but his eyes were sparkling: 'Have you seen our Minister of Foreign Affairs, M de Torcy?' he asked the Duc de Villeroi and several others. 'No', they replied, somewhat surprised. 'He came back in the night from Paris and has brought some gastronomic marvels for his lunch. I don't want to tell you what they are, it's a surprise, but I expect to get my share and you ought to do the same.' So an entire assembly of courtiers, their mouths watering with greed, met at lunchtime in front of Torcy's door. They were surprised to find it shut. They knocked. There was no answer. They knocked again. Silence. Lauzun had been making fun of them again. At fifty-six, the devilish little man still had the heart of a twenty-year-old when it came to practical jokes. A long-standing intriguer, he always knew how to penetrate the best guarded secrets, and was well aware that if Torcy was not there to offer a succulent lunch to his 'guests', it was because, during the night and in secret, he had left under an assumed name for Holland.[12] He had proposed that he should take over from Judge Rouille, and in the situation in which Louis found himself, he could hardly do other than accept.[13]

Louis was less than optimistic about the results of the negotiations and on 8 May 1709 he summoned a council of war, the first in his reign, according to Saint-Simon. For the first time in his life he was not there to give orders, but to ask advice, which amounted to a single question: can we continue the war if negotiations fail? The marshals, Boufflers and Villars, and Harcourt, the former ambassador to Madrid, laid into Chamillart: the frontier fortresses were ill-defended, the troops were in a terrible state, the arms were outdated. The king did not come to the defence of his Minister of War. But Chamillart defended himself, then went over to the attack, won the battle and began to raise his voice so loudly that he was heard in the drawing-room next door. His colleague at Finance, Desmarets, wanted to intervene. The fire then turned on him. The Lifeguards had not been paid for a long time, Boufflers yelled. 'But they have been paid,' the king intervened. 'No, Sire, they have not been paid and I had the honour of telling you so in a memorandum that I wrote to be given Your Majesty.' Suddenly, the king joined in the attack on Desmarets: 'What does this mean? Did you not assure me that they had been paid?' Desmarets 'mumbled' something between his teeth and fell silent, waiting for the storm to pass. Chamillart gently delivered the final blow: 'In fact, not a single regiment has been paid and we shall soon have proof of it.' The king hastened to bring the council to a close.[14] His council had opened a positive Pandora's Box of unpleasant truths and the smell was so bad that he preferred to close it at once. The question of whether to continue the war remained as open as ever.

The Grand Pensionary of Holland, Heinsius, got the surprise of his life when told that no less a person than the Minister of Foreign Affairs of the king of France was awaiting him in his ante-chamber.

Negotiations began at once, but they turned to serious matters only when the true participants, Marlborough and Eugène, were present. Then, in the modest, apparently spartan house, surrounded by a garden of tulips, they sat down around the table. The mouse was the minister of the 'greatest king on earth', who wanted to make his opponents pay through the nose. The three cats were Heinsius, whom Louvois had threatened to throw into the Bastille when he had come to beg in the name of his country; Marlborough, whose services the same Louvois had haughtily rejected; and Eugène, 'the little priest', whom Louis, with ironical contempt, had refused to take on. For each of them, the time of revenge had finally arrived.

On 28 May 1709, they handed Torcy a document signed by the representatives of all the allied powers. The king of France ceded to Holland the protective barrier of the Flemish towns. The king of France renounced sovereignty over Alsace. The king of France handed back to the Duke of Savoy the country of Nice and other trifles. The king of France would join his armies with those of the allies to expel by force his grandson Philip v from the throne of Spain. For this price, he would obtain, not peace, but merely a truce. The conditions of a peace would be discussed later. Torcy's first reaction was to offer four million francs to Marlborough, who rejected them with an ironic smile. The Minister had no alternative but to report back to Louis.[15]

Louis was astounded to learn that he was expected to send his armies against Philip v. 'Since there has to be a war, I would prefer to wage it against my enemies than against my children.'[16] This was one of those historical sayings that he had a talent for coining at the right moment. In short, it was no to the allies.

In that case, Chamillart objected, the enemy would soon be at the gates of Paris. 'Well,' Louis retorted, 'I shall go at the head of my nobility to fight for what remains of my kingdom; I shall retrench from stream to stream, and from town to town, rather than surrender, and we shall see what happens . . .'[17] But while he jousted in this medieval fashion, someone else had to find the money.

The Duchesse de Gramont, who had married the former ambassador in Madrid, now began to show zeal in this direction. She advised her husband to offer the king his silver with a view to having it melted down into coinage. Delighted with this innovation in courtly behaviour, the duke agreed. The Duc de La Rochefoucauld learnt of it and threw a jealous tantrum before the king. How could the king, his friend, accept someone else's silver without having the grace to ask him for his? Thereupon courtier after courtier fell over themselves to be one of the chosen few to offer their silver. Many gibbed at such a sacrifice, but it was also impossible not to be numbered among the donors. 'The most slavish were distressed by a disagreeable imitation all the pleasure of which went to its inventor.'

Surprised by this avalanche of plates and soup tureens, Louis hesitated to accept them. The uselessness of his own gesture, when in 1688 he had sacrificed his own silver, and the criticisms and scorn that it had aroused, were still for him a disagreeable memory. His good sense advised him to refuse but, short as he was of money, he felt unable to resist the trend. Not only did he accept his courtiers' offers, but he sent his own gold and silver tableware to the Mint – he had obviously kept some back from the holocaust of 1688 – thus sweeping away the hesitations of the last courtiers who, out of meanness or prudence were still resisting. When all the porcelain shops in Paris were emptied by the generous donors left without tablewear, when thousands of masterpieces of goldsmith's work had disappeared into the founder's pot, it was realized that the actual money obtained was ridiculously little. The king, regretting being led into this collective stupidity, forbade the continuation of this spoliation.[18] Marlborough and Eugène were not to be beaten with the Duchesse de Gramont's silver plate.

On Sunday morning 9 June 1709, just before entering the council of ministers, the king took the Duc de Beauvilliers to one side. 'This afternoon, he said, 'you will go to Chamillart and ask him to resign his post as Minister of War.' Beauvilliers tried to refuse this disagreeable task. They were interrupted by the entry of the ministers, including Chamillart himself. The council followed its usual course, without giving Chamillart any idea that he had been sacked. The king even asked him to bring an unfinished memorandum to him that evening. Later Beauvilliers persuaded his brother-in-law Chevreuse to go with him to Chamillart's office. Beauvillier wore such a funereal expression that Chamillart understood immediately. He kept calm, put his affairs in order, sent messages of gratitude to the king for the benefits that he had received and went off to his country home.

The king was left with a good deal less peace of mind. He had never had so submissive and docile a minister as Chamillart. And, anyway, he had got used to him and it always cost him a great deal to divest himself of a familiar face. But it was either Chamillart or the State, or at least that was what everyone was telling him. So he bowed before reasons of State, or at least before palace intrigue. Maintenon had a grudge against Chamillart who had never paid quite enough attention to her inventions on behalf of obscure protégés. La Choin, who was increasingly playing the favourite and whom Chamillart had ignored, had turned the Dauphin against him. Lastly, the marshals had continued to denounce his incompetence, whereas it was in fact the master who was responsible, Chamillart having been chosen precisely to carry out the Master's orders. And Louis, once more led by the nose without knowing it, had given himself the luxury of a ministerial crisis at the most dramatic moment of his reign.[19]

With Chamillart dismissed, someone had to be found to replace him – and quickly. Maintenon had someone up her sleeve, called Voysin. He had everything going for him: humble origin, great discretion, remarkable administrative ability, apparent ignorance of politics and intrigue, unlimited devotion to La Maintenon. Mme Voysin chose just the right moment to make the king's delicate wife a present of a padded dressing-gown, and Voysin himself had first come to notice while administering the finances of Saint-Cyr. Voysin, then, was summoned to replace Chamillart. But Saint-Simon noticed the unusual coldness with which the Master received him.[20] Had Maintenon not been persuasive enough or was Louis having doubts? He had certainly told Chamillart that he would always be happy to see him again, but that, for the moment, it would be too painful. And when, on returning from mass, the king caught sight of Chamillart's son M de Cani, he stopped in front of him, looked at him with great tenderness and assured him that he would take care of him. He went into his study, reappeared at the door, looked again at Cani, eyes red with tears, and repeated how solicitous he felt towards him.[21] But if this was how Louis really felt, how does one account for his hypocrisy at the council where, having already decided on Chamillart's dismissal, he treated him as if nothing had happened? It was probably a result of his own doubts, his lack of self-assurance, a touch of bad conscience, an unavowable sadness that unconsciously forced him to behave in that way. It was not a tactic, but weakness.

On 9 June Chamillart was dismissed. On 13 June, Judge Rouille came back to Versailles. After Torcy's return, he had been left in Holland, to try, against all hopes, to obtain some mitigation of the conditions laid down by the allies. The only response he got was an order from the States General to leave within twenty-four hours.[22] Then Louis XIV did an incredible thing: for the first and last time he addressed his people to explain the situation and to justify himself. Not directly – there were, after all, limits to how far he could go – but in a letter to the provincial governors that would be read out in public or pasted up on walls:

'Although the tenderness I feel for my people is no less keen than that I feel for my own children; although I share all the ills that war has inflicted on such faithful subjects, and have shown the whole of Europe that I sincerely desired to allow them to enjoy peace, I am convinced that they would themselves be opposed to receiving it on conditions so contrary to justice and to the honour of the French name.'[23]

If he had realized the impact of such an approach, why had he never used it before? For the first time, he knew that his people were at their wits' end while he himself was in a corner, but he did not really feel he was responsible for either situation. He had wanted neither the war nor the ruin of his country. He was able to express himself because for once he felt confident that he had done nothing wrong. He had always linked the fate of the French with his own – but when things went well there was no need to communicate. Now that the French and he were linked together for worse, they would know it, they should be told. He did not humiliate himself by this approach. His pride was silenced by despair.

'You would be wrong if you thought that we do not hear laments here: night and day one hears nothing else; the famine is such that children have eaten one another.' The Princess Palatine heard these laments, too close for her comfort. Going to the Palais Royal on Tuesday 20 August, she was met by alarming cries: Paris is in revolt, there are already forty dead.[24] Over in the Faubourg Saint–Denis, the (bad) bread that was distributed to the workers had run out while the hungry queue was still very long. There were murmurs and complaints. A woman climbed up on to a milestone and made an inflammatory speech. Archers seized her and put her in the nearest pillory, but the workers beat up the archers and freed the woman. The crowd grew larger, spread into the nearby streets, looted bakeries and cake shops. Shopkeepers hurriedly closed their doors as the riot extended to every quarter of the city with cries of 'Bread, bread!' The Maréchal de Boufflers, who was with his notary, Maître Bérenger, heard the tumult and decided to see what was happening. From every window people urged them not to go on, but to turn back quickly. At the top of the Rue Saint-Denis the crowd was so dense that Boufflers got out of his carriage and continued on foot. He moved forward fearlessly through the shouts and threats. 'What is happening? What do you want?' he cried to the demonstrators. 'Bread, bread!' 'You will have it.' The shouting stopped. He talked, he listened, he made promises and the crowd calmed down. He slowly walked through the nearby street. 'Get us bread.' 'I shall get it.' 'Tell the king about our misery.' 'I shall tell him.' 'Long live the Maréchal de Boufflers!' At this point D'Argenson arrived with regiments of French and Swiss guards, and within a few minutes there was a blood bath. Boufflers meanwhile galloped to Versailles, went up to Maintenon's room, found the king and told them all.[25]

Did 'St Françoise' know of the poverty that reigned? She spent her time succouring the poor. She had doubled the number of her charities, cut out her servants' perks, sold her horses and a precious ring in order to be able to give more away. She fed hordes of families, maintained entire convents, looked after sixteen poor families in Versailles itself and personally took them food parcels, she received all the distressed gentlewomen who appealed to her. On her visits to the poor, she demanded the strictest incognito, terrified one day when she narrowly escaped a coach accident that her identity might have been revealed.[26] Poor Maintenon, spending and exhausting herself unstintingly, so full of good intentions, and so ineffective. She continued to play the role of a charity lady on the tiny scale that had always been hers, with a modesty that was perhaps not so feigned and a sincere discretion, while what was needed was to organize help on a national scale and to give the maximum publicity to her activities, if only to silence public opinion which accused her of stockpiling wheat in order to get rich.[27] (Saint-Simon himself repeated this nonsense.) But she was incapable of conceiving of such a thing. She busied herself tirelessly, but always within a very narrow horizon.

Meanwhile, at Reims, 12,000 poor were living solely off public charity; whole villages had been abandoned in the Charolais; Burgundy and the Nivernais were infested with brigands; 113 inhabitants died of hunger in a single village in the North. Scurvy was rife and accounted for between thirty and forty dead a day at the Hôtel Dieu. The Hôpital Général housed 14,000 patients suffering from ... hunger. 'Half the country will perish,' wrote the Intendant of Lyon. 'I am beside myself with grief at what I see every day. Humanity, let alone Christianity, cannot endure it.'

However, the government did take measures. Public workshops were set up, but several months passed before they were opened and then there were no tools for the workers. An exceptional tax was levied for the poor, but the rich themselves had become poor and 600 parishes out of 830 in the diocese of Sens were unable to contribute: they could no longer pay anything. The private initiatives of the Church sometimes did better. The Cardinal de Noailles managed to get 60,000 *livres* out of the king and princes for the poor. 'We feed 1,300 unfortunates to whom we give soup,' wrote the Bishop of Auxerre. 'I've reduced myself to wholemeal bread in order to make some effort for the poor. I have no other resources but my silverwear; everything else is already mortgaged.' At this point the *parlement* intervened: how dare the Church usurp its privileges and, without reference to them, distribute grain and money! They demanded that the income devoted to charity should be handed over to them so that they could make use of it. Aid ceased abruptly while the quarrel lasted.[28]

Meanwhile, Maintenon wept as she was obliged to gamble away her hard-saved money at the Duchesse de Bourgogne's table. 'My God! How ill-used this money is!' she would remark. But neither would she protest or refuse to play for the king wanted everyone to join in. Luckily fortune smiled on her. Her losses were minimal and she would often put aside some of her gains for the poor. If she had to buy a new dress, the tears would well up. How could one spend on lace and ribbons a sum of money that might save so many from poverty! But there again, she dared not appear in an old dress. She was afraid of ridicule, she admitted it to herself. But since she needed more money for her charities she cut out the harpsichord lessons given her by Mlle d'Aumale who, despite her admiration for her benefactress, thought her evil-minded.[29]

The king, too, was continually hungry, but it was only a tape-worm that was responsible. Trying to relieve his constant nagging hunger gave rise to the now customary attacks of indigestion. He stuffed himself so much with 'peas, fish, oysters, sardines', that he had to get up at night 'to make three stools of moved humour'. After one particularly bad attack of indigestion, he at last agreed to subject himself to a draconian diet of pâté in pastry, pigeon soup and three roast chickens. Believing himself to be cured, he then threw himself upon 'a quantity of new stews'. The result: five stools after dinner. He swallowed a large glass of iced water: this caused 'a very precipitated stool, which gave him so much pain that he almost fainted'. Fagon prescribed cinnamon water, which sent him to his commode twenty-two times in a single day. An excessive intake of peas and meringues 'obstructed the belly, making the matter ferment', and gave His Majesty 'vapours'. These attacks of colic now alternated with constipation, which the learned Fagon attributed to 'many occasions of affliction'. Bad news also had an effect on the royal intestines. Sometimes the day fixed for a purge had to be brought forward because of 'the melancholic humour exalted by subjects of sadness', sometimes it had to be postponed because 'anxiety over the news that might arrive' led to fears that strong emotion might counteract the effect of the purge.

The gout was galloping apace, tying the illustrious invalid to his bed and forcing him to follow mass and to hold his councils of ministers from between the sheets. On top of gout was added gallstones. The 'small ball of sand the size of a grain of wheat' found in the royal urine had caused intolerable pain. He was now more affected than before by bad weather. The transition from the cold outside to the heat of his bedroom, the sometimes over-heated, sometimes icy apartments, the long sermons in the freezing temperature of the chapel, the trying-on of new wigs, which left his shaven head completely bare for too long, gave rise to continual colds. 'Every morning the king had brought up phlegm strongly attached to the throat which becomes detached only by repeated coughing.' As with every other illness, the only remedy for a cold was bleeding, and Fagon was surprised to find, after drawing litres of blood from him, 'the king seemed rather listless'. On top of everything else, the unfortunate man suffered from insomnia, caused mainly by anxiety. 'The king was very gloomy during the council in his study'. Hence his sleep was 'very disturbed' and he would wake up with a start, from 'turbulent dreams'. As if all this were not enough, bugs were found in his bed, 'which much incommoded him'. What with the insects and the bad news, the king lay 'in a languor and dejection great enough to rob him of appetite'.[30]

For Louis xiv to lack appetite, things must really have been going badly. Everybody praised the impassivity and determination with which he weathered the gravest crisis of his reign. Saint-Simon was to laud that Olympian majesty in adversity and Maintenon went into ecstasies over his even temper (which, deep down, she attributed to insensitivity). The *Journal des Médecins du Roi* saw things rather differently. The doctors could only measure the affect of the crisis on the king through his constipation and insomnia: therefore France must be in a bad way, for the king certainly was.

Meanwhile what was happening in Spain? A messenger arrived from Madrid one July morning in 1709 to announce that the Duc d'Orléans' secretary, Renaud, and his aide-de-camp, La Flotte, had been arrested on the orders of the king of Spain while on their way to France. Louis could not understand what was behind it and informed his nephew d'Orléans, who was as surprised as he. The duke pointed out that the arrest of two Frenchmen was an outrage to the king of France and Louis promised to demand an immediate explanation from the Spanish government.

It was at this point that the truth erupted. Renaud and La Flotte had not been going to France at all, but straight to the enemy lines with a proposition from the Duc d'Orléans to Lord Stanhope, the English commander-in-chief. Since the allies had decided to dethrone Philip v, were the English going to give the late Charles ii's twenty-three crowns to the archduke? There was another solution: neither Philip, nor the archduke, but he, the Duc d'Orléans: he had rights over Spain through his grandmother, Anne of Austria, and he would make an excellent king, much better than that simpleton Philip V. The Court, which was all too rapidly informed, turned violently against Philip d'Orléans. It was outrageous that he should deal with the enemy, in the middle of a war, in order to rob a young, unhappy French prince, who was trying against all the odds to hang on to his legitimate heritage. Now that his son was threatened by his own nephew, the Dauphin emerged from his usual apathy and conducted a campaign of incredible virulence against the traitor. That monster deserved nothing less than prison, even if he was a prince of the blood royal, he exclaimed. There should be a trial, an exemplary sentence – even the executioner's axe.

All support for the guilty man fell away. There was nobody left to defend him, except his mother the Palatine, who no one listened to, and his wife. The king was deeply embarrassed, an embarrassment that he took great care to hide. The Spanish affair had been a continual source of anxiety for him from the beginning of the year. The allies would never accept Philip and he, Louis, would never consent to expel him by force. Meanwhile, he had on his back his ruined kingdom and a Europe in coalition against him. What was to be done? The best solution would be for Philip V to give up Spain voluntarily. Louis made discreet appeals to Madrid along these lines. But Philip would have none of it: 'I shall never abdicate'. He had the Spanish people behind him. 'We shall never abdicate,' swore Queen Maria Louisa. She had behind her the Princesse des Ursins who, each morning, strengthened the determination of the young royal couple, undermined by the bad news.

Louis turned the problem over in his mind in search of other solutions. If Philip V were to leave, willingly or no, the allies would have won one of their essential demands and it might be possible to put in place another French prince acceptable to the allies without losing face. With this in view, he slipped a few words in passing, into the ear of his nephew Philippe: if a treaty removed Philip, Philippe would have to be ready to lay claim to the crown of Spain. Meanwhile, it would be a good idea to leave someone he could trust in Madrid who could act, if necessary, when the time came. Philippe swore to Saint-Simon that this was what Louis had whispered to him, and he proved to be telling the truth. La Flotte and Renaud were chosen for the mission. Armed with vague instructions, these two blundering intriguers, La Flotte especially, delightedly threw themselves into their mission: they busied themselves, made contacts and, above all, talked. Perhaps they even imagined they could work out an agreement with the English on their own. But this was a very different matter from getting the Duc d'Orléans to betray his uncle. The fat, shy young man was much too afraid of his uncle to go over his head and concoct so Machiavellian a conspiracy. And, anyway, this profoundly patriotic soldier would never consider dealing with the enemy in the middle of a war. But the terrible accusation had been made and everyone believed it. The Princesse des Ursins had never forgiven Philippe for calling her the '*con*-lieutenant', and though Philippe's betrayal had never been proved it did not prevent the princess from piling calumnies on the suspects.

Louis wanted only one thing: to hush up the whole affair. He knew that the advice that he had slipped to his nephew was the indirect cause of the drama. But, with his eternal mistrust, he had now come to have doubts about his nephew, especially as he allowed himself once again to be deafened by the cries of his family, his ministers and his courtiers. He gave in, and agreed to put Philippe on trial. An order was given to the chancellor to prepare the case. The chancellor, singularly embarrassed, talked about it to Saint-Simon, who was later to claim that he had demonstrated to the chancellor the insurmountable difficulties of such a trial. The chancellor had no difficulty in convincing the king: 'I have looked into this affair, I am surprised that so much has been made of it and I find it very strange that such ill-founded things are said about it,' the king remarked, finally putting an end to Court gossip and suddenly stemming the torrent of horrors being poured on the suspect.[31] Of course, he could have said that at the start. It was bad enough that he should consider replacing his grandson with his nephew – necessity may have the force of law – but it was really too much that the intrigues of underlings should so make him lose his head that he was thinking of putting his own nephew on trial, when he knew in his heart of hearts that he was innocent. As usual, the Sun King had allowed himself to be swayed against his will by the tide of opinion and it was only at the last moment that his good sense brought him to a halt.

Day had not yet broken over Flanders on 11 September 1709, when the Chevalier de Quincy had himself carefully shaved and powdered in readiness for the battle. To the sound of the enemy's trumpets, invisible in the fog, he attended mass and, with his soldiers, received the general absolution for his sins from the chaplain. He then ate a hearty meal, for 'this precaution is always good'. At eight o'clock the fog lifted, to reveal the plain, the village of Malplaquet and the allied army. There were 80,000 of them with 140 cannon. The French had only 70,000 men and 80 cannon. The allied artillery immediately launched a heavy bombardment. The French soldiers who, after a whole day of fasting, had just been given their bread, dropped it to run at the enemy. The enemy fire scythed through whole ranks of the Lifeguards and the French gendarmerie, but they did not retreat. Quincy saw a decapitated Lifeguard being carried on at a mad gallop by his horse, the dead man's spurs stuck in its flanks. In the midst of the deafening noise of rifle and cannon, he heard a young gendarme, eviscerated by a cannonball and writhing in pain a few paces away from him, beg him to finish him off. Quincy, too, was wounded – but only slightly – by the branch of a tree, which, cut off by a cannonball, fell on his hands. More serious for

France was the wounding of the Maréchal de Villars. A cannonball shattered his knee and he fell into a faint. A general gave Quincy the order to retreat. 'Why are we retreating? We have fought all the troops that have attacked us,' Quincy objected. 'Retreat as fast as you can, you're about to be surrounded,' the general replied. 'There's an enemy column marching straight behind you.'

With Villars wounded and his centre breached, the battle of Malplaquet was lost for France. But of the 37,000 killed during the day, the highest single total of the century, it was the allies, with 24,000 dead, who had sustained the greater losses. It was above all the Dutch who had most to complain of. The normally gay, cynical Marlborough remained dumbstruck with horror when he went to visit their trenches, amid the atrocious medley of moans and cries from the wounded, he observed the 12,000 mutilated corpses, stripped bare by thieves, frozen in death in whole ranks. They were packed so tightly in the trenches that no earth was visible.[32] And yet, despite this carnage, which decimated the allies, the French were forced to retreat. Voltaire looked in vain for the cause of this[33] but it was simply because the army, despite its high spirits, was dying of hunger and that there was nothing left to pay it or to feed it with. Villars rubbed his hands with glee as the king had just raised him to the peerage. Saint-Simon was furious; he hated Villars and from the outset of Villars' brilliant career, had bitterly counted the undeserved – in his eyes – honours that the Maréchal had been given: marshal, for a battle that he thought he had lost; duke, for having bargained, unsuccessfully with a brigand (Jean Cavalier), and now a peer for another battle, lost through his own fault.[34]

In the night of 28 October 1709, everyone was asleep in the convent of Port-Royal des Champs. However, the nearby undergrowth was full of furtive movements. Branches snapped, a horse neighed. Hundreds of armed men were approaching the building in silence. They were French and Swiss guards. At dawn, they had completely encircled the convent. In the morning of the 29th, the lieutenant of police, d'Argenson, turned up at the door, surrounded by an imposing posse of constables. Once inside, he posted men at every exit, then gave orders for all the residents of the convent to gather in the chapter hall. At last they would see those dangerous conspirators who made such a deployment of force necessary! Twenty-two elderly nuns – several of them in their eighties – appeared. D'Argenson produced a *lettre de cachet* from the king, declaring that the old women would have to vacate the premises within a quarter of an hour. They were not even given time to wrap up their few belongings before they were hastily put into coaches, each with a woman to look after them, and were taken under military escort to various convents, some as far as a hundred kilometres away. Several of them were so ill that they had to be dragged to their mobile prisons.

The twenty-two elderly women were the last victims of the Jesuits' pitiless struggle for power. Their crime was to be the official remnant of the Jansenists. Jansenism was a school of theology named after the Dutch priest Cornelius Jansen (1585-1638), whose attempt to restore the teachings of St Augustine in Catholic theology brought him into lifelong conflict with the Jesuits. Though anti-Protestant, many of his beliefs resembled those of Calvinism, especially the doctrine that man is innately corrupt and can only be saved by divine grace, not by good works. Jansenism had been persecuted for fifty years with pontifical bulls, condemnations, edicts from the *parlement* and harassment of all kinds. Only the nuns of Port-Royal still held fast, but not because they had been left alone. They had been made to sign innumerable retractions of heresy, the sacraments had been withdrawn from them, then given back to them, but they had been forbidden to receive novices. The nuns had borne it all in silence and had become so inconspicuous that everyone, except the Jesuits and the king, had almost forgotten them. Far too many people went to visit the nuns for their liking. 'I hate that convent for its Jansenism', the king remarked to his friend, the Comtesse de Gramont, whom he had struck off the visiting list at Marly because she had had the audacity to go to Port-Royal.

The nuns were then made to sign a new papal bull condemning Jansenism once and for all. The old women had seen it all before, complied, but with a vague restrictive clause. The Jesuits then seized the opportunity: the words heresy and rebellion began to circulate again. Once more Louis charged at the red rag held out to him by the Fathers. Famine had his kingdom by the throat, the enemy armies were ready to invade, his grandson's throne was toppling, even his own was threatened, but he found time to concern himself with twenty-two elderly women at Port-Royal as if they represented a threat to Church and State. At the instigation of Father Le Tellier the stream of *lettres de cachet* reached flood proportions. An order was issued to raze the convent and all its buildings to the ground so that not a single stone would remain of them. The families of the 3,000 dead buried there were ordered to remove their relations' bones, and another order was issued to throw those skeletons without families to claim them into a ditch in the nearby cemetery. Lastly, an order was issued to plough up the site of the convent and sow it with wheat. Instead of erasing the cursed name from men's memories for all time, these extreme measures led to Port-Royal being talked about everywhere, although no one protested, neither the Cardinal de Noailles, terrified of being accused by the Jesuits yet again of being a Jansenist, nor the pope, whose throne was rocked by the waves from this scandal.[35]

'The courtiers have never been so bored. We are now at Meudon, which is a magnificent palace. Well! One has to go out walking, whether one likes it or not, in a terrible wind, out of respect for the king. One comes back very tired and sits there without in fact knowing what to do to amuse oneself.' Maintenon grumbled in her usual dissatisfied way. She calmly described the courtiers who complained of the regime forced upon them by the king and who were dying of boredom. Yet she herself made no effort to bring any life into that tomb. The worst time was after dinner in her apartment when no one dared to interrupt the king's gloomy silence, and when the ladies of her intimate circle dozed off, impatiently waiting for bedtime.

One evening, however, the Duchesse de Bourgogne suddenly let herself go. She began to jump around the room, dragging her ladies of honour into a wild saraband from one end of the room to the other, chattering away to them in a 'Chinese' of her own invention and laughing madly. In a corner, the king's two bastard daughters, the Duchesse de Bourbon and the Princesse de Conti, shrugged their shoulders and put on contemptuous expressions. Adelaide watched them out of the corner of her eye and, between two *entrechats*, whispered to Saint-Simon's wife: 'Just look at them! I know as well as they that there is no sense in what I say and do, and that is really terrible, but the king needs a bit of noise and things like this amuse him.' And she was off, jumping about and singing to herself. 'La, la! How I laugh at them! How I laugh at them, La, la! How I make fun of them! And I shall be their queen.'[36] It was almost heroic on her part to take it upon herself to entertain the austere king. She pulled it off because she was little more than a child – but an astute child, without any illusions. However, she had to interrupt her bursts of childish choreography because she was pregnant again. On Saturday 15 February 1710, the king was woken up, in violation of his sacrosanct custom, at seven in the morning, to be told that she was in labour. Saint-Simon, his eyes fixed on his watch, noted that at three minutes and three seconds past eight precisely she gave birth to a another son, who would one day be King Louis xv.[37]

'The king seemed to me on that day to be in a state of extraordinary dejection, as if wracked with pain,' his Minister of Foreign Affairs, Torcy, noted one day in the winter of 1709-10. 'It seemed that people were making him mistrustful of his ministers.' It was not that some new catastrophe had struck France, but that the Duc de Beauvilliers had quite simply taken it upon himself to confront Louis with the country's real situation, which other, less courageous individuals had tried to hide from him. The state of France had hardly improved, famine continued to ravage the land and soon the new spring campaign would begin. With what troops, what money, what bread would they face the enemy armies that were preparing to pounce on his kingdom? Maintenon was furious at Beauvilliers' initiative and she conveyed her displeasure to Desmarets.[38] That killjoy had just undone all the work that they had put into maintaining her husband's good humour at all costs, even if it required concealing the truth. Her adversaries denounced her 'crime', but were wrong about her intentions. They imagined Maintenon deceiving the king for her own ends in order to dominate him all the more. They did not understand that this narrow-minded, unintelligent woman constantly confused the man and the head of State. She wanted to protect the man and was unaware that the head of State must know everything. She was not a monster. When it was impossible to hide bad news from the king, she went off to the chapel to pray for courage, then came back and preached Christian resignation to her husband. 'If we knew what God knows, we would want whatever He wants', she would declare. 'Nothing is done without His ordering it and without His permission and it is true that everything He does is good.'[39]

But God, alas, did not rule France and something had to be done. So a new expedition was planned, this time to Scotland. The armies of the European coalition would be invading a defenceless France in the spring and all Louis XIV could come up with was putting the late James II's son on the throne of England, that 'James III' whom Louis had once rashly recognized as the legitimate king. He had been persuaded that the loyal Scots only needed the arrival of their legitimate sovereign to overthrow the ursurper, Anne, and her commander Marlborough, that inveterate enemy of France.[40] This tenacious chimera was bad enough, but the Elector of Bavaria, the only German prince to have remained an ally of France, was invited to the Court. It was the least they could do after he had lost his States as the price of his fidelity. But then the Elector extended his hand to the Dauphin – an unheard of breach of protocol which the king did nothing to discourage. This time, it was too much and Saint-Simon exploded. The misfortunes of that impudent man did not excuse such intolerable behaviour. No catastrophe was on a par with that breach of protocol and none of the king's mistakes – and God knows he had made enough – was the equal to this flagrant disregard of hierarchy. The scandal was so enormous that according to Saint-Simon the entire Court shuddered with horror: 'Everything is demeaned, everything destroyed, everything becomes chaos.' That Paris should be conquered by the enemy and the kingdom divided was a risk, but that the Dauphin of France would give his hand to a mere Elector, that, never![41]

Saint-Simon was not yet at the end of his patience with his master. One evening, after dinner, he saw him cross his study with his most majestic air, observe his courtiers in silence for several seconds, then announce briefly that the children of the Duc de Maine would now enjoy the same rank as their father. Saint-Simon was torn between amazement and anger. So, despite everything, despite the reverses, the misfortunes and the threats, the king was continuing, quietly, step by step, to elevate his bastards almost to his own level. Immediately after making his declaration, the king moved to the corner of the room where the Dauphin and the Duc de Bourgogne were standing. Having never before shown anything but haughty authority towards them, he humbled himself before them for the first time in his life. To Saint-Simon's joy, he begged them to approve the favour that he had just granted to the children of the Duc de Maine. He was old, he went on, he would not be long for this world, he implored them to continue this favour after his death. Son and grandson shook hands and lowered their eyes. The king went to fetch the Duc du Maine, blushing with embarrassment, forced him to kneel before the two future kings and asked them to give their word that they would respect the new rank of the bastard's children. Son and grandson shook hands again. The king, tears in his eyes, made them embrace the Duc de Maine and asked them again to give their word. Son and grandson managed at last to mumble a few incomprehensible words. The king must have been very concerned about the future of his bastards to have to elevate them at every opportunity and then to beg his legitimate children to sanction this incredible breach of custom.[42]

CHAPTER 26

The Incalculable Consequences
of a Woman's Affair

On 1 January 1710, the Minister of Foreign Affairs, Torcy, more pessimistic than ever, dipped his pen in the blackest of ink to confide his anxieties to his journal. Soon the war would begin again. The coffers were empty; the stores were empty; the wheat granaries were empty. People's hopes were in the same state; the enemy was expected at the gates of Paris before the summer.[1] Should they negotiate, then? But they had already been negotiating for two months in the greatest secrecy with Petkum, the official intermediary of the year before. It was simply that no progress had been made. In mid-January, a new benevolent intermediary presented himself in the person of Monsieur Florisson, a merchant at Ypres. He sounded rather more encouraging. Despite their stubbornness, the Dutch seemed more willing to reach a peace. But it was important to get an agreement with them before Marlborough and Eugène arrived at The Hague and made them change their mind. The council went on and on, the minister could not agree, the king could not make up his mind. As usual, they met in Maintenon's bedchamber. She lay in her bed and did not say a word. Suddenly, emerging from her usual reserve, she told her husband that there was only one thing to do: get peace at any price. 'He resisted, he struggled, in the end he gave in.' Torcy put down on paper the 'price' envisaged, for the benefit of Petkum who would take these propositions to Heinsius. The archduke would be recognized as the king of Spain, Philip v abandoned to his fate, Alsace ceded, the fortifications in eastern France and Dunkirk demolished, the barrier of Flemish towns handed over to Holland. It was only on receipt of these written propositions that the Dutch granted their passports to the French representatives, an icy soldier, the Maréchal d'Huxelles, and a voluble prelate, the Abbé de Polignac.

On arrival in Holland, they were confined, almost put under arrest, in an inn in the small town of Gertruydenberg. There were no real negotiations. The Dutch listened in haughty silence to the propositions of the French, left for The Hague to discuss them, came back with counter-propositions, which they announced without comment, then left again. Meanwhile Marlborough and Eugène had arrived in The Hague and, once again, took charge of matters.[2] They were unanimously accused of making any agreement impossible by their demands, certain that they would bring France to her knees in the next campaign.[3] But there was also a suspicion on their part which the Dutch shared, even though they were ready to come to an agreement with France. Louis had deceived people only too often. He declared that he was ready to recognize the archduke, but might he not support Philip v in secret? That he would refuse to assist in dethroning him by force was conceivable, but would he persuade his grandson to abdicate? The allies did not wish to be engaged in a long war in Spain to expel Philip v, while Louis, having withdrawn from the fray, stood by, enjoying the peace that they had given him.

Tired of ruminating about Louis' possible calculations, the allies finally played their master card: the king of France must commit himself to ridding Spain of Philip by force if necessary. 'I shall never promise or even consider agreeing to waging war on my grandson,' Louis cried. Torcy insisted: what should he reply to the allies? 'Play for time,' the king ordered him. So Torcy had to try and find a formula that rejected the allies' demands without breaking off negotiations. The allies agreed to continue negotiations – while starting the war up again.[4]

Marlborough and Eugène calmly marched straight for the lines erected by Villars the previous year. Villars himself might have been able to contain them; despite his swagger and his errors, despite the virulent criticisms that had been levied at him, he was the only possible general to put in against them. But Villars had not recovered from his wounds;[5] he was to be seen every day limping pitiably around Versailles. However, the Chevalier de Quincy remarked that his limping became noticeably more marked as he approached the king's apartments, whereas at home he sometimes managed not to limp at all.[6] The cunning marshal had realized that he could not pull off the success of the previous year again and that his fine lines were sure to be breached by the enemy, so he preferred to let the Maréchal de Montesquiou get defeated in his place. Poor Montesquiou was so badly informed of the enemy's movements that he sent his soldiers looking for forage on the very day the enemy were attacking him. He had no alternative but to order a retreat. The demoralized soldiers made up a little song: 'Montesquiou, montre ton cul.' ('Montesquiou, show your arse.') To cap everything the marshal's secretary disappeared with all his papers and secret codes; he had long been in Eugène's pay and was afraid that he was about to be caught.[7]

On 22 April 1710, the enemies invested Douai and began a siege. Soon Arras and Cambrai were to submit to the same fate. Villars begged the king to accept the enemy's demands, to get peace at any price. If the war continued, the enemy would be at the gates of Paris, the monarchy would be forced to abandon Versailles, France would be given over to anarchy, perhaps to a revolution. Louis kept his imperturbable calm: he had considered all these risks.[8] He decided in view of the urgency of the situation to send Villars in person to head the army. Villars accepted. He had announced unequivocally that the country was on the verge of disaster, so he had cleared himself in advance of the defeats that he was certain he would be subjected to.

He was already driving towards the frontier when he received an urgent message from the king together with a letter from the Maréchal de Montesquiou to His Majesty to the effect that the army was in perfect readiness and would be able to resist the enemy. Villars re-read the very different letter that Montesquiou had just sent him, in which he had admitted that the army was short of everything, the fortifications were not armed, the stores were empty, the troops had neither weapons nor bread. By return messenger, Villars sent Louis the letter that Montesquiou had sent him, asking His Majesty to judge which of the two reports was true.[9]

On 28 May, Torcy received a new proposition from the Dutch: they agreed to persuade their allies to get Sicily and Sardinia for Philip v but, even before discussing peace, the king must agree in writing to remove Philip from the throne of Spain; they left the choice of means to him . . .

On 1 June, Louis made up his mind at last: he would not wage war on his grandson, but he was ready to offer 'a considerable sum' to the allies to assist them in doing so.[10]

On 5 June, at eleven in the evening, Louis learnt that at the Carmelite convent in Paris, Louise de la Miséricorde, one of the lay sisters, had been found in a faint on the cloister flagstones. The Great Winter of 1709-10 appeared to have claimed yet another victim in the person of the former Duchesse de La Vallière. The terrible cold in the convent had combined with hunger to kill off a body already weakened by penances and fasts. The novices were very surprised when told that this skeletal, pale nun, bent almost double by illness, had once been the favourite of the old king back in his twenties. 'I am happy to die,' the old woman murmured as she was taken to the infirmary. The doctor could do nothing to assuage the pains that contracted her body and twisted her face. Not a single complaint left her lips. It was right that a sinner should die in the greatest pain. She died at midday as the Angelus bell was ringing. 'She died for me the day she she joined the Carmelites,' the king remarked. To have preferred God to him – that he could never forgive. And when the daughter that he had had by the dead woman, the Princesse de Conti, came to beg him to allow her to wear mourning for her mother, he gave in to her tears with bitter reluctance.[11]

On 25 June, the city of Douai fell after a heroic siege. The allies went on to take, without a fight, Béthune, Aire and Saint-Venant. A member of the English high command proposed a thrust in the direction of Paris. Villars could have done nothing to stop them; he and his troops were exhausted. His wound began opportunely to trouble him again, and he asked to be recalled.[12]

At Gertruydenberg, Huxelles and Polignac could not contain their impatience. Would the Dutch accept that 'enormous sum' that the king of France proposed to wage war on his grandson? The Dutch demanded guarantees, knowing that France was on the verge of bankruptcy. Huxelles and Polignac named several banks. 'What if they collapsed?' the Dutch persisted.[13]

On 29 June, Torcy read the latest letter from the Dutch to the council of ministers: would the king of France commit himself in writing to expel Philip v of Spain with his own troops, within two months. If so, they would agree to a truce, but if, after two months, Philip v was still in Spain, war would resume. That was all.[14] Then, in front of his ministers, the Sun King wept: 'I can neither continue the war nor obtain peace,' he repeated.[15] In any case, this parody of negotiations could not go on. The Dutch had always claimed that it was the French who had broken off negotiations and indeed, Huxelles and Polignac had left Gertruydenberg on 25 July. Petkum had done all he could to avoid the breakdown, running backwards and forwards between the two camps. On leaving, one of the Frenchmen – we do not know which one – remarked: 'Before long, you'll see the English commander in disgrace, the present minister fallen and parliament dissolved.' Petkum thought he had gone mad.

Marlborough and Eugène pushed the French to breaking point – it is even said that Eugène had a plan up his sleeve to divide France.[16] And yet . . . 'Play for time,' Louis had repeated to Torcy, as if he expected some event that would turn the situation round, as if he expected Marlborough and Eugène to precipitate events. Anyway soon Louis would no longer have to expel his grandson from Spain since the archduke's troops set about doing it for him. On 20 August 1710, they carried off a crushing victory over Philip's miserable troops at Saragossa.

The archduke was bearing down on Madrid. Once again, the time for exodus had come for King Philip. Queen Maria Louisa appeared on the balcony of the royal palace and, holding up her son, the infant Prince of the Asturias, made a moving speech to the huge crowd that had gathered below. Quite spontaneously, the inhabitants of the capital decided to follow their legitimate monarchs on the road to exile. By coach, by cart, even on foot, Grandees, tradesmen, artisans, servants, pregnant women, priests and children left everything behind. 'Illness, old age, poverty, suspicions of infidelity, none of these reasons held anyone back,' noted Torcy. The archduke entered 'his' capital, only to find it empty. The Court retired to Valladolid, but soon the queen was sent to Vitoria, nearer to France, just in case . . . 'We are all dying of cold and a thousand other inconveniences caused by the freezing houses in which we live,' wrote the Princesse des Ursins to Torcy, 'but all this is as nothing when one is as pleased as we are. I wait with the greatest impatience that you do me the honour to tell me that you are too. You would be good for nothing if you did not share these feelings.' Despite the catastrophic situation, morale remained high among the refugees of the Spanish Court. This was because Philip, though deprived of troops, had the vast majority of Spaniards behind him.[17] The Princesse des Ursins hoped that things were the same at Versailles, but her threatening joke to Torcy seems to imply that she did not think that they were. She was right. Morale was even so low that the defeat of Saragossa paradoxically was almost welcome. This was an opportunity to persuade Philip to abdicate at last. At the council of 9 September 1710, Louis did not beat about the bush: he announced that he would send at once some trusted councillor to persuade his grandson to give up his throne.[18]

Throughout those terrible years of 1709-10, historians present a heroic Louis XIV, facing up to a desperate situation, nobly refusing to drop his grandson at the risk of seeing his own kingdom occupied and stripped. In fact, his attitude was much more mysterious, because it was complex and inconsistent. He refused to wage war on his grandson in order to dethrone him but, on several occasions, he advised him discreetly to abdicate. One senses that at the worst moments, Louis wished that Philip might leave of his own accord, but that somehow he refused to give up. Behind his official desire to negotiate, which had even taken in his own ministers, one suspects a delaying tactic. The allies were presented as ogres impatient to devour France, but Louis had actually forced them into this evil role. Marlborough and Eugène may have wanted to take personal revenge on Louis, but they had also sought an accommodation, only to find from the outset that they were up against a brick wall in the person of Louis himself. He offered them enormous concessions but he had always equivocated when confronted with the far less serious concessions demanded of him. So, before this mixture of weakness and obstinancy, their attitude had hardened. For the first time in his reign, Louis XIV was confronted with a situation that he did not control — even if he was ultimately the cause of it — and a tragic situation. For the first time, too, he was alone; the great ministers who used to create his will every day, were dead. So he wavered: on the one hand, essentially weak as he was, he went on deceiving everyone, his ministers as well as his enemies; on the other hand, he changed his mind over and over again. His attitude was often almost incomprehensible, because he himself probably did not fully understand. What did he want? His ministers, his enemies, his grandson all asked themselves this question. Did he even know himself? 'Play for time,' meant wait and see.

He finally made up mind to urge Philip to abdicate just after negotiations had broken down on that very question. The Duc de Noailles was chosen to open up this delicate mission. Noailles arrived at Philip's residence at Valladolid the same day as Vendôme, the disgraced general whom Louis had just sent him as a crumb from the rich man's table. They had been reduced to a terrible state. Instead of an army

367

Vendôme brought with him only the little 'Abbé' Alberoni, son of the Duke of Parma's gardener, who had so cleverly won his heart by outrageous flattery of his backside.

'I always prefer to put myself in God's hands by fighting, rather than to abandon people on whom my misfortunes have produced no other effect than to increase their zeal and their affection for me,' Philip replied firmly. Noailles' mission had failed. On the other hand, Vendôme performed miracles. His presence hardened the determination of the Spanish to resist the invader. Towns, bishops and hidalgos sent money and arms to Valladolid. Volunteers rushed to join up. It was, said Saint-Simon, 'a sudden, universal conspiracy of unshakeable fidelity.'[19] Within a few weeks Philip found himself with an army of 12,000, soon of 15,000, men, well-equipped, well-fed and well-armed. Without wasting time, Vendôme bore down on the imperial and English troops, who hastily retreated. The archduke abandoned Madrid for a second time and Philip v re-entered his capital on 2 December 1710, to the cheers of a deliriously joyful crowd.

In these circumstances there was no longer any question of the Duc de Noailles talking of abdication. Louis put him at the head of the troops that he was sending into Catalonia to support those of his grandson. He had moved without transition from pressure for an abdication to quasi-unconditional support. No wonder the allies could not understand what was happening. Volunteers, equipment and ammunition continued to flow towards Vendôme. He forced the enemy to retreat to Portugal and, hot on their heels, crossed the Tagus behind them, captured the town of Brihuega and took the English commander, Lord Stanhope, prisoner with his 5,000 soldiers, caught up with the imperial troops at Villaviciosa and on 11 December 1710 carried off a crushing victory of them with the effective help of Philip v. The supporters of unconditional peace were disappointed. With a victorious Philip v secure on his throne, there was no longer any question of gently easing him out, no longer any question of an agreement with the allies: France would certainly be invaded. Maintenon herself admitted that she did not know whether she should rejoice or weep over the victory at Villaviciosa.[20] Louis' reaction was even stranger. Publicly he expressed his satisfaction but when Torcy suggested sending someone to congratulate his grandson he flatly refused. To the council which poured praise on Philip, he snapped: 'It was Vendôme who did it all.'[21] Was there a touch of jealousy on the part of the Sun King with regard to his grandson? The unfortunate orphan whom he had nobly protected against all and sundry had been transformed into a victorious and popular king and this, though he did not admit it, was not to Louis' liking. He had refused to get rid of Philip during the negotiations, tried to force him to abdicate when those negotiations broke down, sent the individual who was supposed to get him to abdicate at the head of troops who were supposed to support him, then pulled a face when he crushed the enemy – Louis' fluctuations had reached the limits of incoherence.

With taxes tripled, commodities taxed up to 400 per cent, the currency devalued, the circulation of money interrupted, the insolvent state could pay out only in paper and Saint-Simon floundered among this mass of valueless notes, 'bills of state, currency bills, tax-collectors' bills, toll bills, utensil bills ...' In short, 'chaos' in administration and the ruin of all private citizens reigned supreme. Only speculators and charlatans prospered. Boudin, the Dauphin's first physician, ruined himself in spite of his meanness to pay for the researches of an alchemist, whose work was closely observed by the most serious of the ministers.[22] But there was still no gold.[23] The infernal Desmarets then submitted a project to the king so monstrous that Saint-Simon recoiled in horror: a tax of 10 per cent on the value of the wealth of every Frenchman, a pitiless inventory having been previously drawn up. Louis himself was no less horrified. In the grip of the deepest depression, he hesitated for a week, then confided in his confessor, Le Tellier. The good father ran to consult the doctors of the Sorbonne: 'All the wealth of all his subjects properly belongs to the king and when he takes it, he takes only what is his.' His conscience reassured by the oracle of the professors, Louis at last gave his authorization to Desmarets. 'And so this bloody affair was rushed through, among stifled sobs.'[24]

On the evening of 21 January 1711, the servants of Versailles were surprised to see a poor, simple priest pass through the corridors – he had a dirty beard, thick shoes and threadbare soutane. Was he one of Mme de Maintenon's protégés? No, he was being conducted to the office of the Minister of Foreign Affairs. Torcy did not know him but had been warned of his visit. The Abbé Gaultier had arrived from London in a most roundabout way. 'Do you want peace?' he asked. Torcy managed to remain impassive but, later, was to write in his journal : 'To ask a Minister of Louis XIV if he wished for peace was like asking a dying man if he wished to get well.' This incredible message did not entirely surprise Torcy.[25] They were fairly accurately informed at Versailles as to what was happening on the other side of the Channel, in particular of the misdeeds of the devil in skirts, Sarah Marlborough. Instead of proving conciliatory since her rival Abigail had overtaken her in the queen's favour, she had become even more unpleasant. Behind Abigail, in the shadows, the Tories of the opposition were standing impatiently by. The immense expenditure committed by the Whig government to the war, the loss in human life of the blood-bath battles, the poor advantages that England would derive from a peace treaty had gradually shifted public opinion against the war and brought the isolationist Tories back into power. The delicious champagne suppers to which the Maréchal Tallard, former French ambassador in England who had come back to London as a prisoner of war, invited his English friends made them see France in a more conciliatory light. But nothing could be done as long as Sarah was around. She held the army through her husband, she held the Whigs in power and packed the government with her own creatures, she held the queen through their thirty-year-old relationship and through the key to her apartment. The Tories longed to take that accursed key off her.

'Give me justice and do not reply.' (Signed). Freeman.' But, this time, 'Mrs Morley' (Anne) did not reply to 'Freeman' (Sarah), she did not summon her, she did not beg. Freeman ran to the palace, asked forgiveness, wept. 'You desired no answer and shall have none,' Mrs Morley repeated. And she asked Freeman to give her back the celebrated key. Freeman refused, protested, screamed, fought like a madwoman ... and in the end handed over the key. 'I shall publish that tart's letters,' Sarah repeated throughout London. 'Anyway the queen has secretly received her brother, she is in the pay of France.' The terrible accusation flew from mouth to mouth. Anne, pilloried by public opinion, might be overthrown and the Whigs, who supported the war, become more powerful than ever. The Tories shuddered at the idea of Marlborough and Sarah reigning without challenge.

At about this time an Anglican clergyman, Dr Henry Sacheverell, delivered a sermon in St Paul's Cathedral. His sermons mentioned God and touched on the Gospels, but above all, they were violent attacks on the Whig administration: he used whatever he could lay his hands on – the cost of the war, the loss of human life, the prevarications of the Lord Treasurer Marlborough's depravity. The Tories had chosen their man well. Parliament, shaken by the Whigs, intervened and prosecuted the preacher. The debate turned on the prerogative of the monarchy. Abigail advised Anne to go in person to hear what the Whigs were saying. The queen disguised herself and went, incognito, to the Commons, where she heard Sarah's party ask for a limitation of her powers. Parliament found Sacheverell guilty but failed by one vote to disqualify him from preferment in the Church for three years. The queen, however, had decided – as far as she could – to rid herself of the Whigs. Sarah was forbidden to appear at Court, her son-in-law was dropped from the cabinet and, once by one, Tory ministers supplanted their Whig adversaries.

There was no question, however, of replacing Marlborough – he was still too powerful; or speaking openly of peace – the new government was too weak.[26] So, while affirming his determination to continue the war, he was looking for a way of discreetly opening negotiations with France. It was then that Lord Jersey, a pillar of the Tory party, mentioned the Abbé Gaultier – or rather it was Lady Jersey who did so. As she often went to mass in the private chapel of the emperor's ambassador, Count Gallas, she often noticed the French chaplain. She talked about the Abbé Gaultier to her husband. Lord Jersey talked about him to his friends Shrewsbury and Harley, two Tory ministers. With their consent, he gave Gaultier a mission to go to Versailles. The mission was to be carried out in the utmost secrecy since the two ministers would risk their heads if the truth came out; naturally, they did not inform the other ministers in the cabinet. Gaultier was in fact a dormant spy, left by Tallard. He scarcely moved about, he made his presence as unobtrusive as possible, but he heard interesting things at the embassy and, from time to time, sent information to Versailles by the safest possible route. Of course he accepted the mission and, on the evening of 21 January 1711, found himself opposite Torcy.[27] Torcy ran to inform the king, who had been awaiting this message for months. At last his equivocal attitude during the negotiations at Gertruydenberg had been vindicated. However, he advised caution. Torcy, who distrusted the Abbé Gaultier, repeated this advice to himself. It was too marvellous, too unhoped for, too sudden, and anyway that old priest in his threadbare soutane did not inspire confidence. Gaultier, on the other hand, thought the business was already concluded and asked for an immediate opening of fresh negotiations with the Dutch, whom the English agreed to trick in the interests of peace. Torcy rejected the suggestion out of hand. 'Give me at least a written message for our English friends,' Gaultier persisted. Torcy was as mistrustful as ever. They also worked out ways of communicating in the future. Torcy would write to 'Mr Christopher Bryan at London', Gaultier would write to 'Sieur des Fournelles, compositor at the Gazette, Rotterdam'.

In London the two ministers were disappointed by this display of French prudence. Gaultier wrote many letters to beg Louis XIV at least to make a gesture, but no word came from Versailles. The Abbé was on tenterhooks. Marlborough was about to join up with Eugène and the new campaign would destroy any hope of negotiation. 'Such an opportunity will never present itself again,' he wrote on 27 February ... 'Otherwise the Duke of Marlborough might win another battle, the queen fall back into the hands of the Whigs and God knows where it will all end.' Versailles acknowledged receipt of the message, but made no move. Unable to bear it any longer the Abbé set off on a short pilgrimage – to France. He lingered in the provinces, visited churches and convents and did his best to track down spies. The longest of his pious visits was at Torcy's office, and on 6 April, he could at last announce to the English ministers that France officially proposed opening negotiations with the British government with a view to a general peace.[28]

On Easter Tuesday, 9 April 1711, the Dauphin was dressing for wolf-hunting when he had an attack of dizziness and sank on to his close stool. It was smallpox. The king hurried over to Meudon, though he hated the place, and took up residence there for the duration of the illness. Maintenon was lodged in another small castle nearby. Mlle Choin, Monseigneur's still unofficial wife, was relegated to a barn and Father Le Tellier, whom the King had brought with him in case he was needed, was hidden in another barn. Before long Monseigneur was covered in spots, a sign that the illness was following its most favourable course. The king began to get very bored, irritated at not being at home, and, to pass the time, he held two councils a day instead of one. In the afternoon of 14 April, the council for despatches dragged on and on, while everything was quiet at Meudon. Suddenly, about 4 o'clock, Monseigneur felt very much worse and it was suggested that the king be told. Fagon was strictly against such a step, yelling at everyone to be quiet, while Monseigneur's condition deteriorated by the minute. Not suspecting that anything was afoot, the king sat down to dinner. Meanwhile, in Monseigneur's bedroom, the physicians were beginning to lose their heads, Fagon included, and were indiscriminately getting the patient to swallow whatever remedies lay to hand. The parish priest passed by for news of the Dauphin as was usual each evening. He found a dying man who had already lost the power of speech. Physicians and servants were milling around him in utter confusion. The king was quietly getting up from the table when Fagon dashed in, looking extremely distraught, stammering and shouting: 'All is lost.' The king almost fainted with surprise and hurried to his son's room. His legs would hardly carry him and he collapsed on to a sofa in the antechamber. Maintenon joined him, sat down beside him and tried to weep, for good appearances. An hour later, Fagon appeared on the threshold of the Dauphin's bedroom; everyone understood. Maintenon managed to extricate the king from his lethargy and drag him out to his coach. The bereaved father, looking very haggard, was staggering.[29] But finding at the door of his coach his minister Ponchartrain, he ordered him to tell his colleagues to be at Marly the next morning for the regular session of the council of state. This cold self-control astounded the courtiers present.[30]

Arriving in the middle of the night at Marly, the king found all the gates locked and the castle in complete darkness. In view of the circumstances, everyone had assumed that he would give up spending the week-end in the country and nothing had been prepared. Trying all the doors, servants managed to break open that of Maintenon's antechamber and the king, Maintenon, princesses and ladies of honour piled in, in the dark – it was impossible to find a candle or a brand to light the fire. The few servants who were awake jumped up in terror, running in all directions, jangling enormous bunches of keys. In the darkened antechamber, the king sat beside Maintenon and wept in silence. His wife held his hand and adopted an appropriate expression to conceal her relief – she knew that Monseigneur had never liked her.

Next day, as arranged, the king presided over the council of State. He could hardly speak for emotion. Tears continued to flow down his cheeks. The ministers, not to be outdone, did likewise and the council proceeded in a deluge. Between two sobs, the inconsolable father made the arrangements for his son's funeral: a few ordinary coaches to carry the body to Saint-Denis and an escort of only twelve guards. Ministers objected that the public might be surprised to see the heir to the throne buried like a pauper. 'We must avoid unnecessary expense,'[31] the king replied. The prince, of whom a fortune-teller had predicted, 'son of a king, father of a king and never king',[32] was buried on the cheap.

Saint-Simon devoted some fifty pages to the Dauphin's death and a single paragraph to another death that occurred three days later, that of the emperor Joseph I, in Vienna, on 17 April 1711. And yet having only daughters, the emperor left his crowns to his brother, the archduke Charles. Already king of Spain and the Indies as far as the allies were concerned, Charles hastily accepted the inheritance. The allies had fought against the dangerous concentration of power threatened by the person of Philip v – the possible reunion of the crowns of Spain and France, but were suddenly faced with the same problem in a much more serious way in the person of their own candidate. They had not struggled with such determination to prevent Louis xiv from crossing the Pyrenees in order to allow the complete reconstruction of the empire of Charles v.

'We have a report of secret peace negotiations confirmed by a search that was lately made of some persons as they landed upon coming over from France,' wrote a certain Brydges to Marlborough. The English had stopped one of their compatriots at the frontier. The man, Prior, a tavern-boy turned poet, aroused their suspicions. To the amazement of the police, Prior showed them a passport signed by the English Foreign Secretary in person and they had to free him.[33] Prior was in fact the new negotiator chosen by the British cabinet to discuss terms with Versailles. Torcy listened to him without saying a word as he poured out his exorbitant demands. 'What is France to have from England in return for all this?' Torcy asked abruptly, realizing how anxious the English were to conclude a separate peace behind the backs and at the expense of their allies. 'Spain and the Indies for Philip v,' the poet replied. 'Have you Spain at your disposal, then?' Torcy enquired. Prior was taken aback by this rejoinder. Torcy pursued his advantage. He read the latest batch of Petkum's letters from Holland to Harley's envoy, from which it appeared or was made to appear, fearing an English desertion, that the Dutch were themselves ready to enter into private negotiations with France.

Marlborough, too, wanted to take control of his government by blocking negotiations with victories. He launched an offensive, breached the new lines set up by Villars, and laid siege to the important fortress of Bouchain, one of the last along the northern frontier still held by the French. Villars tried in vain to help the besieged town and to establish supply lines to them. Bouchain surrendered with its garrison on 11 September 1711. There were practically no ramparts between Marlborough and Paris. But Marlborough had other dangers facing him at home in London, so he hastily ended the campaign and returned there.

This time the French chose a Norman negotiator, the Sieur Ménager, to continue talks in London; he was protected from the curiosity of spies by being lodged with a midwife. He was only allowed to go out at night to talk with the ministers. The English still claimed Gibraltar and other Spanish fortresses.[34] But Spain did not belong to Louis xiv and Louis felt obliged to consult his grandson. Anyway, he added, in a note to Philip, there is no alternative but to give in. Philip v let his grandfather know that he found his note excessively harsh but reluctantly gave his authority to make some concessions subject to his previous authority. Given this, Louis lost no time in giving in to the British demands. 'Do not be surprised if I have interpreted your power without consulting you. To have Your Majesty's reply would have meant losing valuable time and I believe I can work usefully for you by ceding the least in order to keep the principal.'[35]

'No one has doubted until now that the Jesuits have been the principal cause of all my present misfortunes.' The Society of Jesus had never agreed to bury the hatchet with Cardinal de Noailles. For several months now bishops, urged on by the king's confessor Father Le Tellier, had flooded France with letters denouncing the iniquities of the Archbishop of Paris. On each occasion Noailles had replied with a bombardment of pastoral letters until he himself had had enough and held fire. In early September he learnt that Le Tellier in person was summoning up the most ignorant bishops he could find to extort from them letters accusing him, Noailles, of having installed heresy at the very heart of the Church of France. Noailles mysteriously obtained written proof of this plot, sent them to Maintenon and asked her to get Le Tellier removed from his position. Maintenon would not be drawn. 'It is not for me to judge and condemn; I can only keep silent and pray for the Church, for the king and for you.'[36] It is clear that Noailles did not know Maintenon's fear, timidity and apathy, in requesting her to take the initiative in attacking Le Tellier and opposing her husband.

Meanwhile Le Tellier, realizing that he had been out-manoeuvred, had so worked upon the king that when Noailles brought the sovereign the evidence, too much time had elapsed and he was given a frosty reception. In fact the proof against Le Tellier's activities was the last straw that finally threw the king's mind into confusion. He knew, deep down, that the whole campaign against Noailles was neither clear nor just. But Le Tellier was there, beside him, present, powerful, brutal. He was afraid of the confessor-dictator as he had been afraid of the minister-dictators. He dared not say anything. In doubt and uncertainty he took refuge behind a mask of haughty majesty. Disconcerted, Noailles did not push his advantage. But then, confident that he was in the right, he suspended three Jesuits, convicted of being the principal architects of the epistolary attacks of the bishops. Howls of indignation rose up from Le Tellier and the Society. The king was indignant. He demanded that Noailles return the powers of confession and preaching to the three Jesuits. At his wits' end, Noailles dared to ask Maintenon to persuade the sovereign to take charge of the situation himself. 'You treat the affair of the Jesuits as a spiritual affair,' Maintenon replied tit for tat, 'and His Majesty regards it as a vendetta.' Once more, Maintenon had dropped a dear friend out of fear of being compromised. Once more, Louis, asked to interfere against dishonesty and injustice but held back by those around him, had not had the courage to intervene. As usual when harassed in this way, his wife pretended she could not hear and her husband assumed the mask of the Sun King.

On 6 October 1711, the English minister, Bolingbroke, was waiting until nightfall to take Ménager through the dark passages of Windsor Castle to the drawing-room where the queen was waiting. 'I hate war and bloodshed,' Anne told him, infinitely relieved that the agreement between France and England could at last be signed. The English were euphoric, for they had got everything they had wanted. 'Of two nations let us make only a single nation of friends,' Harley said to Ménager.[37] One small formality remained: the English would have to inform their allies that they had negotiated behind their backs. They published the agreement. The howls of protest from the allies could be heard in London as their ambassadors did not mince their words. The English ministers, convinced that they were in the right, refused to be intimidated. 'You're a firebrand.' the ambassador of Holland was told; while the emperor's ambassador was quite simply threatened with being thrown out of the window.

Marlborough, threatened by the Tories in power, preferred to leave England with Sarah, and Prince Eugène was in ill-repute with the new emperor Charles VI. With the troublemakers out of the way preparations could quietly go ahead for the international peace conference that was to open at Utrecht in Holland. Queen Anne had already appointed her chief negotiators. and the Dutch had sent their passports to the French, when a difficulty cropped up. Philip wanted Spain to have a place at the conference table and the allies wanted to deal only with Louis XIV.

Philip's mealy-mouthed grandfather wrote back: 'You can count on my tenderest feelings and I shall do nothing to your prejudice.' But his grandson considered that Louis juggled rather too easily with his possessions. 'You have promised,' his grandfather reminded him.[38] A promise is a promise, the grandson bitterly conceded, but on condition that a small part of the territories ceded to Bavaria should be turned into a principality for the Princesse des Ursins. It was right and proper, surely, to guarantee the retirement of a friend who had shown such devotion, such good and loyal service for so many years. Louis agreed to the principality, so his grandson at last gave him the *carte blanche* so long awaited in order to begin the negotiations.[39]

CHAPTER 27

Unexpected Reversals

'I have a feeling that peace will be declared and that I shall die without seeing it,' the Duchesse de Bourgogne declared, for no apparent reason.[1] The guests started. The king, Adelaide and a few female friends were lunching privately in Mme de Maintenon's apartment. Maintenon reassured her, but Louis assumed a serious air. A few days before, Boudin, Adelaide's physician, had warned him that attempts were being made to poison Adelaide and her husband.[2] The same opinion had arrived simultaneously from Spain, from where Philip v had written to his brother, the Duc de Bourgogne, to warn him.[3]

On the evening of 5 February 1712, Adelaide began to shiver violently. She had a fever and pains in her temples. The physician hoped that it was only measles. On the morning of 11 February she was so ill that it was decided to broach the subject of extreme unction. Adelaide was shocked – she did not think she was that ill – but she resigned herself to it and confessed at length. The physicians wanted her to get up so that they could bleed her. 'At least wait until she is sweating more,' advised the Palatine, but Fagon insisted. Maintenon lashed into the Palatine, 'Do you consider yourself to be more skilful than all the doctors here?' 'No, Madame, but one does not have to be very skilful to know that one should follow nature,' that is, let the patient sweat it out. So she was bled – and became deathly pale. The physicians, too ignorant to recognize measles, thus prevented the eruption of the disease and condemned their patient to death. In the evening of 12 February she went into her death throes. Even before she died, the king and Maintenon fled to Marly to hide their grief.[4]

Next morning, Saint-Simon, entering the Duc de Bourgogne's apartments to convey his condolences, was terrified by his appearance. His poor face was covered with red patches. He stood there, motionless as a statue, without saying a word, with the fixed stare of a madman. His gentleman suggested that he go and see the king, who had just woken up. Bourgogne did not move, heard nothing, said nothing. Saint-Simon came up to him and spoke to him quietly, but was answered by the same stare. Saint-Simon took him by the arm. Bourgogne then seemed to awake from a long nightmare and threw a piteous look at Saint-Simon.

The king, also terrified by his grandson's appearance, had his pulse taken by the physicians, who found it bad and sent him to bed. During the next few days, the fever rose. The patient complained of a 'devouring fire' that burned him from within. On Thursday 18 February 1712, at dawn, he was given extreme unction and died at half-past eight in the morning. The physicians had struck a second time.[5]

On Sunday 6 March, the dead couple's two young sons – five and a half and two years old – who had also caught measles were suddenly much worse. The king ordered them to be baptized as a matter of urgency, then abandoned them to their physician-executioners, who took the elder, bled him profusely and brought him to the threshold of death. 'Mother,' the child said to his governess, the Duchesse de Ventadour, 'I dreamt that I was in heaven, and was not too hot there, but all the little angels beat their wings around me to keep me cool.' He died on 7 March at ten in the evening. Meanwhile, the Duchesse de Ventadour had, on her own initiative, snatched the younger brother from the hands of physicians and let the illness follow its normal course, thus saving the life of the future king.[6]

The physicians, however, wanted to justify themselves for wiping out the royal family. When the autopsies were carried out Fagon and Boudin went and told the king that Adelaide and her husband had been poisoned. Louis paled. There it was again, that dreaded word! His surgeon, the faithful Maréchal, interposed: no tangible proof of poison had been found. Fagon and Boudin lost their temper and would not give up their poison theory. In the end the king was convinced, decided to hear no more about it and ordered no second opinion. They must catch the criminal at once. Maréchal tried to reason with him, to stop him sliding further down the slippery slope of suspicion. 'Everyone knows who was responsible,' Maintenon interrupted him. It was the Duc d'Orléans. 'It could only be him,' confirmed the king. Fagon nodded. 'There can be no doubt that it is the duke,' Boudin added.

Maintenon's 'so constantly beloved nurseling', the Duc de Maine, rubbed his hands with glee on hearing the news. So successful was he in repeating it that in a few days the rumour had spread with the speed of lightning through the salons to the street, from Paris to the most distant provinces. The Duc d'Orléans himself heard the terrible accusation thrown at him by a hate-filled crowd when he went to pay his last respects to his dead relation.[7] Maintenon, who had never got over the 'con-capitaine' insult, lost no opportunity of aggravating the king's suspicions. She did not take her revenge coldly, cynically, as the 'con-lieutenant', the Princesse des Ursins, might have done against the same Duc d'Orléans; she was sincerely horrified, she believed the Duc d'Orléans to be a poisoner. Treated by everyone as if he had brought the plague, the Duc d'Orléans went to the king in desperation and offered to put himself in the Bastille. Louis refused to imprison his nephew, but replied with an air of such disgust and contempt that his feelings were made all too clear. Once again, Louis had been misled by his natural mistrust and by those around him. His good sense stopped him on the verge of injustice and scandal, but his weakness prevented him from quietly ordering a proper investigation. So he walled himself up in his silence and suspicion. The rumours abated but, to the end of his life, Louis was to keep his nephew in quarantine and the Duc d'Orléans continued to be subjected even beyond death to the absurd accusation.

Hardly a month had gone by since this cascade of deaths than Louis, at Marly once again, ordered the gaming tables, which had been removed for the period of mourning, to be put back into the drawing-rooms. He himself, in Maintenon's room, resumed his card-playing with his wife's old female friends.[8]

In Spain, everything was going well for Vendôme. He had just been made a 'Highness' and 'he luxuriated in the charms of his new lot'. Before resuming operations against the enemy, which still held the northwest of Spain, he took a rest with a few companions in debauch at Viñeroz, a lonely township on the Valencia coast, famed for its excellent fish. The gourmet indulged himself to such an extent that he died of indigestion on 11 June 1712.[9] Left without a job, the secretary-factotum Alberoni found himself a small niche in the Spanish court, then wormed his way into the favour of the Princesse des Ursins, flattering and amusing her. For the French princess who hated Spanish stews, he prepared the incomparable pasta dishes that had already won him the heart of the late Vendôme. He was so successful that shortly afterwards, when the Duke of Parma felt the need for a representative in Madrid and did not know who to choose, the Princesse des Ursins offered him his compatriot, Alberoni. Already a good cook, he was to become a perfect ambassador. Alberoni had fallen on his feet once more.[10]

'Two trifles occurred in Flanders during March,' Saint-Simon announced. The enemy troops came and bombarded Arras and the future Maréchal de Broglie took Sluys Castle, killing or taking prisoner 800 of the enemy. Hostilities had resumed despite the opening of the peace conference at Utrecht, for Eugène had done his work. From the opening of negotiations, he drove around Utrecht and had the satisfaction of noting the astonishment of the Dutch and imperial representatives at French arrogance. It was inconceivable that an exhausted, moribund, impoverished, unarmed, defenceless France, almost annihilated, had the impudence to dictate its own conditions. There could no longer be any question of recognizing the archduke, who had now become emperor, as king of Spain. Spain belonged to Philip v. The Dutch, furious at having been overtaken by the English, thought only of humiliating France.[11] The emperor may have detested Eugène, but he wanted Spain and he knew that only Eugène alone could give it him by crushing France.[12] Eugène welded the scattered frustrations and desire for vengeance into a common will, collected money and troops from everybody, including the English who, despite their agreement with

France, did not dare to desert their alliance completely – and gathered a formidable army.[13]

To begin with, Louis took his by now ritual measure: in early April 1712, he summoned Villars and put him in command of his army. 'Should any misfortune befall the army that you command, what would your feelings be as to the course I should have to take concerning my person?' the king asked him. An embarrassed Villars did not reply, and Louis replied in his place: 'I know all the reasonings of courtiers: almost everyone thinks that I should retire to Blois and should not wait for the enemy army to approach Paris, which would be possible if mine were beaten ... Personally ... I would expect ... to gather together whatever troops I had and make a final effort with you and either perish with you or save the State, for I shall never consent to let the enemy approach the capital.'[14] It was only after holding out for several years in the worst adversity, it was only when he had just pulled off a major coup in detaching England from the alliance, it was only when the peace conferences were opening that Louis confronted the most desperate situation and envisaged the worst. He knew what Eugène was capable of. One of his lieutenants had already penetrated into eastern France with 2,000 cavalry, looting and devastating the villages of Champagne and Lorraine, and Eugène was moving in the direction of Cambrai. Villars, abandoning his lines on the Scheldt, hurried to the defence of that city. Eugène, having pulled off his feint, calmly crossed the Scheldt at the head of 100,000 men and laid siege to Le Quesnoy, one of the few places still defending Champagne.

On 6 July, Le Quesnoy capitulated. 'The main point is whether England will pass over to the enemy,' Eugène wrote in his report to the emperor.[15] Indeed, the English were quite willing to wage war for appearances' sake, in order to show respect for the alliance that they had betrayed, but they were not at all willing to let Eugène crush France.[16] So after the fall of Le Quesnoy they negotiated a truce with the French. Louis left them Dunkirk by way of a tip and they pulled out of the war. This, it was hoped, would stop Eugène, but they badly misjudged him. After fierce bargaining, he withdrew the foreign contingent, paid for by England and ready to defect with their paymaster.[17] Thanks to this his army maintained a numerical superiority over the French and he laid siege to Landrecies. 'I do not think that Landrecies is capable of stopping the enemy for long,' Louis confided to the Duc d'Harcourt.[18] He was relaxing at Fontainebleau, according to his immutable programme, and listened to the ever-worsening reports. Villars had let the enemy pass the Scheldt, Villars had let Le Quesnoy be taken, Villars was about to let Landrecies fall. Why the devil did he never fight? Villars might have replied, with what? With troops inferior in number, armaments and training? 'All this, Madame, does not make the stay at Fontainebleau as entertaining as one might have expected,' reported the Maréchal de Tessé to the Princesse des Ursins. 'We often go hunting, we gamble a great deal, we eat well. The women, at least some of them, even do what men used to do alone, thirty years ago, that is to say, go riding night and day, drink almost more wine than water and bring as much disorder into their families with gambling as men used to do to please.'[19] Despite the activities of these shameful females, despite the gaiety that the holiday protocol demanded, the atmosphere was heavy and everyone was deeply anxious. The courtiers were convinced that the retreat of the Court to the Loire had already been decided. What is the good of that? the king asked himself. If Landrecies fell, then the enemy were at the gates of Paris; there would be no France left to withstand them. 'The taking of Landrecies and the entry into Champagne will decide the fortune of my kingdom,' he repeated. On 23 July, a messenger informed him that Villars was moving towards Denain. Why Denain? the king exploded in impotent rage. Why not go to the assistance of Landrecies? All was lost.[20]

It was six in the morning, on 25 July 1712. In her room overlooking the courtyard of the Cheval Blanc, the Marquise de Rouvroy was still asleep. The sound of galloping horses suddenly woke her. That's it, she said to herself. Landrecies has fallen and the Court has fled. She rushed to the window and hailed the first person she saw: 'What is happening?' 'The Marquis de Nangis has just arrived from the army. Apparently he brings good news, for the king rose at once and ordered the singing of a *Te Deum* in his chapel.' The Marquise de Rouvroy dressed quickly and ran out for more information. It was then that she learnt the miraculous news. The day before, at Denain, Villars had annihilated Prince Eugène's army.[21]

A week earlier, a councillor from the city of Douai, Le Fèvre d'Orval, walking in the area, had observed the enemy's positions: in order to lay siege to Landrecies, Eugène had left all his supplies at Marchiennes, with an army corps under the command of Lord Albemarle, at Denain between Marchiennes and Landrecies. Two things struck Le Fèvre d'Orval: the line of communication between Marchiennes and Landrecies was too stretched and Albemarle's position at Denain very weak. He conveyed his observations to Villars, who sent a large corps of dragoons to Landrecies in order to trick Eugène, then sent most of his army to Denain. The march took place at night in complete silence in order not to alert Albemarle. Suddenly, shots were fired. An alert – but it turned out to be only a drunken hussar, who had let off his carbine. He was dragged before the colonel, and delivered a long speech in Latin, referring to the colonel throughout as 'my dear patriarch'. The soldiers had laughed, then the order to resume the march had been given. At dawn, they attacked the retrenchments at Denain, sweeping over the defences, killing or taking prisoner Albemarle's seventeen battalions. Furious on learning the news, biting his gloves and lace cuffs, Eugène galloped with his troops to relieve Denain. He was repulsed and had to withdraw again, leaving only dead behind him. Taking advantage of the situation, Villars struck at Marchiennes, taking the posts that had been set up on the line of communication one after another. A siege was organized at once and in three days Marchiennes fell into his hands with all the enormous supplies that had been left there by Eugène. 'The terrible accident that has happened to my battalions must not change the resolutions that we have made,' Eugène wrote to his colleague, Heinsius. 'Political and military reasons demand that we act.' Nevertheless he did not lay siege to Landrecies and no one was taken in: France was saved.[22]

At Utrecht, Heinsius and the imperial forces could only hope for an upheaval in England that would bring Marlborough and the Whigs to power.[23] But there was no upheaval and Villars' troops continued to regain lost ground. Then the Dutch forced Heinsius to ease the path of the negotiations which suddenly began to make progress. One snag remained, however: Philip v. His brother Bourgogne was dead; Adelaide was dead; their elder son was dead. The only survivor of this hecatomb was the younger son, the two-year-old Dauphin, but for how long? Infantile mortality was an accepted fact at the time. And, after so many recent deaths in the royal family, whenever the child coughed he was already seen into his grave. If he died, the king of France would be Philip v, King of France and King of Spain. Never, declared the English, would the two crowns be united over the same head. Louis accepted that, but Philip gibbed at it. His conscience did not allow him to renounce a sacred right that had been vested in him. He was harassed on both sides, by his grandfather and by the English. But he remained stubborn. At Utrecht the negotiations went round and round – and time passed. Suddenly, the young Dauphin fell ill. 'It is nothing, or rather it has passed,' Tessé wrote to the Princesse des Ursins, 'but my God, Madame, what a storm we had to put up with . . .' The fright had been short-lived, but total. If the Dauphin died and Philip would not renounce his claims, everything would have to start all over again. Philip understood the situation and declared himself ready to renounce his right in favour of his younger brother, the Duc de Berry. But if Berry died – the Dauphin had already been eliminated in everyone's mind – if Berry died, the Duc d'Orléans was the next in line and Philip, who hated him, could not accept that at any price. The discussions went on, with quibbling and delay, but finally on 5 November 1712, the king of Spain and of the Indies did solemnly renounce his rights to the crown of France[24] and, at Utrecht, negotiations could be brought to a speedy conclusion. Philip renounced France, but the emperor Charles had not renounced Spain. 'So there remains the emperor,' wrote Tessé, 'who, following the practices of that vexatious House of Austria was to drag out his peace in order to make it with ill-grace, after the others, and as if dragged into it.'[25]

On 11 April 1713, the plenipotentiaries signed the Treaty of Utrecht and put an end to a European war that had lasted for thirteen years. England got Gibraltar, Minorca, a few bits of Canada and commerce with the Spanish American colonies; Holland got her barrier of protective towns. The Duke of Savoy also became king of Sicily. In this way, Philip v was definitively king of Spain and even Louis xiv got a few towns in Flanders. The Emperor had refused to take part in the negotiations; he would not give up his Spain. Without being asked his opinion, he was given the Spanish Netherlands, Lombardy, Naples and Sardinia, and it was felt should have been thankful for it. The war was over at last. For some time an army was still kept on the eastern front as a precautionary measure. Villars was appointed to command it, but since peace had been concluded there was no need of Villars. 'His Majesty thinks that you would not care very much to travel out to Alsace,' the Minister of War Voysin announced to him, wriggling with embarrassment. 'Since peace has been made, we have only to thank God,' Villars replied, rather bitterly.[26]

Two weeks later, Villars was playing cards with the Duchesse de Bouillon when a messenger from the Court brought him an urgent letter. Villars put down the letter without opening it and went on with his game. 'You pay too little attention to letters from the Court,' the duchess said to him, impatient to know its contents. Villars unsealed the letter at last: it was a summons from the king to go to Marly. Villars went and found the king and Voysin, each as embarrassed as the other, not knowing how to speak to him. Villars refrained from saying anything to help them out of their difficulty, so in the end Voysin was forced to ask him, 'Would you refuse to take command of the army in Germany?' 'I have not refused difficult and dangerous tasks, which no one else wanted, so I shall not refuse those that the last campaign makes less embarrassing.' Villars had played his little act of outraged coquetry perfectly, for he knew that they needed him again. The emperor had announced, to universal surprise, that there was no peace as far as he was concerned.[27] The allies had recognized him as king of Spain, then they went and recognized Philip just as easily, and had the effrontery to try and pacify him, the emperor, the legitimate king of Spain, with a few scraps of Italy. If the others were cowards, he was not one and would continue to fight on alone. Eugène, always there at the right moment, was only too pleased to blow on the fire. When it was a matter of attacking King Louis, the two men, who hated one another, got on wonderfully well. The Imperial Diet at Ratisbon, duly softened up, voted the necessary credits and Eugène set out to collect an army of 100,000 men on the Rhine.[28]

Villars set out for the front. 'No peace,' the emperor declared. 'No ratification,' murmured Philip, at the other end of Europe. The Treaty of Utrecht was sent to Madrid for formal ratification, but for Philip, it was no mere formality. He did not like the idea of an English Gibraltar. He hesitated, he shut himself up, he prayed, he confessed, but he did not come to a decision. From Versailles, the Princesse des Ursins was urged to hasten the ratification, she was cajoled, flattered, and reminded that a great deal had been done for her at Utrecht, that she had got her principality at last. In point of fact she had been wondering whether she would ever get it. It certainly existed, there in black and white in the articles of the treaty, but it was in imperial territory and the princess doubted whether the emperor would let her have it. At Versailles, there was a strong suspicion that the delays in the ratification were somehow connected with the princess's principality. Never mind the principality if the peace of Europe is at stake, she repeated to the king and queen of Spain. 'Never!' cried the queen. During the last few months tuberculosis had made terrifying progress in her. Thin, feverish, pasty-faced, she no longer left her bed, the curtains of which were always kept closed; fresh air was never allowed to penetrate her stifling bedroom. She wanted to leave this last present to her friend before dying: 'Never. No principality, no ratification.'

CHAPTER 28

Race against the Clock

Once back in the saddle, Villars did what was expected of him: he gobbled up enemy territory. He took Speyer, Worms and other towns in the Palatinate. Then he took Landau, breached the lines that Eugène had so lovingly placed to stop him and laid siege to Freiburg, to the amazement of Eugène, who did not believe that he could have the audacity to attack such a formidable place. Not only did the troops promised by the provinces of the Empire not arrive to relieve the city, but the imperial coffers were now empty. Freiburg surrendered to Villars on 30 October 1713. Then it was decided to put an end to this trickery – for it is trickery when war is being waged and both sides want nothing more than to stop it. For two months Villars had been empowered by Louis to negotiate peace and for weeks the inter-mediaries – the Elector Palatine and the Intendant of Alsace – had done their best to sound out both parties. But it was the terror of the Swabians after the fall of Freiburg that finally overcame the emperor's stubbornness. Their deputies told him that he had a choice, either to make peace immediately or to allow them to remain neutral. In reply, the Emperor empowered Eugène to negotiate a peace. The small town of Rastadt was chosen for the talks. Villars arrived first at the delightful castle of the dowager Princess of Baden. Then with much rolling of drums and sounding of trumpets, Eugène arrived. Villars rushed down the stairs to welcome him gallantly at the gate. The two illustrious generals, who had fought one another for so long, embraced for the benefit of posterity. Villars immediately put Eugène in the right mood: 'Sir, we are not enemies; your enemies are in Vienna and mine in Versailles.'[1]

'It is said that there is a great deal of talk at Rastadt,' observed the Maréchal de Tessé, 'but no one knows where it will lead, for, with the emperor, peace or war have their days of crisis, like intermittent fevers.'[2]

The French accused the imperial party of being intractable and the imperial party accused the French of piling up monstrous demands. 'This is the tenth day that frequent and very lively arguments have taken place between M le Prince Eugène and myself,' Villars recounts in his report. Louis XIV did not budge: he wanted compensation from the emperor for his loyal allies who had waged war on that same emperor: the Elector of Bavaria should get his States back; Prince Rogotzi, who stirred up the Hungarians against their master, should get something; the Princesse des Ursins should get her celebrated principality. Eugène exploded: 'If the king of Spain demanded a sovereignty for a general to whom he was as greatly indebted as to yourself, the emperor would not be surprised, but to demand it for that lady, you will forgive my astonishment!' In fact Eugène did not quite have his hands free, as he half-admitted to Villars. The important German princes, the emperor's allies, who were fiercely anti-French, set up a hue and cry as soon as there was talk of the slightest concession. Villars did not have his hands free either. He had found his old enemy, the Elector of Bavaria, buzzing in the corridors of the congress, intriguing and confusing every possible issue. More serious still was the intransigence of Versailles. He sent report after report in an attempt to get some concessions. But a categorical no came back each time from Louis.[3] This was because, in the meantime, the king had recovered his spirits. The year before, he had been reduced to contemplating suicide at the head of his troops, but he had soon recovered all the pride of the years of his greatness. He even lent a receptive ear to those of his councillors who suggested that he might resume the war. Villars shuddered. Prince Eugène, abruptly dropping Villars and the negotiations, which were not progressing, went off to Stuttgart to spend the carnival with his friend, the Duke of Würtemberg. Had negotiations been broken off? Versailles woke up with a start. A worried Villars asked for instructions and a much more conciliatory reply came back.

Villars sent one of his officers after Eugène and they all sat down again around the conference table. From now on things went much more quickly and on 6 March 1714, at six in the evening, they began to read over the treaty. The argument went on, with haggling over every article, so that the reading was not finished until seven the next morning. Villars and Eugène, by now both exhausted, put their signatures at the foot of the document, then leapt into their coaches. Louis kept Strasbourg and Landau, the Bavarians recovered their States. There was not a word about the Princesse des Ursins' principality.[4]

'Either I must lose my post or the cardinal his,' remarked Father Le Tellier, declaring war once more on Cardinal de Noailles. Noailles must be forced to back to his last defences; the Vatican must be forced to produce a new, overwhelming, crushing, pitiless condemnation of Jansenism. But the Vatican might not respond as hoped. So, in order to bait the pope Le Tellier decided to present him with a magnificent present: his infallibility. His Holiness should draw up a 'constitution' condemning Jansenism, declaring his infallibility and destroying the foundations of Gallicanism, at one and the same time. Any attack on Gallicanism was an attack on the royal authority, about which Louis had always remained extremely sensitive, but Le Tellier had such a hold over his penitent that this obstacle did not arise. In fact it did not take him long to persuade the king that his reign might draw to a close with the finest, most glorious action of all: the final stamping out of heresy. He persuaded the pope to do what his predecessor had dreamt of doing but had never dared to bring about, namely, to become the 'mouthpiece of God in Rome'. The king used his time, energy and the few millions still at his disposal to press the pope to suppress the independence of the Church of France.

In the secrecy of the papal palace, the final touches were being put to the constitution that came to be known as *Unigenitus*, concocted in Versailles by Father Le Tellier. Le Tellier's creatures had worked so effectively on the pope that the constitution was soon published. There was an outcry from the cardinals. The pope wept, apologized, swore that the document had been published without his consent. Would the Sacred College manage to put its spokes in Le Tellier's wheels? But no, for he soon took the cardinals in hand. Having received the constitution by special messenger, he set about at once publishing it. 'Everything shines in it, except the truth,' declared Saint-Simon, 'Art and audacity reign supreme in it.' Indeed it required a great deal of audacity on the part of its authors to condemn in this masterpiece the writings of the Fathers of the Church and of the apostles. Throughout France these absurdities were greeted with peels of laughter. Jokes at Le Tellier's expense were repeated throughout Paris. 'St Paul and St Augustine were hotheads who would have been thrown into the Bastille,' he was attributed with saying. 'And what about St Thomas?' 'You can imagine what I would do with a Jacobin, when you saw what I did with an apostle.'[5]

It was a particularly cold winter's morning in the desolate plain surrounding Madrid. Insensitive to the icy wind, Philip v was gallop-ing, happy to be out in the open air and free of Court restrictions. At a bend in the road, he halted precipitately, for a funeral procession was moving towards him. Monks, hoods down, holding extinguished torches, hidalgos in black and guards wearing black arm-bands sur-rounded a bier covered with black velvet, bearing a coat of arms surmounted by the royal crown. The Queen of Spain, Maria Louisa of Savoy, was moving to her last resting place in the Escorial. In vain an entire people in prayer had besieged the royal palace night and day, where she had been succumbing to the last assaults of tuberculosis. Her husband, dazed with grief, had refused for weeks to leave her bedside. He had summoned the most famous physician of his time, the Frenchman Helvetius, but she died on 5 February 1714, aged twenty-six. Motionless in the saddle, Philip v watched as the coffin of the woman he had loved so much passed by; for a long time he watched it, without saying a word, without shedding a tear, then he galloped off and resumed his hunt. 'Are princes made like other men?' Saint-Simon wondered.[6]

Soon strange rumours began to reach Versailles. No one could approach the king of Spain; he had shut himself up in a small country palace where the Princesse des Ursins prevented him from going out or receiving anyone. All this was a source of great irritation at Versailles. Philip had still not ratified the Treaty of Utrecht and Catalonia, as always a hotbed of insurrection and separatism, had still not been pacified. No ratification, no troops, Louis retorted when his grandson had asked for his assistance, so Philip ratified the treaty at last and he was sent the Maréchal de Berwick. The Princesse des Ursins had asked for her old friend the Maréchal de Tessé, but her wish had not been gratified, for Versailles was not entirely pleased with her. In fact Louis suspected her of trying to put obstacles in the way of peace, because of that accursed principality – and even Maintenon had been shocked by her friend's claim.

The courtiers, sensing with their infallible intuition a certain cooling off in relations between the old couple on the matter of the princess, did not hesitate to spread the most incongruous gossip about her, which Saint-Simon, who hated her, was only too pleased to write into his *Memoirs*. It was said that the princess had become the king's mistress; that she had decided to marry King Philip. A thirty-one year old king of Spain marrying a mere La Trémoille of seventy-two.[7] The princess was highly embarrassed by all this. She knew that the widower could not do without a legitimate wife to satisfy his demanding desires without sinning. The problem, serious and urgent as it was, also disturbed Versailles: 'One cannot think of the state that he is in without shuddering,' wrote Maintenon to the princess, 'and I understand very well that the king of Spain will remarry. He is too young and too pious to remain in the state in which he is.'[8] Hardly a month had gone by since the death of Maria Louisa before the princess set off in search of the woman who would be capable of replacing the incomparable dead queen. In her perplexity, the princess confided in little Alberoni. He was no help and rejected every name that the princess proposed, on the grounds either of the politics, the age or the physique of the candidate. No solution seemed to be in sight. The princess, having exhausted her candidates remained silent. 'Of course, the Princess of Parma might do,' Alberoni slipped in at last. The Princesse des Ursins was shocked at the prospect of Elizabeth Farnese, the orphan condemned to a country 'barn', practically a pauper but raised via the bed to the duchy of Parma, for the king of Spain and the Indies. 'You serve the duke of Parma very well,' the princess replied sarcastically. But that pauper would be eternally grateful for the good fairy that came round to offering her the unhoped for chance of sitting on the throne of Spain. La Farnese would remain a docile tool in the hands of the woman who married her to a Bourbon. Philip's grandfather at Versailles did not, however, care for the idea. The poor lineage of La Farnese could be overlooked, in view of the lack of candidates and the urgency of the problem, but the empress's own niece and Charles II's widow, that meant putting a 'German' sympathizer, an enemy of France, beside Philip v. It would be La Farnese or nothing, the Princesse des Ursins replied. After considerable delay, Louis gave his approval. He did not like his hand being forced and the princess had lost nothing by waiting.[9]

'We hope that Barcelona will be taken soon,' the Palatine recounted. 'One circumstance I find amusing is the boasting of the governor, Villareal. When called on to surrender he replied that he himself would give the signal for the surrender; he had decided, when he could no longer defend himelf, to put himself on a keg of powder and blow himself up.' Summer came round and still the capital of Catalonia, which Berwick had been besieging for weeks, had not fallen. With the province reconquered, only Barcelona heroically still held out. The determination of the inhabitants to defend it matched the determination of the governor who had stuck black flags bearing skulls on the ramparts. The clergy had joyfully lent a hand to the Palatine's indignation: 'The accursed monks have been preaching in all the streets that they must now surrender; if they followed my advice, those villains would be put in the galleys, instead of the poor protestants who are rotting away in them now.' Despite this desperate determination Barcelona finally surrendered to Berwick.

The triumphant sounds of the *Te Deum* were accompanied by bonfires lit at the crossroads. At the end of April 1714, Paris officially celebrated the peace between France and the empire. More modestly, the king attended a thanksgiving service at his parish church at Marly. Next day, he was informed that his grandson, the Duc du Berry, was sick. He had had a sudden violent fever. He had vomited a great deal of black liquid. 'It's the chocolate he stuffs himself with,' the physicians declared. 'It's blood,' Fagon maintained. Black blood? Immediately the word poison flew from mouth to mouth. 'Ah! I am the sole cause of my death, Father,' murmured the dying man to Father de La Rue, who had come to administer extreme unction. Following a fall from his horse, he had continually vomited blood, but he had threatened his servants to sack them if they said anything about it. He had scarcely made his admission when he fell into a coma. He died at four in the morning, on 4 May 1714. It seemed to be the end of any hopes that Philip v may have had of seeing his brother reign on the – certain – death of the young Dauphin. It also seemed the end of any sort of Louis' hopes of preventing his hated nephew the Duc d'Orléans from taking over the regency.

Late in the morning of Sunday 28 July 1714, Saint-Simon, returning to his apartment at Marly, found a servant from Judge Maisons, begging him to go at once to see him in Paris. Saint-Simon leapt into his coach and drove full speed to Paris. Maisons was with the Duc de

Noailles. Saint-Simon was met by two very dejected men. At last, 'with the air of a dying man', Maisons finally came out with it: the king had decided to raise his two surviving bastards, the Duc du Maine and the Comte de Toulouse, together with their descendants, to the rank and prerogatives of legitimate princes of the blood royal. Crushed by the news, Saint-Simon fell silent, lost in his own thoughts. So 'a Creole, a public woman, a widow living on the charity of a crippled poet' [Maintenon] and 'the first of all the fruits of double adultery' [Maine] had managed to get the king to commit this criminal attack on the laws of monarchy, the laws of the State, the laws of decency in any Court. Saint-Simon saw it as nothing less than a challenge to monarchical absolutism. Were they in France or in the Muscovy of the bloody dictatorship of Peter the Great? Was not France a 'vile slave' to submit in this way to the most arbitrary despotism? For, in truth, 'this crime' completed the task of turning 'this freest of nations' into 'a nation of slaves'.

A noise suddenly woke Saint-Simon from his sombre meditation. Maisons and Noailles, inveighing for all they were worth against the royal decision, were stamping their feet, running around the drawing-room, giving furious kicks to the furniture. The commotion made Saint-Simon want to laugh so much that he forgot his own anger for a moment. He waited for the 'hurricane' to calm down before rushing back to Marly to attend the king's dinner. Everyone was already in the know. The king, haughtier than ever, scrutinized those around him in an attempt to detect their reactions. The 'icy' courtiers looked at one another, not knowing how to react. An unprecedented wave of disapproval then swept through the whole of France and finally reached the Court, only to be transformed by the royal entourage into overwhelming approval. Not for anything in the world would Saint-Simon have missed the session of the *parlement*, on 2 August, when the two royal bastards appeared for the first time in their new status. He almost had pity on the dignified, agreeable Comte de Toulouse who, sensing the enormity of what had been done, could hardly conceal 'his shamefaced modesty'. On the other hand, he took a great delight in the abject appearance of the Duc du Maine, the very image of hypocrisy, limping along, bowing to everyone, almost 'prostrating himself' beside Saint-Simon, appearing to say with his 'gently serious' air, *non sum dignus*, whereas his eyes glittered with delight: why 'this tissue of appalling grandeurs'? Why declare the bastards rightful successors to the throne after the legitimate princes, as if there were any shortage of them, when there was a string of Orléans, Condés and Contis? For Saint-Simon, there was no doubt: the ground was being prepared for the next step,[10] the final step, that is to say, declaring the bastards, and therefore the Duc de Maine, as entitled to succeed before the princes of the blood royal and immediately after the young Dauphin, who was universally expected to die shortly.

★

'Is Mme de Maintenon ill?' her friends asked one another. For over a week, she had remained in her room, down-cast, preoccupied, saying nothing, doing nothing, as if sickening. 'Is my brother sick?' the Comte de Toulouse wondered, for the Duc du Maine seemed as doleful as his dear stepmother. Toulouse tried desperately to thaw the atmosphere: he bravely recounted his hunting exploits, he expatiated at length on the new tree plantings in his park at Rambouillet, he even risked repeating gossip that he had heard from a *valet de chambre*. None of it had the desired effect. The Duc du Maine stood there, silent, at a loss. The physicians watched and grew more and more anxious. Furthermore the king now looked like falling ill. He was also sad, preoccupied, as if some important matter were troubling him. 'No, no, Mme de Maintenon cannot be ill,' her friends told one another. She had no fever, she didn't cough, her complexion looked as healthy as ever. Perhaps she was sulking. That was it, she was sulking about something the king had done – and the Duc de Maine was doing the same, but why? Her ladies had no idea, but accustomed as they were to following the mood of their close friend, they did nothing to relieve it. The silence grew longer and longer, the atmosphere heavier and heavier. 'The gloom thickened', and the king seemed more and more affected by it. The only hours of relaxation that he had, had become a hell for him. Then one morning, to everyone's surprise, Maintenon and the Duc du Maine returned as if by magic to their normal, pleasant selves. Ladies and doctors were as mystified as ever.[11]

Two days later, on Sunday 17 August 1714, Louis summoned to his office the first president of the *parlement* and the procurator-general. He opened a drawer, took out a parcel sealed with seven seals and handed it to them. 'Gentlemen, this is my will. No one knows what it contains, I am giving it to you to keep at the *parlement* ... The example of my predecessors as king, and that of the king my father's will, leave me in no doubt as to what will become of this one; but I have been cajoled and tormented, I have been left no rest, whatever I said. Well! I have now bought my rest. Here it is, take it away. I do not know what will become of it; at least that is the last I shall hear of it.' And, leaving the two magistrates nonplussed, he turned heel and left.[12] Next day, James II's widow visited her friend, Mme de Maintenon. The king then came in and took her to one side: 'Madame, I have made my will. I have been harried into doing so,' he said, giving a long stare at Maintenon, who lowered her eyes. 'I have been forced into it, I have been given no peace until it was done. So, Madame, now it has been done, they may do with it what they will, but it will not trouble me further.' The ex-queen of England, who had scarcely recovered from her amazement, hurried off to recount the king's strong words to her friend Lauzun. Lauzun repeated it immediately to Saint-Simon, who thus had his worst suspicions confirmed.[13]

What explosive articles, then, did this will contain? Certainly something to the advantage of the Duc du Maine, certainly provisions that contradicted monarchical tradition and the fundamental laws of the kingdom and which therefore displeased Louis. He was visibly failing, he would not live for much longer and Maintenon had suddenly taken fright. With Louis XIV dead, the Duc d'Orléans, that debauched poisoner, would become regent and then, on the death of the young Dauphin, which he would no doubt have a hand in bringing about, he would become king. Urged on without knowing it by the secret ambition of the Duc de Maine, stimulated by her own fear, she had done what she had never done before: exerted direct pressure on her husband. It was not by bustling about, by pleading with him, by harassing him, that did not accord with her character: she had her own methods. She simply went on strike. She refused to entertain the king, refused to talk to him, refused any show of affection. Before this emotional blackmail her husband, whose senility now emphasized his natural weakness, gave in without illusion or satisfaction. With very feminine intuition Maintenon knew that by sulking, she would deprive him of what he valued more than anything else: his comforts, his peace, his place by the fireside with his old wife, that last bit of happiness that he needed so much at the end of his life. She had never loved her husband and she never proved it so well as when she pitilessly tortured that old, weakened, and lonely man on the verge of death.

At Parma, the bells rang out and the people put on their holiday clothes. On that day, 16 August 1714, Princess Elizabeth was to marry, by proxy, His Catholic Majesty. In the palace, the duke and his betrothed, his niece, were getting ready for the ceremony, when a killjoy in the shape of a messenger from Spain arrived. A legal difficulty, a canonical impediment stood in the way of the marriage. The ceremony was to be postponed, on orders from the Princesse des Ursins. The uncle, in agreement with his niece, did not hesitate. He seized the messenger and gave him a choice between immediate death and a bag of gold to 'arrive' at Parma officially the next day. The messenger did not hesitate either. He took the gold and Princess Elizabeth was married. Had the Princesse des Ursins suddenly become afraid? 'The longer I live, the more I see that one is never so close to a reversal of fortune than when it is smiling on one,' she wrote, strangely, to her friend Maintenon.[14]

However, the new queen of Spain set out to join the husband that she had not yet met. At Pampeluna, she was joined by her compatriot Alberoni. Suspicious at first, she let herself be won over by his insinuating, subtle wit and soon felt that she could trust him. What was on her mind, then, the Abbé wondered as he watched her, frowning, walking up and down, muttering words to herself. Suddenly, kicking the furniture, she cried angrily: 'I shall get rid of *her* first.' The Abbé was terrified. Elizabeth held his arm tight enough to break it. 'Keep quiet about everything and let nothing that you have heard pass your lips. Say nothing to me. I know what I am doing.' However, the king of Spain set out to meet his wife halfway, accompanied by the Princesse des Ursins, who, without wasting any time, had had herself appointed the queen's '*camarera mayor*', as she had been of the dead queen. They stopped at Guadalajara, near Madrid. The next day, 23 December 1714, the princess put on a magnificent low-cut court dress and jewels and set out to meet Elizabeth at Jadraque. Night was falling. She was at her window, waiting for the queen's procession to arrive. At last, the sound of galloping horses was heard, followed by the sound of drums and trumpets: the queen arrived. The princess was there, standing on a step, very erect, her long train draped around her. Elizabeth jumped out of the coach. The princess made a deep curtsey. Elizabeth mounted the steps. The *camarera mayor* followed her alone to her room. After a moment, the queen's voice was heard shouting. The door was suddenly flung open. Elizabeth, eyes ablaze, her face red with anger, shouted: 'Remove this mad woman!' The lieutenant of the guards in charge of the queen's security appeared. 'I order you to arrest the Princesse des Ursins and not to leave her side until you have put her in a coach and sent her off at once, under military escort, for Bayonne.' 'But, Madame, only the king of Spain . . .' the poor lieutenant protested. 'Have you not a written order from the king of Spain to obey me in everything, unconditionally and without protest?' The princess was immediately put into the coach with two officers and driven at full speed along the icy roads, in the darkness of a winter's night, in which only the feeble reflection of the snow gave relief. The cold was pitiless. The princess, still wearing her low-cut dress, had not been given time to bring with her either a coat to cover herself or a change of linen or money or food. She huddled in the corner of the coach, frozen, silent, lost in thought. They drove on in this way through the night.

Next day, Elizabeth, having put on a robe of silver cloth chosen in advance by the princess, arrived at Guadalajara in the early afternoon. A new nuptial ceremony took place in the church, conducted by the Archbishop of Toledo and twelve mitred bishops. Then at four o'clock, Philip, trembling with impatience, went to bed with the radiant Elizabeth. They did not get up until midnight, exhausted, appeased and happy, when they went down to the chapel to attend midnight mass, for it was Christmas.

For several days and several nights, the Princesse des Ursins' journey continued at appalling speed, to Saint-Jean-de-Luz. 'I do not know how I was able to bear the fatigue of the journey,' she wrote to Maintenon. 'I was made to sleep on straw and to go without the food I am used to . . . I ate only two old eggs a day . . . You must have been very surprised, Madame, on learning of the treatment that I have received from the queen of Spain, when I expected to be treated quite differently.'[15]

But was Maintenon so surprised? Several days before they could have known about the event, the Marquis de Dangeau, a Court gossip who was far from being privy to all secrets, noted in his journal the rumours that were circulating: the queen of Spain was complaining of the lack of respect that the princess had shown to her at a distance. 'It is thought that on her arrival at the king of Spain's, there might well be changes in that Court,' Dangeau predicted.[16] Everyone accepted the accusation of a lack of respect to explain the princess's dismissal. And yet, how could 'a girl from Parma, brought up in a barn', have taken it upon herself suddenly and ignominiously to dismiss the all-powerful friend of her lord and master, before even having met him? The princess was, after all, the ambassador *in partibus* of the Sun King, the omnipresent grandfather. Neither of the two women was ever to provide a satisfactory explanation for the incident. In any case there is little doubt that Elizabeth had planned her action with Philip's full agreement. She clearly hinted as much to Alberoni, who declared that he was surprised, even though he was probably an accomplice. She even showed him a letter from Philip. 'Be quite sure that you pull off your coup at the outset; for if she so much as sees you for two hours she will have you in chains and prevent us from sleeping together, as she did in the case of the late queen.'[17]

These words published in all their crudity in some suspect *Memoirs*, sound false, and yet, on reflection, they are not as incredible as they may appear. Louis and Maintenon could well have been accomplices of the sudden, shameful fall of a woman who, for so long, had been a French instrument in Spain. They had very probably been warned, had acquiesced, and had deliberately not interfered. Elizabeth had soon understood – it was easy enough – that she would never be the true queen of Spain as long as the princess stood between her and her husband. Philip had realized earlier that the princess's yoke suddenly weighed heavily on him, but he went on submitting to it without complaint, out of habit, out of weakness. Louis had seen that his zealous collaborator was also capable of going her own way to the point of disrupting his policy, but he did not want to intervene in the 'internal affairs of Spain'. Maintenon had realized that the submissive friend who proclaimed her to be her guide and model had created a situation, a power and an independence quite in excess of her own, but, true to herself, she had refrained from doing anything about it. So it had been left to the newcomer, Elizabeth to act. Had she been incited, encouraged, or simply allowed to follow her own inclinations, according to everyone's degree of weakness? It hardly matters. Nevertheless, it was with the direct or indirect complicity of Philip, Louis xiv and Maintenon that she got rid of the princess for them. The proof lies in Louis' approval, after the event: 'I would be most displeased if your satisfaction were impaired by the misfortune that befell the Princesse des Ursins in displeasing you.'[18] The princess herself still did not understand what had happened. 'And people are trying to convince me,' she confided to Maintenon, 'that the king has acted in concert with a princess who has had me treated with so much cruelty. So I regard these rumours as proofs of the infamy of a cabal that has sworn to destroy me.' She then assumed the role of Cassandra and predicted a terrible outcome for the Franco–Spanish alliance. In this she was right. Already Philip's French advisers had been replaced by Italians devoted to Elizabeth with Alberoni at their head. Here was another bitter pill for the princess to swallow: the little priest whom she had encouraged at the outset of his career had actually taken her place: 'I am informed that the favour of the Abbé Alberoni is at its height. This is the greatest misfortune that could befall the king. An infinity of unworthy and ungrateful courtiers are attached to him. May God bless them.[19] One was never so well betrayed as by one's friends.

The old couple in Versailles decided at last to receive the princess, perhaps in order to conceal their indirect complicity in her fall. The princess put on her Court dress for the last time, passed through the galleries of Versailles and entered Maintenon's bedchamber, where the king soon joined her. The interview, held in secret, lasted for two hours. The princess reappeared before the curious courtiers, erect, smiling, impenetrable. Her *amour propre* satisfied, they let it be known that her further presence in France would be embarrassing, and she decided to take up residence in Rome. But the pope too, seemed to find objections. The princess exploded. 'This is the last straw,' she wrote to Maintenon. 'Expelled from Spain with indignity, welcomed with kindness[?] by the king, whose subject I have the honour to be, though deprived of the consolation of paying him Court, urged by my best friends to leave his kingdom, as if my presence were an embarrassment to him, all that, in truth, Madame, seems to me incredible.' She still refused to understand that she had become an encumbrance. 'I have not yet received the money that the king was gracious enough to arrange to be delivered to me,' she concluded.[20] In the end, everything was arranged, the money was 'delivered', the pope agreed to take her in and she was able at last to go to Rome. Among other acquaintances she found there the English Pretender 'James III', and the old lady, who had paid dear for her realism, became the inseparable companion of that young man, the living symbol of a chimerical ideal.[21]

CHAPTER 29

The Senile Sun

One morning early in 1715, the Maréchal de Tessé was taking his excited niece, young Victoire de Froulay, to visit Saint-Cyr. They had hardly been travelling for ten minutes along the tree-lined road when, suddenly, their coach stopped in the middle of nowhere. The coachman jumped to the ground, opened the door and lowered the step. 'It's the king,' said the marshal. Everyone got out. Victoire saw the royal coach drawn by eight horses approaching at top speed. She counted only three musketeers and an escort of three light horse. She made out the six pages' blue livery decorated with *fleur-de-lys*. Then she saw the king, sitting alone on the rear seat. Just as the coach reached her, it stopped, as if by magic. The marshal bowed and his niece curtseyed. The king lowered his window, raised his hat and made them a deep bow. When Victoire looked up again the royal coach was already on its way. 'So that is the great king!' the girl cried with emotion. 'You should add,' her uncle retorted, 'the unhappy king.'[1]

Louis certainly was unhappy. His clergy were on the verge of schism, and yet he had been assured – that is to say Father Le Tellier had assured him – that the papal bull *Unigenitus* would be accepted without argument. This exhaustive condemnation of Jansenism, issued by the pope but in fact dictated from Versailles, inflamed public opinion by its extreme intolerance. There was an outcry at once. An assembly of the bishops of France was arranged in the greatest haste to make acceptance of the bull official, but rebellion was in the air. Certain prelates had to be bribed: one had to be promised a cardinal's hat, another the post of Grand Almoner of France, a third large sums of money. Forty bishops agreed, but eight others, including the Cardinal de Noailles, respectfully refused, writing directly to the pope to request changes. Publication of their letter was forbidden, the opponents were sent back to their dioceses and Noailles was told not to appear at Court. The bishops who had accepted were no more pleased. 'The whole affair, from beginning to end, has been a mystery of iniquity against Cardinal de Noailles,' sighed the Bishop of Soissons. He had accepted because he had been promised the archbishopric of Reims. Later, he was seized with remorse. He fell ill, became delirious and began spouting curses against the bull. Everyone was forbidden to approach the possessed man. He died alone shouting so loudly that terrified passers-by heard him in the street. Spurred on by the ecclesiastical authorities, the opposition gave the bull a hard time. The *parlement* had been forced to register it – with innumerable reservations and protests – but, fearing popular reaction, it had not published the fact that it had been registered. At the Sorbonne a majority voted against the bull, but registered it nevertheless. The rebellion reached every section of the State apparatus. 'It's chaos, a tower of Babel,' sighed Saint-Simon. Louis wondered if they were returning to the time of the *Fronde*. He gave Le Tellier and his Jesuits their head. *Lettres de cachet* showered on the land. Large numbers of bishops, priests, nuns, teachers and monks were locked up. 'Write that he resisted the king,' ordered the police officer if anyone refused to accept the bull without reservations. The denunciations multiplied. It was enough to accuse someone of being a Jansenist to have him thrown into prison. Le Tellier had the reports of the cross-examinations of defendants sent to him personally. Fifty years later, Voltaire found them stored away in chests in a Jesuit house. 'We are now living,' said Saint-Simon, 'in a time of persecution, which has depopulated the schools, introduced ignorance, fanaticism and disorder, crowned vice, thrown every community into the utmost confusion, with disorder everywhere, established the most arbitrary and most barbarous inquisition.'[2]

The French had kept one weapon against the inquisition: humour. No one knew where, or how *Les Nouvelles Ecclésiastiques*, a satirical publication of a violence equal to the excesses it denounced, appeared. Copies were to be found throughout France, even in Versailles. Bundles of it were thrown into the carriage of the lieutenant of police d'Argenson, who was trying in vain to track down its authors. Other bundles of the pamphlet were left in the office of Father Le Tellier who, in his fury, struggled impotently against these barbs.[3] It was all the fault of Cardinal de Noailles, he yelled. In the drawing-room of their friend, the Duchesse de Ventadour, the young Dauphin's governess, Cardinal de Rohan declared that they should strike once and for all: 'By order of the king, we must seize Cardinal de Noailles when he goes to Conflans, send him to Rome and hand him over to the papal authorities.' In a corner of the drawing-room, a woman pricked up her ears. This was Mlle de Chausseraye, a rich woman of an original, witty turn of mind, once the king's occasional mistress, who was still received by him and who, above all, was a devoted friend of Noailles. She immediately warned Noailles not to leave Paris under any pretext. Next day, by chance, she had a long audience with the king, who had been working with Le Tellier. She found him sad, preoccupied, lost in thought.

'You don't look so well, Sire, she told him, 'is it your health perhaps ...' 'It is true that I am extremely worried by this matter of the Constitution. People are proposing things to me that I can hardly reconcile myself to. I have spent all morning arguing about it. First I have to listen to one set of people, then another, and I get no peace.' 'It is very good of you to allow yourself to be tormented in this way against your inclination. Those good gentlemen care only for their own business and not at all for your health. In your place, I would think only of living in peace and letting them fight it out among themselves without taking any further part in it.' 'You are right, I shall follow your advice, or those people will surely kill me. I shall forbid them to come tomorrow and speak to me of anything that troubles me in the least way.' Clever Chausseraye! To speak to the king of the question itself would have been to throw him still further into the arms of the vultures in soutanes. On the other hand, to speak to an old gentleman about his health, to advise him to look after himself, that was a feminine masterstroke. Next day, looking her most innocent, she went to lunch with the Duchesse de Ventadour. There she found the Prince de Rohan, the cardinal's brother. 'What can one do against the king's weakness?' he cried sadly. 'Several times he has been about to consent to the seizure of Cardinal de Noailles. Yesterday, he resisted Father Le Tellier on that matter and was ten times ready to give his word, then he suddenly stopped himself and, this morning, he took Father Le Tellier and the cardinal, my brother, to one side, forbidding them so much as to dream of mentioning it to him again.' Chausseraye opened her eyes wide and uttered little cries of surprise.[4] Louis had always had a foundation of good sense that made him resist the good reasons offered by his most unreasonable counsellors. Sometimes, a true word from a friend or a loyal servant enabled that good sense to gain the upper hand and pull him back from the edge of the precipice. More often, his weakness and others' tenacity blinded him and led him on against his better judgment.

Louis soon had a pleasant distraction to extricate him from those torturing ecclesiastical imbroglios. He was preparing to receive in solemn audience the ambassador extraordinary of the Shah of Persia. This pleased him immensely: potentates from the other end of the world still sent him their spokesmen to prostrate themselves before his throne and he was still the greatest king in the world. But a personage as important as His Excellency Mehemet Mira Bey could allow himself to be difficult and, from his arrival in France, he was so to no inconsiderable degree. He had among other things the impudence to postpone the royal audience because his astrologer had informed him that the day chosen was unpropitious. When told that one did not postpone meetings with the Sun King, he completely lost his temper, ground his teeth, brandished his dagger and threatened to kill everybody in sight. The audience was finally fixed for Tuesday 19 February 1715. Louis had decided to dazzle his visitor – to dazzle the Persians, the Court, France, the world and himself, as if this audience was to be the farewell gala of the dazzling 'show' which he had mounted so long ago and which he had played for almost forty years in the theatre that he himself had built for the purpose. The entire Court was ordered to dress itself in jewels from top to toe. No one would be admitted into the Hall of Mirrors, where the audience was to take place. Early in the morning, the glittering courtiers began to fill the galleries and to take up their positions on the stepped platforms especially erected for the purpose. The princes arrived: the Duc du Maine in a costume of pearls and diamonds lent him by the king; his brother Toulouse, in precious stones of various colours; the young Dauphin, held by the Duchesse de Ventadour, wore diamonds from top to toe. The most elegant of all was the Duc d'Orléans – in a costume of blue velvet embroidered with a mosaic of pearls and diamonds. In his state dressing-room, Louis was almost ready. He had ordered that as many diamonds from the crown as possible were to be sewn onto his black and gold coat – 12,500,000 *livres*-worth, Saint-Simon estimated. When the jacket was put round his shoulders bent under the weight. In any case, according to Saint-Simon he looked ill. The great sash of the *Ordre du Saint-Esprit* was passed around his body, then he went out on to the balcony to see the immense crowd that had invaded the avenues of Versailles, the palace courtyards, even the roofs. Thunderous cheering greeted his appearance. Then he moved forward; as he was crossing the great apartments, an enormous pearl came off his coat and fell to the ground. Fortunately it rolled under the foot of the Marquis de Lange who picked it up. Entering the Hall of Mirrors, where the glittering crowd was almost suffocating, Louis made a detour to pass slowly in front of the galleries where four hundred ladies in formal dress were crowded. He mounted the steps of the dais and sat down, his hat on his head, on an immense throne of gilded wood surmounted by the crown. Princes and officers of state stood around him. In a corner, the painter Coypel, brush in hand, was preparing to immortalize the scene. Everything was ready.

His Persian Excellency appeared. The French criticisms poured out at once. He was 'pitiably, miserably' attended. He himself was 'highly embarrassed and very badly dressed', according to Saint-Simon: 'he cut a very poor figure, with the funniest body one could ever see,' according to the Palatine. His speech consisted only of 'a few broken phrases', which were turned into a superb discourse in castrated French for the benefit of the press, which merely exasperated the Persian. The Shah's gifts, which were expected to be of unprecedented magnificence, consisted of a few 'mediocre' pearls, a few 'very ugly' turquoises and a mysterious elixir of life, which was hastily put away in a cupboard and forgotten. After the audience, the ambassador was taken to Paris.

'He's a swindler,' declared the Palatine. 'He has no powers from the king of Persia, nor from any of his ministers,' Saint-Simon maintained. The Court believed him to be an impostor, and he was certainly far from the high dignitary sent specially by the king of kings of Isfahan to bear his respects to the Sun King. But it was of no consequence that Louis XIV was the only one, according to Saint-Simon, to give the ambassador credence. The Persian was for him merely a pretext to mount one of his great spectacles, intended to dazzle his Court, his people and the whole of Europe. A symbolic fate decided that the king of sham should give the last performance of his theatre of illusions for an impostor. Mehemet Mira Bey, having acquired a taste for Paris and above all for the king's munificent hospitality, had to be sent off almost by force . . . eight months later. Among the innumerable items of luggage taken on to his frigate, there was an enormous chest which, the ambassador declared, contained the sacred books of Mahomet. The impure Christians were forbidden to touch or even to come near it. The chest was put in his cabin and he nervously opened it to find . . . the ravishing Marquise d'Espinay. The lady, pregnant by the ambassador, had chosen this uncomfortable way of escaping a jealous husband and a bothersome police and to experience the delights of the Thousand and One Nights.[5]

The Princess Palatine preferred to remain in her apartment than bear the boredom of the Court. These days the king lunched in the company of his wife and a small group of her friends. Then he played cards, if the weather was too bad for him to go out. The afternoons dragged on. From time to time they listened to a little music. But even the concerts were dull. Dinner time never seemed to come round. The king was often three-quarters of an hour late. At table, monastic silence reigned. Moreover it meant eating 'the detestable cooking of that country,' which the Palatine had never got used to. How she yearned for a good *sauerkraut* and a pint of beer! After dinner, everyone met in the king's study. But where was the conversation, the repartee, the wit of the old days? The only topics of conversation allowed were 'the rain and fine weather, cards and clothes'. Everyone was careful not to express the slightest opinion about anything and this general fear exasperated the Palatine's German frankness.[6]

Since Adelaide's laughter no longer echoed through the palace, Maintenon was at a loss to know what might amuse her husband and lift the heavy boredom that had descended on her, too. Certainly neither her few friends, who were as old as she, nor her young protégées, paralysed with shyness, would take the place of the Savoyarde. She had even brought back out of disgrace the king's childhood friend, Villeroi, 'to enliven the evenings with some chat'. But the old marshal, despite his foolish volubility, was not up to the task. Maintenon was also worried about her husband's health. Gallstones gave him 'red, cloudy' urine, containing grains of sand. He constantly had 'broad and luxuriant phlebotomies', insomnia, vapours, tiredness, attacks of giddiness, colds. He was perpetually at the mercy of some illness or other. To remedy all these ills, the physicians alternated bleeding and purgatives, which so weakened his body that the patient, at last beginning to doubt the wisdom of his medical team, refused to subject himself to any more bleedings. They protested. The king was adamant: purgatives, but no bleedings. His doctor complained that 'after purging the king, I had to let him rest for some time.' Above all there were the continual attacks of indigestion caused by his morbid hunger and consequent over-eating, which was as virulent as ever.[7] 'He did not sleep last night, because the peas and strawberries gave him wind,' Maintenon wrote to her friend.

Next day, the king was as fresh as a daisy and Maintenon was almost exasperated. She would have preferred him to be thoroughly ill in order to punish him for his gluttony: 'He cannot expect to grow old without some inconveniences and I admit that I would not be displeased to see him subjected to some of them, for otherwise, he will never restrain his appetite.'[8] Fortunately, he had the young Dauphin to console him. The child's governess, the Duchesse de Ventadour, had become Maintenon's slave. 'He is your beloved child and I have him only from you,' she would say and asked Maintenon for advice on all matters. 'Since you absolutely insist that I give you advice, I shall do so, providing you keep it a secret,' Maintenon replied. They must teach the child discretion and trust, develop humanity, frankness and gratitude in him, never give him an order without explaining the reason for it to him, and so on. With this course of education, Maintenon was drawing up yet another indictment of her husband. The faults that she wanted the Dauphin to avoid – indiscretion, equally blind submission and authoritarianism, inhumanity, ingratitude, selfishness – were precisely those with which she reproached her husband. Even the Palatine, despite her resentments against her family-in-law, was quite won over by the Dauphin: 'He has large, very deep eyes, a round face, a small pretty mouth, a neck so well shaped that it would be difficult to imagine it better, pretty legs and feet.'[9] But if the little boy amused the old lady amid the boredom of Versailles, he was not enough to keep the young people amused.

Scarcely had the king gone to bed at half-past twelve than his daughter, the Duchesse de Bourbon, turned her apartment into a gambling den where cards were played for very high stakes until morning.[10] Her half-sister, the lazy Duchesse d'Orléans, preferred to lie on her *chaise longue* listening to her parrot imitate her own voice, summoning servants and maids. However she was somewhat taken back when the bird interjected: 'Madame, kiss my ass,' a novelty in his vocabulary that he owed to labourers who had been working in her room.[11] Others preferred to abandon Versailles and go and amuse themselves more freely elsewhere. The Duc d'Orléans kept more and more frequently to the Palais Royal with his mistresses and roués for drinking and orgies. But the new great social centre was the Château de Sceaux, 'the Duchesse du Maine's theatre of follies', where, intoxicated by her husband's recent promotion and by the prospects opened up by the king's will, she had turned to extravagant libertinism and carefree ruination.

On the morning of 12 June 1715, a young Englishwoman had taken up position with one of her ladies on the stairs of Versailles to see the king set out for Marly. She was trembling with impatience to see at last the greatest tourist attraction in Europe. The drums began to roll. ' "There he is," my lady exclaimed. "Stand to one side and take good note of Mme de Maintenon ..." Mme de Maintenon appeared, unattended, wearing a plain dress of rust-coloured damask, with no other adornment than a cross studded with four diamonds hanging from her neck ... She sat down at the back of the coach next to the king and as she recognized my lady in passing, she greeted her with one of those serious smiles in which sweetness competes with majesty.' Her ladyship found Maintenon still attractive for her age: 'She appeared quite unconcerned with her greatness and she seemed to concern herself entirely with whether the king was in a comfortable position. As soon as she had sat down, she was brought her work, which was a piece of tapestry; at the same time, she took out her spectacles and, after raising the windows of her coach, set to work.'[12]

At Marly, the immutable rites of those holidays were enacted in their usual way, though in the eyes of Saint-Simon 'the king's health was visibly failing' and he even began to lose his legendary appetite. Fagon, 'much declined in body and in mind', noticed nothing. On the other hand, Maréchal was increasingly concerned. He tried to open Fagon's eyes, but Fagon put him in his place with all the harshness of his arbitrary power. At his wits' end Maréchal decided to go and find Maintenon. 'Fagon is making a serious mistake,' he told her. 'I have often taken the king's pulse. For some time now he has had a slight, slow, internal fever. His body is so resistant that he can still recover with remedies and attention. But if we allow the illness to gain in strength, there will be nothing to be done.' 'But only M Fagon's personal enemies agree with what you say about the king's health,' Maintenon retorted. Exasperated by this blindness, Maréchal exploded: 'Then I have no alternative but to deplore my master's death.' Mme de Maintenon did not see any cause to worry. The king seemed to work as usual with his ministers; that morning, he had the Dutch newspapers read to him by Torcy. Suddenly, the minister stopped in his tracks, stammered, skipped an article and went on with his reading. 'What is the cause of your embarrassment?' the king asked. 'Some impertinence unworthy to be read,' Torcy replied, blushing to the roots of his hair. 'Read it,' the king commanded. 'Sire, it is not necessary.' 'Read it, I tell you.' In the end Torcy did as he was told. 'It is said that bets are being laid in England as to whether the life of the king of France would or would not last until 1 September of this year.' Louis remained impassive, but, at lunch, staring at his courtiers, he suddenly remarked, 'I am told that in England bets are being laid on my imminent death.'[13]

Father Le Tellier was determined to get his papal bull accepted and to get Noailles, condemned before the king died. To this end he concocted an unconditional act of acceptance of the bull, plus an edit forcing the bishops to accept, before it was registered by the *parlement*. But the *parlement* had already proved considerably recalcitrant on the matter. To get his way the king would have to go to Paris and hold a *lit de justice* in person, just like the good old days of the *Fronde*. But Louis was tired, he no longer felt that he had the strength to break off his holiday to go to Paris and listen to the objections of the *parlementaires*, who he had always hated. Instead, he summoned to Marly the procurator-general, d'Aguesseau, and the first advocate-general, Fleury. A few of the king's threatening phrases were repeated to the two lawyers and the ground was prepared.

D'Aguesseau was a small, plump man of amiable disposition, with one eye larger than the other. He appeared before the hollow-cheeked, exhausted king, who made a visible effort to appear more majestic than ever, but condescended at first to be pleasant. D'Aguesseau was sedulously respectful but elusive. The king became more insistent, more direct, more authoritarian. D'Aguesseau, using all the resources of legal jargon drew him into 'verbal convolutions', was careful not to refuse to obey, but still did not come up with the fatal 'yes'. The king became irritated, raised his voice, lost his composure before this tenacious disarming gentleness. But d'Aguesseau held firm. For 'he had three shields (apart from his good conscience): first, his God, the *parlement*; then the large Jansenist party, the persecuted Church; lastly, it has to be said, his wife, who, embracing him as he set out in his coach, had said to him: "Off you go! When faced with the king, forget wife and children. Forget everything except honour." ' By resisting, d'Aguesseau in fact ran the risk of losing his position, his fortune and his freedom, but he also saw that the king would not last much longer. Like the English, he was betting against the clock. Now the king was threatening. Fleury, the advocate-general trembled, already imagining his post being taken from him. D'Aguesseau became even more respectful in his firmness. Then the king, forgetting for once his legendary courtesy, turned his back. The interview was over. The next day there was a royal declaration: 'On my return from Marly, I shall go to Paris to hold a *lit de justice* and see for myself if I have the credit to get the constitution registered without alteration.' At the *parlement*, 'terror spread abroad'.[14] On Saturday 10 August 1715, after walking in the gardens of Marly, Louis returned to Versailles about six in the evening.

On 12 August, he complained of sciatica in one leg. All is well, declared Fagon. On Thursday 15 August, after a 'disturbed' night, he was unable to wash himself, or to go to mass. He could only swallow food with difficulty. There is no cause for concern, Fagon insisted: His Majesty did not have a fever. On 20 August Louis abandoned his efforts to dress for the evening and dined in his bedroom, wearing a dressing-gown. Then he had his wheelchair pushed into his study. On the way, he stopped to say a few words to the Duchesse de Saint-Simon, who had come back that morning from the country at the urgent summons of her husband. 'I would not have recognized the king if I had encountered him anywhere else but at home,' she admitted to her husband. On 22 August the king felt even worse. A conference of physicians was called and the learned doctors listened respectfully to the oracle Fagon: all His Majesty needs is a tonic. The king decided that the Duc de Maine would replace him at the review of the gendarmerie, which he was too weak to attend. Saint-Simon was outraged yet again; for the Duc du Maine to replace the king instead of the Duc d'Orléans, to whom this function fell by right, was an affront. Saint-Simon went to nag the Duc d'Orléans: 'Do something, march up and down at the head of your company, in front of the Duc du Maine, ply him with insulting marks of exaggerated respect, make fun of him, make him feel small. Reduce this cardboard king to terror and embarrassment. Apart from the pleasure of walking all over him in the middle of his triumph, there is everything to be gained by making him afraid.' Orléans hesitated. 'I would have paid a great deal to have been the Duc d'Orléans for twenty-four hours', sighed Saint-Simon. Orléans chose the path of dignity and proceeded therefore before the Duc du Maine, ignoring him and greeting people as a Dauphin should.

On 23 August, the king was working in his study with Father Le Tellier. Knowing that it was perhaps his last opportunity, the confessor threw in all his crude powers of persuasion to get 'those well-known creatures of his with whom his deals were made not in money but in cabals' appointed to ecclesiastical benefices. Louis gibbed: 'I have enough accounts to settle with God without burdening myself further with such appointments and I forbid you to mention them again.'[15]

On 24 August, the king woke up with a violent pain in his leg. The physicians discovered black patches. 'It's gangrene,' they whispered to one another, terrified. They abandoned the pitiful tonic, but did not know what to replace it with.

On 25 August, his feast day, the king took pleasure in listening to the traditional *aubade* played by drums and oboes under his window and ordered his violins to play as usual during lunch. In order to entertain the patient, Maintenon summoned 'familiar ladies' and musicians. As the ladies chatted on, Louis dozed off, then woke up again, in a worse state. The physicians were called. His pulse was very sluggish. The 'familiar ladies' and the physicians were dismissed. Maintenon suggested extreme unction. 'It seems to me that it is still a little early,' her husband protested, 'but I suppose it is always a good thing to do.' Father Le Tellier rushed in to hear his confession, then Cardinal de Rohan, Almoner of France, entered, preceded by eight footmen bearing torches. After the extreme unction, the chancellor presented the king with the codicil to his will, which he had dictated that morning and to which he himself had added a few lines before signing it with a firm hand. Then the king summoned the Duc d'Orléans. 'Nephew, I am making you regent of the kingdom. You will find nothing in my will that should displease you. I recommend the Dauphin to you; serve him as faithfully as you have served me. If he goes, you shall be master and the crown belong to you. I have made the disposition that I believe to the wisest, but, as one cannot foresee everything, if there is anything there that is not good, it will be changed.' There was a pause, then came the final, monumental words: 'You are about to see one king in the grave and another in the cradle. Always remember the memory of the one and the interests of the other.' Overcome with grief, the Duc d'Orléans knelt down and wept. Then the king handed himself over to his physicians. The butchers had decided to make incisions into his leg. They plunged their knives into the bare flesh, cut into it again, reached the bone. The patient bore the appalling pain without a word of complaint. His physicians continued their gory work, only to find gangrened blood; they declared the sickness incurable. They left him in peace at last, watched over by Maintenon, who began her second sleepless night. The king dozed off, woke up again, saw her and said: 'I ask your forgiveness for not having lived well enough with you; I regret that I have not made you happy. But I have always loved and respected you.' He began to weep. Maintenon got up and left the room, 'fearful that he would harm himself if he went on weeping', explained Mlle d'Aumale. It seems an odd therapy to have left her husband dying alone, just when he was becoming more tender. She came back only when he had calmed down. Again he dozed off, again he awoke. Again he looked at Maintenon – when he had an idea he did not let it go. 'What will become of you, Madame, for you have nothing?' 'I am nothing; concern yourself only with God.' Again he seemed agitated, moved. Maintenon got up to leave the room again, took two steps, then came back to the bedside, 'I beg you, Sire, simply to ask M le Duc d'Orléans to have consideration for me.' 'I promise.' She left only half-reassured, for she was still afraid of the revenge that the man she considered a debauched poisoner might wreak on her.[16]

On 26 August, after mass, which he followed from his bed, the king saw Cardinals de Rohan and de Bissy, champions of the papal bull, and before witnesses – Maintenon, Le Tellier, Mlle d'Aumale and the chancellor – declared: 'I die in the faith and in submission to the Church.' The king paused, his eyes on the two cardinals, then resumed. 'It irks me to leave the affairs of the Church in the state in which they are. You know that I have done nothing except what you have wished. It is for you to answer before God on my behalf for everything that has been done.' So, even at the threshold of death, Louis' good sense gained the upper hand. Far from being taken aback by this 'frightful thunder-clap', the cardinals retained their composure and smoothly reassured the king. Louis went on: 'As for Cardinal de Noailles, God is my witness that I do not hate him and have always been angry at what I believed I had to do against him.' In their corner, Fagon and Maréchal looked at one another: 'So they will let the king die without seeing his archbishop.' Louis heard them: 'Not only do I feel no repugnance towards it, but I desire it.' The silence could be cut with a knife, the king broke it, turning to the chancellor: 'Fetch Cardinal de Noailles immediately,' then, gesturing towards Rohan and Bissy, 'If these gentlemen have no objection.' The two cardinals moved away to the window to confer with Le Tellier, then came back to the bedside. 'We agree that Cardinal de Noailles should have the honour of seeing Your Majesty, but on condition that he accept the bull and give his word that he does so.' 'Chancellor, write to the cardinal to this effect.' This blackmail deeply hurt Noailles: he had either to retract or give up seeing the king, his old friend, who was reaching out to him for the last time. Noailles was sick with pain and disgust, but he did not weaken. Le Tellier and his harpies in purple could now withdraw in triumph.[17]

It was time for public farewells. It was the great scene of which the seventeenth century, with its love of noble heroism in the face of death, was so fond. The dying king turned first to his courtiers: 'Gentlemen, I ask your forgiveness for the bad example that I have set you, and I would like to thank you for the way in which you have served me . . . Farewell gentlemen, I hope that you will remember me sometimes.' Then came the turn of the princes of the blood royal, the junior branches. Then the princesses, whom he heard crying in the room next door: his bastard daughter, the Duchesse d'Orléans, the Palatine, the Duchesse de Berry and others. 'I recommend a union between you.' The princesses withdrew, weeping and wailing. The curious, posted under the windows, heard this noisy grief and concluded that the king had just died. 'The king is dead,' the news ran from Versailles to Paris, from Paris to the provinces. In the dying man's bedroom, the king took his leave of the five-year-old boy who was his successor. It was the most famous, the best expressed and most thoroughly prepared of all his speeches: 'Child, you will be a great king; do not imitate me in the taste that I have shown for buildings or for war . . .' The old actor could feel pleased with himself, he had played that poignant scene in a quite dazzling way. He could now let his heart speak. He received the Duc du Maine in private, then the Comte de Toulouse. Then the Duc d'Orléans: there, too, he spoke from the heart; 'Nephew, I recommend Mme de Maintenon to you. You know what consideration and esteem I have always had for her. She has given me nothing but good advice. I would have done well to follow it. She has been useful to me in everything, but above all in my salvation.' Indeed he had loved, he still loved, Maintenon. Returning to his own quarters, the Duc d'Orléans found his apartment so full 'that a pin could not have fallen on the floor'. For several days now, people had thronged the apartment of the former Court pariah, the murderer, the plotter who, at any moment, would become the regent of the kingdom, the master of France.[18]

On 27 August, the king burnt a large quantity of papers, then remained alone with his wife: 'I have always heard it said that it was difficult to reconcile oneself with death. For me, on the point of that moment so feared by men, I do not find that this resolution is so painful to take.' Maintenon, suspicious of her husband's virtues and irritated by his self-satisfaction, replied: 'Yes that resolution is difficult to take when one has attachments to creatures, hatred in one's heart and restitution to be made.' He had a bad, sleepless night, and prayed to pass the time. He struck his breast many times reciting the *Confiteor*.[19]

At seven in the morning, 28 August, he received Father Le Tellier, who for once forgot the bull, the benefices, Cardinal de Noailles and spoke to him only of God and of death. In the mirror over the mantelpiece, Louis XIV caught sight of two servants, sitting at the foot of his bed, weeping: 'Why do you weep,' he asked them, 'did you believe me to be immortal? In view of my age, you should rather have prepared yourselves to lose me.' When he was alone with Maintenon once more he gave her a long, tender look: 'What consoles me in leaving you is the hope that at your age, we shall soon be together again.' Maintenon, who probably had no desire to fulfil this hope too soon, did not look at all pleased. The king's apothecary, Bolduc, swore that he heard her muttering to herself as she left the room: 'Listen to the appointment that he has made for me! That man never loved anyone but himself.' Her duty soon brought her back to her post. She had to complete her mission, for she had doubts about her husband as she had always had. 'Are you concerning yourself with God?' she asked him every quarter of an hour and he, like a good schoolboy replied: 'Yes, I think of Him with all my heart.'[20]

In the morning, a 'very vulgar Provençal churl' called Le Brin arrived at Versailles bringing an elixir that he swore was a miraculous cure for gangrene. Such were the ignorance and impotent despair of the physicians that they agreed to administer the remedy. Scarcely had he swallowed ten drops of the elixir in a glass of Alicante wine than the king felt better, but it proved a short respite. His pulse slowed down even more than before; a second dose of the elixir was administered and the king dozed off.[21]

At seven o'clock in the evening, one of the king's coaches was waiting before a side entrance to the palace. The Maréchal de Villeroi escorted to it a woman whose hair concealed her face. At the coach door, she raised her head. It was Mme de Maintenon. After a sharp, 'Farewell, M le Maréchal', the coach moved off bound for Saint-Cyr.[22] The Court had a great deal to say about this unexplained and premature departure. Maintenon's enemies denounced her appalling lack of feeling, the wife who abandoned her dying husband who needed her presence so much. Maintenon was indeed tired of her husband, to the point of hating him, but her duty, in the absence of affection, would have prevented her from abandoning a dying man. The truth was that she, too, was an old woman, exhausted by a week of sleepless nights. When she saw her husband sleeping calmly, she went to spend a quiet night in the only place where she could find peace. Moreover, she had asked Villeroi to send her a messenger with news every fifteen minutes.[23]

On 29 August, the king, whether because of sleep or the elixir, woke up feeling slightly better. He was even able to swallow two biscuits soaked in Alicante wine. His appetite returned and people began to wonder if he would recover. Entering the Duc d'Orléans' apartment, Saint-Simon found him alone – not a single courtier remained of the crowd of the day before. Orléans openly made fun of those weather-cocks: 'If the king eats a second time, we shall have no one here at all.' Taking advantage of this privacy, Saint-Simon began to sound him out as to what he had decided to do on the king's death. Still somewhat ill at

406

ease before his mentor, whose waspishness he still feared, Orléans made an admission to him. Four days earlier, at Villeroi's own request, he had received the marshal in great secrecy. Villeroi had then revealed to him the tenor of the king's will. In fact, Philippe d'Orléans would be regent only in name: he would merely preside over a council of regency, the members of which had been appointed by Louis XIV and which would decide everything on a majority vote – a majority that belonged in advance to the Duc du Maine. Moreover, the Duc du Maine had been put in charge of the young king's education, with Villeroi as the boy's governor. That was not all. In the codicil that he had dictated to the chancellor, Louis had placed the young king's civil and military household under the orders of the Duc du Maine. By making him absolute master of the sovereign's person, Louis was placing real power in his hands. As might be expected Saint-Simon's first reaction was indignation. 'You will find in my will nothing that will not please you,' Louis had promised his nephew. This monstrous hypocrisy at the very moment of death, made Saint-Simon choke with disgust. But it was less monstrous than the act itself, removing power from its legitimate trustee and giving it to 'that dirty bastard'. This was the explanation of all those mysteries, those incredible precautions to preserve the will from indiscreet eyes. What did the Duc d'Orléans think of it? The Duc d'Orléans thought nothing, or rather he found the king's dispositions perfectly natural. Saint-Simon, who thought them profoundly unnatural, resolved that they must put an end to scandal. They must act quickly and firmly, Orléans' supporters must be gathered together, the *parlement* must be alerted, steps must be taken to summon the States General. 'Do you think so, Monsieur?' inquired the duke. 'I most certainly do, Monseigneur!'[24]

However, the king continued with imperturbable calm to give orders on what should be done after his death, rather like a landlord meticulously putting in order a house that he was going to shut up. That evening he suddenly grew weaker. A new dose of the 'Provençal churl's' elixir was administered, to no effect. 'Where is Mme de Maintenon?' the dying man murmured. A messenger from Villeroi set off at great speed for Saint-Cyr and Louis' wife returned to Versailles without wasting a second. At eleven in the evening, the doctors examined the diseased leg. Gangrene had already eaten into the foot and knee, and was now attacking the thigh. They listened to his heart, palpated him, prodded him, felt his pulse. He lost consciousness.[25]

During the whole of 30 August, the king rarely emerged from a state of semi-consciousness. No one entered the bedchamber except Maintenon, a few servants and Le Tellier, who made brief appearances every now and then. His doctors, knowing that the situation was hopeless, remained in the room next door. Once, when he came round, Louis looked at Maintenon, sitting impassively at his bedside: 'You must have a great deal of courage and friendship for me, Madame, to remain there for so long.' She said nothing. 'Do not stay there any longer, Madame;

it is too sad a spectacle, but I hope that it will end soon.' He went into a coma. Maintenon left the room and went to her own apartment to pack her bags. She sent Mlle d'Aumale to ask her confessor, Father Briderey, to go and see the king. Briderey declared that Louis was dying and came back to his penitent: 'You may leave, you are no longer necessary to him.'[26] Maintenon had her passport at last. The Church had given her the duty of looking after the king and only the Church could tell her when her duty had come to an end; without that permission, she would not have left her post. She was, however, worried about bad feelings if she was recognized in the king's coach. Villeroi lent her his to travel in and had guards posted on the road. She left Versailles at five in the evening with Mlle d'Aumale. When the coach began to move, she burst into tears. 'My worry is great, but somewhat becalmed. I often weep, but they are tears of regret and tenderness. And the king's feelings of piety and his Christian death are great sources of consolation to me.'[27] She did weep over Louis for a while; a woman cannot live with a man for thirty years without weeping over him, even (and perhaps above all) if she did not love him. But at least Maintenon could now tell herself that her mission had been accomplished, for she had saved the king from eternal damnation. She added: 'I have never prayed for his life since he has been ill, only for his salvation.' She cared nothing for Louis XIV's life, but his salvation was her business, her purpose, her victory, after thirty years of effort, trouble and patience. He was dying and she could at last take her rest, her conscience at peace.

During 31 August the king emerged from his coma only for a few short moments. Gangrene had taken over the entire thigh. At eleven in the evening, prayers for the dying began to be said around his bed. At the sound of the voices, he emerged from the coma and gave the responses in a voice so strong that it swamped those of the ecclesiastics: 'O Lord make speed to save us! O God make haste to help us.' He fell back into a coma. He did not emerge from it again during the long agony that dragged throughout the night until quarter past eight the following morning, 1 September 1715: 'He gave up the ghost without any effort, like a candle dying out.'[28] At half-past eight, a messenger arrived at Saint-Cyr. Teachers and pupils hurried to the chapel, and Mlle d'Aumale was given the job of announcing the news to Maintenon: 'Madame, the entire house is at prayer in the church.' Maintenon understood and fell on her knees.[29]

In an apartment on the ground floor at Versailles, a small boy was waiting. The new King, Louis XV, was preparing himself to receive the homage of the Court. He was pale, silent, already grave, like the other small boy who had been in so similar a situation more than seventy years ago. Perhaps he felt close to tears, sensing, despite his five short years, that something immense and terrible was about to happen to him but he bravely held them back. He did not show his fear as he heard the footsteps and the murmur of voices approaching. Up on the floor above, there was a great deal of bustle and excitement; suddenly the

Court, which had slumbered for years, was like an overturned beehive. It was seventy-two years since a king had died in France. Covered in embroidery, lace, jewels, feathers, the courtiers filed into the Hall of Mirrors, led by Monseigneur le Régent. His natural good nature detracted in no way from his dignity, and he was the only one to remain calm and sincerely moved. The boy heard 'a rumble like that of the tides'. The double doors opened, the glittering crowd poured into the room. His uncle moved towards him – a man he hardly knew but about whom his governess and friends had whispered so many terrible things, and whom with a childish instinct he guessed to be an object of hate and repulsion. His dark eyes were fixed on him. Little Louis saw the expression of kindness, tenderness and compassion. The regent went down on one knee: 'Sire, I have come to pay my respects to Your Majesty as the first of your subjects.' And the child smiled.[30]

The next day a memorable session of the *parlement* took place at which Louis xiv's will was solemnly opened. Saint-Simon describes it at length in loving detail, for it marked his triumph. That 'cripple of a bastard', the Duc du Maine, was effectively robbed of all the exorbitant and illegal rights that had been given him by his father. After violent altercations, a good deal of intrigue and bargaining, the *parlementaires*, satiated with the rights that the regent had given them, gleefully voted to annul Louis xiv's will and to deprive the Duc du Maine of his posts one by one. The Duc d'Orléans was regent in fact and no longer in name.[31] It took less than twenty-four hours for Louis xiv's prediction concerning the fate of his will to be fulfilled. A clean sweep was made; the regent summoned Father Le Tellier, whom Louis xiv had appointed his confessor, and announced to him that it was time that he retired. Two men were waiting to accompany the priest at once to the convent of La Flèche.[32] Then the regent, with an unexpected degree of compassion and reconciliation, went, unknown to Saint-Simon, to visit Mme de Maintenon at Saint-Cyr. He was to make sure that the old lady's pension was regularly paid and he begged her, if she needed anything at all, not to hesitate to ask him for it.[33]

'I would wish with all my heart that your state were as happy as mine,' Maintenon wrote to the Princesse des Ursins. 'I saw the king die as a saint and as a hero. I have left the world, which I never cared for, and I am in the pleasantest retirement.' She was no longer in any danger, she was rid at last of her husband, she could now enjoy the rest that she so ardently desired in the setting that she loved so much. The Princesse des Ursins, bitter, exiled, deprived of everything, understood this well and envied it: 'Happy is he who can imitate you, for this world is not worthy of our regard. But one needs your courage and your virtue.'[34]

However, 'the unworthy world' manifested a quite unbridled, indecent relief at being delivered from Louis xiv. It was as if the cage in which the old potentate had for so long imprisoned France had suddenly been opened. Ministers were delighted to escape their slavery; *parlementaires* congratulated themselves on the importance that had been given

409

them; Paris 'breathed in the hope of some liberty'. The exhausted provinces 'trembled with joy', and 'the people, ruined, cowed, desperate, thanked God with scandalous enthusiasm'.

Overt festivities accompanied the funeral procession that took Louis' coffin to its last resting place. One witness of 'that universal joy' was a young man who one day was to be called Voltaire: 'I saw small tents erected on the road to Saint-Denis. People were drinking, singing, laughing. The feelings of the citizens of Paris had even taken hold of the populace.'[35] Appointed to follow his master's remains, one of the dukes of what was already being called 'the old Court' lowered the window of his coach and yelled at the bawling crowd: 'Croak, toads, now that the sun has set.'

Selected Bibliography

The author was able to draw for his research on contemporary sources in private collections and libraries in France not generally open to the public. The following is a short bibliography of works more readily available in English-speaking countries.

ARAGONNIS, Claude: *Madame Louis XIV* (Paris, 1938)

CARRÉ, Henri: *The Early Life of Louis XIV 1638–1661* (Translated by D. Bolton; London, 1951)
Madame de Montespan (Paris, 1939)

CHOISY, Abbé François Timoléon de: *The Transvestite Memoirs of the Abbé de Choisy and the Story of the Marquise-Marquis de Bonneville* (Translated with an introduction by R. H. E. Scott; London, 1973)

CHURCHILL, Rt. Hon. Sir Winston S.: *A History of the English Speaking Peoples* (4 vols; London, 1956–58)
Marlborough, His Life and Times (London, 1938)

DUCASSE, André: *La Guerre des Camisards: La Résistance Huguenots sous Louis XIV* (Paris, 1946)

ERLANGER, Philippe: *Louis XIV* (Translated by Stephen Cox; London, 1970)
'Monsieur', Frère de Louis XIV (Paris, 1974)
Philippe V, Roi d'Espagne (Paris, 1978)

LENÔTRE, Georges: *En France Jadis* (Paris, 1949)
Paris Qui Disparait (Paris, 1937)
Versailles au Temps du Roi (Paris, 1950)

LOUIS XIV: *Oeuvres* (Paris, 1942)

MACAULAY, Baron T. B.: *The History of England from The Accession of James II* (London, 1882)

MICHELET, Jules: *Histoire de France jusqu'au XVIIIe Siècle* (Paris, 1897)

MONGREDIEN, Georges: *La Vie Quotidienne Sous Louis XIV* (Paris, 1948)

NOLHAC, Pierre de: *Versailles et la Cour de France* (10 volumes; Paris, 1925–30)

ORIEUX, Jean: *La Fontaine, ou, La Vie Est un Conte* (Paris, 1976)

POISSON, Georges: *Monsieur de Saint-Simon* (Paris, 1973)

ROBB, Nesca Adeline: *William of Orange: A Personal Portrait* (2 vols; London, 1962–66)

SAINT-GERMAIN, Jacques: *La Reynie et la Police au Grand Siècle* (Paris, 1955)

SAINT-SIMON, Louis de Rouvroy, Duc de: *Memoirs* (Translated by L. Norton. 3 vols; London, 1974)

SPANHEIM, Ézechiel: *Rélations de la Cour de France* (Paris, 1882)

VOLTAIRE, François Marie Arouet de: *The Age of Louis XIV* (Translated by E. Pollack; London, 1950)

ZIEGLER, Gilette: *The Court of Versailles in the Reign of Louis XIV* (Translated by S. Watson-Taylor; London, 1966)

Notes

Chapter 1

1 Madame de Motteville: *Mémoires sur Anne d'Autriche et Sa Cour* (Paris 1886)
2 Louis Henri de Lomenie, Comte de Brienne: *Mémoires* (Paris, 1916)
3 Henri Carré: *The Early Life of Louis XIV, 1638–1661* Trs. D. Bolton. (London, 1951)
4 Comte de Beaucamp: *Correspondance de Louis XIII et de Richelieu*
5 Pierre Adolphe Chéruel: *Histoire de la France Pendant La Minorité de Louis XIV* (Paris, 1879-80); Motteville: *op cit*; Mademoiselle de Montpensier: *Mémoires* (Paris, 1859); Jean Lacour-Gayet: *L'Education de Louis XIV*
6 Motteville: *op cit*
7 *Ibid*
8 Marquis de Chouppes: *Mémoires*
9 Motteville: *op cit*
10 *Ibid*
11 *Ibid*
12 *Ibid*
13 Princess Palatine, Duchesse d'Orléans: *Correspondance* (Paris, 1855)
14 Chéruel: *op cit*
15 Brienne: *op cit*
16 Motteville: *op cit*

Chapter 2

1 Pierre La Porte: *Mémoires* (Geneva, 1756)
2 Mme de Motteville: *Mémoires*
3 Comte de Brienne: *Mémoires*
4 La Porte: *op cit*
5 *Ibid*
6 Motteville: *op cit*
7 La Porte: *op cit*
8 Motteville: *op cit*
9 *Ibid*
10 *Ibid*
11 P. A. Chéruel: *Histoire de la France Pendant la Minorité de Louis XIV*
12 H. Carré: *The Early Life of Louis XIV*
13 Brienne: *op cit*
14 La Porte: *op cit*
15 *Ibid*
16 *Ibid*
17 Motteville: *op cit*
18 La Porte: *op cit*
19 Louis XIV: *Mémoires pour l'Instruction du Dauphin* (Paris, 1860)
20 Brienne: *op cit*
21 La Porte: *op cit*
22 *Ibid*
23 Carré: *op cit*
24 La Porte: *op cit*
25 Mlle de Montpensier: *Mémoires*
26 Motteville: *op cit*; Montpensier: *op cit*; P. A. Chéruel (ed): *Mémoires sur la Vie Publique et Privée de Fouquet, Superintendant de Finances* (Paris, 1862)
27 Motteville: *op cit*
28 Montpensier: *op cit*

29 Motteville: *op cit*
30 *Ibid*
31 *Ibid*; Montpensier: *op cit*

Chapter 3

1 A. Feillet: *La Misére au Temps de la Fronde* (Paris, 1886)
2 Mme de Motteville: *Mémoires*
3 P. A. Chéruel: *Histoire de la France Pendant la Minorité de Louis XIV*
4 Motteville: *op cit*; Mlle de Montpensier: *Mémoires*
5 Motteville: *op cit*
6 Comte de Brienne: *Mémoires*
7 Montpensier: *op cit*
8 Jean Vallé: *Journal*
9 Motteville: *op cit*
10 *Ibid*
11 *Ibid*
12 Brienne: *op cit*
13 Jules, Comte de Cosnac: *Mazarin et Colbert* (Paris, 1892)
14 Montpensier: *op cit*
15 Feillet: *op cit*
16 De Cosnac: *op cit*
17 Chéruel: *op cit*
18 Montpensier: *op cit*

Chapter 4

1 Mme de Motteville: *Mémoires*
2 *Ibid*
3 Louis XIV: *Mémoires pour l'Instruction du Dauphin*
4 Chevalier de Sévigné: *Correspondance avec Christine de France, Duchesse de Savoie* (Paris,
    1911)
5 P. A. Chéruel: *Histoire de la France Pendant la Minorité de Louis XIV*
6 Comte de Cosnac: *Mazarin et Colbert*
7 De Sévigné: *op cit*
8 P. La Porte: *Mémoires*
9 *Ibid*
10 Claude Aragonnis: *Madame Louis XIV* (Paris, 1938)
11 De Sévigné: *op cit*
12 A. Feillet: *La Misére au Temps de la Fronde*
13 *Ibid*
14 Jean Orieux: *La Fontaine, ou, La Vie Est un Conte* (Paris, 1976)
15 P. A. Chéruel (ed): *Mémoires de Fouquet*
16 De Cosnac: *op cit*
17 La Porte: *op cit*
18 *Ibid*
19 Motteville: *op cit*
20 La Porte: *op cit*
21 *Ibid*
22 Motteville: *op cit*
23 De Sévigné: *op cit*
24 Chéruel: *op cit*
25 De Cosnac: *op cit*

Chapter 5

1 Abbe François Timoléon de Choisy: *The Transvestite Memoirs of the Abbé de Choisy and the Story of the Marquise-Marquis de Bonneville* (Trs. R. H. E. Scott, London, 1973)
2 Comte de Cosnac: *Mazarin et Colbert*
3 Mme de Motteville: *Mémoires*
4 Comte de Brienne; *Mémoires*
5 *Ibid*
6 Louis XIV: *Mémoires*
7 P. A. Chéruel (ed): *Mémoires de Fouquet*; Duc de Saint-Simon: *Mémoires* (Paris, 1842)
8 Cosnac: *op cit*
9 Motteville: *op cit*
10 Choisy: *op cit*
11 Saint-Simon: *op cit*
12 Motteville: *op cit*
13 Mlle de Montpensier: *Mémoires*
14 *Ibid*
15 Motteville: *op cit*; Brienne: *op cit*; Montpensier: *op cit*; Cosnac: *op cit*; Princess Palatine: *Correspondance*
16 Motteville: *op cit*; Montpensier: *op cit*
17 Montpensier: *op cit*
18 D'Aquin, Fagon and Vallot: *Journal de la Santé du Roi de l'Année 1647–1711* (Paris, 1862)
19 Montpensier: *op cit*
20 Cosnac: *op cit*
21 Montpensier: *op cit*
22 D'Aquin etc: *op cit*
23 Montpensier: *op cit*
24 *Ibid*
25 Roger de Rabutin, Comte de Bussy: *Correspondance* (Paris, 1858)
26 Motteville: *op cit*; Montpensier: *op cit*; Cosnac: *op cit*
27 Cosnac: *op cit*
28 Montpensier: *op cit*
29 *Ibid*

Chapter 6

1 Comte de Cosnac: *Mazarin et Colbert*
2 P. A. Chéruel (ed): *Mémoires de Fouquet*
3 Jean Héraud de Gourville: *Mémoires* (Paris, 1845)
4 Chéruel: *op cit*
5 Cosnac: *op cit*
6 Mme de Motteville: *Mémoires*
7 Comte de Brienne: *Mémoires*
8 *Ibid*
9 *Ibid*
10 Cosnac: *op cit*
11 Motteville: *op cit*
12 Gabriel Basset d'Auriac: *Les Deux Pénitences de Louise de la Vallière*
13 Motteville: *op cit*
14 Cosnac: *op cit*
15 Abbé de Choisy: *Transvestite Memoirs*
16 Cosnac: *op cit*
17 *Ibid*
18 George Lenôtre: *Le Mariage de Louis XIV*
19 Motteville: *op cit*; Montpensier: *op cit*

20 Montpensier: *op cit*
21 *Ibid*
22 Lenôtre: *op cit*
23 Motteville: *op cit*
24 Claude Aragonnis: *Madame Louis XIV*
25 Chéruel: *op cit*
26 *Ibid*
27 *Ibid*
28 Motteville: *op cit*
29 Brienne: *op cit*
30 Motteville: *op cit*
31 Marquis de Monglas: *Mémoires* (Paris, 1838)
32 Cosnac: *op cit*; Choisy: *op cit*
33 Motteville: *op cit*
34 Duc de Saint-Simon: *Mémoires*
35 Chéruel: *op cit*; Brienne: *op cit*
36 Brienne: *op cit*
37 Duchesse de Navaille: *Mémoires*
38 *Ibid*

Chapter 7

1 Jean de Boislisle (ed): *Mémoriaux du Conseil de 1661* (Paris, 1905)
2 Comte de Brienne: *Mémoires*
3 Mme de Motteville: *Mémoires*
4 Comte de Cosnac: *Mazarin et Colbert*
5 Abbé de Choisy: *Transvestite Memoirs*
6 Motteville: *op cit*
7 *Ibid*
8 François de Salignac de la Mothe Fénélon, Archbishop of Cambrai: *Oeuvres* (Paris, 1826)
9 Louis XIV: *Mémoires pour l'Instruction du Dauphin*
10 P. A. Chéruel (ed): *Mémoires de Fouquet*
11 Louis XIV: *op cit*
12 *Ibid*
13 *Ibid*
14 Duc de Saint-Simon: *Parallèles des Trois Rois Bourbons*
15 Louis XIV: *op cit*
16 Cosnac: *op cit*
17 Louis XIV: *op cit*
18 *Ibid*
19 *Ibid*
20 *Ibid*
21 *Ibid*
22 *Ibid*
23 *Ibid*
24 *Ibid*
25 *Ibid*
26 *Ibid*
27 Mlle de Montpensier: *Mémoires*
28 Jean Lair: *Louise de la Vallière et la Jeunesse de Louis XIV* (Paris, 1881)
29 Louis XIV: *Oeuvres* (Paris, 1942)
30 Motteville: *op cit*
31 Lair: *op cit*; G. Basset d'Auriac: *Les Deux Pénitences de Louise de la Vallière*
32 Basset d'Auriac: *op cit*
33 *Ibid*

34 Lair: *op cit*
35 Chéruel: *op cit*
36 Choisy: *op cit*
37 Saint-Simon: *Mémoires*
38 Choisy: *op cit*
39 Brienne: *op cit*
40 Chéruel: *op cit*
41 J. H. de Gourville: *Mémoires*
42 Chéruel: *op cit*
43 Brienne: *op cit*
44 *Ibid*
45 *Ibid*
46 Chéruel: *op cit*
47 *Ibid*
48 Louis XIV: *Mémoires pour l'Instruction du Dauphin*
49 Chéruel: *op cit*
50 *Ibid*
51 Brienne: *op cit*
52 Voltaire: *Le Siècle de Louis XIV*
53 Louis XIV: *op cit*; Charles Auguste, Marquis de La Fare: *Mémoires et Réflexions sur les Principaux Evenements du Régne de Louis XIV* (Paris, 1838)
54 Saint-Simon: *op cit*
55 J. Lemoine: *Lettres sur la Cour de Louis XIV*
56 Saint-Simon: *op cit*
57 Lair: *op cit*
58 Gilette Ziegler: *The Court of Versailles in the Reign of Louis XIV* (Trs. S. Watson-Taylor, London 1966); Princess Palatine: *Correspondance*
59 Lair: *op cit*
60 *Ibid*
61 *Ibid*

Chapter 8

1 Georges Mongredien: *La Vie Quotidienne sous Louis XIV* (London, 1948)
2 Abbé de Choisy: *Transvestite Memoirs*
3 Louis XIV: *Correspondance Administrative sous le Régne de Louis XIV* (Paris, 1850–1855)
4 P. A. Chéruel (ed): *Mémoires de Fouquet*
5 Voltaire: *Le Siècle de Louis XIV*
6 Chéruel: *op cit*; Duc de Saint-Simon: *Mémoires*
7 Mme de Motteville: *Mémoires*
8 Chéruel: *op cit*
9 Jean Lair: *Louise de La Vallière et la Jeunesse de Louis XIV*
10 Olivier Le Febvre d'Ormesson: *Journal* (Paris, 1860–1862)
11 Gilette Ziegler: *The Court of Versailles in the Reign of Louis XIV*
12 Lair: *op cit*
13 *Ibid*
14 Pierre de Nolhac: *Versailles et la Cour de France; Vol. 1: La Création de Versailles* (Paris, 1925)
15 Motteville: *op cit*
16 Roger de Rabutin, Comte de Bussy: *Histoire Amoureuse des Gaules et la France Galante* (Paris, 1868)
17 *Ibid*
18 Alain Decaux: *Les Grandes Enigmes de l'Histoire*
19 *Ibid*
20 Lair: *op cit*

21 Ziegler: *op cit*
22 *Ibid*
23 Lair: *op cit*
24 Louis XIV: *op cit*

Chapter 9

1 Mlle de Montpensier: *Mémoires*
2 Claude Aragonnis: *Madame Louis XIV*
3 Mme de Caylus: *Souvenirs* (Paris, 1965)
4 Henri Carré: *Madame de Montespan* (Paris, 1939)
5 Gilette Ziegler: *The Court of Versailles in the Reign of Louis XIV*
6 Jean Lair: *Louise de la Vallière et la Jeunesse de Louis XIV*
7 Montpensier: *op cit*
8 Caylus: *op cit*
9 Montpensier: *op cit*
10 J. Lemoine: *Lettres sur la Cour de Louis XIV*
11 G. Basset d'Auriac: *Les Deux Pénitences de Louise de la Vallière*
12 Louis XIV: *Mémoires pour l'Instruction du Dauphin*
13 P. A. Chéruel (ed): *Mémoires de Fouquet*
14 Louis XIV: *op cit*
15 Ezechiel Spanheim: *Rélations de la Cour de France* (Paris, 1882); Voltaire: *Le Siècle de Louis XIV*
16 Montpensier: *op cit*
17 Lair: *op cit*
18 Carré: *op cit*
19 *Ibid*
20 Montpensier: *op cit*; Lair: *op cit*
21 Montpensier: *op cit*
22 *Ibid*
23 Voltaire: *op cit*
24 Duc de Saint-Simon: *Mémoires*
25 *Ibid*
26 Lemoine: *op cit*
27 *Ibid*
28 Roger de Rabutin: *Histoires Amoureuses des Gaules*
29 Lemoine: *op cit*
30 Carré: *op cit*
31 Voltaire: *op cit*
32 Louis XIV: *op cit*
33 *Ibid*
34 Voltaire: *op cit*
35 P. de Nolhac: *La Création de Versailles*
36 Olivier d'Ormesson: *Journal*
37 Montpensier: *op cit*
38 Carré: *op cit*
39 *Ibid*
40 Rabutin: *op cit*
41 Louis XIV: *op cit*
42 Caylus: *op cit*
43 Comte d'Haussonville G. Hanotaux (eds): *Mémoires et Lettres Inédites de Mlle d'Aumale* (Paris, 1902)

Chapter 10

1 Pierre Clément: *Lettres et Instructions de Colbert* (Paris, 1861–1882)
2 Louis XIV: *Mémoires pour l'Instruction du Dauphin*
3 *Ibid*
4 Mlle de Montpensier: *Mémoires*
5 *Ibid*
6 *Ibid*
7 Clément: *op cit*
8 Philippe Erlanger: *Monsieur, Frère de Louis XIV* (Paris, 1972)
9 Montpensier: *op cit*
10 J. Lemoine: *Lettres Sur la Cour de Louis XIV*
11 Montpensier: *op cit*
12 *Ibid*
13 Lemoine: *op cit*
14 Duc de Saint-Simon: *Mémoires*
15 Jean Lair: *Louise de la Vallière et la Jeunesse de Louis XIV*
16 G. Basset d'Auriac: *Les Deux Pénitences de Louise de La Vallière*
17 Louis XIV: *op cit*
18 R. de Vissac: *Antoine de Rourre et la Revolte de 1670* (Paris, 1895)
19 Montpensier: *op cit*
20 H. Carré: *Madame de Montespan*; Montpensier: *op cit*; Saint-Simon: *op cit*
21 Carré: *op cit*; d'Haussonville and Hanotaux: *Mémoires de Mlle d'Aumale*; Primi
     Visconti: *Mémoires sur la Cour de Louis XIV* (Paris, 1909); Lair: *op cit*; Basset
     d'Auriac: *op cit*
22 Roger de Rabutin, Comte de Bussy: *Correspondances*
23 Carré: *op cit*
24 Montpensier: *op cit*
25 Lemoine: *op cit*
26 Princess Palatine: *Correspondance*
27 *Ibid*
28 Montpensier: *op cit*

Chapter 11

1 Joséphe Jacquiot: *Medailles et Jétons de Louis XIV*
2 Abbé de Choisy: *Transvestite Memoirs*; Louis XIV: *Correspondance Administrative*
3 Comte de Brienne: *Mémoires*
4 Nesca Adeline Robb: *William of Orange, A Personal Portrait* (London, 1962–1966);
     Gyel Pieler: *Les Pays-Bas au XVIe Siècle*
5 Louis XIV: *Mémoires pour l'Instruction du Dauphin*
6 Comte Armand de Mormés de Saint-Hilaire: *Mémoires* (Paris, 1903)
7 Marquis de Vogüé (ed): *Mémoires de Louis Hector de Villars, Maréchal de France* (Paris,
     1884)
8 J. Lemoine: *Lettres sur la Cour de Louis XIV*
9 Louis XIV: *Oeuvres*
10 Pieler: *op cit*; Robb: *op cit*
11 J. H. de Gourville: *Mémoires*
12 Robb: *op cit*; Pieler: *op cit*
13 Ezechiel Spanheim: *Rélations de la Cour de France*
14 Louis XIV: *Mémoires*
15 Jean Lair: *Louise de la Vallière et la Jeunesse de Louis XIV*
16 Pieler: *op cit*; Robb: *op cit*; Michel Richard: *Les Oranges-Nassau*
17 Voltaire: *Le Siècle de Louis XIV*
18 Robb: *op cit*
19 P. Clément: *Lettres et Instructions de Colbert*

20 Robb: *op cit*
21 Clément: *op cit*
22 *Ibid*
23 Montpensier: *op cit*; Saint-Simon: *Mémoires*
24 Saint-Simon: *op cit*
25 Roger de Rabutin: *Correspondance*
26 Montpensier: *op cit*
27 H. Carré: *Madame de Montespan*; Françoise d'Aubigné, Marquise de Maintenon
        (Madame de Maintenon): *Correspondance Générale* (Paris, 1865–1866)
28 Lair: *op cit*; G. Basset d'Auriac: *Les Deux Penitences de Louise de la Vallière*
29 Lair: *op cit*; Carré: *op cit*
30 Montpensier: *op cit*
31 *Ibid*
32 Clément: *op cit*
33 Montpensier: *op cit*

Chapter 12

1 Pierre de Nolhac: *La Création de Versailles*
2 Voltaire: *Le Siècle de Louis XIV*
3 Nolhac: *op cit*
4 Gilette Ziegler: *The Court of Versailles in the Reign of Louis XIV*
5 *Ibid*
6 H. Carré: *Madame de Montespan*; d'Haussonville and Hanotaux: *Mémoires de Mlle
        d'Aumale*
7 Mme de Maintenon: *Correspondance*
8 Marquis de Vogüé: *Mémoires du Maréchal de Villars*
9 Carré: *op cit*; d'Haussonville: *op cit*
10 Ziegler: *op cit*
11 J. Lemoine: *La Revolte Dite du Papier Timbre ou des Bonnets Rouges en Bretagne* (Paris,
        1898)
12 Carré: *op cit*; Mme de Caylus: *Souvenirs*; Madame Marie de Sévigné: *Lettres* (Paris,
        1876)
13 Lemoine: *op cit*; Yves-Marie Bercé: *Croquants et Va-nu-pieds: Les Soulevements Paysans
        en France du XVIe au XIXe Siècle* (Geneva, 1970)
14 Sévigné: *op cit*
15 Comte de Saint-Hilaire: *Mémoires*
16 Georges Mongredien: *La Vie Quotidienne sous Louis XIV*; Bercé: *op cit*
17 Saint-Hilaire: *op cit*
18 Sévigné: *op cit*
19 Bercé: *op cit*
20 Sévigné: *op cit*
21 Saint-Hilaire: *op cit*
22 Carré: *op cit*; d'Haussonville: *op cit*; Maintenon: *op cit*
23 Louis XIV: *Oeuvres*
24 N. A. Robb: *William of Orange*
25 Duc de Saint-Simon: *Mémoires*

Chapter 13

1 H. Carré: *Madame de Montespan*; G. Ziegler: *The Court of Versailles*; Primi Visconti:
        Mémoires; Roger de Rabutin: *Correspondance*
2 D'Haussonville and Hanotaux: *Mémoires de Mlle d'Aumale*
3 Mme de Sévigné: *Lettres*
4 Primi Visconti: *op cit*

5 Duc de Saint-Simon: *Mémoires*
6 *Ibid*
7 Sir Winston Churchill: *Marlborough, His Life and Times*
8 Carré: *op cit*
9 Princess Palatine: *Correspondance*
10 Carré: *op cit*
11 P. Erlanger: *Monsieur, Frère de Louis XIV*; N. A. Robb: *William of Orange*; Marquis de
       Saint-Hilaire: *Mémoires*
12 Primi Visconti: *op cit*
13 Louis XIV: *Oeuvres*
14 Carre: *op cit*
15 Rabutin: *op cit*
16 J. Orieux: *La Fontaine*
17 Robb: *op cit*; T. B. Macaulay: *The History of England*
18 Saint-Simon: *op cit*; Robb: *op cit*
19 Princess Palatine: *op cit*
20 Robb: *op cit*; Voltaire: *Le Siècle de Louis XIV*
21 Macaulay: *op cit*
22 Sévigné: *op cit*; Mme de Caylus: *Souvenirs*; Princess Palatine: *op cit*; Saint-Simon: *op cit*
23 Primi Visconti: *Mémoires*
24 *Ibid*
25 Mme de Caylus: *Souvenirs*
26 Saint-Simon: *op cit*
27 Carré: *op cit*
28 *Ibid*
29 Princess Palatine: *Correspondance*
30 Ziegler: *op cit*
31 Princess Palatine: *op cit*

Chapter 14

1 H. Carré: *Madame de Montespan*; Gilette Ziegler: *The Court of Versailles*
2 Carré: *op cit*
3 Roger de Rabutin: *Correspondance*
4 Ziegler: *op cit*
5 Mme de Maintenon: *Correspondance*
6 Carré: *op cit*
7 P. Clément: *Lettres et Instructions de Colbert*
8 Primi Visconti: *Mémoires*
9 Marquis de La Fare: *Mémoires et Réflexions*
10 *Ibid*
11 Ziegler: *op cit*; P. Erlanger: *Monsieur, Frère de Louis XIV*
12 Duc de Saint-Simon: *Mémoires*
13 Louis XIV: *Mémoires pour l'Instruction du Dauphin*
14 La Reynie, Lieutenant de Police de Paris: *Lettres et Notes* (Bibliothèque Nationale,
       Manuscrits Français Nos. 7629-7608); Ziegler: *op cit*
15 J. Orieux: *La Fontaine*
16 La Reynie: *op cit*
17 Primi Visconti: *op cit*; Vogüé: *Mémoires de Marèchal de Villars*
18 Jacques Saint-Germain: *La Reynie et la Police au Grand Siècle* (Paris, 1955); Mme de
       Sévigné: *Lettres*; Saint-Simon: *op cit*; Ziegler: *op cit*
19 Carré: *op cit*
20 *Ibid*
21 D'Haussonville and Hanotaux: *Mémoires de Mlle d'Aumale*
22 Maintenon: *op cit*
23 Primi Visconti: *op cit*; Rabutin: *op cit*; Saint-Germain: *op cit*

24 Saint-Germain: *op cit*
25 Sévigné: *op cit*
26 Mlle de Montpensier: *Mémoires*; Princess Palatine: *Correspondance*; Ziegler: *op cit*;
     Saint-Simon: *op cit*
27 Marquis de Sourches: *Mémoires sur la Cour de Louis XIV* (Paris, 1882); Sévigné: *op cit*
28 D'Haussonville: *op cit*
29 Carré: *op cit*
30 Primi Visconti: *op cit*
31 Maintenon: *op cit*
32 Sévigné: *op cit*; La Fare: *op cit*; Carré: *op cit*; Ziegler: *op cit*
33 Saint-Germain: *op cit*

Chapter 15

1 H. Carré: *Madame de Montespan*; J. Saint-Germain: *La Reynie et la Police*
2 Carré: *op cit*
3 G. Ziegler: *The Court of Versailles*; Princess Palatine: *Correspondance*; Roger de
     Rabutin: *Correspondance*; Saint-Germain: *op cit*
4 Mme de Sévigné: *Lettres*
5 Mme de Maintenon: *Correspondance Générale*
6 Carré: *op cit*
7 Maintenon: *op cit*
8 Carré: *op cit*
9 *Ibid*
10 E. Spanheim: *Rélations de la Cour de Louis XIV*
11 Louis XIV: *Oeuvres*
12 J. Lemoine: *Lettres Sur la Cour de Louis XIV*
13 Duc de Saint-Simon: *Mémoires*
14 Voltaire: *Le Siècle de Louis XIV*
15 Saint-Simon: *Parallèles des Trois Rois Bourbons*; Spanheim: *op cit*; Comte de Saint-
     Hilaire: *Mémoires*
16 Spanheim: *op cit*
17 Saint-Simon: *Mémoires*
18 Voltaire: *op cit*
19 J. H. de Gourville: *Mémoires*
20 N. A. Robb: *William of Orange*
21 Presclin and Jarny: *Histoire de l'Eglise*; Saint-Simon: *op cit*; Voltaire: *op cit*

Chapter 16

1 P. de Nolhac: *La Création de Versailles*
2 Louis XIV: *Oeuvres*
3 G. Lenôtre: *Versailles au Temps des Rois*
4 P. de Nolhac: *Versailles et la Cour de France Vol. 2: Versailles, Résidence de Louis XIV*
     (Paris, 1925)
5 Primi Visconti: *Mémoires*
6 Duc de Saint-Simon: *Mémoires*
7 Nolhac: *op cit*
8 Louis XIV: *Mémoires*
9 *Ibid*
10 Primi Visconti: *op cit*
11 Marquis de Sourches: *Mémoires*
12 Jean Lair: *Louise de la Vallière et la Jeunesse de Louis XIV*
13 G. Ziegler: *The Court of Versailles*; Saint-Simon: *op cit*
14 Princess Palatine: *Correspondance*

15 *Ibid*
16 G. Basset d'Auriac: *Les Deux Pénitences de Louise de la Vallière*
17 Saint-Simon: *op cit*
18 Primi Visconti: *op cit*
19 Louis XIV: *op cit*
20 Comte de Cosnac: *Mémoires*
21 Princess Palatine: *op cit*
22 P. A. Chéruel (ed): *Mémoires de Fouquet*
23 Saint-Simon: *op cit*
24 *Ibid*
25 *Ibid*
26 Mme de Sévigné: *Lettres*
27 Princess Palatine: *op cit*
28 Saint-Simon: *op cit*
29 Primi Visconti: *op cit*
30 Saint-Simon: *op cit*
31 Spanheim: *op cit*
32 *Ibid*
33 *Ibid*
34 *Ibid*
35 *Ibid*
36 G. Lenôtre: *op cit*
37 Princess Palatine: *op cit*
38 J. Lemoine: *Lettres sur la Cour de Louis XIV*
39 Princess Palatine: *op cit*
40 Philippe de Courcillon, Marquis de Dangeau: *Journal de la Cour de Louis XIV* (Paris, 1807)
41 Saint-Simon: *op cit*
42 *Ibid*
43 *Ibid*; Mme de Motteville: *Mémoires*
44 Saint-Simon: *op cit*
45 Arcibal: *Louis XIV et les Protestants*
46 Voltaire: *Le Siècle de Louis XIV*; Arcibal: *op cit*; Jules Michelet: *Histoire de France* (Paris, 1897); J. Marchand: *Un Intendant sous Louis XIV* (Paris, 1889)
47 Louis XIV: *Correspondance Administrative*; Michelet: *op cit*
48 Arcibal: *op cit*; Michelet: *op cit*
49 M. Richard: *Les Orange-Nassau*; T. B. Macaulay: *The History of England from the Accession of James II* (London, 1882)
50 Arcibal: *op cit*
51 *Ibid*
52 *Ibid*
53 D'Haussonville and Hanotaux: *Mémoires de Mlle d'Aumale*
54 Saint-Simon: *op cit*
55 Princess Palatine: *op cit*
56 Abbé de Choisy: *Transvestite Memoirs*
57 Mlle de Montpensier: *Mémoires*
58 H. Carré: *Madame de Montespan*

Chapter 17

1 Abbé Charles Pinot Duclos: *Mémoires Secrets sur la Regne de Louis XIV et Louis XV* (Paris, 1857)
2 Mme de Maintenon: *Correspondance Générale*
3 *Ibid*
4 *Ibid*

5 *Ibid*
6 J. Michelet: *Histoire de France*; Louis XIV: *Correspondance Administrative*
7 André Ducasse: *La Guerre des Camisards: La Résistance Huguenots sous Louis XIV* (Paris, 1946)
8 Duc de Saint-Simon: *Mémoires*
9 Comte de Saint-Hilaire: *Mémoires*
10 Maintenon: *op cit*
11 Voltaire: *Le Siècle de Louis XIV*; Saint-Hilaire: *op cit*; Anonymous: *Histoire du Prince Eugène de Savoie* (Vienna, 1790)
12 Voltaire: *op cit*; *Histoire du Prince Eugène*
13 Voltaire: *op cit*
14 Gyel Pieler: *Les Pays-Bas au XVIIe Siècle*
15 Maintenon: *op cit*
16 Saint-Simon: *op cit*
17 *Ibid*
18 Maintenon: *op cit*
19 *Ibid*
20 D'Haussonville and Hanotaux: *Mémoires de Mlle d'Aumale*
21 Saint-Simon: *op cit*
22 Mme de Caylus: *Souvenirs*
23 Princess Palatine: *Correspondance*
24 Saint-Simon: *op cit*
25 Abbé de Choisy: *Transvestite Memoirs*
26 H. Carré: *Madame de Montespan*
27 D'Haussonville: *op cit*
28 Saint-Simon: *op cit*; Princess Palatine: *op cit*
29 Maintenon: *op cit*
30 N. A. Robb: *William of Orange*
31 Saint-Hilaire: *op cit*; Voltaire: *op cit*
32 Saint-Hilaire: *op cit*
33 Marquis de Dangeau: *Journal*
34 Père Guillon: *Versailles, Palais du Soleil*
35 Pierre de Nolhac: *Versailles, Résidence de Louis XIV*
36 Guillon: *op cit*
37 Saint-Hilaire: *op cit*; Dangeau: *op cit*
38 Saint-Simon: *op cit*

Chapter 18

1 A Ducasse: *La Guerre des Camisards*
2 J. Michelet: *Histoire de France*
3 *Ibid*
4 Abbé Duclos: *Mémoires Secrets*
5 Ducasse: *op cit*
6 Louis XIV: *Correspondance Administrative*
7 Ezechiel Spanheim: *Rélations de la Cour de France*
8 Mme de Caylus: *Souvenirs*
9 Gilette Ziegler: *The Court of Versailles*
10 Michelet: *op cit*
11 *Ibid*
12 Spanheim: *op cit*
13 Sir Winston S. Churchill: *Marlborough: His Life and Times* (London: 1933–38)
14 T. B. Macaulay: *The History of England*
15 Churchill: *op cit*

16 N. A. Robb: *William of Orange*
17 Voltaire: *Le Siècle de Louis XIV*; Comte de Saint-Hilaire: *Mémoires*; Abbé de Choisy: *Transvestite Memoirs*; Marquis de Dangeau: *Journal*
18 Mme de Maintenon: *Correspondance Générale*; Théophile Lavallée: *Madame de Maintenon et la Maison Royale de Saint-Cyr* (Paris, 1862); Choisy: *op cit*
19 Saint-Hilaire: *op cit*
20 Dangeau: *op cit*
21 *Ibid*
22 Chevalier de Quincy: *Mémoires* (Paris, 1848)
23 Saint-Hilaire: *op cit*
24 Choisy: *op cit*; Saint-Hilaire: *op cit*; Voltaire: *op cit*; Duc de Saint-Simon: *Mémoires*
25 *Correspondance Administrative*
26 Voltaire: *op cit*; Saint-Hilaire: *op cit*; Presclin and Jarny: *Histoire de l'Eglise*; La Fontaine: *Oeuvres* (Paris 1824); *Histoire du Prince Eugène*
27 *Histoire du Prince Eugène*; Voltaire: *op cit*; Saint-Hilaire: *op cit*; Robb: *op cit*
28 Princess Palatine: *Correspondance*
29 Macaulay: *op cit*; Churchill: *op cit*; Saint-Simon: *op cit*
30 Saint-Hilaire: *op cit*; Macaulay: *op cit*; Churchill: *op cit*
31 Dangeau: *op cit*
32 Maintenon: *op cit*; Caylus: *op cit*; Claude Aragonnis: *Madame Louis XIV*
33 Aragonnis: *op cit*; Dangeau: *op cit*
34 Princess Palatine: *op cit*

Chapter 19

1 T. B. Macaulay: *The History of England*; Sir Winston Churchill: *Marlborough: His Life and Times*
2 N. A. Robb: *William of Orange*; M. Richard: *Les Orange-Nassau*
3 Marquis de Vogüé: *Mémoires du Maréchal de Villars*; Voltaire: *Le Siècle de Louis XIV*; Princess Palatine: *Correspondance*; Duc de Saint-Simon: *Mémoires*
4 Princess Palatine: *op cit*
5 Saint-Simon: *op cit*
6 F. Gillot: *Le Régne de Louis XIV et l'Opinion Publique en Allemagne*
7 G. Ziegler: *The Court of Versailles*; Macaulay: *op cit*; Voltaire: *op cit*
8 Vogüé: *op cit*; Comte de Saint-Hilaire: *Mémoires*
9 A. Ducasse: *La Guerre des Camisards*
10 Pierre de Nolhac: *Versailles, Résidence de Louis XIV*; Voltaire: *op cit*; Saint-Simon: *op cit*; Primi Visconti: *Mémoires*
11 Louis XIV: *Oeuvres*
12 Saint-Hilaire: *op cit*
13 Saint-Simon: *op cit*; *Histoire du Prince Eugène*
14 *Histoire du Prince Eugène*
15 Chevalier de Quincy: *Mémoires*
16 J. Orieux: *La Fontaine*
17 Voltaire: *op cit*; Macaulay: *op cit*; Churchill: *op cit*
18 Mme de Sévigné: *Lettres*; Robb: *op cit*
19 Macaulay: *op cit*
20 Mme de Maintenon: *Correspondance Générale*
21 Saint-Simon: *op cit*
22 Robb: *op cit*
23 Marquis de La Fare: *Mémoires et Réflexions*
24 Saint-Simon: *op cit*
25 *Ibid*
26 Abbé de Choisy: *Transvestite Memoirs*
27 Princess Palatine: *op cit*

28 Choisy: *op cit*
29 Princess Palatine: *op cit*
30 Maintenon: *op cit*
31 Saint-Simon: *op cit*; H. Carré: *Madame de Montespan*
32 Maintenon: *op cit*
33 Marquis de Sourches: *Mémoires*; d'Haussonville and Hanotaux: *Mémoires de Mlle d'Aumale*; Saint-Simon: *op cit*; Languet de Gercy, Archbishop of Sens: *Mémoires Inédites sur Madame de Maintenon*
34 Saint-Simon: *op cit*
35 D'Haussonville: *op cit*
36 Saint-Simon: *op cit*
37 Princess Palatine: *op cit*
38 Saint-Simon: *op cit*
39 Mme de Caylus: *Souvenirs*
40 Mlle de Montpensier: *Mémoires*
41 Saint-Simon: *op cit*
42 *Ibid*
43 Caylus: *op cit*; Saint-Simon: *op cit*; Ziegler: *op cit*
44 Princess Palatine: *op cit*
45 Maintenon: *op cit*
46 *Ibid*
47 Saint-Simon: *op cit*

Chapter 20

1 Mme de Maintenon: *Correspondance Générale*
2 *Ibid*
3 *Ibid*
4 Marquis de Vogüé: *Mémoires du Maréchal de Villars*; Comte de Saint-Hilaire: *Mémoires*
5 Maintenon: *op cit*
6 J. Michelet: *Histoire de France*; Voltaire: *Le Siècle de Louis XIV*
7 Maintenon: *op cit*
8 Duc de Saint-Simon: *Mémoires*
9 N. A. Robb: *William of Orange*
10 J. Jacquiot: *Médailles et Jetons de Louis XIV*
11 Saint-Simon: *op cit*
12 Voltaire: *op cit*
13 Marquis de La Fare: *Mémoires et Réflexions*
14 Saint-Simon: *op cit*
15 *Ibid*
16 *Ibid*
17 Gyel Pieler: *Les Pays-Bas au XVIIe Siècle*
18 Voltaire: *op cit*
19 Maintenon: *op cit*
20 Georges Lenôtre: *Paris Qui Disparait* (Paris, 1937)
21 J. Saint-Germain: *La Reynie et la Police au Grand Siècle*
22 D'Aquin, Fagon and Vallot: *Journal de la Santé du Roi*
23 Princess Palatine: *Correspondance*
24 D'Haussonville and Hanotaux: *Mémoires de Mlle d'Aumale*
25 Saint-Simon: *op cit*
26 Maintenon: *op cit*
27 Saint-Simon: *op cit*
28 *Ibid*
29 Saint-Germain: *op cit*
30 D'Haussonville: *op cit*

31 Saint-Germain: *op cit*
32 E. Jaloustre: *La Famine de 1694 dans la Basse-Auvergne* (Clermont-Ferrand, 1878)
33 G. Ziegler: *The Court of Versailles*
34 Voltaire: *op cit*; Saint-Simon: *op cit*; Ziegler: *op cit*
35 Saint-Simon: *op cit*; Voltaire: *op cit*
36 *Correspondance Administrative*
37 *Histoire du Prince Eugène*
38 Voltaire: *op cit*; *Histoire du Prince Eugène*; Saint-Simon: *op cit*
39 Voltaire: *op cit*
40 Saint-Simon: *op cit*; Voltaire: *op cit*

Chapter 21

1 Louis XIV: *Oeuvres*
2 Mme de Maintenon: *Correspondance Générale*
3 Duc de Saint-Simon: *Mémoires*
4 Marquis de Dangeau: *Journal*
5 Saint-Simon: *op cit*
6 Dangeau: *op cit;* G. Ziegler: *The Court of Versailles*
7 Saint-Simon: *op cit*; Dangeau: *op cit*
8 Saint-Simon: *op cit*
9 Dangeau: *op cit*
10 Voltaire: *Le Siècle de Louis XIV*
11 Princess Palatine: *Correspondance*
12 Marquis de Vogüé: *Mémoires du Maréchal de Villars*; Comte de Saint-Hilaire: *Mémoires*; Saint-Simon: *op cit*; Voltaire: *op cit*
13 Chevalier de Quincy: *Mémoires*; Saint-Hilaire: *op cit*; Saint-Simon: *op cit*
14 Maintenon: *op cit*
15 Ziegler: *op cit*; Saint-Simon: *op cit*; Voltaire: *op cit*
16 J. Saint-Germain: *La Reynie et la Police au Grand Siècle*
17 Maintenon: *op cit*
18 *Ibid*
19 *Ibid*
20 Voltaire: *op cit*
21 Maintenon: *op cit*
22 *Ibid*
23 *Ibid*
24 Voltaire: *op cit*; Maintenon: *op cit*
25 Maintenon: *op cit*
26 Fénélon: *Oeuvres*; Voltaire: *op cit*
27 Vogüé: *op cit*; Saint-Hilaire: *op cit*; Voltaire: *op cit*; Saint-Simon: *op cit*; Sir Winston Churchill: *Marlborough*
28 Dangeau: *op cit*
29 Ziegler: *op cit*
30 Dangeau: *op cit*
31 *Ibid*
32 *Ibid*
33 *Ibid*
34 Saint-Simon: *op cit*; Princess Palatine: *op cit*; Abbé de Choisy: *Transvestite Memoirs*
35 Dangeau: *op cit*
36 *Ibid*
37 Maintenon: *op cit*
38 *Ibid*
39 *Ibid*

Chapter 22

1 Duc de Saint-Simon: *Mémoires*; Marquis de Vogüé: *Mémoires du Maréchal de Villars*; Voltaire: *Le Siècle de Louis XIV*
2 Vogüé: *op cit*
3 Saint-Simon: *op cit*
4 Marquis de Dangeau: *Journal*
5 Saint-Simon: *op cit*
6 Dangeau: *op cit*; Dangeau: *op cit*
7 Sir Winston Churchill: *Marlborough*; N. A. Robb: *William of Orange*
8 *Histoire du Prince Eugène*
9 Saint-Simon: *op cit*
10 *Ibid*
11 Comte de Saint-Hilaire: *Mémoires*
12 Saint-Simon: *op cit*
13 *Histoire du Prince Eugène*
14 Saint-Simon: *op cit*
15 Robb: *op cit*
16 Mme de Maintenon: *Correspondance Générale*
17 *Ibid*
18 *Ibid*
19 Saint-Simon: *op cit*
20 Chevalier de Quincy: *Mémoires*
21 Robb: *op cit*
22 Saint-Simon: *op cit*
23 Quincy: *op cit*
24 Churchill: *op cit*; Robb: *op cit*
25 Saint-Simon: *op cit*; Mme de Caylus: *Souvenirs*
26 Robb: *op cit*
27 Churchill: *op cit*; Robb: *op cit*
28 Princess Palatine: *Correspondance*
29 Saint-Simon: *op cit*
30 M. Richard: *Les Orange-Nassau*
31 Quincy: *op cit*; Voltaire: *op cit*
32 Maintenon: *op cit*
33 Saint-Simon: *Parallèles des Trois Rois Bourbons*
34 D'Haussonville and Hanotaux: *Mémoires de Mlle d'Aumale*
35 Saint-Simon: *Mémoires*
36 Quincy: *op cit*
37 Saint-Simon: *op cit*
38 Vogüé: *op cit*
39 Saint-Simon: *op cit*

Chapter 23

1 A. Ducasse: *La Guerre des Camisards*; Budonnaux, chef camisard: *Mémoires*; J. Michelet: *Histoire de France*
2 M. M. L. Saint-René Taillandier: *La Princesse des Ursins* (Paris, 1930); Duc de Saint-Simon: *Mémoires*
3 Louis XIV: *Oeuvres*
4 *Ibid*
5 Saint-René Taillandier: *op cit*
6 Chevalier de Quincy: *Mémoires*
7 Comte de Saint-Hilaire: *Mémoires*
8 *Histoire du Prince Eugène*
9 Saint-Simon: *op cit*

10 Marquis de Vogüé: *Mémoires du Maréchal de Villars*
11 *Ibid*
12 George Lenôtre: *En France Jadis* (Paris, 1949); Vogüé: *op cit*
13 Lenôtre: *op cit*
14 Vogüé: *op cit*; Ducasse: *op cit*
15 Marquis de Dangeau: *Journal*; Sir Winston Churchill: *Marlborough*
16 Saint-Hilaire: *op cit*
17 Abbé Duclos: *Mémoires Secrets*
18 Claude Antoine, Comte de Bonneval: *Mémoires* (Paris, 1806)
19 Mme de Maintenon: *Correspondance Générale*
20 Vogüé: *op cit*; Quincy: *op cit*; Saint-Hilaire: *op cit*; Duclos: *op cit*
21 Saint-Simon: *op cit*
22 Vogüé: *op cit*; Ducasse: *op cit*; Michelet: *op cit*
23 Louis XIV: *op cit*; Saint-Simon: *op cit*; Saint-René Taillandier: *op cit*
24 Maréchal de Tessé: *Lettres* (Paris, 1888); Saint-René Taillandier: *op cit*
25 Saint-Simon: *op cit*; Dangeau: *op cit*
26 Saint-Simon: *op cit*; Princess Palatine: *Correspondance*
27 Tessé: *op cit*
28 Voltaire: *Le Siècle de Louis XIV*; Saint-Simon: *op cit*; Saint-René Taillandier: *op cit*;
    Saint-Hilaire: *op cit*
29 Louis, Duc de Bourgogne: *Lettres du Duc de Bourgogne au Roi d'Espagne, Philippe V*
    (Paris, 1912)

Chapter 24

1 Marquis de Dangeau: *Journal*; Duc de Saint-Simon: *Mémoires*
2 Princess Palatine: *Correspondance*; Saint-Simon: *op cit*
3 Mme de Maintenon: *Correspondance Générale*
4 *Ibid*
5 Saint-Simon: *op cit*
6 D'Haussonville and Hanotaux: *Mémoires de Mlle d'Aumale*
7 Mme de Caylus: *Souvenirs*
8 Maintenon: *op cit*
9 Voltaire: *Le Siècle de Louis XIV*; Saint-Simon: *op cit*; Comte de Saint-Hilaire: *Mémoires*
10 Voltaire: *op cit*
11 M. Saint-René Taillandier: *La Princesse des Ursins*
12 *Ibid*
13 Abbé Duclos: *Mémoires Secrets*; Saint-Simon: *op cit*
14 *Histoire du Prince Eugène*; Voltaire: *op cit*; Saint-Simon: *op cit*; Chevalier de Quincy:
    Mémoires; Saint-Hilaire: *op cit*
15 Abbé G. Esnault: *Michel Chamillart, Contrôleur General des Finances* (Le Mans, 1884)
16 Saint-Simon: *op cit*
17 Saint-Simon: *op cit*; J. Michelet: *Histoire de France*; Gilette Ziegler: *The Court of
    Versailles*; Georges Lenôtre: *En France Jadis*
18 Dangeau: *op cit*
19 Princess Palatine: *op cit*
20 Saint-Simon: *op cit*
21 Marquis de Vogue: *Mémoires du Maréchal de Villars*; Voltaire: *op cit*; Saint-Simon: *op cit*
22 *Histoire de Prince Eugène*
23 Voltaire: *op cit*; Maréchal de Tessé: *Lettres*; *Histoire du Prince Eugène*
24 *Ibid*
25 H. Carré: *Madame de Montespan*; d'Haussonville: *op cit*; Saint-Simon: *op cit*
26 Saint-Simon: *op cit*
27 Maintenon: *op cit*
28 Gyel Pieler: *Les Pays-Bas au XVIIe Siècle*

29 Maintenon: *op cit*
30 Saint-Hilaire: *op cit*; Saint-Simon: *op cit*
31 *Histoire du Prince Eugène*
32 Maintenon: *op cit*
33 Michelet: *op cit*; Sir Winston Churchill: *Marlborough*
34 Saint-Simon: *op cit*
35 *Ibid*
36 *Ibid*
37 Duc de Bourgogne: *Lettres au Philippe V*
38 Duclos: *op cit*
39 Saint-Simon: *op cit*
40 *Ibid*
41 *Ibid*
42 *Ibid*

Chapter 25

1 Chevalier de Quincy: *Mémoires*
2 J. Michelet: *Histoire de France*; Sir Winston Churchill: *Marlborough*; Princess Palatine: *Correspondance*; A. de Boilîle: *Le Grand Hiver et la Disette de 1709: Revue de Questions Historiques* (Paris, 1909)
3 Michelet: *op cit*
4 Boislîle: *op cit*
5 Princess Palatine: *op cit*
6 Michelet: *op cit*; J. Saint-Germain: *La Reynie et la Police au Grand Siècle*
7 Duc de Saint-Simon: *Mémoires*
8 Michelet: *op cit*
9 Saint-Simon: *op cit*
10 Marquis de Dangeau: *Journal*
11 Gyel Pieler: *Les Pays-Bas au XVIIe Siècle*
12 Saint-Simon: *op cit*
13 Voltaire: *Le Siècle de Louis XIV*
14 Saint-Simon: *op cit*
15 Jean-Baptiste Colbert, Marquis de Torcy: *Journal Inédit* (Paris, 1884); Voltaire: *op cit*; Churchill: *op cit*
16 Gilette Ziegler: *The Court of Versailles*
17 G. Esnault: *Michel Chamillart*
18 Saint-Simon: *op cit*; Dangeau: *op cit*
19 Saint-Simon: *op cit*
20 *Ibid*
21 Voltaire: *op cit*
22 Marquis de Vogüé: *Mémoires du Maréchal de Villars*
23 Princess Palatine: *op cit*
24 Saint-Simon: *op cit*
25 D'Haussonville and Hanotaux: *Mémoires de Mlle d'Aumale*
26 Saint-Simon: *op cit*
27 Boislîle: *op cit*; Y.-M. Bercé: *Croquants et Va-nu-pieds*
28 D'Haussonville: *op cit*
29 D'Aquin, Fagan and Vallot: *Journal de la Santé du Roi*
30 Saint-Simon: *op cit*; M. Saint-René Taillandier: *La Princesse des Ursins*; Mme de Maintenon: *Correspondance Générale*
31 Churchill: *op cit*
32 Voltaire: *op cit*
33 Saint-Simon: *op cit*
34 Saint-Simon: *op cit*; Abbé Duclos: *Mémoires Secrets*; Voltaire: *op cit*

35 Saint-Simon: *op cit*
36 *Ibid*
37 Marquis de Torcy: *Journal*; Saint-Simon: *op cit*
38 Maintenon: *op cit*
39 Torcy: *op cit*
40 Saint-Simon: *op cit*
41 *Ibid*
42 Maintenon: *op cit*

Chapter 26

1 Marquis de Torcy: *Journal*
2 Torcy: *op cit*; Voltaire: *Le Siècle de Louis XIV*
3 Voltaire: *op cit*; Saint-Simon: *Mémoires*; Marquis de Vogüé: *Mémoires du Maréchal de Villars*
4 Torcy: *op cit*; Vogüé: *op cit*
5 Vogüé: *op cit*
6 Chevalier de Lunicy: *Mémoires*
7 Saint-Simon: *op cit*; Lunicy: *op cit*
8 Vogüé: *op cit*
9 *Ibid*
10 Torcy: *op cit*
11 Saint-Simon: *op cit*; G. Basset d'Auriac: *Les Deux Penitences de Louise de La Vallière*
12 *Histoire du Prince Eugène*; Saint-Simon: *op cit*
13 Torcy: *op cit*
14 *Ibid*
15 Saint-Simon: *op cit*
16 *Histoire du Prince Eugène*; Abbé Duclos: *Mémoires Secrets*; Sir Winston Churchill: *Marlborough*; Voltaire: *op cit*
17 M. Saint-René Taillandier: *La Princesse des Ursins*; Torcy: *op cit*
18 Torcy: *op cit*
19 Saint-René Taillandier: *op cit*
20 Torcy: *op cit*
21 *Ibid*
22 Saint-Simon: *op cit*
23 *Ibid*
24 *Ibid*
25 Torcy: *op cit*; Churchill: *op cit*
26 J. Michelet: *Histoire de France*; Churchill: *op cit*
27 Churchill: *op cit*
28 *Ibid*
29 Saint-Simon: *op cit*
30 Torcy: *op cit*
31 *Ibid*
32 Princess Palatine: *Correspondance*
33 Churchill: *op cit*
34 Michelet: *op cit*; Churchill: *op cit*
35 Louis XIV: *Oeuvres*; Saint-René Taillandier: *op cit*
36 Saint-Simon: *op cit*; Mme de Maintenon: *Correspondance*
37 Michelet: *op cit*; Churchill: *op cit*
38 Louis XIV: *op cit*
39 Saint-René Taillandier: *op cit*

Chapter 27

1 Saint-Simon: *Mémoires*
2 *Ibid*
3 Duc de Bourgogne: *Lettres à Philippe V*
4 D'Haussonville and Hanotaux: *Mémoires de Mlle d'Aumale*; Princess Palatine:
   Correspondance; Duc de Saint-Simon: *Mémoires*
5 Saint-Simon: *op cit*; Marquis de Dangeau: *Journal*
6 D'Haussonville: *op cit*
7 Saint-Simon: *op cit*
8 Dangeau: *op cit*
9 Saint-Simon: *op cit*
10 M. Saint-René Taillandier: *La Princesse des Ursins*; Philippe Erlanger: *Philippe V, Roi
   d'Espagne* (Paris, 1978)
11 *Histoire du Prince Eugène*
12 *Ibid*
13 Marquis de Vogüé: *Mémoires du Maréchal de Villars*
14 *Ibid*
15 *Histoire du Prince Eugène*
16 Vogüé: *op cit*
17 *Histoire du Prince Eugène*
18 Saint-Simon: *op cit*
19 Maréchal de Tessé: *Lettres*
20 Saint-Simon: *op cit*
21 Chevalier de Quincy: *Mémoires*
22 Voltaire: *Le Siècle de Louis XIV*; Vogüé: *op cit*; Saint-Simon: *op cit*; *Histoire du Prince
   Eugène*
23 *Histoire du Prince Eugène*
24 Louis XIV: *Oeuvres*; Saint-René Taillandier: *op cit*; Erlanger: *op cit*; Tessé: *op cit*
25 Tessé: *op cit*
26 Vogüé: *op cit*
27 *Ibid*
28 *Histoire du Prince Eugène*

Chapter 28

1 Marquis de Vogüé: *Mémoires du Maréchal de Villars; Histoire du Prince Eugène*
2 Maréchal de Tessé: *Lettres*
3 Vogüé: *op cit*
4 *Ibid*
5 J. Michelet: *Histoire de France*; Duc de Saint-Simon: *Mémoires*; Abbé Duclos: *Mémoires
   Secrets*
6 M. Saint-René Taillandier: *La Princesse des Ursins*; Saint-Simon: *op cit*
7 Saint-Simon: *op cit*
8 Mme de Maintenon: *Lettres Inédites à Madame des Ursins* (Paris, 1826)
9 Honoré Champion: *Madame des Ursins et la Succession d'Espagne*; P. Erlanger: *Philippe
   V*; Saint-Simon: *op cit*; Duclos: *op cit*
10 Saint-Simon: *op cit*
11 *Ibid*
12 *Ibid*
13 *Ibid*
14 Maintenon: *op cit*
15 Saint-René Taillandier: *op cit*; Erlanger: *op cit*; Saint-Simon: *op cit*
16 Marquis de Dangeau: *Journal*
17 Duclos: *op cit*
18 Louis XIV: *Oeuvres*

19 Maintenon: *op cit*
20 *Ibid*
21 Saint-René Taillandier: *op cit*; Saint-Simon: *op cit*

Chapter 29

1 Marquis de Créqui: *Souvenirs de 1710–1803*
2 Voltaire: *Le Siècle de Louis XIV*
3 Duc de Saint-Simon: *Mémoires*; J. Michelet: *Histoire de France*
4 Abbé Duclos: *Mémoires Secrets*; J. Saint-Germain: *La Reynie et la Police au Grand Siècle*;
      Saint-Simon: *op cit*; Michelet: *op cit*
5 Saint-Simon: *op cit*
6 Duclos: *op cit*; Princess Palatine: *Correspondance*
7 Princess Palatine: *op cit*
8 D'Aquin, Fagon and Vallot: *Journal de la Santé du Roi*
9 Mme de Maintenon: *Correspondance*
10 Princess Palatine: *op cit*
11 Saint-Simon: *op cit*
12 Princess Palatine: *op cit*
13 Claude Aragonnis: *Madame Louis XIV*
14 Saint-Simon: *op cit*
15 Michelet: *op cit*; Saint-Simon: *op cit*; Voltaire: *op cit*
16 Saint-Simon: *op cit*
17 D'Haussonville and Hanotaux: *Mémoires de Mlle d'Aumale*; Saint-Simon: *op cit*
18 *Ibid*
19 *Ibid*
20 *Ibid*
21 Duclos: *op cit*; Marquis de Dangeau: *Journal*; Saint-Simon: *op cit*
22 Saint-Simon: *op cit*
23 Aragonnis: *op cit*
24 D'Haussonville: *op cit*
25 Saint-Simon: *op cit*; Duclos: *op cit*
26 Saint-Simon: *op cit*; d'Haussonville: *op cit*
27 D'Haussonville: *op cit*
28 *Ibid*
29 Dangeau: *op cit*; Saint-Simon: *op cit*
30 D'Haussonville: *op cit*
31 Saint-Simon: *op cit*; Georges Poisson: *Monsieur de Saint-Simon* (Paris, 1973)
32 Saint-Simon: *op cit*
33 Duclos: *op cit*
34 D'Haussonville: *op cit*; Dangeau: *op cit*
35 Mme de Maintenon: *Lettres Inédites à Mme des Ursins*
36 Voltaire: *op cit*; Duclos: *op cit*

Index

Bontemps, *valet de chambre*, 239

Bordeaux, 42, 46–7, 56, 84, 86, 182

Bossuet, Abbé, Bishop of Meaux, 147, 148, 168, 177, 178, 179, 185, 223, 249, 251, 261, 267, 270, 286, 296, 297; 'The Facts about Quietism' by, 296

Bouchain, siege of (1711), 373

Boucher, Dr, 122

Boucherat, M., 107

Boudin, physician, 369, 377

Boufflers, Maréchal de, 264, 295, 316, 349, 353

Bouillon, Cardinal de, 159, 225

Bouillon, Duc de, 37, 44, 46, 201

Bouillon, Duchesse de, 44, 161, 225, 228, 382; accused of poisoning, 199–200

Boulaye, Marquis de, 43

Boulogne, 182

Boulonnais, Lustucru war in, 116–17

Bourbon, Duc de, 151

Bourbon, Duchesse de, 274, 276, 301, 360, 400

Bourdaloue, Father, 174, 179

Bourgogne, Louis, Duc de (son of Dauphin), 235, 295, 296, 300, 302, 312, 324, 329, 361–2; birth of (1682), 223; marriage to Adelaide of Savoy (1697), 291–2, 302, 331; birth of son (1704), 324; appointed C-in-C of French army in Flanders, 340–41, 343; accused of cowardice, 343–4; death of (1712), 376–8

Bourgogne, Adelaide of Savoy, Duchesse de, 310, 324, 330, 331–2, 342, 343, 344, 354; wedding of, 291–2, 302; relations with Mme de Maintenon and king, 291, 330, 331–2, 333–4, 339, 343; social life at Court, 300, 301–2, 324; birth of son (1704), 324; and miscarriage, 339; and birth of Louis xv (1710), 360; death of (1712), 376–8

Boysseulh, army officer, 227–8

Brabant, 134, 333

Bracciano, Mme de *see* Ursins, Princesse des

Brandenberg, Elector of, 162, 252

Bretagne, Duc de, 339

Breteuil, Baron de, 302

Bricmini, queen's dwarf, 154

Briderey, Father, 408

Brienne, Comte de, 8, 83, 107, 109

Brienne, Comtesse de, 18

Brienne, Louis-Henri de, 22–3, 26, 28, 46, 51, 61, 90, 91, 92–3, 107, 108, 157

Brinon, Mme de, 233, 234, 242

Brissac, Duc de, 53

Brissac, Sieur de, 173

Brittany, 171; peasants' revolt in, 178–9, 180–81, 182–3

Broglie, Maréchal de, 378

Broussel, member of *parlement*, 43, 64; imprisonment of (1648), 33–5

Bruges, 340, 343

Brussels, 237, 238, 333; French bombardment of (1695), 281

Bruys, magistrate, 348

Buckingham, Duke of, 124

Burgos, king and queen of Spain's exile in, 335–6

Burgundy, 45, 353

Burnet, Gilbert, 191–2

Bussy-Rabutin, Roger de, 77, 154, 166, 185, 191, 202

Cabours, butchering of garrison, 266

'Cadets of the Cross', 322

Cambrai, 297, 364, 379

Camisards (1702–3), 318–19, 321–4, 325–6

Cani, M. de, 352

Carhaix, 183

Carmelite convent, Paris, La Vallière's retirement at, 167–9, 177, 365

Casal, fortress of: ceded to France (1681), 214–15; and Duke of Savoy's recapture of, 281

Cassel, battle of (1677), 189–90, 191

Castel dos Rios, Marquis, 305, 306, 308

Castel de Rodrigo, Marqués de, governor of the Netherlands, 135, 136–7

Castlemain, Barbara, 187

Catinat, Nicolas, Maréchal de, 215, 265, 281, 312, 315, 316

Cavalier, Jean, 318, 319, 322–4

Caylus, Mme de, 275

Cessac, Marquis de, 199

Cévennes, 234, 318, 325, 337

Chaillot, St Mary's Convent, 114; La Vallière retires to (1671), 153–4

Chambandon, Sieur, 295

Chambre Ardente (royal commission), 196, 199, 206, 207, 208

Chamillart, Michel de, Minister of War and Finance, 315, 316, 322, 323, 332, 335, 342, 343, 348, 349, 350; dismissed by Louis xiv, 351

Champagne, 379, 380

Charleroi, Dutch attack on, 163

Charles i, King of England, 36, 73

Charles ii, King of England, 60, 101, 144, 146, 148, 157, 191–2, 257

Charles ii, King of Spain and the Indies, dispute over successor to, 293–5, 300, 304–10

Charles iv, Duc de Lorraine, 59–60, 122, 300, 301

Charles v, Emperor, 220, 373

Charles vi, Emperor (formerly Archduke Charles), 300, 304, 306, 307, 308, 329, 333, 356, 363, 375, 378, 381; proclaimed king in Madrid, 336; victorious at battle of Saragossa (1710), 366; succeeds Joseph i as Emperor (1711), 373; Treaty of Utrecht (1713) and, 382–3

Charles xii, King of Sweden, 301

Charton, member of *parlement*, 33

434

La Ferté, Duchesse de, 330–31

La Ferté, Maréchal de, 199

La Feuillade, Maréchal de, 184, 255–6, 269, 334

La Filastre, 208

La Flèche, convent of, 409

La Flotte, M., 355, 356

La Fontaine, Jean de, 59, 119, 123, 257, 266–7

La Marck, Comtesse de, 226, 257

La Marsale, battle of (1693), 281

La Meilleraye, Maréchal, 46

La Motte, Maréchal de, 169

La Motte, Mme de, 75, 133

La Motte d'Argencourt, Mlle de, 74–5

La Porte, Pierre, 14, 23, 24, 27, 28, 29, 30, 58, 61

La Reynie, Nicolas de, Poisons Affair and, 196, 199, 202, 206, 207, 211

La Rochefoucauld, Duc de, 38-9, 44, 45–6, 53, 62, 223, 225, 350; *Maximes* by, 66; king's friendship with, 225

La Rochefoucauld, Duc de (*fils*), 202

La Roche-Guyon, Duchesse de, 213

La Roche-sur-Yon, Prince de, 222

La Rue, Father de, 388

La Salle, Mme de, governess, 22–3

La Treaumont, Gilles de, 171, 172, 173

La Tremoille, Duchesse de, 36

La Vallière, Louise de, Duchesse de Vaujours, 84, 120, 123, 132, 135, 199, 223, 270; appointed maid-of-honour to Madame, 101; love affair with king, 102–4, 113–15, 121–2, 124, 125, 131, 132–4, 135–6, 138, 139, 140–41, 142, 148–9, 185; rejects Fouquet's overtures, 103–4; anonymous letter informing on, 121, 127; birth of son (1663), 122, 126; entertainment at Versailles in honour of, 123–4; enemies of, 127–8; La Montespan's friendship with, 132;

made Duchesse de Vaujours, 134; birth of son (Comte de Vermandois), 138; tour of Flanders, 145, 146; expiation of her sins, 148–9; seeks temporary refuge at Chaillot, 153–4; and retires to Carmelite convent, 167–9, 177; death of (1710), 365

La Vertu, Duc de, 345

La Voisin *see* Montvoisin, Catherine

Lalande, Lieutenant-General, 322

Lamoignan, Judge, 118, 249

Landau, 384, 385

Landes, 117

Landrecies, siege of (1712), 379–80, 381

Lange, Marquis de, 398

Langres, Bishop of, 144

Languedoc, 337; repressive measures against protestants in, 234–5; and Camisards, 318–19, 321–4, 326

Laon, Vidame de, 223

Laporte, Pierre (Rolland), 249, 250, 318, 319, 326

Las Fuentes, Marqués de, 110

Launois, *valet de chambre*, 113–14

Lauzun, Comte de, 348–9; betrothel of Grande Mademoiselle to, 150–51; and Louis forbids marriage, 151–2; and Montespan's betrayal of, 152–3; imprisoned at Pignerol, 153, 166, 209; La Montespan's schemes for reunion of Grande Mademoiselle and, 209–11; helps Queen of England escape, and wins pardon, 259; leads French troops into Ireland, 267; death of Grande Mademoiselle, 274

Lavardin, Marquis de, 256–7

Lavienne, *valet-de-chambre*, 281

Law of Devolution, war in Netherlands over, 134–8

Le Balp, Sébastien, 180, 181, 182–3

Le Bourget, 173–4

Le Brin, elixir of, 406, 407

Le Brouage, Maria Mancini sent to, 83–6

Le Brun, Charles, 158, 172, 220, 245

Le Cormier de Sainte-Hélène, 118

Le Féron, Mme, 199

Le Fèvre d'Orval, 380

Le Havre, 48, 51

Le Nôtre, André, 228

Le Pelletier, Minister of Finance, 235

Le Quesnoy, siege of (1712), 379

Le Sage, sorcerer, 196, 206, 207

Le Tellier, Father, 359, 369, 371, 374, 385, 395; appointed king's confessor, 345, 374; *Unigenitus* and, 385–6, 396, 401; and seeks to destroy Noailles, 396–7, 401, 404–5; death of Louis XIV and, 403, 404, 405, 407; and retires to La Flèche, 409

Le Tellier (*père*), Minister of War, 52, 53, 94, 135, 187

Le Tellier, Michel (*fils*) *see* Louvois, Marquis de

Lecuyer, Abbé, 178

Lejeune, Mme, joiner's wife, 178

Lenclos, Ninon de, 74

Lens, battle of (1648), 33

Leopold I, Emperor, 162, 236, 237, 238, 256; Spanish succession and, 293, 294, 304–5, 306

Lerida, siege of, 336

Lery, Mlle, 311

Lescaro, Francesco Imperiali, Doge of Genoa, visits Louis at Versailles, 244–6

Lille, fall of (1708), 343

Lionne, Hugues, Minister of Foreign Affairs, 94, 108, 111–12, 187

lits de justice, 13, 15, 19–20, 31, 32, 401, 402

Livry, *maître d'hôtel* to Queen, 203

Longueville, Duc de, 56, 62; arrest and imprisonment of, 43–4, 47, 48, 49, 51

Longueville (*fils*), 158

Longueville, Anne Geneviève de Bourbon, Duchesse de, 14, 38–9,

44–5, 56, 65
Lorges, Maréchal de, 176,
184, 278
Lorraine, Chevalier de, 188,
189, 222, 225, 273;
relationship with
Monsieur, 143–4;
arrested and exiled to
Montpellier, 144; alleged
implication in death of
Madame, 147–8; recalled
from exile, 155
Lorraine, Duc de *see*
Charles IV
Louis XIII, King, 7–12, 13,
15, 17, 24, 28
Louis XIV, King of France:
birth (1638), 8–9; death
of father and succeeds to
throne (1643), 10–12;
first speech in *parlement*,
20, 21; childhood, 21–54;
and relations with
mother, 22, 23–4, 55,
124–5, 128; and with
Mazarin, 27–8, 52, 61,
68–9, 70–71; education,
28–30, 71; sick with
smallpox, 30–31; attends
lit de justice (1648), 31–2;
flight to Saint-Germain,
36–7; and return to Paris,
40; popularity of, 41,
111; demonstrations at
Palais Royal, 49–50;
coming of age (1651),
53–4, 55–6; *Memoirs*, 55,
110, 199; brother
Philippe's relations with,
56, 58, 113, 142–5, 189–
90; return of Mazarin
and, 57–8; moves into
Louvre, 64; Cardinal de
Retz arrested by, 64;
forbids assemblies of
parlement, 69–70;
Mazarin's education and
supervision of, 70–72;
and Court life, 72–3;
flirtations, 73–5; illness
of, 75–7; love affair with
Maria Mancini, 77, 78,
79, 80, 82–6; and
marriage to Maria
Theresa, 77–80, 82–3,
86–9; death of Mazarin,
91–4; and takes over
government, 94–6;
political philosophy of,
96–100; and his view of
monarchy, 98–100;
flirtation with Princess

Henrietta, 101, 102, 103;
Maria Theresa's relations
with, 101–2, 166–7; 230–
31; and love affair with
Louise de La Vallière,
102–4, 113–15, 121–2,
125, 131, 132–4, 135–6,
138, 140–41; Fouquet
ruined and arrested by,
104–9, 120–21; and
attends entertainment at
Château de Vaux, 105–6;
foreign policy of, 109–
11; victory of protocol
over Spain, 109–10; and
papal legate apologizes
for anti-French riot in
Rome, 110; ministers
chosen by, 111–12; and
mistrust rooted in, 112;
birth of son and heir
(1661), 113; trial of
Fouquet, 118, 120–21;
entertainment at
Versailles, 123–4; death
of mother (1666), 128–
30, 131; Mme de
Montespan's liaison
with, 131–4, 136, 138,
139, 140–41, 149, 154,
175–6, 177–8, 185, 190–
91, 193–4, 243; War of
Devolution in
Netherlands, 134–8; and
conquest of Franche-
Comté, 138–9; and
Treaty of Aix-la-
Chapelle (1668), 139; and
victory entertainment
at Versailles, 139; birth
of son to Montespan
(Duc de Maine), 141;
appoints Colbert
Minister of State, 142;
Philippe quarrels with,
142–5; tour of Flanders
(1670), 145–6; death of
Madame, 147–8; forbids
marriage of Lauzun and
Grande Mademoiselle,
150–52; upset at La
Vallière's retirement,
153–4; clergy's
disapproval of his
liaisons, 154, 177, 178,
179, 181–2; arranges
marriage of Monsieur to
Princess Palatine, 155;
war against Holland
(1672–78), 156–60, 161,
162–3, 165–6; refuses to
see Maria Mancini, 161;

his contempt for William
of Orange, 162; returns
Dutch prisoners-of-war
for ransom, 163; death of
Molière and, 165; fall of
Maestricht (1673), 165–6;
his initial distrust of the
'Widow Scarron', 167,
175, 176; La Vallière
retires to Carmelite
convent, 168–9; conquest
of Franche-Comté
(1674), 170, 172; and
festivities at Versailles,
172, 173; his growing
friendship with Mme de
Maintenon, 177–8, 183–
4, 203–5, 231, 236; and
La Montespan leaves
him, 179; Breton peasant
revolts, 178–9, 180–81,
182–3; and mourns death
of Turenne, 181; La
Montespan returns to
Versailles, 182, 185–6;
omnipotence of, 186–7,
198–9, 220–22, 223–4,
226–7; and sexual
promiscuity, 188, 190;
war in Flanders (1677),
188–9; and mortified at
Monsieur's victory at
Cassel, 189–90; birth of
daughter Françoise
Marie, 190; alarmed at
marriage of William of
Orange and Mary, 192;
tour of Flanders (1678),
192; and Treaty of
Nijmegen, 192–3; birth
of Comte de Toulouse,
192; love affair with Mlle
de Fontanges, 195–6,
197–8, 201, 205, 211;
Poisons Affair and, 196,
199–201, 206, 207–8; his
moral code for Court,
198; Pomponne
dismissed by, 198–9;
accusations of poisoning
against La Montespan,
206, 207–9, 211–12;
criticisms of Colbert by,
213–14; Casal fortress
ceded to, 214–15; and
French occupation of
Strasbourg, 215–16; and
European treaty of
association against, 216;
papal authority
challenged by, 216–17;
takes up permanent

Lustucru war, 116–17
Luxembourg, Maréchal de,
163–4, 189, 275;
implicated in Poisons
Affair, 200, 202; role in
war against Grand
Alliance, 265, 277, 278,
279–80; his passion for
women, 280; and death
of (1695), 280
Luxembourg, 214, 237,
238, 244
Luxembourg, Palais du, 49,
151, 152
Luynes, Duc de, 12, 34
Luzara, battle of (1702), 316
Lyon, Cardinal Archbishop
of, 12

Madame see d'Orléans,
Duchesse de
Maestricht, fall of (1673),
165–6
Maillet, camisard, 326
Maine, Louis Auguste, Duc
de, 141, 168, 175, 182,
212, 270, 280, 343, 344,
361, 390, 398, 400, 402–
3; Mme de Maintenon's
attachment to, 175, 178;
takes the waters at
Barèges, 182, 183; Grand
Mademoiselle agrees to
make him her heir, 209;
and her gifts of
principalities to, 210,
275; cowardice of, 280–
81; king elevates rank
and status of, 361–2, 389;
and king's will, 390–91,
407, 409; death of Louis
XIV and, 405, 407, 409
Maine, Duchesse de, 300,
301, 400
Maintenon, Marquise de
(formerly: Françoise
d'Aubigné: Mme
Scarron), 89, 168, 197,
222, 303, 330, 332, 335,
339–40, 341, 344–5, 351;
her marriage to Paul
Scarron, 58; pension
ceases on death of Queen
Anne, 131; as friend and
confidante of La
Montespan, 131, 136,
165, 167, 175–6; care of
royal bastards by, 141,
167, 175, 178, 182; Louis'
initial distrust of, 167,
175, 176; buys Château
de Maintenon, 176; Louis

XIV's friendship with,
177, 179, 183–4, 203–5,
231, 234, 236, 238–9; and
deteriorating relations
and rivalry between La
Montespan and, 177–8,
179, 182, 185–6, 188,
194, 201–2, 212–13, 270;
accompanies Duc du
Maine to Barèges, 182;
appointed second
Mistress of the Robes to
Dauphine, 203–4;
Queen's friendship with,
230–31; and death of
Queen, 231, 233; Pope
sends present to, 233–4;
Louis' secret marriage to,
238–44; teaches poor
children at Château de
Noisy, 242; blamed for
persecution of
protestants, 249; king has
Saint-Cyr built for, 254;
and performance of
Esther, 260–61; her
influence on Louis, 270–
72, 351–2; war against
Grand Alliance and, 277,
278, 279, 282; Racine's
L'Ombre de M. Scarron
and, 283–4; involvement
with quietism and Mme
Guyon, 285–6, 296–7;
and relations with
Cardinal de Noailles,
286, 287, 298, 339–40,
374–5; at Compiègne
military review, 296;
Duchesse de Bourgogne
and, 291, 330, 331–2,
333–4, 339; rift between
Louis and, 296–8;
Spanish succession and,
306, 309–10; relations
with Louis, 314–15, 325,
331, 340, 360–61; and
with Princesse des
Ursins, 310, 320, 327–8,
336, 387, 391, 392–4;
boredom of Court life,
330–31, 359–60, 399;
death of La Montespan,
338–9; charitable works
of, 353, 354; death of
Dauphin, 372; and death
of Duc and Duchesse de
Bourgogne, 376–8; Louis
makes his will, 390–91;
Louis XIV's last illness
and death, 399–400, 403,
404, 405, 406, 407–8;

retires to Saint-Cyr, 408,
409
Mainz, siege of, 264
Maisonfort, Mlle de, 261
Maisons, Judge, 388–9
Malorte, spy, 326
Malplaquet, battle of
(1709), 357–8
Mancini, Filippo, 72
Mancini, Hortensia, 160–61
Mancini, Maria (Principessa
Colonna), 71; Louis
XIV's affair with, 77, 78,
79, 80, 82–6, 89; and
Louis refuses to see, 160–
61
Mancini, Laura see
Mercoeur, Duchesse de
Mancini, Olympia see
Soissons, Comtesse de
Mancini, Paolo, 28, 51, 61
Mansart, architect, 219, 254
Mantua, Duke of, 214–15
Marais, Abbé des, 272
Marchiennes, battle of
(1712), 380–81
Marcin, Maréchal de, 332,
334
Maréchal, surgeon, 377,
401
Maréchal de l'Hôpital, 63,
73
Margaret Theresa, Infanta,
293
Marguerite, Princess of
Savoy, 77–80
Maria Anna of Austria,
293
Maria Anna of Bavaria-
Neuberg (wife of Charles
II of Spain), 293, 304,
307–8
Maria Anne of Bavaria (La
Dauphine), 203, 204,
212, 276, 293; birth of
son (Duc de Bourgogne),
223
Maria Theresa, Queen of
France, 94, 110, 131, 134,
135, 151, 152, 165, 193,
293; marriage to Louis
XIV, 78–80, 82–3, 86–9;
and Louis' relations with,
101–2, 166–7, 230–31;
birth of son and heir
(Dauphin), 113; Louis'
affair with La Vallière
and, 121, 125–6, 135–6;
birth and death of
premature baby girl, 126;
death of father, Philip IV
of Spain, 129; La

extravagances of, 191,
193; tour of Flanders,
192; birth of Comte de
Toulouse, 192; her
relations with Mlle de
Fontanges, 195–6, 197–
8, 205; becomes duchess
without title, 197;
appointed
Superintendant of
Queen's Household, 201;
anti-Maintenon alliance
with Louvois, 202, 236,
270; accusations of
poisoning against, 206,
207–9, 211–12; schemes
reunion of Grande
Mademoiselle and
Lauzun, 209–11; her
sorrow at death of
daughter, 212–13; and
death of Queen, 232, 233;
and death of Louvois,
270; gives up Versailles
apartment, 270; death of
(1707), 338–9
Montespan, Monsieur de,
132, 133–4, 140, 168
Montesquiou, Maréchal de,
364, 365
Montmorency, Charlotte,
14
Montrevel, Maréchal de,
319, 322–3, 326
Montvoisin, Catherine ('La
Voisin'), 127, 133, 138,
196, 199, 202–3, 206,
207, 208
Morel, Abbé, 288
Mortemart, Duchesse de,
213
Motteville, Mme de, 10,
12, 26, 31, 36, 38, 40, 49,
50, 55, 61–2, 64, 86, 87,
95, 96, 102, 119, 128,
129, 130
Moulay Ismail of Morocco,
Emperor, 301
Mulay Idriss, Sultan of
Morocco, 222

Namur: siege of (1692),
277; and fall of (1695),
280, 281
Nangis, Marquis de, 380
Nantes, Mlle de (daughter
of La Montespan), 212
Nantes: Fouquet arrested
in, 107–8, 119;
demonstrations in (1675),
178–9, 180
Navailles, Duc de, 93

Nazelles, Cauzé de,
conspiracy uncovered
by, 171–2, 173–4
Neerwinden, battle of
(1693), 279, 281
Nemours, Duc de, 62
Netherlands (Spanish), 157,
161, 162, 172, 237, 244,
309; Franco–Spanish War
of 'Devolution', 134–8;
see also Flanders; Holland;
War of Spanish
Succession
New York (formerly New
Amsterdam), 156
Nîmes, 235, 319, 322–3,
326
Noailles, Cardinal de,
Archbishop of Paris, 286,
287, 296, 298, 325, 339,
354, 359; Jesuits accuse
him of Jansenism and
heresy, 298, 339–40,
374–5, 385; refuses to
accept *Unigenitus* papal
bull, 395, 404–5; Le
Tellier seeks to destroy
him, 396–7, 401
Noailles, Duc de, governor
of Languedoc, 234–5,
248, 264, 281, 389;
mission to Philip v of,
367–8
Noailles, Duchesse de, 300
Noailles, Maréchal de, 233,
239
Nogent, Mme de, 151
Nolhac, Pierre de, 265
Nordlingen, battle of, 19
Normandy, 42, 44–5, 171
Notre Dame de Paris, 33,
41, 129
Les Nouvelles Ecclésiastiques,
396

Oeillets, Mme des, 188, 207
d'Olonne, Mme, 77
Orange (Provence), 162,
216, 230, 289, 314
d'Orléans, Duchesse, 37
d'Orléans, Duchesse de
(Mlle de Blois), 270,
273–4, 276, 400, 405
d'Orléans, Princess
Elizabeth Charlotte of
Bavaria, Duchesse de
(the Palatine: Liselotte),
188, 194, 205, 211, 222,
224, 242, 258, 263, 269,
272–3, 276, 294, 330,
352, 388, 398, 399, 405;
marriage to Philippe

(1671), 155; against
marriage of son to Mlle
de Blois, 273–4
d'Orléans, Gaston, Duc,
14, 24, 25, 30, 43, 47–8,
49, 50, 51, 52, 56, 63, 65–
6, 84
d'Orléans, Henrietta Stuart,
Duchesse (Madame), 73,
113–15, 127, 133, 142,
145; marriage to Philippe
(1661), 101; Louis xiv's
flirtation with, 101, 102–
3; affair with Duc de
Guiche, 113–14;
appointed ambassador
extraordinary to
England, 144, 145, 146,
157; and bad relations
with Monsieur, 145,
146–7; death and alleged
poisoning of (1670), 147–
8
d'Orléans, Philippe, Duc
(Monsieur: *père*), 26, 30,
35, 36, 73, 76, 87, 88,
151, 152, 169, 223, 225,
231, 272; birth of (1640),
9; Anne of Austria's
treatment of, 23–4;
homosexuality of, 24, 76,
80, 143; Louis' relations
with, 56, 58, 113, 142–5,
189–90, 311; Louis'
illness and intrigues
centring on, 76–7;
marriage to Henrietta
Stuart, 101; and objects
to Madame's flirtation
with king, 102; deceived
by Madame and de
Guiche, 113–14; New
Year ball given by
(1666), 129; and death of
his mother, 130; La
Montespan's friendship
with, 132, 134; quarrels
with brother Louis, 142–
5; Chevalier de
Lorraine's relationship
with, 143–4; bad
relations with Madame,
145, 146–7; tour of
Flanders with Court,
146; death of Madame
(1670), 147–8; and
marriage to Liselotte,
Princess Palatine, 155;
and king recalls Lorraine
from exile, 155; takes
town of Bouchain, 184;
siege of Saint-Omer by,

188; and battle of Cassel,
189–90; marriage of son
to Mlle de Blois, 273–4;
Grande Mademoiselle
leaves fortune to, 274–5;
death of, 311–12
d'Orléans, Philippe, Duc
(*fils*: Duc de Chartres),
302, 334, 391, 398, 400,
403; marriage to Mlle de
Blois, 273–4; death of
father, 311–12; appointed
C-in-C of Franco–
Spanish troops, 337;
accused of dealing with
enemy, 355–7; and of
poisoning Duc and
Duchesse de Bourgogne,
377–8; made Regent by
Louis, 403–4, 407; and
death of Louis XIV, 405,
406–7, 409; and king's
will annulled in favour
of, 409; visits Mme de
Maintenon, 409
Orléans, rioting in, 116
d'Ormesson, Olivier, 118,
119, 120, 121, 139
d'Ornano, Maréchal, 58
Ottoman Turks, 214, 216,
236–8, 256, 289

Palais Royal, Paris, 22, 25,
31, 33, 34–5, 36, 37, 43,
44, 64, 101, 195, 205,
352, 400; demonstrators
at (1651), 49–50
Palais Royal gardens, La
Vallière's house in, 122
Palais Royal theatre, 164
Palatinate, French invasions
and destruction of, 172,
262–4, 278–9, 384
Palatine *see* d'Orléans,
Elizabeth, Duchesse
Panache, Mme, 227
Paris, 40, 51;
demonstrations and
rioting in, 34–5, 50–51,
58–9, 60, 61–2, 352–3;
and royal family's flight
to Saint-Germain from,
36–7; and blockade of
(1649), 37–9; Hôtel de
Ville massacre (1652),
62–3; Maria Theresa's
procession through (1660),
89; Bonne-Nouvelle
quartier, 127; famine in,
282, 347, 352–3; Great
Winter (1709) in,
347

Paris, Archbishop of, 239
parlement of Guyenne, 230
parlement of Paris, 12, 13–
14, 15, 45, 46, 47, 48, 54,
57, 64, 225, 257, 396,
401–2; Queen's regency
ratified by, 13–14; *lit de
justice* (1645), 19–20, 21;
conflict between Anne of
Austria and, 31–40; and
blockade of Paris, 37–9;
Louis XIV forbids
assemblies of (1655), 69–
70; Louis XIV's will
annulled in (1715), 409
parlement of Provence, 42,
110
parlement at Toulouse, 118
Parma, Duke of, 328
Parma, Princess of, *see*
Elizabeth Farnese, Queen
of Spain
Partition treaties: 1st (1698),
294; 2nd (1699), 300
Pau, 182
Paul, Chevalier, 54
Paul, Vincent de, 18
paulette tax, 31
Paulin, Father, 64, 71
Pérou, Mme de, 242
Peter Alexeyvich, Tsar of
Muscovy, 301
Peterborough, Lord, 336
Petit Bourbon theatre, 72
Petkum, emissary, 348,
363, 366, 373
Phalquon, Konstantine,
Grand Vizir of Siam, 253
Philip II, King of Spain,
221, 230, 333
Philip IV, King of Spain,
78, 86, 87, 88, 121, 134;
Louis' victory of
protocol over, 109–10;
death of (1665), 129, 134
Philip V, King of Spain and
the Indies (Philippe Duc
d'Anjou), 306, 307, 308,
309–10, 316, 326–7, 328,
329, 333, 348, 350, 355,
356, 364, 365, 367, 373–
4, 378; marriage to
Princess of Savoy, 310,
320; retires to Burgos,
336; defeated at battle of
Saragossa (1710), 366;
and retires to Valladolid,
366; rejects Louis'
abdication request, 367–
8; and battle of
Villaviciosa (1710), 368;
Utrecht peace conference

and Treaty, 375, 381–2,
387; and renounce his
rights to crown of
France, 381; death of
wife, 386–7; and
marriage to Elizabeth
Farnese of Parma, 387–8,
391–2; and fall of
Princesse des Ursins,
392–3
Philippe d'Orléans *see*
Orléans, Duc de
Picardy, 52
Pignerol fortress, 287;
Fouquet imprisoned in,
120; and Lauzun's
imprisonment, 153, 209,
210
Pigmental, Don Antonio,
79, 80, 82
Place de Grève, Paris, 203,
284
Place des Victoires, Paris,
255–6, 264
Plaque, Brigadier, 322
'The Pleasures of the
Enchanted Island'
(Versailles
entertainment), 123–4,
295–6
Poison Affair (1679), 196,
199–201, 202–3, 206,
207–9, 211
Poitiers, 57
Poitu, 182
Polignac, Abbé de, 363, 366
Polignac, Mme de, 133, 199
Pomponne, Simon
Arnauld, Marquis de,
Minister of Foreign
Affairs, 198–9
Ponchartrain, Louis
Phélypeaux, Comte de,
343–4, 372
Ponchartrain, President,
120
Pons, Mlle de, 102
Pontivy, peasants' revolt in,
181
Portland, William
Bentinck, Earl of,
mission to Louis XIV of,
292–3, 294
Portocarrero, Cardinal,
307, 308
Port-Royal-des-Champs
convent; nuns accused of
Jansenism, 340, 359; and
turned out of convent,
358–9; and convent razed
to ground, 359
Poussin, Nicolas, 220

445

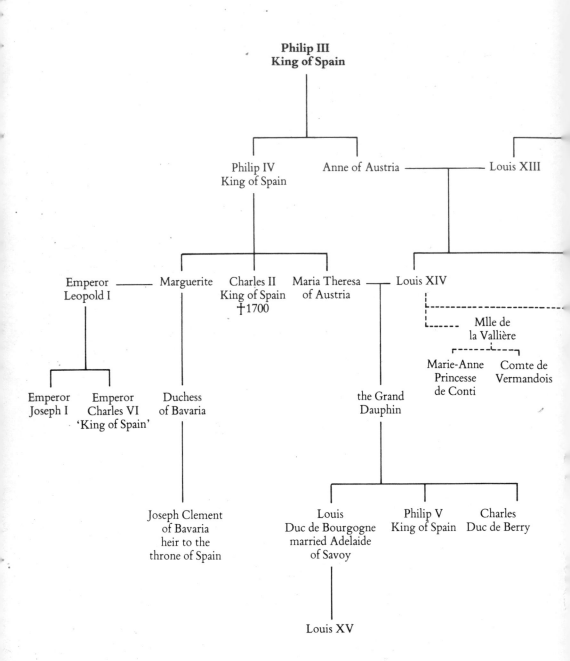

**Philip III
King of Spain**

Philip IV
King of Spain

Anne of Austria ——————— Louis XIII

Emperor ——————— Marguerite   Charles II   Maria Theresa ——— Louis XIV
Leopold I   King of Spain   of Austria
                                  †1700

Mlle de
la Vallière

Emperor   Emperor   Duchess   the Grand   Marie-Anne   Comte de
Joseph I   Charles VI   of Bavaria   Dauphin   Princesse   Vermandois
        'King of Spain'   de Conti

Joseph Clement   Louis   Philip V   Charles
of Bavaria   Duc de Bourgogne   King of Spain   Duc de Berry
heir to the   married Adelaide
throne of Spain   of Savoy

Louis XV